POE

Leaving Certificate

Higher Level 2021

Edited by Niall MacMonagle

Niall MacMonagle has taught English for the Leaving Certificate for many years. A well-known literary commentator on radio, he is the editor of several poetry anthologies, including the best-selling *Windharp: Poems of Ireland since 1916* (Penguin, 2015) and *TEXT: A Transition Year English Reader*. He writes a weekly art column for the *Sunday Independent*. In 2017, he was awarded a Doctorate of Letters, *honoris causa*, by UCD, for services to literature.

' . . . until everything was rainbow, rainbow, rainbow!'

Elizabeth Bishop

First published in 2019 by
The Celtic Press

Ground Floor – Block B, Liffey Valley Office Campus, Dublin 22

ISBN: 978-0-7144-2669-3

Contents

Introduction

'Study is the resting place – poetry the adventure'

– Wallace Stevens

The Leaving Certificate student is already an experienced reader of poetry. For Junior Cycle, you were invited to read a great variety of poems on a wide range of subjects by many different poets. You will have realised that poets use language differently, that poetry is both challenging and rewarding, and in an age of soundbytes and mediaspeak it can hold its own and offer something unique and special; that poetry, in Allison Pearson's words, 'is not in the business of taking polaroids: it should be a long slow developer, raising images that we frame and keep'. You have also had experience of both seen and unseen poems. A similar challenge awaits you at Leaving Certificate level, but there are some important differences. Until now, you might have looked at three or four poems by different poets; in the Leaving Certificate, at Higher Level, you are being invited to read an interesting and representative sample of work by eight poets and you will also be given the opportunity to respond to unseen poetry.

It is worth remembering at the outset that the word for poet in English comes from the Greek word for maker. A good poem is language that has been carefully shaped and well made. Samuel Taylor Coleridge's definition of poetry in the nineteenth century as 'the best words in the best order' still holds. W. H. Auden has described poetry as 'memorable speech'. The *New Princeton Handbook of Poetic Terms* defines a poem as 'an instance of verbal art, a text set in verse, bound speech. More generally, a poem conveys heightened forms of perception, experience, meaning, or consciousness in heightened language, i.e., a heightened mode of discourse.'

But, whichever conception we accept, we will find definitions inadequate and less important than the unique and individual experience when we, as readers, allow ourselves to enter into the world of the poem that the poet has created for us on the page.

'The Voice You Hear When You Read Silently' by Thomas Lux reminds us of the unique, very private, pleasurable experience of reading poetry:

The Voice You Hear When You Read Silently

is not silent, it is a speaking–
out-loud voice in your head: it is spoken,
a voice is saying it
as you read. It's the writer's words,
of course, in a literary sense
his or her 'voice' but the sound
of that voice is the sound of your voice.
Not the sound your friends know
or the sound of a tape played back
but your voice
caught in the dark cathedral
of your skull, your voice heard
by an internal ear informed by internal abstracts
and what you know by feeling,
having felt. It is your voice
saying, for example, the word 'barn'
that the writer wrote
but the 'barn' you say
is a barn you know or knew. The voice
in your head, speaking as you read,
never says anything neutrally – some people
hated the barn they knew,
some people love the barn they know
so you hear the word loaded
and a sensory constellation
is lit: horse-gnawed stalls,
hayloft, black heat tape wrapping
a water pipe, a slippery
spilled chirr of oats from a split sack,
the bony, filthy haunches of cows . . .
And 'barn' is only a noun – no verb
or subject has entered into the sentence yet!
The voice you hear when you read to yourself
is the clearest voice: you speak it
speaking to you.

When we look at a poem for the very first time, we can appreciate and sense how that poem has been made and shaped. This does not only include its actual shape as printed text, though this in itself is extremely important; more importantly, it means that thought, idea, and feeling have been structured and the careful combination produces the living poem.

An open approach brings its own rewards. If we learn to understand how something complex works, then we are aware of its intricacies and can better admire the creative mind that made it possible. The Irish writer Michael Longley says that 'a poet makes the most complex and concentrated response that can be made with words to the total experience of living.' But he also admits that one of the things that studying literature taught him was 'the beauty of things difficult.'

It is an exciting challenge to stand before a painting and discover what it has to say to us, to listen to a piece of music and hear it for the first time, to read a poem unknown to us until that moment. And then to return to these works and to realise how our relationship with them changes and develops as we ourselves change and develop. As we grow and change, so does our response.

We can all remember instances and experiences which we found difficult and challenging initially, but with careful thought and an open, positive approach we gained insight and understanding. Stephen Booth puts it like this: 'Any reader superstitiously fearful that the magic of a poem will vanish with knowledge of its sources need not worry any more than a student of zoology need worry that gazelles will slow down if he investigates the reasons why they run so fast.' Helen Vendler also offers good advice when she says that a reader should not look at a poem 'as if you're looking at the text with a microscope from outside'. For Vendler, the close reader is 'someone who goes inside a room and describes the architecture. You speak from inside the poem as someone looking to see how the roof articulates with the walls and how the wall articulates with the floor. And where are the crossbeams that hold it up, and where are the windows that let light through?'

Poetry can sometimes be difficult and a challenge to understand. But if we reject challenges, our vocabulary, for example, would never grow; the enquiring mind would close down. We need challenges in our lives to sharpen our intellect and keep our minds from dozing off. Sometimes we fall into the trap of saying 'I like this poem because it is easy for me to understand' or 'Why doesn't the poet say what he or she wants to say in an easy-to-understand language?' If we adopt such a position, we are saying that we want a poetry that is at our level only, that if there is an unknown word or a difficult allusion, then the poem should be rejected. If we spoke down to little children throughout their childhood, they would never grow up. Most poetry is written by adults for other adults and as a Leaving Certificate student you are on the threshold of adulthood. Allow the poems in this antology to have their say and you will not be disappointed. And if you come upon a poem in a newspaper, magazine, book, the London Underground, the New York Subway or the DART, you should give that poem a chance. The poem might deserve it and so do you.

Some years ago, the Irish poet Paul Muldoon was asked to judge a poetry competition, in the north of Ireland, which was open to young people up to the age of eighteen. There were hundreds of entries and there were poems, short and long, on all the big subjects – famine, time, death, space travel, nuclear war. Muldoon awarded first prize to an eight-year old boy who wrote the following poem:

The Tortoise

The tortoise goes movey, movey.

There was 'consternation' when 'this little poem about a tiny little subject' was awarded the prize. Muldoon explains that a great deal of the consternation was in the minds of the school teachers in the audience: 'They were upset by the fact that there's no such word in the English language as "movey, m-o-v-e-y". I tried to point out that until recently that there'd been no such word as "movey", but there now certainly was such a word, and I would never again be able to think of a tortoise without seeing it go "movey, movey".' One teacher told Muldoon that the prize-winning poet was illiterate, forgetting that the same boy had an extraordinary fresh and alive imagination.

Consider the poem again. Say it aloud and its atmospheric rhythm is immediate:

The Tortoise

The tortoise goes movey, movey.

Professor Paul Muldoon now teaches creative writing at Princeton University and the first task he sets his students is to write a one-line poem that will change the way he looks at the world. When they have made their poem, he shows them 'The Tortoise', which, for him, does just that. It goes . . .

m-o-v-e-y, m-o-v-e-y.

•

There are many aspects to be considered when it comes to the poem on the page, but let us begin without any set ideas. Consider the following:

In a Station of the Metro

The apparition of these faces in the crowd;
Petals on a wet, black bough.

What have we here? A poem. How can we tell? One of the reasons we can identify it as poetry is by its physical arrangement on the page. Prose is presented within a right and left hand margin on the page, whereas poetry is written in lines, each one causing us to pause, however briefly, before we move on. When we read it through, we can sense a concentration and intensity, a focus, a way of looking, which is one of poetry's hallmarks. What have we here? Three lines, the first of them the title, then two lines separated by a semi-colon; twenty words in all. For accurate understanding, almost all you need is a dictionary: remember Elizabeth Bishop's advice: 'Use the dictionary. It's better than the critics'.

To ask 'What have we here?' is infinitely more rewarding than 'What is this poem about?' And this, I think, is by far the best way of approaching any text. 'What have I here?' means that I, in my own time, will interpret the poem. I will gradually build up an understanding of it in my own mind. A poem is not a static thing. It is in the poet Thomas Kinsella's words 'an orderly dynamic entity'. 'What is this poem about?' is an alienating way of looking at a text, implying as it does that there is only one way of looking at the poem and that I, as reader, must somehow crack some code.

We all bring different things to a text. My way of looking at a poem will be different from yours. The person who has walked Inniskeen Road on a July evening will read Patrick Kavanagh's poetry in a different light from the reader who has never been there. If you have been to Rathlin Island, on the north Antrim coast, then Derek Mahon's description of the place will have different resonances for you than for the person who has never seen the 'rock-face and cliff-top' of Rathlin, just as Emily Dickinson's poetry will be different for those who have been to Amherest, Massachusetts.

Similarly, if you have grown up on a farm you might find yourself reading Seamus Heaney's poetry from a different perspective to the urban dweller. One way is not necessarily better than the other. It is different. What does matter, however, is that interpretation and discussion of the text should be rooted in the text itself. There is such a thing as a wrong interpretation: one which does not take the details of the text into account.

In the short poem by Ezra Pound, the title – 'In a Station of the Metro' – gives us the setting of the poem.

In a Station of the Metro

The apparition of these faces in the crowd;
Petals on a wet, black bough.

We are in Paris, but the actual Metro stop is not named. The title is clinically factual; there is no word in the title to indicate an attitude or a tone. Yet the reader is immediately invited to imagine this particular scene: usually a crowded and very busy underground railway station. In many ways, it is a scene that sums up an aspect of twentieth-century life – urban, anonymous, busy, lacking individuality.

Then the first line of the poem itself speaks of the individual and separate faces in the crowd. Pound on seeing particular faces compares the event to that of experiencing an apparition. The faces are somehow supernatural or ghostly. In a world of concrete and steel, the human being is phantom-like. This is a sense impression. The poem for example has no verb. It is not so much concerned with making a definite statement as with capturing an immediate response to a situation at a particular moment in time.

The second and final line of the poem speaks about the natural world, petals on a tree. The tree itself is wet and black suggesting, perhaps, something unattractive; but the petals are wet too and therefore shiny. They stand out. There are many of them and yet each one is individual and unique. From the way the two lines are arranged on the page, and from the use of the connecting semi-colon, we can tell that Pound is making a link between the nameless faces of people moving through an underground station (with their bright faces) and the petals that stand out against the dull tree bough.

The train in the underground station is a hard, steel object and, it could be argued, bough-like in shape. The faces coming towards Pound are soft, living faces; the petals are soft against the hard surface of the tree, just as the faces are bright against the background of the Metro.

Ezra Pound has defined an image as 'an intellectual and emotional complex in an instant of time' and you can see how this poem is such an image. It captures the idea and the feeling, the intellectual and the emotional, and both are linked together within the one picture.

Pound himself has written of how he came to write this poem. He left the Metro at La Concorde and 'saw suddenly a beautiful face, and then another beautiful woman, and I tried all that day to find words for what this had meant to me, and I could not find any words that seemed to me worthy, or as lovely as that sudden emotion.' Later he wrote a thirty-line poem and destroyed it. Six months after that, he wrote a poem half that length; a year later, he made the haiku-like poem 'In a Station of the Metro'.

The above observations on this poem are far longer than the poem itself, but poetry is compression and intensity. So much is being said in such a short space that any discussion of a poem will require expansion and explanation. What is most important is that you feel comfortable and at ease with poetry. You speak the language in which it is written and this allows us to be closer to poetry and literature than any other art form; the words are ours already or, as we read, they become ours as well as the poet's. There may be no one single, definitive response, explanation or interpretation to a poem, but there are wrongheaded ones. Take care and then the private dialogue between you and the poem, the class discussion, the personal study of the text become rewarding and enriching experiences.

•

The philosophy behind this Leaving Certificate English course is 'knowledge made, not knowledge received'. In other words, you are expected to take an active, not a passive, part in the learning process. The knowledge, insight and understanding gained by you is more enjoyable and memorable than the knowledge presented to you by another. That is to say that if we had the time and inclination a library of books would educate us well if we were willing and enthusiastic readers. However, reality is otherwise. Most of us find a system and a structure, such as classroom and school, necessary, if not vital – initially at any rate. So we go to school and find ourselves in English class studying poems and poets and poetry.

Each year, young people worldwide study poetry in school. Poetry is an art form that exists in every known language. It is also known that only a small percentage of people continue to read poetry throughout their adult life, despite the fact that many enjoy it and remember it from school. But this is changing. Poetry readings now attract very large audiences. More poetry books are being sold; occasionally, poetry books even become best-sellers. *Birthday Letters* by Ted Hughes, for example, sold over 120,000 copies in one year, while 200,000 hardback copies of Seamus Heaney's translation of *Beowulf* were bought in 2000.

•

Silence and slow time are not things that we associate with the way we live today. Yet silence and slow time are probably the two most important things when it comes to the intensely private experience of reading poetry. There are specifically public poems as well of course. When President Mary McAleese was inaugurated, she quoted from Christopher Logue's poem 'Come to the Edge'. On 11 November 2004 in her Re-Inaugural speech, President McAleese ended with a quotation from a poem by Seamus Heaney, a poem which had been written especially to mark the expansion, six months earlier, of the European Union on 1 May: 'Move lips, move minds and make new meanings flare'. Michael D. Higgins, Ireland's ninth president, is himself a published poet. His *New and Selected Poems* was published in 2011.

Poetry does not offer easy answers or solutions, but it does allow us to experience emotions. It does not lessen our fear and confusions and anger, but it helps us to accept our anger, confusions and fears, and, in Richard Bernstein's words, we find in literature 'a difficult sort of comfort' because great literature 'refuses to provide comfort that is 'false' or 'saccharine''. Likewise, it heightens our experience of positive feelings and, at its best, is life-affirming.

In the film *Invictus*, Nelson Mandela, played by Morgan Freeman, tells the captain of the Springboks rugby team Francois Pienaar that his favourite poem is William Ernest Henley's 'Invictus'. When one remembers that Mandela was imprisoned for twenty-seven years for opposing apartheid, eighteen of which were spent on Robben Island, it is easy to see why such a poem sustained him during his imprisonment:

Invictus

Out of the night that covers me,
Black as the Pit from pole to pole,
I thank whatever gods may be
For my unconquerable soul.

In the fell clutch of circumstance
I have not winced nor cried aloud.
Under the bludgeonings of chance
My head is bloody but unbowed.

Beyond this place of wrath and tears
Looms but the horror of the shade,
And yet the menace of the years
Finds, and shall find me, unafraid.

It matters not how strait the gate,
How charged with punishments the scroll,
I am the master of my fate:
I am the captain of my soul.

William Ernest Henley (1849–1903)

This book provides you with the texts, the most important things of all. You may find the critical apparatus of some use, but absolutely nothing can replace the lively, engaged, discursive atmosphere in a classroom where poems and poets are discussed between teacher and student and student and student, or the careful reading of the poems and thinking done by you in private. It is hoped that you will return again and again to these wonderful poems and that long after you have left school, a poet's way of seeing, a poet's way of saying will remain with you. In an age such as ours, where we often demand and expect instant gratification, the reading and re-reading of poetry is sometimes viewed as an unusual and strange activity. It is also one of the most valuable, enriching and stimulating things you could do. And it can be, as Wallace Stevens reminds us, an adventure.

Niall MacMonagle

How To Use This Book

There are two compulsory poetry questions on **Paper II** of the Leaving Certificate English course: **Prescribed Poetry** and the **Unseen Poem**. Read the prescribed poems closely, preferably aloud. Then read the poems again (with the aid of the dictionary or glossary if necessary). Think about the poems and talk about the poems. Re-read the poems until you feel comfortable with them. There is no substitute for knowing the poems well; reading the poems and thinking about the poems is the most important of all. The questions beneath each poem will direct you towards some important aspects of the text. Later, you may wish to read the Biographical Notes and the Critical Commentary. These might help clarify your own thinking. Finally, you should find writing on the texts a very good way of finding out how much you understand.

There has been a long and interesting discussion regarding the relevance of biographical detail, glossary, background and so on to the poem. In 1929, I. A. Richards published an important and influential book called *Practical Criticism*. It was based on an experiment in which he gave his students at Cambridge a series of unsigned poems for comment. Such an exercise produced some misreadings, but in itself was valuable and promoted a close and careful reading of the poem. As a result, 'practical criticism' became a standard classroom exercise throughout the English-speaking world.

You might wish to adopt this method and, simply by ignoring the critical apparatus in this textbook, such an approach is possible. But the teaching of literature also allows for other approaches. If you met a person during the course of a long journey and that person withheld details regarding background, place of birth, nationality, religion, politics, influences, then your knowledge and understanding of the individual would be constrained and incomplete. So too with a poem. The more we know, the greater our understanding. Professor Declan Kiberd thinks that every text should have a context and that to stay with the 'practical criticism' approach is to become the ostrich that sticks its head in the sand and looks at one grain, then another and then attempts to make a connection between them.

For the Unseen Poetry question, you might find the response to 'A Blessing' by James Wright of interest. There is also an Appendix which includes an outline of various strategies when responding to any poem and a Glossary of Literary Terms.

Eight poets are prescribed for Higher Level. Students will be expected to have studied **at least six poems** by each poet.

American spelling has been retained where appropriate.

Prescribed Poets and Poems
at Higher Level
Part I

Elizabeth Bishop
(1911–1979)

Contents Page

The Overview

These ten poems by Elizabeth Bishop reveal many of the most striking characteristics of her work: her eye for detail, her interest in travel and different places (Brazil; Nova Scotia; Worcester, Massachusetts), her apparently conversational tone, her command of internal rhyme, her use of repetition, her interest in strict poetic forms (the sonnet and the sestina), childhood memories, identity, loss.

The world which Bishop describes in her poetry is vivid and particular. Colm Tóibín says of Elizabeth Bishop that 'She began with the idea that little is known and that much is puzzling' (*On Elizabeth Bishop*, Princeton University Press, 2015). She is so intent on accurate description that often a detail is qualified and clarified within the poem. In Mexican-British poet Michael Schmidt's words, 'the voice affirms, hesitates, corrects itself; the image comes clear to us as it came clear to her, a process of adjusting perception until the thing is seen. Or the feeling is released.' For example, in 'The Fish' she tells us 'his gills were breathing in/ the terrible oxygen/ — the frightening gills,' fresh and crisp with blood,/ that can cut so badly' or that the eyes of the fish 'shifted a little', and then the more precise observation: ' — It was more like the tipping/ of an object toward the light'.

Bishop is a sympathetic observer and it has been remarked that she asks us 'to focus not on her but *with* her'. She looks at the fish, imagines its insides – 'the coarse white flesh/ packed in like feathers,/ the big bones and the little bones'; she sings hymns to the seal in 'At the Fishhouses'; she is concerned for the 'piercing cry/ and panic' of the armadillo; she finds love is present in the unlikely setting of a dirty filling station. When she uses 'I' in her poetry, it is never alienating or distancing. Somehow she makes the reader feel at ease. The poems as we read them are working out something.

The poetry is not always explicitly autobiographical but Bishop, an outsider for much of her life, writes indirectly in 'The Prodigal' of the outsider and later, in the explicitly autobiographical 'In the Waiting Room', she names herself ('you are an *Elizabeth*') and charts the sense of her child's mind realising her uniqueness and identity. 'Sestina' is also autobiographical, in that it tells of a home without a mother and father. Bishop only wrote about her childhood experiences late in life: 'Sestina', 'First Death in Nova Scotia', and 'In the Waiting Room' all date from when Bishop was in her fifties. She captures in them the confusion and complexities of childhood, its terror, panic and alienation. In 'First Death in Nova Scotia', she pieces together, as a child's mind would, the details, in order to understand them: 'Arthur's coffin was/ a little frosted cake,/ and the red-eyed loon eyed it/ from his white, frozen lake.'

Bishop preferred geography to history. It is significant that she remembers reading *National Geographic* in 'In the Waiting Room'. The title of her first book, *North & South*, contains the idea of opposites, but opposites that co-exist. Yet her descriptions of place are never just descriptions of place. Morality, history and politics are also evident in Bishop's landscapes. In 'Questions of Travel', Brazil and its otherness prompt Bishop to ask if it's right to watch strangers in another country. She dwells on the country's traditions ('In another country the clogs would all be tested'), religious influences ('a bamboo church of Jesuit baroque'), history ('the weak calligraphy of songbirds' cages').

Not only Bishop's eye but also her ear is finely attuned to the nuance of language. For example, she makes music in unusual and interesting rhyme patterns. In the closing lines of 'The Bight', the ear responds to sounds:

> and brings up a dripping **jawful** of marl.
> All the untidy activity continues,
> **awful** but cheer**ful**.

Rhyme (end rhyme, internal rhyme) and repetition are also used effectively. Bishop's tone is immediate ('Be careful with that match!'), often seemingly conversational ('There are too many waterfalls here'), relaxed ('He was curious about me. He was interested in music') or self-deprecating ('What childishness is it that while there's a breath of life/ in our bodies, we are determined to rush/ to see the sun the other way around?'). Bishop once wrote in a notebook that 'our nature consists in motion; complete rest is death.'

In Elizabeth Bishop's poetry, there is self-discovery, a sense of difference, moments of heightened awareness, a strong sense of here and now, an absence of any religious belief but a belief in the mystery of knowledge 'flowing and flown'. In 'At the Fishhouses', what begins as accurate and gradual description of landscape gives way to a downward movement towards the dark, cold centre of meaning, here imagined as deep beneath the ocean surface and something which we can never know or understand fully.

In Bishop, the act and the art of writing bring shape and order to experience. In 'Questions of Travel', she describes the traveller taking a notebook and writing. The use of 'we' in the poem and the way in which every traveller is contained in 'the traveller' allows everyone to enter into the experience. This record of thought and feeling is what Bishop herself does in her poems. She was interested in form: the sonnet and the sestina are very formal, but in other poems where the structure and rhythm may not be obvious at first, there is often a very fine command and control.

Biographical Notes

An only child, Elizabeth Bishop was born on 8 February 1911, in Worcester, Massachusetts, and her father died of Bright's disease the following October, when she was eight months old. Her mother was deeply affected by the death and spent the following five years in and out of nursing homes and mental hospitals, moving between Worcester, Boston, and Great Village, her hometown, in Nova Scotia, Canada. In 1916, when Elizabeth Bishop was five, her mother was permanently confined in Dartmouth Hospital in Nova Scotia and she never saw her again.

Bishop was brought up by relatives. First by her maternal grandparents in Nova Scotia (from spring 1916 to September 1917, returning every summer for two months until 1923), and later by relations in Massachusetts.

Bishop's Nova Scotia childhood is captured in 'First Death in Nova Scotia' and 'Sestina', both written when she was in her fifties. Though 'Sestina' describes childhood anxiety, Bishop, elsewhere, has spoken kindly of her grandparents who were simple, loving and conservative people. Her grandfather was a deacon in the Baptist church and her grandmother used to sing hymns to the young Elizabeth. These were her first introduction to poetry. Later she stayed with her father's relations in Worcester and her aunt Maud, her mother's sister, in Boston. It was here that she first read the Victorian poets and learnt many poems by heart during the many days she spent ill in bed. It was here too, at the age of eight, that Bishop began to write poetry and prose. Looking back, she described her early years with relatives as a time when she was 'always a sort of guest', adding, 'I think I've always felt like that.'

As a child she had weak lungs and suffered from eczema, bronchitis and asthma. These and other lung-related illnesses were to bother her for much of her adult life. Her wealthy paternal grandparents paid for Elizabeth to attend boarding school but Bishop, when she stayed with them, was always uncomfortable in their luxurious home and it was here that she first suffered asthma attacks.

In 1928, Elizabeth Bishop published her first poems in the school's literary magazine. She was seventeen. In her school essays from this time she wrote about things that were to matter to her for the rest of her life: her love of the sea, islands, the seashore, and the need to travel. When she was twelve, Bishop won a $5 gold piece, awarded by the American Legion for an essay on 'Americanism'.

The opening sentence was quoted by Bishop in 1961 and she said of it that it seems to have been prophetic, indicating directions taken later in life and work: 'From the icy regions of the frozen north to the waving palm trees of the burning south....'

After high school, in the autumn of 1930, Bishop went to Vassar intending to be a composer but, at Vassar, music meant that you had to perform in public once a month and this terrified her. She gave up the piano and majored in English literature instead. Her other subjects included music, history, religion, zoology and Greek.

On 16 March 1934, the Vassar College Librarian arranged for Bishop, a young and enthusiastic admirer of Marianne Moore ('I hadn't known poetry could be like that; I took to it immediately'), to meet the poet on the right-hand bench outside the reading-room of the New York Public Library. It was the beginning of an important literary friendship. Moore became Bishop's mentor. She was, says one of Bishop's biographers, 'the most important single influence on Elizabeth Bishop's poetic practice and career'. What has been called Moore's 'meticulous taste for fact' was certainly an influence. The seventeenth-century poet George Herbert, Protestant hymns, Cowper and Wordsworth are other important influences. Like Wordsworth's, many of her poems contain a solitary figure, but George Herbert (1593–1633) was the poet she admired most and it is thought that Herbert strongly influenced Bishop's purity of line.

She left Vassar in June 1934 (Bishop's mother had died that May) and, determined to be a writer, moved to New York. She kept a notebook and that summer her entries record several trips to the sea and anticipate many of her poems, including 'The Fish' and 'At the Fishhouses'.

In December 1934, Bishop was so ill with asthma that she spent two weeks in bed. Alone on New Year's Eve she sat on the floor of her apartment, a map of the North Atlantic before her, and she wrote her poem 'The Map'. It is the first poem in her first collection, *North & South*, first in *The Complete Poems*, and it marks her first real signature as a poet.

Between 1935 and 1951, Elizabeth Bishop led an unsettled, restless life. In the poet Andrew Motion's words, Bishop was 'energetically nomadic'. Mark Strand, the American poet, says that for Bishop there was 'always the possibility of finding a place for herself', adding that 'if we have a home why travel?' She travelled to Europe (Belgium, France, England, Spain, Ireland, Italy), visited North Africa, spent a year in Washington as poetry consultant at the Library of Congress, lived in Key West in Florida, lived in Mexico and New York, but from 1952 to 1971 she considered Brazil her home, where she lived with her partner Lota de Macedo Soares. They lived in Rio de Janeiro and Petropolis, and Bishop eventually bought a house of her own in Ouro Preto. It was an eighteenth-century colonial house and she named it Casa Mariana after Marianne Moore.

She gave very few readings: once in 1947 at Wellesley College, two months after her first book appeared, when she was sick for days in anticipation; again in Washington in 1949, when she was sick again. And then she didn't read publicy for twenty-six years. She survived on grants, fellowships and the generosity of friends and, when she returned to the United States from Brazil in 1970, she took a teaching post at Harvard and later at New York University. She returned permanently to the United States in 1972, living for a time in Seattle and San Francisco. She spent her final years in Boston.

Bishop won the Pulitzer Prize in 1956, the National Book Award in 1969, and the Neustadt International Prize for Literature in 1976, but, in Eavan Boland's words, Bishop 'disliked the swagger and visibility of literary life'. In an interview in 1978 Bishop remarked that 'There's nothing more embarrassing than being a poet really... There must be an awful core of ego somewhere for you to set yourself up to write poetry. I've never felt it, but it must be there'. Her friend, the American poet James Merrill, speaking of Elizabeth Bishop, spoke of her 'instinctive, modest, lifelong impersonations of an ordinary woman, someone who during the day did errands, went to the beach, would perhaps that evening jot a phrase or two inside the nightclub matchbook before returning to the dance floor. Thus the later glimpses of her playing – was it poker? – with Neruda in a Mexican hotel, or pingpong with Octavio Paz in Cambridge, or getting Robert Duncan high on grass – "for the first time" – in San Francisco, or teaching Frank Bidart the wildflowers in Maine.'

Elizabeth Bishop, always a traveller, spent the last years of her life in her native Massachusetts, where she taught at Harvard. She was alone in her apartment on Lewis Wharf when she died of a cerebral aneurysm on 6 October 1979.

Elizabeth Bishop disapproved of biography; she considered it 'finally just unpleasant'. In Eavan Boland's words, she was 'shy and hidden' and preferred to remain that way. 'Elizabeth Bishop was known for not wishing to be known' was how Ian Hamilton put it; and Marianne Moore said that Bishop was 'spectacular in being unspectacular'. 'The shy perfectionist with her painter's eye' is how the writer Derek Mahon described her. Helen Vendler thought Elizabeth Bishop 'A foreigner everywhere, and, perhaps, with everyone.' But the poems are born of the life, and biographical details can deepen our understanding and appreciation of the poems and our admiration for the poet.

In one of Elizabeth Bishop's finest poems, 'Crusoe in England', she imagines Robinson Crusoe lonely for his island and Friday; and, remembering his time there, she writes:

> The sun set in the sea; the same odd sun
> rose from the sea,
> and there was one of it and one of me.

Here we have the voice of Robinson Crusoe, and the voice of Bishop, and the voice of all other lonely, observing, travellers. It is significant that Bishop was attracted to a figure like Crusoe, an isolate, someone ill-at-ease having returned to society. Bishop's sexuality and her struggle with alcohol were part of her own sense of isolation. In a letter written in 1948 to Robert Lowell, she said 'When you write my epitaph, you must say I was the loneliest person who ever lived.' Her later work suggests a happier person, but her life was never uncomplicatedly happy.

One other thing – read Bishop's poem called 'Poem' sometime. It maps a reader's experience of the reading of poetry itself – that initial distance between reader and poem, possibly indifference, then the gradual, awakening recognition and the final realisation that both reader and poet share a common humanity.

Bishop's *The Complete Poems 1927–1972* contains just over 140 poems and some thirty of these are translations from French, Spanish and Portuguese. She wrote very slowly, very carefully, sometimes pinning bits of paper on her walls, leaving blank spaces ('with gaps / and empties for the unimagined phrases' is how Robert Lowell described it in a poem for her), waiting for the right word. Some of her poems were several years in the making. She worked on 'The Moose' for over twenty-five years, yet it seems effortless as all good poetry does. She writes a poetry which echoes the rhythms of natural speech and her rhymes are not always easy to detect. End rhymes and cross rhymes or slant rhymes create a special and effective music. And what Yeats says of all true poetry is true of Bishop:

> 'A line will take us hours maybe;
> Yet if it does not seem a moment's thought,
> Our stitching and unstitching has been naught.'

POEMS

Dates refer to the year of composition. The poems as they are printed here, are in the order in which they were written.

The Fish

I caught a tremendous fish
and held him beside the boat
half out of water, with my hook
fast in a corner of his mouth.
He didn't fight.
He hadn't fought at all.
He hung a grunting weight,
battered and venerable
and homely. Here and there
his brown skin hung in strips
like ancient wallpaper,
and its pattern of darker brown
was like wallpaper:
shapes like full-blown roses
stained and lost through age.
He was speckled with barnacles,
fine rosettes of lime,
and infested
with tiny white sea-lice,
and underneath two or three
rags of green weed hung down.
While his gills were breathing in
the terrible oxygen
— the frightening gills,
fresh and crisp with blood,
that can cut so badly —
I thought of the coarse white flesh
packed in like feathers,
the big bones and the little bones,
the dramatic reds and blacks
of his shiny entrails,
and the pink swim-bladder
like a big peony.

I looked into his eyes
which were far larger than mine
but shallower, and yellowed,
the irises backed and packed
with tarnished tinfoil
seen through the lenses
of old scratched isinglass.
They shifted a little, but not
to return my stare.
— It was more like the tipping
of an object toward the light.
I admired his sullen face,
the mechanism of his jaw,
and then I saw
that from his lower lip
— if you could call it a lip —
grim, wet, and weaponlike,
hung five old pieces of fish-line,
or four and a wire leader
with the swivel still attached,
with all their five big hooks
grown firmly in his mouth.
A green line, frayed at the end
where he broke it, two heavier lines,
and a fine black thread
still crimped from the strain and snap
when it broke and he got away.
Like medals with their ribbons
frayed and wavering,
a five-haired beard of wisdom
trailing from his aching jaw.
I stared and stared
and victory filled up
the little rented boat,
from the pool of bilge
where oil had spread a rainbow

around the rusted engine
to the bailer rusted orange,
the sun-cracked thwarts,
the oarlocks on their strings,
the gunnels — until everything
was rainbow, rainbow, rainbow!
And I let the fish go.

Glossary

Line 1 tremendous: it may seem unnecessary to explain the word tremendous, but poets are attuned to the nuance of words and the dictionary is a vital companion for the reader of poetry. Tremendous does not only mean immense; more accurately, it means that which excites trembling or awe from the Latin *tremere* to tremble, tremble at; awe-inspiring.

Line 8 venerable: worthy of reverence, aged-looking.

Line 9 homely: familiar or plain/ugly (in American English).

Line 17 rosettes: rose shaped patterns – knots of radiating loops of ribbon or the like in concentric arrangement.

Line 25 crisp: firm.

Line 31 entrails: the internal parts of the fish.

Line 33 peony: a large showy crimson or white globular flower.

Line 40 isinglass: a whitish semi-transparent gelatin substance used for windows, originally got from the swim bladders of some freshwater fish.

Line 45 sullen: showing irritation or ill humour by a gloomy silence or reserve.

Line 52 leader: short piece of wire connecting fishhook and fishline.

Line 53 swivel: a ring or link that turns round on a pin or neck.

Line 54 five big hooks: Bonnie Costello, in her book *Elizabeth Bishop: Questions of Mastery*, says, 'Five wounds on a fish make him a Christ figure but the epiphany he brings the poet has nothing otherworldly about it.'

Line 59 crimped: shrunk and curled.

Line 68 bilge: filth that collects in the broadest part of the bottom of a boat.

Line 71 bailer: bucket for scooping water out of the boat.

Line 72 thwarts: the seats or benches for rowers.

Line 73 oarlocks: a rowlock – metal devices to hold the oars, attached by 'string' to the boat itself.

Line 74 gunnels: or gunwale – the upper edges of a boat's side.

In a letter, Bishop wrote: 'With "The Fish", that's exactly how it happened. It was in Key West, and I did it just as the poem says. That was in 1938. Oh, but I did change one thing; the poem says he had five hooks hanging from his mouth, but actually he had only three. Sometimes a poem makes its own demands. But I always try to stick as much as possible to what really happened when I describe something in the poem.'

Questions

1. Between the opening line, 'I caught a tremendous fish', and the poem's final line, 'And I let the fish go', is a detailed and interesting account of Bishop's response to the incident. How does the speaker feel about catching this 'tremendous fish'? Which words and phrases, in your opinion, best capture her feelings? Comment on Bishop's use of 'him' and 'he'.
2. How does the fish react when caught this time? How and why does the poet empathise with the fish?
3. Comment on Bishop's use of language. What is the effect of repetition? Which lines or images are particularly vivid? Discuss images such as 'ancient wallpaper' and 'big peony' and say what they contribute to the poem.
4. 'I looked into his eyes ...', says the poet in line 34. What happens?
5. How would you describe the speaker's tone? Look particularly at lines such as '– It was more like ...' or '– if you could call it ...'
6. What do you think Bishop means by 'victory' in line 66? How would you describe the poet's mood in the closing line?
7. Does the ending of the poem come as a surprise? Give reasons for your answer. Why do you think the speaker 'let the fish go'? What does this poem say about power and control?

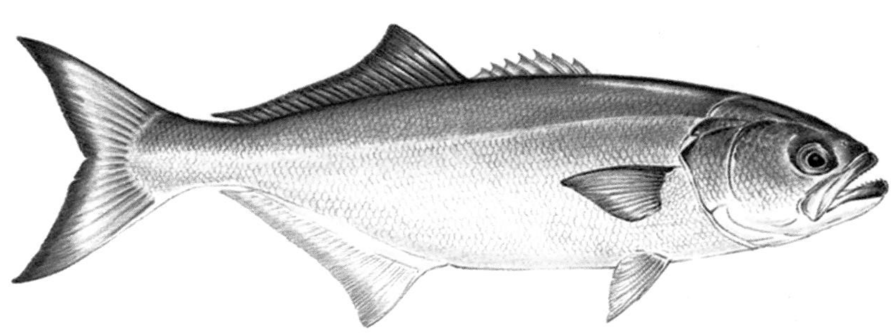

At the Fishhouses

Although it is a cold evening,
down by one of the fishhouses
an old man sits netting,
his net, in the gloaming almost invisible,
a dark purple-brown,
and his shuttle worn and polished.
The air smells so strong of codfish
it makes one's nose run and one's eyes water.
The five fishhouses have steeply peaked roofs
and narrow, cleated gangplanks slant up
to storerooms in the gables
for the wheelbarrows to be pushed up and down on.
All is silver: the heavy surface of the sea,
swelling slowly as if considering spilling over,
is opaque, but the silver of the benches,
the lobster pots, and masts, scattered
among the wild jagged rocks,
is of an apparent translucence
like the small old buildings with an emerald moss
growing on their shoreward walls.
The big fish tubs are completely lined
with layers of beautiful herring scales
and the wheelbarrows are similarly plastered
with creamy iridescent coats of mail,
with small iridescent flies crawling on them.
Up on the little slope behind the houses,
set in the sparse bright sprinkle of grass,
is an ancient wooden capstan,
cracked, with two long bleached handles
and some melancholy stains, like dried blood,
where the ironwork has rusted.
The old man accepts a Lucky Strike.
He was a friend of my grandfather.

We talk of the decline in the population
and of codfish and herring
while he waits for a herring boat to come in.
There are sequins on his vest and on his thumb.
He has scraped the scales, the principal beauty,
from unnumbered fish with that black old knife,
the blade of which is almost worn away.

Down at the water's edge, at the place
where they haul up the boats, up the long ramp
descending into the water, thin silver
tree trunks are laid horizontally
across the gray stones, down and down
at intervals of four or five feet.

Cold dark deep and absolutely clear,
element bearable to no mortal,
to fish and to seals . . . One seal particularly
I have seen here evening after evening.
He was curious about me. He was interested in music;
like me a believer in total immersion,
so I used to sing him Baptist hymns.
I also sang 'A Mighty Fortess Is Our God.'
He stood up in the water and regarded me
steadily, moving his head a little.
Then he would disappear, then suddenly emerge
almost in the same spot, with a sort of shrug
as if it were against his better judgment.
Cold dark deep and absolutely clear,
the clear gray icy water . . . Back, behind us,
the dignified tall firs begin.
Bluish, associating with their shadows,
a million Christmas trees stand
waiting for Christmas. The water seems suspended
above the rounded gray and blue-gray stones.

I have seen it over and over, the same sea, the same,
slightly, indifferently swinging above the stones,
icily free above the stones,
above the stones and then the world.
If you should dip your hand in,
your wrist would ache immediately,
your bones would begin to ache and your hand would burn
as if the water were a transmutation of fire
that feeds on stones and burns with a dark gray flame.
If you tasted it, it would first taste bitter,
then briny, then surely burn your tongue.
It is like what we imagine knowledge to be:
dark, salt, clear, moving, utterly free,
drawn from the cold hard mouth
of the world, derived from the rocky breasts
forever, flowing and drawn, and since
our knowledge is historical, flowing, and flown.

Glossary

Line 4 gloaming: twilight, dusk.

Line 6 shuttle: an instrument used for shooting the thread of the woof between the threads of the warp in weaving.

Line 10 cleated: having pieces of wood nailed on to give footing.

Line 10 gangplank: a long, narrow, movable wooden plank/walkway.

Line 15 opaque: dark, dull, cannot be seen through, not transparent.

Line 18 translucence: when light shines through.

Line 24 iridescent: coloured like the rainbow, glittering with changing colours.

Line 28 capstan: a machine with a cylindrical drum around which rope is wound and used for hauling.

Line 32 Lucky Strike: an American brand of cigarette.

Line 37 sequins: small, circular, thin, glittering, sparkling ornament on a dress.

Line 52 total immersion: a form of baptism practised by certain Christian groups.

Line 63 associating: uniting.

Line 74 transmutation: a change from one form into another.

Line 77 briny: very salty water.

Line 83 historical: pertaining to the course of events.

? Questions

1. This poem begins with a particular place and then it becomes a poem which explores many complex and abstract ideas such as knowledge and meaning. Identify the words and phrases that allow the reader to picture the fishhouses in detail. Comment on Bishop's use of colour.

2. Can you suggest why Bishop has divided 'At the Fishhouses' into three sections? How would you sum up what is happening in each section? Which of the three sections is the most personal?

3. There are three solitary figures in the poem: the fisherman, the speaker and the seal. Imagine the poem without the fisherman and the seal and discuss what would be lost.

4. The poem moves from description towards meditation. Is it possible to identify where the poem becomes meditative or philosophical? Explain your answer.

5. 'Cold dark deep and absolutely clear,/the clear gray icy water . . .' (lines 60–61) refer not only to the ocean. What similarities, according to Bishop, are there between water and knowledge?

6. There are many religious references in the poem. Identify these and say whether you think the poem is religious or not.

7. What do you think Bishop means when she writes 'and then the world' (line 70)?

8. The poem ends with an image of knowledge. How would you describe Bishop's understanding of human experience as it is revealed to us in this poem?

The Bight

[On my birthday]

At low tide like this how sheer the water is.
White, crumbling ribs of marl protrude and glare
and the boats are dry, the pilings dry as matches.
Absorbing, rather than being absorbed,
the water in the bight doesn't wet anything,
the color of the gas flame turned as low as possible.
One can smell it turning to gas; if one were Baudelaire
one could probably hear it turning to marimba music.
The little ocher dredge at work off the end of the dock
already plays the dry perfectly off-beat claves.
The birds are outsize. Pelicans crash
into this peculiar gas unnecessarily hard,
it seems to me, like pickaxes,
rarely coming up with anything to show for it,
and going off with humorous elbowings.
Black-and-white man-of-war birds soar
on impalpable drafts
and open their tails like scissors on the curves
or tense them like wishbones, till they tremble.
The frowsy sponge boats keep coming in
with the obliging air of retrievers,
bristling with jackstraw gaffs and hooks
and decorated with bobbles of sponges.
There is a fence of chicken wire along the dock
where, glinting like little plowshares,
the blue-gray shark tails are hung up to dry
for the Chinese-restaurant trade.
Some of the little white boats are still piled up
against each other, or lie on their sides, stove in,
and not yet salvaged, if they ever will be,
        from the last bad storm,
like torn-open, unanswered letters.

The bight is littered with old correspondences.
Click. Click. Goes the dredge,
and brings up a dripping jawful of marl.
All the untidy activity continues,
awful but cheerful.

Glossary

Title The Bight: a bay formed by a bend in a coastline, a wide bay. The bight here is Garrison Bight in Key West, Florida.

Subtitle: 'on my birthday' – 8 February 1948 – Bishop was 37. Personal details in Elizabeth Bishop's poetry are rare and most often not explicitly expressed. By placing 'On my birthday' beneath a title that names a place, Bishop is suggesting both place and the passing of time.

Line 1 sheer: transparently thin; smooth, calm; bright.

Line 2 marl: deposit consisting of clay and lime.

Line 3 pilings: sharp posts or stakes, a heavy timber driven into the ground, especially under water, to form a foundation.

Line 7 Baudelaire: French poet (1821–1867).

Line 8 marimba: African xylophone adopted by Central Americans and Jazz musicians.

Line 9 ocher dredge: yellowish-brown machine used to scoop/draw up silt.

Line 10 claves: wooden percussion instruments; small wooden cylinders held in the hand and struck together to mark Latin American dance rhythm.

Line 16 man-of-war birds: the frigate-birds – large tropical sea bird with very long wings.

Line 17 impalpable: not perceivable by touch, imperceptible to the touch, not perceptible by the watching poet.

Line 17 drafts: currents of air.

Line 19 wishbones: forked bones in front of the breasts of some birds.

Line 20 frowsy: ill-smelling, offensive, unkempt.

Line 21 retrievers: dogs who have been trained to find and fetch.

Line 22 jackstraw: a short staff, usually set upon the bowsprit or at the bow of a ship on which the flag called the jack is hoisted.

Line 22 gaffs: hooks used especially for landing large fish.

Line 22 hooks: the hooks on a sponge-catching boat to hold the catch.

Line 25 plowshares: the part of a plough that cuts and turns the soil.

Line 27 Chinese-restaurant trade: shark tails are used in Chinese cooking. Shark-tail soup is a delicacy.

Line 29 stove in: broken – especially in the hull or lowermost portion.

Line 32 old correspondences: cf. line 7 – Baudelaire wrote a sonnet 'Correspondences' in which he speaks of man as one who, while wandering among Nature, wanders among symbols. Baudelaire says that the perfumes of Nature are as sweet as the sound of the oboe, as green as the prairies, as fresh as the caress of a child. Bishop responds in a similar way to the natural world in her poem. Baudelaire in his theory of correspondences promised connections or links by means of poetry between the physical and spiritual worlds.

This is a Bishop poem which, like 'At the Fishhouses', begins with objective description and gradually gives way to a more personal, private world. The objective and subjective are side by side in the poem's title and subtitle. A bight is a public place; a birthday is personal and an occasion for thinking more intensely about oneself, one's birth, one's life and death. In the poem, Bishop is on her own; she celebrates her birthday by celebrating the bight. The poem overall may not seem that personal, but the choice of subject matter, the way of seeing, the words used, the mood conveyed, all convey Bishop's personal view.

? Questions

1. Like 'At the Fishhouses', this is another place poem. What is usually associated with a birthday? Why do you think Bishop included the detail of her birthday here? Does it alter the poem? Explain.
2. In many of her poems, Bishop describes in an atmospheric way a particular place. Discuss how she does that in 'The Bight'. Pay particular attention to lines 7 and 8.
3. Is Bishop enjoying what she sees? Support your answer by reference to the text. Does it matter that she is alone in the poem?
4. Consider all the action and movement described in the poem. What is the significance of the dredge? What do you think Bishop means by the phrase 'untidy activity' in the closing lines?
5. Some sentences here are four or five lines long; others consist of one word. Examine and discuss how the sentence length and sentence organisation contribute to the poem's movement.
6. Is the bight in any way symbolic?

The Prodigal

The brown enormous odor he lived by
was too close, with its breathing and thick hair,
for him to judge. The floor was rotten; the sty
was plastered halfway up with glass-smooth dung.
Light-lashed, self-righteous, above moving snouts,
the pigs' eyes followed him, a cheerful stare –
even to the sow that always ate her young –
till, sickening, he leaned to scratch her head.
But sometimes mornings after drinking bouts
(he hid the pints behind a two-by-four),
the sunrise glazed the barnyard mud with red;
the burning puddles seemed to reassure.
And then he thought he almost might endure
his exile yet another year or more.

But evenings the first star came to warn.
The farmer whom he worked for came at dark
to shut the cows and horses in the barn
beneath their overhanging clouds of hay,
with pitchforks, faint forked lightnings, catching light,
safe and companionable as in the Ark.
The pigs stuck out their little feet and snored.
The lantern – like the sun, going away –
laid on the mud a pacing aureole.
Carrying a bucket along a slimy board,
he felt the bats' uncertain staggering flight,
his shuddering insights, beyond his control,
touching him. But it took him a long time
finally to make his mind up to go home.

Glossary

Title: The poem was originally referred to by Bishop as 'Prodigal Son'.

The Prodigal: A reference to the story of the Prodigal Son in the Bible as told by St. Luke, Chapter 15: A certain man had two sons and the younger of them said to his father, Father, give me the portion of goods that falleth to me. And he divided unto them his living. And not many days after the younger son gathered all together and took his journey into a far country, and there wasted his substance with riotous living. And when he had spent all, there arose a mighty famine in that land; and he began to be in want. And he went and joined himself to a citizen of that country; and he sent him into his fields to feed swine. And he would fain have filled his belly with the husks that the swine did eat: and no man gave unto him. And when he came to himself, he said, How many hired servants of my father's have bread enough and to spare, and I perish with hunger! I will arise and go to my father, and will say unto him, Father, I have sinned against heaven, and before thee, and am no more worthy to be called thy son: make me as one of thy hired servants. And he arose, and came to his father. But when he was yet a great way off, his father saw him, and had compassion, and ran, and fell on his neck, and kissed him. (King James Version).

Title prodigal: wasteful, extravagant.

Line 2 close: stifling, unventilated, oppressive.

Line 10 two-by-four: timber with cross-section, 2 inches by 4 inches.

Line 20 companionable: happily together.

Line 23 aureole: the halo or celestial crown round the head of a pictured martyr or divine figure.

Questions

1. What immediately comes to mind when the words 'prodigal' or 'prodigal son' are mentioned? (Bishop's original title was 'Prodigal Son'.)

2. Look at how the poem is organised and shaped (metre, line length, end-rhyme). Can you suggest a reason why Bishop chose this form?

3. How does Bishop imagine the life of the prodigal son in the first section of the poem? Is it all ugly and hopeless? Give reasons for your answer and quote from the text to support the points you make.

4. What is the effect of the use of 'But' in lines 9, 15 and 27?

5. Comment on the significance of 'sunrise', 'star', 'aureole' and the Biblical reference to the Ark.

6. What is meant by tone? How would you describe the tone in the opening lines? Is there a change of tone in the poem?

7. How do you respond and how do you think Bishop wanted her reader to respond to line 21: 'The pigs stuck out their little feet and snored' (a perfect example of an iambic pentameter)?

8. Comment on Bishop's choice of adjectives: 'enormous', 'glass-smooth', 'cheerful', 'overhanging', 'companionable', 'slimy', 'staggering', 'shuddering' and the power of the last word in the poem. Write a note on any four of these.

Filling Station

Oh, but it is dirty!
– this little filling station,
oil-soaked, oil-permeated
to a disturbing, over-all
black translucency.
Be careful with that match!

Father wears a dirty,
oil-soaked monkey suit
that cuts him under the arms,
and several quick and saucy
and greasy sons assist him
(it's a family filling station),
all quite thoroughly dirty.

Do they live in the station?
It has a cement porch
behind the pumps, and on it
a set of crushed and grease-
impregnated wickerwork;
on the wicker sofa
a dirty dog, quite comfy.

Some comic books provide
the only note of color –
of certain color. They lie
upon a big dim doily
draping a taboret
(part of the set), beside
a big hirsute begonia.

Why the extraneous plant?
Why the taboret?
Why, oh why, the doily?
(Embroidered in daisy stitch
with marguerites, I think,
and heavy with gray crochet.)

Somebody embroidered the doily.
Somebody waters the plant,
or oils it, maybe. Somebody
arranges the rows of cans
so that they softly say:
ESSO-SO-SO-SO
to high-strung automobiles.
Somebody loves us all.

Glossary

Line 5 translucency: shiny, glossy quality.

Line 8 monkey suit: dungarees, overalls.

Line 18 impregnated: saturated.

Line 24 doily: a small ornamented napkin, often laid under dishes (from Doily or Doiley, a famous haberdasher).

Line 25 taboret: a low seat usually without arms or back/a small drum.

Line 27 hirsute: shaggy, untrimmed.

Line 27 begonia: plant with pink flowers and remarkable unequal-sided coloured leaves.

Line 28 extraneous: of external origin, not belonging, not essential.

Line 31 daisy stitch: a design pattern.

Line 32 marguerites: ox-eye daisies.

Line 33 crochet: knitting done with hooked needle forming intertwined loops.

Questions

1. What details immediately strike the reader on a first reading? Is this a typical or an atypical Bishop poem? Give reasons for your answer.
2. Lines 1 and 6 end with exclamation marks. How would you describe the tone of the opening stanza? Dismissive? Cautious? Both? Identify the other tones in the poem.
3. How does Bishop convince her reader that the place is indeed 'oil-soaked, oil-permeated' and 'grease-impregnated'?
4. Bishop has been described as a very accurate observer. Where in the poem is this evident? Quote from the poem in support of your answer.
5. Choose any stanza from the poem and show how Bishop creates an inner music in her use of language. Your answer should include a discussion of alliteration, assonance, slant or cross-rhyme.
6. Discuss Bishop's use of repetition in the poem, especially the repetition of 'why' and 'somebody'.
7. Were you surprised by the final line in the poem? How is the line justified within the context of the poem as a whole?

Questions of Travel

There are too many waterfalls here; the crowded streams
hurry too rapidly down to the sea,
and the pressure of so many clouds on the mountaintops
makes them spill over the sides in soft slow-motion,
turning to waterfalls under our very eyes.
— For if those streaks, those mile-long, shiny, tearstains,
aren't waterfalls yet,
in a quick age or so, as ages go here,
they probably will be.
But if the streams and clouds keep travelling, travelling,
the mountains look like the hulls of capsized ships,
slime-hung and barnacled.

Think of the long trip home.
Should we have stayed at home and thought of here?
Where should we be today?
Is it right to be watching strangers in a play
in this strangest of theatres?
What childishness is it that while there's a breath of life
in our bodies, we are determined to rush
to see the sun the other way around?
The tiniest green hummingbird in the world?
To stare at some inexplicable old stonework,
inexplicable and impenetrable,
at any view,
instantly seen and always, always delightful?
Oh, must we dream our dreams
and have them too?
And have we room
for one more folded sunset, still quite warm?

But surely it would have been a pity
not to have seen the trees along this road,
really exaggerated in their beauty,

not to have seen them gesturing
like noble pantomimists, robed in pink.
— Not to have had to stop for gas and heard
the sad, two-noted, wooden tune
of disparate wooden clogs
carelessly clacking over
a grease-stained filling-station floor.
(In another country the clogs would all be tested.
Each pair there would have identical pitch.)
— A pity not to have heard
the other, less primitive music of the fat brown bird
who sings above the broken gasoline pump
in a bamboo church of Jesuit baroque:
three towers, five silver crosses.
— Yes, a pity not to have pondered,
blurr'dly and inconclusively,
on what connection can exist for centuries
between the crudest wooden footwear
and, careful and finicky,
the whittled fantasies of wooden cages.
— Never to have studied history in
the weak calligraphy of songbirds' cages.
— And never to have had to listen to rain
so much like politicians' speeches:
two hours of unrelenting oratory
and then a sudden golden silence
in which the traveller takes a notebook, writes:

'Is it lack of imagination that makes us come
to imagined places, not just stay at home?
Or could Pascal have been not entirely right
about just sitting quietly in one's room?

Continent, city, country, society:
the choice is never wide and never free.
And here, or there . . . No. Should we have stayed at home,
wherever that may be?'

Glossary

Title: Not only this particular poem but the title of Bishop's third collection.

Line 1 There: Brazil.

Line 11 hulls: framework or body of boats.

Line 22 inexplicable: unable to be explained.

Line 37 disparate: dissimilar, discordant.

Line 45 baroque: an exuberant kind of European architecture which the Jesuits in the seventeenth century introduced into Latin America.

Line 51 finicky: overdone.

Line 52 fantasies: fanciful design.

Line 54 calligraphy: a style of writing but here refers to the style of construction of the cages.

Line 57 unrelenting: persistent.

Line 57 oratory: public speaking.

Line 61 Pascal: French mathematician, physicist and philosopher (1623–1662) who in his *Pensées* wrote: 'I have often said that the sole cause of man's unhappiness is that he does not know how to stay quietly in his room'.

Questions

1. In the opening section of the poem, Bishop describes a Brazilian landscape. How is a state of flux conveyed? How would you describe her response to it? Give reasons for your answer.

2. In the second section, she uses the pronoun 'we'. Who is she including here? Why is she uneasy about certain aspects of travel? Why does she think travel invasive and childish?

3. Which images do you find striking or interesting in the poem? Does the poem focus on the particular or the general or both? What is the effect of this?

4. 'But surely it would have been a pity ...' begins her justification for travel. Examine how she argues her point. Which details justify her point? Look at her use of the dash and repetition. Is the argument convincing? Why or why not? Is the speaker a sympathetic observer?

5. Bishop suggests that Pascal (line 61), who believed that 'the sole cause of man's unhappiness is that he does not know how to stay quietly in his room', might not have been entirely right. Which viewpoint would you agree with? Give reasons for your answer. Does Bishop put forward a convincing argument?

6. The poem's final italicised section takes the form of an entry in the traveller's notebook, written during 'a sudden golden silence'. What does the traveller conclude in this notebook entry? Why do you think the poem ends with a question mark?

The Armadillo

For Robert Lowell

This is the time of year
when almost every night
the frail, illegal fire balloons appear.
Climbing the mountain height,

rising toward a saint
still honored in these parts,
the paper chambers flush and fill with light
that comes and goes, like hearts.

Once up against the sky it's hard
to tell them from the stars —
planets, that is — the tinted ones:
Venus going down, or Mars,

or the pale green one. With a wind,
they flare and falter, wobble and toss;
but if it's still they steer between
the kite sticks of the Southern Cross,

receding, dwindling, solemnly
and steadily forsaking us,
or, in the downdraft from a peak,
suddenly turning dangerous.

Last night another big one fell.
It splattered like an egg of fire
against the cliff behind the house.
The flame ran down. We saw the pair

of owls who nest there flying up
and up, their whirling black-and-white
stained bright pink underneath, until
they shrieked up out of sight.

The ancient owls' nest must have burned.
Hastily, all alone,
a glistening armadillo left the scene,
rose-flecked, head down, tail down,

and then a baby rabbit jumped out,
short-eared, to our surprise.
So soft! — a handful of intangible ash
with fixed, ignited eyes.

Too pretty, dreamlike mimicry!
O falling fire and piercing cry
and panic, and a weak mailed fist
clenched ignorant against the sky!

Glossary

Title: the armadillo is a chiefly nocturnal, burrowing animal whose body is encased in bony plates. It is found in southern United States and in Latin America. When captured it rolls itself into a ball and while curled tight it is protected from everything except fire. It is pronounced 'armadeeo' in Spanish. When this poem was first published – in *The New Yorker* on 22 June 1957 – it was called 'The Armadillo – Brazil'. Her friend the American poet Robert Lowell, to whom the poem is dedicated, considered the title wrong at first but later thought 'The Armadillo' right: 'the little creature, given only five lines, runs off with the whole poem'.

Line 1 time of year: June, particularly 24 June which is St. John's Day. This is the shortest day of the year in the Southern Hemisphere, a holy day, and as part of the celebrations balloons are released on St. John's Night and the nights before and after. These were fire balloons and supposedly illegal. The house mentioned in the poem is the house in Petropolis which Bishop shared with Lota de Macedo Soares.

Line 13 the pale green one: the planet Uranus, perhaps.

Line 16 kite sticks: the kite-like formation of the constellation.

Line 16 Southern Cross: constellation visible only in the southern hemisphere.

Line 35 intangible: cannot be touched/cannot be grasped mentally.

Line 37 mimicry: imitating, imitative, especially for amusement.

Questions

1. The poem describes St. John's day, a religious feast in Brazil, and the practise of releasing fire balloons. Discuss how in the first five stanzas Bishop describes the balloons. Are they viewed as beautiful, or dangerous, or both?
2. Consider line length, stanza and rhyme. What is the effect of the short sentence at line 21 and the short line at line 30?
3. Does our attitude towards the fire balloons change when we read of the owls, the armadillo and the rabbit?
4. The balloons are described, at first, as 'paper chambers ... like hearts'. What does Bishop think of the balloons by the end of the poem? Where is this most evident?
5. Why do you think Bishop chose 'The Armadillo' as her title?
6. The armadillo and the other creatures have been interpreted symbolically as the oppressed, the victimised. Look particularly at lines 39–40. Do you think this is a valid interpretation? Give reasons for your answer.
7. What is being signalled, in your opinion, by the change to italics in the last stanza?
8. How would you describe the poet's tone? Does the tone change?

Sestina

September rain falls on the house.
In the failing light, the old grandmother
sits in the kitchen with the child
beside the Little Marvel Stove,
reading the jokes from the almanac,
laughing and talking to hide her tears.

She thinks that her equinoctial tears
and the rain that beats on the roof of the house
were both foretold by the almanac,
but only known to a grandmother.
The iron kettle sings on the stove.
She cuts some bread and says to the child,

It's time for tea now; but the child
is watching the teakettle's small hard tears
dance like mad on the hot black stove,
the way the rain must dance on the house.
Tidying up, the old grandmother
hangs up the clever almanac

on its string. Birdlike, the almanac
hovers half open above the child,
hovers above the old grandmother
and her teacup full of dark brown tears.
She shivers and says she thinks the house
feels chilly, and puts more wood in the stove.

It was to be, says the Marvel Stove.
I know what I know, says the almanac.
With crayons the child draws a rigid house
and a winding pathway. Then the child
puts in a man with buttons like tears
and shows it proudly to the grandmother.

But secretly, while the grandmother
busies herself about the stove,
the little moons fall down like tears
from between the pages of the almanac
into the flower bed the child
has carefully placed in the front of the house.

Time to plant tears, says the almanac.
The grandmother sings to the marvellous stove
and the child draws another inscrutable house.

Glossary

Title Sestina (meaning song of sixes): a rhymed or unrhymed poem with six stanzas of six lines and final triplet, each stanza having the same words to end its lines but in a different order. Lines may be of any length. The final three lines, the triplet, must introduce the six words which end the six preceding stanzas – in this instance, 'tears', 'child', 'almanac', 'stove', 'grandmother', 'house'. The sestina was supposedly invented by Arnaut Daniel in the twelfth century.

The order in which the end-words are re-used is prescribed by a set pattern which is very formal and it has been argued that such rules are so inhibiting that the poem becomes artificial and strained. But, on the other hand, if a poet chooses six key words or ideas or images, then they become vitally important throughout the poem and the accomplished poet can explore in great detail the important relation among all six. The six key words in Elizabeth Bishop's 'Sestina' are: house; grandmother; child; stove; almanac; tears, and many of these are highly charged, significant words in themselves. They become even more powerful in the context of what we know of Bishop's parents and early childhood. This poem was originally titled 'Early Sorrow'.

Line 5 almanac: a register of the days, weeks, months of the year, with astronomical events, anniversaries *et cetera*.

Line 7 equinoctial: at the time of the autumn equinox.

Line 37 inscrutable: that which cannot be searched into and understood.

Questions

1. Having read the poem through a number of times, study the end word in every line. What is the effect of this? How does Bishop convey sorrow in 'Sestina'?

2. The sestina is a very strict poetic format. Try writing one yourself. What do you learn from the exercise?

3. The poem offers a view of the world from a child's perspective. What details are being pieced together in the child's mind? How can you tell that things are being seen from a child's point of view?

4. Of the six key words in the sestina, which would you consider more important? Give reasons for your choice.

5. The almanac becomes a sinister presence – it 'hovers'. What does this poem say about the passing of time? Why do you think Bishop uses the present tense throughout?

6. Choose any one example of very ordinary language (e.g. 'It's time for tea now') and one example of unusual language and comment on both.

7. What is the significance of the child's drawing in stanza 5? Why does the child draw 'another inscrutable house'?

8. What image of the grandmother emerges from the poem?

9. Discuss what is said and what is left unsaid in this poem.

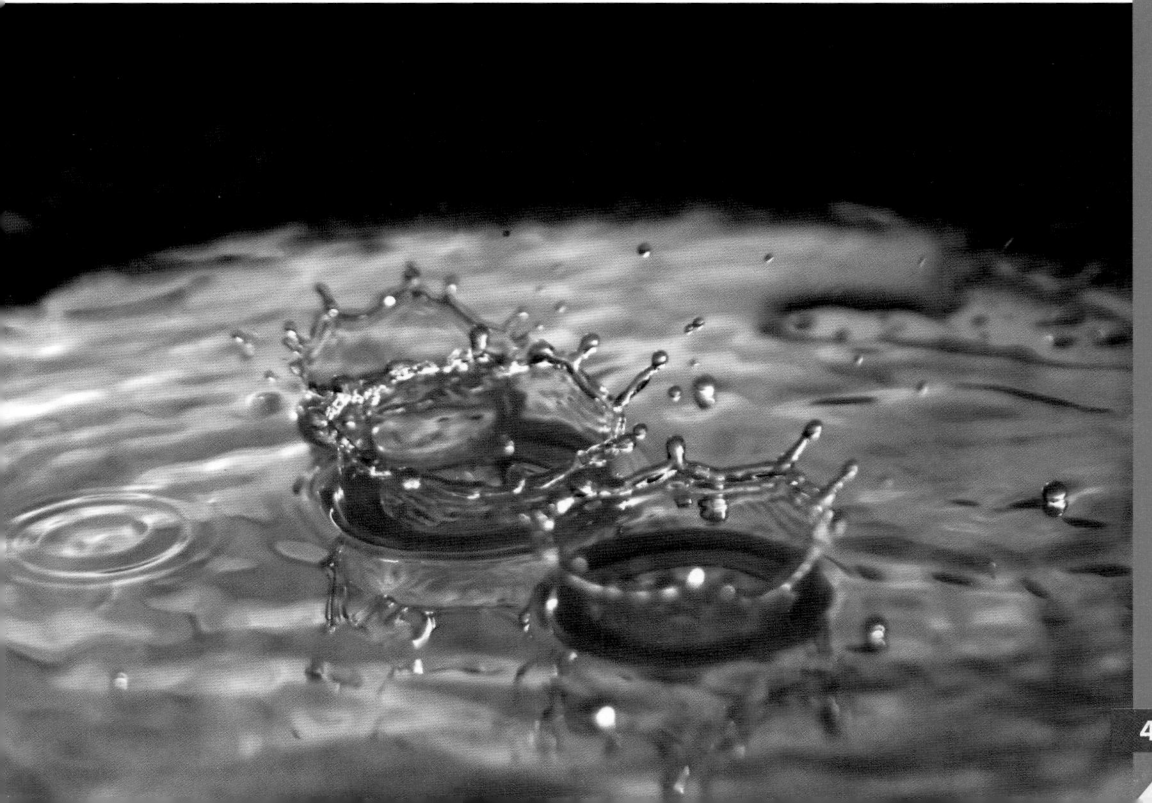

First Death in Nova Scotia

In the cold, cold parlor
my mother laid out Arthur
beneath the chromographs:
Edward, Prince of Wales,
with Princess Alexandra,
and King George with Queen Mary.
Below them on the table
stood a stuffed loon
shot and stuffed by Uncle
Arthur, Arthur's father.

Since Uncle Arthur fired
a bullet into him,
he hadn't said a word.
He kept his own counsel
on his white, frozen lake,
the marble-topped table.
His breast was deep and white,
cold and caressable:
his eyes were red glass,
much to be desired.

'Come,' said my mother,
'Come and say good-bye
to your little cousin Arthur.'
I was lifted up and given
one lily of the valley
to put in Arthur's hand.
Arthur's coffin was
a little frosted cake,
and the red-eyed loon eyed it
from his white, frozen lake.

Arthur was very small.
He was all white, like a doll
that hadn't been painted yet.
Jack Frost had started to paint him
the way he always painted
the Maple Leaf (Forever).
He had just begun on his hair,
a few red strokes, and then
Jack Frost had dropped the brush
and left him white, forever.

The gracious royal couples
were warm in red and ermine;
their feet were well wrapped up
in the ladies' ermine trains.
They invited Arthur to be
the smallest page at court.
But how could Arthur go,
clutching his tiny lily,
with his eyes shut up so tight
and the roads deep in snow?

Glossary

Title First Death: not only does the phrase suggest Bishop's first experience of death, but also the death of the very first person to die in the province of Nova Scotia.

Line 3 chromographs: pictures obtained by means of chromo-lithography – a method of producing coloured pictures by using stones with different portions of the picture drawn upon them in inks of different colours, so arranged as to blend into the complete picture.

Line 4 Edward: (1841–1910) Prince of Wales, eldest son of Queen Victoria and Prince Albert, later Edward VII.

Line 5 Alexandra: beautiful Danish Princess who married Edward VII in 1863.

Line 6 King George with Queen Mary: George V (1865–1936) and Mary (1867–1953), Queen consort of George V.

Line 8 loon: bird, the great northern diver.

Line 14 kept his own counsel: keeps to oneself secret opinions or purposes.

Line 28 frosted: iced.

Line 36 Maple Leaf: symbol of Canada. 'Maple Leaf Forever' is a phrase from the Canadian national anthem.

Line 42 ermine: a white fur (from the stoat's winter coat in northern lands).

Line 46 page: a boy attendant.

'First Death in Nova Scotia' was first published in *The New Yorker*, 10 March 1962, and was included in her third collection, *Questions of Travel*, in the section entitled 'Elsewhere'. The poem remembers a moment in Bishop's childhood, but she didn't write the poem until she was in her fifties. Elsewhere, Bishop wrote of other early deaths, many of them in Nova Scotia.

'First Death in Nova Scotia' remembers the winter funeral of Bishop's cousin Arthur (whose real name was Frank) circa 1914, when Bishop was almost four. It was first published when Bishop was fifty-one.

Questions

1. What is suggested by the title of this poem? How does it capture a child's experience, a child's way of thinking?
2. In this poem, Bishop is remembering a winter funeral of a cousin almost half a century before. What details of the experience are being remembered here? How does Bishop give the sense of a child's confused mind? In your answer, you should discuss the significance of repetitions, confusions and connections.
3. Religion plays no part in the death of little cousin Arthur as it is described in this poem. What is the significance of the royal personages? Consider the colours and their clothes in your answer, quoting from the text to support your answer.
4. Identify and list all the references that give the poem a chilling quality.
5. How would you describe the speaker's mood in the closing stanza? What details help to create that mood? Do you think death is seen here as mysterious and frightening?
6. Compare the speaker's view of 'my mother' and 'Uncle Arthur' with the other adults mentioned in the poem – the figures in the chromographs.

In the Waiting Room

In Worcester, Massachusetts,
I went with Aunt Consuelo
to keep her dentist's appointment
and sat and waited for her
in the dentist's waiting room.
It was winter. It got dark
early. The waiting room
was full of grown-up people,
arctics and overcoats,
lamps and magazines.
My aunt was inside
what seemed like a long time
and while I waited I read
the *National Geographic*
(I could read) and carefully
studied the photographs:
the inside of a volcano,
black, and full of ashes;
then it was spilling over
in rivulets of fire.
Osa and Martin Johnson
dressed in riding breeches,
laced boots, and pith helmets.
A dead man slung on a pole
— 'Long Pig,' the caption said.
Babies, with pointed heads
wound round and round with string;
black, naked women with necks
wound round and round with wire
like the necks of light bulbs.
Their breasts were horrifying.
I read it right straight through.
I was too shy to stop.
And then I looked at the cover:
the yellow margins, the date.

Suddenly, from inside,
came an *oh!* of pain
— Aunt Consuelo's voice —
not very loud or long.
I wasn't at all surprised;
even then I knew she was
a foolish, timid woman.
I might have been embarrassed,
but wasn't. What took me
completely by surprise
was that it was *me*:
my voice, in my mouth.
Without thinking at all
I was my foolish aunt,
I — we — were falling, falling,
our eyes glued to the cover
of the *National Geographic*,
February, 1918.

I said to myself: three days
and you'll be seven years old.
I was saying it to stop
the sensation of falling off
the round, turning world
into cold, blue-black space.
But I felt: you are an *I*,
you are an *Elizabeth*,
you are one of *them*.
Why should you be one, too?
I scarcely dared to look
to see what it was I was.
I gave a sidelong glance
— I couldn't look any higher —
at shadowy gray knees,
trousers and skirts and boots

and different pairs of hands
lying under the lamps.
I knew that nothing stranger
had ever happened, that nothing
stranger could ever happen.
Why should I be my aunt,
or me, or anyone?
What similarities –
boots, hands, the family voice
I felt in my throat, or even
the *National Geographic*
and those awful hanging breasts —
held us all together
or made us all just one?
How — I didn't know any
word for it — how 'unlikely'...
How had I come to be here,
like them, and overhear
a cry of pain that could have
got loud and worse but hadn't?

The waiting room was bright
and too hot. It was sliding
beneath a big black wave,
another, and another.

Then I was back in it.
The War was on. Outside,
in Worcester, Massachusetts,
were night and slush and cold,
and it was still the fifth
of February, 1918.

Glossary

Line 1 Worcester, Massachusetts: where Elizabeth Bishop was born on 8 February 1911.

Line 2 Consuelo: Aunt Florence in real life.

Line 9 arctics: an American expression for waterproof overshoes/galoshes.

Line 21 Osa and Martin Johnson: a well-known and popular husband and wife team of explorers and naturalists; Osa Johnson (1894–1953) and Martin Johnson (1894–1937) wrote several travel books.

Line 23 pith helmets: sun helmets made from dried pithy stemmed swamp plant.

Line 25 'Long Pig': the name given by Polynesian cannibals to a dead man to be eaten.

Line 53 February 1918: this poem, though first published in 1971, was written in 1967. She included it in a letter to her friend, the American poet Robert Lowell. The setting of the poem is precisely dated – 5 February 1918 – 'three days and you'll be seven years old' – she writes in lines 54–55. Bishop waited 49 years before she wrote about the experience.

Line 61 Elizabeth: this is the first poem in which Elizabeth Bishop names herself.

Though it remembers and recalls a moment from 1918, Elizabeth Bishop did not write so directly about early childhood until she was in her fifties.

Questions

1. What does the title suggest? Can it be interpreted in different ways?

2. Like 'First Death in Nova Scotia', 'In the Waiting Room' is a poem, also written in her fifies, where Elizabeth Bishop recalls a moment from early childhood, a very precise moment in this instance: 5 February 1918. What does the adult remember of her childhood in the opening lines of the poem?

3. Prompted by her reading of the *National Geographic*, the location of the poem shifts (at line 17) to an altogether different and unfamiliar world. Describe what the young Elizabeth Bishop reads and sees and discuss her reaction to it.

4. What does the young girl think of her aunt? Why? Consider the women in the poem – Aunt Consuelo, Osa Martin, the black, naked women, the women in the waiting room.

5. Why does Bishop write 'I — we — were falling, falling'. Why does she think that she becomes her foolish aunt? And why 'foolish'?

6. In the poem's third section, why does the speaker focus on herself?

7. In the poem as a whole, 'I' is used twenty-six times. Considering that in some of Bishop's poems the personal pronoun is never used, why is it used so often here?

8. What do you think is meant by lines 72–74: 'I knew that nothing stranger/ had ever happened, that nothing/ stranger could ever happen.'

9. Discuss this poem as an exploration of childhood and adulthood. Use the text to support your answer.

10. Of the ten poems by Elizabeth Bishop on your course, which one is your favourite? Which one do you admire most? Give reasons for your answer.

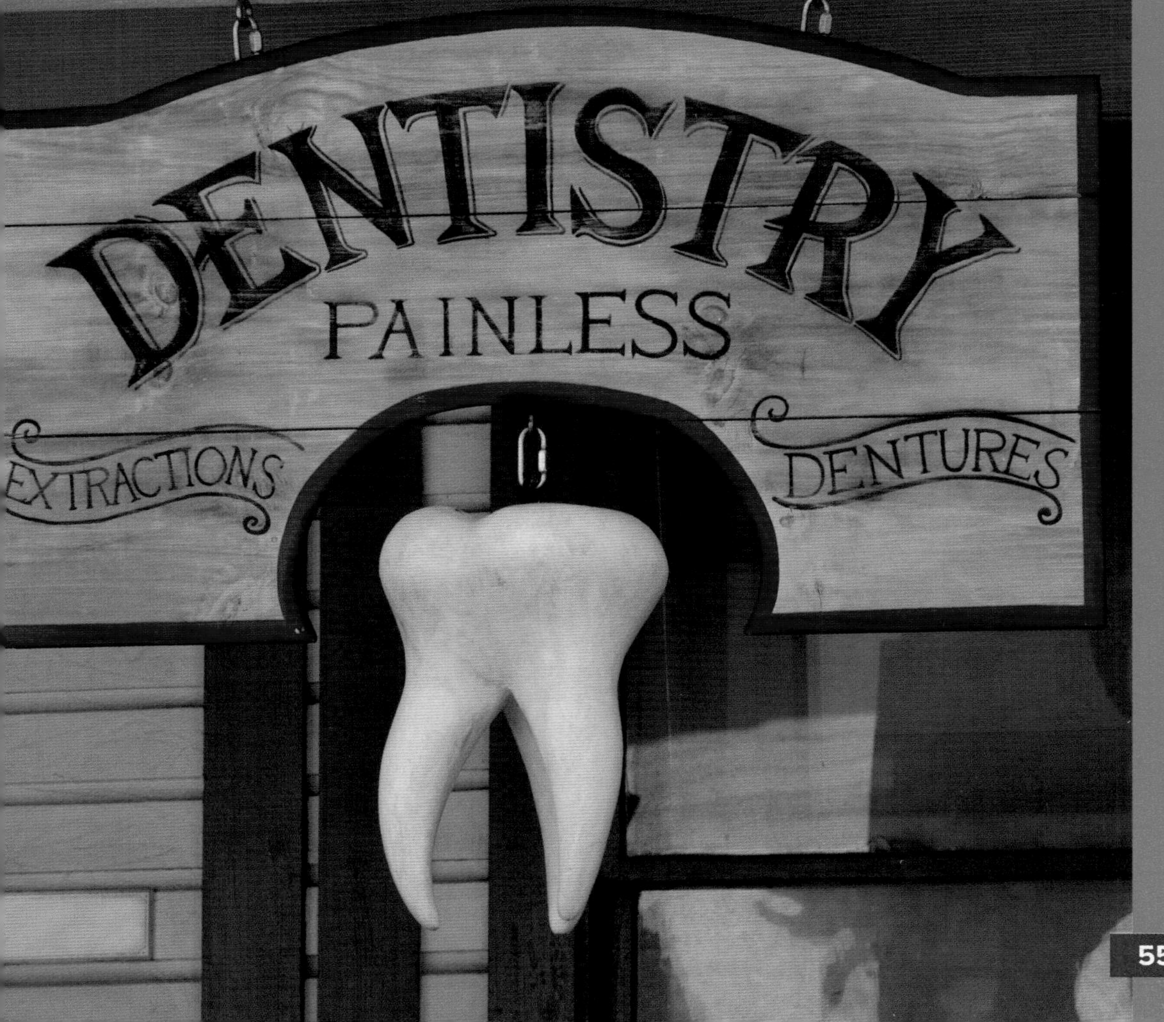

General Questions

A. 'Bishop, in her poetry, writes about the familiar and the unusual and does so in an interesting and unusual way.' Discuss this view, supporting your answer by relevant quotation from or reference to the poems by Elizabeth Bishop on your course.

B. 'The full complexity of childhood and adulthood is effectively evoked by Elizabeth Bishop in her poetry.' Discuss this view, supporting your answer by appropriate quotation from or reference to at least six of the poems by Bishop on your course.

C. 'In her poetry Elizabeth Bishop is a curious and sympathetic observer.' Discuss this view, supporting your answer by quotation from or reference to the poems by Bishop on your course.

D. 'In Elizabeth Bishop's poetry, description is never mere description; her poetry is a moral landscape, an emotional journey.' Discuss this statement, supporting your answer by relevant quotation or reference to the poems by Elizabeth Bishop on your course.

E. 'Bishop's poetry through both natural speech rhythms and formal patterns achieves an extraordinary immediacy and musical quality.' Discuss this view, supporting your answer by reference to the poems by Bishop on your course.

F. Discuss how Bishop uses images from Nature (water, fire, snow, for example) in her poetry, supporting your answer with reference to or quotation from the poems by Bishop on your course.

G. Randall Jarrell, the American poet, said of Elizabeth Bishop's work: 'all of her poems have written underneath, "I have seen it"'. Discuss what Bishop sees and explores in her poetry and how her descriptions and insights are vividly conveyed. You should refer to the poems on your course in your answer.

H. Bishop, according to Craig Raine, has 'a plain style in which the images appear like sovereigns'. Would you agree with this estimate of Elizabeth Bishop's poetry in the light of your reading the poetry by Bishop on your course? Support your answer with suitable quotation or reference to the poems.

I. Bishop herself said that 'I like painting probably better than I like poetry'. Discuss the painterly qualities of Elizabeth Bishop's work. In your answer you should refer to or quote from the poems by Bishop on your course.

J. 'Elizabeth Bishop's poems are not poems that begin with conclusions nor do they reach conclusions and yet we learn a great deal from them.' Would you agree with this statement? Support your answer by relevant quotation or reference to the poems by Bishop on your course.

K. Bishop, in her poetry, 'asks us to focus not on her but with her.' Would you agree with this statement? Support your answer with suitable quotations or reference to the poems by Bishop on your course.

Critical Commentary

The Fish

Elizabeth Bishop loved Florida and settled in Key West between 1939 and 1948. There Bishop discovered her love of fishing and, days after pulling in a sixty-pound amberjack, she began recording in her notebook descriptions which would later become part of her poem 'The Fish'. In Brett Millier's words, it is a poem of 'remarkable clarity and straightforwardness'. The form of the poem is the trimeter line interspersed at times by the dimeter. This is a form often suited to storytelling.

The fish of the poem is the enormous Caribbean jewfish which Bishop caught at Key West. Though the opening line is direct, 'I caught a tremendous fish', the adjective adds interest and excitement immediately. The fish isn't just described as 'large' or 'huge', though it is both. Instead, Bishop chooses the more powerfully subjective word 'tremendous', meaning immense and something that causes one to tremble. That first sentence is almost matter-of-fact:

> I caught a tremendous fish
> and held him beside the boat
> half out of water, with my hook
> fast in the corner of his mouth.

Yet it is 'my hook'. That detail, along with 'half out of water' (the fish is out of his element, between worlds) and 'fast', adds to the dramatic quality of the opening lines.

The focus shifts with the second sentence, line 5, 'He didn't fight', from Bishop to the fish, from fisher to the thing caught. Now we are told something about this fish and the personality which the poet attributes to it.

> He hadn't fought at all.

The fish submitted. The description of it as a 'grunting weight' is the first of many vivid pictures:

> He hung a grunting weight,
> battered and venerable
> and homely.

'Grunting', 'battered' and 'homely' (meaning, in American English, plain-looking) capture the exhausted and ugly state of the fish, but then Bishop's use of 'venerable' casts a different light on things. It means both aged looking and worthy of reverence.

Bishop is an extraordinary observer. The fish, once caught, is not just cast aside. She looks at it in great detail. Line 9 begins this thorough examination and observation of the fish:

> Here and there
> his brown skin hung in strips
> like ancient wallpaper:
> shapes like full-blown roses
> stained and lost through age.

Throughout the poem there is a very definite sense of Bishop as participant and observer: 'I caught', 'I thought', 'I looked', 'I stared and stared', but the poem is so much more than a matter-of-fact account of catching a fish. The fish intrigues her; it fascinates and frightens her, teaching her something about the fish and something about herself.

The simile in line 14, 'like full-blown roses', is a beautiful image, even if the shapes on the fish are 'stained and lost through age'. Here the fish becomes less 'homely' but, as Bishop looks more closely, a less attractive aspect of this fish is revealed:

> He was speckled with barnacles,
> fine rosettes of lime,
> and infested
> with tiny white sea-lice,
> and underneath two or three
> rags of green weed hung down.

These physical details are such that the texture (speckled, infested, rags) and the colours (lime, white, green) vividly help to create the complete picture.

The fish exists between the two elements of air and water: 'his gills were breathing in/the terrible oxygen'. The fish will die if its gills drink in the air, not water, and the gills are 'frightening': they are 'fresh and crisp with blood', they 'can cut so badly'.

In line 27, there is a shift in emphasis signalled by the phrase 'I thought'. Here Bishop imagines the insides of the fish, that aspect of the fish invisible to the fisherman or fisherwoman. By speaking now of

the coarse white flesh
packed in like feathers,
the big bones and the little bones,
the dramatic reds and blacks
of his shiny entrails,
and the pink swim-bladder
like a big peony.

we have a sense of the whole fish, outside and inside. The image of the feathers, the use of 'little', the colours red, black and pink signal Bishop's sympathetic imaginative response.

The 'big peony' is a startling and beautiful image. The guts of a fish are not often viewed in this delicate, imaginative manner. And this peony image sends us back to line 14, where the fish's skin was also described in terms of flower imagery – the shapes of full-blown roses.

In some respects, the fish is familiar – his skin is compared to 'ancient wallpaper' – but the fish is also 'infested', 'coarse' and 'weapon-like'. She admires him, but she also recognises something disgusting in the fish. Yet the fish is ugly only to the careless observer; Bishop recognises that the fish is beautiful too.

When, in line 34, Bishop tells us that she 'looked into his eyes', a more immediate relationship between the poet and the fish is being established. The captor is now looking straight into the eyes of the captive. The eyes of the fish are then described in typical Bishop style: a style which seems objective at first but in fact reveals Bishop's unique and subjective eye. First, the eyes are described in terms of size, shape, colour:

his eyes
which were far larger than mine
but shallower, and yellowed.

Then we are given more detailed imagery; the irises are

backed and packed
with tarnished tinfoil

and even this image is overlain with another image – the image of the irises

seen through the lenses
of old scratched isinglass.

The fish does not return her look, her stare. The eyes, we are told,

shifted a little, but not
to return my stare.

The fish not looking, not returning Bishop's stare, suggests the separateness, the independence, the dignity and yet the vulnerability of the fish. When the stronger captures the weak, it does not mean that the weaker one surrenders everything.

As in much of Bishop's poetry, the writing is such that, as we read through the poem, it is as if we are reading her thoughts directly as they are being formed.

The use of the dash at line 43 (she also uses the dash elsewhere in the poem at lines 24, 49 and 74) suggests a considered, explanatory addition; it indicates Bishop's attempt at getting it right. She has spoken of how the eyes shifted slightly and then we are given the further explanation or clarification:

> – It was more like the tipping
> of an object toward the light.

'I caught' (line 1), 'I thought' (line 27) and 'I looked' (line 34) have already marked certain stages in the poem. Now, with line 45, we have a new development: Bishop tells us that

> I admired his sullen face,
> the mechanism of his jaw.

Sullen is not a quality usually or often admired, but Bishop attributes a resolute quality to the fish and senses a gloomy and unresponsive state. It is at this point that she mentions how she saw 'five pieces of fish-line', each one indicating a former struggle and unsuccessful catch. The struggle was powerful and determined, and the fish still bears the evidence to prove it:

> A green line, frayed at the end
> where he broke it, two heavier lines,
> and a fine black thread
> still crimped from the strain and snap
> when it broke and he got away.

Here the adjectives and the verbs achieve the convincing effect: frayed, broke, heavier, crimped, broke, got away – that of a long, determined struggle. This fish has had an interesting and vivid past.

Bishop is clearly impressed. She sees the hooks as victory medals, while the gut lines are like the ribbons attached to such medals and they form a five-haired beard of wisdom. The fish, personified, has survived the wars – in this instance the fight with the fisherman's hook.

Earlier in the poem (line 46), Bishop has spoken of 'the mechanism of his jaw'; in line 64 we read of the fish's aching jaw. Bishop has become more engaged with the plight of this tremendous, battered and venerable fish. There is also, of course, the sense of the fish as male, as conqueror – it has battled with the hook and won. Now it is well and truly caught, but Bishop, female, does not play conqueror, as the last line of the poem indicates.

All the details so far lead us to the poem's conclusion. The second last sentence begins with the line 'I stared and stared'. It is a moment of triumph and victory; Bishop speaks of how

> victory filled up
> the little rented boat.

Everything seems transformed. The boat is 'little' and 'rented': nothing remarkable there. The fish, however, was 'tremendous' and 'victory' seems to belong to Bishop for having caught the fish, but also to the fish itself for having survived five previous hooks.

She mentions no other person in this poem; Bishop, it would seem, is alone in the boat. One person in a little boat floating on the sea conjures up a small scene, but the feeling which she is experiencing is an expansive feeling, a feeling which begins within and spreads to embrace and include the very ordinary details of the boat. 'The 'pool of bilge', the 'rusted engine', 'the bailer', 'the sun-cracked thwarts', 'the oarlocks', 'the gunnels' are transformed. In the pool of bilge at the bottom of the boat, Bishop notices where oil had 'spread a rainbow'. And that rainbow spreads everywhere

> – until everywhere
> was rainbow, rainbow, rainbow!

The poem's final line is one of the shortest sentences in the poem. By the poem's end, we ask what has happened between line 1 ('I caught a tremendous fish') and line 76. 'And I let the fish go' is not surprising. The word 'and' suggests that everything has led to this conclusion.

Bishop's use of rhyme in the final couplet (rainbow/go; elsewhere in the poem she prefers to use internal rhymes) also adds to the mood of exultation with which the poem ends:

> – until everything
> was rainbow, rainbow, rainbow!
> And I let the fish go.

This is the moment of epiphany and revelation, a visionary moment. (An *epiphany* is an extraordinary moment of heightened awareness, insight and understanding.)

The poem not only describes the fish, but also tells us a great deal about Elizabeth Bishop. The poet Randall Jarrell admired this poem for its moral quality.

The speaker sets out to catch a fish: it is a battered creature and in the end the fish is let go. The fish has escaped the hook five other times – the 'five big hooks' have 'grown firmly in his mouth' to remind us, but this time it is literally being let off the hook. Bishop admires the fish for its individual self; as the American writer and literary critic David Kalstone observed, 'victory belongs both to the wild survivor and his human counterpart'.

Bishop's 'The Fish' can also be seen as an allegorical poem: in other words, it gives us a narrative that can be understood symbolically or at a level other than the literal or actual one. It is but one of several poems by Bishop which Andrew Motion has called 'arguifying, Metaphysical and fabling'. Between that opening and closing line, not only is there, in Craig Raine's words, an 'unhurried, methodical, humane' response to the fish but 'she pronounces a true but merciful verdict on our precarious existence'.

These closing lines can also be read as a reversal of the macho stance. American literature has memorable examples of the fisherman in search of the fish. Melville's great novel *Moby Dick* (1851) and Ernest Hemingway's *The Old Man and the Sea* (1952) reveal a man's determined and ambitious attempt to conquer. But this is not a poem about the fish that got away: 'I let the fish go'.

At The Fishhouses

There is almost something anti-poetic or non-poetic about the words 'At the Fishhouses'. But Elizabeth Bishop was to make and shape her poetry from what might be termed the very opposite of the traditional sources of poetic inspiration. 'Filling Station' and 'In the Waiting Room' are other such titles which suggest the apparently unpoetic. Fishhouses are functional buildings, reeking of fish. Fishhouses are also places linked with death in that all the fish stored and processed are dead. The fishhouses of the title are fishhouses on Cuttyhunk Island, Massachusetts, by the cold Atlantic, though the notebooks Bishop kept while at Lockeport Beach in Nova Scotia in 1946 also found their way into this poem.

The poem begins unassertively, almost apologetically:

> Although it is a cold evening
> down by one of the fishhouses
> an old man sits netting,
> his net, in the gloaming almost invisible,
> a dark purple-brown,
> and his shuttle worn and polished.

The only other person beside the poet is 'an old man'. He 'sits netting, / his net, in the gloaming almost invisible'. There are echoes of Wordsworth here, in that William Wordsworth often wrote about ordinary working people and the lives they lived against a background of 'the goings on of earth and sky'. The fisherman is a solitary figure. So too is Bishop.

The opening section of the poem describes the five fishhouses and her conversation with the old fisherman while he is waiting for a herring boat to come in. The language, though conversational, is also very musical. Within the opening lines, for example, are alliteration and internal rhyme, two of Bishop's favourite techniques. The long 'o' sound of 'although' is echoed in the word 'gloaming'; 'cold' and 'old' rhyme; the words 'brown', 'worn', 'strong', and 'run', together with 'sits', 'nets', 'purple' and 'polished', all add to this musical effect.

Feeling the cold, seeing the fisherman and smelling the codfish establish immediately a world created through the senses:

> The air smells so strong of codfish
> it makes one's nose run and one's eyes water

And again:

> The five fishhouses have steeply peaked roofs
> and narrow, cleated gangplanks slant up
> to storerooms in the gables
> for the wheelbarrows to be pushed up and down on.

These lines illustrate the music of poetry. In 'five' and 'fish. . .' the poet uses alliteration and assonance and the rhyming 'steep ly' and 'peak ed'; alliteration again with 'slant' and 'storerooms'. The 'up' of 'pushed up' echoes the 'up' at the end of the line two lines earlier and everything goes to create what seems both a very natural sounding utterance and a musical quality which is typical of Elizabeth Bishop.

The initial effect of the place on the poet is physical. Bishop, in lines 7 and 8, tells us that

> The air smells so strong of codfish
> it makes one's nose run and one's eyes water

but her use of 'one's' rather than 'my' makes it more impersonal. What the opening lines offer us is, according to Seamus Heaney, 'the slow-motion spectacle of a well-disciplined poetic imagination'. Everything is presented to us without fuss.

Line 13 announces that 'All is silver'. This is the cold opaque silver of the sea, the apparently translucent silver

> of the benches
> the lobster pots, and masts, scattered
> among the wild jagged rocks.

Such detail is characteristic of Bishop. She watches everything closely. In many of her poems, she will begin with a description (a particular place, a particular time, an object) and from description, through imagination, she moves towards understanding and insight.

What Seamus Heaney called Bishop's 'lucid awareness' is clearly at work in lines 21 and following:

> The big fish tubs are completely lined
> with layers of beautiful herring scales
> and the wheelbarrows are similarly plastered
> with creamy iridescent coats of mail,
> with small iridescent flies crawling on them.

Her eye picks out the tiny detail of the 'small iridescent flies' crawling on the silvered, rainbowed wheelbarrows. For Bishop there is a beauty here in the sensory details she describes. She uses the word 'beautiful' in line 22, and the 'creamy iridescent coats of mail' is an example of that beauty.

The poem's focus then moves, camera-like, from the minute, the flies in line 25, to the wide-angle shot captured in line 26:

> Up on the little slope behind the houses,
> set in the sparse bright sprinkle of grass,
> is an ancient wooden capstan,
> cracked, with two long bleached handles
> and some melancholy stains, like dried blood,
> where the ironwork has rusted.

The capstan, cracked and rusted, is a reminder of the work done over the years. This detail and precision is, yet again, giving us the exterior world. Bishop does not hurry us through the poem, though the poet's main preoccupation, or that which forms one of the poem's main themes (how to make sense of the world), is not yet arrived at.

Up until now, Bishop has been describing what she sees, but line 32 ('The old man accepts a Lucky Strike') marks the human encounter and conversation. Bishop enters into the poem in a more obvious way. The detail that the old man 'was a friend of my grandfather' creates a human and personal story. The final lines in this first section of 'At the Fishhouses' give the reader the factual, outward, public world:

> We talk of the decline in the population
> and of codfish and herring
> while he waits for a herring boat to come in.

And Bishop's own private observations:

> There are sequins on his vest and on his thumb.
> He has scraped the scales, the principal beauty,
> from unnumbered fish with that black old knife,
> the blade of which is almost worn away.

The old man in these four lines is described as expert at his task but one who is also coming to the end of his life. His 'blade is almost worn away'. The literary critic Bonnie Costello sees the fisherman as a divine agent. Bishop herself said of these four lines (37–40) that they came to her in a dream.

To see the fishscales as sequins is another example of Bishop's ability to bring a word with such specific connotations and associations (glittering ballgowns, glamour) and to give it a new life and appropriateness. The man, both times he is mentioned, is spoken of as old. The awareness of mortality is never explicitly stated, but, in the third section of the poem, Bishop confronts her own mortality.

Meanwhile, in the second section, lines 41–46, the picture is of the water's edge:

> Down at the water's edge, at the place
> where they haul up the boats, up the long ramp
> descending into the water, thin silver
> tree trunks are laid horizontally
> across the gray stones, down and down
> at intervals of four or five feet.

Bishop has shifted her focus from the details of the old man's hands (he is not mentioned again in the poem) and 'that black old knife' to that in-between world of land and sea:

> the place
> where they haul up the boats, up the long ramp
> descending into the water.

The phrase 'down and down' in line 45 suggests not only the angle of the tree trunks but the direction of the poem, in that Bishop, in the third and final section, goes deep beneath the surface of the moment, deep into her own consciousness and this leads her to a fuller understanding and awareness of her own aloneness and mortality.

Section 3 begins with the line:

> Cold dark deep and absolutely clear

Seamus Heaney refers to this line as 'a rhythmic heave which suggests that something other is about to happen'. Eavan Boland recognises its 'serious music', and we are reminded of its importance when the same line is repeated 13 lines later. The four adjectives present us with the chilling reality of the water of the North Atlantic, an 'element bearable to no mortal'. It is in this third section that the seal makes his appearance. In an earlier draft of this poem, Bishop speaks of seals; in the final draft of 'At the Fishhouses', the seal is solitary, just as the old man and Bishop herself are.

Bishop is drawn to this sea shore 'evening after evening', to this curious seal. In his element, the seal believes in total immersion and Bishop says that she too believes in it. Total immersion can refer to a baptism by water and this is why Bishop adds 'so I used to sing him Baptist hymns', but the phrase can also mean a state of deep absorption or involvement, a meaning which is also interesting in this context. The seal belongs to another world and a different world.

The seal appears in line 49 and disappears in 59, but it is more than a charming, distracting and delightful interlude.

> One seal particularly
> I have seen here evening after evening.
> He was curious about me. He was interested in music;
> Like me a believer in total immersion,
> so I used to sing him Baptist hymns.
> I also sang 'A Mighty Fortress Is Our God'.
> He stood up in the water and regarded me
> steadily, moving his head a little.
> Then he would disappear, then suddenly emerge
> almost in the same spot, with a sort of shrug
> as if it were against his better judgement.

Though Bishop here refers to religion and belief she finds no comfort or consolation there. God may be a fortress but one to which Bishop does not belong.

Seals belong to sea and land; they are often seen as ambiguous creatures. In the water, the seal is in its element, 'a believer in total immersion', and it allows Bishop to imagine more fully the element to which it belongs. Total immersion for Bishop is immersion of herself in knowledge, and what she imagines knowledge to be is this 'Cold, dark deep and absolutely clear' water before her.

Immediately after the seal disappears from the poem, Bishop repeats the line which began this third section:

> Cold dark deep and absolutely clear,

bringing us again to the more serious concerns of the poem, namely that, like the 'cold dark deep' water there are, in Eavan Boland's phrase, corresponding 'cold interiors of human knowledge'.

That passage in the poem from line 60 to the end marks a very different order of experience. The thinking within these lines is at a different level from the earlier part of the poem. Before Bishop is 'the clear gray icy water', like knowledge. Behind,

> ... Back, behind us,
> the dignified tall firs begin.
> Bluish, associating with their shadows,
> a million Christmas trees stand
> waiting for Christmas.

It has been suggested that the Christmas trees are behind her in more than one sense. These have been interpreted as the traces of Christianity which Bishop herself has put behind her. Here the Christmas trees are waiting not for Christ's birth, but to be cut down.

There is also the use of 'us' here, the only time Bishop uses it in the poem. The 'us' refers to Bishop, the seal and the old man, but it has been argued that she could also be including us, the readers, here.

It is only in this third section of 'At the Fishhouses' that Elizabeth Bishop uses the personal pronoun 'I'. What fascinates her and what makes her human is knowledge. She has seen the water 'over and over, the same sea' and it is

> icily free above the stones,
> above the stones and then the world.

The sea of knowledge is a familiar phrase. Bishop's sea of knowledge is cold, dark and painful.

The final section of the poem is more private and more difficult to grasp. Yet Bishop in this very passage speaks directly to the reader, using 'you' (line 71). The water is bitterly cold:

> If you should dip your hand in,
> Your wrist would ache immediately,
> your bones would begin to ache and your hand would burn
> as if the water were a transmutation of fire
> that feeds on stone and burns with a dark gray flame.
> If you tasted it, it would first taste bitter

> then briny, then surely burn your tongue.

Bishop herself makes her meaning clear. To dip into this bitterly cold water and to taste it

> is like what we imagine knowledge to be:
> dark, salt, clear, moving, utterly free.

Knowledge, the poet tells us, is 'drawn from the cold hard mouth / of the world, derived from the rocky breasts / forever'. Knowledge, in other words, hurts. The 'cold hard mouth' and 'the rocky breasts' are uncomfortable images. The source is part maternal, but Mother Nature here is cold and forbidding.

What began seemingly as an objective descriptive poem has become a personal and private poem. Yet, 'At the Fishhouses' is a poem in which the reader can enter into the experience and share the poet's understanding. When she writes 'It is like what we imagine knowledge to be', Bishop is speaking for herself, the reader and everyone.

What we know, our knowledge, is drawn from the past, but knowledge is also something which is ongoing, never static and flowing. Knowledge, as Bishop puts it in those closing lines, is

> forever, flowing and drawn, and since
> our knowledge is historical, flowing, and flown.

We have moments of insight and understanding that might enrich or unsettle us and we have witnessed one such moment in this poem. The moment is 'flowing', in that it belongs to the present, and it is 'flown', in that it becomes part of our past. As humans we are part of flux and we cannot hope to control or to stop it.

The poem ends with this heightened moment of insight. In *Elizabeth Bishop: An Oral Biography*, we learn that Bishop told her friend Frank Bidart that 'when she was writing it she hardly knew what she was writing, knew the words were right, and (at this she raised her arms as high straight above her head as she could) felt ten feet tall.'

The Bight

The poem begins with description and in fact most of the poem describes a place. Yet the poem is much more than a place-picture; it becomes a romantic meditation. The phrase 'it seems to me' (line 13) and the final line are the most personal, though in fact what Bishop chooses to describe and how she describes it reveals her personality everywhere.

The opening lines are both plain and sensuous, in that the bight is described in terms of sight, touch, smell and hearing. And though the place is neither remarkable nor beautiful, Bishop makes it interesting and almost beautiful through her choice and control of language.

The very first line – 'At low tide like this how sheer the water is' – achieves an immediacy with the phrase 'like this', and Bishop's sense of engagement or awe is expressed in the words 'how sheer the water is'. Here and elsewhere, Elizabeth Bishop often writes a line which is almost entirely composed of monosyllabic words (lines 1, 9, 16, 26, 33 are other examples in 'The Bight'). It is a spare, simple and strong style.

What is remarkable about these opening lines, and it is one of Bishop's identifying characteristics, is her ability to bring a particular place alive. Marl isn't just marl:

> White, crumbling ribs of marl protrude and glare

Details – the adjectives and verbs – give it a vivid presence.

The dry boats, the dry pilings and the water in the bight that doesn't wet anything create a very distinctive atmosphere. Bishop describes the colour of the water as 'the color of the gas flame turned as low as possible' and this accurate image is followed by the surreal when Bishop says:

> One can smell it turning to gas; if one were Baudelaire
> one could probably hear it turning to marimba music.

The use of 'one' here, not 'I', includes rather than excludes the reader, and yet the use of 'one' is more impersonal than 'I'. This imagined transformation of water 'turning to gas', 'turning to marimba music', involves the senses. Smell allows us to imagine water as gas; our sense of hearing can turn the water into vibrant jazzy sounds. As Bishop reminds us, this is a way of thinking or of viewing the world that can be found in Baudelaire's poetry. Unusual and marvellous connections are being made. Bishop herself, in lines 9 and 10, is now thinking in this way when she hears a Latin American dance music in the sounds of the dredging machine:

> The little ochre dredge at work off the end of the dock
> already plays the dry perfectly off-beat claves.

The poem is a busy one. There is a great deal of activity. Lines 11 to 19 describe the pelican and man-of-war birds. A phrase like 'humorous elbowings' catches the pelicans' movements; the man-of-war birds are also caught: they 'open their tails like scissors on the curves / or tense them like wishbones'.

The next section of the poem has sponge boats, the shark tails and the little white boats, but they are not simply listed. The sponge boats are 'frowsy', coming in 'with the obliging air of retrievers', and the words 'bristling' and 'decorated' give them energy; the shark tails are 'blue-gray' and are 'glinting like little plowshares'; and the damaged little white boats are 'like torn-open, unanswered letters'. In a letter to Robert Lowell, Bishop had written, 15 January 1948, that the harbour was a mess – boats piled up, some broken by a recent hurricane – and that it had reminded her a little of her desk. Here the image from the letter reappears in the poem, not as Bishop's untidy writing desk, but in the phrase 'old correspondences'.

'The bight is littered with old correspondences', but the personal detail of Bishop's own desk is made less personal and the word 'correspondences' also has the literary echo of Baudelaire's sonnet 'Correspondances'. The bight is not only a place that resembles a paper littered desk; it is also a place where interesting, unusual connections or correspondences can be found.

The poem ends with the sound of the dredger, first mentioned in line 9. The 'little ocher dredge' continues its digging. Bishop spoke of the pelicans crashing into the water and 'rarely coming up with anything to show for it'. The dredge comes up with something:

> Click. Click. Goes the **d**redge,
> and brings up a **d**ripping *jawful* of marl.
> All the untidy activity continues,
> *awful* but cheer*ful*.

The sounds here are spot on. First, the mechanical sharpness of the 'Click. Click.', each one given a definition of its own with those full stops. The sound contained in the phrase 'a dripping jawful of marl' is the sound of heavy wetness. And the movement of that line – 'and brings up a dripping jawful of marl' is awkward and staggered, just as the dredger's digger would be as it gouges out, scoops and lifts up the clayey, limey wet soil. Apart from rhythm and individual sounds, there is another music also, which Bishop captures in the use of alliteration, assonance and cross or slant rhyme. Look again. Listen.

> Click. Click. Goes the **d**redge,
> and brings up a **d**ripping *jawful* of marl.
> All the untidy activity continues,
> *awful* but cheer*ful*.

The second last line in the poem refers to all that is going on before her in the bight, but it could also be read as a description of life itself. Life goes on, but life can be random, chaotic, disorganised. It is a poem that she associates with her thirty-seventh birthday, and every birthday is a moment of natural reflection on the passing of time and the nature of one's life.

That famous last line, 'awful but cheerful', sums up much about Elizabeth Bishop. Towards the end of her life she herself asked that those words be inscribed on her tombstone in the Bishop family plot in Worcester, Massachusetts. The accepted and most usual meaning for 'awful' is 'very bad, terrible, unattractive', but there is also its original meaning of 'inspiring awe, solemnly impressive'. This bight and its untidy activity are not conventionally pretty. It has, of course, been the inspiration for this very poem. The first and more common interpretation of the word is probably the more valid in the context of the 'untidy activity' in the preceding line. Bishop has clearly enjoyed observing. Life does go on and it can be both 'awful' and 'cheerful'. Bishop does say 'awful but cheerful', suggesting perhaps that the birds, the 'frowsy sponge boats' and the dredger all continue their activity with good humour, as we should and must. It is perhaps the only way to go on.

The Prodigal

It is worth asking at the outset why Bishop should be drawn to such a figure as the prodigal; she often felt like an outsider, someone away from home, and, like the prodigal son of the poem, she also engaged in drinking bouts.

The structure of the poem consists of a double sonnet and the irregular but ordered rhyming scheme is as follows: abacdbcedfeggf

A different sound rhyme and a different rhyming scheme is used in stanza 2: abacdbecfedfgh. An identical rhyming scheme is used in the first six lines of each stanza. The American literary critic David Kalstone spoke of 'two nicely rhymed sonnets' and how the 'air of sanity' in the poem is what makes it frightening, 'its ease and attractiveness only just keeping down panic and fear'.

The poem, though based on the biblical story of the Prodigal Son, chooses to focus on the lowest and ugliest part of that man's life – his time minding pigs. The ugliness and unpleasantness is presented immediately in the opening line: 'The brown enormous odor' captures the colour and the impact of the stench. This is the world he knows now. It is 'too close', too close for comfort, and so close that he does not judge. Not judging in this context could mean he has lost all sense of a world other than this one. It could also mean that this man does not judge – in other words, he is not thinking whether he deserves this life or not. Later there will come a time when he will judge it wise or best to go home and ask his father for forgiveness, but Bishop is suggesting at this point that the world of the pigs is so overwhelming that he does not judge. The phrase 'he lived by' in line 1 can mean that the prodigal son lived next to this horrible smell or it could also be interpreted to mean that he lived by it in the sense that it allows him to survive. The presence of the pigs is there before us in the two details 'breathing and thick hair'.

The first part of the poem brings us within the pig shed. 'The floor was rotten; the sty / was plastered halfway up with glass-smooth dung.' The vivid ugliness of 'glass-smooth' is all the more effective in that 'glass-smooth' is more often associated with the surface of a calm, beautiful lake. That the dung is 'halfway' up the wall reminds us of its prevalence and liquid state.

Lines 5 to 8 focus on the pigs themselves, their heads, more specifically their eyes, their snouts. As everywhere in Bishop, the observations are exact: the eyes are 'light-lashed' and 'self-righteous'. Who gives the 'cheerful stare' – the pigs or the prodigal? The dash at the end of line 6 suggests that the stare belongs to the pigs' eyes and that the pigs even stare in a cheerful manner at the 'sow that always ate her young'. The 'always' is frightening. Whether it is intentional or not, line 7 does prompt the reader to consider this sow's behaviour towards its offspring and the comparison between that and the subsequent attitude of the father towards his prodigal son.

The pigs follow their carer and, even though he feels sickened by it all, something eventually ('till' – line 8) in the prodigal causes him to offer a gesture of comfort or affection:

> sickening, he leaned to scratch her head.

In line 9, we are given a sense of the prodigal's meaningless life and secret drinking bouts but something else, something other, is also introduced. Bishop reminds us that there is a world beyond the pigsty. There is the sunrise, and the morning sun transforms the ordinary and everyday. In this instance, the barnyard mud is glazed with red. Earlier in line 4 we read that the ugly smelly pigsty walls were glazed with dung; here the mud and the puddles are made beautiful by the sunrise and, seeing them, the heart seems to be reassured.

Such a moment of passing beauty sustains him in his suffering and loneliness and exile:

> And then he thought he almost might endure
> his exile yet another year or more.

The use of 'But' at the beginning of line 9 indicates hope. And Bishop also uses 'but' to begin the second section of 'The Prodigal', this time to signal a change of direction.

> But evenings the first star came to warn.

Perhaps Bishop is using 'star' here as a signal of fate or destiny. If it is spoken of in terms of warning then the prodigal is being told that he must act or make decisions. Then follows such a comforting picture of order and safety (the farmer tending to his cows and horses and seeing that they are safe for the night) that

Bishop speaks of it in terms of it being

> safe and companionable as in the Ark.

Lines 18 and 19 give only some details of the inside of the barn in lantern light:

> beneath their overhanging clouds of hay,
> with pitchforks, faint forked lightnings, catching light,
> yet these few details allow the reader of the poem to picture it clearly.

'Clouds of hay' and the words 'safe and companionable' suggest warmth and a dry place, a contrast with the wet, dung-covered pigsty where the prodigal works. Line 21 is one sentence. It returns us to the world of the pigs and gives us both their vulnerability – 'their little feet' – and their ugly side – they snored.

The farmer shuts the barn door and goes home, but Bishop, imagining the life of the prodigal, never speaks of him as having a home separate from the animals. The farmer's lantern is observed: its light 'laid on the mud' forms a moving or 'pacing aureole', and this interpretation of light on mud is similar to the earlier lines in which the early morning sun colours the mud and puddles. The lantern light becomes an aureole or halo and this too, like the glazed mud in stanza 1, sustains him.

We are given another very vivid description of the prodigal at work before the poem ends. It is as if the time spent among the pigs is so long and the drudgery so great that Bishop returns to it again to remind us of its awfulness. With

> Carrying a bucket along a slimy board,
> he felt the bats' uncertain staggering flight

we are once again in the wet and smelly dark. The prodigal's private, inner self is spoken of in terms of 'shuddering insights'. We know from the biblical story what he is thinking, what conclusions he is reaching. These insights are 'beyond his control, / touching him'. This is the disturbed, aware Prodigal Son. But Elizabeth Bishop does not give us a simple, quick ending. St. Luke says 'And when he came to himself. . .'. Bishops charts the journey towards that difficult decision with words such as 'shuddering', 'touching him' and the final sentence in the poem. Here again she uses 'But' with great effect; it wasn't an easy or sudden decision:

> But it took him a long time
> finally to make his mind up to go home.

The final word resonates particularly because the word does not hark back to an obvious rhyme and because of what it implies within the poem as a whole. The loner, outsider, exile is returning to the place where he will be forgiven and loved.

Our knowing the ending of this biblical story adds to the poem's effect. However, our knowing that Bishop's mother was confined to a hospital for the insane and that Bishop herself grew up never having a home to go to also adds to the poem's power and effect.

In a letter to Robert Lowell, dated 23 November 1955, Bishop herself said that in 'The Prodigal' the technique was like a spiritual exercise of the Jesuits – where one thinks in great detail about how the thing happened. In another letter to U. T. and Joseph Summers, dated 19 October 1967, she tells of how 'The Prodigal' suggested itself. It 'was suggested to me when one of my aunt's stepsons offered me a drink of rum, in the pigsties, at about nine in the morning, when I was visiting her in Nova Scotia'.

Filling Station

'Oh, but it is dirty!' There is no introduction, no explanation. The title sets the scene and there is an immediacy in that opening line. The 'Oh' is spontaneous, the word 'dirty' given extra force with that exclamation mark. In this, as in many of Bishop's poems, we begin with a place and Bishop's description of it but, by the end of the poem, the experience has expanded to include wider, deeper issues. It is a poem that moves towards a wonderful and, in the end, an unsurprising last line.

The place is black, glistening and disturbing because it can also be dangerous:

> oil-soaked, oil permeated
> to a disturbing, over-all
> black translucency.
> Be careful with that match!

That final line in stanza 1 – 'Be careful with that match!' – is very ordinary and everyday. It certainly isn't a line one might associate with the language of poetry, but poetry is the living, speaking voice of the time. This opening stanza combines a language that is exact ('black translucency', for example) with an equally effective the language which may seem throwaway or commonplace, but which in the context of the poem is perfectly right.

A masculine place, usually, the filling station is given a human and domestic dimension in the second stanza. Father and sons give it a family feeling, as do details later in the poem such as the wicker sofa, the dog, the doily. The word 'dirty' occurs in the first three stanzas. The place is dirty, the father dirty, the sons dirty; the dog is a 'dirty dog'.

The dirt is fascinating. Every aspect of it is noted: the father's clothes are so black they resemble an

> oil-soaked monkey suit
> that cuts him under the arms

The 'several quick and saucy' sons are 'greasy'. 'All', Bishop tells us, is 'quite thoroughly dirty'.

Stanza 3 draws us in further with the question 'Do they live in the station?'

The comic books are the only things which seem to have retained their original, 'certain color'. Bishop's humorous eye suggests that the plant is oiled, not watered; the doily is 'dim', yet the plant on the doily-covered taboret fascinates her. The doily is improbable and unexpected, totally unnecessary, it could be argued, and it is dirty:

> Why, oh why, the doily?

This question is both simple and crucial. The doily reminds us that there are such things as creativity, grace, manners; it is a gesture towards elegance. Filling stations are naturally oily and dirty, and we've already seen how the father, the sons, the furniture and the dog are filthy. The doily is not as fresh as the day it was made, but it was created to decorate and to enhance. It was also most likely embroidered and crocheted by a woman, which may be another interesting consideration. A woman brought something special to this place and it is a woman who is reminding us of this in the very act of writing the poem.

The cans of oil have also been attended to in a special way:

> Somebody
> arranges the rows of cans
> so that they softly say:
> ESSO—SO—SO—SO
> to high-strung automobiles.

Whoever embroidered the doily, whoever waters the plant, whoever arranges the oil cans, is a 'somebody' never named. There is, it would seem, always someone doing small, almost unnoticeable little acts of kindness or acts which reflect our ability as humans to care, to shape, to bring order or to create. They are not always named and they do not need to be named, but the world is a better place because of them. Andrew Motion thinks the filling station 'the small theatre for a degraded life which stubbornly refuses to give up the effort to decorate and enjoy'. No matter where we live, we try to make it home.

The oil cans so arranged say musically and comfortingly 'SO-SO-SO', which was, according to Bishop herself, a phrase used to calm and soothe horses. This little detail adds a further interesting perspective to the poem. 'High-strung' automobiles refers to the tension and busyness of the cars' occupants more than the cars themselves, but the 'so-so-so' is doubly effective in that it was once used to comfort horses and now the phrase is read by those who sit in automobiles whose power is often described in terms of horse-power. The word 'high-strung' is also applied to thoroughbred horses; Bishop is describing the cars in terms of horses.

The last line is astonishing and wonderful and totally justified.

> Somebody loves us all.

It is a short sentence, a line complete in itself and gains the power of proverb. It is a wise, true, and marvellously comforting thought with which to end, all the more effective and powerful when we see how the dirty filling station, observed closely, reveals this truth and makes possible this insight.

Questions of Travel

The poem begins with the description of a place and its climate, movement and flux. Unlike, say, the opening lines of 'At the Fishhouses', Bishop's presence is more evident:

> 'There are too many waterfalls here'

This gives both a sense of the landscape and her opinion of it. Bishop speaks of her travels in the opening section. There are clouds and mountain tops and movement. A scientist would talk about the hydrological cycle, but Bishop, a poet, sees it differently. She is clearly engaged with the 'too many waterfalls'; the water is described as 'those streaks, those mile-long, shiny, tearstains' becoming waterfalls. This is what she sees on her travels, and she even imagines more and more water falling and waterfalls:

> the pressure of so many clouds on the mountaintops
> makes them spill over the sides in soft slow-motion,
> turning to waterfalls under our very eyes.

Not only is Bishop the traveller, the 'streams and clouds' (line 10) 'keep travelling, travelling' too. It is as if the mind cannot take everything in. This first section ends with yet another example of how Elizabeth Bishop can make us see:

> the mountains look like the hulls of capsized ships,
> slime-hung and barnacled.

In section 2, Bishop's mood, her preoccupation, becomes more complex and philosophical. Should we travel? Why do we travel? What if we were to stay at home? What right have we to be here in a strange, foreign place?

Section 2 is made up of nine sentences, eight of which end with question marks, and these questions become the questions of travel. First, there is the invitation to

> Think of the long trip home.

and then the sequence of eight questions.

> Should we have stayed at home and thought of here?
> Where should we be today?
> Is it right to be watching strangers in a play
> in this strangest of theatres?
> What childishness is it that while there's a breath of life
> in our bodies, we are determined to rush
> to see the sun the other way around?
> The tiniest green hummingbird in the world?
> To stare at some inexplicable old stonework,
> inexplicable and impenetrable,
> at any view,
> instantly seen and always, always delightful?

Bishop is clearly intrigued by the whole concept of travel and is disoriented and a little uneasy about it. She wonders, in line 18, if it is childishness that causes us 'to rush / to see the sun the other way round?' (Brazil being below the Equator). Her focus has been on landscape and the natural world, but people and their work are also included. The people are 'strangers in a play'; the old stonework is 'inexplicable'. Bishop is in a place and yet feels separate and outside of it.

The American academic Brett Millier thinks that 'Questions of Travel' is concerned with 'the limitations of one's knowledge and understanding of a foreign culture'. It is a poem that admits to difference: the view may be 'inexplicable and impenetrable', yet the traveller is forever looking. To the questions

> Oh, must we dream our dreams
> and have them, too?
> And have we room
> for one more folded sunset, still quite warm?

the answers are implied but never given. The traveller did not stay at home and think or dream of here. The dream became a reality. There is a human need to see for oneself. The traveller has not grown weary of collecting sunsets. The image is that of folded, ironed clothes being packed away in a suitcase.

Bishop reinforces this viewpoint in the third section, which begins:

> But surely it would have been a pity
> not to have seen the trees along the road,
> really exaggerated in their beauty,
> not to have seen them gesturing
> like noble pantomimists, robed in pink.

Here Bishop is clearly enthralled and captivated, as a child is at the pantomime. She notices and delights in the tiniest of details, such as the clacking sounds of the petrol pump attendant's clogs:

> the sad, two-noted, wooden tune
> of disparate wooden clogs
> carelessly clacking over
> a grease-stained filling station floor.

Bishop adds in brackets the observation that the clogs are imperfectly made:

> (In another country the clogs would all be tested.
> Each pair there would have identical pitch.)

Is this in praise of Brazil? She prefers the disparate music of these clogs to the perfectly made, perfectly pitched clogs of a more precise and efficient country. Such an observation and such a response is typical of Elizabeth Bishop. She can focus on the ordinary and the inconsequential and find them interesting and engaging. She is a poet who tells of things as they are.

In this third section, Bishop continues to give reasons to justify travel. She presents us with other enjoyed aspects of her journey: the music of the fat brown bird, the ornate, church-like, wooden songbird's cage, the pounding rain and the subsequent 'sudden golden silence'.

> – A pity not to have heard
> the other, less primitive music of the fat brown bird
> who sings above the broken gasoline pump
> in a bamboo church of Jesuit baroque:
> three towers, five silver crosses.

These are the details which Bishop notes and remembers, details which most tourists wouldn't notice, let alone remember, and it isn't a mere list. In this section we are shown how Bishop ponders the connection, if any, between the making of wooden clogs and the making of wooden cages. Why do these people put their efforts into ornate impractical objects, and not bother about perfecting the practical ones? It doesn't matter that the connection between clogs and cages is pondered 'blurr'dly and inconclusively' (she playfully blurs the very word blurr'dly). The form of the cage, with its 'weak calligraphy', encapsulates the colonized history of Latin American. The traveller who views the cage is seeing history.

She reveals herself to be good-humoured, curious, open-minded and tolerant when she writes:

> – Yes a pity not to have pondered,
> blurr'dly and inconclusively,
> on what connection can exist for centuries
> between the crudest wooden footwear
> and, careful and finicky,
> the whittled fantasies of wooden cages.
> – Never to have studied history in
> the weak calligraphy of songbirds' cages.
> – And never to have had to listen to rain
> so much like politicians' speeches:
> two hours of unrelenting oratory
> and then a sudden golden silence...'

Section 3 began with Bishop saying that 'it would have been a pity' not to have witnessed or experienced what she then describes, and each time a new aspect of her travels is added to the list, the phrase 'a pity' is repeated or implied: It would have been a pity 'Not to have had to stop for gas ...' (line 34); 'A pity not to have heard' (line 42); '– Yes, a pity not to have pondered' (line 47); 'Never to have studied ...' (line 53); '– And never to have had to listen to rain ...' (line 55).

The uncertainty of line 14, 'Should we have stayed at home and thought of here?', is now answered. And it is answered also in the final eight lines of the poem when Bishop imagines 'the traveller' (all travellers?) writing in a notebook, during 'a sudden golden silence', a philosophical musing on the nature of travel. There is no 'I' in this poem. Bishop has used 'we' five times already, and she also uses 'we' in the traveller's notebook, suggesting that the questions she has asked and the conclusions she has reached are shared with all travellers.

There is still some unease and some uncertainty in the traveller's notebook entry, despite the many convincing reasons given in section three in support and in praise of travel. The reference to the seventeenth-century French philosopher Blaise Pascal is a dramatic touch. Pascal was famous for staying at home. Elizabeth Bishop, his opposite, spent her life travelling, and 'Questions of Travel', dated 1965, when Bishop was in her mid fifties, asks questions which Bishop asked her entire life. She wonders whether the impulse or the need to travel is due to a lack of imagination:

> *'Is it lack of imagination that makes us come*
> *to imagined places, not just stay at home?'*

The imagined places, however, once visited, as we have seen from the poem, do not disappoint. This is what allows her to suggest (Bishop is never dogmatic):

> *'Or could Pascal have been not entirely right*
> *about just sitting quietly in one's room?'*

The italicised final lines, like section 2, consists of questions, and the poem 'Questions of Travel' appropriately ends with a question mark. There are eleven known drafts or versions of this poem and the statement in line 65:

> *the choice is never wide and never free*

originally read as 'the choice perhaps is not great . . . but fairly free', proving that Bishop changed her mind during the writing of this poem (like many Bishop poems it was written over a period of time). For the traveller the world seems varied and huge. Does one choose 'continent, city, country, society'? (line 63). Does one choose 'here, or there'? Is one still restricted?

> Con*tinent, city, country, society:*
> *the choice is never wide and never free.*
> *And here, or there... No. Should we have stayed at home,*
> *wher*ever that may be?

The placing of the word 'No' is important here, and the poem suggests that the restrictions need not invalidate the experience. The question 'Should we have stayed at home?' has already been answered.

Throughout this poem, there is the implied sense of a place called home, the place from which the traveller set out and to which the traveller returns. 'The Prodigal' also explores this idea. In Bishop's case, she lost home after home (an idea she writes about in her poem 'One Art'), and her final question in 'Questions of Travel' is shadowed by her own sense of homelessness. The speaker in the poem is a traveller. Beyond the questions of travel is the ultimate question of belonging:

> *'Should we have stayed at home,*
> *wherever that may be?'*

In Bishop's case, the question suggests that she has never felt at home.

The Armadillo

On the page, the structure and shape of 'The Armadillo' are ordered: ten four-lined stanzas. The rhyming scheme in the first stanza – abab – is not strictly observed throughout, but the second and fourth lines in each stanza rhyme.

The armadillo itself does not appear until line 30, and for most of the poem Bishop describes the balloon offerings associated with the religious festival. The balloons are 'frail, illegal', dangerous, fascinating and beautiful. Their delicacy is captured in a phrase such as 'paper chambers', and the simile 'like hearts' suggests that they are an expression of love.

From her house, Bishop watches the fire balloons rising towards 'a saint / still honored in these parts'. Bishop, though living in Brazil, is the observer, not the participant. The poem traces their movement as they move skywards, 'climbing the mountain height'. The balloons are offerings, forms of prayer, and they drift heavenwards. Bishop does not dwell on their religious source and symbolism, but their beauty is captured in stanza 3:

> Once up against the sky it's hard
> to tell them from the stars –
> planets, that is – the tinted ones:
> Venus going down, or Mars,
> or the pale green one.

They have become part of the night sky, the constellations where there is even a star group known as the Southern Cross. When she uses the phrase 'steadily forsaking us' in line 18, Bishop gives us a sense of our earth bound selves. The people who released these balloons watch them drift upwards and away. If we are forsaken, we are being abandoned or left behind. We cannot go with them. But they are also dangerous if caught in a downwind and line 21 introduces this other aspect:

> Last night another big one fell.
> It splattered like an egg of fire
> against the cliff behind the house.

The human world is threatened, as is the natural world. The house and its inhabitants, the owls, the armadillo and the rabbit are all threatened, and Bishop has seen the birds and animals suffer. 'Whirling', 'stained bright pink' and 'shrieked' all suggest confusion, pain and suffering. Fire that was once contained and distant has become destructive.

The armadillo makes its brief appearance in line 30: it is frightened and alone and can protect itself from almost everything, except fire. 'Glistening' and 'rose-flecked, head down, tail down' give the reader a vivid sense of the animal's presence. It has been suggested that the armadillo, a threatened creature on the edge of the human and the natural world, resembles the artist who has to discover a means of survival.

The owls, and the rabbit which appears suddenly in line 33, are even more vulnerable creatures. The birds flee their burning nest; the 'baby' rabbit, 'so soft!', is also frightened. Bishop's use of the dash in line 35 suggests that the rabbit is or will become 'a handful of intangible ash'; its eyes are 'fixed, ignited', yet she notices with surprise that the rabbit is 'short-eared'. The balloons have now become sources of threat and violence.

The last stanza is italicised, not only for emphasis and force:

> *Too pretty, dreamlike mimicry!*
> *O falling fire and piercing cry*
> *and panic, and a weak mailed fist*
> *clenched ignorant against the sky!*

These last four lines dismiss the earlier stanzas in a way, in that Bishop says that her descriptions of the fleeing animals are 'too pretty'. What the poem has presented to the reader so far is a 'dreamlike mimicry!'

Those closing lines emphasise the horrible reality:

> *O falling fire and piercing cry*
> *and panic*

Here, it is as if Bishop is questioning language and poetry itself; is poetry capable of conveying ugly, frightening reality? The italics and the exclamation marks in the final stanza add an urgency to the moment of suffering which has already been described in stanzas 7, 8 and 9. The final idea in the poem, which is that of

> *a weak mailed fist*
> *clenched ignorant against the sky!*

suggests both defiance and helplessness. The '*mailed fist*' could be taken to refer to the armadillo's coat of mail, its defensive armour. Here Bishop does not offer just the accurate, objective description of the armadillo. She has done that in lines 30 to 32. The last two lines of the poem describe the armadillo, but now from a different and sympathetic perspective – that of the armadillo itself. The animal is spoken of as clenching its weak mailed fist, but clenching it nonetheless. And it is 'clenched ignorant against the sky!' The word 'ignorant' in line 40 reminds us that the armadillo does not understand the origins of this threatening fire and, since fire is the one thing from which the armadillo's outer coat cannot protect him, we are asked perhaps to consider the objects of supposedly religious worship in another light.

The owls, the armadillo and the rabbit are all victims, but the armadillo is the most striking presence among the creatures mentioned. It is the armadillo that gives the poem its title and it is to the armadillo that Bishop, clearly moved, returns in that final stanza. These closing lines of the poem have also been interpreted as symbolic of an ignorant and victimised working class, society's underdog, and the attempt by the working classes to strike for and assert their rights.

Sestina

The first lines of the poem establish a mood. It is as if the world itself is in mourning: the September rain and the failing light suggest sorrow and dying; it is the dying of the year and the dying of the day, but what is at the heart of the stanza is the human sorrow of the grandmother holding back her tears. In Bishop's story 'In the Village', the grandmother is crying openly; in the poem, those tears are stifled.

The last word in the first line is the word 'house'. This being a sestina, the word will occur in every stanza and occur seven times in all; it is the word with which the poem ends. This house has a grandmother and child and, as Seamus Heaney points out, 'the repetition of grandmother and child and house alerts us to the significant absence from this house of a father and a mother'.

The scene in stanza 1 is part cosy and comfortable, part dark and painful. There is the grandmother sitting in the kitchen with the child. It is warm; they sit 'beside the Little Marvel Stove' and the grandmother is reading jokes from the almanac. However, the grandmother's laughter and talking hide her tears.

The speaker in 'Sestina' is the adult Bishop, but she records her own experience as if she were an observer at a play. Bishop also interprets what is going on. In stanza 2, for example, Bishop allows us to glimpse the workings of the child's mind.

There is a significant difference between the grandmother and the young girl: the grandmother thinks that her autumn tears and the rain beating on the roof were known about and recorded in the almanac. Sorrow and the autumn rain seem inevitable. This is experience. The grandmother

> thinks that her equinoctial tears
> and the rain that beats on the roof of the house
> were both foretold by the almanac...

Normality keeps returning to the poem. Lines 11, 12 and 13 are pictures of domestic ordinariness and harmony:

> The iron kettle sings on the stove.
> She cuts some bread and says to the child,
>
> *It's time for tea now...*

But then the child transfers the unwept tears of the grandmother to the drops, falling from the kettle on to the stove. As in 'First Death in Nova Scotia', the child's mind is attempting to connect and make sense of the world. In the Nova Scotia poem, the first person is used; here Bishop stands outside or apart from the experience by writing about herself and her childhood in the third person. The two people in the poem are never given personal names.

She knows that the grandmother has held back her tears and now the child

> is watching the teakettle's small hard tears
> dance like mad on the hot black stove,
> the way the rain must dance on the house.

To the child, it now seems as if the tears are everywhere and they are 'hard' tears; they 'dance like mad', and she imagines them dancing on the house. In these lines Bishop returns us again to the child's thinking, the child's inner world.

Line 17 switches back to the everyday and ordinary:

> Tidying up, the old grandmother
> hangs up the clever almanac
> on its string.

This domestic busyness and organisation indicates that life must go on, even if a life is overshadowed by great sadness. The almanac was said to have foretold this sorrow, in lines 7–10. In lines 19 and 20, the almanac is seen as a sinister presence, but this time it is not the child or the grandmother who thinks it, but Bishop, the adult poet.

> Birdlike, the almanac
> hovers half open above the child,
> hovers above the old grandmother
> and her teacup full of dark brown tears.

The future that the almanac represents hovers above child and grandmother. The tea in the teacup, like the water from the kettle, is described in terms of tears. Stanzas 2, 3 and 4 associate the ordinary things of the household with tears, but end with the business of the house. The 'tidying up' in stanza 3 and the building of the fire in stanza 4:

> She shivers and says she thinks the house
> feels chilly, and puts more wood in the stove.

Stanza 5 begins with a sense of inevitability and even the stove seems to have become a part of that inevitability:

> *It was to be,* says the Marvel Stove.
> *I know what I know,* says the almanac.

The italicised phrases are highly charged. The ordinary, familiar domestic world is no longer ordinary and familiar. The child withdraws by drawing an imaginary house, but that house is 'rigid' or tension filled and can only be reached by a 'winding pathway'.

> With crayons the child draws a rigid house
> and a winding pathway. Then the child
> puts in a man with buttons like tears
> and shows it proudly to the grandmother.

It is hardly straining the interpretation to see the presence of the man as a father figure; Elizabeth Bishop never knew her father. She, the child, does not shed any tears in the poem, but there are tears everywhere, even in the drawing.

The child is proud of her representation of a house, but the adult, in this instance the grandmother, the grown-up Elizabeth Bishop, and the reader, sees the drawing with a different understanding.

The grandmother is busy again while the little girl looks at the sun, moon and stars on the open pages of the almanac. She imagines 'little moons' fall secretly, and the description of these as tears reveals yet again the enquiring, puzzled, yet perceptive mind of the child. Reality and fantasy merge. Those same tears fall into the child's world of the flower beds.

The closing three lines tighten up: the six words focused on in the previous stanzas were each given a line of their own. Here, in the final stanza, the ideas which those same six words represent must be brought even closer:

> *Time to plant tears,* says the almanac.
> The grandmother sings to the marvellous stove
> and the child draws another inscrutable house.

What is past is past was how the literary critic David Kalstone interpreted those italicised words. The almanac, more often associated with future events, seems to declare the time of tears is over. The grandmother pretends to be cheerful in the same spirit in which she hid her tears in stanza 1. The child draws another house. The actual house in which the child lives with her grandparents is the only home she has really known. A child instinctively draws a house; it should be a familiar, comfortable and comforting place. But this house she draws is 'another inscrutable house'.

First Death in Nova Scotia

The poem 'First Death in Nova Scotia' is told from a child's point of view. The very title suggests this. It is as if no one had ever died in Nova Scotia before now. This is the child's first experience of death, and in the poem the child attempts to understand reality and, in doing so, makes confused, extraordinary, and sometimes almost fairytale connections. The fairytale element is most clearly seen, for example, when the child-speaker in the poem imagines that the royal presences in stanza 1 invite little Arthur in the final stanza to become 'the smallest page at court'. American academic Helen Vendler says that the poem 'goes steadily, but crazily, from little Arthur in his coffin to the royal pictures to the loon to Arthur to the child-speaker to the loon to Arthur to the royal pictures. This structure, which follows the bewildered eye of the gazing child trying to put together all her information (sense data, stories of an afterlife, and the rituals of mourning) is a picture of the mind at work.'

An elegy does not usually begin in such a stark manner, but in this poem it is the young uncomprehending child who speaks. It is as if Bishop can present us immediately with a grim picture. The repetition is chilling:

> In the cold, cold parlor
> my mother laid out Arthur

Bishop's mother is seldom mentioned in her poems, and she is mentioned here in a matter-of-fact way. The little body is spoken of in line 2, but the rest of the stanza describes the furnishings in the room. The royal presences lend the moment importance and dignity.

In line 7, the attention shifts to the stuffed bird on the table beneath the pictures. The stuffed loon, like Arthur, is dead. It has been

> shot and stuffed by Uncle
> Arthur, Arthur's father.

The room is 'cold, cold', and to the child observer it is as if everything has been frozen in time: the lifeless corpse, the still photographs, the stuffed loon. The use of repetition throughout the poem reflects the mind of a child attempting to make sense of the world it is describing.

In stanza 2 the child is wholly preoccupied with the bird, the violence of its death its silence, its cold stance and, contradicting everything else, its attractiveness ('caressable' and 'much to be desired' red glass eyes). Little Arthur is forgotten. Attention has shifted to the object:

> on his white, frozen lake,
> the marble-topped table.

The bird hasn't said a word since it was shot (nor of course has little Arthur since his death, but this is implied, never stated), and there is a sense of mystery, power and separateness in Bishop's phrase 'He kept his own counsel' in line 14. The child's mind works by association: an idea in stanza 1 recurs later; a phrase, 'deep and white', used once to describe the loon's breast, is later echoed in Bishop's description of the snow; and the red of the loon's eye recurs in the red of the Maple Leaf, little Arthur's red hair and the red royal clothes.

The child's gaze is broken by her mother's words:

> 'Come,' said my mother,
> 'Come and say good-bye
> to your little cousin Arthur.'

She is lifted up to place a lily of the valley in Arthur's hand. The poem's setting is the familiar, domestic world of the parlour, but death and the coffin turn the familiar into the strange. The mother asks the child to look on death and to put 'one lily of the valley' in her dead little cousin's hand. The coffin becomes in the child's mind 'a little frosted cake' and the loon is now seen almost as predator, as something alive:

> Arthur's coffin was
> a little frosted cake,
> and the red-eyed loon eyed it
> from his white, frozen lake.

Stanza 4 focuses on little Arthur. The language also marks the simplicity of childhood grappling with a first death:

> Arthur was very small.
> He was all white, like a doll
> that hadn't been painted yet.
> Jack Frost had started to paint him
> the way he always painted
> the Maple Leaf (Forever).

She imagines first that the body is like an unpainted doll, then that Jack Frost had 'started to paint him'. The child-speaker knows how Jack Frost always 'paints' the leaves red in autumn, specifically the maple leaf, and this thought is immediately connected with her being in Canada and the maple leaf as it is mentioned in the Canadian national anthem: 'the Maple Leaf (Forever).' The reference to the hair as red strokes/brush strokes is another indication of how the child's mind can process and transfer ideas: she imagines that hair on the white body has been painted red.

The 'Forever' associated with the Maple Leaf is the forever of Canadian patriotism.

The 'forever' in the last line of the stanza is the same word but with a different meaning; this time it signifies the finality of death:

> Jack Frost had dropped the brush
> and left him white, forever.

The poem ends with an imagined royal court, but there is no trace of a Christian or religious consolation. And the child invents this world, more fairytale than paradise; the mother does not offer one.

The cold is felt throughout the poem. Words such as 'cold, cold', 'white, frozen', 'marble-topped', 'white, cold', 'lily of the valley', 'frosted cake', 'white, frozen lake', 'all white', Jack Frost', 'white, forever' and the effect of repetition turn the parlour white and cold. But the last stanza brings warmth, pomp and ceremony:

> The gracious royal couples
> were warm in red and ermine;
> their feet were well wrapped up
> in the ladies' ermine trains.

Even the white of the ermine seems warm. The gracious presences of the two couples in the two pictures are warm, comfortable, welcoming. They invite little Arthur to join them; it is they who make possible his future.

> They invited Arthur to be
> the smallest page at court.

This, in the eyes of the observing child, is how and where little Arthur will live now that he has died.

In the closing lines, however, the speaker's fears return: Arthur is in his coffin. It is winter. How can Arthur escape from his coffin in the 'cold, cold parlor' and join the faraway royal court?

> But how could Arthur go,
> clutching his tiny lily,
> with his eyes shut up so tight
> and the roads deep in snow?

The details here ('clutching', 'tiny', 'tight', 'deep') suggest vulnerability, terror and fear. The final image in the poem is of Arthur, a child all alone in the world, incapable of reaching safety and a place he could call home.

Instead of heaven as Arthur's destination or Christian consolation, it is Bishop's imagination that makes possible and gives new life to the dead little boy; she imagines him, frightened, and wonders how he will travel 'roads deep in snow'.

Death is a powerful displacer. Of course there is a danger that biographical details will colour our reading of a poem too much, but the reader, realising that this poem was written by a woman whose father had died when she was eight months old and whose mother disappeared from her life when she was five, may see how fully 'First Death in Nova Scotia' reflects Bishop's uncomprehending childhood and her attempts to come to terms with absence and death.

In the Waiting Room

The poem begins with a place, a location, in this instance Elizabeth Bishop's own birthplace; it focuses on her place in the world and the distances between the personal world and the wider world beyond. There are references to 'in' and 'outside' throughout the poem.

In February 1918, Elizabeth Bishop was but a few days from her seventh birthday and the poem is spoken in the innocent, naive, unaffected voice of a seven year old. There is a matter-of-factness about it:

> In Worcester, Massachusetts,
> I went with Aunt Consuelo
> to keep her dentist's appointment
> and sat and waited for her
> in the dentist's waiting room.

The setting consists of unglamorous places: a waiting room suggests a form of displacement. In the waiting room one is neither here nor there. The ordinary world has been left behind: it is outside the door and can only be re-entered through that same door. The fact that it is a dentist's waiting room adds another dimension: waiting often involves tension, uneasiness and it often anticipates pain, but Bishop is not attending the dentist, merely accompanying her aunt. Later in the poem, a painful cry is heard from the dentist's room. The poem also explores how childhood can sometimes view adulthood harshly.

The scene is built up gradually. Bishop begins with town, state, waiting room, then the time of year.

Elizabeth Bishop sees herself as the odd-one-out. Everyone else in the waiting room is an adult:

> The waiting room
> was full of grown-up people,
> arctics and overcoats,
> lamps and magazines.

The adults in the room are never given personalities or individuality and are described in terms of what they wear. She is so shy of them that in line 64 she says 'I scarcely dared to look'.

The child-speaker in the poem retreats into the world of the *National Geographic* and carefully studies photographs of places and people very far away. Everything she sees in the magazine is different. The volcanic landscape with its black ashes and 'rivulets of fire' is different and in sharp contrast with a New England town in winter. The people she sees are also different: first the two explorers Osa and Martin Johnson in their travellers' attire and then 'the dead man slung on the pole', black women, black babies. The women have mutilated themselves in order to be sexually attractive. That this is a form of enslavement is not fully grasped by the seven-year-old child: it is certainly not articulated in the poem, but the reader recognises Bishop's genuine revulsion on seeing what they have done. 'In the Waiting Room' records Bishop's early and growing awareness of herself and the choices that await her, especially as a woman.

The language is simple and clear. The reader is presented with no difficulty in understanding what the child describes, but what is more important and interesting is Bishop's response.

> A dead man slung on a pole
> – 'Long Pig,' the caption said.
> Babies with pointed heads
> wound round and round with string;
> black, naked women with necks
> wound round and round with wire
> like the necks of light bulbs.

The dead man or 'Long Pig' will be eaten by the Polynesian cannibals; the babies have had their heads reshaped and the women's necks have been elongated, 'their breasts were horrifying.' This is inflicted and self-inflicted violence, and the child in the waiting room finds it repulsive and yet:

> I read it right straight through.
> I was too shy to stop.

Her emotions on reading the magazine are not shared or discussed with anyone in the room, and, having read and having been horrified, she attempts to objectify the experience by closing the magazine and observing mundane details:

> And then I looked at the cover:
> the yellow margins, the date.

The child has entered into an experience and, though not unmoved, she has retreated from it.

The child's gaze is abruptly broken at line 36. There is the cry of pain from the dentist's room. The dentist is unintentionally causing Aunt Consuelo to suffer:

Suddenly from inside,
came an *oh!* of pain
– Aunt Consuelo's voice –
not very loud or long.

The attitude to the pain in the next room is not Bishop's attitude to the pain of head shaping and neck lengthening she saw a moment before in the *National Geographic*. Instead, she sees her aunt as foolish and timid; she is neither surprised nor embarrassed:

I wasn't at all surprised;
even then I knew she was
a foolish, timid woman.
I might have been embarrassed,
but wasn't.

However, the poem takes an interesting and unexpected direction when Bishop, the seven-year-old girl sees herself as a grown woman and as foolish as her aunt.

What took me
completely by surprise
was that it was me:
my voice, in my mouth.

Her aunt's cry becomes the speaker's own cry. The woman and the girl are one. It is as if the girl has no option but to grow up to become the kind of woman she does not want to be.

The child-speaker imagines, 'without thinking at all', that 'I was my foolish aunt', and, in a surreal leap of the imagination, both the aunt 'from inside' and the girl 'in' the waiting room are falling:

I – we – were falling, falling,
our eyes glued to the cover
of the *National Geographic*,
February, 1918.

The eyes are 'glued' to reality, to the magazine, the month and year, and then the aunt is forgotten about for 21 lines. The 'I' takes over and the defining 'I' is used nine times. Like Alice, she is falling but there is no Wonderland as such. It is, however, she says at lines 72–73, the strangest thing that could ever happen.

She hangs on to hard facts: her imminent birthday in three days.

> I was saying it to stop
> the sensation of falling off
> the round, turning world
> into cold, blue-black space.

The date of the experience recorded in the poem and given in the poem itself, in the closing lines, is 5 February and the facts give way to intense feeling:

> But I felt: you are an *I*,
> You are an *Elizabeth*

What she discovers with a sharp perceptiveness is that there is only one Elizabeth Bishop, separate, unique, but that that unique individual self is also one of womankind and destined perhaps to become like the women she has been thinking about – the trapped black women, the foolish Aunt Consuelo:

> you are one of *them*.
> *Why* should you be one, too?

Here the child-speaker wants to hang on, to stay on earth, and not to tumble into space or unknown territory.

Line 64 brings a lull. The language is no longer so insistent (the 'you are', 'you are' of the previous lines) and Bishop attempts to take her bearings:

> I scarcely dared to look
> to see what it was I was.
> I gave a sidelong glance
> – I couldn't look any higher –
> at shadowy gray knees,
> trousers and skirts and boots
> and different pairs of hands
> lying under the lamps.

This return to the familiar is comforting, and yet she is still shy, uneasy, and deeply aware that this moment has somehow altered and clarified her understanding of herself, that it is a moment of such insight and understanding that it will affect the rest of her life:

> I knew that nothing stranger
> had ever happened, that nothing
> stranger could ever happen.

And this sends her back to the earlier question (line 63 – '*Why* should you be one, too?') which Bishop now repeats with a different emphasis. The question at line 63 implies that Bishop resisted becoming a certain kind of woman. Now the question opens out into a question that explores the mystery of existence, the very strangeness of being alive:

> Why should I be my aunt,
> or me, or anyone?

It then opens out further to include the questions whether and how there are connections between people so obviously different:

> What similarities –
> boots, hands, the family voice
> I felt in my throat, or even
> the *National Geographic*
> and those awful hanging breasts –
> held us all together
> or made us all just one?

The child, almost seven, has been unnerved by the black women and their 'horrifying' breasts, their 'awful hanging breasts'. This is the outside world. She is also unnerved by the aunt's cry 'from inside',

> a cry of pain that could have
> got loud and worse but hadn't?

The poem ends with Bishop feeling faint and her sense of the waiting room

> sliding
> beneath a big black wave,
> another, and another.

The fainting spell is a loss of consciousness and then she is back in the waiting room. In the short closing section of the poem, there is an intense awareness again of place, outside and inside, and the specifics of time. In the first section of the poem, outside meant winter (line 6); later outside includes Polynesian culture and, in the final reference to a world beyond the waiting room, we are told that a war is being fought.

The young Elizabeth Bishop has waited in the waiting room. The place could be read as a symbol of childhood, a time spent waiting for adulthood, but everything that is spoken of in relation to the world beyond the immediate one is frightening, strange, confusing (what the academic Brett Millier calls 'the awful otherness of the inevitable world'). Elizabeth Bishop's relationship with that world and her feeling of not belonging to it recurs in many of her poems.

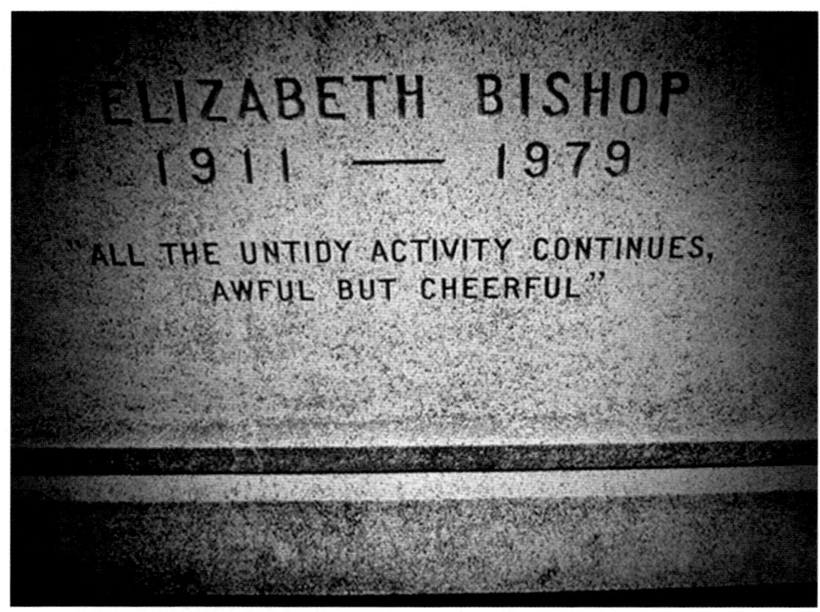
ELIZABETH BISHOP
1911 — 1979
"ALL THE UNTIDY ACTIVITY CONTINUES,
AWFUL BUT CHEERFUL"

Eavan Boland

Born 1944

Contents Page

POEMS

Dates refer to the year of composition. The poems as they are printed here, are in the order in which they were written.

The War Horse

This dry night, nothing unusual
About the clip, clop, casual

Iron of his shoes as he stamps death
Like a mint on the innocent coinage of earth.

I lift the window, watch the ambling feather
Of hock and fetlock, loosed from its daily tether

In the tinker camp on the Enniskerry Road,
Pass, his breath hissing, his snuffling head

Down. He is gone. No great harm is done.
Only a leaf of our laurel hedge is torn –

Of distant interest like a maimed limb,
Only a rose which now will never climb

The stone of our house, expendable, a mere
Line of defence against him, a volunteer

You might say, only a crocus, its bulbous head
Blown from growth, one of the screamless dead.

But we, we are safe, our unformed fear
Of fierce commitment gone; why should we care

If a rose, a hedge, a crocus are uprooted
Like corpses, remote, crushed, mutilated?

He stumbles on like a rumour of war, huge,
Threatening. Neighbours use the subterfuge

Of curtains. He stumbles down our short street
Thankfully passing us, I pause, wait,

Then to breathe relief lean on the sill
And for a second only my blood is still

With atavism. That rose he smashed frays
Ribboned across our hedge, recalling days

Of burned countryside, illicit braid:
A cause ruined before, a world betrayed.

Glossary

Title: War Horse – historically, a war horse is a powerful horse ridden in war by a knight or cavalryman. Tennyson, for example, in 'The Lady of Shalott' says of Sir Launcelot: 'His broad clear brow in sunlight glowed;/On burnished hooves his war-horse trode'. In Boland's poem, the war horse is a large horse that has strayed from a Travellers' camp into her ordered, man-made suburban garden and neighbourhood.

'The War Horse' was written during a time of renewed political violence in the North of Ireland.

Line 4 mint: a machine used for coining.

Line 4 coinage: a reference to the circular-shaped, iron horse-shoe as it makes its print on the level, unpatterned earth.

Line 5 ambling: moving at a smooth or easy pace.

Line 6 hock: the joint in the hinder leg of the horse.

Line 6 fetlock: that part of the horse's leg where the tuft of hair grows.

Line 6 tether: rope fastening.

Line 7 tinker: a word no longer used, tinker originally meant a craftsman, usually itinerant, who mended pots, kettles etc. In Ireland, tinkers referred to Travellers until it came to be considered a patronising or insulting term.

Line 8 snuffling: means to draw air into the nostrils in order to smell something and to express dislike or disdain.

Line 13 expendable: can be done without.

Line 20 mutilated: deprived of a limb or organ of the body.

Line 22 subterfuge: a device to which a person resorts in order to escape or avoid argument or debate.

Line 27 atavism: a resemblance to remote ancestors.

Line 27 frays: ravels out.

Line 29 illicit braid: the smashed rose is like a plait, disturbing the neatness of the hedge. Braid (archaic) also means a sudden movement of sword; perhaps Boland intends a pun here where 'illicit braid' could also mean an unlawful sudden sword movement.

'The War Horse' was first published in the *Irish Times*, 28 October 1972, when Eavan Boland was twenty-eight. In a chapter of *Object Lessons* entitled 'Writing the Political Poem in Ireland', Boland gives the background to 'The War Horse':

> I married in my mid-twenties and went to live in a suburban house at the foothills of the Dublin mountains. The first winter in the suburb was harsh. The weather was cold; the road was half-finished. Each morning the fields on the Dublin hills appeared as great slates of frost. At night the street lamps were too few. And the road itself ran out in a gloom of icy mud and builders' huts.
>
> It was the early '70s, a time of violence in Northern Ireland. Our front room was a cold rectangle with white walls, hardly any furniture, and a small television chanting deaths and statistics at teatime.
>
> One evening, at the time of the news, I came into the front room with a cup of coffee in my hand. I heard something at the front door. I set down the coffee and went to open it. A large, dappled head – a surreal dismemberment in the dusk – swayed low on the doorstep. Then reattached itself to a clumsy horse and clattered away.
>
> There was an explanation. It was almost certainly a traveller's horse with some memory of our road as a travelling-site and our garden as fields where it had grazed only recently. The memory withstood the surprises of its return, but not for long. It came back four or five times. Each time, as it was startled into retreat, its huge hooves did damage. Crocus bulbs were uprooted. Hedge seedlings were dragged up. Grass seeds were churned out of their place.
>
> Some months later I began to write a poem. I called it 'The War Horse'. Its argument was gathered around the oppositions of force and formality. Of an intrusion of nature – the horse – menacing the decorous reductions of nature that were the gardens. And of the failure of language to describe such violence and resist it.
>
> I wrote the poem slowly, adding each couplet with care. I was twenty-seven years of age. At first, when it was finished, I looked at it with pleasure and wonder. It encompassed a real event. It entered a place in my life and moved beyond it. I was young enough in the craft to want nothing more.

? Questions

1. Where is this poem set? Which details convey this?
2. How does the poet feel about the presence of the horse outside her window in a Dublin suburb? Which words and phrases best capture her thoughts and feelings? Do her feelings change?
3. The torn leaf and the broken crocus are compared to 'a maimed limb', 'one of the screamless dead'. What is the poet suggesting here?
4. Would you agree that there is a movement in this poem from the particular to the general? Why has the episode of the horse prompted the poet to think of other times and other places?
5. Towards the end of the poem the poet says 'my blood is still/ With atavism'. What is the poet thinking of here?
6. Is this a private, personal poem or a public, political poem? Or both?
7. Compare the opening lines of the poem with the closing lines. What has happened? How have the pictures in the reader's mind changed?
8. What is the effect of the way the poem is presented to the reader on the page? Consider the poet's use of two-line stanzas, rhyme and spacing.
9. The horse in the poem belongs to the 'tinker camp on the Enniskerry Road'.
   Why does Boland refer to it as the War Horse? What does it symbolise? Why?
10. What is the difference between the poet's response to the incident and the way in which her neighbours respond? Is the poet a watcher? An interpreter? Or both?

Child of our Time

for Aengus

Yesterday I knew no lullaby
But you have taught me overnight to order
This song, which takes from your final cry
Its tune, from your unreasoned end its reason;
Its rhythm from the discord of your murder
Its motive from the fact you cannot listen.

We who should have known how to instruct
With rhymes for your waking, rhythms for your sleep,
Names for the animals you took to bed,
Tales to distract, legends to protect
Later an idiom for you to keep
And living, learn, must learn from you dead,

To make our broken images, rebuild
Themselves around your limbs, your broken
Image, find for your sake whose life our idle
Talk has cost, a new language. Child
Of our time, our times have robbed your cradle.
Sleep in a world your final sleep has woken.

17 May 1974

Glossary

Line 11 idiom: a particular form of speech.

This poem was written in response to the death of a child who was killed in a Dublin bombing in May 1974. It was prompted specifically by a newspaper photograph which showed a fireman tenderly lifting a dead child from the bomb-blast debris. In all, twenty-two people died and a hundred were injured. During that same time when Boland worked on the poem, a friend's baby died a cot death and that baby is the Aengus of the dedication. By combining the two different and terrible deaths of young children, Boland manages to write a poem in response to the sudden and unexpected deaths of all young children. 'Child of our Time' was first published in *The Irish Times*, 25 May 1974.

Questions

1. This poem was prompted by a newspaper photograph which showed a dead child being carried from the rubble of a bomb explosion in Dublin in May 1974. Why is the child a child of our time?

2. Is this poem a lullaby or a different kind of song? Why does the poet feel that such a song should be made?

3. The poet begins in the first person, 'I', but uses 'We' at the beginning of stanza two. Why do you think she does this? What is its effect?

4. In the second stanza, the poet speaks of what she and other adults 'should have known'. What does she mean by this? What is the effect of the references to 'rhymes for your waking, rhythms for your sleep,/Names for the animals you took to bed …'?

5. What is the poet's mood in the final stanza? Which lines capture that mood best?

6. Examine carefully the poem's closing line. Do you think it a suitable ending?

The Famine Road

'Idle as trout in light Colonel Jones
these Irish, give them no coins at all; their bones
need toil, their characters no less.' Trevelyan's
seal blooded the deal table. The Relief
Committee deliberated: 'Might it be safe,
Colonel, to give them roads, roads to force
from nowhere, going nowhere of course?'

one out of every ten and then
another third of those again
women – in a case like yours.

Sick, directionless they worked fork, stick
were iron years away; after all could
they not blood their knuckles on rock, suck
April hailstones for water and for food?
Why for that, cunning as housewives, each eyed –
as if at a corner butcher – the other's buttock.

anything may have caused it, spores,
a childhood accident; one sees
day after day these mysteries.

Dusk: they will work tomorrow without him.
They know it and walk clear. He has become
a typhoid pariah, his blood tainted, although
he shares it with some there. No more than snow
attends its own flakes where they settle
and melt, will they pray by his death rattle.

You never will, never you know
but take it well woman, grow
your garden, keep house, good-bye.

'It has gone better than we expected, Lord
Trevelyan, sedition, idleness, cured
in one; from parish to parish, field to field;
the wretches work till they are quite worn,
then fester by their work; we march the corn
to the ships in peace. This Tuesday I saw bones
out of my carriage window. Your servant Jones.'

Barren, never to know the load
of his child in you, what is your body
now if not a famine road?

Glossary

Title: The Famine Road – During the Great Famine of 1845–52 the Irish Board of Works created extra employment by making new roads for the provision of famine relief. The districts where distress was greatest were poor, uncultivated and boggy and many of the roads which were built were of limited use.

The stanzas in standard typeface refer to a public and political world, that of the nineteenth-century Irish famine, whereas the stanzas in italics belong to a different world, the private world of the sterility of woman. By placing each concern side by side, Eavan Boland is recognising a similarity or parallel between the racist attitude of the English towards the Irish and the attitude of the doctor towards the female patient. Eavan Boland sees 'The Famine Road' as a poem about imperialism, its command and absolute power.

Line 1 Colonel Jones: Colonel Harry Jones, a distinguished English officer of the Royal Engineers who had been appointed Chairman of the Board of Works in Ireland. (cf Chapter III *The Great Hunger* by Cecil Woodham-Smith)

Line 3 Trevelyan: Sir Charles Edward Trevelyan (1807–1886) oversaw Irish relief. He defended the export of food from Ireland during the famine and in 'The Irish Crisis', published in *The Edinburgh Review*, January 1848, writing anonymously, hinted that the famine was God's way of dealing with overpopulation. (cf Roy Foster's *Modern Ireland, 1600–1972*, Chapter 14)

Line 4/5 Relief Committee: the first Relief Commission began work in November 1845 and the first and most important plan was to form committees of local landowners, or their agents, magistrates, clergy and residents of importance. In *The Great Hunger*, Woodham-Smith writes that these committees 'would raise subscriptions, out of which food was to be bought for resale to distressed persons, or, in urgent cases, given free.'

Line 5 deliberated: thought it over carefully.

Line 17 spores: minute germs or organisms.

Line 22 typhoid: an infectious fever that can cause a delerious stupor.

Line 22 pariah: a social outcast.

Line 22 tainted: contaminated.

Line 25 death rattle: a sound in the throat of a dying person and usually caused by that person's last breath.

Line 30 sedition: mutiny, revolt, a concerted movement to overthrow an established government.

Line 33 fester: putrefy, rot.

Line 33/34 corn to the ships: a reference to how corn was exported from Ireland during the famine.

This is a poem of several voices and there are two poems with apparently different topics within one. The first, in standard typeface, is concerned with the nineteenth-century Irish famine and is framed by two letters, one from Trevelyan to Jones, the other from Jones to Trevelyan; the second poem, in italics, focuses on sterility or barrenness and it is spoken by a doctor to a patient. The italicised stanzas refer to no one particular period of time, though the image of the famine road would suggest that it could be seen within a nineteenth-century context also.

For clarity and impact, it is worth reading the standard typeface and the italicised lines separately and then as interlinked poems.

? Questions

1. Two narratives can be heard in this poem, an historical and a personal, a public and a private. With the aid of the glossary, work out who is speaking in each section. What is the connection between them?
2. How would you describe the tone in stanza one? Is there a similar tone to be found in the italicised lines?
3. The famine roads go nowhere. Is this significant? How does the childless woman resemble the famine road?
4. What picture emerges of the famine victims in the section beginning 'Sick, directionless they worked...'? Which phrase suggests that it is survival of the fittest?
5. Comment on the use of 'never' in the sixth section. Which words and phrases suggest indifference and cruelty?
6. In the closing lines of the letter (lines 29–35), what is the tone used by Colonel Jones to Lord Trevelyan?
7. Who is speaking the final lines of the poem? Is it the barren woman? The poet?
8. Do you think the comparison between the plight of the woman and the plight of the Irish people is a valid one?
9. How does this poem differ from 'The War Horse' and 'Child of Our Time'?

The Black Lace Fan My Mother Gave Me

It was the first gift he ever gave her,
buying it for five francs in the Galeries
in pre-war Paris. It was stifling.
A starless drought made the nights stormy.

They stayed in the city for the summer.
They met in cafés. She was always early.
He was late. That evening he was later.
They wrapped the fan. He looked at his watch.

She looked down the Boulevard des Capucines.
She ordered more coffee. She stood up.
The streets were emptying. The heat was killing.
She thought the distance smelled of rain and lightning.

These are wild roses, appliquéd on silk by hand,
darkly picked, stitched boldly, quickly.
The rest is tortoiseshell and has the reticent,
clear patience of its element. It is

a worn-out, underwater bullion and it keeps,
even now, an inference of its violation.
The lace is overcast as if the weather
it opened for and offset had entered it.

The past is an empty café terrace.
An airless dusk before thunder. A man running.
And no way now to know what happened then –
none at all – unless, of course, you improvise:

The blackbird on this first sultry morning,
in summer, finding buds, worms, fruit,
feels the heat. Suddenly she puts out her wing –
the whole, full, flirtatious span of it.

Glossary

Line 13 appliquéd: a trimming cut out in outline and laid on another surface.

Line 15 tortoiseshell: the shell of a tortoise used in ornamental work.

Line 15 reticent: given to silence or concealment (as the tortoise itself is).

Line 17 bullion: convex-curved ornament; gold or silver treasure.

Line 18 an inference of its violation: a conclusion drawn about its having been treated with violence.

Line 20 offset: set off as an equivalent against something else.

Line 24 improvise: invent on the spur of the moment.

Line 25 sultry: oppressively hot and moist weather.

Line 28 flirtatious: sudden; playfully flirting.

Line 28 span: measure.

The title refers to an object and a relationship. The words, black lace fan, may suggest a woman, elegance, grace, beauty, times past, something both romantic and clichéd, something erotic. In this instance it may also suggest the relationship between man and woman. Is this a power relationship between them and is the man in giving the woman the fan somehow controlling and subordinating the woman? With this object, is he turning her into an object of sexual desire? Her father had given the fan to Boland's mother in a heatwave in Paris in the 1930s and the giving of this delicate and precious object by mother to daughter could be interpreted as a symbol of love and continuing love. Boland, however, also sees the fan as a reminder of the passing of time, the ageing body, the complex relationship between man and woman.

Questions

1. The first three stanzas describe a particular summer which the poet's mother and father spent in Paris. Using the details in the text, discuss how Boland evokes that time.

2. What is the significance of the father's gift of a black lace fan to the poet's mother? What does it say about their relationship?

3. Can you suggest why Boland uses so many short sentences? What does it contribute to the mood of the opening stanzas?

4. In stanza four, Boland looks at the black lace fan in detail. Why is the object associated with beauty and violence?

5. The poet speaks of one moment in the past, a moment she herself did not witness. Yet her imagination allows her to create a picture in her mind and to improvise beyond that moment. What does the last stanza tell us about how Boland viewed 'what happened then'?

6. What is the effect of the transformation of fan into blackbird in the closing lines of the poem?

7. The fan dates from another time. It is 'worn-out', 'overcast'. Boland herself has said that the fan is a sign of suffering. Tease out how this might be.

8. Why does Boland never say 'my father' and why does she say 'my mother' only in the title?

9. In Boland's own words, this is a 'back-to-front love poem'. How do you interpret this?

The Shadow Doll

They stitched blooms from the ivory tulle
to hem the oyster gleam of the veil.
They made hoops for the crinoline.

Now, in summary and neatly sewn –
a porcelain bride in an airless glamour –
the shadow doll survives its occasion.

Under glass, under wraps, it stays
even now, after all, discreet about
visits, fevers, quickenings and lusts

and just how, when she looked at
the shell-tone spray of seed pearls,
the bisque features, she could see herself

inside it all, holding less than real
stephanotis, rose petals, never feeling
satin rise and fall with the vows

I kept repeating on the night before –
astray among the cards and wedding gifts –
the coffee pots and the clocks and

the battered tan case full of cotton
lace and tissue-paper, pressing down, then
pressing down again. And then, locks.

Glossary

Title: The Shadow Doll – This was sent to the bride-to-be in Victorian times, by her dressmaker. It consisted of a porcelain doll, under a dome of glass, modelling the proposed wedding dress.

Line 1 tulle: a fine silk bobbin-net.

Line 3 crinoline: a petticoat made of stiff fabric (originally horsehair and cotton) worn under the skirt to support and spread it.

Line 8 discreet: well-behaved, cautious.

Line 12 bisque: unglazed white porcelain.

Line 14 stephanotis: fragrant white flowers.

Questions

1. As in 'The Black Lace Fan my Mother Gave me', 'The Shadow Doll' is a poem that looks at the past and present, in this instance Victorian times and the late twentieth century, side by side. What is being said here about the Victorian doll and by implication the Victorian woman?
2. Stanzas one and two are given over to a description of the actual doll. What does Boland associate with the shadow doll? Is it positive or negative or a mixture of both?

3. In stanza three, something other than description enters the poem. How did the Victorian bride-to-be view the shadow doll? What happens to the flow of thought in the poem from stanza three on? Look at the punctuation.
4. What sense do you get of the poet as she reveals herself to us in this poem?
5. What do you think is suggested by the definite gesture with which the poem ends?
6. How does Eavan Boland suggest the differences between the Victorian bride-to-be and herself? Are there similarities? Explain.

White Hawthorn in the West of Ireland

I drove West
in the season between seasons.
I left behind suburban gardens.
Lawnmowers. Small talk.

Under low skies, past splashes of coltsfoot,
I assumed
the hard shyness of Atlantic light
and the superstitious aura of hawthorn.

All I wanted then was to fill my arms with
sharp flowers,
to seem, from a distance, to be part of
that ivory, downhill rush. But I knew,

I had always known
the custom was
not to touch hawthorn.
Not to bring it indoors for the sake of

the luck
such constraint would forfeit –
a child might die, perhaps, or an unexplained
fever speckle heifers. So I left it

stirring on those hills
with a fluency
only water has. And, like water, able
to re-define land. And free to seem to be –

for anglers,
and for travellers astray in
the unmarked lights of a May dusk –
the only language spoken in those parts.

Glossary

Title: Hawthorn – a thorny, spring-flowering shrub of the rose family with white or pink flowers and small pome fruits or haws. A sprig of hawthorn was proof against storms at sea, lightning ashore; and in the house it was proof against spirits and ghosts. But it is an Irish folk custom and belief that whitethorn should not be carried indoors; if it does it will bring misfortune and illness, and in some localities it even brought death. In Ireland, hawthorns are believed to be frequented by fairies and are therefore sometimes called 'gentle bushes'. To cut one down brings death upon the cattle or the children, and loss of memory to the feller. Their scent is sometimes said to have the sweet, enchanting scent of death. The boughs are fastened to the outside of barns on May Day to keep out evil spirits and ensure plenty of milk during the summer.

Line 5 coltsfoot: so named because of the shape of the leaves, coltsfoot is a common weed in waste or clayey ground, with large spreading heart-shaped leaves, and yellow flowers that appear in early spring before the leaves.

Line 6 assumed: to take into the body, to pretend to possess.

Line 8 superstitious aura: the uneasy feeling associated with, or surrounding, the hawthorn.

Line 18 forfeit: lose or give up.

'White Hawthorn in the West of Ireland' is poem IV in a sequence of poems called 'Outside History'. 'Writing about the lost, the voiceless, the silent' is how Boland describes the sequence. Eavan Boland has described herself as 'an indoor nature poet' but in 'White Hawthorn in the West of Ireland' she celebrates the light and landscape of the west of Ireland.

Questions

1. This poem tells of a car journey west, but at what point does the reader sense that it is something much more than this?

2. Look at how often the poet uses the pronoun 'I'. What is the effect of this?

3. The poet leaves behind suburban gardens, lawnmowers, small talk. Contrast this world with the world of the west of Ireland as revealed to us in the poem.

4. What would you say is the central theme of the poem? What is the significance of the white hawthorn? Is it symbolic?

5. How would you describe the poet's mood? Does the mood change as one reads through the poem?

6. Why does the poet refer to anglers and travellers in the final stanza? What do such references contribute to the poem as a whole?

7. How does Eavan Boland in this poem convey a sense of expansion? How does she convey a sense of place, folklore, longing?

Outside History

There are outsiders, always. These stars –
these iron inklings of an Irish January,
whose light happened

thousands of years before
our pain did: they are, they have always been
outside history.

They keep their distance. Under them remains
a place where you found
you were human, and

a landscape in which you know you are mortal.
And a time to choose between them.
I have chosen:

out of myth into history I move to be
part of that ordeal
whose darkness is

only now reaching me from those fields,
those rivers, those roads clotted as
firmaments with the dead.

How slowly they die
as we kneel beside them, whisper in their ear.
And we are too late. We are always too late.

Glossary

Line 2 inklings: hints.

Lines 17/18 roads clotted as/firmaments: Boland imagines the roads covered with clusters of dead bodies just as the sky has clusters of stars.

Line 18 firmaments: the sky – a reference to the stars in the night sky.

This is the final poem in the sequence 'Outside History'. The phrase 'outside history' is often associated with Eavan Boland; it is the title of a sequence of poems, the title of a collection, and the phrase was quoted by President Mary Robinson in her inauguration speech in December 1990. In her writing, Boland has responded powerfully and imaginatively to those who never had a voice, to those who never made their way into the history books. In Boland's words, these are 'the lost, the voiceless, the silent' and her work explores how women, for example, have been marginalised throughout history. (Feminist historians have suggested that a glance at the 18-page Index of Names in Roy Foster's *Modern Ireland, 1600–1972* would suggest that women hardly existed.)

In Eavan Boland's early work, the making of the poem frequently included regular line length, stanza length and rhyme. Eavan Boland sees very little technical experiment in 'Outside History' but by then she had mastered free verse and a poem which was not dependent on end-rhyme. 'Outside History' is divided into seven three-line, unrhymed stanzas where the line length and the line break are important qualities in the poem.

Questions

1. Why does the poet see the stars as outsiders? Why is the word 'Irish' in line two important within the context of the poem? What do you understand by Boland's reference to 'our pain'?
2. To what does Boland compare the light of the stars reaching earth in sections five and six? What does such an image tell us about Boland's relationship with the past?
3. What do you think the poet means when she says 'I move to be/part of that ordeal'?
4. Would you agree that the language here is both general and particular, abstract and vivid? Choose examples of both kinds and discuss their effect.
5. What do the words 'fields', 'rivers', 'roads' in section six conjure up in your mind? Comment on the lines 'those roads clotted as/firmaments with the dead'. How does it fit in with the overall imagery of the poem?
6. Can you explain how the sense of pity and helplessness is conveyed in the final section of the poem? What is the significance of 'we' here?

This Moment

A neighbourhood.
At dusk.

Things are getting ready
to happen
out of sight.

Stars and moths.
And rinds slanting around fruit.

But not yet.

One tree is black.
One window is yellow as butter.

A woman leans down to catch a child
who has run into her arms
this moment.

Stars rise.
Moths flutter.
Apples sweeten in the dark.

Questions

1. How does Boland get the reader to move through this poem very slowly? Look at sentence length. Count the full stops.
2. What would you say is the central theme of the poem? What connection is there between the world of nature and the human world?
3. Which words are particularly effective in conveying atmosphere?
4. At the centre of the poem is the tender, caring image of mother and child. How does Boland achieve a timelessness in her description of this particular moment?
5. What is the effect of the references to stars and moths and fruit?
6. Would you consider this a personal or an impersonal poem?
7. Compare lines 6 and 7 with lines 14 to 16. Why has a change taken place in your opinion?

Love

Dark falls on this mid-western town
where we once lived when myths collided.
Dusk has hidden the bridge in the river
which slides and deepens
to become the water
the hero crossed on his way to hell.

Not far from here is our old apartment.
We had a kitchen and an Amish table.
We had a view. And we discovered there
love had the feather and muscle of wings
and had come to live with us,
a brother of fire and air.

We had two infant children one of whom
was touched by death in this town
and spared: and when the hero
was hailed by his comrades in hell
their mouths opened and their voices failed and
there is no knowing what they would have asked
about a life they had shared and lost.

I am your wife.
It was years ago.
Our child is healed. We love each other still.
Across our day-to-day and ordinary distances
we speak plainly. We hear each other clearly.
And yet I want to return to you
on the bridge of the Iowa river as you were,
with snow on the shoulders of your coat
and a car passing with its headlights on:

I see you as a hero in a text –
the image blazing and the edges gilded –
and I long to cry out the epic question
my dear companion:

Will we ever live so intensely again?
Will love come to us again and be
so formidable at rest it offered us ascension
even to look at him?

But the words are shadows and you cannot hear me.
You walk away and I cannot follow.

Glossary

Line 1 mid-western town: Iowa in Iowa State, United States where Boland and her husband, the novelist Kevin Casey, were both teaching at the International Writing Programme at Iowa University in 1979.

Line 2 myths: fictitious stories usually involving supernatural persons, objects or events.

Line 6 the hero: Aeneas, the hero of Virgil's *The Aeneid*. In *Object Lessons* (1995), Boland writes of how she studied Book VI of *The Aeneid* at school: 'The story line was clear and uncomplicated. Aeneas, Virgil's hero, had already travelled through other lands in other books. He has courted and betrayed Dido in Carthage. He has left her to commit suicide and sailed with the Trojan fleet to Libya and on to Sicily. Now the Sixth Book opens, and Aeneas visits the Cumaean sibyl in Italy. Once he has got the Golden Bough, she descends with him to the underworld and to the river Styx, and on the far shore of it they see the dead.'

In 'Love', Boland merely alludes to *The Aeneid* and it is pointless to try and find too many parallels between Boland's poem and Virgil.

Line 8 Amish: plain, simple, unadorned (the Amish community in Pennsylvania live a strict religious life and choose to do without many modern inventions including electricity and motor cars).

Line 31 epic: great, important.

Line 35 formidable: giving cause for fear or alarm.

Line 35 ascension: a sense of uplift.

This is a poem which remembers a time in Boland's life when she and her husband and their two children under three were in Iowa in the late 1970s. While there, their youngest daughter, eleven-month old Eavan Frances, contracted meningitis and almost died. Eavan Boland and her husband watched by their baby as she lay in hospital attached to tubes and machines. Their daughter was spared and years later Boland wrote about that time in 'Love'.

The poem contains two intertwining stories, Boland's own and the story of Aeneas from Virgil's *The Aeneid* who goes down into the underworld and is greeted by his friends and enemies. Love is one of poetry's great themes. It has been written about thousands of times but there are very few poems entitled 'Love', the most famous of all being a series of poems by George Herbert.

? Questions

1. This is a poem that contains two narratives. One tells of how Boland's young daughter became very ill and nearly died; the other tells of how she is remembering meeting her husband during that difficult time and how it reminds her of Virgil's *Aeneid* where Aeneas meets with ghosts from his past in the underworld. How does Eavan Boland connect naturalistic and mythic elements?
2. What do you think the poet means by the phrase 'when myths collided'? How is the sense of mystery and danger conveyed in the opening section of the poem?
3. Parts of the poem are very direct and immediate, other parts difficult and mysterious to grasp. Staying with the more accessible parts, read the poem through, omitting the more challenging sections. Then read it through again. What does the poem gain by the allusions to the hero and hell?
4. The poem is a memory poem. Consider how the poet uses the present and past tense. What is the effect of this?
5. What is the poet's mood in the closing section (lines 29 and following) of the poem? Why does she feel like this?
6. Look back over the poem and note how Boland creates an expression of great emotional intensity. Consider the use of the full stop. Why is the shorter sentence sometimes more appropriate? Why does she sometimes use a run-on line?
7. What is the nature of love as it is revealed to us in this poem?
8. Boland has said of this poem that it 'is really a poem about the underworld of memory'. How is this revealed to us in the poem?

The Pomegranate

The only legend I have ever loved is
the story of a daughter lost in hell.
And found and rescued there.
Love and blackmail are the gist of it.
Ceres and Persephone the names.
And the best thing about the legend is
I can enter it anywhere. And have.
As a child in exile in
a city of fogs and strange consonants,
I read it first and at first I was
an exiled child in the crackling dusk of
the underworld, the stars blighted. Later
I walked out in a summer twilight
searching for my daughter at bed-time.
When she came running I was ready
to make any bargain to keep her.
I carried her back past whitebeams
and wasps and honey-scented buddleias.
But I was Ceres then and I knew
winter was in store for every leaf
on every tree on that road.
Was inescapable for each one we passed.
And for me.
                    It is winter
and the stars are hidden.
I climb the stairs and stand where I can see
my child asleep beside her teen magazines,
her can of Coke, her plate of uncut fruit.
The pomegranate! How did I forget it?
She could have come home and been safe
and ended the story and all
our heart-broken searching but she reached
out a hand and plucked a pomegranate.

She put out her hand and pulled down
the French sound for apple and
the noise of stone and the proof
that even in the place of death,
at the heart of legend, in the midst
of rocks full of unshed tears
ready to be diamonds by the time
the story was told, a child can be
hungry. I could warn her. There is still a chance.
The rain is cold. The road is flint-coloured.
The suburb has cars and cable television.
The veiled stars are above ground.
It is another world. But what else
can a mother give her daughter but such
beautiful rifts in time?
If I defer the grief I will diminish the gift.
The legend will be hers as well as mine.
She will enter it. As I have.
She will wake up. She will hold
the papery flushed skin in her hand.
And to her lips. I will say nothing.

Glossary

Title: Pomegranate – the word literally means an apple having many seeds; the pomegranate is a large, roundish, many-celled berry, with many seeds, each enveloped in a pleasantly acid juicy reddish pulp, enclosed in a tough rind of a golden colour tinged with red. The pomegranate referred to here is from the Greek myth which tells of a mother's love for her daughter.

Among other things, this poem tells of Eavan Boland's relationship with her eldest daughter, Sarah. In the myth the child could have come back if it hadn't eaten the pomegranate, a story which is, according to Boland, 'psychologically so accurate of teenagers as anyone who has ever had teenage children will know'. 'The Pomegranate' was written when Sarah was seventeen years old; it is one of Boland's own favourite poems.

Line 4 gist: the substance of a matter, the essence.

Line 5 Ceres and Persephone: In mythology, Ceres was the goddess of the corn-bearing earth, the harvest and agriculture. Persephone was the daughter of Ceres and Zeus, the greatest of the Greek gods. In the myth, Persephone, while gathering flowers on the vale of Enna in Sicily, was carried off by Hades the god of the underworld and there made his queen. Heartbroken, Ceres wandered the earth in search of her beloved daughter and while she did so nothing grew on earth. Ceres begged Zeus to help her and he agreed to return Persephone on condition that she had eaten nothing while in the underworld. But she had eaten six pomegranate seeds and a condition was laid down. Persephone would only be allowed to return to earth for six months of the year and the other six months would be spent underground with Hades. The symbolism in the myth refers to the burying of the seed in the ground and the growth of the corn. It also explains the seasons. When Persephone comes back to earth to join her mother, the world celebrates with spring, when she departs each year, the world mourns with Ceres and winter approaches.

The eating of the pomegranate by Persephone brought about suffering and exile. There are some similarities between Persephone eating the pomegranate seeds and the eating of the apple by Eve in the Garden of Eden in the Genesis myth. The African-American poet Rita Dove uses the myth in her book *Mother Love* (1995). Dove in her Introduction says that the ancient story is 'a tale of a violated world' and she continues: 'It is a modern dilemma as well – there comes a point when a mother can no longer protect her child, when the daughter must go her own way into womanhood'.

(In Greek the names are Demeter and Persephone, in Latin Ceres and Proserpine. Eavan Boland has used the Greek form and a Latin form of the names in what could be termed poetic licence).

Line 9 strange consonants: the different accent which Boland heard as a girl when she lived in London.

Line 11 crackling: sharp dry sounding.

Line 39 rocks full of unshed tears: a place of sorrow.

Line 48 rifts: chinks, openings (in Middle English it meant a cleft or chasm in the earth, rock).

Line 49 defer: to put off to some later time.

Questions

1. The myth which serves as a backdrop to this poem is about separation and recovery. What is the nature of that recovery? In the myth, why can that recovery never be total or absolute recovery? What is Boland implying about the relationship between herself and her own daughter?

2. How does 'the story of a daughter lost in hell' apply to the young Eavan Boland? What picture of her childhood does she paint in lines 8–12?

3. Eavan Boland sees in the myth of Ceres and Persephone both an image of herself as a young girl and of herself as a woman and mother. Explain why this is so. Why does she see herself as Persephone? In what way does Boland resemble her?

4. When she sees herself as Ceres at line 19 ('But I was Ceres then ...') what are her main thoughts, feelings, preoccupations? What does she mean when she speaks of winter being inescapable?

5. What is the significance of the break between the two sections of this poem? What might this chasm between 23 and 24 represent in the actual myth?

6. When the poet sees her sleeping teenage daughter in section two, what does she think about? Why is the separation inevitable? What do the details of 'can of Coke' and 'teen magazines' suggest? What is the effect of such references as cars and cable television in a poem that also tells of a myth thousands of years old?

7. Why did her daughter reach out a hand and pluck a pomegranate? What does the pomegranate symbolise in the myth? In her daughter's story, as Eavan Boland sees it?

8. What is Eavan Boland's wish for her daughter? What does she hope to give her? What is meant by the phrase 'beautiful rifts in time'?

9. How would you describe the poet's mood in the closing lines? In the final sentence of the poem?

10. What close connection between mother and daughter is revealed to us in this poem? Can 'The Pomegranate' be read as a poem about every mother and every daughter? Every parent and every child?

General Questions

A. 'The place of the past is always an important aspect of the poetry of Eavan Boland.' Discuss this view, quoting from or referring to the poems by Eavan Boland on your course.

B. 'In her poetry Boland explores the public and the private: Ireland's violent and troubled history and her own personal story.' Would you agree with this view? Support your answer with relevant quotations or reference to the poems by Eavan Boland on your course.

C. 'Eavan Boland's poetry uses striking and vivid imagery.' Discuss this statement, supporting your answer by quotation from, or reference to, the poems by Boland on your course.

D. 'Boland's voice is that of the detached observer, the outsider, yet her poetry does not lack feeling.' Consider this view, supporting your answer by quotation from, or reference to, the poems by Eavan Boland on your course.

E. 'Her command of sentence and structure are striking features of Eavan Boland's poetry.' Discuss this view, supporting your answer with suitable quotation or reference. In your answer, you should refer to the poems by Eavan Boland on your course.

F. 'The titles of Boland's poems are powerful and evocative and capture the central preoccupations of the poet.' Would you agree with this view? In your answer, you should quote from, or refer to, the poems by Eavan Boland on your course.

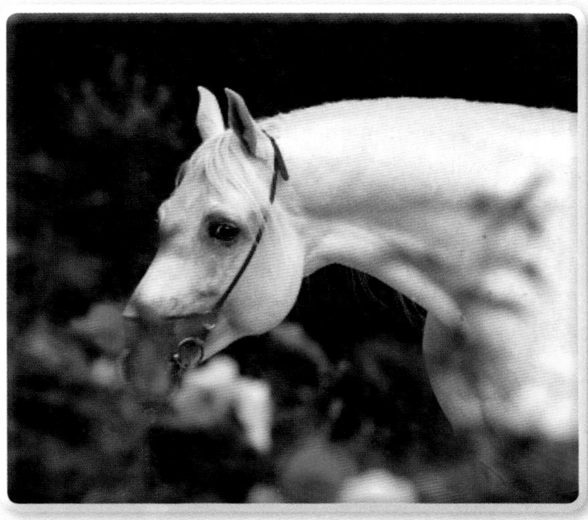

Critical Commentary

The War Horse

One of the very first things that strikes the reader of 'The War Horse' is the poet's technical discipline and control. Here is a poem in thirty lines, divided into fifteen couplets, and each couplet rhymes. Boland has chosen to use a space between each couplet: this gives a particular sense of the thinking process and the making of the poem. If the poem were printed as one thirty-line block, it would work differently; the spaces allow the poem to make its own deliberate and considered structure.

The strong and powerful title may conjure up images of conflict, violence, strength, a former age, but the opening line dispels such colourful pictures, when Boland describes the horse which she sees outside her suburban window.

> This dry night, nothing unusual
> About the clip, clop, casual
>
> Iron of his shoes as he stamps death
> Like a mint on the innocent coinage of earth.

The opening phrase, 'This dry night', with its clipped vowel sounds, sets the scene immediately. The use of 'This' gives the moment focus and Boland thinks the sound of the horse's hoofs 'nothing unusual'. In line 2, the onomatopoeia of 'the clip, clop' gives the very sounds. Yet these not-so-unusual sounds are stamping death on the lawns and flowerbeds outside her window.

The very act of iron hoof on earth is captured in 'stamps' and in the sharp rhymes of 'mint' and 'innocent'; the imprint is vivid. The horse itself, its presence still not explained, is seen as confident and at ease. His relaxed movements are conveyed in an adjective: the

> casual
> Iron of his shoes

Though Boland speaks of there being 'nothing unusual' about the 'clip, clop, casual/Iron of his shoes', she then shows how those very shoes can stamp death on the earth. The size, weight and force of the horse causes some damage and destruction, though of a very minor nature.

In line 5, Boland uses first-person narration. She is an interested observer:

> I lift the window, watch the ambling feather
> Of hock and fetlock, loosed from its daily tether
>
> In the tinker camp on the Enniskerry Road,
> Pass, his breath hissing, his snuffling head
>
> Down. He is gone. No great harm is done.

Here we have a fine sense of the horse's presence and an explanation for how he came to be 'ambling' in Boland's neighbourhood. In the flow and check of these lines, Boland follows the horse's movement. For example:

> loosed from its daily tether
>
> In the tinker camp on the Enniskerry Road

is long and flowing, a run-on line unhindered by punctuation, and its movement is the free movement of the horse's sense of release. Whereas the punctuation in

> his breath hissing, his snuffling head
>
> Down. He is gone. No great harm is done.

captures both the abrupt movements of the horse and Boland's own sense of anxiety, then relief.

'The War Horse' begins with a particular incident. By line 9 it seems that the horse has gone and Boland in a practical and sensible manner surveys the result:

> Only a leaf of our laurel hedge is torn –
>
> Of distant interest like a maimed limb,
> Only a rose which now will never climb
>
> The stone of our house, expendable, a mere
> Line of defence against him, a volunteer
>
> You might say, only a crocus its bulbous head
> Blown from growth, one of the screamless dead.

She speaks of how rose and crocus have been destroyed, but the rose is 'expendable'; they can and will get on without it. There is also the comparison of a torn leaf with a maimed limb. This damaged leaf is a small inconvenience, of 'distant interest', and the simile 'like a maimed limb' (presumably on an actual battlefield) suggests that the speaker somehow has become so removed from war and conflict that it too, like the torn leaf, is only of 'distant interest'.

What is also interesting here is the language which Boland uses to speak of both rose and crocus. The rose was 'a mere/Line of defence', the crocus 'a volunteer', its 'head/Blown from growth, one of the screamless dead', and this terminology of war indicates the direction the poem is going to take, as Boland meditates on threat and violence and war.

There is no real threat from this particular horse: it isn't a war horse in the true sense of that word, though it symbolises potential destruction and reminds Boland of what fear can be. Once Boland realises that her place is safe, she marks a turning point in the poem.

The 'But we' of line 17 introduces Boland's sense of having escaped violence and her awareness of safety, but it doesn't prevent her from questioning attitudes and from thinking of other times when war was a real threat, when real destruction occurred:

> But we, we are safe, our unformed fear
> Of fierce commitment gone; why should we care
>
> If a rose, a hedge, a crocus are uprooted
> Like corpses, remote, crushed, mutilated?

War calls for 'fierce commitment'. If war is not threatened, then there is no need for such commitment. Boland in line 17 speaks of an 'unformed fear' of commitment. In a war, one is called on to take sides, to commit oneself, and this can be frightening. The suburban incident calls for nothing because the moment of danger has passed. It can be seen as a war in microcosm in that the horse, capable of brute force, has entered foreign territory. Boland asks 'why should we care' about a damaged rose, a crushed crocus. The tone here suggests that we do not care. It is a question asked, not by an 'I', but a 'we'. The suburban community should not care as long as the danger has passed, but Boland, by posing the question and implying the answer, is highlighting the dangers perhaps inherent in the unconcerned response.

Boland sees a similarity between this lack of concern for the flowers which are innocent victims and man's indifference to corpses crushed and mutilated in war. The poem posits an important question about our involvement, our commitment or our lack of it, when Boland asks:

why should we care

If a rose, a hedge, a crocus are uprooted
Like corpses, remote, crushed, mutilated?

And the question implies a further question: what are the consequences of our not caring?

The horse enters the poem again at line 21. He is both horse and symbol and some have chosen, or have pretended, to ignore the threatening presence on their doorstep:

He stumbles on like a rumour of war, huge,
Threatening; neighbours use the subterfuge

Of curtains; he stumbles down our short street
Thankfully passing us, I pause, wait.

The clumsy sounding word 'stumbles' is used twice, imitating the very movements of the horse; 'subterfuge' identifies a certain attitude, an attitude which does not involve itself in debate or argument. Boland is not making value judgements here. Instead, she is but recognising a different response. Her neighbours have chosen to stay hidden behind their curtains: she herself lifted the window. Boland is grateful that this 'huge, threatening' presence has passed her door. There is a moment of tension as 'I pause, wait.' Then, the relief.

The closing six lines of the poem belong both to the actual present moment of Boland's relief and to the past. The poem ends with a sense of history, communal suffering and a huge historical perspective. She sees a connection between herself, this suburban woman, and her Irish ancestors:

Then to breathe relief lean on the sill
And for a second only my blood is still

With atavism. That rose he smashed frays
Ribboned across our hedge, recalling days

Of burned countryside, illicit braid:
A cause ruined before, a world betrayed.

The horse's presence, its size and momentary threat, has awakened, 'for a second only', in this woman in late twentieth-century suburban Dublin, a feeling which she thinks was felt by the Irish long ago when their land was in flames, when their lives were threatened unlawfully by blow or sword.

The smashed rose on the hedge outside her window reminds her of former destruction. The poem's last line is a complex one. Boland and her neighbours did not confront the horse because they didn't have to, but it would seem that her ancestors also did not fight the unlawful presence of the enemy, when that enemy came and destroyed. There was a reason for fierce commitment there, but it was not summoned up.

This is why the final image in the poem is one of ruination. The horse smashed the rose; the enemy ruined and destroyed and the Irish were betrayed by colonial powers. The predominant mood at the end of the poem is one of loss, and Boland's tone is one of regret that those other 'war horses' in the past were not challenged successfully. Though the war horse of the title and the war horse of the past are very different, there is never a sense of blame in either situation; Boland does not blame her neighbours for remaining behind their suburban curtains nor does she blame her ancestors for not winning their wars.

'The War Horse' is an example of how poems can be written from unexpected circumstances. When Eavan Boland was a student and then a lecturer at Trinity College Dublin, she was a visible presence in Dublin's literary life. After her marriage, there followed the wrongheaded notion that she had disappeared. Commenting on this, Boland herself says:

> I didn't disappear. Of course not. What really happened was that, as far as poets were concerned, I went off the radar screen. I went to the suburbs. I married. I had two small children.

But, as much of Boland's poetry testifies, she made a poetry that was prompted by her experience of living in the suburbs but went far beyond suburbia in its range and scope.

Child of Our Time

The title 'Child of Our Time' combines private and public worlds. A child belongs first to a family, but every child also inherits a whole social and cultural context. This child dies in a bomb explosion in the centre of Dublin and this makes him a victim of his time. The poem focuses on the death of a child and this intensifies the sense of loss, for a child should symbolise love, continuity, tomorrow.

Boland was twenty-nine when she wrote this poem, and she had as yet no children of her own:

> Yesterday I knew no lullaby

The lullaby, with all its connotations of peace, gentleness and sleep, was unknown to Boland yesterday; today, 17 May 1974, calls for a different kind of song. A soothing lullaby will not suit this moment. What Boland feels she must make is a song that will not betray the anguish of the child's death.

> Yesterday I knew no lullaby
> But you have taught me overnight to order
> This song, which takes from your final cry
> Its tune, from your unreasoned end its reason

The child's violent death needs a different kind of song. The child's 'final cry' is one of pain, anguish and confusion. This she will take as the poem's tune and she says in line 4 that she will make the song's reason from the child's 'unreasoned end'. She recognises the appropriateness of a discordant rhythm; the poem will take

> Its rhythm from the discord of your murder

and she knows that she needs to speak this poem so that others can hear it:

> Its motive from the fact you cannot listen.

The poem's mood is both sad and aware – Boland can understand clearly the implications of such a death, and the poem ends with a mood of guilt and prayer. There is a sadness in the poem's long lines, in the way its four sentences are structured. The poem's tone is formal but not distant: Boland is writing a poem about a public catastrophe and a private death, but the death of someone she has never known. The three six-line stanzas follow a rhyming scheme of abacbc, defdef, ghigih, and many of the end-rhymes are slant or half-rhymes (instruct/protect or idle/cradle) which prevent the poem from becoming inappropriately melodious.

In stanza two, Boland no longer uses the 'I' and 'me' of stanza one. Instead, she introduces the collective 'we' and there is an awareness and admission of failure. 'We', the public, the community, the adults, should have made possible and fostered a safe environment for that murdered child:

> We who should have known how to instruct
> With rhymes for your waking, rhythms for your sleep,
> Names for the animals you took to bed,
> Tales to distract, legends to protect,

have failed. In these lines, she evokes a happy and caring world in which the infant is cherished and nourished, but there is also the sense of how useless such instruction is in the face of random death by bombing.

Boland is speaking here on behalf of caring adults. But the reader will realise that the dead child had parents who most likely did instruct their son or daughter in the very way which Boland describes in lines 7–10. The death of the child is therefore all the more moving, the fact that we cannot guarantee safety for our children all the more frightening.

The language of lullaby and the world of tales and legends should later give way to a particular language, a particular way of speaking which the child inherits and keeps as he or she grows up:

> Later an idiom for you to keep
> And living, learn

This is the natural course of events which the child, living, will learn; this is as it should be, but this sudden, violent death has destroyed that natural process of child growing to adulthood. Instead, in this poem, Boland sees herself in the light of the dead child and knows that she and others

> must learn from you, dead,
>
> To make our broken images rebuild
> Themselves around your limbs, your broken
> Image

Out of the destruction of the child's death by bombing, the poet grasps at the possibility of learning and rebuilding. Out of 'our broken images', Boland says we must rebuild. All that she once believed in, the need to instruct with rhymes and rhythms, tales and legends, has been momentarily shattered and broken by the bombing atrocity. And yet it is the broken image of the child that will inspire her to rebuild and to believe in those images again.

This final stanza is concerned with a way forward and Boland's need to find a new language, to

> find for your sake whose life our idle
> Talk has cost, a new language. Child
> Of our time, our times have robbed your cradle.

Here she implicates herself and others in the child's death. 'Child of Our Time' is a poem about public violence in which Boland explores the relationship between the private and the public voice. 'Yesterday I knew no lullaby' is how she begins. She uses 'we' in stanza two and by the final stanza Boland is searching for a new language to replace 'our idle/Talk'. The poem moves from a single to a collective voice.

Nowhere in the poem does she engage with sectarian issues or party politics. She does not attempt to diagnose or explain the political circumstances of the bomb. She mentions no place-names, no person's name, and by doing so one act of violence becomes a symbol for every act of violence in which innocent people are killed. But she does admit to 'our idle/Talk'. Boland is recognising the need for empty, useless talk to be replaced with a new language, a language which may prevent a bomb from exploding, a child from dying. This child has been robbed, 'our times have robbed your cradle', but if a new language can be found then that child may not have died in vain.

The final line of the poem is both a prayer and a hope:

> Sleep in a world your final sleep has woken

and it can be interpreted in different ways.

One reading could suggest that the child has slept its final sleep in this world and has woken up to a world beyond this one where it will sleep peacefully and undisturbed.

Or 'Sleep in a world your final sleep has woken' could mean that the child's final sleep has woken the world up to an awareness of the need for change, for a 'new language'. Eavan Boland wishes for the child the possibility of sleep in a world which knows no violence and terrorism. There is no indulgent sentimentalism in Boland, nor does she find comfort in spiritual consolation. As a poet, her medium is language and it is language, a new language, which will make possible or bring about an end to innocent deaths. Both readings should be discussed but, whatever the final interpretation, it should be seen within the context of the poem as a whole.

The Famine Road

This poem uses many of the devices of the dramatist: the different voices, a situation involving conflict, suspense. Eavan Boland has absented herself from the poem in one sense. There is no personal 'I', but Boland's presence is felt everywhere – in her choice of subject matter, her sympathetic response to suffering, in her shaping and making of the poem.

'The Famine Road' begins with a letter from Charles Edward Trevelyan written to Colonel Jones and being read by Jones before a Relief Committee. The mid-nineteenth-century language is very archaic, and, though the phrasings resemble ordinary speech, what distinguishes it are its simile, its vividness, its use of balance.

> 'Idle as trout in light Colonel Jones,
> these Irish, give them no coins at all; their bones
> need toil, their character no less.'

The dismissive tone is clearly heard in these lines as Trevelyan claims to know the Irish and to know what's good for them. He insults a people, both physically and mentally. Then Boland dramatically sets the scene:

> Trevelyan's
> seal blooded the deal table.

The red wax seal on the letter has become a death warrant, the striking verb 'blooded' hinting at the devastation and suffering to come. There is tension and possibility in lines 4–5:

> The Relief
> Committee deliberated:

and Boland gives them a tentative but concerned sentence which counteracts Trevelyan's implacable one.

> 'Might it be safe,
> Colonel, to give them roads, roads to force
> from nowhere, going nowhere of course?'

The suggestion is both compassionate and absurd.

In this first stanza, Boland has vividly re-enacted a crucial moment from one of Ireland's most difficult times: in three sentences she has allowed us a glimpse of the enormity of the crisis and the fate of thousands. People around a table are determining a people's future.

The italicised verse which follows is addressed to a particular woman and it is introduced without explanation. The speaker is a doctor. It does not begin with a capital letter; the voice is in mid-sentence and it abruptly cuts across the first stanza. The woman is being evaluated and judged, just as the Irish people were judged and evaluated in the previous stanza:

> *'one out of every ten and then*
> *another third of those again*
> *women – in a case like yours.'*

The individual is reduced to a statistic in a tone of voice that is matter-of-fact, objective, and that we do not know exactly what is being spoken of here creates a sense of unease. What we do know is that we are hearing an unwelcome, upsetting diagnosis.

The third section of Boland's poem describes the famine road itself.

> Sick, directionless they worked; . . .

By placing the two adjectives at the beginning of the line, Boland achieves greater emphasis and these two adjectives sum up the basic plight of the people and the nature of the enterprise. 'Directionless' could apply not only to the road but to those making it and Boland is a sympathetic imaginative witness to their condition:

> Fork, stick
> were iron years away

But then another, more detached, and outrageously insensitive voice is heard in line 12:

> after all could
> they not blood their knuckles on rock, suck
> April hailstones for water and for food?

And their starvation, which is famine, is caught in a grim but realistic image suggestive of cannibalism:

> Why for that, cunning as housewives, each eyed –
> as if at a corner butcher – the other's buttock.

What is particularly frightening here is Boland's use of a familiar, everyday situation – housewives examining butcher's meat with a careful, knowing eye – and then comparing this to the desperate plight of the famine victims as they watch each other's bodies and see 'the other's buttock' as a potential meal.

In stanza four, the attention shifts again from the making of the famine road scene to the italicised impersonal doctor's voice addressing a sterile woman. The diagnosis continues; the tone is still casual, almost off-hand, the voice unsympathetic:

> *'anything may have caused it, spores,*
> *a childhood accident; one sees*
> *day after day these mysteries.'*

The blame here is being levelled at anything. The woman is a victim of chance or fate. A remedy seems impossible. All the time, one is aware of the distance between authority and helplessness.

Boland once again returns to the broader picture at line 20:

> Dusk: they will work tomorrow without him.

The end of the day brings the end of a life and these makers of the famine road know that tomorrow those who survive the night will go on working. If one of them falls to death

> they will work tomorrow without him.
> They know it and walk clear;

Disease and illness pervade the poem at this point. The man who has died is impassively viewed by those who still survive:

> He has become
> a typhoid pariah, his blood tainted, although
> he shares it with some there. No more than snow
> attends its own flakes where they settle
> and melt, will they pray by his death rattle.

The first line in this fifth stanza ends with a full stop, but all the other end-lines run on until 'death rattle'. Here the focus is on a disease taking its course and on the inevitability of death. Each one becomes 'a typhoid pariah' or fevered outcast and, though the individual mentioned in lines 21–23 is in a worse state than others, those who can continue on for longer will not even pray by his death bed. The image of the snow being indifferent to individual melting snowflakes is Boland's image here for man's inhumanity to man. The syntax is a little strained, but the rhymed 'snow' and 'although' seem to determine the structure. It is an image which conjures up a sense of the collective and the isolated.

When we return to the italicised voice, it has become even more hurtful and negative. The woman is addressed, but not by name; she is but 'woman'. The double 'never' and the false consolations of gardening and housekeeping ring hollow:

> *'You never will, never you know*
> *but take it well woman, grow*
> *your garden, keep house, good-bye.'*

Here the woman is dismissed, just as the Irish in general were dismissed by those who served the British Empire and, as we read through the poem, we can see how Eavan Boland is drawing our attention to two stories – one public, one private – and how both interconnect.

The poem ends with Jones's reply to Trevelyan and with the woman's own voice in which she compares her own sterility to a famine road.

Colonel Jones's letter is smug in tone. He is pleased to report that the famine road scheme has worked. Trevelyan's recommendation in his letter (lines 2–3) was hard work and Jones points out that the building of the famine roads exhausted the people and prevented them from rebelling.

> 'It has gone better than we expected, Lord
> Trevelyan, sedition, idleness, cured
> in one; from parish to parish, field to field,
> the wretches work till they are quite worn,
> then fester by their work;

The Irish are seen as either seditious or idle and Boland lets the voice of imperialism speak for itself. There is no need for her to comment.

Hard-heartedly, and without irony, Jones reports:

> we march the corn
> to the ships in peace.

But Boland has ensured that the irony has not been lost on the reader.

The closing words of Jones's letter, so insensitive towards the dead and so formally ingratiating towards Trevelyan, are probably the most offensive of all, especially to an Irish reader:

> this Tuesday I saw bones
> out of my carriage window, your servant Jones.'

The death of the starving, diseased Irish is offered as an after-thought and the juxtaposition of 'bones' and 'carriage' highlights how separate from each other are those who rule and those who are ruled.

The final voice is given to the woman who has been baldly told that she will never bear children and her grief on knowing this:

> 'Barren, never to know the load
> of his child in you, what is your body
> now if not a famine road?'

The woman, in seeing her own body and the life it has yet to live as a famine road, is recognising both an imposed sterility on a people and her own barrenness or sterility.

'The Famine Road' is a poem that works at several levels, the public and private, the historical and the personal, the male and the female.

The Black Lace Fan My Mother Gave Me

In line 1, Boland tells us that the gift from her father to her mother early in their relationship is even more special because

> It was the first gift he ever gave her

That very straightforward opening line turns the fan into an expression of a young man's love for a woman; the fan is also a practical object in a heatwave. The gift belongs to a time which Boland can only know second-hand. The fan itself is a gift, but the story surrounding the fan is also passed on and in the first three stanzas Boland recreates, imagines, reinvents this story:

> It was the first gift he ever gave her,
> buying it for five francs in the Galeries
> in pre-war Paris. It was stifling.
> A starless drought made the nights stormy.

The precise cost, the setting, the weather all create an atmosphere. The very short sentence 'It was stifling' is a sentence that could have been spoken by her mother in the telling of the story; the sentence is brief – it is as if the oppressive heat is preventing elaboration.

The poem does not follow a regular rhyme throughout, though Boland does use end-rhyme for effect in the final stanza. The first stanza has a music in its rhythm (the long, run-on first sentence, then the very short one followed by a longer) and alliteration ('gift'/'gave'; 'five francs', 'stifling'/'starless'/'stormy').

Stanza two pieces together a scene that took place fifty years ago and its seven crisp sentences become part of a jigsaw puzzle. There are facts and there are imaginings. Boland imagines her father waiting while the fan was being wrapped, knowing that he was late:

> They stayed in the city for the summer.
> They met in cafes. She was always early.
> He was late. That evening he was later.
> They wrapped the fan. He looked at his watch.

Boland does not attempt to describe the young man and the young woman in any physical detail, but we are given a glimpse of their personalities in half a line:

> She was always early.
> He was late.

And stanza three focuses on her mother waiting, not knowing that he had bought her his first gift. The technique here is visual, cinematic, sensuous:

> She looked down the Boulevard des Capucines.
> She ordered more coffee. She stood up.
> The streets were emptying. The heat was killing.
> She thought the distance smelled of rain and lightning.

Again, short sentences here show us Boland carefully attempting to construct the past. Her use of repetition ('They stayed', 'They met', 'They wrapped'; 'He was late', 'He looked' and 'She looked', 'She ordered', 'She stood', 'She thought') gives the scene a distance and a tension.

Having pictured it, Boland leaves the scene incomplete. She does not describe the man arriving with the wrapped fan. Instead, in stanza four, she turns to the object itself. The poem shifts from the imagined past to the present. The scene in Paris may be vague or incomplete, but the fan itself is vividly before her. The eye no longer imagines a Parisian street or a distance smelling of rain and lightning; the word 'These' in line 13 indicates the eye is now focusing on the particular:

> These are wild roses, appliquéd on silk by hand,
> darkly picked, stitched boldly, quickly.
> The rest is tortoiseshell and has the reticent,
> clear patience of its element. It is
>
> a worn-out, underwater bullion and it keeps,
> even now, an inference of its violation.
> The lace is overcast as if the weather
> it opened for and offset had entered it.

This is present time and this is Boland contemplating the black lace fan her mother gave her. The poem moves from fragments of narrative to an interesting and complex consideration of the fan before her. The descriptive technique in stanzas four and five is richly imaginative as she contemplates the making of the fan and the sentences from here on in the poem become longer and more expansive, matching her exploratory mind at work.

First the floral design of 'wild roses' is described. The artistry of the creator is captured in verbs and adverbs: 'darkly picked, stitched boldly, quickly'. Boland sees a contrast between the fabric and the hard shell:

> The rest is tortoiseshell and has the reticent,
> clear patience of its element. It is
> a worn-out, underwater bullion and it keeps,
> even now, an inference of its violation.

The object is now given a different dimension; the tortoiseshell is associated with a sense of silence or concealment and the sense of having been violated or abused. There is a contrast between 'darkly picked, stitched boldly, quickly' and the submissive tortoiseshell.

What was ostensibly a romantic or erotic object, an object expressing human love, is now being seen and understood in terms of its origins, which involved destruction and violence. The shell of the tortoise has had to be broken and carved; its colour now reminds Boland of 'a worn-out, underwater bullion'. She recognises in the tortoiseshell, despite its ornamental context, 'an inference of its violation'; it is as if the shell itself, now supporting black lace and wild roses, is aware of its former self and how it has been violated.

Such an interpretation is the opposite of romantic, but Boland herself says in *Object Lessons* that she sees the fan, a traditional erotic object, not as a sign of triumph and acquisition, but as a sign of suffering. In other words, the fan, given by a man to a woman, is not an emblem of power and control and possession, but one of the passing of time. In Boland's words: 'ordinary objects seemed to warn me that the body might share the world but could not own it.'

The thought pattern here, when teased out, reveals a woman looking at a black lace fan in an unsentimental way. The emotionally charged moment belongs to the past, but the object remains, and in her telling of the story there is an attempt to gather the facts. Boland, however, does not enter into a description of the emotional bond, the love relationship between her father and mother. Boland has described 'The Black Lace Fan My Mother Gave Me' as a 'back-to-front love poem'.

The past and the present are there throughout the poem but Boland knows that the only way of reconstructing the past is through improvisation. She says so in line 24. First she gave us a story as she pictured it, then she contemplates an emblem from that story, the black lace fan, in stanzas four and five. In stanza six, she returns to that Paris café and sets in motion a scene, but it is a scene whose ending she does not and cannot know.

The scene itself is essentially romantic: a man hurrying to meet the woman he loves in Paris and bringing with him her first gift:

> The past is an empty café terrace.
> An airless dusk before thunder. A man running.
> And no way now to know what happened then –
> none at all – unless, of course, you improvise:

Here is drama, excitement, expectation and Boland knows that the moment belongs to someone else, not to her. There is a tone of wonder in her use of 'no way now' and 'none at all'. The word 'airless' in line 22 echoes the 'starless' of line 4. The lovers met and the fan was given, but Eavan Boland was not part of their private emotional experience and, therefore, she must invent it if she is to know it.

This is why 'now' and 'then' (line 23) are key words. The past is the past, but Boland ends the poem by recreating the earlier sensation, perhaps of intense delight, known to her mother when she first saw the fan in Paris in stifling heat fifty years before. The fan itself is 'worn-out' and 'faded' now, hinting perhaps that the relationship between those lovers in Paris has also grown old, but Boland, in a marvellous concluding stanza, sees it afresh in the span of a blackbird's wing outside her window:

> The blackbird on this first sultry morning,
> in summer, finding buds, worms, fruit,
> feels the heat. Suddenly she puts out her wing –
> the whole, full, flirtatious span of it.

In this way, from the fan in Paris in the past to the blackbird's wing in the present, there is connection and continuity. When her mother gave her the fan, it was a gesture of love and continuity, but Boland could only, at first, piece things together and could only guess at 'what happened then'. The fan could be handed on, but the emotion associated with the fan and experienced by her mother could never be fully communicated to her daughter. That is not to say that Eavan Boland did not sense that emotion and she glimpses something akin to it in the blackbird's wing.

The fan is old; she thinks of the occasion when it was given and of how it had been made. The fan is altered by the passing of time; it grows old just as the lovers do, but in an altogether different context Boland sees the fan afresh. She finds in nature's blackbird an equivalent for the black lace fan. The 'first gift he ever gave her' is remembered now on 'this first sultry morning/in summer'. The bird is as free as a bird. The blackbird's fan is 'whole, full', unlike the broken tortoiseshell in the ornamental fan; it is natural and beautiful and in its element. The sense of summer and the use of 'Suddenly' and 'flirtatious' make for a flourishing celebratory ending.

The final line, 'the whole, full, flirtatious span of it', refers to the blackbird's wing, but it could also be a description of the black lace fan when her mother first opened it in Paris all those years ago. Waiting for the man, she was bored, impatient, but when the gift was given, when the fan was opened, the boredom and impatience disappeared.

The subject matter of the poem is a black lace fan but its themes include time and memory; how the past can or cannot live in the present; the ageing body; the understanding of man and woman; and their relationship to each other.

Among other things, this is a poem that invites its readers to imagine an emotion, a life story other than our own. It reminds us that this is not always possible, but it also reminds us that in our own experience we can find a moment, a mood, an image, which allows us to imagine and to know what others knew. It is a complex, intricate poem and one that becomes more and more rewarding on subsequent readings.

The Shadow Doll

As with 'The Black Lace Fan My Mother Gave Me', 'The Shadow Doll' is a poem that sets past and present side by side. In this poem, Boland is remembering the night before her wedding in the early 1970s and she is also remembering a Victorian wedding-custom from a hundred years before.

The earlier stanzas describe the object: the shadow doll, a miniature bride, in its dome of glass. It begins in the past tense with a description of the making of the wedding dress:

> They stitched blooms from ivory tulle
> to hem the oyster gleam of the veil.
> They made hoops for the crinoline.

Boland here imagines something beautiful and delicate and special. The details, 'blooms', 'oyster gleam' and 'crinoline', suggest elegance, and in the second stanza the poem moves into the present tense when Boland looks at the object, the shadow doll.

> Now, in summary and neatly sewn –
> a porcelain bride in an airless glamour –
> the shadow doll survives its occasion.

This wedding dress in miniature or summary is a relic from an age long gone. The bride is porcelain and its lifeless quality is emphasised further in Boland's use of 'airless glamour'. The dress and the Victorian bride who wore it belong to the past, but the shadow doll survives.

Boland's awareness of past and present is highlighted again in stanza three with the phrase 'even now'. The poem began with two self-contained stanzas, but at line 7 the poem flows through five stanzas down to the final line. It is as if Boland's focused and concentrated attention on the object gives way to her own eventual subjective response.

The third stanza begins with Boland's awareness of how the glass-domed shadow doll was part of a busy world of social interaction, illnesses, impulses. It would be kept by the married woman and would witness life going on. But Boland thinks of it as knowing but not telling:

> Under glass, under wraps, it stays
> even now, after all, discreet about
> visits, fevers, quickenings and lusts

This shadow doll was once viewed by a bride-to-be and Boland considers what it must have been like for this Victorian woman to view an effigy of herself;

> and just how, when she looked at
> the shell-tone spray of seed pearls,
> the bisque features, she could see herself
>
> inside it all, holding less than real
> stephanotis, rose petals, never feeling
> satin rise and fall with the vows

Here Boland has the Victorian bride-to-be envisaging herself 'inside it all' and the image becomes almost one of imprisonment: the woman is reduced to a miniature, what it depicts is 'less than real', and the woman becomes the lifeless doll 'never feeling/satin rise and fall' as she speaks her marriage vows.

Stanza six into stanza seven shifts from Boland picturing the Victorian woman contemplating her shadow doll before her wedding to Boland herself on the night before her own wedding. She thinks of the doll, the other bride-to-be, her vows and Boland's vows which, she tells us,

> I kept repeating on the night before –
> astray among the cards and wedding gifts –
> the coffee pots and the clocks . . .

The poem has now moved into Boland's present. She repeats the vows that she will declare in public tomorrow. She is surrounded by the happy clutter of wedding presents; she speaks of herself as 'astray' or wandering, but the poem ends with a decisive gesture. The final stanza describes an object:

> the battered tan case full of cotton
> lace and tissue-paper, pressing down, then
> pressing down again. And then, locks.

This, presumably, is either the case that she will carry on honeymoon or a case containing a wedding-gift of cotton lace. At any rate, what is important here is the gesture of

> pressing down, then
> pressing down again. And then, locks.

The words here in these closing lines precisely capture the gesture itself; 'pressing down' is repeated as is 'then' and 'then' and 'again' rhyme: the punctuation and the final verb click the case and the sentence into place.

Eavan Boland has not been sent a shadow doll. She is presented with no such image of herself, and that which emerges from the poem is one of a determined woman who is in control of her future. The sense of the 'astray' of line 17 has become a woman closing and locking a suitcase.

The shadow doll was locked inside an airless dome of glass and Boland imagined the Victorian woman viewing the object as a possible representation of her situation. Boland herself locks the wedding case, in a gesture that captures difference and change in women's lives.

White Hawthorn in the West of Ireland

The line length and where the line breaks are important for every poet. This poem is written in free verse; the line length and the arrangement of lines follow no distinct or definite pattern, but in line 1, for example, the line break allows for emphasis on 'West'.

There is a sense of release and expansion in the opening stanzas as Boland describes her journey west. The first line is factual; line 2 gives the sentence atmosphere and colour. It is neither quite the end of spring nor the beginning of summer. There is the sense of a world opening up before her and a smaller, contained world being left behind:

> I drove West
> in the season between seasons.
> I left behind suburban gardens.
> Lawnmowers. Small talk.

This contrast is more fully realised in the second section; the wild landscape is different from the enclosed, neat suburban gardens, and Boland takes in a different kind of light, a different way of thinking and speaking.

> Under low skies, past splashes of coltsfoot,
> I assumed
> the hard shyness of Atlantic light
> and the superstitious aura of hawthorn.

First-person narration is central to the poem ('I' occurs in each of the first five sections) and the poem charts not only the journey west, but also the effect the journey has on the poet.

The poem is structured in such a way that the first two sections end with a full-stop (a technique which Boland also uses in 'The Shadow Doll') and then the poem is shaped so that it moves from section to section without pausing: this gives the poem a sense of expansion suited to the feeling of longing which is introduced in line 9:

> All I wanted then was to fill my arms with
> sharp flowers,
> to seem, from a distance, to be part of
> that ivory, downhill rush. . .

There is a feeling here of becoming one with the landscape, of embracing not only the flowers of the white hawthorn but of entering into, of being 'part of' the light and the movement of the west; 'to seem, from a distance' that she has merged with the landscape. The lyrical and poetic 'ivory, downhill rush' are miles removed, in every sense, from 'Lawnmowers. Small talk.'

But the fulfilment of desire is hindered by knowledge and by caution:

> But I knew,
> I had always known
> the custom was
> not to touch hawthorn.
> Not to bring it indoors for the sake of
> the luck
> such constraint would forfeit –

The 'superstitious aura' of line 8 has prevented Boland from filling her arms with white hawthorn flowers, yet it was all she wanted then.

She imagines how desire is checked and restrained by inherited folk beliefs. She thinks of how

> a child might die, perhaps, or an unexplained
> fever speckle heifers. So I left it

What the poem succeeds in doing, however, is allow Eavan Boland to fill her mind and imagination with the white hawthorn. She has had to leave it, but has brought it with her in the poem:

> So I left it
> stirring on those hills
> with a fluency
> only water has. And, like water, able
> to re-define land. And free to seem to be –
>
> for anglers,
> and for travellers astray in
> the unmarked lights of a May dusk –
> the only language spoken in those parts.

The lines themselves here achieve a fluency. The 's' and 'f' sounds flow into each other and there is movement in the imagery she uses: 'stirring on those hills', 'like water', 'free'.

The poem begins with an awareness of the suburban world it is leaving behind. It then focuses on the individual and her desire to lose herself in an open, free landscape, while the closing section speaks of people against a darkening rural background, anglers and travellers for whom the white hawthorn seems to be 'the only language spoken in those parts'. The anglers and travellers do not belong to this place; for them the whitethorn seems to be 'the only language spoken in those parts', a language different from the 'Small talk' of line 4.

'White Hawthorn in the West of Ireland' is a poem that explores freedom and constraint, desire and language (small talk, superstition and the language of landscape) and the uniqueness of place. It is part of Boland's sequence 'Outside History' in which she writes about the lost, the voiceless, the silent. These themes are not, however, particularly evident in this poem, except perhaps in the implied sense of loss through the unpeopled landscape of the west.

Outside History

'Outside History' begins with a recognised truth:

> There are outsiders, always

and every reader can supply interpretations and examples. In that same line, Boland offers one such example. She sees the stars as outsiders, they are at a great remove:

> There are outsiders, always. These stars –
> these iron inklings of an Irish January,
> whose light appeared
> thousands of years before
> our pain did: they are, they have always been
> outside history.

What is clearly established in these opening lines is a sense of the cosmos and the planet Earth, the macrocosm and the microcosm, the great world or universe and the little world of human nature. Poem VII in the 'Outside History' sequence is called 'We Are Human History. We Are Not Natural History' and Boland is making this distinction here. The life of the stars is immense. They are natural history. Their presence now is conveyed in images ('iron', 'Irish January') which suggest cold and distant presences that contrast with the human history, the particular, 'our pain'. Pain may refer to human suffering in general or how the Irish have suffered throughout history.

Boland's voice here is the collective voice; she is speaking for the Irish people. As a woman, Boland may see herself as someone outside history, but here she is also saying that she has chosen to become part of human history. The stars are outside history, they do not get involved:

> They keep their distance. Under them remains
> a place where you found
> you were human, and
>
> a landscape in which you know you are mortal.

The 'you' of line 8 would seem to refer to all of us beneath the stars, but perhaps more specifically it refers to the people of Ireland, the Irish in their landscape. Or perhaps it refers to an individual who is mortal, who knows pain and suffering.

In the central stanza, Boland speaks of 'a time to choose' and what it seems she is choosing between is the stars on the one hand and the human story or history on the other. Or the lines could also be read to mean that she is choosing between 'a place where you found/you were human' and 'a landscape in which you know you are mortal'. Under the stars, there remains a place

> And a time to choose between them.
> I have chosen:

This decisive line, 'I have chosen', marks a turning point in the poem. Boland explains the direction she is taking:

> out of myth into history I move to be
> part of that ordeal
> whose darkness is
>
> only now reaching me from those fields,
> those rivers, those roads clotted as
> firmaments with the dead.

This movement from myth into history is a movement from a world where woman is often the victim or the object, to a world where woman could become the subject, the maker of history, the maker of the poem.

In this poem, Boland is possessing a past which she did not know. It is her past, a painful ordeal, and, in the act of writing the poem, she is finding a voice to honour the silent voices of the past.

The imagery of the stars and their light, which has been travelling for thousands and thousands of years, becomes an image of darkness travelling through time from Ireland's past. Boland sees the light of the stars and is aware of the darkness of ordeal and pain; she has chosen to write about human history, not natural history.

The details of 'fields', 'rivers', 'roads' suggest countryside and the clusters of dead on the road hint at the Great Irish Famine. Boland, in the lines 'clotted as/ firmaments with the dead', has effectively taken the language associated with the stars of stanza one and transferred the image to the human story that is of greater interest to her now.

The closing stanza once again uses 'we'.

> How slowly they die
> as we kneel beside them, whisper in their ear.
> And we are too late. We are always too late.

The poem began with a reference to 'our pain'; then Boland spoke of how 'I have chosen' and 'I move to be part of that ordeal'. She returns to an inclusive voice at the end, indicating perhaps that she herself may once have felt that, as a woman and as a woman poet, she was outside history, but that she has now entered into history. The poem has focused on Irish history and on the need to know and remember it.

The tone in the final lines is one of pity, helplessness and deep regret. The poem remembers 'that ordeal', those dreadful deaths on the roads. They are dead and dying and cannot be saved. All Boland can offer is words of comfort when it is too late, and the repetition in the poem's last line

> And we are too late. We are always too late.

highlights the idea contained in the poem's title. Is Boland saying here that she has responded too late to the plight of those who belong to history or is she saying that as a poet, as an Irish poet, she has not marked or remembered before now, and perhaps might never fully mark, the lives of all those who died and have been forgotten. The poem itself, of course, succeeds in conveying to the reader that those who are outside history, 'the lost, the voiceless, the silent,' should never be forgotten.

This Moment

In this short, lyric poem, Boland is writing about a place and a feeling. She is the observer and her technique is such that every detail, every mood, is presented carefully and very slowly. The poem has twelve full stops and ten of the individual lines of the poem end with a full-stop. Several sentences are just two or three words long.

'A neighbourhood' (line 1), 'A woman . . . a child' (line 11) would suggest the impersonal; but Boland, in writing 'A neighbourhood', not 'this' or 'the' or 'my' neighbourhood, and 'A woman', 'a child' allows the poem to become any neighbourhood, every woman, every child. She does not use 'I', but the experience is hers as well as an experience which becomes ours.

The moment of the poem is created in terms of place and time:

> A neighbourhood.
> At dusk.

Boland's decision here not to observe conventional grammatical rules achieves far greater effect than if she were to present neighbourhood and dusk within complete sentences.

Dusk, a shadowy time, creates a mood of quietness and closure. (In each of the poems 'This Moment', 'Love', 'The Pomegranate' from *In a Time of Violence*, the word 'dusk' occurs.) The day is almost at an end. There is a sense of secrecy and mystery in nature. There is the sense of anticipation:

> Things are getting ready
> to happen
> out of sight.
> Stars and moths.
> And rinds slanting around fruit.

The stars will soon shine, the moths flutter, the fruit expand, become plumper. The darkness is non-threatening, mysterious. Here the eye moves from the brightening stars in the expanse high above to the softness of moths, to the detail of the slanting rinds and the richness of the fruit. Such sensory details together evoke harmony and fulfilment.

Having given the reader a sense of what is getting ready to happen, having shown us things we will not see, things that will 'happen/out of sight', Boland holds the poem a moment and prevents it from going forward. The pacing is as gradual and slow as the coming on of night. These things will happen, she tells us,

> But not yet.

These words, in a line on their own in the centre of the poem, mark a delicate pause, and then Boland gives us two striking images that have all the simplicity and beauty of a child's painting:

> One tree is black.
> One window is yellow as butter.

The strong, single colours here create vivid pictures; the simile is homely, familiar and appropriately domestic.

Towards the poem's end, the focus is on the human world. The neighbourhood was introduced in line 1, but it was a neighbourhood without people. Now at line 11, we find the image of woman and child, presumably a mother and child, one of the most potent images in the world:

> A woman leans down to catch a child
> who has run into her arms
> this moment.

This last phrase gives the poem its title; it is the central event for Boland. This moment is the moment of expressive action. All other movement in the poem is slow compared to this one just past when the child 'has run' into its mother's arms. It is a precious loving gesture between mother and child, and it is as if nature itself is celebrating and blessing the moment, for it is then that

> Stars rise.
> Moths flutter.
> Apples sweeten in the dark

and this beautifully musical, harmonious ending gives the moment its special quality.

The poem's gentle, quiet, reflective mood is partly achieved by the 's' sounds and repetition in 'dusk', 'sight', 'Stars', 'moths', 'rinds', 'slanting', 'leans', 'arms', 'rise', 'Moths', 'Apples' and 'sweeten', but also in the way the line and space are controlled on the page.

'This Moment' is a poem in which there is a poetry in the words and what they say, and there is also a poetry in the spaces and silences between them. Imagine for a moment the poem presented in a prose format:

> This Moment. A neighbourhood. At dusk. Things are getting ready to happen out of sight. Stars and moths. And rinds slanting round fruit. But not yet. One tree is black. One window is yellow as butter. A woman leans down to catch a child who has run into her arms this moment. Stars rise. Moths flutter. Apples sweeten in the dark.

Clearly, the writing here is too concentrated to be mistaken for prose, but if you were asked to rearrange the paragraph on a page using line, line breaks and spaces, how would you go about it? Such an exercise would focus your attention on how these aspects are important in the making of a poem.

Love

The poem remembers the past and was written years after the time it describes. In the poem's opening lines, that past is remembered and made present again on a return visit by Boland to Iowa:

> Dark falls on this mid-western town
> where we once lived when myths collided.

The experience and the memory of it are immediately enriched and made complex by the phrase 'when myths collided'. A dictionary will define myth as a fabulous tale, a fiction containing strange, supernatural characters and events; myth can also be something extraordinary and wonderful and something that you believe in; or it could mean something else entirely. Boland does not spell out her meaning here. One of the myths is from *The Aeneid*, but even that is never directly referred to. Instead, Boland works through allusion:

> Dusk has hidden the bridge in the river
> which slides and deepens
> to become the water
> the hero crossed on his way to hell.

In her mind, the bridge which she herself crosses and the bridge where she and her husband meet later in the poem becomes a bridge that leads towards hell. Aeneas is on his way to the underworld. Boland does not compare her crossing of the bridge to Aeneas's journey to hell, but the difficult circumstances of her daughter's illness and Boland's daily journey to her hospital bed may be shimmering behind the image.

The language at times is particular, accurate, crisp:

> Not far from here is our old apartment.
> We had a kitchen and an Amish table.
> We had a view.

and it is also charged with metaphor:

> And we discovered there
> love had the feather and muscle of wings
> and had come to live with us,
> a brother of fire and air.

These two languages reflect two areas of experience, one ordinary and everyday, the other emotional and imaginative. One is an outer, visible world, the other a world which is felt from within.

The time Boland speaks of in Iowa was a very difficult time for her family, but in that time of anxiety they discovered something new about the nature of love: that it was an almost palpable, physical thing, both gentle and strong; that it had 'the feather and muscle of wings'; that love was 'a brother of fire and air'. Earth, water, fire and air are the four elements, but Boland sees love not in terms of the physical reality of earth and water but as the powerful and invisible presences of 'fire and air'.

In the third section, Boland speaks of that dramatic time:

> We had two infant children one of whom
> was touched by death in this town
> and spared:

and a link is clearly established between this fact and the moment in *The Aeneid* that Boland returns to throughout the poem. The colon gives way to

> and when the hero
> was hailed by his comrades in hell
> their mouths opened and their voices failed and
> there is no knowing what they would have asked
> about a life they had shared and lost.

This is a difficult passage. Boland presumes that her readers will be familiar with Virgil and that they will make the connection between the two worlds. The moment referred to has to do with the attempt to find out, discover something. Aeneas's comrades, on seeing him again, want to cry out, but they cannot speak. His comrades once shared Aeneas's life and then they lost it. What Boland tells us is that there is no knowing what these comrades would have asked at this crucial time. The moment finds a parallel later in the poem when Boland herself longs to cry out to her husband but her voice, too, fails.

'Love' is complex, so complex perhaps that Boland herself does not always find the language to capture the thought or feeling. But there are sections which are very clear, such as these lines which make up section four:

> I am your wife.
> It was years ago.
> Our child is healed. We love each other still.
> Across our day-to-day and ordinary distances
> we speak plainly. We hear each other clearly.

In six short sentences, Boland compresses a time-span and gives a sense of her continuing life: the time when death touched one of her children is over; love is what has sustained past and present.

There is the recognition of the wonderful in the ordinary. She and her husband 'love each other still', but she wants to return to that extraordinary, difficult and intense time.

And yet I want to return to you
on the bridge of the Iowa river as you were,
with snow on the shoulders of your coat
and a car passing with its headlights on:

I see you as a hero in a text –
the images blazing and the edges gilded –
and I long to cry out the epic question
my dear companion:

Will we ever live so intensely again?
Will love come to us again and be
so formidable at rest it offered us ascension
even to look at him?

But the words are shadows and you cannot hear me.
You walk away and I cannot follow.

Here the tone is one of longing. The poem begins with 'we' ('we once lived', 'we had a kitchen', 'we had a view', 'we discovered', 'We had two infant children'), but at line 20, almost at the poem's centre, Boland speaks as 'I':

I am your wife

and the 'I' voice ('I want to return', 'I see you', 'I long to cry out', 'I cannot follow') is heard in the second half of the poem.

Boland here is searching for the intense and heightened moment she once knew; the image is 'blazing' and 'gilded', but she also knows that it can never be repeated. The love they knew then was so 'formidable at rest' that it offered 'ascension'. Love was an imposing and impressive presence; it gave Boland and her husband a sense of transcendence. The word 'ascension' is often associated with Christ's ascension into heaven on the fortieth day after the resurrection and, though that is not mentioned specifically in this poem, 'ascension' here does have a spiritual resonance.

The questions which Boland asks

Will we ever live so intensely again?
Will love come to us again and be
so formidable at rest it offered us ascension
even to look at him?

are asked even though it is as if she knows that the answers to both questions are no. She can only imagine herself asking these question; she does not ever get to speak them.

> But the words are shadows and you cannot hear me.
> You walk away and I cannot follow.

The references to the hero, the underworld, the voices attempting to speak, voices failing and not being heard, the allusions to Virgil and the hero in the underworld though complex, enrich the poem.

When Boland speaks of the comrades in hell and their not being able to speak, she is recognising a moment in literature where there is both an intensity of feeling and an inability to express it. In her own life, Boland experienced one such moment all those years ago in Iowa. She cannot relive that time as it was once lived. She can remember it and return to it in this very poem, but there are emotions and experiences which can never be articulated in words and which cannot be shared. This is why Aeneas's comrades cannot ask their hero 'about a life they shared and lost' and Boland similarly cannot ask her husband, whom she sees 'as a hero in a text', about the life they lived so intensely and the love they knew. It is something that she never will forget, nor will her husband ever forget it. However, it isn't just that the moment belongs to the past. Feelings are sometimes so deep that they can only be experienced and never fully articulated or explained. Their love now belongs to a different order of experience – they speak plainly, hear each other clearly – but Boland is realistic enough to know that she cannot find the words for that other experience of love; the words are shadows and her husband cannot hear her.

The Pomegranate

'The Pomegranate' looks different from Boland's other poems in this selection. There are no stanza divisions as such, no spacings, and it is written in blank verse: this is verse without rhyme in an iambic five-beat line, with considerable variation. Blank verse achieves a natural sounding utterance or speaking voice. Shakespeare's plays were written in blank verse.

The focus of the poem is the mother/daughter relationship and Boland begins by remembering her own first encounter with the mother/daughter myth of Ceres and Persephone when she was a girl and daughter. She responded to it strongly:

> The only legend I have ever loved is
> the story of a daughter lost in hell.
> And found and rescued there.
> Love and blackmail are the gist of it.
> Ceres and Persephone the names.

The technique here is descriptive summary; Boland writes in a straightforward style, announcing the facts which lead her to a more subjective and personal response.

The thing she likes best about this particular myth is that it allows her to become part of it. When she was a girl, she could respond to it and identify with it, and later as a woman and as a mother she can still see a powerful significance in this ancient story.

> And the best thing about the legend is
> I can enter it anywhere. And have.
> As a child in exile in
> a city of fogs and strange consonants,
> I read it first and at first I was
> an exiled child in the crackling dusk of
> the underworld, the stars blighted.

Here Boland is remembering a childhood spent in London. She did not feel at home in 'a city of fogs and strange consonants'; both the place and the language seemed foreign. For Boland, it was as if she, like Persephone, were living in an underworld with its unsettling sounds ('the crackling dusk') and hopeless atmosphere ('blighted stars').

From childhood memory, Boland moves directly to a time when she was now mother to a daughter and living in Dublin, the city of her birth. Once Persephone, she is now Ceres:

> Later
> I walked out in a summer twilight
> searching for my daughter at bed-time.

In the myth, Ceres frantically searches and searches for her daughter. Here in suburbia, a woman 'in a summer twilight' is simply going out to call her young daughter home, but Boland draws a parallel. The similarity is obviously not one of circumstance but of emotion. In Boland's case, her daughter will grow up to live her own life and one of the tests of Boland's love for her daughter is in letting her go.

This, of course, does not make the letting go any easier.

> When she came running I was ready
> to make any bargain to keep her.
> I carried her back past whitebeams
> and wasps and honey-scented buddleias.
> But I was Ceres then and I knew
> winter was in store for every leaf
> on every tree on that road.
> Was inescapable for each one we passed.
> And for me.

Just as Ceres knew, when her 'daughter came running', that she would lose her to winter and the underworld, Boland realistically knows that her daughter will move away from her mother; the girl will have to take on, and to know for herself, the difficulties and complexities of adulthood. There is also in these lines the knowledge that we must all face our own growing old and dying, that 'winter was in store for every leaf/on every tree on that road . . .'

Line 24 marks a divide in the poem as it shifts from past to present, from summer to winter. The daughter she once carried home in a summer twilight is now seventeen; she has her own identity, her own world, and is like any teenager with her 'teen magazines,/her can of Coke'. Boland watches her sleeping daughter whom she loves and she knows that she is losing her:

> It is winter
> and the stars are hidden.
> I climb the stairs and stand where I can see
> my child asleep beside her teen magazines,
> her can of Coke, her plate of uncut fruit.

The moment suddenly reveals its significance. She is Ceres, her daughter Persephone, and the 'uncut fruit' becomes the pomegranate.

> The pomegranate! How did I forget it?

If Ceres were to forget about the pomegranate, she would think that her daughter was returning to her forever. When Boland forgot the pomegranate, she forgot that her daughter would be distant from her, lost to her. But she remembers and is startled that she could have forgotten it. Line 29, with its exclamation mark and question mark, captures that mood.

This leads Boland to imagine what would have happened if Persephone had not eaten the pomegranate. It would have made for a happy ending, an ending which wouldn't know sorrow or loss:

> She could have come home and been safe
> and ended the story and all
> our heart-broken searching

Here, through the use of 'our', Boland is speaking for Ceres and herself and by implication every mother and she knows that the relationship between mother and daughter must give way to change. It is inevitable:

> but she reached
> out a hand and plucked a pomegranate.
> She put out her hand and pulled down
> the French sound for apple and
> the noise of stone

The gesture here is decisive: 'she reached out', she 'plucked', 'She put out her hand and pulled down'; and Boland sees in the word itself something of the future. It has both softness and harshness, beauty and sorrow: pomme, 'the French sound for apple' and granite, 'the noise of stone'.

The gesture is sympathetically understood. It is only natural that a child is hungry, be it in the world of legend or in the actual world where her own daughter lives.

> and the proof
> that even in the place of death,
> at the heart of legend, in the midst
> of rocks full of unshed tears
> ready to be diamonds by the time
> the story was told, a child can be
> hungry.

The child cannot resist hunger. The child in this instance does not know the consequences of eating; the mother does. By speaking of 'the place of death', Boland is perhaps also suggesting that somewhere deep within us there is a impulse, an urge, an appetite which will be met and which will become an acceptance of dying and death. The child on eating the pomegranate leaves childhood behind, enters adulthood and all that adulthood eventually implies, growing old and dying.

Boland knows and understands this as the child's mother and she imagines herself Ceres-like telling her daughter not to eat of the fruit, for it will only bring sorrow and separation:

> I could warn her. There is still a chance.

The late twentieth-century world that Boland and her daughter belong to is summoned up in stark, vivid images, set down one by one. Four sentences, each beginning with 'The' make for a plain, unadorned style:

> The rain is cold. The road is flint-coloured.
> The suburb has cars and cable television.
> The veiled stars are above ground.

This is not the world where Persephone spends winter:

> It is another world.

And Eavan Boland asks, wonders, what else can she do for her daughter as she cannot warn her. By warning her daughter of what lies ahead, she can give her rifts or openings in time, moments which will postpone or defer grief.

> But what else
> can a mother give her daughter but such
> beautiful rifts in time?

But grief is seen by Boland to be inevitable. It is something that every mother and every daughter will know. By warning her daughter, she will postpone the grief and the gift will be diminished.

> If I defer the grief I will diminish the gift.
> The legend will be hers as well as mine.
> She will enter it. As I have.

If Ceres could have told her daughter not to eat the pomegranate, she and Persephone would never have been separated, but Persephone wasn't warned and she came to know grief.

If Boland warns her daughter not 'to eat of the pomegranate', which becomes at this point in the poem a symbolic act of entering adulthood, she will have her daughter for longer, but paradoxically she knows that by deferring the grief she will diminish the gift, the gift of letting go, of allowing her teenage daughter to enter womanhood. The gift could also refer to her daughter's sense of knowing that her freedom involves choices and decisions. The Ceres and Persephone myth serves as a powerful and haunting background to the poem, but the reader should remember that to search too closely for parallels between the Greek myth and the relationship between Boland and her daughter could only confuse and detract from the poem's power.

Just as Boland herself grew to know the legend that told of sorrow, disappointment and separation, so, too, Boland's daughter must know that world someday:

> The legend will be hers as well as mine.

Boland's daughter will enter the myth of Ceres and Persephone, just as Boland herself entered that world when she was younger:

> She will enter it. As I have.
> She will wake up. She will hold
> the papery flushed skin in her hand.
> And to her lips. I will say nothing.

The poem ends with a slow-motion dramatic unfolding of what is to be. Boland's use of 'she' in 'She will', 'She will', 'She will' recognises and acknowledges the distance between mother and daughter, and the repetition of 'will' highlights the inevitability and the need for such an act. Her daughter will make her own decisions. Boland imagines her eating the imagined pomegranate, while Boland herself withdraws into silence.

This is a private and personal poem and yet, like the myth which it echoes, it speaks to every parent and every child because it is a poem about growing up and growing old.

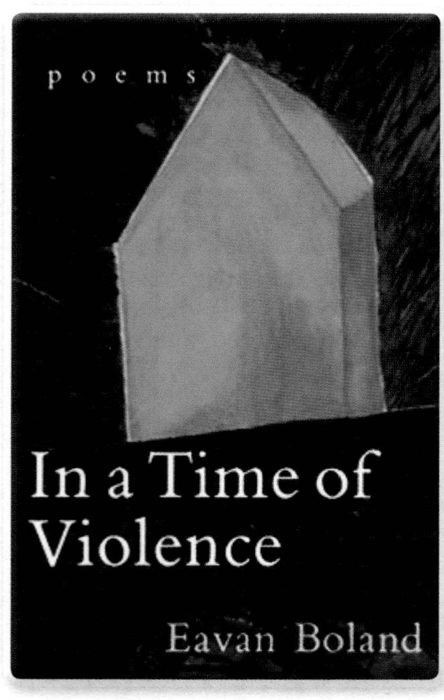

He continued:

> 'What you should experience as a reader is that sense of the truth of reality conveyed through the form of the poem. So much of it is free verse, yes, but I feel it's every bit as strict a form as the sonnet. There is only one right word. You must find that word. The other part is music. All art aspires to the condition of music, so what you hear must sound right.'

And Durcan quotes T. S. Eliot who believed that poetry must find the music 'latent in common speech'. He also professed that a line from his poem 'The Nun's Bath' sums it all up: '"My job is to be present, which I am." That's it.'

Reviewing *Life is a Dream* in *The Irish Times*, Harry Clifton says that 'Paul Durcan, like all real poets, is a street wanderer, constantly looking through the lit windows of the ordinary, wishing to get back in.' Pat Crotty says that 'Durcan's ear for colloquial speech vindicates Durcan's belief that poetry must grow out of ordinary life'.

Durcan, says Ruth Padel (in *52 Ways of Looking at a Poem*), 'has crafted a unique, manically confidential voice which puts a surreal (or maybe super-real) imagination to work through self-deprecating tragic-comic narrative and social observation which shows us every detail in a bizarre and surreal light. He brings out the madness of what everyone takes for normal.'

In an essay titled 'Passage to Utopia', Durcan wrote: 'My work as a poet has always been searching for the other place. The notion of "utopia" is fundamental to something about myself, and I think, about human nature . . . All my life I have been looking for a Mont Saint Victoire. And it is no accident that most of my books have the names of places in them.' In his poem 'The Difficulty that is Marriage', Durcan confides 'I have my troubles and I shall always have them' while in 'A Cold Wind Blew in from Lake Geneva', he says that his two mottos are 'Provincials to The Wall/ And – Never Conform'.

Paula Meehan reviewing *Life is a Dream* wrote that this is 'a poetry for the befuddled, the disorganized, the demented, the muddling through, the most of us. His songs celebrate our small mercies and tender decencies in a world that favours the corrupt, the greedy, the alpha-gobshites.'

Biographical Notes

Paul Durcan was born in Dublin, on 16 October 1944, of County Mayo parents. His father, John Durcan, a barrister and later a judge, grew up in Turlough and his mother, Sheila MacBride, was the famous John MacBride's niece. Major John MacBride was married to Maud Gonne, the love of Yeats's life, and was executed in 1916 for his part in the Rising. Paul Durcan, as a young boy, was brought to see Gonne, now old and gaunt. This family background meant that Durcan grew up with a strong awareness of Irish history, place and culture.

Durcan was educated at Gonzaga College. He took classes in painting and acting, went to UCD to study economics, dropped out after a year and went to London in search of work. He worked for Securicor, washed dishes, worked for the North Thames Gas Company which was five minutes from the Tate Gallery and which he visited every lunchtime. In the end, he couldn't stand the gas job (he remembers how a sign by the entrance read 'Look Ahead With Gas') and returned to Dublin, in 1967, where he met Patrick and Katherine Kavanagh and spent many days in their company.

That same year he met Nessa O'Neill at a wedding at the Shangri-La Hotel in Dalkey. They went to London where Nessa was working but Durcan returned to Dublin where he was to start work as a sports sub-editor on *The Irish Press*. He left after a day, went back to London and Nessa and then they shifted to Barcelona where Durcan taught at the Casa Ingles. They stayed until Christmas before returning to London where he and Nessa got married. Nessa was the bread-winner; Durcan wrote reviews and looked after their children.

The couple returned to Ireland, Cork this time, when their two daughters were one and two, and Durcan studied archaeology and medieval history at University College Cork. He had studied English in his First Year at UCC and intended to take it to degree level but was told by a lecturer at the end of First Year that he 'did not have a proper understanding of poetry'. In 1973, Durcan was awarded a first-class honours degree in archaeology and history. He was greatly influenced by Professor M. J. O'Kelly, an expert on Newgrange, who brought his students on trips to ancient sites in Munster.

Paul Durcan won the Patrick Kavanagh Award for poetry in 1974 for his collection *O Westport in the Light of Asia Minor* and since then has published over twenty titles including *Teresa's Bar* (1976); *Sam's Cross* (1978); *Jesus, Break His Fall* (1980); *Cries of an Irish Caveman* (2001) and *Life is a Dream* (2009). He has written about his personal life in his poetry: the day he met his future wife, married life, fatherhood, marriage break-up, birth of grandchildren and his work also explores public themes and concerns such as the Catholic Church, the Government, politics and violence. When *The Selected Paul Durcan* was published in 1982, he was widely and critically acclaimed. Two years later, 160 post-primary schools in Ireland were sent Durcan's books by Raven Arts Press for their libraries. Among them was his 1980 collection *Jesus, Break His Fall* and following a newspaper report some TDs, teachers and parents – and more than a few who hadn't even read the book – wanted it banned.

Durcan has given poetry readings all over the world and considers these very important. Over forty years, he has given 'hundreds, perhaps thousands' of readings – in Russia, Australia, America, Japan, Brazil and many other places.

Here's how an *Irish Times* profile from 1987 described his riveting, charismatic readings:

> 'He stands in the spotlight, legs apart, his body slightly swaying, a book held close to his thigh and rarely consulted (except as a signal that a poem is over). As he prepares to speak, his eyes blink with the tension, his lips curve into strange shapes of concentrated, nervous energy, into anger or melancholy – you can't tell which – and then *the voice*.'

In *Paul Durcan's Diary*, Durcan himself says of his readings:

> 'Every poetry recital is a Beecher's Brook and in the days leading up to it there are nightmare glimpses of that Himalayan crevasses as it comes galloping out to devour you. No matter how many times you may have jumped it before, each time is always the first time and you try not to think about it and, when you've jumped it, you wonder how you did it and the sense of relief purifies.'

In a piece written in 1987 and entitled 'Birth of a Poet', Paul Durcan, remembering a formative day in 1956, wrote:

> 'I was twelve years of age. It was winter and it was a Saturday afternoon. I should have been playing football for my school that afternoon but due to the heavy rain the game had been cancelled. I was sitting at the breakfast table in our basement livingroom in our home in Dublin city, attempting to engage myself in my weekend English essay. Before me on the table lay one of those sixpenny school exercise copybooks with redbrick covers. The open page got blanker and blanker.
>
> I stared at my mother who was sitting silently at the fireside, knitting. I stared at the flames of the coal fire. I stared at the relentless downpour outside.
>
> I could think of nothing to write for this English essay. The title was 'Give In Your Own Words An Imaginary Account Of The Kidnapping Of St Patrick In Wales By Irish Pirates.' I felt choked by boredom and self-pity. What had I done to deserve this fate?

I had no interest in writing essays, least of all about obscure and dubious goings on in Wales all of two thousand years ago. What I was interested in was Adventure – the Adventure of the sports field and the Adventure of girlfriends. As for reading – only adventure, murder and love stories were of any interest to me. R.L. Stevenson, Sir Walter Scott, Mrs Belloc Lowndes.

At least half an hour, an hour, an hour and a quarter maybe, went by. The pages blank. My Osmiroid pen poised in vindictive futility. Gazing into the flames of the fire, the sunflower flames, I fell into a state of daydreaming, and on the celluloid film, so to speak, of the actual flames I saw unfold before me the actual kidnapping of this young boy in Wales. All I had to do now was to write down what I had just seen with my own eyes, and in less than twenty minutes I had filed a four-page report on the kidnap.

I was not a conceited boy but I recognized the quality of direct unadorned reportage in my essay and I knew that my teacher, who was strict about marking, would give it 10/10.

Sure enough, when I got back my copy book, there in his unmistakeable Bic biro logo, the magic 10/10. From that time on I wrote for my own pleasure, tales of imaginary adventure and romance. About a year later I began to write in the form of verse (as distinct from prose) because I had got the feeling that poetry was itself the supreme form of adventure and romance. I came to see poetry as being a valid form of social protest and liberation.

However it was the writing itself which lay at the heart of the adventure: the day to day, year-in year-out struggle to achieve the primordial state of daydreaming out of which all true poetry gets written, and simultaneously the struggle with the material itself – the hard slog with words and their silences.

One of the truest poems I ever wrote was a poem called 'Aughawall Graveyard', which is situated in the lea of the pilgrimage mountain of Croagh Patrick in Co. Mayo. My grandfather Joseph McBride lies buried there under a cairn of stones. For six months or more my completed poem stood at 42 lines and while I knew that the poem was 90% right, I knew also that it was a massive 10% off beam. Until one day, preoccupied with minding my infant children, I was in a daydream – the very same as when I had gazed into the flames and daydreamed the kidnap of St Patrick – I saw that my 42-line poem was 40 lines too long. In the exhilaration of true poem-making – which is akin to the ecstasy of hailing a friend from the other side of the street, or of Sherpa Tenzing waving from the top of Mount Everest – I took out my black Bic biro sickle and slashed off the 40 redundant lines of 'Aughawall Graveyard':

> Lonely Lonely Lonely Lonely:
> The story with a middle only.

In an *Irish Times* interview in 2012, Durcan, on being asked about the process involved in the writing of a poem that was deeply rooted in the present moment, said that it was essential to make notes at the time: 'I once heard Dervla Murphy (travel writer) say on the wireless – about 30 years ago – that if she didn't write down what she had heard and seen within 24 hours, it was no good. That was music to my ears, because that's how it has to be. And the next 24 or 48 hours are crucial for me. If the first draft doesn't get written then, it won't have what it should have – the actuality of that utterly unique and fleeting moment. The exact words some person used. I like that phrase of Wallace Stevens: "The poem is the cry of its occasion".'

Paul Durcan lives in Dublin and on Achill Island.

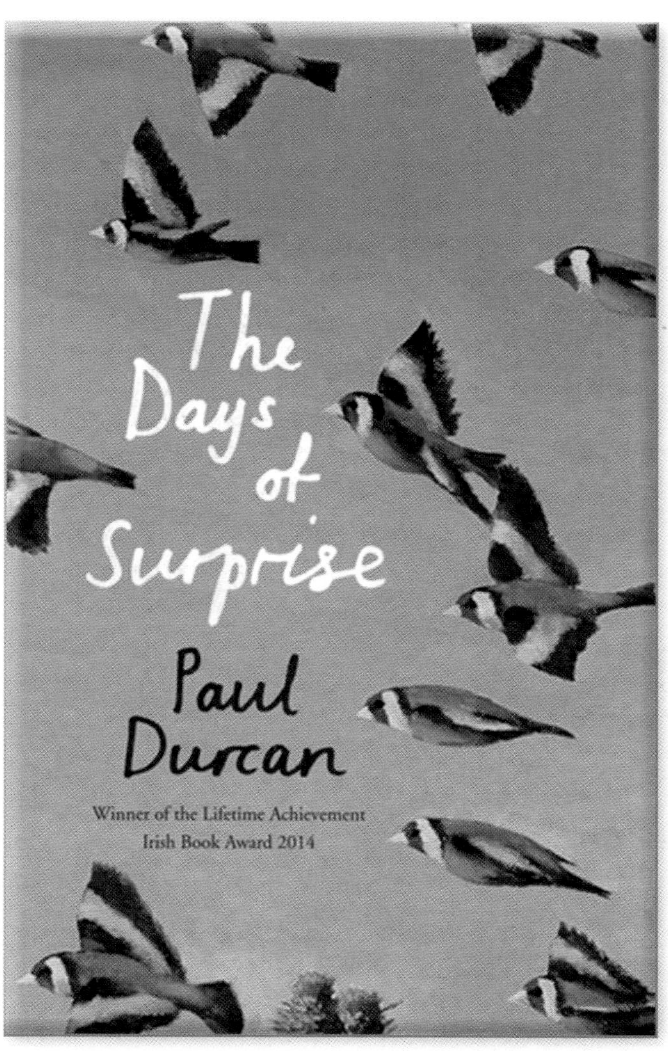

POEMS

(The poems, as they are printed here, are in the order in which they appear in *Life is a Dream: 40 Years Reading Poems, 1967–2007.*)

Nessa

I met her on the first of August
In the Shangri-La Hotel,
She took me by her index finger
And dropped me in her well.
And that was a whirlpool, that was a whirlpool,
And I very nearly drowned.

Take off your pants, she said to me,
And I very nearly didn't;
Would you care to swim? she said to me
And I hopped into the Irish Sea.
And that was a whirlpool, that was a whirlpool,
And I very nearly drowned.

On the way back I fell in the field
And she fell down beside me,
I'd have lain in the grass with her all my life
With Nessa:
She was a whirlpool, she was a whirlpool,
And I very nearly drowned.

O Nessa my dear, Nessa my dear,
Will you stay with me on the rocks?
Will you come for me into the Irish Sea
And for me let your red hair down?
And then we will ride into Dublin City
In a taxi-cab wrapped up in dust.
Oh you are a whirlpool, you are a whirlpool,
And I am very nearly drowned.

Glossary

Title Nessa: Paul Durcan married Nessa O'Neill. At the outset, it is worthwhile to ask if the personal names and references are autobiographical. It is even more useful to ask if it matters. In some poems, the speaker refers to himself as 'Paul' but it may or may not be the Paul Durcan who wrote the poem.

Line 1 first of August: Lughnasa, the Celtic Harvest Festival; Lugh is the Celtic god of light and *nasád* means a gathering.

Line 2 Shangri-La Hotel: Shangri-La is another word for paradise; it's the name given to the hidden place where a Buddhist or Tibetan monk leader lives. The Shangri-La Hotel in this instance is a hotel 'on the hill of Dalkey'. Paul Durcan's poem 'Waterloo Road' from his 1999 collection *Greeting to Our Friends in Brazil* tells of first meeting Nessa O'Neill at a wedding that he and Patrick Kavanagh attended. In Durcan's poem 'Waterloo Road', we read of how the speaker 'sitting at the bar, found/ myself beside a beautiful woman/With long red hair, green eyes, freckles./Nessa O'Neill was her name and she invited me/ To go for a swim with her at the bottom of the garden./The Shangri-La backed on to the Irish Sea./There was an Indian Summer that year in Ireland/And in October she and I set up home in London./We lived together sixteen years,/Rearing two golden girls.'

Line 5 whirlpool: a quickly rotating mass of water.

'Nessa' is from Paul Durcan's 1975 collection *O Westport in the Light of Asia Minor.*

Questions

1. This poem remembers the speaker's first and eventful meeting with the woman he later married. It was a special moment. Which details strike you as special?
2. Do you think this poem paints a realistic picture? Are there fairytale elements in the poem? Give reasons for your answer.
3. What does the image of 'a whirlpool' suggest? Each stanza ends with the same line. What is the effect of this? Does its meaning change as you read through the poem?
4. Look at the different places, real or imagined, mentioned in the poem. Comment on 'Shangri-La Hotel', 'Irish Sea', 'the field', 'on the rocks', 'Dublin City', 'taxi-cab'. What do they reveal to us about the speaker?
5. How would you describe the tone of voice in the poem? Does the poem change?
6. This is a love poem. Did you enjoy it? Did you like it? Did you admire it?
7. A reading aloud of this poem gives a very strong sense of the poem's rhythm. How would you describe it? How important is the rhythm in terms of the overall effect of the poem?
8. Durcan is a very popular, best-selling poet. Based on your reading of this and other Paul Durcan poems in this anthology, can you suggest why?

The Girl with the Keys to Pearse's Cottage

To John and Judith Meagher

When I was sixteen I met a dark girl;
Her dark hair was darker because her smile was so bright;
She was the girl with the keys to Pearse's Cottage;
And her name was Cáit Killann.

The cottage was built into the side of a hill;
I recall two windows and cosmic peace
Of bare brown rooms and on whitewashed walls
Photographs of the passionate and pale Pearse.

I recall wet thatch and peeling jambs
And how all was best seen from below in the field;
I used sit in the rushes with ledger-book and pencil
Compiling poems of passion for Cáit Killann.

Often she used linger on the sill of a window;
Hands by her side and brown legs akimbo;
In sun-red skirt and moon-black blazer;
Looking toward our strange world wide-eyed.

Our world was strange because it had no future;
She was America-bound at summer's end.
She had no choice but to leave her home –
The girl with the keys to Pearse's Cottage.

O Cáit Killann, O Cáit Killann,
You have gone with your keys from your own native place.
Yet here in this dark – El Greco eyes blaze back
From your Connemara postman's daughter's proudly mortal
face.

Glossary

Title Pearse's Cottage: Patrick/Pádraic Pearse (1879–1916), iconic Irish historical figure, nationalist, revolutionary, educator, poet and writer. He joined the Gaelic League when he was seventeen and founded St Enda's Irish-speaking school in Ranelagh first, then Rathfarnham, a boarding school for boys, in 1909. Cuchulainn was presented as the boys' model and their motto was drawn from the Fianna: 'Courage in our hands, truth in our tongues and purity in our hearts'.

Pearse was commander-in-chief during the Easter Rising, a signatory of the Proclamation of the Republic. He was court-martialled and executed by firing squad on 3 May 1916. A complex, powerful, charismatic figure, Michael Collins said: 'Connolly I'd follow into hell: Pearse I'd have to think about.' Pearse loved the west of Ireland. He visited first in 1898, aged nineteen, and as a twenty-three year old he went to Rosmuc as an examiner for Conradh na Gaeilge (Gaelic League). He then bought a site overlooking Loch Eiliarach and had a two-bedroomed thatched cottage built. It was here, in 1915, that Pearse wrote the oration that he gave at the grave of O'Donovan Rossa in Glasnevin Cemetery, a speech which in Brian Crowley's words 'was to confirm him as the face and voice of the coming revolution'. The restored cottage (Teach an Phiarsaigh) at Inbhear, Rosmuc, is open to the public for four months of the year.

Line 6 cosmic peace: an out-of-this-world peace; cosmos means the universe.

Line 9 jambs: the side posts of the doorway.

Line 11 ledger-book: usually a large, hard-backed book used for financial accounts.

Line 14 akimbo: with hands on the hips and elbows turned outwards.

Line 23 El Greco: 'The Greek' – Domenico Theotocopoulos (1541–1614); artist born in Crete, of Greek descent, studied in Italy and settled in Toledo in the late 1570s; a distinctive portrait painter of elongated figures.

'The Girl with the Keys to Pearse's Cottage' is from Paul Durcan's 1975 collection *O Westport in the Light of Asia Minor.*

Questions

1. Here is a poem that tells of a youthful infatuation. How do we know that the speaker is infatuated with Cáit Killann. What is her attraction?

2. What is the significance of the girl's summer job? What does this historical backdrop contribute to the poem?

3. What do details such as 'wet thatch and peeling jambs' suggest?

4. Why is the world 'strange' according to the speaker in the poem?

5. This is a personal poem but it also has a social and political dimension. What is the effect of this? Is this a poem that could be read and appreciated anywhere in the world? Give reasons for your answer.

6. We are told that the girl is 'America-bound at summer's end' and that she has gone 'with your keys from your own native place'. How does this colour one's reading of the poem?

7. Both 'Nessa' and in 'The Girl with the Keys to Pearse's Cottage' are love poems. Is one more personal than the other? Why? Is one darker than the other? Give reasons for your answer.

8. What do you understand by the closing two lines? Is the dark actual or metaphorical?

9. Comment on 'passionate and pale' and 'proudly mortal face'.

10. Paul Durcan is passionately interested in painting. Is this evident in this particular poem?

The Difficulty that is Marriage

We disagree to disagree, we divide, we differ;
Yet each night as I lie in bed beside you
And you are faraway curled up in sleep
I array the moonlit ceiling with a mosaic of question marks;
How was it I was so lucky to have ever met you?
I am no brave pagan proud of my mortality
Yet gladly on this changeling earth I should live for ever
If it were with you, my sleeping friend.
I have my troubles and I shall always have them
But I should rather live with you for ever
Than exchange my troubles for a changeless kingdom.
But I do not put you on a pedestal or throne;
You must have your faults but I do not see them.
If it were with you, I should live for ever.

Glossary

Line 4 array: arrange in a neat or impressive way.

Line 4 mosaic: a pattern.

Line 6 pagan: someone holding beliefs other than those of the main world religions.

Line 7 changeling: In Irish folklore, a changeling is a child believed to have been secretly substituted by fairies for the parents' real child in infancy; here, perhaps Durcan, in saying 'changeling earth', is suggesting that the world he shares with his wife is something other, different and one that he would like to last forever. There is, however, an obsolete definition of the word in the Oxford English Dictionary dating from 1646 where changeling means 'changeable, variable, inconstant'.

Line 12 pedestal: a raised structure; the base on which a statue is mounted.

Line 12 throne: an ornate seat for a royal person, bishop, etc.

> 'The Difficulty that is Marriage' is from Durcan's 1976 collection *Teresa's Bar.*

Questions

1. The words 'Difficulty' and 'Marriage' occur in the title. Tease out the connection.
2. What picture of a relationship in conjured up in the opening line? What is the effect of the poet's use of alliteration?
3. How would you describe the speaker's mood in the opening lines? Lonely? Grateful?
4. Do you pity the speaker? Why? Why not?
5. What impression do you have of the speaker's wife?
6. Comment on the contrast in the poem between waking and sleeping.
7. Listen to the sounds and the rhythm of the poem. Are they different, do they change as you read through the poem? Comment on the poet's use of punctuation. Compare and contrast, for example, the use of the comma in line 1 with the use of the run-on line later in the poem.
8. Is this poem realistic? Depressing? Necessary?
9. Why do you think Paul Durcan chose the sonnet form for this particular poem?

Wife Who Smashed Television Gets Jail

'She came home, my Lord, and smashed in the television;
Me and the kids were peaceably watching Kojak
When she marched into the living room and declared
That if I didn't turn off the television immediately
She'd put her boot through the screen;
I didn't turn it off, so instead she turned it off –
I remember the moment exactly because Kojak
After shooting a dame with the same name as my wife
Snarled at the corpse – Goodnight, Queen Maeve –
And then she took off her boots and smashed in the television;
I had to bring the kids round to my mother's place;
We got there just before the finish of Kojak;
(My mother has a fondness for Kojak, my Lord);
When I returned home my wife had deposited
What was left of the television into the dustbin,
Saying – I didn't get married to a television
And I don't see why my kids or anybody else's kids
Should have a television for a father or mother,
We'd be much better off all down in the pub talking
Or playing bar-billiards –
Whereupon she disappeared off back down again to the pub.'
Justice Ó Brádaigh said wives who preferred bar-billiards to family television
Were a threat to the family which was the basic unit of society
As indeed the television itself could be said to be a basic unit of the family
And when as in this case wives expressed their preference in forms of violence
Jail was the only place for them. Leave to appeal was refused.

Glossary

Title: The title sounds like a headline in a tabloid newspaper. Many of Paul Durcan's poems and books have striking, intriguing and memorable titles: 'The Archbishop Dreams of the Harlot of Rathkeale'; 'Making Love Outside Áras an Uachtaráin; 'Backside to the Wind'; 'The Man Whose Name Was Tom-and-Ann'; *The Berlin Wall Café*; 'On Falling in Love with a Salesman in a Shoe Shop'; *Going Home to Russia*; 'On Giving a Poetry Recital to an Empty Hall'; *Greetings to Our Friends in Brazil*; 'The Day Kerry Became Dublin'; 'The Man with a Bit of Jizz in Him'; 'To Dympna Who Taught Me Online Banking'; 'The Annual January Nervous Breakdown'; *Praise in Which I Live and Move and Have my Being.*

Line 2 Kojak: a popular American TV show from the 1970s (1973–1978); Kojak (played by Telly Savalas) was a bald, lollipop-sucking New York detective.

Line 9 Queen Maeve: a goddess in Irish mythology who was also Queen of Connacht; she married several times and conferred kingship on her spouses.

'Wife Who Smashed Television Gets Jail' is from Durcan's 1976 collection *Teresa's Bar.*

Questions

1. Does the title strike you as a typical title for a poem? Give reasons for your answer.

2. Who is speaking in this poem? What is the setting? What kind of a picture is being painted of domestic life?

3. The woman in this instance is the aggressor, the violent one. Does this poem explore gender reversal? Where has the wife and mother come from and where does she go? Comment on this in relation to stereotypes of men and women.

4. Even though this poem describes a scene of anger and violence, do you think Paul Durcan succeeds in turning it into a humorous poem? If so, how?

5. What do you think of the wife's anti-television arguments?

6. This is a poem written about Ireland. Do you think it has universal appeal or significance? Give reasons for your answer.

7. Comment on the judge's decision. Do you agree with it?

8. Paul Durcan's father was a judge. Is this a relevant detail?

9. Seamus Heaney, commenting on Durcan's poetry from the 1970s, says that what Heaney calls 'a disappointment and impatience at the abdication and vacuities of public life in Euro-Ireland' in Durcan's poetry 'got transformed into comedy, litany, the melody of panic and loss'. Explain what is meant by this in your own words.

Parents

A child's face is a drowned face:
Her parents stare down at her asleep
Estranged from her by a sea:
She is under the sea
And they are above the sea:
If she looked up she would see them
As if locked out of their own home,
Their mouths open,
Their foreheads furrowed –
Pursed-up orifices of fearful fish –
Their big ears are fins behind glass
And in her sleep she is calling out to them
    Father, Father
    Mother, Mother
But they cannot hear her:
She is inside the sea
And they are outside the sea.
Through the night, stranded, they stare
At the drowned, drowned face of their child.

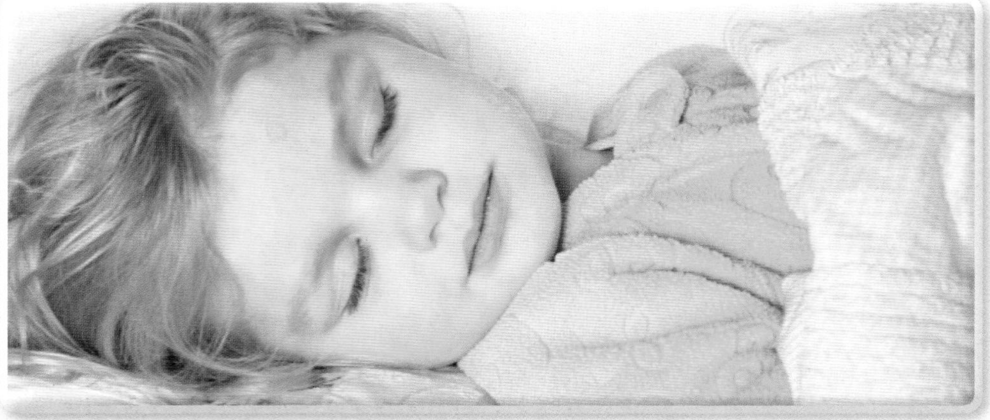

Glossary

Line 3 Estranged: feeling cut off, alienated.

Line 10 orifices: openings.

'Parents' is from Durcan's 1978 collection *Sam's Cross*.

Questions

1. This is a portrait of a family – a mother and father and child. Were you surprised by it? Why? Why not?
2. The opening line introduces the image of being drowned. Trace this image of water and drowning through the poem. What is the effect of this?
3. How would you describe the dominant mood or feeling within the poem? How is this mood created?
4. How would you describe the relationship between the young girl and her mother and father?
5. How do you interpret the 'sea' that this child is 'under' and 'inside'?
6. How do the parents feel about their daughter? Which details capture this best in your opinion?
7. Consider the shape of the poem on the page. What is the effect of lines thirteen and fourteen?
8. Comment on words such as 'estranged', 'locked out', 'furrowed', 'stranded' and 'drowned'.
9. Identify the poet's use of contrast and repetition in the poem and say what it contributes to the poem as a whole?
10. Imagine you are the daughter mentioned in the poem. How would you feel if you read it years later? Do you think the experience the poet has described is an accurate, convincing one? Why? Why not?

En Famille, 1979

Bring me back to the dark school – to the dark school of childhood:
To where tiny is tiny, and massive is massive.

Glossary

Title En Famille: a well-known French phrase meaning 'at home', 'in or with one's family' and it usually has warm associations/connotations.

'En Famille, 1979' is from *Jesus, Break His Fall* (1980).

Questions

1. The two-line poem expresses a desire. What is revealed of the speaker? What does the speaker want?

2. How is childhood portrayed in this poem? Why, according to the speaker, is the school of childhood dark?

3. What do you think is meant or implied by the title?

4. Do you think a two-line poem works? Why? Why not?

Madman

Every child has a madman on their street:
The only trouble about our madman is that he's our father.

'Madman', like 'En Famille', is from *Jesus, Break His Fall* (1980).

Questions

1. What was your first reaction to this poem?
2. What is meant by black humour? Is this an example?
3. Comedy can be deadly serious. Is the story contained within this tiny poem comic or tragic? Funny or frightening?

'Windfall', 8 Parnell Hill, Cork

But, then, at the end of day I could always say –
Well, now, I am going home.
I felt elected, steeped, sovereign to be able to say –
I am going home.
When I was at home I liked to stay at home;
At home I stayed at home for weeks;
At home I used sit in a winged chair by the window
Overlooking the river and the factory chimneys,
The electricity power station and the car assembly works,
The fleets of trawlers and the pilot tugs,
Dreaming that life is a dream which is real,
The river a reflection of itself in its own waters,
Goya sketching Goya among the smoky mirrors.
The industrial vista was my Mont Sainte-Victoire.
While my children sat on my knees watching TV
Their mother, my wife, reclined on the couch
Knitting a bright-coloured scarf, drinking a cup of black coffee,
Smoking a cigarette – one of her own roll-ups.
I closed my eyes and breathed in and breathed out.
It is ecstasy to breathe if you are at home in the world.
What a windfall! A home of our own!
Our neighbours' houses had names like 'Con Amore',
'Sans Souci', 'Pacelli', 'Montini', 'Homesville'.
But we called our home 'Windfall'.
'Windfall', 8 Parnell Hill, Cork.
In the gut of my head coursed the leaf of tranquillity
Which I dreamed was known only to Buddhist Monks
In lotus monasteries high up in the Hindu Kush.
Down here in the dark depths of Ireland,
Below sea level in the city of Cork,
In a city as intimate and homicidal as a Little Marseilles,
In a country where all the children of the nation
Are not cherished equally
And where the best go homeless, while the worst
Erect block-house palaces – self-regardingly ugly –

Having a home of your own can give to a family
A chance in a lifetime to transcend death.

At the high window, shipping from all over the world
Being borne up and down the busy, yet contemplative, river;
Skylines drifting in and out of skylines in the cloudy valley;
Firelight at dusk, and city lights;
Beyond them the control tower of the airport on the hill
A lighthouse in the sky flashing green to white to green;
Our black-and-white cat snoozing in the corner of a chair;
Pastels and etchings on the four walls, and over the mantelpiece
'Van Gogh's Grave' and 'Lovers in Water';
A room wallpapered in books and family photograph albums
Chronicling the adventures and metamorphoses of family life:
In swaddling clothes in Mammy's arms on baptism day;
Being a baby of nine months and not remembering it;
Face-down in a pram, incarcerated in a high chair;
Everybody, including strangers, wearing shop-window smiles;
With Granny in Felixstowe, with Granny in Ballymaloe;
In a group photo in First Infants, on a bike at thirteen;
In the back garden in London, in the back garden in Cork;
Performing a headstand after First Holy Communion;
Getting a kiss from the Bishop on Confirmation Day;
Straw hats in the Bois de Boulougne, wearing wings at the seaside;
Mammy and Daddy holding hands on the Normandy Beaches;
Mammy and Daddy at the wedding of Jeremiah and Margot;
Mammy and Daddy queueing up for Last Tango in Paris;
Boating on the Shannon, climbing mountains in Kerry;
Building sandcastles in Killala, camping in Barley Cove;
Picnicking in Moone, hide-and-go-seek in Clonmacnoise;
Riding horses, cantering, jumping fences;
Pushing out toy yachts in the pond in the Tuileries;
The Irish College revisited in the Rue des Irlandais;
Sipping an orange pressé through a straw on the roof of the
    Beaubourg;
Dancing in Père Lachaise, weeping at Auvers.
Year in, year out, I pored over these albums accumulating,

My children looking over my shoulder, exhilarated as I was,
Their mother presiding at our ritual from a distance –
The far side of the hearthrug, diffidently, proudly.
Schoolbooks on the floor and pyjamas on the couch –
Whose turn is it tonight to put the children to bed?

Our children swam about our home
As if it was their private sea,
Their own unique, symbiotic fluid
Of which their parents also partook.
Such is home – a sea of your own –
In which you hang upside down from the ceiling
With equanimity while postcards from Thailand on the mantelpiece
Are raising their eyebrow markings benignly:
Your hands dangling their prayers to the floorboards of your home,
Sifting the sands underneath the surfaces of conversations,
The marine insect life of the family psyche.
A home of your own – or a sea of your own –
In which climbing the walls is as natural
As making love on the stairs;
In which when the telephone rings
Husband and wife are metamorphosed into smiling accomplices,
Both declining to answer it;
Initiating, instead, a yet more subversive kiss –
A kiss they have perhaps never attempted before –
And might never have dreamed of attempting
Were it not for the telephone belling.
Through the bannisters or along the bannister rails
The pyjama-clad children solemnly watching
Their parents at play, jumping up and down in support,
Race back to bed, gesticulating wordlessly:
The most subversive unit in society is the human family.

We're almost home, pet, almost home . . .
Our home is at . . .
I'll be home . . .
I have to go home now . . .
I want to go home now . . .

Are you feeling homesick?
Are you anxious to get home? . . .
I can't wait to get home . . .
Let's stay at home tonight and . . .
What time will you be coming home at? . . .
If I'm not home by six at the latest, I'll phone . . .
We're nearly home, don't worry, we're nearly home . . .

But then with good reason
I was put out of my home:
By a keen wind felled.
I find myself now without a home
Having to live homeless in the alien, foreign city of Dublin.
It is an eerie enough feeling to be homesick
Yet knowing you will be going home next week;
It is an eerie feeling beyond all ornithological analysis
To be homesick knowing that there is no home to go home to:
Day by day, creeping, crawling,
Moonlighting, escaping,
Bed-and-breakfast to bed-and-breakfast;
Hostels, centres, one-night hotels.

Homeless in Dublin,
Blown about the suburban streets at evening,
Peering in the windows of other people's homes,
Wondering what it must feel like
To be sitting around a fire –
Apache or Cherokee or Bourgeoisie –
Beholding the firelit faces of your family,
Beholding their starry or their TV gaze:
Windfall to Windfall – can you hear me?
Windfall to Windfall . . .
We're almost home, pet, don't worry anymore, we're almost home.

Glossary

Title 'Windfall', 8 Parnell Hill, Cork: Durcan lived with his wife and children in Cork in the 1970s but this is not an actual address.

Line 3 elected: blessed, lucky, made, chosen.

Line 3 steeped: soaked/bathed in liquid – an image of relaxation, ease.

Line 3 sovereign: royal, special.

Line 10 pilot tugs: small powerful vessels for towing others.

Line 13 Goya: celebrated Spanish artist (1746–1848).

Line 14 Mont Sainte-Victoire: a mountain in Provence, southern France which the French artist Paul Cézanne (1839–1906) painted again and again – over sixty times.

Line 21 windfall: a piece of good luck, unexpected good fortune.

***Lines 22/23*: 'Con Amore', 'Sans Souci', 'Pacelli', 'Montini'**: Italian words meaning 'With Love'; French words meaning 'Without Care'; Italian word meaning Pacelli was the surname of Pope Pius XII; the family name of Pope Paul VI.

Line 28 lotus: a large water-lily plant associated with calmness; lotus monasteries would suggest places of meditation and ease.

Line 28 Hindu Kush: a mountain range between central Afghanistan and northern Pakistan.

Lines 32/33 where all the children of the nation/Are not cherished equally: The 1916 Irish Proclamation (Poblacht na hEireann) states: 'The Republic guarantees religious and civil liberty, equal rights and equal opportunities to all its citizens, and declares its resolve to pursue the happiness and prosperity of the whole nation and of all its parts, cherishing all the children of the nation equally.'

Line 46 'Van Gogh's Grave' and 'Lovers in Water': interesting, unusual images for over the mantelpiece in a family home.

Line 48 metamorphoses: complete changes.

Line 51 incarcerated: confined.

Line 58 Bois de Boulougne: a large public park in Paris.

Line 61 Last Tango in Paris: a controversial Bernardo Bertolucci film from 1972 starring Marlon Brando and Maria Schneider. It was considered obscene by some on its release.

Line 63 Killala ... Barley Cove: seaside places in Counties Mayo and Cork.

Line 66 Tuileries: public gardens in Paris.

Line 68 orange pressé: freshly squeezed orange juice.

Line 68 Beaubourg: also known as the Centre Georges Pompidou, an art gallery in Paris.

Line 69 Père Lachaise: the largest graveyard within the city of Paris where Oscar Wilde, Jim Morrison, Edith Piaf, Balzac, Colette, Chopin, Proust, Gertrude Stein et al are buried.

Line 69 Auvers: in north-west Paris and famous for its Vincent van Gogh association; one of his famous paintings is of the church there.

Line 73 diffidently: shyly.

Line 78 symbiotic fluid: symbiosis, a biological term, meaning a close interaction between two different organisms; here, the words 'symbiotic fluid' suggest a close, warm relationship between the speaker's two children; echoing perhaps amniotic fluid which is the fluid surrounding the foetus.

Line 119 eerie: frightening and strange.

Line 121 ornithological analysis: ornithology is the scientific study of birds; in this context, home is seen as a kind of nest that the speaker can no longer return to.

Line 124 Moonlighting: under moonlight; doing a second job, especially secretly and at night.

Line 132 Apache or Cherokee: Native American people.

Line 132 Bourgeoisie: the middle classes.

'"Windfall", 8 Parnell Hill, Cork' is from Paul Durcan's *The Berlin Wall Café* (1985).

? Questions

1. Home is everything to the speaker in this poem. The word 'home' occurs thirty-five times and it is the poem's final word. Homesick and homeless are also key words here. Having read through the poem's six sections, which words best sum up the gist of this poem?

2. How would you describe the speaker's tone in the opening section? Comment on the effect of the opening words, 'But, then ...'

3. This poem is the portrait of a family in a home they named 'Windfall'. Why did they name the house 'Windfall'. The speaker remembers a special, happy time in his life with his wife and two daughters. What made possible that happiness?

4. Which images best convey a feeling of home in lines 1–37?

5. The list is frequently a very effective, rhetorical/persuasive technique. Explore the poet's use of the list in the poem's second section (lines 38–75). Comment on the use of repetition and pick out those images that you found particularly effective and say why.

6. The poem captures a world within and without: the domestic world and the world beyond 'Windfall'. What do the many place names contribute to the overall effect?

7. The third section focuses on the intimate – the children and the relationship between husband and wife. Look closely at the images here, especially the images of sea and sand and of freedom. Is it a happy, self-contained world?

8. The first word in this third section (lines 76–101) is 'Our'. Later, the speaker moved from the first person to the third person. What, in your opinion, is the effect of this?

9. Section four (lines 102–113) looks different. Why do you think the shape of the poem on the page changes at this point?

10. In lines 102–113, the word 'home' occurs on every line (in line 107 'home' is contained within 'homesick). Why this emphasis?

11. How would you describe the speaker's mood at the beginning of section five? The speaker admits that 'with good reason/ I was put out of my home'. Do you feel sympathy for the speaker? Compare his way of life now with his earlier life as husband and father and family man.

12. Is loneliness the dominant mood throughout the poem?

13. How would you describe the poet's technique here? Is it like watching a film?

14. Look at Durcan's use of language. What aspects of the language of poetry do you recognise and discover here?

15. Comment on the phrase 'the dark depths of Ireland' (line 29).

Six Nuns Die in Convent Inferno

To the
happy memory of six Loreto nuns
who died
between midnight and morning of
2 June 1986

I

We resided in a Loreto convent in the centre of Dublin city
On the east side of a public gardens, St Stephen's Green.
Grafton Street – the paseo
Where everyone paseo'd, including even ourselves –
Debouched on the north side, and at the top of Grafton Street,
Or round the base of the great patriotic pebble of O'Donovan Rossa,
Knelt tableaus of punk girls and punk boys.
When I used pass them – scurrying as I went –
Often as not to catch a mass in Clarendon Street,
The Carmelite Church in Clarendon Street
(Myself, I never used the Clarendon Street entrance,
I always slipped in by way of Johnson's Court,
Opposite the side entrance to Bewley's Oriental Café),
I could not help but smile, as I sucked on a Fox's mint,
That for all the half-shaven heads and the martial garb
And the dyed hair-dos and the nappy pins
They looked so conventional, really, and vulnerable,
Clinging to warpaint and to uniforms and to one another.
I knew it was myself who was the ultimate drop-out,
The delinquent, the recidivist, the vagabond,
The wild woman, the subversive, the original punk.
Yet, although I confess I was smiling, I was also afraid,
Appalled by my own nerve, my own fervour,
My apocalyptic enthusiasm, my other-worldly hubris:
To opt out of the world and to
Choose such exotic loneliness,
Such terrestrial abandonment,
A lifetime of bicycle lamps and bicycle pumps,
A lifetime of galoshes stowed under the stairs,
A lifetime of umbrellas drying out in the kitchens.

I was an old nun – an aged beadswoman –
But I was no daw.
I knew what a weird bird I was, I knew that when we
Went to bed we were as eerie an aviary as you'd find
In all the blown-off rooftops of the city:
Scuttling about our dorm, wheezing, shrieking, croaking,
In our yellowy corsets, wonky suspenders, strung-out garters,
A bony crew in the gods of the sleeping city.
Many's the night I lay awake in bed
Dreaming what would befall us if there were a fire:
No fire-escapes outside, no fire-extinguishers inside;
To coin a Dublin saying,
We'd not stand a snowball's chance in hell. Fancy that!
It seemed too good to be true:
Happy death vouchsafed only to the few.
Sleeping up there was like sleeping at the top of the mast
Of a nineteenth-century schooner, and in the daytime
We old nuns were the ones who crawled out on the yardarms
To stitch and sew the rigging and the canvas.
To be sure we were weird birds, oddballs, Christniks,
For we had done the weirdest thing a woman can do –
Surrendered the marvellous passions of girlhood,
The innocent dreams of childhood,
Not for a night or a weekend or even a Lent or a season,
But for a lifetime.
Never to know the love of a man or a woman;
Never to have children of our own;
Never to have a home of our own;
And for why and for what?
To follow a young man – would you believe it –
Who lived two thousand years ago in Palestine
And who died a common criminal strung up on a tree.

As we stood there in the disintegrating dormitory
Burning to death in the arms of Christ –
O Christ, Christ, come quickly, quickly –

Fluttering about in our tight, gold bodices,
Beating our wings in vain,
It reminded me of the snaps one of the sisters took
When we took a seaside holiday in 1956
(The year Cardinal Mindszenty went into hiding
In the US legation in Budapest.
He was a great hero of ours, Cardinal Mindszenty,
Any of us would have given our right arm
To have been his nun – darning his socks, cooking his meals,
Making his bed, doing his washing and ironing.)
Somebody – an affluent buddy of the bishop's repenting his affluence –
Loaned Mother Superior a secluded beach in Co. Waterford –
Ardmore, along the coast from Tramore –
A cove with palm trees, no less, well off the main road.
There we were, fluttering up and down the beach,
Scampering hither and thither in our starched bathing-costumes.
Tonight, expiring in the fire, was quite much like that,
Only instead of scampering into the waves of the sea
Now we were scampering into the flames of the fire.

That was one of the gayest days of my life,
The day the sisters went swimming.
Often in the silent darkness of the chapel after Benediction,
During the Exposition of the Blessed Sacrament,
I glimpsed the sea again as it was that day.
Praying – daydreaming really –
I became aware that Christ is the ocean
Forever rising and falling on the world's shore.
Now tonight in the convent Christ is the fire in whose waves
We are doomed but delighted to drown.
And, darting in and out of the flames of the dormitory,
Gabriel, with that extraordinary message of his on his boyish lips,
Frenetically pedalling his skybike.
He whispers into my ear what I must do
And I do it – and die.

Each of us in our own tiny, frail, furtive way
Was a Mother of God, mothering forth illegitimate Christs
In the street life of Dublin city.
God have mercy on our whirring souls
Wild women were we all –
And on the misfortunate, poor fire-brigade men
Whose task it will be to shovel up our ashes and shovel
What is left of us into black plastic refuse sacks.
Fire-brigade men are the salt of the earth.
Isn't it a marvellous thing how your hour comes
When you least expect it? When you lose a thing,
Not to know about it until it actually happens?
How, in so many ways, losing things is such a refreshing
experience,
Giving you a sense of freedom you've not often experienced?
How lucky I was to lose – I say, lose – lose my life.
It was a Sunday night, and after vespers
I skipped bathroom so that I could hop straight into bed
And get in a bit of a read before lights out:
Conor Cruise O'Brien's new book The Siege,
All about Israel and superlatively insightful
For a man who they say is reputedly an agnostic –
I got a loan of it from the brother-in-law's married niece –
But I was tired out and I fell asleep with the book open
Face down across my breast and I woke
To the racket of bellowing flame and snarling glass.
The first thing I thought of was that the brother-in-law's married
niece
Would never again get her Conor Cruise O'Brien back
And I had seen on the price tag that it cost £23.00:
Small wonder that the custom of snipping off the price
As an exercise in social deportment has simply died out;
Indeed a book today is almost worth buying for its price,
Its price frequently being more remarkable than its contents.

The strange Eucharist of my death –
To be eaten alive by fire and smoke.

I clasped the dragon to my breast
And stroked his red-hot ears.
Strange! There we were, all sleeping molecules,
Suddenly all giving birth to our deaths,
All frantically in labour.
Doctors and midwives weaved in and out
In gowns of smoke and gloves of fire.
Christ, like an Orthodox patriarch in his dressing gown,
Flew up and down the dormitory, splashing water on our souls:
Sister Eucharia; Sister Seraphia; Sister Rosario;
Sister Gonzaga; Sister Margaret; Sister Edith.
If you will remember us – six nuns burnt to death -
Remember us for the frisky girls that we were,
Now more than ever kittens in the sun.

II

When Jesus heard these words at the top of Grafton Street
Uttered by a small, agèd, emaciated, female punk
Clad all in mourning black, and grieving like an alley cat,
He was annulled with astonishment, and turning round
He declared to the gangs of teenagers and dicemen following him:
'I tell you, not even in New York City
Have I found faith like this.'

That night in St Stephen's Green
After the keepers had locked the gates,
And the courting couples had found cinemas themselves to die in,
The six nuns who had died in the convent inferno,
From the bandstand they'd been hiding under, crept out
And knelt together by the Fountain of the Three Fates,
Reciting the Agnus Dei: reciting it as if it were the torch song
Of all aid – Live Aid, Self Aid, Aids, and All Aid –
Lord, I am not worthy
That thou should'st enter under my roof;
Say but the word and my soul shall be healed.

Glossary

Title: The English poet and priest Gerard Manley Hopkins (1844–1889) wrote a poem called 'The Wreck of the Deutschland' dedicated 'To the happy memory of five Franciscan nuns exiles by the Falck Laws drowned between midnight and morning of Dec. 7th, 1875.'

Line 3 paseo: public walkway for leisurely strolling.

Line 5 Debouched: having emerged from a confined space into a wide open area.

Line 6 pebble: the very large memorial resembles an upright small smooth stone.

Line 6 O'Donovan Rossa: a Fenian, born Rosscarbery, Co. Cork 1831, died 1915; imprisoned 1865–71, then left for America where he edited *The United Irishman*; at his funeral in Glasnevin, Patrick Pearse gave an oration.

Line 7 tableaus: (plural of tableau, usually spelt tableaux) living pictures; silent and motionless groups.

Line 7 punk: a late 1970s trend in music and fashion.

Line 8 scurrying: moving quickly with short quick steps.

Line 17 conventional . . . vulnerable: acceptable . . . exposed to risk.

Line 20 recidivist: convicted criminal who reoffends.

Line 21 subversive: one who undermines authority, an established institution or system.

Line 24 apocalyptic: momentous/catastrophic.

Line 24 hubris: excessive pride or self-confidence.

Line 27 terrestial abandonment: the permanent leaving of earth/the world.

Line 29 galoshes: waterproof rubber overshoes.

Line 31 beadswoman: a reference in this instance to a woman who uses rosary beads.

Line 32 I was no daw: a daw is a person who is stupid or easily fooled. *Brewer's Dictionary of Irish Phrase and Fable* (ed MacMahon and O'Donoghue) says that the disclaimer 'I'm no daw!' refers to the presumed stupidity of the jackdaw.

Line 34 eerie: strange and frightening.

Line 34 aviary: large enclosure for keeping birds in.

Line 38 in the gods: a term that usually refers to the gallery of a theatre; the upper floor/balcony.

Line 45 vouchsafed: here, graciously granted.

Line 47 schooner: a sailing ship with two or more masts.

Line 48 yardarms: the outer extremity of a cylindrical spar/stout pole.

Line 50 Christniks: those who follow Christ and his teaching (as in 'beatnik' – young people who rejected conventional society in the 1950s–early 1960s).

Line 54 Lent: the period preceding Easter – from Ash Wednesday to Holy Saturday in the Christian church.

Line 61 Palestine: the Holy Land, Christ's birthplace.

Line 65 O Christ, Christ, come quickly, quickly: in Gerard Manley Hopkins's poem 'The Wreck of the Deutschland', stanza 24 contains the line 'O Christ, Christ, come quickly'.

Line 70 Cardinal Mindszenty: Hungarian Cardinal (1892–1975) who acquired international fame in 1948–9 when he was charged with treason by the Communist government in Budapest. Mindszenty was sentenced to life imprisonment in 1949 but was released in October 1956 on condition that he not leave Hungary; in 1956, at the end of the Hungarian Uprising he was granted asylum in the US legation where he remained a voluntary prisoner until 1971. When things eased in Hungary he travelled abroad and spent his final years in Vienna.

Line 85 gayest: carefree, light-hearted.

Line 87 Benediction: Catholic service where the congregation is blessed with the Blessed sacrament.

Line 96 Gabriel: one of the archangels, sometimes regarded as the angel of death, the prince of fire and thunder, but more frequently as one of God's chief messengers.

Line 100 furtive: secretive, guilty.

Line 115 vespers: a service of evening prayers.

Line 118 Conor Cruise O'Brien: Dublin-born writer, intellectual, politician, journalist (1917–2008). He published several books including *The Seige: The Saga of Israel and Zionism* in 1986.

Line 120 agnostic: person who believes that nothing is known or can be known of the existence or nature of God.

Line 132 Eucharist: the Christian sacrament in which the bread and wine are consecrated and consumed.

Line 136 molecules: the smallest portion to which a substance can be reduced by subdivision without losing its chemical identity.

Line 141 Orthodox patriarch: the Orthodox Church is the Eastern or Greek Church separated from the Western Church in the ninth century, the Patriarch/Father of Constantinople its head.

Line 143 Eucharia . . . Seraphia: in Greek eucharistos means grateful; Seraphim is the highest order of angels; traditionally, nuns gave up their names on being professed as brides of Christ.

Line 151 annulled: from the Latin words 'ad' + 'nullum' meaning 'to nothing'.

Line 152 dicemen: Thom McGinty (1954–95), a street artist and actor best known as 'The Diceman' and well-known especially on Grafton Street. His most famous costume was that of a dice. McGinty died of AIDS aged forty-one.

Line 153 'I tell you . . .': echoes Christ's words in Matthew Ch 8 v 10 where Jesus says of the centurion in Capernaum, 'Verily I say unto you, I have not found so great faith, no, not in Israel.'

Line 160 the Fountain of the Three Fates: a fountain in Stephen's Green, Dublin, very near the Loreto Convent. It was presented to the Irish nation by Germany in gratitude for Ireland's kindness after World War II. The inscription in German, Irish and English reads 'With gratitude for the help given to German children by the Irish people after World War II. Roman Herzog, President of the Federal Republic of Germany 23.03.1997'. The Three Fates are three female figures, Clotho, Lachesis and Atropos, whom the Greeks believed controlled the birth, life and death of everyone and were considered cruel in that they paid no regard to the wishes of anyone.

Line 161 Agnus Dei: Latin meaning 'Lamb of God' – that part of Mass that begins Agnus Dei, qui tollis peccata mundi (Lamb of God that takest away the sins of the world ...)

Line 161 torch song: a sad song of unrequited love.

Line 162 Live Aid: a fundraising endeavour by Bob Geldof, rock singer and Developing World activist; his Live Aid concerts, held simultaneously in London and Philadelphia on 13 July 1985, raised £50 million; the protest song 'Do They Know It's Christmas' which Geldof organized earned £8 million for the Ethiopia appeal.

Lines 163/5 Lord ... healed: the words spoken at communion during mass which echo Matthew 8.9.

'Six Nuns Die in Convent Inferno' is the first poem in Durcan's 1987 collection *Going Home to Russia.*

Questions

1. How would you describe this poem's title? Does it read like a newspaper headline? Consider, for example, *The Irish Times* heading, 'Gardai still seek cause of convent fire disaster'. Compare and contrast the two.

2. Comment on the use of the word 'happy' in the poem's dedication. In Hopkins's nineteenth century ode, which remembers the death of five Franciscan nuns by drowning in the sea, the dedication also reads 'To the happy memory ...'

3. The poem is in two sections and eight parts. Part I has six stanzas; part II has two. In stanza one, we are introduced to the voice of an unnamed old nun. She uses a 'We' voice to begin but moves to an 'I' voice. How would you describe her personality? Were you surprised? How would you describe her tone? Chatty? Sympathetic? Singular? Confident? How would you describe the way she lives her life? Odd? Courageous?
4. What is the speaker's attitude to 'punk girls and punk boys'. What connection is suggested between punks and nuns? Why are the punks considered 'so conventional ... and vulnerable'? Why does this nun see herself as 'the ultimate drop-out'?
5. Stanza one focuses on the world beyond the convent – Stephen's Green, Clarendon St Church, the punks and ends with a picture of convent life, a lifetime of bicycle lamps, galoshes and umbrellas. What do these images suggest? Are they images of 'exotic loneliness'?
6. The poem's second stanza describes life within the convent and the dormitory. Why do you think the speaker – though realising that there are 'No fire-escapes outside, no fire-extinguishers inside' – speaks of a 'happy death'?
7. Do you think the ship and sea imagery is effective here? Explain your answer.
8. 'O Christ, Christ, come quickly, quickly' is a powerful utterance. Read the glossary note for line 65. Is this, in your judgement, crucial to one's understanding of the poem as a whole?
9. At the moment of crisis in stanza three (lines 63–84) how does the speaker's mind work? Do you think it realistic? Convincing? Effective? Comment on the word 'scampering' in lines 84 and 85.
10. What is the effect of the contrast between 'one of the gayest days of my life,/ The day the sisters went swimming' and 'the fire in whose waves/ We are doomed but delighted to drown'. How can the speaker be 'delighted' to drown? What does that tell us about the speaker?
11. In an unfinished Gerard Manley Hopkins's poem, 'Epithalamium', Hopkins writes 'What is water? Spousal love.' – words which Paul Durcan has frequently written beneath his own name at book signings. Consider this in relation to lines 91–2 of this poem: 'I became aware that Christ is the ocean/ Forever rising and falling on the world's shore.'
12. Is this a frightening poem? Is it a poem of celebration? Can it be both?
13. How would you describe the speaker's tone in lines 109–14? How is such an attitude possible?

14. Stanza five (lines 109–31) describes the horror of the fire – 'the racket of bellowing flame and snarling glass' – but it also contains humour. Explore how Paul Durcan achieves this. Do you think it adds to the poem's achievement?

15. Discuss how stanza six (lines 132–47) uses imagery of birth and death in an interesting way.

16. In Part II, the voice is different; it's in the third person. Is it possible to say who is speaking here? How would you describe the mood in the opening lines? Is this a calm after a storm?

17. What is your response to the poem as a whole? Does it interest you? How does Durcan's response to a disastrous fire and the deaths of six nuns differ from that of a newspaper report? Why will this poem be read long after the event?

18. In Part II, would you agree that the poem moves from the particular to the global? What is the effect of this?

19. Consider the words the speaker uses to describe herself throughout the poem beginning with 'drop-out', 'delinquent', 'recidivist', 'vagabond', 'wild woman', 'subversive', 'the original punk', 'frisky girls'. Why does she see herself as such?

20. What is meant by surreal? Are there surreal elements to the poem and, if so, do you think them a strength or a weakness.

21. When Patrick Crotty included this Durcan poem in *Modern Irish Poetry* (Blackstaff Press, 1995) he did not include Part II, which is only eighteen lines long. Would you agree with his editorial decision? Why? Why not? Give reasons for your answer.

22. Based on your reading of this poem, what characteristics define Paul Durcan's poetry? Choose three adjectives and then justify your choice.

23. If you were asked to choose eight objects that you associate with this poem (e.g. galoshes; the book by Conor Cruise O'Brien; palm trees; black plastic refuse sacks . . .), which six would you choose? Justify your choice for each one.

24. Look at the opening and closing lines of the poem: compare the reference to the tableau of kneeling punk girls and boys around the base of the O'Donovan Rossa monument with the kneeling nuns by the Fountain of the Three Fates. Does this, in your opinion, make for a striking and effective structure? Explain your answer.

Sport

There were not many fields
In which you had hopes for me
But sport was one of them.
On my twenty-first birthday
I was selected to play
For Grangegorman Mental Hospital
In an away game
Against Mullingar Mental Hospital.
I was a patient
In B Wing.
You drove all the way down,
Fifty miles,
To Mullingar to stand
On the sidelines and observe me.

I was fearful I would let down
Not only my team but you.
It was Gaelic football.
I was selected as goalkeeper.
There were big country men
On the Mullingar Mental Hospital team,
Men with gapped teeth, red faces,
Oily, frizzy hair, bushy eyebrows.
Their full forward line
Were over six foot tall
Fifteen stone in weight.
All three of them, I was informed,
Cases of schizophrenia.

There was a rumour
That their centre-half forward
Was an alcoholic solicitor
Who, in a lounge bar misunderstanding,

Had castrated his best friend
But that he had no memory of it.
He had meant well – it was said.
His best friend had had to emigrate
To Nigeria.

To my surprise,
I did not flinch in the goals.
I made three or four spectacular saves,
Diving full stretch to turn
A certain goal around the corner,
Leaping high to tip another certain goal
Over the bar for a point.
It was my knowing
That you were standing on the sideline
That gave me the necessary motivation –
That will to die
That is as essential to sportsmen as to artists.
More than anybody it was you
I wanted to mesmerize, and after the game –
Grangegorman Mental Hospital
Having defeated Mullingar Mental Hospital
By 14 goals and 38 points to 3 goals and 10 points –
Sniffing your approval, you shook hands with me.
'Well played, son.'

I may not have been mesmeric
But I had not been mediocre.
In your eyes I had achieved something at last.
On my twenty-first birthday I had played on a winning team
The Grangegorman Mental Hospital team.
Seldom if ever again in your eyes
Was I to rise to these heights.

Glossary

Line 27 schizophrenia: a mental disorder involving breakdown in the relation between thought, emotion, and behaviour, leading to a faulty perception, inappropriate actions and feelings, and withdrawal from reality into fantasy and delusion (from Gk skhizein 'to split' + phren 'mind').

Line 32 castrated: to remove a man's testicles.

Line 38 flinch: draw back/give way.

Line 50 mesmerize: capture the whole attention of.

Line 56 mesmeric: causing a person to become transfixed and unaware of their surroundings.

Line 57 mediocre: of only average quality.

'Sport' is from Paul Durcan's 1990 collection *Daddy, Daddy* which won the Whitbread Award for poetry.

Questions

1. The poem's title will prompt images in every reader's mind. How does the game of football described here compare with your expectations of sport in general and this game in particular?

2. This is a father and son poem. How would you describe their relationship?

3. Identify the speaker's tone in the opening lines and trace that tone through the poem. Does it change and why?

4. What is meant by black humour? What does humour contribute to the poem? Give examples.

5. Pick out three significant details such as 'my twenty-first birthday', 'Fifty miles' and comment on them.

6. How would you describe the speaker's mood in stanza two?

7. Section three paints a strange, unsettling picture. What does this contribute, in your opinion, to the poem as a whole? How did you respond to this stanza? With shock? Uneasy laughter? Disgust? Do you think males would respond differently to this poem than females? Explain your answer.

8. What is the high point or the happiest moment in the poem? What is meant, do you think, by the phrase (line 47) 'the will to die'? What connection is there between 'sportmen' and 'artists' (line 48)?

9. The poem remembers a moment of triumph and happiness. Is this the mood with which the poem ends? How would you describe the speaker's mood in the closing two lines?

10. In his poetry, Paul Durcan writes in a number of different voices and it is sometimes difficult and sometimes impossible to say whether the poems are autobiographical or not. Do you find this unsatisfactory, unusual, interesting?

Father's Day, 21 June 1992

Just as I was dashing to catch the Dublin-Cork train,
Dashing up and down the stairs, searching my pockets,
She told me that her sister in Cork wanted a loan of the axe;
It was late June and
The buddleia tree in the backyard
Had grown out of control.
The taxi was ticking over outside in the street,
All the neighbours noticing it.
'You mean that you want me to bring her down the axe?'
'Yes, if you wouldn't mind, that is – '
'A simple saw would do the job, surely to God
She could borrow a simple saw.'
'She said that she'd like the axe.'
'OK. There is a Blue Cabs taxi ticking over outside
And the whole world inspecting it,
I'll bring her down the axe.'
The axe – all four-and-a-half feet of it –
Was leaning up against the wall behind the settee –
The fold-up settee that doubles as a bed.
She handed the axe to me just as it was,
As neat as a newborn babe,
All in the bare buff.
You'd think she'd have swaddled it up
In something – if not a blanket, an old newspaper,
But no, not even a token hanky
Tied in a bow round its head.
I decided not to argue the toss. I kissed her goodbye.

The whole long way down to Cork
I felt uneasy. Guilt feelings.
It's a killer, this guilt.
I always feel bad leaving her
But this time it was the worst.

I could see that she was glad
To see me go away for a while,
Glad at the prospect of being
Two weeks on her own,
Two weeks of having the bed to herself,
Two weeks of not having to be pestered
By my coarse advances,
Two weeks of not having to look up from her plate
And behold me eating spaghetti with a knife and fork.
Our daughters are all grown up and gone away.
Once when she was sitting pregnant on the settee
It snapped shut with herself inside it,
But not a bother on her. I nearly died.

As the train slowed down approaching Portarlington
I overheard myself say to the passenger sitting opposite me:
'I am feeling guilty because she does not love me
As much as she used to, can you explain that?'
The passenger's eyes were on the axe on the seat beside me.
'Her sister wants a loan of the axe . . . '
As the train threaded itself into Portarlington
I nodded to the passenger 'Cúl an tSúdaire!'
The passenger stood up, lifted down a case from the rack,
Walked out of the coach, but did not get off the train.
For the remainder of the journey, we sat alone,
The axe and I,
All the green fields running away from us,
All our daughters grown up and gone away.

Glossary

Title Father's Day: the third Sunday in June.

Title 21 June: Summer solstice, the longest day of the year.

Line 22 bare buff: naked.

Line 53 Cúl an tSúdaire!: literally, the Tanner's Recess (Irish for Portarlington).

'Father's Day, 21 June 1992' is from Paul Durcan's 1993 collection *A Snail in My Prime.*

Questions

1. Sum up the 'story' of the poem in a sentence. Now reread the poem and say what's lost in summary.
2. What kind of a scene is created in the opening lines of the poem? Look at words such as 'dashing', 'searching', 'ticking'.
3. Who is the 'She' of line 3? Is the request an unusual one? Why? How does the speaker respond? How would you describe the relationship between him and her?
4. Look at lines 14 and 15. What does their inclusion contribute to the poem?
5. Lines 17 and those following paint vivid pictures. Examine each image in turn and comment on its effect.
6. What happens in the second section? What emerges from these lines in terms of a self-portrait? How would you describe the speaker's tone and mood?
7. The settee is mentioned in sections one and two. Comment on this.
8. In the third and final section, the speaker addresses the passenger sitting opposite him on the train. It could be argued that the poem, at this point, combines heartbreak and humour. Would you agree?
9. How did the passenger react to the speaker's confession?
10. How would you describe the atmosphere in the poem's closing lines? What created this mood? What is your attitude towards the speaker in lines 56 to 59? Has your attitude towards the speaker changed throughout the poem? If so, why?

The Arnolfini Marriage

after Jan van Eyck

We are the Arnolfinis.
Do not think you may invade
Our privacy because you may not.

We are standing to our portrait,
The most erotic portrait ever made,
Because we have faith in the artist

To do justice to the plurality,
Fertility, domesticity, barefootedness
Of a man and a woman saying 'we':

To do justice to our bed
As being our most necessary furniture;
To do justice to our life as a reflection.

Our brains spill out upon the floor
And the terrier at our feet sniffs
The minutiae of our magnitude.

The most relaxing word in our vocabulary is 'we'.
Imagine being able to say 'we'.
Most people are in no position to say 'we'.

Are you? Who eat alone? Sleep alone?
And at dawn cycle to work
With an Alsatian shepherd dog tied to your handlebars?

We will pause now for the Angelus.
Here you have it:
The two halves of the coconut.

Glossary

Title The Arnolfini Marriage after Jan van Eyck: van Eyck (1385?–1441?), a Flemish painter, was born near Maastricht. 'The Arnolfini Marriage' (also known as 'The Arnolfini Betrothal') is a portrait of Giovanni Arnolfini and his wife Jeanne de Cename, dated 1434, and is in the National Gallery, London. Painted on wood, it measures thirty-three inches by twenty-two and a half inches. On the wall above the mirror, van Eyck has painted 'Johannes de Eyck fuit hic 1434: Jan van Eyck was here 1434'. The setting is an upper room in a house on Coopers Street in Bruges. Van Eyck was employed by Arnolfini so as to provide his patron with a formal certificate of marriage. At that time, any Catholic man and woman could contract a valid marriage as long as they could, by 'mutual consent expressed by words and actions', fulfill their intentions. Thus, Arnolfini, in his stockinged feet, stands with his right hand raised, Jeanne's right hand in his left hand. Above them, the chandelier with its single lit candle symbolizes the Light of the World. The wooden pattens (wooden overshoes) on the floor in the left foreground echo the text: 'Put off the shoes from thy feet, for the place whereon thou standest is holy ground.' The dog, a terrier, suggests fidelity. On the armchair by the bed, there is a carving of St Margaret, patron saint of married women. The convex mirror, diameter two inches, on the far wall, allows the viewer to see the painter and another witness. On the mirror's frame, there are ten coloured miniatures depicting the Passion of Christ. It is a painting that contains the past, present and future.

Line 5 erotic: tending to arouse sexual desire or excitement (from Greek *erotikos*, sexual love).

Line 7 plurality: being plural, meaning being more than one; in this instance being husband and wife, being 'we'.

Line 8 Fertility: the ability to conceive and produce offspring.

Line 8 domesticity: home/family life.

Line 15 minutiae: the small/precise details.

Line 15 magnitude: importance, great size.

Line 22 Angelus: a Roman Catholic prayer that commemorates the incarnation of Jesus (Latin *Angelus domini* – The Angel of the Lord – are the opening words of the prayer). The words 'We will pause now for the Angelus' are frequently used by presenters at noon on RTÉ Radio 1, weekdays.

? Questions

1. How does this differ from the other Paul Durcan poems in this book?

2. Who is speaking in this poem?

3. Why is the word 'We' – it occurs seven times – central to the poem? And the portrait?

4. Which details from the painting are explored in the poem? Explore how 'bed', 'reflection', 'terrier' are significant to both artist and poet.

5. Are there details in the poem that shock or surprise you? Comment on line 13. What do you make of line 21?

6. Do you think Paul Durcan's response enhances van Eyck's painting? Give reasons for your answer.

7. Look at the poet's use of repetition. Does it affect the poem? Explain your answer.

8. This poem is from *Give Me Your Hand* (1994) which contains 49 poems by Paul Durcan written in response to 49 paintings in the National Gallery, London. In an Introduction to the book, Bryan Robertson says 'these beautiful and constantly surprising poems have poetic self-sufficiency and keep the paintings firmly in their place.' Would you agree with this view?

9. Who is being addressed in the second last stanza? Contrast the picture that lines 19–21 conjure up with the picture of the couple as described in the poem.

10. Do you think the ending a suitable one? Explain your answer.

Ireland 2002

Do you ever take a holiday abroad?
No, we always go to America.

? Questions

1. What is meant by the term 'mid-Atlantic culture'? Has Ireland, in your opinion, become mid-Atlantic?
2. There is a saying in the west of Ireland, 'Next parish, America'. Explore the relationship between Ireland and the US. Consider the girl's plans in Paul Durcan's poem 'The Girl with the Keys to Pearse's Cottage' in the light of this little poem.
3. The couplet enacts a tiny little drama. Who, do you think, could be speaking here?
4. Is this a depressing poem or a funny poem or could it be a bit of both? Explain your answer.
5. In a piece entitled 'Home from Italy' in *Paul Durcan's Diary*, Durcan writes: 'The hinterlands of the minds of we Irish are the UK on the one hand and the USA on the other hand.' Comment on this observation in relation to 'Ireland 2002'.
6. If this is a snapshot of Ireland in 2002, what does it tell us about that particular time? Could it refer to Ireland today?

Rosie Joyce

I

That was that Sunday afternoon in May
When a hot sun pushed through the clouds
And you were born!

I was driving the two hundred miles from west to east,
The sky blue-and-white china in the fields
In impromptu picnics of tartan rugs;

When neither words nor I
Could have known that you had been named already
And that your name was Rosie –

Rosie Joyce! May you some day in May
Fifty-six years from today be as lucky
As I was when you were born that Sunday:

To drive such side-roads, such main roads, such ramps, such roundabouts,
To cross such bridges, to by-pass such villages, such towns
As I did on your Incarnation Day.

By-passing Swinford – Croagh Patrick in my rear-view mirror –
My mobile phone rang and, stopping on the hard edge of
P. Flynn's highway,
I heard Mark your father say:

'A baby girl was born at 3,33 p.m.
Weighing 7 and a ½ lbs in Holles Street.
Tough work, all well.'

II

That Sunday in May before daybreak
Night had pushed up through the slopes of Achill
Yellow forefingers of Arum Lily – the first of the year;

Down at the Sound the first rhododendrons
Purpling the golden camps of whins;
The first hawthorns powdering white the mainland;

The first yellow irises flagging roadside streams;
Quills of bog-cotton skimming the bogs;
Burrishoole cemetery shin-deep in forget-me-nots;

The first sea pinks speckling the seashore;
Cliffs of London Pride, groves of bluebell.
First fuchsia, Queen Anne's Lace, primrose.

I drove the Old Turlough Road, past Walter Durcan's farm,
Umbrella'd in the joined handwriting of its ash trees;
I drove Tulsk, Kilmainham, the Grand Canal.

Never before had I felt so fortunate
To be driving back into Dublin city;
Each canal bridge an old pewter brooch.

I rode the waters and the roads of Ireland,
Rosie, to be with you, seashell at my ear!
How I laughed when I cradled you in my hand.

Only at Tarmonbarry did I slow down,
As in my father's Ford Anglia half a century ago
He slowed down also, as across the River Shannon

We crashed, rattled, bounced on a Bailey bridge;
Daddy relishing his role as Moses,
Enunciating the name of the Great Divide

Between the East and the West!
We are the people of the West,
Our fate is to go East.

No such thing, Rosie, as a Uniform Ireland
And please God there never will be;
There is only the River Shannon and all her sister rivers

And all her brother mountains and their family prospects.
There are higher powers than politics
And these we call wildflowers or, geologically, people.

Rosie Joyce – that Sunday in May
Not alone did you make my day, my week, my year
To the prescription of Jonathan Philbin Bowman –

Daymaker!
Daymaker!
Daymaker!

Popping out of my daughter, your mother –
Changing the expressions on the faces all around you –
All of them looking like blue hills in a heat haze –

But you saved my life. For three years
I had been subsisting in the slums of despair,
Unable to distinguish one day from the next.

III

On the return journey from Dublin to Mayo
In Charlestown on Main Street
I met John Normanly, organic farmer from Curry.

He is driving home to his wife Caroline
From a Mountbellew meeting of the Western Development
Commission
Of Dillon House in Ballaghadereen.

He crouches in his car, I waver in the street,
As we exchange lullabies of expectancy;
We wet our foreheads in John Moriarty's autobiography.

The following Sunday is the Feast of the Ascension
Of Our Lord into Heaven:

Thank you, O Lord, for the Descent of Rosie onto Earth.

Glossary

Title Rosie Joyce: Durcan's granddaughter.

Line 6 impromptu: unplanned or unrehearsed.

Line 6 tartan: a pattern of coloured checks and intersecting lines.

Line 15 Incarnation Day: a term used to describe the embodiment of the Son of God, in human flesh as Jesus Christ.

Line 16 Croagh Patrick: a mountain in County Mayo (765 m or 2,510 feet); it is said that St. Patrick fasted for the 40 days of Lent on its summit in 441. Croagh is from the Irish *cruach*, meaning haystack or rick; each year on the last Sunday in July a pilgrimage to the top of Croagh Patrick is held and many of the pilgrims – thousands of them – climb the mountain in their bare feet.

Line 17 P. Flynn's highway: Pádraig 'Pee' Flynn (born 1939), a former Fianna Fail politician and minister based in Castlebar; he was European Union commissioner for social affairs from 1993 to 1999. The entry in *Brewers Dictionary of Irish Phrase and Fable* reads as follows: 'Able but arrogant, Flynn is remembered for two major PR gaffes: the first when he referred to Mary Robinson's alleged new-found family values ('the new interest in her family') in a lunchtime radio discussion on 3 November 1999 during the presidential election campaign; the second when, on *The Late Late Show* of 15 January 1999, he referred patronisingly to property developer Tom Gilmartin, who had claimed to have given £50,000 to Flynn for Fianna Fail in 1989. On the same show, he forfeited all public sympathy by appealing for public understanding of the difficulty of maintaining three residencies in Castlebar, Dublin and Brussels.'

Line 20 Holles Street: the National Maternity Hospital in Dublin.

Line 24 Arum Lily: a plant with arrow shaped leaves with a spike of minute flowers (wild arum is the cuckoo pint).

Line 25 Sound: a narrow stretch of water connecting two larger bodies of water.

Line 25 rhododendrons: a shrub or small tree with large evergreen leaves and large clusters of bell-shaped flowers (in Latin via Greek, *rhodon* is rose and *dendron*, tree).

Line 26 whins: furze, gorse.

Line 30 Burrishoole cemetery: on the north shore of Clew Bay.

Line 32 London Pride: low growing plant with rosettes of fleshy leaves and stems of pink starlike flowers.

Line 33 fuchsia: a shrub with drooping red and purple flowers; named in honour of a 16th century German botanist Leonhard Fuchs; in Irish, it's known as deora Dé – God's tears.

Line 33 Queen Anne's Lace: cow parsley, a wildflower with white, lacelike blossom.

Line 36 Tulsk, Kilmainham, the Grand Canal: Tulsk is a village in County Roscommon; Kilmainham and the Grand Canal are in Dublin; naming these places signifies the speaker's happy journey from west to east. In Paul Durcan's poem 'Going Home to Mayo, Winter 1949', the speaker describes the childhood sensation of returning to 'the daylight nightmare of Dublin City' with his father and 'each lock-gate' on the Grand Canal 'tolled our mutual doom'.

Line 39 pewter brooch: a copper and silvery-white semimetal ornament pinned to clothing.

Line 43 Tarmonbarry: a village in County Roscommon.

Line 46 Bailey bridge: a temporary bridge of lattice steel designed for rapid assembly from prefabricated standard parts.

Line 47 Moses: Hebrew prophet and law giver from circa 15th century BC. He led the Hebrews from Egypt, established the worship of Jehovah and gave his people the basic Jewish law, including the Ten Commandments. The story of Moses is found in the Book of Exodus.

Line 48 Great Divide: the river Shannon but referring to Moses who raised his hand and parted the Red Sea (*Exodus* 14. 16 ff).

Line 51 go East: 'Go West Young Man' is a well-known phrase meaning 'Go in search of a better life, adventure'. It originally referred to the expansion of the U.S. westward.

Line 52 Uniform: same, without variation.

Line 60/61 the prescription of Jonathan Philbin Bowman/Daymaker!: on 'A Living Word' on RTÉ Radio 1, the journalist Jonathan Philbin Bowman (1969–2000) spoke of how emails from friends 'made his day'. In *Paul Durcan's Diary*, dated 7 March 2001, Durcan says 'unasked-for, unexpected sweetness makes my day. And I think of Jonathan Philbin Bowman who went home to God just a year ago and that beautiful concept of his: "daymaker". Jonathan – Jonathan said – Jonathan wanted to be a "daymaker": to make your day and my day. And he did, oh he did...'

Line 78 We wet our foreheads in John Moriarty's autobiography: discussed, praised, found sustenance in John Moriarty's autobiography; wetting one's forehead with Holy Water is a Catholic custom on entering a church – a gesture of respect; John Moriarty (1938–2007) was a writer, philosopher, mystic and much admired by Paul Durcan. On 21 March 2001, his diary column on RTÉ Radio 1 was called 'The Autobiography of John Moriarty'. *Nostos* (meaning 'homecoming') is the first volume and was published in 2001. It is, says Paul Durcan, 'one of the most remarkable autobiographies I have ever read in my life'.

Line 79 Feast of the Ascension: in the Christian calendar, the day, a Thursday and the 40th day after Easter – when the faithful believe that Jesus Christ ascended from earth to heaven.

Line 81 Descent: the suggestion here is that Rosie has been sent from heaven to earth; the Descent of the Holy Spirit upon the Apostles refers to the moment at Pentecost when the Holy Spirit under the form of tongues of fire appeared and filled the hearts of the Apostles with love, empowered and prepared them to bear witness to Jesus – a very special and spiritual moment.

'Rosie Joyce' is from Paul Durcan's 2004 collection *The Art of Life*.

? Questions

1. Like many of Paul Durcan poems, this one tells a story, the story of the birth of the poet's granddaughter and his driving across Ireland, from Achill to Dublin, to see her, and his returning to Mayo. Biographical facts would suggest that the speaker here is Paul Durcan himself, not an adopted persona. What does his writing this poem tell us about him?

2. This poem has been carefully divided into three parts and 27 stanzas (7;16;4), each containing three lines. Can you suggest why a poet chooses a certain form and technique for certain poems?

3. Look at the images in the opening lines, especially the images of the sun and sky. Consider too the images used in the opening lines of Part II (lines 22–33). Why are these images of birth and growth appropriate here?

4. How would you describe the speaker's mood in Part I? Which words and phrases best capture that feeling?

5. In stanza five (lines 13–15), why does the speaker list the details of the journey? What is revealed here of the speaker?

6. The birth of the speaker's granddaughter is announced via mobile phone. How would you describe the father's message?

7. 'That Sunday in May' is emphasised in the poem. Having announced the baby's birth in Part I, what does the poet do in Part II time-wise? Trace the movement of the day and the speaker's movement as described in the poem. How do present, future and past intermingle in the poem? Look, for example, at line 42.

8. What is the speaker's attitude towards the Ireland that Rosie has been born into? Why do you think the speaker says 'No such thing, Rosie, as a Uniform Ireland/And please god there never will be'.

9. Though this is a poem of joy and celebration, there are dark moments too. Consider lines 67–69.

10. The poem includes what might be called random details – the meeting with John Normanly, organic farmer from Curry, who is driving home to his wife Caroline. How do such details work within the poem as a whole?

11. Comment on the phrase 'lullabies of expectancy' (line 77) and 'We wet our foreheads' (line 78). Link these to the poem's central theme.

12. The final stanza contains references to Ascension and Descent, to Christ and to Rosie. Is this a spiritual poem? What other adjectives would you use to describe this poem?

13. The speaker is clearly ecstatic at the birth of his granddaughter. Which aspects of her birth does the speaker celebrate?

14. Is this more than a personal poem? Consider the references to aspects of Ireland and say how these colour our understanding of the poem.

15. If you were Rosie Joyce, would you be pleased to have a poem such as this written for you? Which aspects would please you best?

16. Do you think that the poet has created a sense of continuity? How has this been achieved? Refer to the text in your answer.

The MacBride Dynasty

What young mother is not a vengeful goddess
Spitting dynastic as well as motherly pride?
In 1949 in the black Ford Anglia,
Now that I had become a walking, talking little boy,
Mummy drove me out to visit my grand-aunt Maud Gonne
In Roebuck House in the countryside near Dublin,
To show off to the servant of the Queen
The latest addition to the extended family.
Although the eighty-year-old Cathleen Ní Houlihan had taken
to her bed
She was keen as ever to receive admirers,
Especially the children of the family.
Only the previous week the actor MacLiammóir
Had been kneeling at her bedside reciting Yeats to her,
His hand on his heart, clutching a red rose.
Cousin Séan and his wife Kid led the way up the stairs,
Séan opening the door and announcing my mother.
Mummy lifted me up in her arms as she approached the bed
And Maud leaned forward, sticking out her claws
To embrace me, her lizards of eyes darting about
In the rubble of the ruins of her beautiful face.
Terrified, I recoiled from her embrace
And, fleeing her bedroom, ran down the stairs
Out onto the wrought-iron balcony
Until Séan caught up with me and quieted me
And took me for a walk in the walled orchard.
Mummy was a little but not totally mortified:
She had never liked Maud Gonne because of Maud's
Betrayal of her husband, Mummy's Uncle John,
Major John, most ordinary of men, most
Humorous, courageous of soldiers,
The pride of our family,
Whose memory always brought laughter
To my grandmother Eileen's lips. 'John,'
She used cry, 'John was such a gay man.'

Mummy set great store by loyalty; loyalty
In Mummy's eyes was the cardinal virtue.
Maud Gonne was a disloyal wife
And, therefore, not worthy of Mummy's love.
For dynastic reasons we would tolerate Maud,
But we would always see through her.

Glossary

Title MacBride: John MacBride, nationalist revolutionary, born in Westport, County Mayo on 7 May 1865, was Paul Durcan's grand-uncle. He fought in the Boer War against the British in 1899, he married Maud Gonne in 1903 and was executed in May 1916 for his part in the Rising. Durcan's mother was Sheila MacBride Durcan (1915–2004). Séan MacBride (1904–88), politician, human-rights campaigner, winner of the Nobel Peace Prize (1974) and the Lenin Peace Prize (1977) was the son of John MacBride and Maud Gonne.

Title Dynasty: a line of hereditary leaders.

Line 1 vengeful: vindictive; disposed to revenge; seeking to harm someone in return for a perceived injury.

Line 3 1949: Paul Durcan was born in 1944; he was five years old in 1949.

Line 5 Maud Gonne: (1866–1953) an iconic figure in Irish nationalism; born in Aldershot, Surrey, the daughter of an army colonel she moved to Ireland when she was sixteen; considered very beautiful, W. B. Yeats was infatuated with her; she was unconventional, a political activist for which she was imprisoned, a convert to Catholicism; she died aged 87.

Line 6 Roebuck House: in Clonskeagh, opposite the back gates of UCD – suburban now, countryside in 1949.

Line 7 servant of the Queen: Maud Gonne's autobiography was called *A Servant of the Queen* (1938).

Line 9 Cathleen Ní Houlihan: a name for Ireland in which the country is personified as a woman; it's also the name of a play which Yeats, assisted by Lady Gregory, wrote for Maud Gonne. Maud Gonne also acted the part of the old woman who was trying to recover her four green fields from a stranger.

Line 12 MacLiammóir: the actor and director Mícheál MacLiammóir (1899–1978).

Line 13 Yeats: W. B. Yeats proposed several times to Maud Gonne; she refused him and then Yeats proposed to her daughter Iseult who also rejected him.

Line 15 Cousin Séan: he was 45 at the time; Paul Durcan was five; Maud Gonne was 83.

Line 15 Kid: Catalina 'Kid' Bulfin (born Buenos Aires) whom Séan MacBride married on his 21st birthday, on 26 January 1925, in secret, as both were on the Irish Government's 'wanted' list for their republican activities.

Line 26 mortified: humiliated.

Lines 27–28 Maud's/ Betrayal of her husband, Mummy's Uncle John: In 1900, Maud Gonne met John MacBride and married him in 1903. Their son Séan MacBride was born in 1904; in 1905 the marriage was dissolved. Earlier, Maud Gonne had two children with French journalist Lucien Millevoye. The first did not survive infancy and the second, Iseult, was conceived on the grave of the first for spiritual reasons.

Line 34 gay: light-hearted, carefree (only in recent decades did gay meaning homosexual supersede its other, centuries-old meaning).

Line 36 cardinal virtue: the chief/fundamental/important moral attributes of scholastic philosophy – justice, prudence, temperance, fortitude, faith, hope, charity; Mummy thought loyalty more important than those other seven virtues.

'The MacBride Dynasty' is from Paul Durcan's 2007 collection *The Laughter of Mothers*.

? Questions

1. This poem remembers a time in the speaker's childhood when as 'a walking, talking little boy' he visited a relative (his grand-aunt) who happened to be one of the most famous people in Ireland. What is the speaker's dominant memory?
2. According to the opening two lines, why did the mother bring her son to visit Maud Gonne? Consider 'vengeful', 'spitting', 'motherly'.
3. How is the aged Maud Gonne portrayed in the poem? Consider her personality and the physical description.
4. The poem contains striking images of the old woman in the bed. Comment on the poet's use of 'claws', 'lizards', 'rubble'.
5. 'This poem does much more than tell a story.' Would you agree with this view? Explain your answer.
6. You can read about the people mentioned here in history books. What does this poem do that the history book cannot do?
7. The speaker is on the side of John MacBride. Why?
8. Is 'The MacBride Dynasty' the most appropriate title for the poem? Why? Give reasons for your answer. Consider the importance of the speaker's mother and grandmother within the context of the poem.
9. The poem ends with a condemnation, a strong verdict. How would you describe the Durcan family's judgement on Maud Gonne? Is it biased? Fair? Justified?
10. Irish politics and family history combine here. Explore how this is both a public and a private poem. How would you describe the speaker's tone and mood as you read through the poem?

General Questions

A. 'Reading Paul Durcan's poetry is both entertaining and challenging.' To what extent do you agree with this statement? Support your answer with suitable reference to the poems by Durcan on your course.

B. 'Paul Durcan explores people and situations in his own distinctive style.' Write your response to this statement, supporting your points with the aid of suitable reference to the poems you have studied.

C. 'Paul Durcan's original approach to poetry results in interesting, thought-provoking moments in his work.' Do you agree with this assessment of his poetry? Write a response, supporting your points with the aid of suitable reference to the poems on your course.

D. 'Though an Irish poet, Paul Durcan's poetry speaks to people everywhere.' Write your response to this statement, supporting your answer with suitable reference to the poetry by Durcan on your course.

E. 'Durcan's poems often reveal moments of humour which lessen the loneliness and suffering found in much of his work.' To what extent do you agree with this statement? Support your answer with suitable reference to the poetry of Paul Durcan on your course.

F. 'Different voices in Paul Durcan's poetry offer varied and memorable insights.' Give your response to the poetry of Durcan in the light of this statement. Support your points with the aid of suitable reference to the poems you have studied.

G. 'In terms of theme and technique, Paul Durcan in his poetry is a unique voice.' You have been asked by your local newspaper to write an article on the poetry of Paul Durcan. Write the article in response to the above title. You should refer to both style and subject matter. Support the points you make by reference to the poetry on your course.

H. 'Paul Durcan appeals to many readers including those who are indifferent to poetry.' Using the above title, write an essay outlining what you consider to be the appeal of Paul Durcan's poetry. Support the points you make by reference to the poetry by Paul Durcan on your course.

I. 'With Paul Durcan's poetry, you don't know whether to laugh or cry', says Colm Tóibín. Would you agree with this statement? Give reasons for your answer, supporting the points you make by reference to the poetry on your course.

Critical Commentary

Nessa

This love poem tells of a momentous day in the speaker's life – the day he met the woman whom he later married. The poem contains dates and facts: he tells us that he met her on the first of August in a hotel in Dalkey, but the poem by line 3 becomes more magical. The speaker tells us that he was in thrall from the beginning; he was captivated. There is a surreal and fairytale-like quality in the images used – 'She took me by the index finger/ And dropped me in her well.' It would seem that she, Nessa, is mesmerizing. It is she who is manipulating him and the experience is a dangerous, thrilling and exciting one.

The image of the whirlpool (the word is used eight times) occurs and is repeated at the end of each of the four stanzas, and in that image the speaker expresses not only his awareness of the danger involved but also his lack of control. He tells us that 'I very nearly drowned'. The repetition here adds to the speaker's sense of awe, wonder, helplessness: 'And that was a whirlpool, that was a whirlpool'.

In stanza two, Nessa addresses the speaker in a tone that is both an order and an invitation: 'Take off your pants, she said to me'. The following line – 'And I very nearly didn't' – reveals the speaker's shyness and relief. If he hadn't taken off his pants and if he hadn't gone swimming, he might not have experienced love.

In stanza one, 'her well' is the whirlpool; in stanza two, the sea becomes the whirlpool and the sensation conveyed is one of intense excitement and movement. Nessa's tone is different when she says, 'Would you care to swim?' – more invitation than order. And the speaker in line 10 – 'And I hopped into the Irish Sea' – conveys an ease and friskiness. The speaker is more and more interested and involved as the story unfolds.

The poem moves in terms of setting from 'the Shangri-La Hotel' to the 'Irish Sea' to 'the field'. Shangri-La means paradise, while water is often associated with cleansing and rebirth. The speaker undergoes a sea-change and in stanza three when he and she, the speaker and Nessa, are together in the field, there is a strong feeling of their being together.

The use of the word 'fell' is interesting. The words 'falling in love' are familiar ones. 'On the way back I fell in the field/ And she fell down beside me' suggests a falling without hurt or danger, a falling in love. In this third stanza, something interesting happens in terms of the arrangement of the poem on the page. The poem consists of four stanzas, three of which are six lines long and the concluding stanza runs to eight lines. The lines are of similar length in all four stanzas except for line 16 which contains only two words: 'With Nessa'. Nessa is at the heart of the poem and the two-word line emphasizes her importance not only visually but also in terms of the poem's rhythm. Reading through the poem, the reader has to pause at line 16.

The speaker tells us at the end of each stanza: 'And I very nearly drowned'. Drowning is a frightening situation; it suggests an ending, a death. But, in this instance, the speaker is grateful that he hasn't drowned, that somehow Nessa has saved him from drowning.

'O Nessa my dear, Nessa my dear' is a very tender and intense expression of his love for her. The poem's title is her name and Nessa is repeated three times, twice in this fourth and final stanza's opening line. When the speaker asks his lover 'Will you stay with me on the rocks?' and 'Will you come for me into the Irish Sea?', the rocks and sea could be taken to mean difficulties and uncertainty. The speaker is opening himself to her in a direct and immediate way. He is clearly infatuated with Nessa and dependent on her.

The closing image is one of togetherness. He and she are in a taxi-cab 'wrapped up in dust' and heading into Dublin City. It has been pointed out by the critic John Redmond that in this poem '(w)ithin a short space, Durcan covers an enormous distance'. From hotel to sea to field but also, of course, it is an emotional journey as well as an actual one.

Redmond calls the poem a 'casual aisling', aisling being an eighteenth-century Irish poem in which the speaker addresses a beautiful woman. He comments too on how the word Lughnasa rhymes with Nessa. Lughnasa is celebrated on the first of August, mentioned in line 1 of the poem, but it is difficult to say whether this is intended or not.

The Girl with the Keys to Pearse's Cottage

Like 'Nessa', this poem tells of an encounter between the speaker and an interesting, attractive young woman. Pearse is an iconic, central figure in Irish history and his summer cottage in County Galway has become a tourist attraction. This poem was published in 1975, almost sixty years after Pearse was executed in May 1916. The speaker talks of Pearse's cottage as a special, tranquil place, but the main focus of the poem is the speaker's love for this local girl, Cáit Killann, the girl with the keys to Pearse's cottage.

The memorable title brings together two interesting ideas. The young woman's summer job is as tour guide to this place, a place with significant historical associations. Having the key to something is a phrase or concept that suggests understanding at a deeper level but the poem's portrait of the girl would seem to suggest that she is not very busy, not that interested and is preparing to emigrate to America at the end of the summer.

The opening line – 'When I was sixteen I met a dark girl' – tells us that this records a youthful experience. He and she are both teenagers and the details are factual. We are told what this dark girl does, we are given her name. We also sense that she is beautiful:

> 'Her dark hair was darker because her smile was so bright'.

The second stanza paints a clear picture of the physical cottage and the atmosphere around it – 'bare brown rooms . . . whitewashed walls' and its 'cosmic peace'. The description of the photographs of Pearse as 'passionate and pale' is succinct, while the use of alliteration forges a memorable image.

The speaker is remembering details and the use of 'recall' here suggests that this is a memory poem. He is writing about his 16-year-old self but the details are vivid:

> I recall wet thatch and peeling jambs
> And how all was best seen from below in the field;
> I used sit in the rushes with ledger-book and pencil
> Compiling poems of passion for Cáit Killann.

The cottage itself has been neglected, is in need of repair – 'wet thatch and peeling jambs' – and this could be a symbol of Ireland's relationship with its past. Is modern Ireland indifferent to Pearse's legacy? The speaker believes that Pearse's cottage is best seen from a distance, best seen when the 'peeling jambs' cannot be discerned. The speaker is more interested in the girl than in the cottage and he is engaged in what is considered typical or familiar adolescent behaviour: he is in love and he is writing her 'poems of passion'. Pearse was 'passionate' in his commitment to free Ireland from colonial power; the speaker is passionate in his love for the girl with the keys to Pearse's cottage.

The poem focuses on a place and a relationship, but in stanza four it begins to become a poem with wider implications. Here is a young Irish woman in a uniform of 'sun-red skirt and moon-black blazer' and we read that she is 'Looking toward our strange world wide-eyed'. She is not busy as a tour-guide. We know this from line 13: 'Often she used linger on the sill of the window'. She is lingering, she is waiting and then the poem offers us the grim detail:

> Our world was strange because it had no future;
> She was America-bound at summer's end.
> She had no choice but to leave her home

The tone here is flat. 'She was' and 'She had' make for two statements that are without hope. The images 'sun-red' and 'moon-black' in the previous stanza are interesting, imaginative and colourful, but stanza five is deliberately lacking such rich language. The situation that the girl finds herself in is more sad than happy, more hopeless than hopeful.

The poem ends with a passionate expression on the speaker's part as he addresses the girl to whom he has been writing poems:

> O Cáit Killann, O Cáit Killann

She has left Connemara, her own native place, she has left her job as the girl with the keys to Pearse's cottage, but the speaker comments:

> You have gone with your keys from your own native place

The poem's final two lines create a sense of darkness. When the speaker says 'here in this dark', the line could refer to his feeling of loneliness now that she has gone. Line 2 spoke of her 'dark hair' and her 'bright smile, but now though she has gone the speaker still sees her eyes blazing back. We are also given a new detail in the closing line. We discover that the girl is a 'Connemara postman's daughter'; he is now the father of an emigrant.

She no longer has the keys to Pearse's cottage, but 'You have gone with the keys from your own native place'. This, perhaps, means that she has gone but she still has the ability to work things out, to discover things for herself. The final detail – that she has a proud mortal face – reminds us that though she is young, though she is living a new and different life in another country, she is also going to die. Such a detail is realistic, true and overshadows the young life that was so vividly captured in the opening stanzas of the poem.

The Difficulty that is Marriage

The title announces the poem's central idea: that marriage can be a complex, challenging and difficult situation to be in. In line 1, the speaker paints a picture of a marriage where both husband and wife have reached a way of life, a *modus vivendi*, a compromised position:

We disagree to disagree, we divide, we differ

Eight words, four of them beginning with 'd' and the play on the familiar phrase 'we agree to differ' suggest a complex relationship.

The speaker's tone in the opening line is one of resigned acceptance. It states the facts. But lines 2 to 5 present us with an image of a couple together and separate and the tone is one of wonder and gratitude:

Yet each night as I lie in bed beside you
And you are faraway curled up in sleep
I array the moonlit ceiling with a mosaic of question marks;
How was it I was so lucky to have ever met you?

Though he and she are together in bed, she is 'faraway curled up in sleep'. The speaker, it would seem, is unable to sleep and yet the images are soft and beautiful. The choice of 'array', meaning 'to arrange in a neat or impressive way', and the moonlight create an attractive image in the reader's mind. The slow rhythm contained within the question 'How was it I was so lucky to have ever met you?' creates a thoughtful mood. A more usual phrasing would be 'How was I so lucky?' but the 'How was it I was so lucky?' adds emphasis.

The poem, a sonnet, becomes more direct and confessional at line 6. When the speaker admits that 'I am no brave pagan proud of my mortality', the tone is humble. He describes his situation as difficult. He is not arrogant; he knows that his mortality is a reality and yet he would happily, gladly stay alive on earth for ever were it meant that he could spend it with his wife. 'Changeling earth' is difficult to tease out. The adjective chosen is not changeable nor changing earth and changeling refers to a substitution. Perhaps the speaker is interpreting the world and seeing the world as a substituted one, a more challenging one. And yet the husband here says he would happily 'live for ever/ If it were with you my sleeping friend'.

One of the most striking and memorable lines in the poem is line 9:

I have my troubles and I shall always have them

This is very direct and accepting. The speaker, in being so honest, is, it could be said, making himself vulnerable but his pleading tone is sincere. He would prefer a world with his troubles rather than a world that was changeless, as long as he could live his life with his wife.

The poem ends on a very quiet note. The speaker admits that he knows his wife must have faults but he cannot see them and, yet, he clearly does not want to portray her as some kind of saint or hero. 'You must have your faults but I do not see them.'

The final line of the sonnet contains ten words, every one of them a monosyllable except for the last one:

> If I were with you, I should live for ever.

This gives that line a quiet power. It is a line that is filled with loneliness and longing and with a deep love for his wife.

Wife Who Smashed Television Gets Jail

The very dramatic title grabs our attention. Why did this wife smash the television? Why was she jailed for doing so? The poem is a mini-drama, a dramatic episode in the life of this family of husband, wife and kids.

It begins with the immediacy of the husband's voice addressing a judge in a courtroom. A story is being told. The situation is explained. The language is that of violence and threat – 'smashed', 'marched', 'declared', 'put her boot through the screen'. It's a domestic situation where it could be argued that the expected is reversed or upside down: it is the mother and wife who is the aggressive one and the judge's verdict regarding 'a threat to the family' is also unusual and unexpected.

One of the most striking things about this poem is its humour. 'Wife Who Smashed Television Gets Jail' is from Durcan's 1976 collection and at the time television was still a relatively new but a very definite presence in Irish homes. Watching television was a family event. Parents and children sat down together in the one room and watched the same programmes.

Kojak, in this poem, is the TV programme of choice. There is humour in the use of 'peaceably' in line 2:

> Me and the kids were peaceably watching *Kojak*

when one considers that the programme features not-so-peaceful actions: we discover that this particular episode features Kojak 'shooting a dame'. The words 'Me and the kids' as opposed to 'My kids and I' suggests a more informal, relaxed tone.

This topsy-turvy portrait of family life contrasts with conventional images of Irish family life such as contained in the phrase 'The family that prays together stays together' or a family where father, mother and children live in harmony.

There is nothing harmonious about this family scene. The husband refuses to turn off the television, the wife reacts violently, the television is smashed and the husband and kids head over to his mother's place to catch the end of the programme.

Everything is seen from the husband's point of view: lines 1–21 comprise a monologue spoken before the judge and the remaining five lines offer the reported words of the judge's verdict. This first part has a 'when, when and what' quality to it. The language is colloquial and colourful. The zany humour is found in such details as having the woman whom Kojak has just shot 'the same name as my wife'. That Kojak snarls the words 'Goodnight, Queen Maeve' clearly resonates in an Irish reader's mind in that Queen Maeve in Irish mythology is a devious, selfish queen. The 'dame' in the television programme has been shot but the other Maeve, the wife in the poem, seems to be getting her own way. That is until the husband and wife end up in court arguing their point of view.

There is humour also in the wife's argument when she says

> I don't see why my kids or anybody's else's kids
> Should have a television for a father or mother

but the alternative which she proposes is equally odd:

> We'd be much better off all down in the pub talking
> Or playing bar-billiards

And that 'she disappeared off back down again to the pub' adds to the humour.

The verdict too when the judge pronounces the television 'a basic unit of the family' adds more humour to the poem. The judge, named as Justice Ó Brádaigh, is given a distinctly Irish surname and yet his judgement in a country where the mother or mammy is often revered is strange. People who are violent are sometimes sent to jail, but the violence in this instance, the kicking in of a television, is not the conventional kind.

Many of Paul Durcan's poems reflect a changing Ireland. They respond to current events, newspaper stories, public figures. They offer a picture of Ireland that can be unsettling, odd, funny, dark, memorable.

Parents

Paul Durcan frequently writes about family life and often employs a narrative technique when doing so. A story is being told. In 'Parents', the story is less important than the expression of an intense, private and deep emotion.

The title, 'Parents', unites mother and father and, though the poem is told in the third person, the effect is very direct. The poem's subject matter – two parents watch their sleeping child – is often regarded as heart-warming and charming but the opening line is disturbing:

> A child's face is a drowned face

A child belongs to its parents, yet is separate from them. In this poem, the speaker explores the mystery of identity, the mystery of parent-child relationship and the strangeness and loneliness of it all.

The drowning and sea imagery that pervades the poem suggests estrangement. The sleeping child is in a different, separate world and seems lost to her parents. The focus of attention contains an intense preoccupation and awareness. The word 'stare' in line 2 captures that strong sense of fascination the parents have with their sleeping daughter. The word 'estranged' in the third line, however, captures a sense of disconnection between mother and father and their child.

The separation isn't deliberate or intentional. There is, nonetheless, a feeling of loss, perhaps even hurt, brought about by this sense of two different worlds. The tone is calm and accepting when we read that:

> She is under the sea
> And they are above the sea

And then the poem shifts to give us the child's perspective. The middle section speaks of what this sleeping child would see were she to look up at her parents. Continuing the sea imagery, her parents are presented as fish-like with their 'Pursed-up orifices' and 'fins'. Language such as 'big ears' is suitably child-like. The word 'fearful' is important. It reminds us of the nervousness, the unease and the feeling of helplessness that parents can feel. They love their child but they are nervous for her.

The shortest lines in the poem define the child's parents and the daughter's relationship with them. The child names them and repeats what they are to her:

> Father, Father
> Mother, Mother

These are simple lines but powerful in their expression of a daughter 'calling out' to her parents.

Words in the closing lines such as 'cannot', 'outside', 'night', 'stranded' and the repeated use of 'drowned' (in the final line) create a mood of sadness, an unavoidable, inevitable sadness prompted by the realisation that communication and relationships are complicated and complex.

En Famille, 1979

Paul Durcan was thirty-five in 1979. The title suggests togetherness, a feeling of belonging. The poem's opening words are a request. The speaker, it would seem, would prefer an earlier time in his life to the life he knows now.

In two lines, the speaker longs to return to childhood which he views as a strange time. Childhood is seen as a school, a dark school, a place where one learns and experiences things for the very first time.

Childhood is frequently seen as a time of playful innocence, happiness and freedom. The speaker here doesn't dwell on those aspects. Instead, we are given a glimpse into the mind and the imagination of a child who sees the world in an intense and interesting way. In this speaker's childhood, what is very small seemed very small and what was very big seemed very big: a time when 'tiny is tiny, and massive is massive'. In other words, it was a time of certainty.

Madman

This two-line poem manages to be funny and frightening at once. The title, 'Madman', announces danger and the use of 'Every' suggests that all children are in danger of encountering a mad man. This is unsettling in itself but the poem's second line brings the sense of danger and threat closer to home. When the speaker announces that 'The only trouble about our madman is that he's our father', the tone is not boastful; it's more self-pitying and accepting.

The interaction between adults and children is a subject that is frequently discussed and featured in the media. A little poem like this alerts the reader to the need on children's part, especially, to be cautious and careful.

'Windfall', 8 Parnell Hill, Cork

This poem is 137 lines long. Durcan's poem 'Six Nuns Die in Convent Inferno' is 165 lines long. These are among the longest poems on the Leaving Certificate course, but their length is not daunting. Their story-telling power and their emotional charge cast a spell.

The speaker in '"Windfall", 8 Parnell Hill, Cork' tells of a very challenging and difficult time in his life – the breakup of his marriage, his leaving the family home and his move from Cork to Dublin where he ends up homeless. The poem celebrates the importance of home, the sense of belonging and family life, and it laments their loss.

The title, an address, roots the speaker's experience in a particular place. It's a memory poem and a sorrowful mood is there at the outset, captured in the opening lines:

> But, then, at the end of day I could always say –
> Well, now, I am going home

'But, then' suggests that the speaker is revisiting a different time in his life and the reader soon realises that it was a better time. The speaker then remembers the glorious feeling of belonging, how being able to say 'I am going home' creates a warm feeling.

Home is of vital importance in the poem. The word 'home' occurs eleven times in the opening section and this first section (lines 1–37) describes in vivid detail an easy and comfortable domestic scene. In the poem as a whole, 'home' is mentioned thirty-five times.

The poem focuses on interiors and exteriors, on inside and outside worlds. The living room and the cityscape are described in great detail. Not only are we presented with what the speaker sees, we also discover how he feels. The language is rich in allusion. Artists Goya and Cezanne are invoked to convey the speaker's sensation of his being with his family. Scents and colours combine to make for a scene that the speaker loves. At line 11, the speaker says that he is

> Dreaming that life is a dream which is real

A dream has become a reality. There is a mood of contentment, ease and happiness.

The sense of domestic harmony is captured in details such as

> While my children sat on my knees watching TV
> Their mother, my wife, reclined on the couch
> Knitting a bright-coloured scarf, drinking a cup of black coffee
> Smoking a cigarette . . . .

and the emphasis on easy breathing adds to this relaxed feeling:

> I closed my eyes and breathed in and breathed out.
> It is ecstasy to breathe if you are at home in the world.

The choice of 'Windfall' as a name for their home is also significant: 'What a windfall!' He relishes his situation and confesses that the feeling of tranquillity that he has come to know was one he believed only Buddhist monks experienced.

'Windfall' suggests great good luck, a blessing and the poem's second section (lines 38–75) moves from the present to the past. The reader is presented with a sequence of images from scenes of family life. The river Lee below the speaker's window is described as 'busy, yet contemplative', a description that could suit this second section.

It is a catalogue of memories, a family photograph album 'Chronicling the adventures and metamorphoses of family life'. Reading through this section, which begins with birth and baptism (line 49), we notice that it moves through class photo, 'First Infants', to 'on a bike at thirteen'; from First Holy Communion to Confirmation, holidays in France and Kerry, weddings and movies, boating on the Shannon and mountain climbing and building sandcastles. Again and again, we are presented with images that many families would find familiar. The list includes many places – 'Felixstowe, Ballymaloe, London, Cork, the Bois de Boulougne, the Normandy Beaches, the Shannon, Kerry, Killala, Barley cove, Moone, Clonmacnoise, the Tuileries, the Beaubourg, Père Lachaise, Auvers – and each location is associated with emotions: 'Dancing in Père Lachaise, weeping at Auvers'. And the speaker tells us that:

> Year in, year out, I pored over these albums accumulating

In other words, these photograph albums held a record of happy, busy varied lives:

> My children looking over my shoulder, exhilarated as I was,
> Their mother presiding at our ritual from a distance –

This second section ends with a return to the immediate present:

> Schoolbooks on the floor and pyjamas on the couch –
> Whose turn is it tonight to put the children to bed?

Section three also focuses on the speaker's family, but this time the emphasis is on a family behind closed doors who are totally at ease with each other, so much at ease that there is a freedom unique to that particular family.

The image of the sea and swimming is used here to capture the fluid, easy movement and outlook of the husband, wife and their two daughters. 'Such is home – a sea of your own' at line 80 is echoed again at line 87 – 'A home of your own – or a sea of your own'. This picture of family life is free and easy and filled with energy; they're all in this together. The speaker says it's a world:

> In which you hang upside down from the ceiling a world
> In which climbing the stairs is as natural
> As making love on the stairs

It is a self-contained world. When the telephone rings, we are told that:

> Husband and wife are metamorphosed into smiling accomplices,
> Both declining to answer it;
> Initiating, instead, a yet more subversive kiss –
> A kiss they have perhaps never attempted before –

The 'pyjama-clad' children observe their parents not answering the phone and we are told that they watch 'solemnly', jumping up and down in support. The family unit in this instance is a united one and the final line in section three honours and celebrates the family as the 'most subversive unit in society':

> The most subversive unit in society is the human family.

This poem is a private and intimate portrait of a particular family. Every family is individual in its own way. Both the ordinary and the special, the usual and the unusual are contained within the poem and, having presented us with such a picture, the poem's closing section tells of a much sadder situation.

The husband and father who speaks the poem is now estranged from his family, is now in Dublin and has been put out of his home. He accepts his situation in that he tells us that 'with good reason/ I was put out of my home'.

We saw how section one contained the keyword 'home' eleven times. In section three, 'home' occurs four times. Now in the closing sections (lines 102–36), the word reappears with emphasis. Section four riffs on the word; 'home' occurs in every line except one where the word 'homesick' occurs. In the opening and closing lines of this section, 'home' is used twice:

> We're almost **home**, pet, almost **home** . . .
> Our **home** is at . . .
> I'll be **home** . . .
> I have to go **home** now . . .
> I want to go **home** now . . .
> Are you feeling *homesick*?
> Are you anxious to get **home**? . . .
> I can't wait to get **home** . . .
> Let's stay at **home** tonight and . . .
> What time will you be coming **home** at? . . .
> If I'm not **home** by six at the latest, I'll phone . . .
> We're nearly **home**, don't worry, we're nearly **home** . . .

The language here belongs to ordinary and different situations. They are familiar and everyday but, orchestrated in this way, these colloquial utterances become a musical and patterned sequence of significant ideas.

The dramatically changed status of the speaker is summed up in the image in line 116: 'By a keen wind felled'. The generous, expansive descriptions in the three earlier and longer sections have been replaced by three shorter, more fragmented sections.

The picture of 'Having to live homeless in the alien, foreign city of Dublin' is grim, lonely and without hope:

> It is an eerie enough feeling to be homesick
> Yet knowing you will be going home next week;
> It is an eerie feeling beyond all ornithological analysis
> To be homesick knowing that there is no home to go home to

The bird reference ('ornithological analysis') conjures up an image of nesting, roosting and warmth.

The speaker's tone is accepting; he blames no one but himself. In the final section (lines 126–37), the portrait painted is one of wandering the streets, of being an outsider, not belonging and envying the world glimpsed through 'the windows of other people's homes'.

The final three lines call out the name 'Windfall' repeating the word again and again. The last line echoes an earlier line (line 113) in which the speaker imagines that things are all right, that things are better, that he has a home to go to:

> We're almost home, pet, don't worry anymore, we're almost home

This is a line that is spoken to a loved one ('pet'), a comforting, calming line. It is also an ironic line in the context of the homeless speaker longing to belong, longing to be part of a family that he cherished.

Six Nuns Die in Convent Inferno

The title states the horrific facts. The word 'Inferno' means hell, a conflagration. The subtitle announces that the poem is dedicated to the 'happy memory' of these nuns who experienced terrible deaths. The reader's attention is immediately engaged.

In Part I, the poem uses a persona and an 'I' or first person voice; in Part II, a third-person voice is used. The poem, overall, is divided into eight separate sections: Part I contains six; Part II, two. For practical purposes, here is a brief overview of the poem:

Part I

(i) A description of the convent on St Stephen's Green and surroundings.

(ii) A meditation on the nuns' way of life.

(iii) The fire itself and a memory of a summer holiday by the sea.

(iv) Swimming in the sea and the sea as a metaphor for Christ.

(v) The nun's thoughts on losing her life and her bedtime reading and the borrowed book that will never be returned.

(vi) The moment of death itself – six nuns burnt to death and how she would like to be remembered.

Part II

(vii) Jesus responds. He speaks and comments on the faith of these nuns.

(viii) A description of the dead nuns coming back to life and praying in St. Stephen's Green.

The story of these nuns' lives and deaths is told from the perspective of one of the nuns – 'an old nun – an aged beadswoman' – and the opening lines begin in a matter-of-fact way. The tone is descriptive:

> We resided in a Loreto convent in the centre of Dublin city
> On the east side of a public gardens, St Stephen's Green

And then an exotic and colourful detail is introduced in line 3 when nearby Grafton Street is described as 'the paseo'. The speaker paints a picture of Grafton Street as a place where people meet, gather and interact.

The 'punk girls and punk boys' (line 7), it would seem, are very different from the nuns but the speaker, this old nun, thinking about these 'half-shaven heads' in their 'martial garb', their 'dyed hair-dos and nappy pins', announces that it is she who is the 'ultimate drop-out'.

Little details such as 'scurrying' to mass, 'I sucked on a Fox's mint' and

> A lifetime of bicycle lamps and bicycle pumps,
> A lifetime of galoshes stowed under the stairs,
> A lifetime of umbrellas drying out in kitchens

summon up a picture of a simple, austere life. There is nothing glamorous about this life but there is something extraordinary about it. Punks are outrageously different in their style but this nun sees herself as odd and eccentric:

> The delinquent, the recidivist, the vagabond,
> The wild woman, the subversive, the original punk

The mood here is that of someone quietly proud of her own life choice. She is both happy and fearful: 'I was smiling, I was also afraid'. She chose to opt out of the world and has not regretted it, but it is a life filled with challenges.

Words such as 'loneliness' and 'abandonment' suggest something negative and yet the adjective chosen to qualify loneliness is fresh and startling. This old nun sees her loneliness as 'exotic', although the repetition in lines 28–30 ('A lifetime of . . . A lifetime of . . . A lifetime of . . .') emphasises an aspect of their lives that is modest, ordinary and dull.

She is an open-minded nun. She is sympathetic to the punks, seeing them as 'so conventional, really and vulnerable'; she is content with her own lot.

Part I section (ii) (lines 31–62) dwells on death. The use of the past tense reminds us that this nun has met an horrific end; she had been burnt to death in a fire. The bird and aviary images follow on from the nun's description of herself as 'a weird bird'. The horror is contained in words such as 'wheezing, shrieking, croaking'.

Here, the awfulness of smoke and fire and the difficulty of breathing and the screams are clearly evident.

Side-by-side with this suffering the poet introduces a light-hearted, humorous touch when the nun speaks of

> our yellowy corsets, wonky suspenders, strung-out garters

and then there follows the reality of old age – 'a bony crew' aboard a 'nineteenth-century schooner'.

This ship image is powerful. It sails on and the nuns are the ones who see to it that it does. The 'rigging and the canvas' are in need of repair and these nuns take risks.

> We old nuns were the ones who crawled out on the yardarms
> To stitch and sew the rigging and the canvas

Moreover, the speaker, a voice for the old nuns, acknowledges and admits that she and her fellow nuns are 'weird birds, oddballs, Christniks'.

This second section, Part I, ends with a meditation on the way they live their lives. They have:

> done the weirdest thing a woman can do –
> Surrendered the marvellous passions of girlhood,

They have given a whole lifetime to Christ. The use of 'Never' at the beginning of three consecutive lines (lines 56–58) creates a series of negatives and reminds the reader of all they have sacrificed:

> Never to know the love of a man or a woman;
> Never to have children of our own;
> Never to have a home of our own

And the question then asked is courageous, straightforward and clear-sighted:

> And for why and for what?

This poem is inspired by an event in 1986 and Ireland at the time was becoming more and more materialistic, secular and open-minded. All the more reason then to reflect on the strangeness of their lives.

Those lines with which the second section ends are all the more remarkable for their strangeness in the modern era. The speaker, in outlining some biographical facts about Jesus, is clearly reminding us of the choice made by these nuns:

> To follow a young man – would you believe it –
> Who lived two thousand years ago in Palestine
> And who died a common criminal strung up on a tree.

The tone is one of astonishment and incredulity and yet the mood is one of commitment and belief.

Part I, (iii) (lines 63–84) focuses on the fire in the dormitory, but the description of the 'disintegrating dormitory' does not dominate. There is the desperation in the cry

> O Christ, Christ, come quickly, quickly

and the plea for it all to be over. The old nuns are transformed into angels, it would seem, through imagery. They are:

> Fluttering about in our tight, gold bodices,
> Beating our wings . . .

But the chaos of the fire gives way to an easy, relaxed, casual tone of voice when the speaker is reminded of holiday snaps. The free association here provides respite from the imagined horror of being burnt to death. The flames of fire become the waves of the sea.

Rather than expiring in the fire, the poem resurrects a moment of freedom and pleasure. The speaker is reminiscing. 'Scampering' is used twice. It is a lively, fun-filled word and by juxtaposing the sea and the fire it is as if this nun and her fellow nuns accept God's will. 'Tonight' at the beginning of line 81 roots the experience in the present moment; against that is the vista of secluded beach, cove and palm trees. And even here there is humour in the observation that:

> Somebody – an affluent buddy of the bishop's repenting his
> affluence –
> Loaned Mother Superior a secluded beach in Co. Waterford

The next section (lines 85–108) continues this account of what the nun calls:

> one of the gayest days of my life

The sea imagery is elaborated further when we read that the speaker

> became aware that Christ is the ocean
> Forever rising and falling on the world's shore

and this makes possible the realisation:

> Now tonight in the convent Christ is the fire in whose waves
> We are doomed and delighted to drown

This line, 'We are doomed and delighted to drown', is notable for what it says and for the way it says it. The alliterative 'doomed, delighted, drown' is musical and the idea it expresses is a striking example of a paradox: a contradictory statement that, once teased out, makes sense. Here and elsewhere we are presented with an unwavering expression of the speaker's deep religious faith.

That the word 'tonight' occurs in line 82 that it is repeated in line 93 gives immediacy to a momentous time in the lives of these nuns. The passage then describes the presence of the angel Gabriel in the dormitory. This is a moment of pure poetry. Gabriel, the most important of angelic messengers, is portrayed as brilliant, energetic and charismatic:

> Gabriel, with that extraordinary message of his on his boyish lips,
> Frenetically pedalling his skybike.

An earlier and extraordinary message from Gabriel was that to Mary announcing that she was to be the mother of God. That this should shimmer behind this other moment adds to its significance. His message to this old nun is whispered:

> He whispers into my ear what I must do
> And I do it – and die.

And the speaker then makes specific reference to Gabriel's message to Mary. This nun sees herself and her fellow nuns as Mothers of God:

> Each of us in our own tiny, frail, furtive way
> Was a Mother of God, mothering forth illegitimate Christs
> In the street life of Dublin city

This is a traditional Gabriel and a modern Gabriel side-by-side. It also locates the presence of Christ in a contemporary setting. These nuns see themselves as living the Christian life and the phrase 'illegitimate Christs' brings to mind how Christ belongs everywhere. Nuns are not expected to give birth and the word 'illegitimate', at the time of the poem's composition, was often associated with those who might be considered outsiders or looked down on. These nuns are involved in bringing Christ's message to everyone, especially the poor and those who have little social standing.

The nun prays:

> God have mercy on our whirring souls
> whirring conveying a sense of the heightened excitement of the moment.

This fourth section ends with a very generous thought. The speaker sees the nuns who died that night as 'wild women' – 'Wild women were we all' and then she, with Christian charity, thinks of the firemen who fought the fire and attempted to save them. She asks that God have mercy

> on the misfortunate, poor fire-brigade men
> Whose task it will be to shovel up our ashes and shovel
> What is left of us into black plastic refuse sacks.

The time-frame here contains the present and the future. She describes what will happen and concludes that:

> Fire-brigade men are the salt of the earth.

The fifth section is relaxed and curious in tone. In the friendly, opening lines (lines 109–13), the speaker muses on the nature of existence.

> Isn't it a marvellous thing how your hour comes
> When you least expect it? When you lose a thing,
> Not to know about it until it actually happens?

The questions need no answers. The speaker is accepting of how things are and how things will be.

This is a challenging and unusual way of looking at life. The act of losing is something that this speaker accepts and the word 'lucky' is used to describe what many would see as a traumatic event:

> How lucky I was to lose – I say, lose – lose my life

'Lose', used here three times in the one line, becomes a positive rather than a negative. The old nun is grateful for her death. The fire is referred to as an 'Inferno' in the poem's title and, though inferno means hell and the conflagration was terrible, there is in the nun's account of the fire a sense of freedom and release.

And then the rest of section five contains a quirky and revealing detail. Lines 115–31 are an account of the nun's bedtime reading and her anxiety about not being able to return a borrowed book now that she and the book perished in the fire. Here, again, we find an example of Paul Durcan's humour. That an old nun tells us:

> I got a loan of it from the brother-in-law's married niece

The complicated family connection, the mention of the cost of the book, the reference to snobbishness and social deportment add a sense of absurdity to the poem that contrasts sharply with the 'racket of bellowing flame and snarling glass'. The Conor Cruise O'Brien book is one of those details in the poem that simply becomes unforgettable. And it is a revealing detail. The nun in her final moments is worried that she is inconveniencing somebody else. She is a kind, sympathetic, caring person to the end.

Part I ends with a powerful sixth section. The language becomes heightened and is rich with emotional charge and imagery. At line 132, the nun refers to

> The strange Eucharist of my death

And the eucharist, the Christian sacrament in which bread and wine are consecrated and consumed, is here interpreted in an interesting way: 'To be eaten alive by fire and smoke'. In this instance, the nun is being consumed by fire and she willingly gives herself to death in a ritual that turns death into birth.

> I clasped the dragon to my breast
> And stroked his red-hot ears.

The word 'clasped' and the stroking gesture create a positive, welcoming atmosphere in the midst of the chaos of the burning convent.

There is a very dramatic, paradoxical and vivid description of how this nun sees the situation:

> Strange! There we were, all sleeping molecules,
> Suddenly all giving birth to our deaths,
> All frantically in labour.

And the birth imagery is followed through when we read:

> Doctors and midwives weaved in and out
> In gowns of smoke and gloves of fire

This is a powerful image, filled with movement and its surreal quality – 'gowns of smoke and gloves of fire' – engages the imagination.

Gabriel appeared earlier in the poem, at line 96, and now Christ appears:

> Christ, like an Orthodox patriarch in his dressing gown,
> Flew up and down the dormitory, splashing water on our souls

The Christ figure here is magnificently authoritative, magnificently busy – the simile is both grand ('Orthodox patriarch') and a little absurd ('dressing gown'). The energy contained within the words 'splashing water on our souls' creates a healing effect.

Section six ends very simply and effectively. The six nuns who died in the convent inferno are named, one by one:

> Sister Eucharia; Sister Seraphia; Sister Rosario;
> Sister Gonzaga; Sister Margaret; Sister Edith

These names remind the reader of the six human beings who died. We are also reminded of their dedication to Christ – they abandoned their own names when they entered the convent and professed themselves to be brides of Christ.

The nun who has spoken in Part I ends with a gentle and humble request. There is no presumption here:

> If you will remember us – six nuns burnt to death –
> Remember us for the frisky girls that we were,
> Now more than ever kittens in the sun.

These lines contain the harsh truth that 'six nuns burnt to death', but also present us with a happy, carefree, playful, life-filled image.

•

Part II of the poem, in two sections, has a serious tone. The voice shifts from the first person to the third person, from the nun's voice to a voice that now offers a commentary and interpretation of Part I. The voice of Jesus is also heard.

He speaks in response to what:

> a small, aged, emaciated, female punk
> Clad all in mourning black, and grieving like an alley cat

Jesus himself is depicted as a figure whom 'gangs of teenagers and dicemen' follow. Jesus is clearly impressed – 'He was annulled with astonishment'. The nun's voice is heard at the top of Grafton Street and her voice is now a voice that is 'grieving like an alley cat'.

The final section (lines 155–65) brings us to the next night, the night following the fire. The setting is an empty St Stephen's Green except for the six nuns. The reference to the 'courting couples' who are now locked out and who have 'found cinemas themselves to die in' is a grim detail. The message is that others will die in fires.

The nuns' collective voice has the final word. They kneel 'together by the Fountain of the Three Fates' and recite the *Agnus Dei*. They recite it fervently and the speaker links this passionate utterance of a prayer that is seeking help and forgiveness to all those who seek aid – 'all aid – Live Aid, Self Aid, Aids and All Aid'. This list contains a range of experiences and is global in its reach.

The poem has recounted the horrors of six terrible deaths and its closing words are the words of the *Agnus Dei*, part of the Catholic mass. The mood is calm and calming. The tone is one of supplication and longing. The final word is comforting – 'healed' – and the final picture in the reader's mind is of six dead nuns brought back to life – a resurrection.

Sport

The word sport has many happy, positive and thrilling associations. Paul Durcan, in this poem, explores a father-son relationship and a game of football is used to enhance our understanding of that relationship.

The speaker is despondent in the opening stanza. He expresses his belief that his father expects little of him:

> There were not many fields
> In which you had hopes for me

In the context of the poem as a whole, the opening line puns on the word 'field' for it is on the football field that the speaker proves himself and wins his father's admiration and respect.

The reader, early on in the poem, senses that this is no ordinary game, nor is it an ordinary day:

> On my twenty-first birthday
> I was selected to play
> For Gangegorman Mental Hospital
> In an away game
> Against Mullingar Mental Hospital.

Being twenty-one is an important milestone but mental illness, a reality for many people, adds a challenging dimension to the situation. Some readers may find a black humour in the idea of two mental hospital teams playing each other, some may not.

Comedy, it is said, can be deadly serious and if this poem has comic elements it also focuses on very serious ones.

The poem is told from the son's point of view, a son who is fearful, anxious and unsure. His wish is that he will not let down his father, a father who has driven 'all the way down,/ Fifty miles' to watch his son play. The descriptions of the men on the opposing team are economical and effective:

> There were big country men
> On the Mullingar Mental Hospital team,
> Men with gapped teeth, red faces,
> Oily, frizzy hair, bushy eyebrows

We also learn that the three full forwards are schizophrenic and this could be considered blackly humorous or not depending on the view of the reader or audience member. Is one sympathetic or cruel?

More unsettling details are found in stanza three with its dramatic and random information. These details, however, are presented as a rumour and this diminishes the horror somewhat.

> There was a rumour
> That their centre-half forward
> Was an alcoholic solicitor
> Who, in a lounge bar misunderstanding,
> Had castrated his best friend
> But that he had no memory of it.
> He had meant well – it was said.
> His best friend had had to emigrate
> To Nigeria.

The game itself is centre stage in stanza four and the speaker, who plays in goal, creates a feeling of triumph and success. The expert manoeuvring is captured in the following lines:

> I did not flinch in the goals.
> I made three or four spectacular saves,
> Diving full stretch to turn
> A certain goal around the corner,
> Leaping high to tip another certain goal
> Over the bar for a point

and the son tells us that this success and triumph were possible because of his father's presence on the sideline.

Sport is often seen as a bonding and character-building experience for the players but it can also, as portrayed here, strengthen the bond between father and son. The speaker in 'Sport' is very conscious of his father's presence and this brought out the best performance in the son:

> It was my knowing
> That you were standing on the sideline
> That gave me the necessary motivation –
> That will to die

There follows a one-line observation on the nature of commitment and achievement. 'That will to die', he says,

> That is as essential to sportsmen as to artists.

'I' occurs thirteen times in the poem; seven lines in this poem begin with the pronoun 'I'; in the final and shortest stanza 'I' is used five times. Clearly it is the son's story but the father's voice is heard at line 55. Just three words:

> 'Well played, son'

However, they are of huge significance. The mood in the closing stanza is one of quiet pride and grateful realisation – 'In your eyes I had achieved something at last'. The speaker knows that he gave it his all and being on the winning team on his twenty-first birthday was marvellous. He is on a high – the image of 'heights' occurs at line 62. And yet the final two lines are tinged with sadness:

> Seldom if ever again in your eyes
> Was I to rise to these heights

There is a feeling of disappointment and loneliness here. The poem tells of a complex situation and relationship, a crucial time in that relationship and how father and son, at that moment, are closer than usual. Though the speaker longs for such moments again, he knows that the father's demanding, exacting standards are such that he will 'Seldom if ever' impress or please him again.

Father's Day, 21 June 1992

At one level, this is a mad, daft and funny poem. Summarise the 'plot' and it reads like a wacky mini-drama: On Father's Day a man in Dublin rushing to catch a train to Cork is told by his wife/partner that his sister-in-law in Cork needs to borrow an axe to cut back a buddleia tree and he reluctantly brings it with him; he is met with suspicion from the passenger opposite him who moves to another seat. But it is also a portrait of a marriage and a family, an exploration of guilt and loneliness.

The opening section is filled with busyness, commotion, activity – 'dashing', 'Dashing up and down', 'searching my pockets', 'the taxi was ticking' – and the dialogue between the man and woman all add to the sense of drama. The thin plot revolves about the bringing of a large axe to Cork. Practical considerations (Are there no axes in Cork?) are irrelevant here. The speaker is consumed with anxieties. He tries to propose an argument filled with common sense:

> 'A simple saw would do the job, surely to God
> She could borrow a simple saw'
>
> He gives in to the idea 'She said that she'd like the axe'.

Despite the subject matter, the exchanges between husband and wife are captured convincingly in ordinary language, question marks, half-finished sentences and adding to the scene is the 'Blue Cabs taxi ticking over outside'. The atmosphere is the opposite to relaxed.

The axe itself – 'all four-and-a-half feet of it' – makes its dramatic entrance at line 17 and the speaker, uncomfortable at the idea of having to bring it with him, is even more uncomfortable that it's given to him just as it is – no wrapping, no covering:

> She handed the axe to me just as it was,
> As neat as a newborn babe
> All in the bare buff.

Critical Commentary

There is humour in the following observation:

> You'd think she'd have swaddled it up
> In something – if not a blanket, an old newspaper,
> But no, not even a token hanky
> Tied in a bow round its head.

The poem contains two settings: home and train. Stanza one describes the domestic scene. The second and third stanzas describe the train journey and the speaker's thoughts and feelings about his wife and children.

The speaker, in stanza two, confesses to a feeling of unease and guilt. His relationship with his wife is troubled.

> I always feel bad leaving her
> and yet the realisation that
> I could see that she was glad
> To see me go away for a while

This creates a sympathetic response in the reader. We are presented with a series of different images – their bed, eating a meal, his partner pregnant on the settee. These remembered moments upset the speaker and in the middle of this reflection there is a line (line 42) on its own which highlights the loneliness of the speaker's life:

> Our daughters are all grown up and gone away

The phrase 'my coarse advances' is used to describe the speaker's sense of himself. He lacks confidence, he feels inadequate and his partner seems to be the more together of the couple:

> Once when she was sitting pregnant on the settee
> It snapped shut with herself inside it,
> But not a bother on her.

When the speaker adds 'I nearly died', it reveals his anxiety, his concern, his sense of helplessness.

Most often, laughter is a result of being delighted and happy, but sometimes laughter is a result of being frightened and shocked. The image of a pregnant woman snapped shut inside a settee is a frightening, upsetting image but one that can elicit black humour. Again and again in Paul Durcan's poetry, the world of the poem can surprise you with something that is not intrinsically funny and yet the response can be laughter.

From a moment from several years back – his pregnant partner snapped shut inside the settee – the poem returns to the present in stanza three. The speaker with the axe confides in the passenger sitting opposite him. He speaks his private thoughts and feelings, and convention dictates that people should behave in a particular or expected way, especially in public. This outpouring of guilt, this expression of loneliness, the question asked makes for a very uncomfortable situation for his fellow passenger:

> As the train slowed down approaching Portarlington
> I overheard myself say to the passenger sitting opposite me:
> 'I am feeling guilty because she does not love me
> As much as she used to, can you explain that?'

This is intimate, confessional talk and the stranger in whom he confides is understandably made uneasy. There is humour in the line:

> The passenger's eyes were on the axe on the seat beside me

And when the speaker explains the presence of the axe beside him, an explanation the reader knows to be true, we sense the passenger is becoming more and more uneasy.

The move by the passenger to another seat in another coach adds to the loneliness of the speaker and yet can be seen as darkly humorous. The speaker's announcement, as the train 'threaded itself into Portarlington', of the town's Irish name is interpreted as odd. The use of an exclamation mark – 'Cúl an tSúdaire!' – suggests a spontaneous utterance and at this the passenger leaves his company but not the train.

The poem ends with a striking picture: a man and an axe sitting alone.

> All the green fields running away from us

The poem's final line (line 59) echoes an earlier one (line 42):

> All our daughters grown up and gone away.

The rhythm here is beautifully cadenced; the repeated 'All' and 'away' add to the loneliness and the regular rhythm could be said to resemble the rhythm of the train. This quiet ending is very different from the frenetic opening lines. The image with which the poem finishes is a lonely one and the poem's title deepens that sense of loneliness. Father's Day is supposedly a family day, a day when wife and children can express their love and appreciation for the father of the family. In this poem, however, the father is increasingly isolated and alone.

The Arnolfini Marriage

Paul Durcan has published two books, *Crazy About Women* and *Give Me Your Hand*, which feature poems he wrote in response to paintings in the National Art Galleries in Dublin and London. The technical term for a poem written in response to a painting is *ekphrasis*.

Unlike many Paul Durcan poems, this one is spoken in the plural voice. The man and woman, the husband and wife tell their story. It's a very confident, self-contained 'we' voice. 'We' is the first word in the poem (it occurs eight times in all) and the use of the full-stop here creates a definite sense of self:

> We are the Arnolfinis.

The tone is very confident and assertive:

> Do not think you may invade
> Our privacy because you may not.

The poem refers to details in the painting such as their standing position, the bed, the mirror, the terrier and these details are linked to the poem's theme of 'married love'. The poem focuses on how wonderful it is to find a loving relationship.

The speakers tell us that their portrait is 'The most erotic portrait ever made'. In other words, they see their portrait as relating to, or tending to arouse, sexual desire or excitement. The painting of a man and woman in their bedroom might suggest a very different kind of picture than the one van Eyck painted. In this portrait, their stance is formal, they are fully clothed and yet they see their portrait as 'erotic'. Its eroticism lies in its capturing

> the plurality
> Fertility, domesticity, barefootedness
> Of a man and woman saying 'we'.

The marriage bed is central to their world. This is clearly stated. It is, we are told,

> our most necessary furniture

Another key word is 'our': it is used seven times and their world as depicted here is a world where he and she are in harmony with each other.

Though very happy together, in stanza seven the poem addresses the reader; it goes beyond the portrait, beyond the bedroom. It reaches out to the reader.

This man and this woman are grateful to be in a relationship where

> The most relaxing word in our vocabulary is 'we'.

And they ask:

> Imagine being able to say 'we'.
> Most people are in no position to say 'we'.

The tone in the first six stanzas, from lines 1 to 18, is ordered and stately; the mood is grateful. The structure of the line then changes and so too does the rhythm. Four questions follow and these lines paint a picture of loneliness. The speakers ask to know if you, the reader, are in a position to say 'we'.

This direct, concerned voice asks if you are in such a position:

> Are you? Who eat alone? Sleep alone?

Then there follows another question: the reader is asked if he/she is someone who fits the description of a lonely individual at dawn cycling to work.

> With an Alsatian shepherd dog tied to your handlebars?

The 15th century painting with its formal elegance, its ornate details is suddenly replaced by a lonely cyclist. The 15th century meets a more modern time. The questions challenge us to understand our own situation against a background of happily married love.

The closing stanza seems odd and random. The words 'We will pause now for the Angelus' are usually associated with RTE Radio 1 where the Angelus is still sounded at twelve noon on weekdays. Perhaps the reference to this Catholic prayer, which remembers the angel Gabriel telling Mary that she is going to have a baby, is deliberately intended as a link to the fertility mentioned earlier in line 8.

The second-last line is both matter-of-fact and conclusive:

> Here you have it:

And what have we? The poem's final line contains a simple but memorable image of separateness and union, a perfect fit:

> The two halves of the coconut.

It is worth remembering the words of the art critic Bryan Robertson who says – in his Introduction to *Give Me Your Hand* containing the van Eyck portrait and Durcan's poem – that Durcan 'projects himself into the personages, the situations; imagines a development in the action, treats the paintings like kites in the gusty air of his imagination'.

There is a playfulness and freedom in Durcan's response to particular paintings. He brings you on many different journeys and in directions initiated by the artwork. It is an invitation to the viewer/reader to interpret his response and the connections made with an open mind.

Ireland 2002

Of the fifteen poems on your course, this is the one poem which Paul Durcan himself asked to be on the Leaving Certificate course. It is a deceptive poem. It seems slighter than it is.

> Do you ever take a holiday abroad?
> No, we always go to America.

There's an obvious and important contradiction here. Ireland is a large island off the north-west coast of continental Europe. Leaving the island of Ireland means going abroad and heading west across three thousand miles of Atlantic Ocean is certainly going abroad.

But, no. That 'No' at the beginning of the second line is definite in tone. America is seen by the speaker as part of Ireland.

This little poem contains an interesting idea and a different way of looking at things.

Rosie Joyce

This is a happy poem, an exuberant poem about a life-changing event. It is a grandfather celebrating the birth of his granddaughter. Arranged in three parts: Part I contains seven stanzas; Part II, sixteen stanzas; Part III, four stanzas; and each stanza is three lines long.

Part I: describes the speaker's joy on being told of Rosie's birth.

Part II: describes the drive from Achill to Dublin to visit newborn Rosie and the significance of her birth.

Part III: the return journey and the joy felt.

Paul Durcan is not often thought of as a nature poet but the natural world is of vital importance here. It is late spring, a Sunday in May, and the speaker connects the birth of his granddaughter with sunshine. The opening words capture the significance of the event in the speaker's mind. The use of 'that' twice creates this emphasis:

> That was that Sunday afternoon in May
> . . . .
> And you were born!

But the in-between line, while refering still to nature, contains a covert image of birth:

> When a hot sun pushed through the clouds

The glorious sense of the sun pushing through and the exclamation mark after 'born!' create an intensely happy mood in stanza one.

The west-of-Ireland landscape on this bright Sunday afternoon mirrors the speaker's mood. The 'blue-and-white' of the sky is compared to china and the varied changing and shadowed colours of the landscape are likened to tartan rugs. Blue, white and such colours as green, purple, brown are summoned up but the phrase 'impromptu picnics' captures a sense of delight, ease and freedom:

> I was driving the two hundred miles from west to east,
> The sky blue-and-white china in the fields
> In impromptu picnics of tartan rugs

The language in that first line is factual and functional, but the imagery in the following lines reminds us what the language of poetry can achieve.

The name Rosie Joyce is not only the title of the poem. 'Rosie' and 'Rosie Joyce' occur several times throughout. The naming of his granddaughter clearly gives the speaker great joy and his wish and prayer for her is that she will live to feel as lucky as her grandfather feels on this special day. He thinks ahead fifty-six years (presumably the speaker's age) and hopes that Rosie will feel as blessed at fifty-six as he does today.

The car journey east is described with lyrical energy. Place names and details and the use of 'such' create an exuberant feeling of anticipation. The day itself is accorded dignity and holiness when the speaker refers to Rosie's birth date as 'Incarnation Day'.

This poem draws on real events. Rosie Joyce was born; Mark Joyce is her father; Paul Durcan is Rosie's grandfather. However, the poet's art transforms actual facts into an emotionally charged, imaginative, shaped experience that becomes the poem on the page.

The musical flow is clearly heard in stanza five:

> To drive such side-roads, such main roads, such ramps, such
> roundabouts,
> To cross such bridges, to by-pass such villages, such towns
> As I did on your Incarnation Day.

Ramps and roundabouts are not often celebrated in poetry but everything in the world is viewed differently because of the speaker's joy as he looks forward to the birth of the as yet unnamed baby. The repetition ('such') and the rhyme ('side-roads . . . main roads') and alliteration ('ramps . . . roundabouts') contribute to this feeling of happiness.

Part I ends with the announcement by mobile phone of Rosie's birth. The message contains everything one would want to hear. Mother and 'A baby girl' are safe and healthy; the baby is unnamed but we know her name from the poem's title and stanza three. Stanza one referred to 'afternoon'; stanza seven gives us the precise time – '3.33 p.m.' – that made that afternoon so special.

Part II brings us back to earlier in the day and to Achill Island. The poem plays with time sequencing and this time-flow aspect of the poem lends it a fluidity and adds to the speaker's delight at this momentous time.

Stanza seven describes a May Sunday in Mayo before daybreak. Stanza one focused on the afternoon of that very same day, stanza seven brings us back in time and in Part II the poem contains a number of stanzas (lines 22–33) that celebrate the beauty of the unspoilt natural world. Plants are named – Arum Lily, rhododendrons, whins, hawthorns, yellow irises, bog-cotton, forget-me-nots, sea pinks, London Pride, bluebell, fucshia, Queen Anne's Lace, primrose – and the list conveys a beautiful range of colour. The sound, seashore, cliffs, mainland, streams, bogs all add up to a beautiful picture.

This is nature at its best. In these stanzas, the only reference to man's presence is 'Burrishoole cemetery'; that the flowers mentioned in association with the graveyard are 'forget-me-nots' is a tender detail. Overall, there is an atmosphere of expectation, new beginnings, energy. Words (mainly participles) such as 'pushed', 'purpling', 'powdering', 'flagging', 'skimming', 'speckling' are dramatic and filled with life.

On this particular day, the landscape is vivid to the speaker as he drives through it and he names places, mentioning 'the old Turlough Road, past Walter Durcan's farm'. Though Paul Durcan was born in Dublin his family background is County Mayo and Walter Durcan, though it is not said, could be a relation. The description of the Walter Durcan's farm as

> Umbrella'd in the joint writing of its ash trees

is a lovely fresh, imaginative one.

The lyrical, expansive world of County Mayo gives way (at line 36) to a one-line summary of the journey from Mayo to Dublin:

> I drove Tulsk, Kilmainham, the Grand Canal

The speaker confesses how

> Never before had I felt so fortunate
> To be driving back to Dublin city

and the birth of this baby girl 'saved my life'. Part II ends with a dark admission:

> For three years
> I had been subsisting in the slums of despair,
> Unable to distinguish one day from the next

However, the lines leading up to that lonely, hopeless situation contain great joy and laughter.

A line such as 'I rode the waters and the roads of Ireland' belongs to a narrative of high adventure, heroic tales and the metaphor chosen to describe Rosie – 'seashell at my ear' – is one that captures the perfect, delicate, finely-shaped baby so well.

Line 42, 'How I laughed when I cradled you in my hand', is the present moment and then the poem returns to the journey from Mayo and an earlier journey with the speaker's father travelling across Ireland, west to east. He uses the phrase 'half a century ago' to capture that long-ago sense of time. It was a magical moment from the speaker's childhood and remembered now on this day when he made another magical journey.

There is a family feeling in the lines 'We are the people of the West,/ Our fate is to go East.' The speaker is remembering his father and addressing his granddaughter. There is a sense of purpose and destiny, and he rejoices in the east to west direction, symbolic here of going against the more familiar direction of heading west. At this point in the poem, the speaker also wants to advise the newborn baby.

> No such thing, Rosie, as a Uniform Ireland
> And please God there never will be

The birth of a baby intensifies one's sense of life, continuity, belonging, family. Here the poet looks to the landscape of Ireland its

> River Shannon and all her sister rivers
>
> And all her brother mountains and their family prospects

for inspiration and meaning, seeing more significance and more power in 'wildflowers . . . people' than in politics.

Rosie Joyce has made possible all these happy thoughts. She has banished and counteracted the despair felt by the speaker. She makes his day: 'Daymaker! Daymaker! Daymaker!' These three words ring with celebration. Rosie has changed the speaker's world and his outlook on life. The mood is one of deep happiness, the tone is one of praise and gratitude.

The poem's final section is four stanzas long. This is the return journey, east to west, and in casual, familiarly everyday language we are given a picture of an encounter in Charlestown with a friend. It's an at-ease meeting and includes details such as his being an 'organic farmer from Curry' and that:

> He is driving home to his wife Caroline
> From a Mountbellew meeting of the Western Development
> Commission
> Of Dillon House in Ballaghadereen.

These practical details belong to a life-goes-on scenario. They do not concern Rosie Joyce but the speaker (the grandfather) is returning to the ordinary world having witnessed the excitement of Rosie's arrival. He is engaging with ordinary life and ordinary concerns. But there is in the phrase 'lullabies of expectancy' an allusion to the baby, future and hope.

Towards the end, the factual details are left behind. The philosopher John Moriarty is mentioned. John Normanly and Paul Durcan are at ease in each other's company – 'we exchange lullabies of expectancy; We wet our foreheads in John Moriarty's autobiography'.

Wetting foreheads could be interpreted as a religious gesture and the following stanza, the final one, glows with religious imagery. The Sunday following Rosie's birth is 'the Feast of the Ascension/ Of Our Lord into Heaven'. Christ ascends, Rosie descends. The idea of Rosie, 'the Descent of Rosie onto Earth', lends her

Robert Frost
(1874–1963)

modern american poet

Contents Page

The Overview

Robert Frost once said that 'the four things I most wanted to go into in life' were 'archaeology, astronomy, farming, and teaching Latin', but he also 'went into' poetry. 'I want to reach out to all sorts and kinds', said Frost and it would seem that, in his poetry, he succeeded. As a young man, he was advised by the Reverend William E. Wolcott to write a more elevated kind of poem. Wolcott thought that Frost's poetry was too much like the speaking voice but, in fact, this speaking voice – ordinary speech – poetry that talked, was what Frost preferred. Years later, Frost was to see that advice as pivotal to his development as a poet: 'I'm sure the old gentleman didn't have the slightest idea he was having any effect on a very stubborn youngster who thought he knew what he knew. But something he said actually changed the whole course of my writing. It all became purposeful.' In a letter written in 1914, Frost commented that 'Words exist in the mouth not books' and, whenever Frost gave a poetry reading, he used the word 'say' rather than 'read'. At one such reading in the grand ballroom of the Waldorf-Astoria hotel in New York, for instance, he told his audience: 'I have a feeling you didn't understand that poem. I'll say it again.'

W.H. Auden thought that in Frost '(t)he music is always that of the speaking voice, quiet and sensible, and I cannot think of any modern poet, except Cavafy, who uses language more simply'. An early reviewer of Frost's work admired his ability to get 'poetry back again into touch with the living vigours of speech...the rise and fall, the stressed pauses and little hurries, of spoken language.' His friend Edward Thomas said: 'All Frost insists on is what he believes to find in all poets — absolute fidelity to the postures which the voice assumes in the most expressive intimate speech...He has trusted his conviction that a man will not easily write better than he speaks when some matter has touched him deeply...His poems are revolutionary because they lack the exaggeration of rhetoric. Many, if not most, of the separate lines and separate sentences are plain and in themselves nothing. But they are bound together and made elements of beauty by a calm eagerness of emotion.'

Yet, though Frost was always interested in the rhythms of natural speech, he was also very interested in formal patterning and rhyme. Free verse (unrhymed, irregular verse) was rejected by Frost. He said that writing free verse was like playing tennis without a net. In other words, he enjoyed the discipline and restrictions of the net – for example, 'The Tuft of Flowers' is written in heroic couplets and he also wrote blank verse and liked the sonnet form ('Design').

Frost chose to write in a language that was close to and inspired by ordinary, everyday speech. But it was not only the language that made him a very popular and accessible poet; it was also his subject matter. Frost's poems are rooted in the natural world. He himself was careful to point out that in his poetry man is almost always part of the landscape. He made New England his own and wrote about ordinary people living ordinary lives. The subject matter of the poems – turning the hay, mending a wall, swinging from birch trees, spring pools, picking apples, a farmyard accident, a spider, walking at night – is described, but the poems go beyond description. In 'The Road Not Taken' and many other Frost poems, the speaker explores moral and philosophical ideas, so that suggestion is as important as what is being described. 'You don't want to say directly what you can say indirectly,' according to Frost.

Robert Penn Warren said of Frost that 'It's as though he were dropped into the countryside north of Boston from outer space, and remained perpetually stunned by what he saw. I don't think you can overemphasise that fact of Frost. A native takes, or may take, a place for granted; if you have to earn your citizenship, your locality, it requires a special focus.' Henry David Thoreau (1817–1862) claimed that 'a true account of the actual is the purest poetry' and, as an old man, Frost frequently quoted Thoreau: 'I went to the woods because I wished to live deliberately, to front only the essential facts of life, and see if I could not learn what it had to teach, and not, when I came to die, discover that I had not lived.'

The world of Frost's poetry is beautiful but it is also harsh. Frost wrote that 'Man has need of nature, but nature has no need of man'. At a dinner in Frost's honour in New York on the poet's eighty-fifth birthday (26 March 1959), Lionel Trilling said Frost's best poems represented 'the terrible actualities of life' and, in an essay published in *Partisan Review*, Summer 1959, Trilling described the world of Frost's poetry as a 'terrifying universe' and one of loneliness, doubts, disappointment and despair. Frost's biography reveals that his life was a troubled, anxious, sorrowful one.

•

In 1936, when asked to name some of his favourite books, Frost chose *Robinson Crusoe* and *Walden*: 'Robinson Crusoe is never quite out of my mind. I never tire of being shown how the limited can make snug in the limitless. Walden has the same fascination. Crusoe was cast away: Thoreau was self-cast away. Both found themselves sufficient.' Peter Jones thinks that 'the will to be sufficient in himself was strong in Frost; his poems reveal the impossibility of that will ever being finally expressed in action.'

The voice we imagine when we read Frost is a warm, inviting, gentle voice. Lines such as 'I went to turn the grass once', 'I am done with apple-picking now', 'I shall be telling this with a sigh', 'But I was going to say', 'I have outwalked the furthest city light' are immediate, even colloquial, in tone. In 1939, Frost wrote: 'No tears in the writer, no tears in the reader. No surprise for the writer, no surprise for the reader. For me the initial delight is in the surprise of remembering something I didn't know I knew...A poem may be worked over once it is in being, but may not be worried into being. Its most precious quality will remain its having run itself and carried away the poet with it. Read it a hundred times: it will forever keep its freshness as a metal keeps its fragrance. It can never lose its sense of a meaning that once unfolded by surprise as it went'.

•

At a dinner in Amherst on the day of his eightieth birthday, Frost said: 'all I've wanted to do is to write a few little poems it'd be hard to get rid of.' He also commented: 'We rise out of disorder into order and the poems that I make are little bits of order. It's as if I made a basket or a piece of pottery or a vase or something and if you suffer any sense of confusion in life the best thing you can do is make little poems. Or cigarette smoke rings. Even those have form.'

At the beginning of many volumes of his poems, and also at the beginning of his *Collected Poems*, is a poem called 'The Pasture'. It serves as both introduction and invitation. Frost is going out to attend to everyday jobs on the farm but he invites us to look at the world through his eyes, the eyes of a poet:

The Pasture

I'm going out to clean the pasture spring;
I'll only stop to rake the leaves away
(And wait to watch the water clear, I may):
I shan't be long. — You come too.

I'm going out to fetch the little calf
That's standing by the mother. It's so young
It totters when she licks it with her tongue.
I shan't be gone long. — You come too.

Biographical Notes

Though Robert Frost is most often associated with New England, more specifically the states of New Hampshire and Vermont, he was born in San Francisco, California on 26 March 1874, in a small apartment on Washington Street. His father, Will Frost, a New Englander, worked for *The San Francisco Post* and later became business manager of the newspaper; he named his son Robert in honour of General Robert E. Lee, a civil war hero. His mother, Belle Moodie, was born in Scotland but, from the age of eleven, grew up with relatives in Ohio. Robert was their eldest child; a daughter, Jeanie, was born in 1876, but by then the marriage was in difficulty, due to Will Frost's heavy drinking. His father rejected organised religion but his mother became more and more religious. She brought Robert Frost to many churches in his childhood, so much so that in later life Frost was to describe his religious progression as: 'Presbyterian, Unitarian, Swedenborgian, Nothing.'

Robert Frost did not care for school and pretended to be sick so as to avoid going. This disrupted pattern continued: he attended both Dartmouth and Harvard but dropped out of both and never cared for organised, conventional education. His mother and a family friend, who lived with the Frosts, educated Robert and Jeanie at home in the mornings and Robert was free in the afternoons. In a small back garden, Robert kept chickens; he also walked the city and fell in with a local gang. Petty theft and fist fights were common. This fighting instinct appalled his mother but Will Frost felt it would strengthen his son's character.

Tuberculosis eventually destroyed Will Frost. He regularly coughed up blood and, in a desperate attempt at a cure, he once brought the eleven-year-old Robert Frost to a slaughterhouse where he drank cups of fresh steer blood. Frost's father died in May 1885, at the age of thirty-four. He had failed to keep up payments on a life-insurance policy and shortly before he died he wrote to his parents in Massachusetts asking them to look after his wife and two children.

Robert Frost had lived on the west coast, in an urban Californian setting, until he was eleven. Then in 1885, the family travelled east, from San Francisco to Massachusetts, accompanying Will Frost's coffin; in Robert Frost's words, it was 'the *longest, loneliest* train ride he ever took.'

Belle Frost took a teaching job in Salem, New Hampshire, and lived in a small apartment with her two children. They got to know a Scottish couple who had a farm and Frost worked on the farm and in a cobbler shop attached to the farm after school and at weekends. Frost liked school in Salem and having his mother as teacher. He loved baseball and he also began to read voraciously – Walter Scott, Longfellow, Emerson, Poe, Bryant – and learnt many poems by heart which he used to recite while he worked.

At high school, Frost studied Latin, Greek and Roman history and worked summers on the farm learning haymaking and wall building.

At school, Frost met Carl Burell, a man in his twenties who had returned to school to complete his education. The friendship was an important one: they exchanged books; Burell introduced Frost to botany; moreover, when Burell published verse in the high school paper, Frost decided that he would also try writing poetry. In April 1890, a sixteen-year old Robert Frost published his first verse, 'La Noche Triste', a poem inspired by a book he had been reading on the conquest of Mexico. In his final year at school, he was elected chief editor of the *High School Bulletin* and that same year he and Elinor White became friends. She was a very brilliant student. While still students they entered into a secret marriage – they were married, publicly, in 1895.

After high school, Frost went to Dartmouth on a scholarship where he took courses in Homer, Latin prose and mathematics. He would walk for hours along mountain trails and used to go into the woods on his own at night. It was also at Dartmouth that he bought Palgrave's *Golden Treasury* and began serious reading of the English poets. He wrote first drafts of his poems 'My Butterfly' and 'Now Close the Windows' at Dartmouth, and these he included in his first collection *A Boy's Will*. However, Frost published nothing in Dartmouth publications and left the college suddenly when examinations approached.

He taught for a short while, using a rattan cane to gain control in class, and decided that teaching was not for him. He wrote to Elinor, who was at St. Lawrence University, and announced that he was going to write poetry. He worked at Woollen Mills in Arlington, read Shakespeare during breaks and worked at his poetry in the evenings: he re-worked 'My Butterfly' and later called it his 'first real poem.'

Frost's life as a young man was unstable in terms of jobs but his devotion to poetry was total. He tried teaching again, studied Greek, asked Elinor to marry him and, in November 1895, when it seemed she was rejecting him, Frost left home and set off for Dismal Swamp on the Virginia/North Carolina border. He returned home however and decided that he would settle to a job and community living and this would, perhaps, help him win Elinor. He tried journalism, tutoring, then returned, yet again, to teaching. By this time Elinor was teaching in Frost's mother's school but the relationship between Frost and Elinor was stormy and strained. However, they did marry in December 1895; her father, thinking Frost unsuitable, refused to attend the ceremony. Frost was twenty-one, she was twenty-three.

They had no money and lived with Belle Frost for a while; Jay Parini describes it as 'a dire beginning to married life'. Their first child, a son, Elliott, was born in September 1896 and, in another effort to support his family, Frost enrolled at Harvard. He did extremely well, winning a prize for excellence in classical studies, but did not complete his degree. Suffering from nervous exhaustion, he abandoned formal education and was advised by a doctor, who recommended farming, to abandon a sedentary life. Shortly after the birth of their second child,

Lesley, in April 1899, the Frosts moved to a rented farm where Frost's mental and physical health improved but the following year, three-and-a-half year-old Elliott died of typhoid fever, their daughter was unwell and Frost's mother was admitted to a sanatorium, ill with cancer.

A change of fortune came about with a change of location. With help from Frost's grandfather, a thirty-acre farm was purchased in Derry, in Rockingham County, New Hampshire, and on 30 October 1900 Robert Frost began what has been termed the most important phase in his long life. Frost himself said that 'it all started in Derry, the whole thing'; 'There was something about the experience at Derry which stayed in my mind, and was tapped for poetry in the years that came after.'

Frost devoted himself to farming – eggs and apples supplied an income – and, though he wrote throughout this time, he published very little. His mother died; his sister suffered from a nervous condition; his grandfather died and in his will Frost was guaranteed a small income; a son, Carol, was born in 1902; a daughter, Irma, in 1903, another, Marjorie, in 1905. The children were educated at home during their early years.

Frost wrote late into the night and suffered bouts of depression; at times he was moody and difficult, at other times playful, kind and caring. But that period at Derry was 'a time when my eyes and ears were open, very open.'

He turned yet again to teaching. At Pinkerton Academy, he was a popular if unconventional teacher, who emphasised grammatical accuracy and learning by heart, and he had a boy expelled for writing an insult ('hen-man') on the blackboard. He worked hard but unfortunately contracted pneumonia; his pregnant wife nursed him in the spring of 1907, becoming ill herself, and their baby girl died soon after she was born in June. That summer the Frost family went to Bethlehem, New Hampshire, and moved to the village of Derry, two miles from the farm, in the autumn, before Frost resumed teaching. About this time, he addressed a group of teachers on teaching methods and focused on the need for teachers to develop their own minds first, saying that students should be made to feel dependent on books to avoid loneliness and that writing should put things into memorable, concrete language. His reputation as a teacher grew but he gave up teaching at Pinkerton because of overwork and sold the neglected farm in 1911. He taught again, this time in Plymouth at a teacher-training college, but 1912 marked a turning-point: Frost had realised that he could not devote himself to both teaching and poetry and he gave up teaching. At thirty-eight, and without having published a book, Frost and his family moved to England.

Frost lived in England from September 1912 to February 1915, first settling in Beaconsfield, a village twenty miles north of London, and later in Little Iddens, Gloucestershire, and in Ryton in Warwickshire. Frost wrote in the morning and explored the countryside in the afternoon. His first two collection, *A Boy's Will* (1913) and *North of Boston* (1914), were published in England and within months he had written 'Mending Wall', 'After Apple-Picking' and 'Birches'. In London, Frost became acquainted with literary London and met many writers, including Ezra Pound, W. B. Yeats and Edward Thomas. An American publisher expressed an interest in publishing his work and his reputation was growing. This prompted the poet to think of returning home.

Back in the United States, Frost bought a little farm at Sugar Hill, New Hampshire, and enjoyed a greater awareness and interest in his work. By the following year, *North of Boston* had sold 20,000 copies in America. In a newspaper interview soon after his return, Frost spoke of the importance of 'writing with your ear to the voice' and named Wordsworth as an significant influence: 'This is what Wordsworth did himself in all his best poetry.'

Settled to farm life once more, Frost was both poet and farmer and continued writing. 'Out, Out —', based on a farming accident, five years earlier, in 1910, dates from this period. He was now lecturing widely and joined the faculty at Amherst College for a spring semester in 1917. Later he was appointed professor but resigned in order to focus on his writing, though a link between Frost and Amherst lasted for the rest of his life.

The Frost family's next move was to a ninety-acre farm in southern Vermont. Jeanie, his sister, who had suffered mental health problems for years, became so ill about this time that she was confined to hospital permanently. This troubled Frost greatly, for he also saw in himself and his children traces of insanity.

Other university connections followed, including a visiting fellowship at the University of Michigan at Ann Arbor, but Frost again realised that academic life was keeping him from poetry. He returned to southern Vermont in June 1922 and one morning, while sitting at the kitchen table, he wrote his most famous poem, 'Stopping by Woods on a Snowy Evening'. That same summer, Frost and his children did a 200-mile trek through the wilderness.

In 1923, Frost moved back to Amherst and his third collection, *New Hampshire*, was published; he won the Pulitzer Prize for poetry in 1924 and went on to win it three more times. He was becoming more and more famous, was awarded several honorary degrees and had many invitations to read his work. In the spring of 1927, while still at Ann Arbor, he wrote 'Spring Pools' and 'Acquainted with the Night'. Soon after this, he gave up Ann Arbor for Amherst where he would teach ten weeks per year; his teaching was informal – 'What I teach is myself, my way of seeing the world, of knowing the world'. It also meant he would be closer to his farm home, which was being run by his son.

His public life was one of extraordinary popularity but his private world was increasingly overshadowed by many sorrows: illnesses, a daughter's instability, his son's financial difficulties.

In 1928, Frost, his wife and daughter Marjorie travelled to Europe: France and England. Frost went to Ireland on his own for five days where he met the poet Padraic Colum and the writer George Russell, known as AE. In Dublin, Frost stayed with another Irish poet, Constantine Curran, at Garville Avenue in Rathgar, and spent one evening at a literary gathering that included Yeats. Frost said of AE and Yeats's conversation that 'nowhere else on earth have I ever heard the like' and that 'these men took ordinary conversation and lifted it into the realm of pure literature.' Back in London, he had dinner with fellow-American T.S. Eliot but Frost disliked Eliot's English accent and manners, thinking him a snob and a fake.

The trip proved exhausting for all three Frosts and they returned home to Vermont to discover that his other two daughters were having marital problems. Frost bought a new farm of 153 acres for he felt that Carol, who worked the other one, deserved it for himself.

A *Collected Poems* was published in 1930 and it won for Frost another Pulitzer Prize. That same year he was elected to the American Academy of Arts and Letters. But the 1930s also brought poor health to the Frost family. Frost's daughter Marjorie contracted tuberculosis and so too did his daughter-in-law; Marjorie recovered, fell in love and married but died of puerperal fever very soon after giving birth to a daughter. That same year his wife suffered a serious heart attack. Frost found himself supporting his children financially and he himself was often ill and for long stretches could not work at his writing or teaching.

The family went to Florida in December 1934 where Frost met Wallace Stevens. He delayed his return to Amherst in the spring because Elinor was ill and the summer was spent on the farm. They travelled west in July to visit Marjorie's grave and Frost read at the Rocky Mountain Writers' Conference in Colorado to a huge crowd. He also went to Santa Fe, New Mexico and read to another huge audience. Sometimes, Frost would read a poem twice, saying, 'I'll say that one again, in case you missed it the first time round.'

The winter was spent in Miami and in March 1935 Frost delivered the Charles Eliot Norton lectures at Harvard before a thousand students. He was also invited to write a poem in celebration of Harvard's tercentenary; he accepted but was uneasy about having to write a poem to order: 'You don't know when a poem will come, or from where. And that's a good thing. A poet doesn't want to know too much, not while he's writing anyway. The knowing can come later.'

It was about this time that Frost described himself as 'a family man, a professor, a farmer, a lecturer, a contributor to magazines, a publisher's author, and a diner-out when I am where they have dinners.'

June 1936 saw the publication of *A Further Range*, Frost's sixth collection, and, like the previous five, it was dedicated to his wife, Elinor. Some of the reviews were negative and Frost cancelled many public appearances, including the delivery of the Harvard poem. Mental and physical illnesses followed. The book, however, won a Pulitzer Prize in 1937 and Frost returned to public life. There was a family gathering in Florida at Christmas and Frost planned to buy a house in Gainesville which he hoped to use as a winter home. Unfortunately, Elinor, his wife of forty-three years, died suddenly in Florida. Frost was sixty-four and her death left him deeply depressed.

He resigned from Amherst and for the rest of his life lived on the farm in Ripton, Vermont, and in a flat in Boston/Cambridge, spending winters in Florida.

Kay Morrison now became a very important presence in Frost's life. She visited Frost in Vermont during the summer of 1938 and became his secretary and closest companion for the next twenty-five years of his life, until his death in 1963. Though she was married and a mother, Frost asked her to marry him; she refused and their relationship soon settled into a companionable one and Kay became invaluable. She was Frost's business manager, agent, typist and best friend. His 1942 collection, *A Witness Tree*, was dedicated to K. M.

Travelling and readings were resumed, but the next great sorrow in Frost's life came with his son Carol's suicide in October 1940. In 1942, he won his fourth Pulitzer prize for *A Witness Tree* and also began an informal teaching commitment at Dartmouth. He was extraordinarily popular there even if he once, on taking up some writing from students, asked if anyone considered their papers 'of permanent value', even to themselves. When no one said yes, he replied: 'I'll be damned if I'll be a perfunctory reader of perfunctory writing' and threw the lot into the waste paper bin.

He wrote plays during the 1940s which were based on the Old Testament but these were not considered successful. Another volume of poems, *Steeple Bush*, was published in 1947. More personal troubles came Frost's way when his daughter, Irma, now separated from her husband, came with her son to live near him in Cambridge. In the wider world, his fame was consolidated. He went to California to be presented with another honorary doctorate, this time from Berkeley, and a lavish birthday dinner – he was seventy-two – was held in his honour in San Francisco. This included a huge chocolate birthday cake with 'Stopping by Woods on a Snowy Evening' displayed in white icing.

Later that year, Irma's state was such that she was admitted to a mental hospital. Anxious about money, he renewed his ties with Amherst. The *Complete Poems* was published in 1949 and in 1950 *Time* magazine reported that in the US alone Frost's work had sold 375,000 copies, a huge figure for books of poetry. All the while, however, Frost was torn between the private and the public domain. At a reading in Berkeley, 2,500 people turned up and his largest audience was 10,000 at the University of Detroit. Frost had become a superstar in the world of literature. He needed time to write but he also enjoyed the world of lectures, dinners and awards. He suffered from depression and there was no new book of poems until his final one in 1962: *In the Clearing*.

During the 1950s, he travelled widely. He visited Brazil, England, Ireland (where he was given an honorary degree by the NUI), Israel, Greece and Russia (where he met Khrushchev). More honours were bestowed and a friend had a quilt made from the twenty-five plus doctoral hoods that had been presented to him.

One of Frost's most famous public appearances was at the inauguration of John F. Kennedy in 1961, where he read 'The Gift Outright'. His final collection, published on his eighty-eighth birthday, was a best-seller.

Despite his illnesses, he had extraordinary energy. He travelled right up to the end. He gave his last reading in Boston on 2 December 1962, was hospitalised the next day and died there on 29 January 1963 in his eighty-ninth year.

Summing up his life, Jay Parini says of Frost: 'His family life was not often happy, and he experienced some extremely bad luck with his children. On the other hand, he was a man of immense fortitude, an attentive father, and an artist of the first order who understood what he must do to create a body of work of lasting significance, to "lodge a few poems where they can't be gotten rid of easily". Robert Frost did what was necessary, for him, to achieve what he did, at times risking the welfare of others, even his own. Each major poem was, in the complex circumstances of his life, a feat of rescued sanity as well as a "momentary stay against confusion," as he memorably put it.'

Robert Frost as a young man.

POEMS

Dates refer to the year of composition. The poems as they are printed here, are in the order in which they were written.

The Tuft of Flowers

I went to turn the grass once after one
Who mowed it in the dew before the sun.

The dew was gone that made his blade so keen
Before I came to view the leveled scene.

I looked for him behind an isle of trees;
I listened for his whetstone on the breeze.

But he had gone his way, the grass all mown,
And I must be, as he had been — alone,

'As all must be,' I said within my heart,
'Whether they work together or apart.'

But as I said it, swift there passed me by
On noiseless wing a bewildered butterfly,

Seeking with memories grown dim o'er night
Some resting flower of yesterday's delight.

And once I marked his flight go round and round,
As where some flower lay withering on the ground.

And then he flew as far as eye could see,
And then on tremulous wing came back to me.

I thought of questions that have no reply,
And would have turned to toss the grass to dry;

But he turned first, and led my eye to look
At a tall tuft of flowers beside a brook,

A leaping tongue of bloom the scythe had spared
Beside a reedy brook the scythe had bared.

The mower in the dew had loved them thus,
By leaving them to flourish, not for us,

Nor yet to draw one thought of ours to him,
But from sheer morning gladness at the brim.

The butterfly and I had lit upon,
Nevertheless, a message from the dawn,

That made me hear the wakening birds around,
And hear his long scythe whispering to the ground,

And feel a spirit kindred to my own;
So that henceforth I worked no more alone;

But glad with him, I worked as with his aid,
And weary, sought at noon with him the shade;

And dreaming, as it were, held brotherly speech
With one whose thought I had not hoped to reach.

'Men work together,' I told him from the heart,
'Whether they work together or apart.'

Glossary

Title Tuft: a bunched cluster or clump.

Line 6 whetstone: a stone for sharpening edged instruments – in this instance, a scythe.

Line 18 tremulous: trembling, quivering.

'The Tuft of Flowers' was written by Frost in his early twenties and was first published in *The Derry Enterprise* newspaper on 9 March 1906. When it was first published in book form, Frost said of it that it was 'about fellowship'. It is from Frost's first collection *A Boy's Will*.

Questions

1. At first glance, this is a narrative poem. Tell in your own words the story of the poem.
2. The subject matter of this poem is an account of turning the grass. What would you say is the poem's theme?
3. Lines 9–10 and 39–40 express opposite ideas within the same poem. Why did the speaker change his mind?
4. What is the significance of the butterfly, in your opinion? If the poem omitted the butterfly's presence, if the speaker had come upon the tuft of flowers on his own, what would have been lost?
5. The American poet Lawrence Ferlinghetti says that 'the poet like an acrobat/ climbs on rhyme/ to a high wire of his own making.' How would you describe Frost's use of rhyme in this poem?
6. Frost said of his poetry that 'I was after poetry that talked. If my poems were talking poems – if to read one of them you heard a voice – that would be to my liking!' Consider this view in the light of your reading of all the poems by Frost on your course.
7. Frost said of this poem, 'The Tuft of Flowers', that it spoke of 'my position . . . between socialism and individualism.' How do you interpret Frost's statement?
8. How would you describe the poem's rhythm? How does Frost achieve that rhythm? Consider rhyme, line length, the use of monosyllables.

Mending Wall

Something there is that doesn't love a wall,
That sends the frozen-ground-swell under it
And spills the upper boulders in the sun,
And makes gaps even two can pass abreast.
The work of hunters is another thing:
I have come after them and made repair
Where they have left not one stone on a stone,
But they would have the rabbit out of hiding,
To please the yelping dogs. The gaps I mean,
No one has seen them made or heard them made,
But at spring mending-time we find them there.
I let my neighbor know beyond the hill;
And on a day we meet to walk the line
And set the wall between us once again.
We keep the wall between us as we go.
To each the boulders that have fallen to each.
And some are loaves and some so nearly balls
We have to use a spell to make them balance:
'Stay where you are until our backs are turned!'
We wear our fingers rough with handling them.
Oh, just another kind of outdoor game,
One on a side. It comes to little more:
There where it is we do not need the wall:
He is all pine and I am apple orchard.
My apple trees will never get across
And eat the cones under his pines, I tell him.
He only says, 'Good fences make good neighbors.'
Spring is the mischief in me, and I wonder
If I could put a notion in his head:
'*Why* do they make good neighbors? Isn't it
Where there are cows? But here there are no cows.
Before I built a wall I'd ask to know
What I was walling in or walling out,

And to whom I was like to give offense.
Something there is that doesn't love a wall,
That wants it down.' I could say 'Elves' to him,
But it's not elves exactly, and I'd rather
He said it for himself. I see him there,
Bringing a stone grasped firmly by the top
In each hand, like an old-stone savage armed.
He moves in darkness as it seems to me,
Not of woods only and the shade of trees.
He will not go behind his father's saying,
And he likes having thought of it so well
He says again, 'Good fences make good neighbors.'

Glossary

Line 1 Something there is that doesn't love a wall: frost – with a pun on Frost's own name.

Line 4 abreast: side by side and facing the same way.

Line 27 'Good fences make good neighbors': a proverbial saying often found in nineteenth-century almanacs such as *Poor Richard's Almanac* but the wording here is Frost's own. The word 'good', according to the American critic William Harmon, may mislead readers into thinking that the poem is about being a good neighbour in the biblical or socio-political sense: helping, caring, sharing, loving. But, Harmon argues, a good fence is a strong barrier to keep people apart; the better the fence, the less you see of your neighbour. The American phrase 'spite fence' suggests a spirit far from good and neighbourly.

Line 36 Elves: small supernatural beings in human form; usually considered more harmful than fairies.

'Mending Wall' was written in the autumn of 1913 in England. It is the first poem in Frost's second collection *North of Boston* (1914). North of Boston refers to northern New England, and New Hampshire is known as the Granite State. When the early European settlers cleared the land to farm it, the loose stones were made into walls.

Years after writing the poem, Frost said 'I wrote the poem "Mending Wall" thinking of the old wall that I hadn't mended in several years and which must be in a terrible condition. I wrote that poem in England when I was very homesick for my old wall in New England.'

The poem is written in blank verse (unrhymed iambic pentameter).

Questions

1. What does the activity of mending a wall suggest? Can it be interpreted in different ways?

2. 'Something there is that doesn't love a wall'. What might that something be? Could there be more than one answer?

3. There are two speakers in this poem. Frost himself said that the poem 'contrasts two types of people'. How would you describe each one? Which one in your opinion is the wiser of the two? What does the speaker suggest about the neighbour in lines 41–42? 'He moves in darkness as it seems to me,/ Not of woods only and the shade of trees.'

4. The speaker in this poem has a sense of humour. Where is this evident? How would you describe his personality?

5. Each spring the wall needs to be repaired. Who reminds whom that it needs to be done, the speaker or the neighbour? Is this ironic?

6. 'Good fences make good neighbors' is repeated by the neighbour. Why? The speaker also says something twice. Identify what this is and comment on its significance.

7. The language here seems ordinary, everyday, colloquial. What sets it apart as poetry?

8. When Robert Frost visited Russia in 1962, he read this poem to a Russian audience and quoted the poem to Khrushchev at the time of the Cuban missile crisis. Could this poem be viewed as symbolic or political in any way?

9. What perspective do you think this poem offers on custom, tradition, togetherness, separateness, communication between people, positive and negative outlooks, living in general?

10. Frost describes the business of mending the wall as 'just another kind of outdoor game'. Is this a serious poem or a light-hearted one? Give reasons for your answer.

After Apple-Picking

My long two-pointed ladder's sticking through a tree
Toward heaven still,
And there's a barrel that I didn't fill
Beside it, and there may be two or three
Apples I didn't pick upon some bough.
But I am done with apple-picking now.
Essence of winter sleep is on the night,
The scent of apples: I am drowsing off.
I cannot rub the strangeness from my sight
I got from looking through a pane of glass
I skimmed this morning from the drinking trough
And held against the world of hoary grass.
It melted, and I let it fall and break.
But I was well
Upon my way to sleep before it fell,
And I could tell
What form my dreaming was about to take.
Magnified apples appear and disappear,
Stem end and blossom end,
And every fleck of russet showing clear.
My instep arch not only keeps the ache,
It keeps the pressure of a ladder-round.
I feel the ladder sway as the boughs bend.
And I keep hearing from the cellar bin
The rumbling sound
Of load on load of apples coming in.
For I have had too much
Of apple-picking: I am overtired
Of the great harvest I myself desired.
There were ten thousand thousand fruit to touch,
Cherish in hand, lift down, and not let fall.
For all
That struck the earth,

No matter if not bruised or spiked with stubble,
Went surely to the cider-apple heap
As of no worth.
One can see what will trouble
This sleep of mine, whatever sleep it is.
Were he not gone,
The woodchuck could say whether it's like his
Long sleep, as I describe its coming on,
Or just some human sleep.

Glossary

Line 7 essence of winter sleep: here the essence of sleep can mean both the ultimate nature of sleep and the scent of apples.

Line 12 hoary: frost-covered.

Line 20 russet: reddish-brown colour.

Line 34 stubble: cut stalks of cereal plants left sticking up after harvest.

Line 40 woodchuck: a stocky, burrowing, bushy-tailed North American animal that hibernates in the winter.

'After Apple-Picking' is from Frost's collection *North Of Boston*. Writing of this collection, Frost said that 'One thing to notice is that but one poem in the book will intone and that is "After Apple-Picking." The rest talk.'

And the American author Joyce Carol Oates says of 'After Apple-Picking': 'It's beautifully nuanced, haunting, and profound in its suggestion of a life so passionately lived, or a career so energetically mined, that it has utterly satiated its original appetite. But what mystery in Frost's rhythms and words!' The Belfast-born poet and novelist Ciaran Carson wrote that 'After some thirty years of reading it off and on, I'm not entirely clear what it's all about, though the ordinary speech rhythms lull you into thinking that you know. The last lines are especially mysterious. Memory, anticipation, art, time . . . the big themes are all in there: emotion recollected in tranquillity.'

Questions

1. Frost said that 'Poetry provides the one permissible way of saying one thing and meaning another.' Like many of Robert Frost's poems, 'After Apple-Picking' illustrates this idea. What do you think the speaker is saying here and what do you think he means? In other words, there's the actual experience of apple-picking but how has that task a symbolic role?
2. When do you first realise that the poem is more than description, that it is about more than actual apple-picking? What happens after apple-picking? Trace the movement of the poem from morning to night.
3. At line 18, the speaker describes a dream. What troubles him in his dream? What does the speaker admit to in this poem about his life? How would you describe the speaker's tone?
4. Look at the rhyming scheme in the poem. Is the rhyme noticeable immediately? Does the rhyming pattern surprise you? It has been said of this poem that 'Frost uses rhymes to organise his thoughts, emphasise important words and thus convey the speaker's view of his own existence and of life in general.' Comment on this statement, quoting from the poem to support the points you make.
5. Is it significant that apples are being picked and not some other fruit? Are there echoes here, do you think, of the Tree of Knowledge in the Garden of Eden, for example?
6. Memory and the past, the present and the future, all play a part in this poem. Examine how past, present and future are viewed by the speaker.
7. How would you describe the dominant mood in the poem? Which words and phrases, in your opinion, best capture that mood?
8. Why do you think the speaker refers to the woodchuck?
9. What effect is achieved in the closing lines of the poem? How does the poet achieve this effect? Consider, for example, the use of repetition.
10. What do you understand 'essence of winter sleep' (line 7) to mean? Why is it a central image in the poem?

The Road Not Taken

Two roads diverged in a yellow wood,
And sorry I could not travel both
And be one traveler, long I stood
And looked down one as far as I could
To where it bent in the undergrowth;

Then took the other, as just as fair,
And having perhaps the better claim,
Because it was grassy and wanted wear;
Though as for that, the passing there
Had worn them really about the same,

And both that morning equally lay
In leaves no step had trodden black.
Oh, I kept the first for another day!
Yet knowing how way leads on to way,
I doubted if I should ever come back.

I shall be telling this with a sigh
Somewhere ages and ages hence:
Two roads diverged in a wood, and I—
I took the one less traveled by,
And that has made all the difference.

Glossary

Line 18 I —: an earlier version of the poem had no dash after 'I'; William H. Pritchard says: 'presumably Frost added it to make the whole thing more expressive and heartfelt'.

The four five-line stanzas follow a regular but unusual rhyme scheme: abaab, cdccd, efeef, ghggh. Frost placed 'The Road Not Taken' as the first poem in his collection *Mountain Interval* (1916).

Questions

1. Can you suggest reasons why this is one of the best known of Robert Frost's poems? How is it that almost every reader everywhere can identify with 'The Road Not Taken'?

2. Explain how the poem works at two different levels, the actual and the symbolic.

3. The speaker chooses 'the road less traveled'. What does this tell us about the speaker? What is the significance of lines 9–10?

4. The language in a Frost poem sometimes appears 'casual and even rambling'. Would you agree? Identify and write out seemingly 'casual' or 'rambling' language in this and other poems by Frost on your course.

5. How would you describe the effect the decision has had on the speaker?

6. The phrase 'yellow wood' suggests autumn. Is the season significant in your opinion? Give reasons for your answer.

7. In line 2, the poet is 'sorry'; in line 16, he speaks of how 'I shall be telling this with a sigh'. How would you sum up the mood of the poem?

Birches

When I see birches bend to left and right
Across the lines of straighter darker trees,
I like to think some boy's been swinging them.
But swinging doesn't bend them down to stay
As ice storms do. Often you must have seen them
Loaded with ice a sunny winter morning
After a rain. They click upon themselves
As the breeze rises, and turn many-colored
As the stir cracks and crazes their enamel.
Soon the sun's warmth makes them shed crystal shells
Shattering and avalanching on the snow crust —
Such heaps of broken glass to sweep away
You'd think the inner dome of heaven had fallen.
They are dragged to the withered bracken by the load,
And they seem not to break; though once they are bowed
So low for long, they never right themselves:
You may see their trunks arching in the woods
Years afterwards, trailing their leaves on the ground
Like girls on hands and knees that throw their hair
Before them over their heads to dry in the sun.
But I was going to say when Truth broke in
With all her matter of fact about the ice storm,
I should prefer to have some boy bend them
As he went out and in to fetch the cows —
Some boy too far from town to learn baseball,
Whose only play was what he found himself,
Summer or winter, and could play alone.
One by one he subdued his father's trees
By riding them down over and over again
Until he took the stiffness out of them,
And not one but hung limp, not one was left
For him to conquer. He learned all there was
To learn about not launching out too soon

And so not carrying the tree away
Clear to the ground. He always kept his poise
To the top branches, climbing carefully
With the same pains you use to fill a cup
Up to the brim, and even above the brim.
Then he flung outward, feet first, with a swish,
Kicking his way down through the air to the ground.
So was I once myself a swinger of birches.
And so I dream of going back to be.
It's when I'm weary of considerations,
And life is too much like a pathless wood
Where your face burns and tickles with the cobwebs
Broken across it, and one eye is weeping
From a twig's having lashed across it open.
I'd like to get away from earth awhile
And then come back to it and begin over.
May no fate willfully misunderstand me
And half grant what I wish and snatch me away
Not to return. Earth's the right place for love:
I don't know where it's likely to go better.
I'd like to go by climbing a birch tree,
And climb black branches up a snow-white trunk
Toward heaven, till the tree could bear no more,
But dipped its top and set me down again.
That would be good both going and coming back.
One could do worse than be a swinger of birches.

Glossary

Line 9 crazes their enamel: produces small cracks in the glassy, enamel-like, ice-coated birches; the verb 'to craze' means to shatter or crack.

Lines 37/38 a cup/ Up to the brim: a reference, perhaps, to 'my cup runs over', meaning my blessings overflow. Cf. Psalms XXIII in the Bible – 'my cup runneth over'.

Line 43 considerations: careful, serious thinking.

It was on his uncle's farm in Amherst, New Hampshire, that the twelve-year-old Frost first climbed birch trees. In adulthood, Frost said that swinging birches, 'climbing a birch tree till it bent, till it gave and swooped to the ground', was 'almost sacrilegious' and added 'but that's what boys did in those days'. The poem was written when Frost was living in England and was originally called 'Swinging Birches'.

The poem is written in blank verse and is from his collection *Mountain Interval* (1916).

Questions

1. Why do you think the speaker says that when he sees birch trees he likes to think 'some boy's been swinging them', that he prefers 'to have some boy bend them' and not the ice storm?
2. What do you think the speaker means here when he refers to the swinging of birches?
3. At line 21, the poet says that 'Truth broke in'. What does he mean by 'Truth' here and how does it alter things? What is the opposite of 'Truth'?
4. What relationship does the poet see between man and nature? Is a similar relationship evident in other poems by Frost in this selection?
5. In lines 32–35, the boy learns something important about birch-swinging. What do you understand by these lines?
6. How is earth described in this poem? Why does the speaker prefer it to heaven?
7. Commenting on 'Birches', the poet C. S. Lewis said that 'it is solidly constructed of seasoned materials, is carefully sited, is shapely, and a spirit of sober joy inhabits it.' Consider this view in the light of your reading of the poem.
8. How does the poet convey the difficulties, disappointments and frustrations of adult life? In your opinion, is this a poem of celebration or regret?
9. How would you describe the speaker as he reveals himself to us in this poem? What does the last line reveal of the speaker?
10. Many years after writing 'Birches', Frost said that the poem was 'two fragments soldered together so long ago I have forgotten where the joint is'. Can you detect the two parts of the poem and where Frost joined them together?

'Out, Out —'

The buzz saw snarled and rattled in the yard
And made dust and dropped stove-length sticks of wood,
Sweet-scented stuff when the breeze drew across it.
And from there those that lifted eyes could count
Five mountain ranges one behind the other
Under the sunset far into Vermont.
And the saw snarled and rattled, snarled and rattled,
As it ran light, or had to bear a load.
And nothing happened: day was all but done.
Call it a day, I wish they might have said
To please the boy by giving him the half hour
That a boy counts so much when saved from work.
His sister stood beside them in her apron
To tell them 'Supper'. At the word, the saw,
As if to prove saws knew what supper meant,
Leaped out at the boy's hand, or seemed to leap—
He must have given the hand. However it was,
Neither refused the meeting. But the hand!
The boy's first outcry was a rueful laugh,
As he swung toward them holding up the hand,
Half in appeal, but half as if to keep
The life from spilling. Then the boy saw all—
Since he was old enough to know, big boy
Doing a man's work, though a child at heart—
He saw all spoiled. 'Don't let him cut my hand off—
The doctor, when he comes. Don't let him, sister!'
So. But the hand was gone already.
The doctor put him in the dark of ether.
He lay and puffed his lips out with his breath.
And then—the watcher at his pulse took fright.
No one believed. They listened at his heart.
Little—less—nothing!—and that ended it.
No more to build on there. And they, since they
Were not the one dead, turned to their affairs.

Glossary

Title from Shakespeare's *Macbeth*, Act V, sc v. Macbeth's wife has committed suicide; his castle is surrounded and is about to be taken. Macbeth is at his lowest when he says:

> Tomorrow, and tomorrow, and tomorrow,
> Creeps in this petty pace from day to day,
> To the last syllable of recorded time;
> And all our yesterdays have lighted fools
> The way to dusty death. Out, out, brief candle!
> Life's but a walking shadow, a poor player
> That struts and frets his hour upon the stage,
> And then is heard no more; it is a tale
> Told by an idiot, full of sound and fury,
> Signifying nothing.

Line 4 lifted eyes: Marie Borroff thinks that Frost is alluding to Psalm 121, verse 1, of the Christian Bible here: 'I will lift up mine eyes unto the hills, from whence cometh my help. My help cometh from the Lord which made heaven and earth.' Borroff comments that '"raised their eyes" would have been equally satisfactory metrically, and perhaps more idiomatic but "lifted eyes" echoes Psalm 121. The point is that "they" do not lift their eyes; the sunset is ignored.'

Line 19 rueful: regretful, sorrowful.

Robert Frost would never read this poem aloud because he thought it was 'too cruel'. It is from his third collection *Mountain Interval* (1916).

The poem was prompted by a newspaper article in *The Littleton Courier*, 31 March 1901, which was headed 'Sad tragedy at Bethlehem, Raymond Fitzgerald, a victim of fatal accident, 'Raymond Tracy Fitzgerald, one of the twin sons of Michael G. and Margaret Fitzgerald of Bethlehem, died at his home Thursday afternoon, March 24, as a result of an accident by which one of his hands was badly hurt in a sawing machine. The young man was assisting in sawing up some wood in his own dooryard with a sawing machine and accidentally hit the loose pulley, causing the saw to descend upon his hand, cutting and lacerating it badly. Raymond was taken into the house and a physician was immediately summoned, but he died very suddenly from the effect of the shock, which produced heart failure . . .'

Questions

1. Read the passage, quoted in the glossary, which gives the poem its title. What does the extract from Shakespeare's *Macbeth* contribute to your understanding of the poem?

2. This poem was inspired by a real event, the accidental death of a boy, which was reported in a newspaper. Read the newspaper account in the box above and re-read the poem. How different is Frost's account of the accident?

3. Identify the ordinary, everyday details in the poem and the horrific. What is the effect of both within the one poem?

4. Discuss how the poet uses repetition and comment on its effect.

5. Robert Frost, in many of his poems, uses the personal pronoun 'I' frequently. In 'Out, Out—' it occurs once (line 10: 'I wish'). Do you think this significant? How would you describe the poet's tone throughout? How would you describe the attitude contained in the closing lines of the poem – callous, heartless, realistic?

6. Comment on how boyhood is portrayed in 'Birches' and 'Out, Out—'. Are there similarities and differences?

7. Comment on the sounds and the silence in the poem. Write a note on lines 1 and 32.

8. Suggest an alternative title for the poem.

Spring Pools

These pools that, though in forests, still reflect
The total sky almost without defect,
And like the flowers beside them, chill and shiver,
Will like the flowers beside them soon be gone,
And yet not out by any brook or river,
But up by roots to bring dark foliage on.

The trees that have it in their pent-up buds
To darken nature and be summer woods —
Let them think twice before they use their powers
To blot out and drink up and sweep away
These flowery waters and these watery flowers
From snow that melted only yesterday.

'Spring Pools' was first published on 23 April 1927 in *The Dearborn Independent* and it is the first poem in Frost's fifth collection *West-Running Brook*, published in 1928 when Frost was fifty-four.

'Spring Pools' has been described by Jay Parini as one of Frost's 'most intricate pieces of verse making'; the stanzas are identically patterned, mirroring the way the pools mirror the sky.' It has also been read as a poem about poetry itself and the creative process and water is seen as inspirational.

Questions

1. What is remarkable about the spring pools according to the poet? Is it significant that they are forest pools?
2. How does the speaker suggest a connection between the disappearing pools and the 'dark foliage' of the forest? What cycle is being described?
3. Why does the speaker think that the trees should 'think twice' as spring becomes summer?
4. Consider the effect of such words as 'dark', 'darken', 'blot out', 'drink up' and 'sweep away'. What do these words suggest?
5. 'You don't want to say directly what you can say indirectly' is how Frost commented on his poetry. Do you think that something is being said in this poem directly and indirectly?
6. How does this poem compare with the other poems by Frost on your course?
7. How would you describe the speaker's relationship with nature, as revealed to us in this poem?
8. It has been suggested that this a poem about poetry itself and the creative process. Do you think such an interpretation convincing and valid?

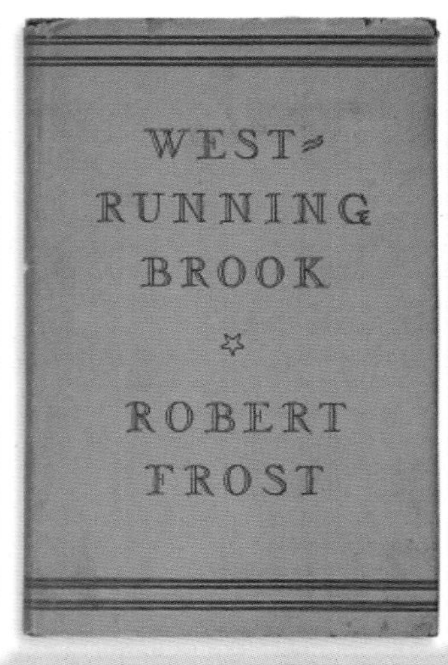

Acquainted with the Night

I have been one acquainted with the night.
I have walked out in rain—and back in rain.
I have outwalked the furthest city light.

I have looked down the saddest city lane.
I have passed by the watchman on his beat
And dropped my eyes, unwilling to explain.

I have stood still and stopped the sound of feet
When far away an interrupted cry
Came over houses from another street,

But not to call me back or say good-by;
And further still at an unearthly height
One luminary clock against the sky

Proclaimed the time was neither wrong nor right.
I have been one acquainted with the night.

Glossary

Line 12 luminary clock: luminary means giving light, shining, lighted; the clock, Frost said, was in the old Washtenaw County Courthouse, Ann Arbour, Michigan, where the poem was written. However, some critics have read 'luminary clock' to mean the moon.

This sonnet is divided neither into three quatrains and a couplet (3x4+2) nor an octet and a sestet (8+6). Frost here opts for the terza rima format, a three line rhyming stanza plus a couplet.

Questions

1. In this fourteen-line poem, seven of the lines begin with 'I'. What is the effect of this?

2. What can you tell about the speaker in this poem? Which details do you think convey the speaker most effectively?

3. Do you think the rain, is significant? Why? Give reasons for your answer.

4. Other people are mentioned or suggested by the poet: 'the watchman,' 'the sound of feet,' 'an interrupted cry'. What images are suggested by these words?

5. Examine how the poet uses repetition. Can you suggest why repetition plays an important part here?

6. Frost said of this poem that it was 'written for the tune'. How would you describe the music this poem makes?

7. This poem has been described as 'a descent into darkness'. Would you agree with this description?

8. Unusually for Robert Frost, this poem has an urban setting. Is it a typical or atypical Frost poem?

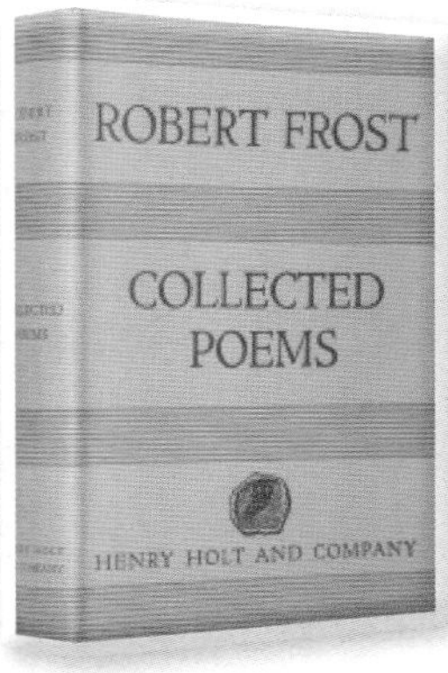

ROBERT FROST
COLLECTED POEMS
HENRY HOLT AND COMPANY

Design

I found a dimpled spider, fat and white,
On a white heal-all, holding up a moth
Like a white piece of rigid satin cloth—
Assorted characters of death and blight
Mixed ready to begin the morning right,
Like the ingredients of a witches' broth—
A snow-drop spider, a flower like a froth,
And dead wings carried like a paper kite.

What had that flower to do with being white,
The wayside blue and innocent heal-all?
What brought the kindred spider to that height,
Then steered the white moth thither in the night?
What but design of darkness to appall?—
If design govern in a thing so small.

Glossary

Title Design: it is often argued that the presence of order in nature is proof of God's existence.

Line 1 dimpled spider: the spider has a small hollow on the surface of its body.

Line 2 heal-all: a plant, also known as 'self-heal'; it has tightly clustered violet-blue flowers and was once used for medicinal purposes. Though usually blue, here it is white.

Line 3 rigid satin cloth: Susan MacDonald explains this as follows – satin cloth is used to line a coffin.

Line 4 blight: usually plant disease but can also mean a malignant influence.

Line 13 appall: to make pale is the literal meaning.

Lines 13/14: Frost biographer Jay Parini reads these two lines as an expression of the idea that God is not in heaven and all is not right with the world. According to Parini, the two lines refer to 'a small aberration in the natural order that he has observed – a white spider with a dead white moth on a white (instead of blue) heal-all'.

As a teenager, Frost read *Our Place Among Infinities* by Richard A. Proctor, which focuses on the evolution of the universe, theology and cosmology. Jay Parini, one of Frost's biographers, points out that it was in Proctor that Frost first came across the 'argument from design'; this became a subject in 'Design,' which, according to Parini, is 'one of Frost's most ferocious, and original poems.'

This sonnet was originally called 'In White' and an earlier version of the poem, written in 1912, reads as follows:

In White

A dented spider like a snow drop white
On a white Heal-all, holding up a moth
Like a white piece of lifeless satin cloth —
Saw ever curious eye so strange a sight? —
Portent in little, assorted death and blight
Like the ingredients of a witches' broth? —
The beady spider, the flower like a froth,
And the moth carried like a paper kite.

What had that flower to do with being white,
The blue prunella every child's delight.
What brought the kindred spider to that height?
(Make we no thesis of the miller's* plight.)
What but design of darkness and of night?
Design, design! Do I use the word aright?

(*miller's plight = miller-moth's plight.)

'Design' was first published in *American Poetry* in 1922, when Frost was forty-eight. Jay Parini says that this poem reflects on the conflict between idealism and natural science. Frost did not publish it in book form until fourteen years later. 'Design' is a sonnet, one of the most designed of poetic structures.

? Questions

1. The American scholar Lionel Trilling says that the universe Frost conceives is a 'terrifying universe.' Read the poem called 'Design', says Trilling, and see if you sleep the better for it. Do you find it a disturbing poem?
2. Once, having read this poem, Robert Frost told his audience: 'I always wanted to be observing. But I have always been afraid of my own observations.' What could have frightened Frost about this poem?
3. In this poem, the speaker describes a fact: a spider kills a moth. How do you interpret 'Mixed' in line 5? Would you agree that complex meanings are found in this simple fact?
4. Does the spider strike you as attractive or unattractive? Give reasons for your answer.
5. What is meant by the title? How have the spider, the moth and the flower come together?
6. It has been suggested that this poem poses the two-fold question 'Is there an overall plan or is life random; are we all on our own in a terrifying way?' What do you think of this interpretation and can you suggest how such an interpretation came about?
7. How does the octave differ from the sestet? How would you describe the speaker's tone in the closing lines of the poem?
8. Comment on the significance of 'in the night' and 'darkness'. Do you think it possible to say whether this is an optimistic or a pessimistic poem?

Provide, Provide

The witch that came (the withered hag)
To wash the steps with pail and rag
Was once the beauty Abishag,

The picture pride of Hollywood.
Too many fall from great and good
For you to doubt the likelihood.

Die early and avoid the fate.
Or if predestined to die late,
Make up your mind to die in state.

Make the whole stock exchange your own!
If need be occupy a throne,
Where nobody can call *you* crone.

Some have relied on what they knew,
Others on being simply true.
What worked for them might work for you.

No memory of having starred
Atones for later disregard
Or keeps the end from being hard.

Better to go down dignified
With boughten friendship at your side
Than none at all. Provide, provide!

Glossary

Line 3 Abishag: a beautiful young woman who comforted the biblical King David in his old age. This is a reference to the Book of Kings (1) in the Old Testament, 1: 1–4. 'Now King David was old and stricken in years; and they covered him with clothes, but he gat no heat. Wherefore his servants said unto him, Let there be sought for my lord the king a young virgin: and let her stand before the king, and let her cherish him, and let her lie in thy bosom, that my lord the king may get heat. So they sought for a fair damsel throughout all the coasts of Israel, and found Abishag a Shunammite, and brought her to the king. And the damsel was very fair and cherished the king, and ministered to him: but the king knew her not.'

Line 12 crone: withered old woman.

Line 17 Atones: make amends/make up for.

Line 20 boughten: bought.

Questions

1. 'Make the whole stock exchange your own!' This poem focuses on the need for holding on to our money. The speaker urges the readers to hold on to enough money so that they will die in comfort. But how would you describe the tone of the poem?

2. 'Too many fall from great and good.' What lesson is being taught here?

3. What is the effect of putting Abishag, an Old Testament figure, and Hollywood side by side?

4. Do you think there are elements in the poem that resemble fable or fairy tale?

5. Do you agree or disagree with the ideas contained in the final stanza? Give reasons for your answer.

6. How does this poem compare and contrast with the other Robert Frost poems on your course?

General Questions

A. 'Frost himself said that a poem 'begins in delight and ends in wisdom'. Discuss this view, supporting your answer by reference to, and quotation from, the poems by Frost on your course.

B. Robert Frost's poetry has been described, by Amy Lowell, as 'photographic'. 'The pictures, the characters, are reproduced directly from life'. Would you agree with this description? Support the points you make with the aid of suitable quotation or reference.

C. 'The poetry of Robert Frost is a poetry of deep feeling and sharp observation.' Would you agree with this assessment of the poet's work? In your answer, you should refer to, or quote from, the poems by Frost on your course.

D. 'In Frost's poetry, nature is a teacher and a source of inspiration.' Discuss this view and support your discussion by quotation from, or reference to, the poems by Robert Frost you have studied.

E. Write a short essay on the aspects of Robert Frost's poems that you found most interesting. Support your discussion by reference to, or quotation from, the poems you have studied.

F. 'Though place is important, Robert Frost, in his poetry, is more interested in human nature rather than Mother Nature.' Discuss this view, supporting your answer by reference to, or quotation from, the poems you have studied.

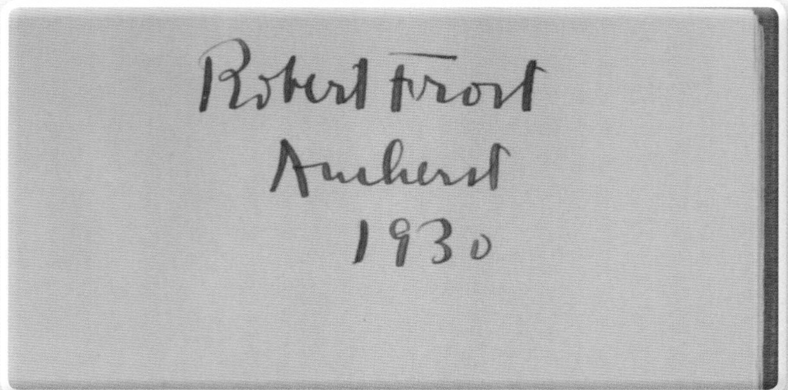

Frost's signature

Critical Commentary

The Tuft of Flowers

'Nature Poet' is a well-known literary category and Robert Frost has sometimes been termed a Nature Poet. Titles such as 'The Tuft of Flowers', 'Mending Wall', 'After Apple-Picking', 'Birches' suggest rural, pastoral scenes. But 'Nature Poet' does not do Frost's poetry justice and Frost himself said: 'I'm not a Nature Poet. I've only written two poems without a human being in them. Only two. All my poems have got a person in them.' Frost also believed that nature is cruel.

The ten poems here depict country scenes and country landscapes, but they also explore moral landscapes; they explore the nature of friendship, choice, isolation, loneliness and death. Poets, Frost once said, 'like to talk in parables and in hints and in indirections' and what may appear as a simple, straightforward poem rewards repeated readings. He also said that his poems were 'written in parable so the wrong people won't understand and so be saved'.

'The Tuft of Flowers', forty lines in all, consists of twenty couplets, each one perfectly rhymed, and the opening line captures something quintessential about Robert Frost: the personal voice, the casual, easy tone, the idea of man in the landscape.

> I went to turn the grass once . . .

This is the common man speaking a language close to natural speech. And yet the rhyming couplets give the poem a formality and an ordered, steady rhythm.

The title 'The Tuft of Flowers' suggests flowers in the landscape – growing, not cut, flowers. Frost begins with a gesture of fellowship. The speaker is going to help his neighbour who has mowed the grass early that morning:

> I went to turn the grass once after one
> Who mowed it in the dew before the sun.

Every word here is simple; almost every word is a monosyllable. The opening couplet begins the story of the poem and the narrative can be summed up as follows: 'The Tuft of Flowers' tells of how a man goes to help his neighbour only to discover that his neighbour, who had worked alone, has gone and now the speaker is alone. He sees a butterfly and watches as it flies, leading him eventually to a tall tuft of flowers which the mower had spared earlier.

But Frost's poem is so much more. He understands and interprets beyond the surface level; he learns and he teaches and he ends with a moralising couplet. The poem moves at a leisurely pace. The rhythm of the speaker's voice is unhurried and straightforward verbs such as 'I went', 'I came', 'I looked', 'I listened' convey this measured, relaxed tone:

> I went to turn the grass once after one
> Who mowed it in the dew before the sun.
>
> The dew was gone that made his blade so keen
> Before I came to view the leveled scene.
>
> I looked for him behind an isle of trees;
> I listened for his whetstone on the breeze.

The slow pace is also achieved by the comma and the full stop. Each couplet ends with a pause.

The speaker's neighbour is noted for his absence. The mower is not to be seen or heard; the dew has disappeared and so has he. The speaker looks and listens.

> But he had gone his way, the grass all mown,
> And I must be, as he had been — alone

The mower worked alone in the meadow; the speaker now finds himself alone in the same meadow; 'alone' becomes a key word in that Frost is not just talking about being alone in this particular place at a particular time. He dwells on the idea of being alone, whether we are on our own or not. When the poet does realise that he is alone, he recognises that being alone is essentially a part of the human condition:

> 'As all must be,' I said within my heart,
> 'Whether they work together or apart.'

The phrase 'within my heart' would suggest that it is a felt experience. He knows himself that there is an inescapable loneliness in man 'Whether they work together or apart'. The use of 'they' here, not 'we', widens the poem into a sense of all mankind, not just the poet and his neighbour.

And yet that loneliness is qualified by the world of nature. Just as the poet is recognising and admitting that he must be alone, a butterfly appears:

> But as I said it, swift there passed me by
> On noiseless wing a bewildered butterfly,
>
> Seeking with memories grown dim o'er night
> Some resting flower of yesterday's delight.

The butterfly is perplexed, confused, bewildered because it is searching for a flower it visited yesterday. The busyness of the butterfly contrasts with the 'resting flower'; yesterday, the butterfly found calm and it seeks it out again. The memories of the flower that delighted the butterfly the previous day, the poet suggests, have grown dim overnight. Frost's use of 'o'er' is quaint and archaic and sounds out of place in a poem whose language is close to natural speech, but if 'over' were used it would break the iambic pentameter. The butterfly, faintly remembering and seeking 'yesterday's delight', becomes an image of a memory and a search for happiness.

Initially, the butterfly flies 'round and round' and only finds a flower 'withering on the ground'; it then flies on only to return trembling.

> And once I marked his flight go round and round,
> As where some flower lay withering on the ground.
>
> And then he flew as far as eye could see,
> And then on tremulous wing came back to me.

At this point, the poet admits that the butterfly, seeking and not finding, prompts him to think of unanswerable questions:

> I thought of questions that have no reply,
> And would have turned to toss the grass to dry

The speaker would have turned to the business in hand, the ordinary and necessary work that needs to be done, but the butterfly draws his eye and attention to the tuft of flowers:

> But he turned first, and led my eye to look
> At a tall tuft of flowers beside a brook,
>
> A leaping tongue of bloom the scythe had spared
> Beside a reedy brook the scythe had bared.

All around is the mown grass, lying flat, and the image of the 'leaping tongue of bloom' is all the more singular and powerful by contrast. The image of 'leaping tongue' may echo the tongues of fire representing the Holy Spirit in the Bible, suggesting perhaps a spiritual dimension.

The butterfly entered the poem at line 11 and its activity and presence are central to the poem as a whole. This poem, says Frost, is about fellowship and it is the butterfly that unites the mower and the speaker. The butterfly connects yesterday with today in that the poet imagines that the butterfly is returning to that same tuft of flowers it visited yesterday. And, earlier that morning in the dew, the tuft of flowers was spared by the mower because he had loved them. Had the butterfly not appeared the speaker might not have noticed that these flowers, left standing, symbolise the mower's kindness and eye for beauty. Just as somebody in Elizabeth Bishop's poem 'Filling Station' arranged the oil cans in an orderly fashion and the apparently insignificant gesture was seen by Bishop as life-enhancing, so, too, is the gesture here of sparing the tuft of flowers. These flowers were considered special by the mower and the following lines were singled out by Frost himself as crucial:

> The mower in the dew had loved them thus,
> By leaving them to flourish, not for us,
>
> Nor yet to draw one thought of ours to him,
> But from sheer morning gladness at the brim.

But the speaker here claims no connection with his fellow worker, nor any connection in the mower's mind between him and the speaker. The mower spared the flowers and allowed them to flourish 'not for us' and not so that someone might think of the mower. Instead, he, in his early morning happiness, spared them for themselves. There is a spiritual rather than a physical connection between the two.

The poet welcomes the butterfly and the flowers. The experience has allowed him to imagine vividly the dawn and the presence of the mower:

> The butterfly and I had lit upon,
> Nevertheless, a message from the dawn,
>
> That made me hear the wakening birds around,
> And hear his long scythe whispering to the ground

There's a double time-scheme at work here in that the dawn, with its sounds of wakening bird song and whispering scythe, is brought alive in the poet's imagination later that same day. He thinks of the mower working earlier as 'a kindred spirit' and his loneliness is dispelled. He feels

> a spirit kindred to my own;
> So that henceforth I worked no more alone

In the closing lines, there is no sense of aloneness. In fact, the earlier lines 'alone/ "As all must be," . . . "Whether they work together or apart."' are now contradicted. The closing couplet says the exact opposite and leading towards that conclusion he offers a warm sense of companionable ease. This is particularly seen in such words as 'glad', 'aid', 'brotherly', 'together':

> But glad with him, I worked as with his aid,
> And weary, sought at noon with him the shade;
>
> And dreaming, as it were, held brotherly speech
> With one whose thought I had not hoped to reach.
>
> 'Men work together,' I told him from the heart,
> 'Whether they work together or apart.'

The ending is idyllic. Two men take a break from working together and rest in the shade at noon; their speech is 'brotherly' and there is a sense of ease and understanding between the two. But the word 'dreaming' reminds us that the speaker did not meet with the mower, nor did he sit and relax with him and hold 'brotherly speech'. It was a desire, a dream that does not become a reality within the poem. But the mood with which the poem ends is, nonetheless, a mood of ease and calm, made possible by the poet's new understanding. The academic William H. Pritchard says that 'the poem asks us to believe that things do come together in wonderful and surprising ways'.

'I told him from the heart' (line 39) echoes 'I said within my heart' (line 9) and both heartfelt statements are preoccupied with fellowship and the possibility of fellowship. But between line 9 and 39, he has changed his mind. The poet concludes that there is a bond between men, 'Whether they work together or apart'. This bond is possible but, as the poem proves, it is something which the poet experiences on his own. In this instance, he is working apart, but he feels close to his fellow man and what made that feeling possible was the tuft of flowers. The poem seems relatively straightforward: Frost explores an everyday, familiar landscape and this gives way to a meditation on the relationship between man and his fellow man. Frank Lentricchia, the American literary critic, sees 'The Tuft of Flowers' as a poem in which Frost 'dramatises the urge of self to move out of isolation and toward community'.

Mending Wall

The opening line in this poem reads more like a conclusion. It has the power of a proverb and sums up a way of viewing the world, an outlook on life; it serves, it could be argued, as a definition of the human spirit. The phrase 'Something there is' is more effective than 'There is something . . .' Line 1, on its own, could mean that there is a feeling or an attitude that does not like coming up against a wall, a barrier or meeting with opposition:

> Something there is that doesn't love a wall

However, lines 2–4 are more specific and we discover that the poet is referring to frost:

> Something there is that doesn't love a wall,
> That sends the frozen-ground-swell under it
> And spills the upper boulders in the sun,
> And makes gaps even two can pass abreast.

The frost is powerful and destructive; it can destroy the man-made wall, but we are also told that the same frost can make a gap whereby two can pass abreast. This detail may suggest that the broken wall which separated man from man can now be passed by two abreast. The wall is a solid, substantial one – it contains boulders – and yet it comes tumbling down. The use of 'spills' captures the power of nature and, though the poet does not name the 'something' that 'sends the frozen-ground-swell under it', it is the power of frost.

But there is another reason for the broken wall. Line 5 suggests that hunters often destroy a wall and the speaker has had to repair the damage. That they can be so careless and yet so calculating is referred to in lines 5–9:

> The work of hunters is another thing:
> I have come after them and made repair
> Where they have left not one stone on a stone,
> But they would have the rabbit out of hiding,
> To please the yelping dogs.

Speaking of the poem, Frost said that it 'contrasts two types of people' and it tells of how two farmers repair a wall. The speaker of the poem is the one who initiates the mending; he is the one who wants to maintain the wall. These two farmers meet in spring-time and their meeting and walking the wall is described as easy, natural, a kind of ritual:

> I let my neighbour know beyond the hill;
> And on a day we meet to walk the line
> And set the wall between us once again.
> We keep the wall between us as we go.

The wall is both itself and is a metaphor. As so often in Frost's poetry, it is the everyday and ordinary – a road in a wood or, in this instance, a wall – that reveal deeper meanings. His imagery is not remote or esoteric, but the American writer Jay Parini thinks that here, as in so many of Frost's best poems, 'various levels in the poem may be discerned and these are often contradictory'. The language could hardly be simpler and yet it contains layers of both meaning and understanding. Frost uses repetition and a slant rhyme in 'line'/'again'; 'the wall between us' is the central idea and that the lines do not rhyme perfectly may suggest the necessary but not ideal connection between the speaker and his neighbour. The re-building of the wall, though, does allow the 'I' and the 'he' of the poem to become 'we' – 'We wear our fingers rough . . .'

There is humour in the way the speaker describes the boulders on either side as 'loaves' and 'nearly balls' and in how he thinks of them as having minds of their own:

> We have to use a spell to make them balance:
> 'Stay where you are until our backs are turned!'

The humour is found also in his seeing the wall-mending as a game.

> We wear our fingers rough with handling them.
> Oh, just another kind of outdoor game,
> One on a side

And there is more humour in the playful way he imagines his apple trees moving into his neighbour's territory to eat the pine-cones. The wall is not necessary for the entire length of the boundary; there are places where 'we do not need the wall', but his neighbour disagrees and deploys a maxim:

> There where it is we do not need the wall:
> He is all pine and I am apple orchard.
> My apple trees will never get across
> And eat the cones under his pines, I tell him.
> He only says, 'Good fences make good neighbors.'

The neighbour is taciturn, reserved, uncommunicative; the speaker becomes mischievous and wonders

> If I could put a notion in his head:
> 'Why do they make good neighbors? . . .'

And then there follows the thoughts the speaker would like his neighbour to think. The speaker was the one who set this wall-mending in motion and the neighbour contradicts him in this imagined monologue. But it is the poet who has thought these thoughts; there is an implied wish that both men would think the same. There is no need for a wall, he suggests. If there were cows on the land, a wall would be necessary, 'But here there are no cows'.

It is at this point that the poem opens out to become a philosophical or questioning work. The *idea* of the wall, more than an actual wall, is more interesting when he asks:

> Before I built a wall I'd ask to know
> What I was walling in or walling out,
> And to whom I was like to give offense.

This interest in knowing, this way of seeing a wall as both exclusion and inclusion and the speaker's sensitivity to others all indicate a deep-thinking individual. The speaker is also, perhaps, punning when he says 'offense'. The reader is only told one thing that the neighbour says. The poet attributes a philosophical dimension to his neighbour in lines 30–36, but he actually never speaks those lines. That the poet imagines the neighbour speaking the poem's opening line would suggest that both men are in agreement:

> Something there is that doesn't love a wall,
> That wants it down.

The speaker's playful, imaginative suggestion of elves is never spoken either. It is as if the neighbour is too dull to understand ('he moves in darkness'). Indeed, the poem contains much that is left unsaid:

> I could say 'Elves' to him,
> But it's not elves exactly, and I'd rather
> He said it for himself.

And the poem ends with a portrait of this neighbour as some form of prehistoric man, a savage from the stone age:

> I see him there,
> Bringing a stone grasped firmly by the top
> In each hand, like an old-stone savage armed.
> He moves in darkness as it seems to me,
> Not of woods only and the shade of trees.

But one who, nevertheless, has a deep belief in continuing an age-old tradition:

> He will not go behind his father's saying,
> And he likes having thought of it so well
> He says again, 'Good fences make good neighbors.'

Therefore, there is no change. The wall is repaired and will continue, it would seem, to be repaired. Yet much of the poem is directed against the proposition that 'Good fences make good neighbors'.

For Jay Parini it is 'as if civilisation depends upon the collective activity of making barriers. There is a lot of "making" and "mending" in this poem, and it is more than a wall that is erected. One senses a profound commitment to the act of creating community in the speaker, who allies his voice with the "something" that sends frozen ground swells under the walls to disrupt it.' And Parini adds that 'The energy of the speaker's imagination unsettles and builds at the same time, a paradoxical motion that would seem to lie at the heart of the creative process itself.'

'Mending Wall', in unrhymed iambic pentameter (blank verse), appears on the page as a solid block, forty-five lines long. The text itself could be a wall and the words themselves explore the building up and the breaking down of the wall. Twenty-five years after writing this poem, Frost described himself as 'both wall-builder and wall-destroyer'. He also added, in a tone as mischievous as that in the poem, that regarding the closing line, 'People are frequently misunderstanding it or misinterpreting it. The secret of what it means I keep.'

After Apple-Picking

This is what the Irish poet Seamus Heaney called a 'gift poem' and he went on to explain how Frost made and wrote out the poem without fumbling a line. Heaney added that 'it does have that sense of something willowy and yielding. The rhythmic principle there is in the slight sway of the ladder on the yielding bough'.

Autumn and the apple harvest, especially in New England, conjure up a time of beauty and plenty. The English writer D. M. Thomas thinks this poem is 'a celebration of abundance' and, though the opening lines are matter-of-fact, they also capture a dreamy feeling with their references to 'heaven' and 'winter sleep' and the 'scent of apples' and the sweet tiredness that comes with the bringing in of the harvest:

> My long two-pointed ladder's sticking through a tree
> Toward heaven still,
> And there's a barrel that I didn't fill
> Beside it, and there may be two or three
> Apples I didn't pick upon some bough.

The sentence flows through these five lines in a tone that suggests tiredness and completion. The two-pointed ladder is not pointing towards the sky but 'toward heaven' and the mention of heaven suggests a place beyond the ordinary, but he does not dwell on it; the activity of apple-picking goes on between heaven and earth; in other words, apple-picking is half-way to heaven.

The second sentence is one line long and it slows down the poem:

> But I am done with apple-picking now.

That this is part of a rhyming couplet adds to the effect. The mood of the speaker here is one of quiet acceptance. There are some apples still on the tree and 'there's a barrel that I didn't fill', but the speaker is content to stop. The activity of apple-picking is drawing to a close. He is tired, drowsing off, and the poem becomes an image for life itself and its drawing to an end. Maurice Woolman, commenting on the poem, says that 'the concrete experience of apple-picking is communicated firmly and realistically, but the task has a more universal application. The task of apple-picking is any task; it is life.' The harvest could be seen here as the creative and imaginative work of the poet.

The speaker drowsily remembers a moment earlier that day when he looked at the world through a sheet of ice. Actual happenings and sensations combine in the speaker's mind:

> Essence of winter sleep is on the night,
> The scent of apples: I am drowsing off.
> I cannot rub the strangeness from my sight
> I got from looking through a pane of glass
> I skimmed this morning from the drinking trough
> And held against the world of hoary grass.

The ice melted; he let it fall and break, but the strangeness remains. His way of viewing the world, then, remains with him. Though it was morning, the speaker connects morning with night-time in his awareness of how morning inevitably leads to night and sleep:

> But I was well
> Upon my way to sleep before it fell,
> And I could tell
> What form my dreaming was about to take.

These lines would seem as if the speaker has a sense of what is to come and everything seems relaxed and easy. 'I am drowsing off' is in the present tense; then it moves to the past – 'I skimmed . . . It melted . . .' and then the speaker imagines the future – 'I could tell/ What form my dreaming was about to take'. This drifting from present to past and his awareness of what is about to happen reflect the speaker's meditative mood.

The dream itself, with its strange almost surreal imagery, begins in line 18. The once familiar apples change size, seem bigger, appear and disappear:

> Magnified apples appear and disappear,
> Stem end and blossom end,
> And every fleck of russet showing clear.

The apples appear before him, both ends, and their colours intense and vivid. The speaker is haunted by his time picking apples; he still aches; the sensation of apple-picking is still felt:

> My instep arch not only keeps the ache,
> It keeps the pressure of a ladder-round.

He dreams not only of what he saw (the russet apples) and what he felt (the movement of the ladder against the trees):

> I feel the ladder sway as the boughs bend.

The dream is one that will not go away – 'I keep hearing' – and line 24 introduces a mood of tired fulfilment. First there is the plentiful harvest, but this is described as a 'rumbling sound' as the 'load on load of apples' reach the cellar bin:

> And I keep hearing from the cellar bin
> The rumbling sound
> Of load on load of apples coming in.

Then lines 27–31 tell of the speaker's exhaustion. He once desired a great harvest, as captured in the hyperbole 'ten thousand thousand fruit'; he wanted once to hold each apple carefully, to lift it down and not damage it, but now he has reached a stage where this is no longer his desire:

> For I have had too much
> Of apple-picking: I am overtired
> Of the great harvest I myself desired.
> There were ten thousand thousand fruit to touch,
> Cherish in hand, lift down, and not let fall.

However, not every apple was 'not let fall'. There are spoilt apples, 'bruised or spiked', and these end up as useless or 'no worth'. Heaven figured in the opening lines, but the cider-apple heap is, according to some interpretations, in a way the opposite to heaven.

> For all
> That struck the earth,
> No matter if not bruised or spiked with stubble,
> Went surely to the cider-apple heap
> As of no worth.

Jay Parini, the writer and academic, considers 'After Apple-Picking' as a meditation on the art of poetry itself. The poet draws on memory and Parini sees a parallel between the store of apples and the poet's remembering. The cellar bin is full and Parini argues that there is 'a bin stored with imagery that he could draw on. There seemed no end to the poems he might fashion from this experience, and even that material which had not yet been transformed into poetry was still there, waiting, like the apples that had struck the earth and been transported to the cider-apple heap – a hoard that would create a certain amount of anxiety in the poet that time until he found the creative energy to raid it.'

That some apples ended up in this way troubles the speaker: he knows that his sleep will be disturbed by his realisation that, while some apples were put to good use, others were spoilt, that he did not use them all to best advantage.

He also knows that he is heading towards sleep and his description of it as 'whatever sleep it is' would suggest that it is his final, long sleep.

> One can see what will trouble
> This sleep of mine, whatever sleep it is.

The speaker is all alone in this poem. Even the woodchuck has gone into hibernation. The speaker wonders if his sleep will be like that of the woodchuck:

> Were he not gone,
> The woodchuck could say whether it's like his
> Long sleep, as I describe its coming on,
> Or just some human sleep.

These closing lines achieve a special quality – quiet, sleep-inducing and drawing slowly to a close.

'After Apple-Picking' contains both whimsical and serious observations about man's relationship with nature: whimsical when he speaks of 'ten thousand thousand' apples, serious when he confesses his tiredness, his troubled mind and his longing for sleep.

It is also said to be a poem that explores the way the imagination works. Reuben A. Brower, American academic and former student of Frost's, saw 'After Apple-Picking' as a 'lyric-idyll'. It is musical in its rhymes and cadences, but idyllic implies an attractive picture of rustic life, whereas Frost offers more than a pretty picture.

For the most part, in 'After Apple-Picking', Frost uses iambic pentameter and it is used here, in D. M. Thomas's words, with 'exquisite naturalness and lyricism'. And unlike 'Mending Wall' or 'Birches', which are written in unrhymed iambic pentameter or blank verse, 'After Apple-Picking' is in perfectly rhymed iambic pentameter. Every end-word in every line is rhymed but the run-on line and the varying rhyme scheme make for a subtle music. For example, the opening twelve lines have the following rhyme scheme: abba cc ded fef. Later in lines 14–16, there is a three-line rhyme. The rhymes emphasise important words.

Seamus Heaney cautioned that if 'After Apple-Picking' is 'taught in a melodramatic way, saying that it's a poem about death, it robs it of all its life'.

The Road Not Taken

This, together with 'Stopping by Woods on a Snowy Evening', is Frost's best-known poem. At poetry readings, Frost sometimes advised his audience that it was a tricky one. The setting is immediately grasped: a traveller comes to a fork in a woodland path in autumn and has to choose one road. He chooses the one which fewer, it seems, have chosen; the other road intrigues him and he imagines that he will regret not having travelled that road in years to come. However, there's a mischievous, contradictory and somewhat unsatisfactory aspect to this poem. The speaker, in line two, wishes that he could have travelled both roads, then chooses the one supposedly less travelled and concludes that both roads were well-travelled, both were 'worn . . . really about the same'; and yet he returns to the idea, in line nineteen, that he took the one less-travelled by. William H. Pritchard, author of *Frost: A Literary Life Reconsidered* (1984), thinks that the poem sounds noble but is really mischievous. In his view, 'The Road Not Taken' is a poem 'which announced itself to be "abc[illegible] important issues in life: about the nature of choice, of decision, of how to go in one direction rather than another and how to feel about the direction you took and didn't take'.

The poem begins with an exceptionally long sentence that flows through two stanzas and comes to a full-stop at line 12. There is no difficult or unusual word here and the idea is one that every reader can respond to. The idea of a journey is a familiar one; an actual journey is frequently used by writers and becomes a metaphor for life's journey.

The image here is a beautiful one. An autumn woodland is simply and effectively evoked in the word 'yellow' and the mood is one of regret. The speaker is 'sorry' that he 'could not travel both'. If it were possible to travel both roads, to 'be one traveler', then he would have had both experiences, but he acknowledges this impossibility. He has to make a choice. The poem focuses on our having to choose and the significance of the choice made. The tone is measured and calm, the rhyming scheme unusual and regular (abaab cdccd efeef ghggh). The poem is personal; the speaker uses 'I' nine times but the poem's subject matter invites the reader in, rather than excludes.

To Frost, it doesn't seem to matter much which road he took, or didn't take. Some critics think that it is that indifference which should have been the real subject of the poem. And yet it could be argued that the journey intrigues him and he considers the choice important:

> . . . long I stood
> And looked down one as far as I could
> To where it bent in the undergrowth

So much so that he carefully examines one road before taking the other. He chooses the road less-travelled; both roads are attractive but the one which drew him was the one

> . . . having perhaps the better claim,
> Because it was grassy and wanted wear

The realisation that this road is 'really about the same' comes immediately. He thinks it less-travelled in line 8; in lines 9 and 10, he tells us that he was wrong.

Line 11 refers to morning, which suggests beginnings, and 'yellow wood' suggests autumn, the dying of the year. The poet, therefore, it could be said, captures both beginnings and endings within the one poem. The speaker is young in that he imagines a time 'ages and ages hence' when he will look back on this important morning when he had to make a choice that 'made all the difference'. The mood of regret in the poem's final stanza echoes that same mood from the opening lines:

> I shall be telling this with a sigh
> Somewhere ages and ages hence:
> Two roads diverged in a wood, and I—
> I took the one less traveled by,
> And that has made all the difference.

He does not specify the nature of that difference and nor could he, in that it belongs to the realm of philosophical speculation.

The poem's penultimate line contradicts lines 9 and 10 which, in turn, had contradicted lines 7 and 8 which described the poet's first impressions of the two roads. If you were to read these lines in succession, the contradiction becomes evident: one was less-travelled; it was not less-travelled; I took the less travelled road. William H. Pritchard, in his study of Frost, says that 'the mischievous aspect of "The Road Not Taken" is what makes it un-boring'. Pritchard argues that the large moral meaning which 'The Road Not Taken' seems to endorse – go, as I did, your own way, take the road less travelled by, and it will make 'all the difference' – does not maintain itself when the poem is looked at more carefully.

Frost himself said that he was 'fooling my way along' in 'The Road Not Taken' and that he had written it for his friend, the English poet Edward Thomas, because, when they walked together, Thomas always chastised himself for not taking the other path than the one they took. When Frost sent the poem to Thomas, he replied saying 'I doubt if you can get anybody to see the fun of the thing without showing them and advising them which kind of laugh they are to turn on.'

Birches

'Birches', like 'Mending Wall' and 'After Apple-Picking', is what has been termed a 'meditative lyric'. It begins with an easy, relaxed tone and with a description of birches against 'straighter darker trees', an image of freedom and movement against rigidity, stasis, darkness. This poem has what the Irish poet and publisher Peter Fallon calls Frost's 'simple, pure, attractive music and a narrative that contains mysteries and complexities':

> When I see birches bend to left and right
> Across the lines of straighter trees,
> I like to think some boy's been swinging them.

The image is one of man and nature and man in nature, or rather boy in nature. The boy's presence is seen in the bent birches and, though the speaker does not know for certain that the birches have been swung, he likes to think 'some boy's been swinging them'. Nature, as represented by 'lines of straighter darker trees', is a distant, forbidding presence, but the image of the boy swinging on birches is a much warmer, sensuous, more inviting, more involving one.

The speaker then dwells on how the birches' movements are affected not only by man but by ice storms. Such storms have an even greater effect on the trees in that the ice bends them down 'to stay':

> But swinging doesn't bend them down to stay
> As ice storms do.

The reader is invited to share in, and agree with, this observation. The tone is welcoming; the reader is addressed directly in 'you':

> Often you must have seen them
> Loaded with ice a sunny winter morning
> After a rain

And in the following two expansive sentences, Frost describes in atmospheric detail the sounds and shapes of these birches. It is as if the trees have energies and personalities of their own:

> They click upon themselves
> As the breeze rises, and turn many-colored
> As the stir cracks and crazes their enamel.

The clicking, cracking, crazing sounds here are accurate and effective, creating an onomatopoeic description of the ice-coated trees moving very gradually in the breeze. A more dramatic movement follows, accompanying the thaw:

> Soon the sun's warmth makes them shed crystal shells
> Shattering and avalanching on the snow crust—-
> Such heaps of broken glass to sweep away
> You'd think the inner dome of heaven had fallen.

The trees' icy coatings or shells break up and fall from the birches, but Frost, in the image of the avalanche, creates a huge drama in miniature. The cracked and shattered ice is given a domestic touch in the metaphor of 'broken glass to sweep away' and then the emphasis shifts from the domestic to the cosmic when he imagines that the inner dome of heaven has shattered and collapsed upon earth in the form of these icy splinters among the birch trees.

The effect of the winter ice-storms is long-term: the birches are dragged down by the weight of the ice, so much so that they never right themselves, and years later their arching trunks reveal their history:

> They are dragged to the withered bracken by the load,
> And they seem not to break; though once they are bowed
> So low for long, they never right themselves

Frost shares his observations with his reader in a gentle and inviting way:

> You may see their trunks arching in the woods
> Years afterwards, trailing their leaves on the ground

Nature itself has altered and distorted these trees and, even though the birches have been affected by winters, Frost, in a natural and attractive simile, conveys a sense of how these trees are still youthful, fluid and feminine. The trees, Frost says, in an image which turns nature human, are

> Like girls on hands and knees that throw their hair
> Before them over their heads to dry in the sun.

and immediately follows this image with what Jay Parini calls 'the rambling quality of everyday speech': 'But I was going to say when Truth broke in / With all her matter of fact about the ice-storm . . .' This introduces a distinctly casual touch and the poet is differentiating between what he calls 'Truth' (the ice-storms) and imagination. The birches are bent, in reality by the ice, but Frost prefers to conjure up a different reason:

> I should prefer to have some boy bend them
> As he went out and in to fetch the cows—

At the heart of the poem is this image of the boy. Lines 23–40 summon up a freedom-loving, daring, physical, lonely boy whom Frost sees as his former and younger self. The boy is a solitary, resourceful figure:

> Some boy too far from town to learn baseball,
> Whose only play was what he found himself,
> Summer or winter, and could play alone

And in his own way rebellious:

> One by one he subdued his father's trees
> By riding them down over and over again
> Until he took the stiffness out of them

The boy subdues and conquers all the birches:

> And not one but hung limp, not one was left
> For him to conquer.

The pleasure of being a swinger of birches is charted in stages. There is, in Parini's words, anticipation, exhilaration, fulfilment and the letting down at the end. The isolated boy learns how to delay the pleasure by 'not launching out too soon' and, after careful, controlled planning, there is a great sense of delight, captured especially in the words 'flung', 'feet first', 'swish', 'Kicking':

He learned all there was
To learn about not launching out too soon
And so not carrying the tree away
Clear to the ground. He always kept his poise
To the top branches, climbing carefully
With the same pains you use to fill a cup
Up to the brim, and even above the brim.
Then he flung outward, feet first, with a swish,
Kicking his way down through the air to the ground.

This poem falls into three sections. First, the speaker, in the opening twenty lines, focuses on the distinctive qualities of birches; in the second section – lines 21–40 – the poet imagines a boy at play, swinging birches; and in the final section the speaker reminisces on his own boyhood and meditates on his life. This third section begins with two self-contained lines (the final two lines in the poem use a similar technique); each one is a sentence and the punctuation and the short line slow down the poem's movement:

So was I once myself a swinger of birches.
And so I dream of going back to be.

The repetition of 'so' and the use of 'once', 'dream' and 'going back' suggest a wistful, nostalgic mood. Frost longs for the freedom of that boy he once was and he uses an image of a wood to convey his understanding of adult life, with its difficulties and uncertainties. Life, for the adult speaker, is 'too much like a pathless wood' and the experience of travelling through this wood hurts. He dreams of going back when life becomes oppressive, when he is weighed down by thinking. The freedom of the imagination is preferred and so he dreams of again becoming a swinger of birches:

It's when I'm weary of considerations,
And life is too much like a pathless wood
Where your face burns and tickles with the cobwebs
Broken across it, and one eye is weeping
From a twig's having lashed across it open.

This is a harsh, uncomfortable, troubling landscape. The trees here are seen as negative, their twigs minor irritants. The speaker, for a moment, forgets the birches that he associates with happier times and expresses a desire to leave Earth behind. He longs to escape but only for a while:

I'd like to get away from earth awhile
And then come back to it and begin over.

But he wants to make things clear. He is not rejecting Planet Earth; there is what Seamus Heaney refers to as a 'seesawing between Earth and Heaven' but he thinks Earth, in the end, 'the right place for love':

> May no fate willfully misunderstand me
> And half grant what I wish and snatch me away
> Not to return. Earth's the right place for love:
> I don't know where it's likely to go better.

These lines, unlike so much of the poem which is vivid and atmospheric, are philosophical. The poet has moved from physical to spiritual, from earth to heaven. But earth is chosen over heaven and then, in a playful conclusion, the poet imagines birches as a journey heavenwards. He may aspire heavenwards but he prefers being down to earth. The italicised 'Toward' emphasises his awareness of the birch trees as somewhere between earth and heaven. His wish is simple and there is the pleasure in both the journeying heavenward and returning:

> I'd like to go by climbing a birch tree,
> And climb black branches up a snow-white trunk
> *Toward* heaven, till the tree could bear no more,
> But dipped its top and set me down again.

The sense of exultation here, the movement heavenward and the subsequent down to earth movement, parallels the flight of the imagination and Jay Parini thinks that 'Frost's commonplace theme of the wish to escape, to get away from his earthly troubles, is given perfect symbolic form in the trope [figure] of the boy climbing to heaven on the slender birch.'

Frost in his poetry, according to the British writer and critic Ian Hamilton, has 'confidence in his freedom to ramble on, in order to achieve the triumphs of concentrated and subtle naturalness' that one finds in a poem such as 'Birches'. Here, Hamilton argued, Frost achieves 'the extraordinarily difficult task of both mounting the scene, pictorializing it in vivid and exact detail, and at the same time convincing us that he is – *at this moment* – pursuing a complex and precarious course of feeling, a course of feeling which we can observe shifting and developing as the local drama unfolds. What sustains the tension is the poem's achieved state of presentness, and this is made convincing by the authenticity of Frost's spoken rhythms.'

And Hamilton added that 'The art in the poem "Birches" is in the apparent ease and naturalness of style: the simple narrative contains a parable of human aspiration, evolving through a progression of metaphors so apparently inevitable to the mind and ear that the poem has done its work before one is conscious of it.'

It is worth remembering that, for Frost, a poem 'begins in delight and ends in wisdom'. In 'Birches', the reader by the closing lines has arrived at wisdom, but Frost's wise conclusion is presented not in a self-important or self-conscious or dogmatic way but with quiet perceptiveness:

> That would be good both going and coming back.
> One could do worse than be a swinger of birches.

'Out, Out—'

Seamus Heaney remarked that this was one of the first Frost poems that he read and that his 'primary attraction was a sense of familiarity with the world that was in the poem – a world of actual, hard, rattling, buzz-saw, snarling action of a farmyard'. Heaney, on encountering Frost's poetry, felt that 'Here was a poet who touched things as they are, somehow.'

The subject matter of the poem is horrific and the unexpected, violent death of a boy shocks every reader. The title implies suddenness, abruptness, harshness, as well as the fragility and vulnerability of life. The image, from Shakespeare's *Macbeth*, of a candle being blown out signals the feeling of helplessness that pervades the poem.

In just thirty-four lines, Frost tells a very dramatic and unforgettable story. Line 1 describes the scene with its onomatopoeic 'buzz', 'snarled' and 'rattled'. It's a functional, practical world where work has to be done but, by line 3, the poet reminds us that there is a beauty there too in the scent of cut wood:

> The buzz saw snarled and rattled in the yard
> And made dust and dropped stove-length sticks of wood,
> Sweet-scented stuff when the breeze drew across it.

Phrases such as 'stove-length' root the poem in the real world and Frost's choice of the word 'stuff' is almost a deliberate put-down, following the more poetic, sensuous 'Sweet-scented'. The scene is a practical, everyday one.

The speaker is aware of the landscape and reminds us that the people work against a beautiful, picturesque scene. If they were to look up from their work, they would see mountains and sunset:

> And from there those that lifted eyes could count
> Five mountain ranges one behind the other
> Under the sunset far into Vermont.

But this natural, lyrical beauty is framed by the practical and the necessary. Line 7 returns to the saw and the repetition of its sounds captures the harsh reality. The agressive noise of the saw destroys the silence:

> And the saw snarled and rattled, snarled and rattled

The deliberate repetition imitates the repeated movement of the saw:

> As it ran light, or had to bear a load.

The ordinariness of it all is emphasised when the speaker says:

> And nothing happened: day was all but done.

By line 10, however, there is a sense of unease, a sense of foreboding, of coming danger, when we read:

> Call it a day, I wish they might have said
> To please the boy by giving him the half hour
> That a boy counts so much when saved from work.

The poem now centres on this boy and unlike 'Birches', where the boy enjoyed a release and freedom from work, the boy in 'Out, Out—' is doing a man's job. He is not saved from work this particular evening; 'they' are to blame for his having to work on and the poem describes the fatal accident in an appropriately jagged, nervous language. The lines no longer flow easily. The abrupt sentence, 'But the hand!', expresses the shock, the fright, a sense of the incredible.

The central episode is introduced in words that suggest the family, the domestic – 'His sister stood beside them in her apron'. Ironically, it is when his sister announces 'Supper' that the boy loses control of the saw:

> His sister stood beside them in her apron
> To tell them 'Supper.' At the word, the saw,
> As if to prove saws knew what supper meant,
> Leaped out at the boy's hand, or seemed to leap—
> He must have given the hand.

The episode which prompted this poem was reported in a local newspaper on 31 March 1910. In the newspaper report, Frost read that 'the young man was assisting in sawing up some wood in his own dooryard with a sawing machine and accidentally hit the loose pulley, causing the saw to descend upon his hand . . .'

Frost deliberately changes the factual account and creates for the reader a much more humanly engaged and imaginative account; he includes the boy's sister and suggests that the saw and the hand were destined to meet:

> He must have given the hand. However it was,
> Neither refused the meeting. But the hand!

The buzz saw, a symbol of technological advancement, is the boy's enemy and some critics think that Frost here is reacting to the industrialisation of farming.

The first reaction of the boy is to laugh but it is 'a rueful laugh'. Jay Parini says that 'the "rue" in the boy's laugh is a familiar Frostian note: a wincing grin in which the fate of the boy is seen – by himself as much as the reader – as painfully ironic. The nakedness of the boy's gesture is at once pathetic and appalling.'

> The boy's first outcry was a rueful laugh,
> As he swung toward them holding up the hand,
> Half in appeal, but half as if to keep
> The life from spilling.

The total sense of devastation, fright and helplessness is captured in every detail. They, to whom he turns, were the ones who had him work. He is no longer one of 'them'; he is wounded and dying and he looks to the others there beside him 'half in appeal' but also knowing that his life is 'spilling'. The use of 'spilling' conveys how quickly it is happening and how unstoppable it is. The speaker's tone is both urgent and helpless in the sudden short outburst, 'But the hand!'

The grim reality is known to the boy almost immediately:

> Then the boy saw all—
> Since he was old enough to know, big boy
> Doing a man's work, though a child at heart—
> He saw all spoiled

The boy's only utterance is a desperate plea. The world he belongs to is a world of work where the hand is vital and he does not turn to it now but to his sister:

> 'Don't let him cut my hand off—
> The doctor, when he comes. Don't let him, sister!'

Together with his sister's 'Supper' (line 14), these are the only spoken works in the poem. The first is unremarkable; the second is urgent, dramatic, out of the ordinary.

The closing lines are among the most striking in Frost's poetry. First, the one-word sentence 'So', then the difficult truth 'But the hand was gone already', expressing the inevitability of what has happened. Details are recorded:

> The doctor put him in the dark of ether.
> He lay and puffed his lips out with his breath.

And the 'brief candle' (from Shakespeare) is extinguished forever. The confusion and shock of those watching are contained in the abrupt sentences that lead towards 'nothing!' with its exclamation mark:

> And then – the watcher at his pulse took fright.
> No one believed. They listened at his heart.
> Little—less—nothing!

The nothing here, perhaps, echoes the nothing in Macbeth's speech where he speaks of the futility of life.

The closing lines which then follow are unforgettable and sobering:

> — and that ended it.
> No more to build on there. And they, since they
> Were not the one dead, turned to their affairs.

Critics have viewed these closing lines differently. The words 'since they were not the one dead' suggest a matter-of-fact attitude. It seems, according to William H. Pritchard, that 'the survivors skipped away because in fact they were still alive. And that, the poem says, is what happened. What is there to say – by anyone, including the poet – in the face of such a finality? The answer is that we are powerless, except to change the subject.'

Ian Hamilton says that there is 'a nerveless, anaesthetized cynicism here that one can only believe to be calculated and – in a subtle, disguising but revealing sense – self-examining'. Peter Jones says of these same lines that they capture 'a frightening, inexorably bitter pattern of acceptance.' The Shakespeare speech, from which the words of the title are taken, says that life is 'a tale/ Told by an idiot, full of sound and fury,/ Signifying nothing'. Marie Borroff thinks the speaker 'far from indicating approval of "their" stoical acceptance of bereavement, dismisses them with contempt as they turn to their "affairs".' Seamus Heaney speaks of the poem's 'grim accuracy' and 'documentary weight' and says that he 'did not mistake the wintry report of what happened at the end for the poet's own callousness'.

The Greek poet Homer (c. 8th century B.C.) said that the greatest tribute that you can pay your dead friend is to eat your next meal. Life must go on; life does go on, even after the dreadful and premature death of this boy. Which attitude do you think is conveyed by Frost in the closing lines of this horrifying poem?

Spring Pools

This lyric poem is preoccupied with reflections and, appropriately, both stanzas are of equal length and have similarly patterned rhyming schemes. The speaker is observing how pools of water in the forest mirror the sky overhead and, unlike many of Frost's poems in this selection, it is not a narrative poem but a meditation on the spring.

Each stanza is one sentence long. Stanza one meditates on the passing of time, change and how the pools of water on the forest floor will 'soon be gone'. These pools mirror the 'total sky almost without defect' and the speaker compares the pools to the flowers beside them. Both pools and flowers 'chill and shiver' and both will soon disappear. The flowers will wither and die, but the poet focuses on the disappearing pools, not the flowers. He reminds us that these pools will not disappear 'by any brook or river' and creates a sense of the natural and the mysterious when he speaks of how the water from spring pools is absorbed and drawn upwards through the roots of trees, making possible the dark foliage in late spring and summer. There is an awareness of order here and continuity. The sky gave the snow that formed the pools on the ground and the water in the pools is then drawn into the trees. The speaker does not dwell on scientific fact; he observes and is interested in the quiet workings of nature. The meditative note is captured in the slow line created by commas and by words such as 'though', 'yet', 'but' and the repetition of 'like the flowers beside them':

> And like the flowers beside them, chill and shiver,
> Will like the flowers beside them soon be gone

The American literary critic and novelist Frank Lentricchia says of this first stanza that the 'tiny forest pools and the flowers of spring growing beside them, both magnetizing the poet's loving attention, enjoy only a precarious existence' and he sees the poem as 'a lament for the transience of precarious things'.

The pools in stanza one are bright, open reflections of the wide expanse of sky and the flowers suggest beauty and colour. By contrast, the trees, with their 'dark foliage', dominate stanza two. Frost offers some advice to the trees which are described in terms of having a controlling, selfish nature with words such as 'pent-up', 'darken', 'powers', 'blot out', 'drink up', 'sweep away'. The trees are dependent on the spring pools and, in drawing the water up through their roots, they are drying up the pools and the flowers are made wither and die. The advice given

Let them think twice before they use their powers

of course cannot and will not be heeded. What Frost is observing here is how the passive (pools) and the weak (flowers) do not control their own destiny but are part of the necessary work of the seasons. The trees cannot produce their foliage unless they destroy the spring pools and the phrase 'darken nature' suggests something negative. The trees in leaf will darken the forest floor, that same place which was once bright with pools reflecting the sky. The observer under leafy trees in the forest is no longer able to view the sky.

It is a poem of regret. The speaker prefers the present to the future and the short-lived nature of the spring pools is captured in the poem's final word. Frank Lentriccia thinks this poem is rooted in a vision of violence, in that the dark wood controls and dominates. The poem moves from spring woods to summer woods and, though it is never stated explicitly, the speaker, it seems, prefers the woods in spring. Summer woods have become what they are by powerful, destructive forces.

Jay Parini reads 'Spring Pools' as a poem about poetry and the creative process, and says that water can be taken to mean 'a substance into which one dips for inspiration'. The poet's imagination takes the beautiful world and remakes it, just as the trees suck the pools dry so that they can create their summer leaves.

Acquainted with the Night

The world of this poem is different from so many of Frost's other poems: it is urban, a cityscape. It has been called 'Frost's quintessential dramatic lyric of homelessness' by Frank Lentricchia and Frost himself commented that it was 'written for the tune'. Seamus Heaney described 'Acquainted with the Night' as a 'dark poem' and the darkness is not only the actual darkness of night but the inner darkness and loneliness that the speaker is admitting to. It has also been suggested that 'the night' might symbolise death.

Introducing this poem, Peter Forbes writes in *Scanning the Century: The Penguin Book of the Twentieth Century in Poetry* (1999), that 'The century of mass consumption, mass killing and social upheaval has also been the century of the individual – often alienated, lonely and confused. Poetry has always been a medium for the still small voice and in the twentieth century the range of expression of stubborn or disturbed individuality is greater than ever. The loss of certainties and the comforts of traditional belief has made us all existentialists now.'

This is an intensely personal poem and the direction the poem takes is interestingly summed up by the American poet Robert Pack as follows: 'The speaker's movements outward in body and inward in thought both lead to the same darkness'.

It is a sonnet where seven of the poem's fourteen lines begin with 'I' and the opening line is repeated as the closing line:

> I have been one acquainted with the night

However, the layout on the page is not that of a conventional sonnet. In fact, this is a terza rima sonnet and the terza rima (a three-lined rhyming stanza) was used by the Italian poet Dante in his 'Divine Comedy'. In that particular poem, Dante at one stage describes, using the terza rima, his descent into hell. It has been suggested that Frost uses the terza rima here in his own journey into his own circle of hell.

Night-time is often viewed as a time of romance, a time for lovers. Here there is nothing to suggest romance or happiness. The details suggest loneliness, isolation, separation. The speaker lives in a city but conveys no sense of community or togetherness:

> I have been one acquainted with the night.
> I have walked out in rain—and back in rain.
> I have outwalked the furthest city light.

The deliberate repetition here creates a listless effect and the rainy city streets, the never-ending rain ('out in rain—and back in rain') convey a gloomy mood. The nightwalker has walked into the darkness beyond 'the furthest city light', which adds to the sense of desolation. If one were to picture this, some of Edward Hopper's paintings might come to mind.

The poet has outwalked the furthest city light into the darkness beyond and in line four we are given another example of the extreme:

> I have looked down the saddest city lane.

The rhythm of the poem is imitative of a slow walking movement. Frost uses the iambic pentameter, the closest rhythmic pattern to the speaking voice in English, throughout and this measured flow, combined with images, suits the melancholy mood of the speaker.

The speaker is alone and remains alone. The watchman is the only other person identified, but there is no communication between them:

> I have passed by the watchman on his beat
> And dropped my eyes, unwilling to explain.

Other people in the poem are shadowy presences, known only by the sound of feet or an interrupted cry.

We are never given a reason for the speaker's loneliness and restlessness. His night walks are symptomatic of his inner state, but he is unwilling to explain to the watchman on his beat and he is also unwilling to explain to the reader. And yet there is no doubt that the speaker is fully aware of his plight. The world of 'another street' is unknown or does not matter to him. He hears 'an interrupted cry'; however, there is no connection between him and another. The cry does not 'call me back or say good-bye', thus highlighting his separateness.

In stanza one, the speaker went beyond the city light into the darkness. In stanza four, the light of the clock 'at an unearthly height' is interpreted by the nightwalker to mean that 'the time was neither wrong nor right'. Frost himself has said that the 'luminary clock' is an actual clock tower, but some readers have interpreted it to mean the moon. Both readings are valid, in that both remind us of the passing of time. If the time is 'neither wrong nor right', there is a sense of uncertainty, a feeling of confusion. And the poem ends where it began. The speaker has come full circle and there seems to be no escaping his situation. However, the word 'acquainted' is not the same as 'know'; perhaps there is hope in that an acquaintanceship is not the strongest of bonds. He may succeed in breaking his link with 'the night'.

Design

Both 'Design' and 'Provide, Provide' were chosen by the American poet Randall Jarrell as poems that would remove the slightly 'sugary' taste from the palates of readers who had been brought up wholly on 'Birches'. Jarrell viewed 'Design' as a dark, disturbing poem, where nature is portrayed as frightening and terrifying.

The title implies a plan, something deliberately intended, but the dictionary also defines 'argument from design' in terms of deducing the existence of a God from evidence of purpose or scheme in the universe. The actual text of the poem is carefully designed. The sonnet is divided into octet and sestet, with the following rhyming scheme: abbaabba, acaacc. The first eight lines focus on a problem and the sestet attempts to answer that problem in a series of questions.

The opening words, 'I found a dimpled spider', are straightforward; the word 'dimpled' suggests something attractive, but it is an unusual way of describing a spider. The two other adjectives in line 1 are even more unusual:

> I found a dimpled spider, fat and white

The word 'white' occurs five times in the poem and, though white is often associated with innocence and purity, it has a different purpose in this context. Spiders are more often black and the heal-all flower where the spider rests, though usually blue, is also white. The spider had killed a moth and its victim is also white. The opening lines, therefore, have been drained of colour:

> I found a dimpled spider, fat and white,
> On a white heal-all, holding up a moth
> Like a white piece of rigid satin cloth—

There's almost a nursery-rhyme feeling at first to the rhythm, but the meaning, once grasped, is grim. Susan MacDonald points out that even the detail of the 'rigid satin cloth' adds to the effect, in that this is the cloth used in a coffin.

The speaker, having come across this deliberate and calculated killing of a moth, sums up the scene in line 4:

> Assorted characters of death and blight

But their coming together in this way – blight in this instance could refer to the diseased flower, causing it to be white not blue but it could also mean 'malignant influence' – gives way to an ironic observation in the following line, when the speaker suggests that this is the right way to begin the day:

> Mixed ready to begin the morning right

Morning is a time of new beginning, but the evil image contained in the simile 'Like ingredients of a witches' broth' would suggest that the morning is a time of evil.

The first section ends with another description of the white spider, the white flower, the moth:

> A snow-drop spider, a flower like a froth,
> And dead wings carried like a paper kite.

A snow-drop is attractive in itself, but, when used to describe the killer spider, the fragile, beautiful flower image is given a different charge. The flower, like a froth, is of the moment, and the paper kite image is an ironic description of how the spider plays with the dead moth. Overall, these eight lines are presenting us with an unattractive and unexpected aspect of nature.

The sestet questions why. Why was the blue flower white? How did the spider and the moth happen to meet on the white flower at a particular moment in time? The strong verbs 'brought' and 'steered' imply a guiding force and the repeated 'What' at the beginning of three lines in the sestet reinforces the speaker's questioning tone ('What had . . .'; 'What brought . . .'; 'What but . . .')

> What had that flower to do with being white,
> The wayside blue and innocent heal-all?
> What brought the kindred spider to that height,
> Then steered the white moth thither in the night.

The unusually white spider and the unnaturally white flower are 'kindred'; it is as if they are both contriving to kill the moth. However, the moth had to be steered there, 'thither in the night', according to the speaker.

The poem ends with an argument from design, but the tone is questioning. In an earlier draft of this poem, Frost asked 'What but design of darkness and of night?' and in the revised version he ends:

> What but design of darkness to appall?—
> If design govern in a thing so small.

The flower was an ordinary one – it was a 'wayside blue' and 'innocent'. Its name 'heal-all' is ironic, in that it was here that the moth was killed and the flower itself, being white, camouflaged the spider and so helped kill it. This strange sight perplexes the speaker and the dominant mood is unease and uncertainty. Why should it happen? How could it happen? The phrase 'design of darkness' suggests a creator that cannot be easily understood. The final word in the poem reminds us of the world we have witnessed here. If a higher, greater force has a plan for spider, flower and moth, then the implied question is whether we are also part of a plan. Are our lives designed, predestined, or are our lives governed by chance?

Provide, Provide

Even on a first reading, the reader quickly picks up on this poem's central themes: change is the only certainty; disasters could befall everyone of us; and we should plan ahead. The exclamation mark with which the poem ends captures the spirit of the piece. The speaker is not altogether serious and the advice offered is too vague to be truly helpful. Frost, who loved to read this poem aloud, and almost growl the final stanza, often added an extra line at the end: 'Or somebody else'll provide *for* ya'. This biographical detail sheds light on how Frost thought the poem should be interpreted.

The title of the poem strongly urges or commands the reader to make preparation for the future and stanza one illustrates why. The witch was once a beauty; now that same beauty, Abishag, is a withered hag and survives by washing steps. How can we know what is to be?

> The witch that came (the withered hag)
> To wash the steps with pail and rag
> Was once the beauty Abishag

The poem looks to the future, but the reference to Abishag, a character from the Old Testament, suggests that what the speaker is observing here is true in every age. From the Old Testament to Hollywood is a huge leap, but the connection is made: the young and beautiful do not stay young and beautiful and we do not have to be reminded that the fortunes of many change for the worse. In Hollywood, there are Abishags too.

> The witch that came (the withered hag)
> To wash the steps with pail and rag
> Was once the beauty Abishag,
> The picture pride of Hollywood.

The speaker appeals to our common knowledge of life to prove his point about the fickle nature of fortune:

> Too many fall from great and good
> For you to doubt the likelihood.

Line 7, in a directive, suggests that the grim possibility can only be avoided by dying young:

> Die early and avoid the fate.

But another solution is offered immediately, should fate decide that you are to live long:

> Or if predestined to die late,
> Make up your mind to die in state.

Then the poem becomes an extravagant imagining in line 10, when inestimable wealth can be yours if you make up your mind to become wealthy:

> Make the whole stock exchange your own!

This emphasis on materialism is unusual in Frost's poetry and the voice is different, too. The speaker never uses 'I' and the voice resembles a public, impersonal one. The person addressed is 'you' and the frequency of 'you' (three times) and 'your' (three times) creates a focused, urgent directive:

> Make the whole stock exchange your own!
> If need be occupy a throne,
> Where nobody can call *you* crone.

The image of the throne is quaint and that italicised *you* adds to the unreal nature of the piece. It is more fantasy than reality, but the speaker continues in the same tone. There is a vagueness about stanza five, though the vagueness is inevitable. There is no one formula for success.

> Some have relied on what they knew,
> Others on being simply true.
> What worked for them might work for you.

What matters here is that 'you' avoid what happened to Abishag. No matter how wonderful your early life may be, no matter how happy your memories, they do not make up or compensate for the misery you might have to suffer later:

> No memory of having starred
> Atones for later disregard
> Or keeps the end from being hard.

The poem can joke about the future, but it is a form of black humour, especially in line 7 ('Die early and avoid the fate.'). It speaks of disregard and suffering, and offers no real solution as to how one might avoid a hard end. And, in what might be taken for an upbeat, reckless tone, the final stanza, as a last resort, suggests that it is

> Better to go down dignified
> With boughten friendship at your side
> Than none at all.

This should be contradictory. How can 'you' find dignity in bought friendship and how can you buy friendship? Is the speaker suggesting that while 'you' are young you should use your powers to provide for the future, no matter how insincere it might be? The speaker does not dwell on this. Peter Jones says that in the closing stanza, bitterly and uncompromisingly, Frost confronts himself with himself and his disillusion. The final two words of the poem seem to sum up its main thrust and capture everything that matters here:

> Provide, provide!

If this were the only poem by Robert Frost in this anthology, it would give no real sense of what truly interested him in his poetry, nor does 'Provide, Provide' represent Frost's typical poetic voice. That said, it does look, though this time in a light-hearted way, at life's darker side and other poems by Frost in this group of ten also explore life's downside.

Stopping by Woods on a Snowy Evening

Whose woods these are I think I know.
His house is in the village though.
He will not see me stopping here
To watch his woods fill up with snow.

My little horse must think it queer
To stop without a farmhouse near
Between the woods and frozen lake
The darkest evening of the year.

He gives his harness bells a shake
To ask if there is some mistake.
The only other sound's the sweep
Of easy wind and downy flake

The woods are lovely, dark and deep.
But I have promises to keep,
And miles to go before I sleep —
And miles to go before I sleep.

Robert Frost

Handwritten manuscript by Robert Frost.

Biographical Notes

Seamus Heaney was born on 13 April 1939 in a farmhouse on a forty-acre farm called Mossbawn, at Castledawson in the townland of Tamniarn, Co. Derry. In a poem such as 'Personal Helicon', Heaney gives us a glimpse of his childhood: 'As a child, they could not keep me from wells./And old pumps, with buckets and windlasses./I loved the dark drop, the trapped sky, the smells/Of waterweed, fungus and dank moss.'

In his poem 'A Peacock's Feather', he says 'I come from scraggy farm and moss, Old patchworks that the pitch and toss/Of history have left dishevelled'.

He was the eldest of nine children, two girls and seven boys, one of whom, Christopher, died very young as the result of a road accident. Between 1945 and 1951, Seamus Heaney attended Anahorish Primary School and later boarded at St Columb's College in Derry. His background was Catholic and what has been described as quietly nationalist in a predominantly Protestant Northern Ireland. Heaney's childhood in a small rural community was exclusively Catholic; his 'country of community. . . was also a place of division'. Mass, confession, the rosary, Gaelic football and the Catholic Village Hall all played an important part in his development. 'The culture I grew up in was Catholic, folk, rural, Irish' is how Heaney himself put it.

After St Columb's, Heaney went to Queen's University, Belfast, in 1957 to study English and, while studying for a degree, greatly admired the Elizabethan dramatist John Webster and especially the poetry of Keats and Hopkins. He was awarded a first in English and after graduating in 1961 spent a year at St Joseph's College of Education in Andersonstown, Belfast, training to be a teacher; having qualified he taught in a secondary school, St Thomas's Intermediate School in Ballymurphy, Belfast, from 1962 to 1963. While there, the headmaster Michael McLaverty, the short-story writer, introduced Heaney to the poetry of Patrick Kavanagh, which was to have a deep and lasting influence on him. It was during that year that Seamus Heaney published his poem 'Tractors' in the *Belfast Telegraph*, though earlier poems, 'Reaping in Heat', 'October Thought', 'Nostalgia in the Afternoon', were published during his third year at university under the pseudonym 'Incertus' ('uncertain' in Latin). One evening in February 1963, Heaney wrote 'Mid-term Break' as his brother Christopher's anniversary approached. When it was first published in the *Kilkenny Magazine* Heaney felt that from 'down in the great unknown in the South' came confirmation of his beginnings as a poet.

After a year's teaching, Heaney returned to St. Joseph's College of Education as a lecturer in English; at that same time, he was meeting as part of a poetry discussion group which Philip Hobsbaum, recently appointed as a lecturer at Queen's, had organised. This 'Belfast Group' included Michael Longley, Edna Longley, Bernard MacLaverty, Stewart Parker, James Simmons and Seamus Heaney; their work was promoted as part of the Belfast Festival of 1965. In November 1965, Heaney published his first small collection. It was called *Eleven Poems*.

In August 1965, Heaney and Marie Devlin from Ardboe, Co. Tyrone, were married and that same summer Faber and Faber accepted his first full-length collection. *Death of a Naturalist* appeared in May l966 when Heaney was 27; in 1966, he was appointed as a lecturer in English at Queen's.

Those years in Belfast were also the years of civil unrest in the North. In Derry, October 1968, 2,000 marched and protested against discrimination in housing allocations; 88 were injured and when the television pictures were shown around the world there was international outrage. Months of violence followed. In August 1969, the street fighting in Derry, known as the Battle of the Bogside, took place and two days later the British Army was sent in. In January 1970, the Provisional IRA was officially formed in Dublin. All of this was to have a profound effect on the work of Seamus Heaney. He himself said in his essay 'Feeling into Words' that poetry would now have to find images and symbols to match the predicament of the people in the North. At this time, Heaney was also reading the Danish archaeologist P.V. Glob's book *The Bog People*, a study of ritual killings, of victims of fertility rituals during the Iron Age in Jutland, and he found similarities and parallels between these other deaths and the killing in the North of Ireland. These ideas were explored in a poem such as 'The Tollund Man' from *Wintering Out* (1972) and in his sequence of bog poems which can be found in *North*.

In June 1969, *Door into the Dark* had been published and his third collection *Wintering Out* came out in 1972. In the early 1970s, Heaney had been writing explicitly political poems and these were published in various literary journals but some were omitted (for example, the 1970 'Intimidation') from *North*, his most political book to date, which was published in 1975.

The academic year 1970–1971 was spent in Berkeley, California, 'the most important year of my life maybe', and as a result Heaney has said that American poetic forms, 'a loosening' and 'that California spirit' were beginning to reveal themselves in his poetry. He read American poets such as William Carlos Williams. He also read Gary Snyder, Robert Bly and Robert Duncan, whose protest poetry about the Vietnam war influenced him. While in California, Heaney began a sequence of 21 prose poems which were completed in 1974 and published the following year as *Stations* by Ulsterman Publications in booklet form; the majority of them have not been reprinted since. These prose poems include descriptions of a young boy being kicked by a horse ('Branded'); playing in muck and water ('Waterbabies'); the 'Sweet William Flower' in which the very words Sweet William have 'the silky lift of a banner on the wind'; the drumming on the twelfth of July ('July'); first night in the Gaeltacht; and sectarian tension ('Inquisition').

'The Forge' is from Seamus Heaney's second collection, published in 1969, and the title of the collection is taken from the opening line of this sonnet. *Door into the Dark* is not only the actual doorway of the forge; it signals an awareness of mystery and complexities, the darkness of the subconscious, an exploration of those feelings through poetry. Heaney put it this way in his essay 'Feeling into Words': 'When I called my second book *Door into the Dark,* I intended to gesture towards this idea of poetry as a point of entry into the buried life of the feelings or as a point of exit for it'; Heaney also said of the title: 'Words themselves are doors, Janus to a certain extent their deity, looking back to a ramification of roots and associations and forward to a clarification of sense and meaning.'

It has also been pointed out that, just as the blacksmith works the metal and shapes it within his forge, the poet makes and shapes the poem within his head. The imagination has been described by Shakespeare in *Henry V* as 'the quick forge and working-house of thought'.

? Questions

1. In this sonnet, in which Heaney remembers his childhood, why is the boy both frightened and fascinated by the forge? Which details capture fear and fascination?
2. How has Heaney described the blacksmith?
3. The poem is about change – 'old axles and iron hoops' are rusting and the motor cars are 'flashing in rows'. Which side is Heaney on would you say from your reading of this poem? Or is it possible to say? Give reasons for your answer.
4. What the poet sees, hears and imagines are all important in the poem. Trace how Heaney uses visual and aural details to build up an overall picture of the forge. Comment on the word 'altar' in line 8 and the phrase 'shape and music' in line 9.
5. What are the effects of the present tense, the iambic pentameter and sonnet form?
6. Can this be read as a poem about the writing of poetry, the creative process, the sacred nature of art? Explain.

Bogland

for T. P. Flanagan

We have no prairies
To slice a big sun at evening —
Everywhere the eye concedes to
Encroaching horizon,

Is wooed into the cyclops' eye
Of a tarn. Our unfenced country
Is bog that keeps crusting
Between the sights of the sun.

They've taken the skeleton
Of the Great Irish Elk
Out of the peat, set it up
An astounding crate full of air.

Butter sunk under
More than a hundred years
Was recovered salty and white.
The ground itself is kind, black butter

Melting and opening underfoot,
Missing its last definition
By millions of years.
They'll never dig coal here,

Only the waterlogged trunks
Of great firs, soft as pulp.
Our pioneers keep striking
Inwards and downwards,

Every layer they strip
Seems camped on before.
The bogholes might be Atlantic seepage.
The wet centre is bottomless.

Glossary

Line 1 prairies: grassland, without trees, of great extent; applies chiefly to the grassy plains of North America.

Line 3 concedes: gives way to, admits to.

Line 4 encroaching: intruding.

Line 5 wooed: tempted, invited.

Line 5 cyclops' eye: in Greek mythology, the cyclops were a race of one-eyed giants.

Line 6 tarn: a small mountain lake.

Line 23 pioneers: diggers; pioneers originally referred to foot-soldiers who preceded the main army with spade or pickaxe, hence a digger. In *Hamlet I*, (v), the word is used to describe the ghost burrowing in the earth (beneath the stage).

'Bogland' is the final poem in *Door into the Dark* (1969) and looks forward to what would become a sequence of bog poems such as 'The Tollund Man' in *Wintering Out* (1972) and 'Bog Queen', 'The Grauballe man' and 'Punishment' in *North* (1975). Unlike the later poems, however, there is no pain or suffering associated with 'Bogland'. T. P. Flanagan, the artist to whom Heaney has dedicated the poem, has given an account of the poem's happy origins:

'Seamus and I and our families had spent Hallowe'en together in McFaddens Hotel at Gortahork in County Donegal. And he came with me when I went out sketching in the car. It was a dry luminous autumn, and after the hot summer of that year the bogland was burnt the colour of marmalade. We all stood on the beach watching marvellous sunsets, and, in the twilight, let off fireworks from the sand dunes to please our children. The poem is a celebration for me of a very happy and creative time in both our lives.'

On completing this poem, Heaney told an interviewer that he felt that it was 'one of the most important poems I had written because it was something like a symbol. I felt the poem was a promise of something else, I wasn't quite sure what... I like the notion of the bog, which, incidentally, we call the moss in the North of Ireland. Bog is a slightly literary word for me. It's a very beautiful, benign place. I associate that quiet, still, otherness with the bog. When you go there, as a child, you go with older people. It's the only place I ever saw my father actually lighting a fire, you know. Grown men boiled water. You stayed the whole day, and usually it was the summer. There was a sense of being in migration. It was physically attractive, fragrant with heather, the ground was springy. There was that seepage of water. It was just a beautiful place physically. And emotionally, then, in memory, it represented a free place for me.' (Interview with Kate O'Callaghan, *Irish America*, May 1986)

And in his essay called 'Feeling into Words' in *Preoccupations,* Heaney wrote:

'. . . the best moments are those when your mind seems to implode and words and images rush of their own accord into the vortex. Which happened to me once when the line "We have no prairies" drifted into my head at bedtime, and loosened a fall of images that constitute the poem "Bogland". . .

'I had been vaguely wishing to write a poem about bogland, chiefly because it is the landscape that has a strange assuaging effect on me, one with associations reaching back into early childhood. We used to hear about bog-butter, butter kept fresh for a great number of years under the peat. Then when I was at school the skeleton of an elk had been taken out of a bog nearby and a few of our neighbours had got their photographs in the paper, peering out across its antlers.

So I began to get an idea of bog as the memory of the landscape, or as a landscape that remembered everything that happened in and to it. In fact, if you go round the National Museum in Dublin, you will realise that a great proportion of the most cherished material heritage of Ireland was "found in a bog". Moreover, since memory was the faculty that supplied me with the first quickening of my own poetry, I had a tentative unrealized need to make a congruence between memory and bogland and, for the want of a better word, our national consciousness. And it all released itself after "We have no prairies..." – but we have bogs.'

And elsewhere, Heaney has said that the bog, in a way, represented the collective unconscious of a people, a phrase often associated with the Swiss psychologist and psychiatrist Carl Jung (1875–1961). Jung believed that as a people we share a collective unconscious, that there is a primal force which we all share and that we ought to discover within ourselves:

'The allusion was that the bog was a kind of Jungian ground or landscape in that it preserved traces of everything that had occurred before. It had layers of memory. The objects, the material culture by which the nation identifies itself, were mostly found in the bogs and are now in museums. I remember when we were children, they used to tell us not to go near the bog because there was no bottom to it.'

(Heaney, quoted in *Dictionary of Irish Literature*, ed. Robert Hogan, Gill & Macmillan, Dublin 1979.)

? Questions

1. What are the characteristics of Irish bogland as revealed to us in this poem? Consider the significance of 'prairies', 'Cyclops' eye', 'pioneers' in your answer.

2. According to Patrick Kavanagh, 'A turf bog is a history of the world from the time of Noah'. How is the sense of the past evoked? Which particular aspects of history are evoked?

3. The poem is more than a landscape poem. It is in one sense about bogland – digging deep and discovering. Does it also work on another level? Explain.

4. How would you describe Heaney's tone in 'Bogland'? How has the tone changed from the opening to the closing stanza?

5. How does Heaney create a sense of mystery in this poem? Which words capture this sense of mystery?

6. The senses play an important part in this poem. Trace how Heaney uses the senses to convey to his reader his own response to bogland. How does this poem differ from 'The Tollund Man'?

The Tollund Man

I
Some day I will go to Aarhus
To see his peat-brown head,
The mild pods of his eye-lids,
His pointed skin cap.

In the flat country nearby
Where they dug him out,
His last gruel of winter seeds
Caked in his stomach,

Naked except for
The cap, noose and girdle,
I will stand a long time.
Bridegroom to the goddess,

She tightened her torc on him
And opened her fen,
Those dark juices working
Him to a saint's kept body,

Trove of the turfcutters'
Honeycombed workings.
Now his stained face
Reposes at Aarhus.

II
I could risk blasphemy,
Consecrate the cauldron bog
Our holy ground and pray
Him to make germinate

The scattered, ambushed
Flesh of labourers,
Stockinged corpses
Laid out in the farmyards,

Tell-tale skin and teeth
Flecking the sleepers
Of four young brothers, trailed
For miles along the lines.

III
Something of his sad freedom
As he rode the tumbril
Should come to me, driving,
Saying the names

Tollund, Grabaulle, Nebelgard,
Watching the pointing hands
Of country people,
Not knowing their tongue.

Out there in Jutland
In the old man-killing parishes
I will feel lost,
Unhappy and at home.

Glossary

Line 3 pods: seed-vessels, usually dry.

Line 7 gruel: a light, liquid food made by boiling ground grain in water or milk.

Line 10 noose: a loop, with a running knot, which tightens as the rope is pulled.

Line 10 girdle: a belt worn about the waist.

Line 13 torc: Irish word for torque – a collar, necklace, consisting of a twisted narrow band or strip, usually of precious metal.

Line 14 fen: low land covered wholly or partly with shallow water.

Line 17 Trove: a valuable find as in treasure-trove.

Line 18 honeycombed: a reference to the patterned way in which the turfcutters cut through the peat.

Line 21 blasphemy: profane or irreverent speaking of holy things.

Line 22 Consecrate: to dedicate, to set apart as sacred.

Line 22 cauldron bog: here refers to the shape of the bog (the other associations with cauldron, such as evil, may also be intended).

Line 24 germinate: to sprout, put forth shoots; here, to bring to life.

Line 25 ambushed: attacked, waylaid.

Line 34 tumbril: a cart so constructed that the body tilts backwards so as to empty out the load; a dung cart.

Line 37 Tollund, Grabualle, Nebelgard: places in Jutland associated with corpses from the Iron Age which had been sacrificed in ritual death ceremonies.

Line 41 Jutland: The region where the 2,000 year old bodies were found.

On 8 May 1950, the body of the Tollund man was discovered by two farmers who were digging peat in a Danish bog. He had been so well preserved by the peat that the farmers thought he had been recently killed. The body, from the Iron Age, was some 2,000 years old. The man had died by hanging, the rope was still around his neck and in his stomach were found the remains of his last meal – a gruel made of barley, linseed, 'gold-of-pleasure' (*Camelina sativa*), knotweed and other sorts of common weeds. The Tollund Man and others, it is thought, had been sacrificed to the spirit of the earth, a fertility goddess named Nerthus. They were found naked, strangled or with their throats cut; they had been murdered in winter to bring back the spring, so that there would be renewal, fertility, and that the seasons would continue. Heaney, quoting P. V. Glob, says in *Preoccupations* that 'This mother Goddess needed new bridegrooms each winter to bed with her in her sacred place, in the bog, to ensure the renewal and fertility of the territory in the spring.' P. V. Glob's book *The Bog People* (Faber, 1969) which was the inspiration for this poem, gives more details and includes some remarkable photographs. It was the photographs rather than Glob's text which moved him most, though he said that 'When I read [Glob] . . . I experienced feelings normally evinced by the charms of poetry.'

(The discoveries in Denmark are not isolated occurrences. Remains of an ancient human body, the Lindow Man, were found in a bog at Lindow Moss, near Wilmslow, Cheshire, in 1984. Apparently ritually slaughtered, he was felled with an axe, garrotted with a thin 'cord', and then his throat was cut open. The Lindow Man can be seen in the British Museum in London.)

Unlike 'Bogland' this bog poem is, in Heaney's own words, 'complicated by Jutland bog burials, archaeology'. It is also a poem in which Heaney contemplates the Iron Age and what was happening in the North of Ireland side by side: Iron Age victims and the contemporary victims of sectarian violence in Northern Ireland. In his essay 'Feeling into Words', he speaks of the pattern linking the Iron Age ritual killings for an Earth Goddess and the tradition of Irish political martyrdom for Mother Ireland.

In the *Paris Review* interview, Heaney says of 'The Tollund Man': 'Essentially, it is a prayer that the bodies of people killed in various actions and atrocities in modern Ireland, in the teens and twenties of the century as well as in the more recent past, a prayer that something would come of them, some kind of new peace or resolution. In the understanding of his Iron Age contemporaries, the sacrificed body of Tollund Man germinated into spring, so the poem wants a similar flowering to come from the violence in the present.'

Questions

1. The poem focuses on ancient burial rites in Jutland in Part I and contemporary violence in Northern Ireland in Part II. Why is Heaney drawn to the Tollund man? How does he know that, once there, he 'will stand a long time' (line 11)?
2. Heaney first saw the Tollund man in a photograph. Discuss the vivid detail used by Heaney to imagine the exhumed body.
3. What is the relationship between the burial place and the buried (lines 11–15) as Heaney sees it?
4. Why does Heaney say he 'could risk blasphemy' in line 21? How is the Tollund man viewed in Part II? What does such a line tell us about Heaney and his attitude to the North of Ireland?
5. In Part II, the poem describes a sectarian killing of four brothers in the 1920s. Which words capture the grotesque violence? What is Heaney's tone here?
6. Discuss how this poem is both public and private, political and personal.
7. What do you think is meant by the phrase 'sad freedom' in line 33?
8. Comment on the closing lines of the poem. Why does Heaney feel both 'Unhappy and at home'?
9. 'The Tollund Man' speaks of particular killings in particular places at particular times. Do you think the poem transcends the particular and becomes a universal utterance? Why?

Tollund Man

Mossbawn: Two Poems in Dedication
for Mary Heaney

1. Sunlight

There was a sunlit absence.
The helmeted pump in the yard
heated its iron,
water honeyed

in the slung bucket
and the sun stood
like a griddle cooling
against the wall

of each long afternoon.
So, her hands scuffled
over the bakeboard,
the reddening stove

sent its plaque of heat
against her where she stood
in a floury apron
by the window.

Now she dusts the board
with a goose's wing,
now sits, broad-lapped,
with whitened nails

and measling shins:
here is a space
again, the scone rising
to the tick of two clocks.

And here is love
like a tinsmith's scoop
sunk past its gleam
in the meal-bin.

Glossary

Title: Mossbawn – Heaney's birthplace. In *Preoccupations,* Heaney writes: 'Our farm was called Mossbawn. Moss, a Scots word probably carried to Ulster by the Planters, and bawn, the name the English colonists gave to their fortified farmhouses. Mossbawn, the planter's house on the bog. Yet in spite of this Ordnance Survey spelling, we pronounced it Moss bann, and bán is the Gaelic word for white. So might not the thing mean the white moss, the moss of bog-cotton? In the syllables of my home, I see a metaphor of the split culture of Ulster.'

Mary Heaney, to whom the poem is dedicated, is Heaney's aunt and she is at the heart of this poem. She lived with the family and there was a special bond between her and Seamus Heaney, the eldest child. Heaney has described her as 'a woman with a huge well of affection and a very experienced, dry-eyed sense of the world'. There are in fact two poems in dedication under the general heading 'Mossbawn': 1 is 'Sunlight'; 2 is 'The Seed Cutters'.

Line 7 griddle: round-shaped, home-made bread cooked on a griddle or gridiron or the round-shaped griddle itself – a flat iron plate for baking cakes.

Line 10 scuffled: moved quickly, touching lightly in passing.

Line 13 plaque: ornament; here, patch of intense heat.

Line 21 measling: ageing, spotted.

Line 24 the tick of two clocks: not only the actual clocks in the kitchen but a reference perhaps to the two time sequences in the poem – the past and the present.

Line 28 meal-bin: a wooden container with a lidded top for flour, ground grain.

This poem is from Heaney's fourth collection, *North* (1975), which has his first political book-title; it not only refers to his northern roots, but poems in this book also address the political situation in the North. However, the book opens with 'Two poems in Dedication for Mary Heaney'; the scene is Mossbawn. 'Sunlight' is a marvellously atmospheric, lyrical, domestic, love poem for his aunt. The two dedicatory poems, in Helen Vendler's words, 'show people living ordinary lives in peaceful and coherent ways'.

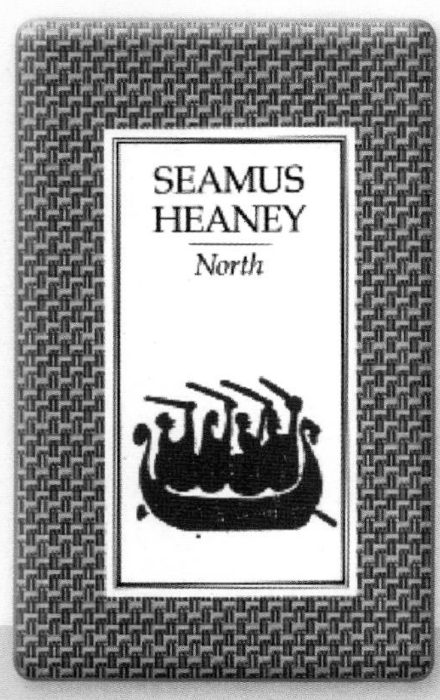

Questions

1. How would you describe the atmosphere in this poem and how does Heaney convey this atmosphere so effectively? Which details convey the slow passing of time?

2. Pick out three examples of Heaney's command and control of language and say why you think them effective or not.

3. What image do you have of Mary Heaney as revealed to us in the poem? Which details has the poet focused on?

4. Can you explain the final image in the poem? Why is the gleam of love almost invisible? Do you think it an appropriate image within the context of the poem as a whole? Give reasons for your answer.

5. Do you think Heaney succeeds in turning the ordinary into the extraordinary in this poem? How is this transformation achieved?

6. Look at the sounds in the poem. Identify Heaney's use of alliteration, assonance and onomatopoeia and comment on how the words create a music of their own within the text.

A Constable Calls

His bicycle stood at the window-sill,
The rubber cowl of a mud-splasher
Skirting the front mudguard,
Its fat black handlegrips

Heating in sunlight, the 'spud'
Of the dynamo gleaming and cocked back,
The pedal treads hanging relieved
Of the boot of the law.

His cap was upside down
On the floor, next his chair.
The line of its pressure ran like a bevel
In his slightly sweating hair.

He had unstrapped
The heavy ledger, and my father
Was making tillage returns
In acres, roods, and perches.

Arithmetic and fear.
I sat staring at the polished holster
With its buttoned flap, the braid cord
Looped into the revolver butt.

'Any other root crops?
Mangolds? Marrowstems? Anything like that?'
'No.' But was there not a line
Of turnips where the seed ran out

In the potato field? I assumed
Small guilts and sat
Imagining the black hole in the barracks.
He stood up, shifted the baton-case

Further round on his belt,
Closed the domesday book,
Fitted his cap back with two hands,
And looked at me as he said goodbye.

A shadow bobbed in the window.
He was snapping the carrier spring
Over the ledger. His boot pushed off
And the bicycle ticked, ticked, ticked.

Glossary

Line 2 cowl: hood-shaped covering.

Line 5 'spud': potato shaped.

Line 8 the boot of the law: not only the actual boot but a phrase which suggests power, control and threat.

Line 11 bevel: here, a narrow, double-lined impression.

Line 14 ledger: a book containing records; a register.

Line 15 tillage returns: the amount harvested from cultivated land.

Line 19 braid: interwoven.

Line 30 domesday book: the name of the record of the *Great Inquisition or Survey of the lands of England, their extent, value, ownership, and liabilities, made by order of William the Conqueror* in 1086. It also refers to the day of judgement when all will be judged.

Line 33 bobbed: an ironic echo perhaps of the word 'Bobby' – the English friendly term for a policeman.

'A Constable Calls' is poem number two from a six-poem sequence called 'Singing School' which comes at the end of *North*. The poem that precedes 'A Constable Calls' is 'The Ministry of Fear'. In this, Heaney remembers his schooldays in the 1950s, growing up, being stopped and interrogated by policemen who crowded round 'The car like black cattle, snuffing and pointing / The muzzle of a Sten-gun in my eye'. Immediately following 'A Constable Calls' is 'Orange Drums, Tyrone, 1966' which captures the pounding of the drums, an anti-Catholic feeling. The six-poem sequence is explicitly political at times; 'A Constable Calls' seems one of the least political, but even here Heaney is commenting on his family and their relationship with the law. The Heaneys were Catholic; a constable would be a member of the Royal Ulster Constabulary and, therefore, Protestant.

? Questions

1. Briefly describe in your own words what is happening in this poem. What details in the poem are both actual and symbolic?
2. How is the presence of the constable conveyed in the first three stanzas? Look at how often the word 'his' is used throughout the poem. What is the effect of this? Does Heaney convey to his reader the sense of being part of a Catholic minority in Northern Ireland in this poem?
3. How does the young boy react to the constable? Does the speaker here regret not admitting to 'a line of turnips'? Why does he feel guilt and fear? What do we learn from this poem of the relationship between Heaney and his father?
4. Which details in the poem give an uneasy feeling? Pick out individual words and phrases. Why is the bicycle viewed as something dangerous?
5. 'A Constable Calls' has been described as 'a directly political and committed' poem. Would you agree with this view? How is this a political poem? Explain, giving reasons for your answer.

The Skunk

Up, black, striped and damasked like the chasuble
At a funeral mass, the skunk's tail
Paraded the skunk. Night after night
I expected her like a visitor.

The refrigerator whinnied into silence.
My desk light softened beyond the verandah.
Small oranges loomed in the orange tree.
I began to be tense as a voyeur.

After eleven years I was composing
Love-letters again, broaching the word 'wife'
Like a stored cask, as if its slender vowel
Had mutated into the night earth and air

Of California. The beautiful, useless
Tang of eucalyptus spelt your absence.
The aftermath of a mouthful of wine
Was like inhaling you off a cold pillow.

And there she was, the intent and glamorous,
Ordinary, mysterious skunk,
Mythologized, demythologized,
Snuffing the boards five feet beyond me.

It all came back to me last night, stirred
By the sootfall of your things at bedtime,
Your head-down, tail-up hunt in a bottom drawer
For the black plunge-line nightdress.

Glossary

Title: Skunk – a North American animal of the weasel kind.

Line 1 damasked: a surface variegated pattern usually on linen, silk.

Line 1 chasuble: an ecclesiastical vestment; a sleeveless mantle covering the body and shoulders, worn over the alb and stole by the celebrant at Mass or the Eucharist.

Line 5 whinnied: made a gentle, low, recurring sound.

Line 6 verandah: an open roofed gallery along the front of a building to protect from sun or rain.

Line 8 voyeur: one who spies (usually for sexual thrills).

Line 12 mutated: undergone a change.

Line 13 useless: useless because his wife is not there with him to share the evocative, sensuous scent of the eucalyptus? Another explanation perhaps is that in the nineteenth century the eucalyptus tree was imported into Berkeley, California from Australia. This fast-growing tree was intended as building material on an expanding university campus. It was discovered, however, that the eucalyptus tree was particularly unsuited as building material and so it was deemed useless.

Line 14 Tang: penetrating scent.

Line 14 eucalyptus: the eucalyptus tree, native to Australia, growing in Berkeley, California.

Line 15 aftermath: here, lingering taste.

Line 19 Mythologised: converted into fable.

Line 24 plunge-line: low-cut.

Questions

1. In terms of setting, this is an atypical Heaney poem. Are there other aspects of the poem that strike you as unusual?
2. Consider the dramatic qualities in the poem and discuss their effect. Look at the opening and closing stanzas in particular.
3. In this poem, Heaney is comparing his wife to a skunk. What memory prompted the comparison? Does the image work?
4. What tones can you identify in 'The Skunk'? Is it a humorous poem? A love poem? Can it be both?
5. Discuss how Heaney creates a sensuous atmosphere in 'The Skunk'. Which words and phrases contribute to this sensuousness?
6. Examine how the poem presents the reader with separate, different but inter-connecting pictures. List the different colours in 'The Skunk'. Comment on the use of colour and its significance in the poem.
7. Is the poem itself, as Heaney himself says of the skunk, ordinary and mysterious?

The Harvest Bow

As you plaited the harvest bow
You implicated the mellowed silence in you
In wheat that does not rust
But brightens as it tightens twist by twist
Into a knowable corona,
A throwaway love-knot of straw.

Hands that aged round ashplants and cane sticks
And lapped the spurs on a lifetime of game cocks
Harked to their gift and worked with fine intent
Until your fingers moved somnambulant:
I tell and finger it like braille,
Gleaning the unsaid off the palpable,

And if I spy into its golden loops
I see us walk between the railway slopes
Into an evening of long grass and midges,
Blue smoke straight up, old beds and ploughs in hedges,
An auction notice on an outhouse wall —
You with a harvest bow in your lapel,

Me with the fishing rod, already homesick
For the big lift of these evenings, as your stick
Whacking the tips off weeds and bushes
Beats out of time, and beats, but flushes
Nothing: that original townland
Still tongue-tied in the straw tied by your hand.

The end of art is peace
Could be the motto of this frail device
That I have pinned up on our deal dresser —
Like a drawn snare
Slipped lately by the spirit of the corn
Yet burnished by its passage, and still warm.

Glossary

Title: Harvest Bow – the harvest bow was part of the harvest celebrations and symbolised a fruitful harvest. Traditionally, the cutting of the last sheaf of the grain-crop was taken home in triumph and placed on the beams of the kitchen during an end-of-harvest feast. Harvest knots were woven from this last sheaf and worn by the harvesters. The harvest bow itself is a decorative twist of wheat, made in a fine plait of two straws tied into loops or interlaced. They were offered as love tokens long ago and, more recently, were worn as buttonholes for the harvest fair.

In folklore, there was an ancient belief that the last sheaf was the spirit of growing grain incarnate, but this has given way to the last sheaf as an emblem of abundance.

Line 2 implicated: intertwined; implied or indirectly expressed.

Line 2 mellowed: soft, matured, genial.

Line 5 corona: circle of light.

Line 8 lapped: wrapped, bound.

Line 8 spurs: sharp, hard projections to be attached to the back of the bird's leg.

Line 8 game cocks: the males of the common domestic fowl used in cock-fighting.

Line 9 harked: responded.

Line 10 somnambulant: instinctively (literally, as if moving in sleep).

Line 11 braille: the system of printing for the blind, in which the characters are represented by tangible points or dots. Named after the blind French educator Louis Braille, who developed it.

Line 12 Gleaning: to gather or pick up – originally it referred to the gathering of ears of corn left by the reapers.

Line 12 palpable: what can be touched, felt.

Line 15 midges: as a boy Heaney learnt Keats's ode 'To Autumn' by heart, but he has said that his vague satisfaction from 'the small gnats mourn' would have been complete if it had been midges mourning. In 'The Harvest Bow', Heaney wrote his own ode to autumn and included the midges.

Line 22 flushes: here, sends nothing rushing out suddenly (such as an animal hiding in the weeds and bushes).

Line 25 The end of art is peace: a line from Coventry Patmore (1823–1896) originating with Horace (65–8 B.C.), which Yeats also used (as an epigraph to *Explorations*) before it was taken up by Heaney. Yeats also speaks of 'Art whose end is peace' in his poem 'To a wealthy Man who promised a second Subscription to the Dublin Municipal Gallery if it were proved the People wanted Pictures' (line 26).

Line 26 device: invention; also means emblematic or heraldic design which with 'motto' and 'burnished' suggest heraldry, nobility and tradition. 'The end of art is peace' is interesting and complex in the way that Keats's 'Beauty is truth, truth beauty' is. A further complexity is introduced if the word 'end' is read as a pun. End means 'goal or achievement' but it can also mean 'extinction'.

In an interview, Heaney has commented in detail on this line: '["The end of art is peace"] is a quoted statement. I enjoy the triple take because Coventry Patmore said it, Yeats used it and I used Yeats using it. Obviously, no matter how turbulent, apocalyptic, vehement or destructive art's subject is or that which is contained with art, no matter how unpeaceful the thing previous to art is – once it has been addressed and brought into a condition called art, it is, if not pacified, brought into equilibrium. For a moment, the parallelogram of forces is just held. The minute after art, everything breaks out again. Art is an image. It is not a solution to reality, and to confuse the pacifications and appeasements and peace of art with something that is actually attainable in life is a great error. But to deny your life the suasion of art-peace is also an unnecessary Puritanism. It is an unnecessary extreme.

All the same, I am very attracted to that extreme of denial. In post-Holocaust, and post-nuclear conditions, the seeming smarminess of offering art as peace, the slightly sanctimonious, unearned "Let's go out and enjoy the alibi of art" – the indulgence is a possible affront. But to carry that denial too far, to demean the possibility of art and say that is all art is capable of is also a great error. The greatest art confronts every destructiveness that experience offers it and in Thomas Kinsella's terms, "digests it". So, when we salute art with joy, we acknowledge that it has managed to overcome all the dice that were loaded against it. Can you write a poem that gazes at death, or the western front or Auschwitz – a poem that gives peace and tells horror? It gives true peace only if the horror is satisfactorily rendered. If the eyes are not averted from it. If its overmastering power is acknowledged and unconceded, so the human spirit holds its own against its affront and immensity. To me that is what "the end of art is peace" means and understood in those terms, I still believe in it.'

Line 28 snare: trap.

Line 30 burnished: gleaming, shining.

This is an intricately made poem: the six-lined stanzas, the longer line and the rhyme scheme mirror the intricacies involved in the making of the harvest bow itself.

'The Harvest Bow' from *Field Work* (1979) is a more sympathetic and loving poem. In the 1996 interview with Patricia Harty in *Irish America* magazine, Heaney spoke of his father's 'majesty' and his father having 'the country farmer's silence and hauteur'.

Questions

1. This has been described as a poem that 'sanctifies the common'. In what way is the ordinary made special and transformed?
2. The harvest bow is richly symbolic. Discuss its various meanings and its place within the poem.
3. What image of the poet's father emerges from these lines? What does the poem reveal to the reader of the relationship between father and son?
4. Trace the references to hands and touch and action through the poem. Would you agree that the poem is structured in a masterful way?
5. Is the poem celebrating the past? The present? Both? Explain your answer.
6. Comment on this poem in relation to the phrase quoted within the poem: 'The end of art is peace'. You may find it useful to consider both the harvest bow itself as a work of art and the poem on the page.
7. Would you agree or disagree that Heaney in 'The Harvest Bow' has created a beautiful and musical movement? Examine how rhyme, rhythm, sentence structure and stanza divisions all contribute to this effect. Look back over the poems that you have read so far by Seamus Heaney. Why do you think the longer line and the six-line stanza are more appropriate here?

The Underground

There we were in the vaulted tunnel running,
You in your going-away coat speeding ahead
And me, me then like a fleet god gaining
Upon you before you turned to a reed

Or some new white flower japped with crimson
As the coat flapped wild and button after button
Sprang off and fell in a trail
Between the Underground and the Albert Hall.

Honeymooning, mooning around, late for the Proms,
Our echoes die in that corridor and now
I come as Hansel came on the moonlit stones
Retracing the path back, lifting the buttons

To end up in a draughty lamplit station
After the trains have gone, the wet track
Bared and tensed as I am, all attention
For your step following and damned if I look back.

Glossary

'The Underground' is the first poem in Heaney's 1984 collection *Station Island* and remembers, as Heaney himself says in *Stepping Stones* (2008), 'running through a tunnel from the South Kensington tube station towards the Albert Hall, late for a BBC Promenade Concert'.

Title: The Underground – the London Tube, but it could also refer to the underworld that is frequently mentioned in Greek and Roman myth.

Line 1 vaulted: arched.

Line 2 going-away coat: a coat bought especially to wear immediately following a wedding reception.

Line 3 fleet: fast and nimble, swift.

Line 4 reed: in mythology, the idea of a chase occurs often. Apollo chased Daphne and Daphne, fleeing, sought help from the gods and was changed into a bay tree; Pan chased the nymph Syrinx who prayed to be changed into a reed.

Line 5 japped: dashed, splashed.

Line 5 crimson: rich deep red.

Line 8 Albert Hall: the Royal Albert Hall, one of the world's most famous performing centres, opened 1871.

Line 9 Honeymooning: the honeymoon refers to the first month after marriage. The word dates from the 16th century and is explained as a reference to the affections of married people changing with the moon.

Line 9 mooning: behaving or moving in a listless or dreamy manner.

Line 9 Proms: Prom(enade) Concerts held in London's Royal Albert Hall every summer. So named because some of the audience stand in an open area near the platform. The London Proms began in 1838 and were held at different venues including Queen's Hall which was destroyed by enemy action in 1941. Following wartime interruption, the Proms were resumed at the Albert Hall.

Line 11 Hansel: Hänsel and Gretel – a fairy story by the brothers Grimm.

Line 16 damned if I look back: in the Greek myth, 'Orpheus and Eurydice', Orpheus, poet and musician, goes down into the Underworld to rescue his wife whom he loves. She is allowed return with him under one condition: that Orpheus who leads the way does not look back until he reaches the light of the Upperworld. He does look back and he loses Eurydice forever. This line, says Heaney in *Stepping Stones*, 'takes us well beyond the honeymoon. In this version of the story, Eurydice and much else gets saved by the sheer cussedness of the poet up ahead just keeping going.'

? Questions

1. Heaney calls his poem 'The Underground'. Explore its different meanings.
2. How would you describe the mood as captured in the opening two stanzas? Which details best convey that feeling?
3. This is a honeymoon poem, a love poem. What do you associate with love and romance? Do you think this is a romantic poem? Why? Why not?
4. Comment of the details such as 'speeding', 'japped with crimson', 'Bared and tensed'.
5. How would you describe the speaker's understanding of his situation?
6. A young married couple on their honeymoon in London in the 1960s are linked with characters from fairy tale and myth. Why do you think the speaker is inviting us to make connections between the two worlds? What is the effect of this?

The Pitchfork

Of all implements, the pitchfork was the one
That came near to an imagined perfection:
When he tightened his raised hand and aimed with it,
It felt like a javelin, accurate and light.

So whether he played the warrior or the athlete
Or worked in earnest in the chaff and sweat,
He loved its grain of tapering, dark-flecked ash
Grown satiny from its own natural polish.

Riveted steel, turned timber, burnish, grain,
Smoothness, straightness, roundness, length and sheen.
Sweat-cured, sharpened, balanced, tested, fitted.
The springiness, the clip and dart of it.

And then when he thought of probes that reached the farthest,
He would see the shaft of a pitchfork sailing past
Evenly, imperturbably through space,
Its prongs starlit and absolutely soundless –

But has learned at last to follow that simple lead
Past its own aim, out to an other side
Where perfection – or nearness to it – is imagined
Not in the aiming but the opening hand.

Glossary

Title: Pitchfork – a farm tool with a long handle and, usually, two sharp metal prongs, used for lifting hay.

Line 1 implements: tools, utensils.

Line 4 javelin: a long, light spear thrown by hand in a competitive sport.

Line 6 chaff: chopped hay and straw used as fodder.

Line 7 tapering: reduced in thickness towards one end.

Line 8 satiny: smooth (satin is a silk-like fabric).

Line 9 Riveted: fastened.

Line 9 turned: shaped.

Line 10 sheen: soft shine on a surface.

Line 12 clip: smart strike.

Line 12 dart: quick movement.

Line 13 probes: exploratory devices.

Line 14 shaft: the long, narrow handle.

Line 15 imperturbably: not diverted, impeded.

Line 16 prongs: the projected pointed parts.

In *Stepping Stones* interviews with Seamus Heaney, Dennis O'Driscoll comments that 'The Pitchfork' suggests that Heaney was very much in his element when it came to making hay. And Heaney replied: 'Well, yes, I was. I loved handling the fork and the rake, their lightness and rightness in the hand, their perfect suitedness to the jobs they had to do . . . Using the pitchfork was like playing an instrument. So much so that when you clipped and trimmed the head of a ruck, the strike of the fork on the hay made it a kind of tuning fork.'

Questions

1. This is poem that celebrates the nature and nobility of work and especially a well-made implement. List the qualities that the speaker admires about the pitchfork.
2. Many readers will neither have seen nor handled a pitchfork. Does this poem bring alive the experience of handling a pitchfork in your opinion?
3. The man handling the pitchfork in the poem sees himself as more than a farmer. How is this achieved? Which details in the poem suggest that he sees himself as more than a farmer?
4. How would you describe the speaker's tone?
5. How can you tell that the speaker admires and identifies with the handler of the pitchfork?
6. Does this poem tie in with your idea of the farming life? Give reasons for your answer.
7. Examine the poem's movement, paying special attention to key words such as 'When', 'So', 'And then when', 'He would see', 'But has learned'.
8. What is the effect of 'the opening hand', the poem's final words?

Lightenings viii

The annals say: when the monks of Clonmacnoise
Were all at prayers inside the oratory
A ship appeared above them in the air.

The anchor dragged along behind so deep
It hooked itself into the altar rails
And then, as the big hull rocked to a standstill,

A crewman shinned and grappled down the rope
And struggled to release it. But in vain.
'This man can't bear our life here and will drown,'

The abbot said, 'unless we help him.' So
They did, the freed ship sailed, and the man climbed back
Out of the marvellous as he had known it.

Glossary

Line 1 annals: historical records; The *Annals of Clonmacnoise* (originally in Irish, now lost) was translated into English in 1627. It is one of the earliest translations from Irish into English.

Line 2 oratory: a place for private prayer.

Line 6 hull: the body or frame of the ship.

Line 7 shinned: climbed.

Line 7 grappled: gripped, seized.

Line 10 abbot: male head of an abbey.

The Nobel Prize citation made specific reference to 'Lightenings viii': 'A poem like "Lightenings viii", on the miracle of Clonmacnoise, is a crystallisation of much of Heaney's imaginative world: history and sensuality, myths and the day-to-day – all articulated in Heaney's rich language.'

And Patricia Harty, in an interview with Heaney, asked him if he was surprised that 'Lightenings viii' was cited by the Nobel Committee. 'You mean the one about the monks at Clonmacnoise having the vision of a boat in the air above them? I was delighted with that, because the thing is a kind of image of poetry itself. It's about the negotiation that goes on in everybody's life between what is envisaged and what is endured – between the dream up there and the doings down here. It has the mysterious purchase of a good story but also it's pregnant with suggestion. I think it's about poetry, maybe that is why they cited it.'

Questions

1. What does the word 'annals' suggest? Does the story told here form part of real or imagined experience?

2. The ship and the sailors are out of their element. How does Heaney suggest this? What is the link between the monks and the people on board the ship? Is it significant that the vision occurs when the monks are at prayer?

3. Once again in a Heaney poem, the power of the verbs is striking. Comment on their effect. Consider also the effect of distance, of the distance between high and low in the poem. Explore how the senses are used in the text.

4. Why can the crewman not bear the other life, 'our life here'?

5. Do the abbot and monks view their life as 'marvellous'? Why does the crewman view it as such?

6. Compare and contrast this poem with 'Field of Vision' as poems that capture special moments.

7. What is the overall effect of this poem? Can it be read as a metaphor for experience, the ordinary and the extraordinary? Can it be read as a poem about poetry?

8. The title 'Lightenings' means 'being unburdened and being illuminated'. Why is this an appropriate title?

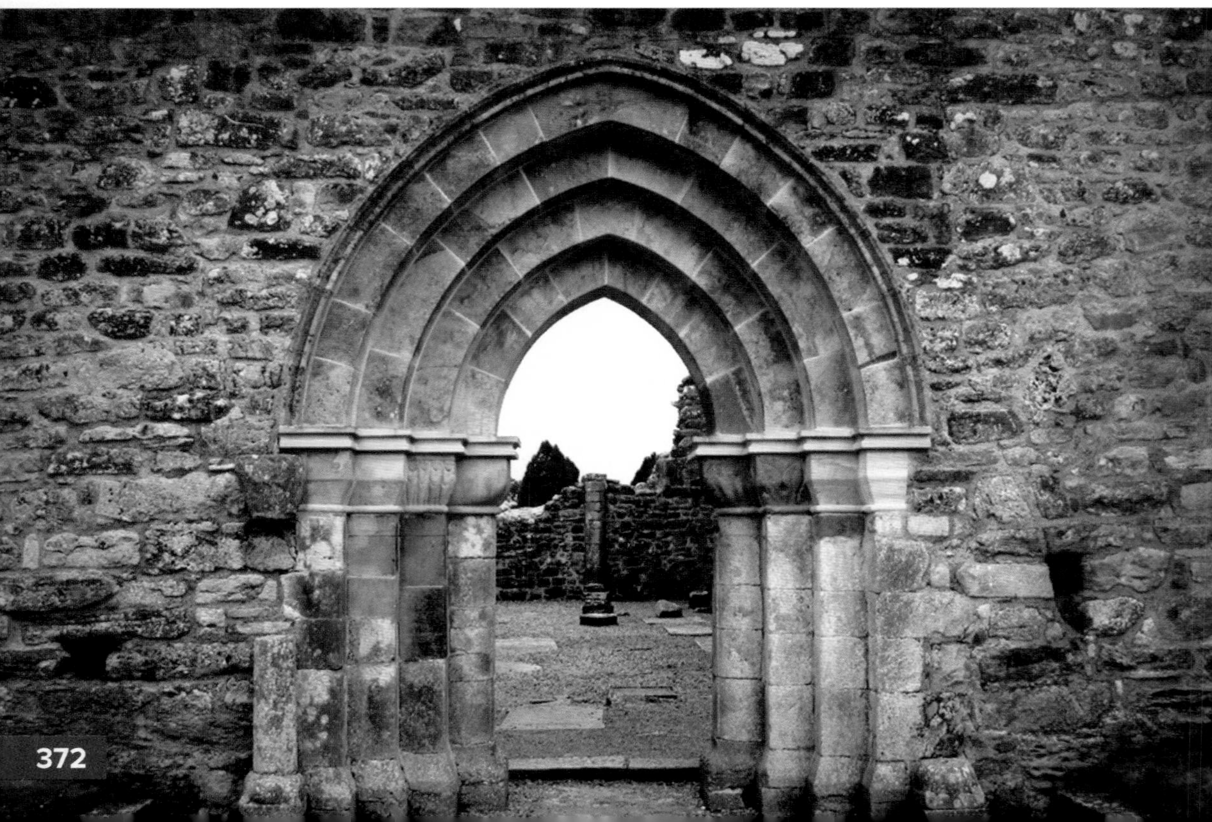

A Call

'Hold on,' she said, 'I'll just run out and get him.
The weather here's so good, he took the chance
To do a bit of weeding.'
So I saw him
Down on his hands and knees beside the leek rig,
Touching, inspecting, separating one
Stalk from the other, gently pulling up
Everything not tapered, frail and leafless,
Pleased to feel each little weed-root break,
But rueful also . . .
Then found myself listening to
The amplified grave ticking of hall clocks
Where the phone lay unattended in a calm
Of mirror glass and sunstruck pendulums . . .

And found myself then thinking: if it were nowadays,
This is how Death would summon Everyman.

Next thing he spoke and I nearly said I loved him.

Glossary

Title: A Call – A telephone contact but the word 'Call' also has more significant and serious connotations. The word call sometimes refers to a call from God.

Line 5 rig: a northern word for ridge.

Line 10 rueful: expressing regret but usually with a touch of humour.

Line 12 amplified: increased (sound).

Line 12 grave: serious, but a play on burial place.

Line 14 pendulums: free-swinging weights in a clock regulating the clock's mechanism.

Line 16 Everyman: the main character in the fifteenth century morality play (author unknown) of the same name.

The fifteenth-century *Everyman* play tells of the hero's journey towards death. Characters, such as Knowledge, Beauty, Goods, Kindred, personify these qualities. Everyman turns to them for help but in the end only Good Deeds is willing to accompany him to the grave. The well-known lines 'Everyman I will go with thee and be thy guide, In thy most need to be by thy side' are spoken by Good Deeds.

Questions

1. Heaney, introducing this poem at a reading, said, 'Death interrupts life; Death calls on everyone of us'. How does this poem, in your opinion, reflect that idea?
2. The poem's opening lines contain everyday, ordinary speech. What is the effect of this? Comment on the similarities and differences between ordinary language and the language of poetry.
3. Line 4 begins with the word 'So', a word frequently used by Heaney. What does the word 'So' create here? What mood does it introduce into the poem? How does it compare with the mood in the opening section?
4. The poem's second section paints a vivid picture of his father gardening. Which details, in your opinion, bring the scene to life?
5. Comment on the use of the word 'rueful' in line 10.
6. What connection does the speaker make between the image of his father weeding and the speaker's intense awareness of the ticking of clocks? Comment on the link between the word 'So' in line 4 and the word 'Then' in line 11. Why did the clock prompt the listener to think about death?
7. Comment on the use of 'grave' in line 12 and the image 'the phone lay unattended' in the following line.
8. Sections 2 and 3 end with an ellipsis [...]. What is the effect of this?
9. The arrangement of the poem on the page is such that the opening section is three lines long, followed by a seven-line section and then another seven lines divided into four, two and one. Why do you think the poet chose to arrange the poem in this particular way?
10. Explore and comment on how the poet invites you to imagine, to see and to hear in this poem.
11. The use of the word 'nowadays' highlights the contrast between the medieval play *Everyman* and the world the speaker inhabits. How does the poem capture a modern and different death summons?
12. What do you think of the poem's final line? How does it change what has gone before? How would you describe the language in the closing line? How would you describe the emotion it contains?

Postscript

And some time make the time to drive out west
Into County Clare, along the Flaggy Shore,
In September or October, when the wind
And the light are working off each other
So that the ocean on one side is wild
With foam and glitter, and inland among stones
The surface of a slate-grey lake is lit
By the earthed lightning of a flock of swans,
Their feathers roughed and ruffling, white on white,
Their fully grown headstrong-looking heads
Tucked or cresting or busy underwater.
Useless to think you'll park and capture it
More thoroughly. You are neither here nor there,
A hurry through which known and strange things pass
As big soft buffetings come at the car sideways
And catch the heart off guard and blow it open.

Glossary

Title: Postscript – an afterthought, an addition to a book after it is written; 'Postscript' is the final poem in Heaney's *Opened Ground*: *Poems, 1966–1996.*

Line 2 Flaggy Shore: an area of the burren. It is a half-mile of coastline between New Quay and Finvarra in County Clare.

Line 11 cresting: head high.

Line 15 buffetings: blows.

Line 16 off guard: unexpectedly.

Questions

1. The poem is full of sound and movement. Identify these and look at how the poem's three-sentence structure captures the feelings of the speaker.
2. Comments on the time of year and the colours in the poem.
3. Choose three details from the poem which, in your opinion, are particularly effective and interesting. Give reasons for your choice.
4. Why do you think is it 'Useless to think you'll park and capture it'?
5. Do you think this a get-away-from-it-all poem? Or is it something more than that?
6. 'You are neither here nor there' says the poet at line 13. What do you think he means by 'here' and 'there'? Where is the speaker if not either here or there?

Tate's Avenue

Not the brown and fawn car rug, that first one
Spread on sand by the sea but breathing land-breaths,
Its vestal folds unfolded, its comfort zone
Edged with a fringe of sepia-coloured wool tails.

Not the one scraggy with crusts and eggshells
And olive stones and cheese and salami rinds
Laid out by the torrents of the Guadalquivir
Where we got drunk before the corrida.

Instead, again, it's locked-park Sunday Belfast,
A walled back yard, the dust-bins high and silent
As a page is turned, a finger twirls warm hair
And nothing gives on the rug or the ground beneath it.

I lay at my length and felt the lumpy earth,
Keen-sensed more than ever through discomfort,
But never shifted off the plaid square once.
When we moved I had your measure and you had mine.

Glossary

Title: Tate's Avenue – in Belfast; an address associated with the speaker's student days.

Line 1 fawn: a light yellowish brown, sandy colour.

Line 3 vestal: pure, virginal, chaste (from Vesta, a Roman goddess, vowed to chastity and who shared charge of a sacred fire).

Line 3 comfort zone: a place where one feels at ease. The phrase has become a buzz word in the twenty-first century but Heaney uses it here without any trace of cliché.

Line 4 sepia-coloured: brown-coloured.

Line 5 scraggy: ragged or untidy.

Line 6 salami rinds: the tough outer layers of a highly-seasoned, preserved sausage originally from Italy.

Line 7 torrents: strong, fast-moving streams of water.

Line 7 Gaudalquivir: a river in Andalusia, in southern Spain; the name, from Arabic, means 'the Great Valley'.

Line 8 corrida: bullfight.

Line 9 locked-park Sunday Belfast: referring to a time when strict religious beliefs insisted the public parks were closed on a Sunday. It was thought that children should not play on the Lord's Day.

Line 10 high: here, 'high' refers to the whiff or the strong smell from the dustbins.

Line 15 plaid: chequered or tartan rug.

Line 16 your measure: body length and also a pun. The measure of you also means the value of you.

> Heaney himself, introducing this poem, has said that it is about a romantic scene in an unromantic setting; in *Stepping Stones,* he says that the erotic is present in 'Tate's Avenue' in 'an abstinent kind of way'.

? Questions

1. The image is of a young man and woman happy being in each other's company but shy at first and interested in each other. How does the speaker convey these details?

2. The poem moves back through time, to a sea-side scene, to a picnic in Spain to decades ago when he and she were young. What is the effect of 'not' at the beginning of the first and second stanzas?

3. Which of the three scenes is the most important to the speaker? How can you tell? What connects all three scenes?

4. How would you describe the Belfast setting? What is unattractive and what is attractive about it?

5. Why did the speaker not mind the 'lumpy earth', the 'discomfort' in stanza 4?

6. The poem contains many sensuous details. List these and explain what such details contribute to the poem.

7. Compare and contrast the scenes depicted in stanzas 2 and 4. How can one tell that they're from very different periods in the speaker's life?

8. Look at how 'I', 'we', 'your' and 'mine' work in the final stanza. Comment on the use of the phrase 'keen-sensed'.

General Questions

A. 'Many of Heaney's poems capture moments of insight in a striking and memorable way.' Discuss this view, supporting your answer by quotation or reference to the poems by Heaney on your course.

B. 'Heaney in his poetry often combines private and public worlds.' Discuss this statement, supporting your answer by quotation from or reference to the poems by Heaney on your course.

C. In the *Field Day Anthology of Irish Writing,* Heaney's poetry is said to be 'excavatory in every sense, reaching down into the ground and back into the past'. Examine this statement in the light of your reading of some of the poems by Heaney. In your answer, you should quote from or refer to the poems by Seamus Heaney on your course.

D. 'Heaney's language is sensuously evocative and rich in imagery.' Would you agree with this view? In your answer, you should quote from or refer to the poems by Seamus Heaney on your course.

E. 'Relationships, personal or otherwise, are at the heart of Seamus Heaney's poetry.' Discuss this view, supporting your answer by quotation or reference to the poems by Heaney on your course.

F. 'Place, its significance and resonances, plays a vitally important part in Seamus Heaney's poetry.' Discuss this view supporting the points you make with quotation or reference to the poems by Heaney on your course.

G. Identify and discuss what, in your opinion, are the distinctive qualities of Seamus Heaney's poetry. In your answer, you should refer to the poems by Heaney on your course.

H. 'Seamus Heaney is both a personal and a political poet.' Discuss this view, supporting your answer by quotation or reference to the poems by Heaney on your course.

Critical Commentary

The Forge

The sonnet's opening line is the five-foot, iambic pentameter. Eight of the words in line 1 are monosyllabic which gives the line the quality of statement, but the phrase 'All I know' suggests both humility and certainty. Heaney has not crossed the threshold. Though drawn to the forge, and its dark and strange interior, he examines and explores it from without.

The outside is familiar and can be seen clearly in daylight:

> Outside, old axles and iron hoops rusting

The following line focuses on the dark and interesting world within:

> Inside, the hammered anvil's short-pitched ring

The contrast here is clearly established. Heaney begins line 2 with 'Outside', line 3 with 'Inside'. Everything outside is lifeless: the axles are 'old', the iron hoops 'rusting', things falling apart, whereas there is great energy, strength and action associated with the inside of the forge. There things are being made. The anvil is being 'hammered' and the sound heard is a ringing 'short-pitched' one.

Lines 3 to 9 imagine the blacksmith's workplace. Heaney is fascinated by the place and he captures vividly and accurately what is going on. An image like that in line 4,

> The unpredictable fantail of sparks

gives the reader a fine sense of the irregular, unexpected shower of sparks. The metaphor of the fanshaped flow of sparks in 'fantail' brings the blacksmith's activity alive and gives it a beautiful quality.

Line 5 offers yet another aspect of the blacksmith's work and a contrast to the description in the previous line of sparks flying through the darkness. The image in lines 3 and 4 is one of sound and sight, this next image

> Or hiss when a new shoe toughens in water

is sound and sight also, but, instead of the clear metallic sounds of the 'short-pitched ring' (the very vowel sounds in 'pitched' and 'ring' creating an onomatopoeic effect) and the sparks flying through the air, there is now the hissing sound of the red-hot metal horse-shoe plunged in water. The word 'toughens' in line 5 conjures up strong solid metal contrasting with the airy, light sparks. Onomatopoeia, once again, is effective: the abrupt and short-lived 'hiss'. If you look at the words on the page this closely, you will see how Heaney offers so much accurately and imaginatively observed detail, how the senses are brought into play and how the Heaney voice is a musical one. He hears more than he sees. In line 6, he can only guess that:

> The anvil must be somewhere in the centre

But it is something special, legendary, a fixed presence. The anvil is:

> Horned as a unicorn, at one end square,
> Set there immoveable

When Heaney likens it to an altar, it also becomes something sacred. It is here that the blacksmith 'expends himself', using up his energy and his materials. The word 'expend' means both and both meanings are relevant here. The nuance and resonance of language, a word's several and different meanings, are often sounded out in a Heaney poem.

The phrase 'shape and music' is used to describe the blacksmith's work, though it could equally well be applied to Heaney's own skill, that of poetry making. The blacksmith is never named nor is the word blacksmith or farrier ever used. 'He' is how Heaney refers to him, a particular individual, but also perhaps a symbol of all blacksmiths and the end of a way of life.

The sonnet does not follow a conventional structure, either that of three quatrains and a couplet or an octet and sestet, but the closing five lines do signal a shift within the poem. Lines 1 to 9 describe the dark forge and Heaney's fascination with its sounds and activities. Lines 10 to 14 describe the blacksmith 'leather-aproned, hairs in his nose' coming out from the dark:

> He leans out on the jamb, recalls a clatter
> Of hoofs where traffic is flashing in rows

And, in two phrases, 'a clatter of hoofs' and traffic 'flashing in rows', Heaney puts an age-old way of life against the modern.

The motor car marks the end of the blacksmith's way of life. Cars are flashing by in rows: they are modern, gleaming creations and there are many of them, but the blacksmith is not impressed; instead he remembers and prefers 'a clatter / Of hoofs' and horses in their hey-day. 'Flashing' means moving at speed, but its other meaning of superficially brilliant or showy is also appropriate here.

The final two lines are noticeable for their strong sounds: grunts, goes, slam, flick, beat, work, the verbs especially giving the line a power and strength. The poem ends with the blacksmith at work in his forge, the world he knows best. There is a defiance and fighting spirit in his dismissive grunt. Our final image of him is one of a man at the height of his powers, strong, determined and hard at work. The poem began with 'All I know is a door into the dark' and the Irish literary critic John Wilson Foster says that 'at the sonnet's end he has yet to open that door, and stands transfixed upon the threshold, dumbly witnessing the blacksmith return to his grotto-like forge.' Another critic, Henry Hart, suggests that 'The door is knowable but the dark beyond blinds him [Heaney] to a creative process that is ultimately unknowable'.

Heaney as observer does not reveal his own attitude towards what is known as progress, the age of the horse giving way to the age of the motor car, but the poem clearly reveals Heaney's focused fascination with the forge.

Bogland

This poem is, first of all, about landscape. Later it becomes a poem about the past, memory and poetry itself. It begins with what the landscape is not: it is not flat and empty and extensive.

> We have no prairies
> To slice a big sun at evening –

The 'prairies' and 'big sun' conjure up images of a wild and adventurous west, the world of rich grasslands and cowboys. Heaney's tone is low-key, almost apologetic. Perhaps he is thinking of Theodore Roethke's poem 'In Praise of Prairie'.

The bogscape is first described with a painter's eye: there is horizon and foreground.

> Everywhere the eye concedes to
> Encroaching horizon,
> Is wooed into the cyclops' eye
> Of a tarn.

Instead of a landscape that opens up, the bogland Heaney describes is one that closes in; the eye, wherever it looks, gives way to an encroaching or intruding horizon or is drawn towards a small mountain lake. Like the prairies, this bogland is unfenced, but the ground is different from the prairie grasslands.

> Our unfenced country
> Is bog that keeps crusting
> Between the sights of the sun.

Bogland is mostly wet and soft and as Irish people it is ours.
His description of the tarn as 'the cyclops' eye' brings an interesting dimension to the landscape suggesting, as it does, power, strangeness and mystery.

Heaney's voice in this poem is closer to a speaking than a singing voice. The tone in the opening lines is full of awareness. There is very little end rhyme in the seven four-line stanzas, but a music emerges with alliteration (slice/sun, sights/sun, black/butter) internal rhyme (evening/Encroaching, taken/skeleton, Melting/opening) and his use of the run-on line.

The poem began by saying what this Irish landscape was not; there is the suggestion that, perhaps, the wide open prairies are more exciting. Heaney then goes on to describe and create a very dramatic and interesting landscape. Stanza 3 remembers the past: the poem now opens up to reveal history.

> They've taken the skeleton
> Of the Great Irish Elk
> Out of the peat, set it up
> An astounding crate full of air.

The image of the discovered and exhumed skeleton is an image of release and freedom; it is 'full of air', having been buried in the heavy bogland for centuries. The bog had held the elk until now; its appearance is 'astounding'.

Butter, something less strange than an elk, in fact something very domestic or close to home, is also found in the bog:

> Butter sunk under
> More than a hundred years
> Was recovered salty and white.

This is the palpable human link with the past. The elk is of the animal world; someone, sometime has made that butter with his or her own hands. On recovering it, the past is also being recovered.

The bogland holds the past. 'A turf bog', said Patrick Kavanagh, 'is a history of the world from the time of Noah', and Heaney in lines 16 to 19 is aware of that huge timespan, million of years:

> The ground itself is kind, **b**lack **b**utter
> **M**elting and open*ing* underfoot,
> **M**iss*ing* its last definition
> By **m**illions of years.

And these same lines reveal Heaney's masterful creation of sound:

> The ground itself is kind, black butter
>
> Melting and opening underfoot,
> Missing its last definition
> By millions of years.

The bogland is described as a living presence, 'melting and opening'; it lacks solidity. Heaney adds that 'They'll never dig coal here' and the poem ends with a description of what bogland is best known for, digging turf. The soft 'waterlogged trunks/of great firs' are dug and in a reference back to the opening lines of the poem Heaney speaks of Irish pioneers who, unlike their American counterparts who travelled westward and opened up new territory, 'kept striking/ Inwards and downwards', a vertical rather than a horizontal discovery. This image becomes a metaphor: the digging for turf becomes an image of the Irish people and their digging into the past and discovering more about themselves, layer after layer. The word 'pioneer' brings with it excitement, risk, adventure and new discoveries. That they are 'our' pioneers suggests a collective activity. The past should be actively explored; they will come upon other lives, traces of their ancestors:

> Every layer they strip
> Seems camped on before.

The closing lines, Heaney realised months after the poem was written, refer to 'a warning that older people would give us about going into the bog. They were afraid we might fall into the pools in the old workings, so they put it about (and we believed them) that *there was no bottom* to the bog-holes'. Interestingly, Edna Longley sees the bog as a door into 'the dark rich places of the human psyche'. and Michael Parker speaks of these lines,

> The bogholes might be Atlantic seepage.
> The wet centre is bottomless.

as celebrating the primacy of water, and the endless potential, the bottomless well of the imagination. Heaney himself draws a direct link between the digging down deep into the bog and the act of making a poem when he says: 'I have always listened for poems, they come sometimes like bodies out of a bog, almost complete, seeming to have been laid down a long time ago, surfacing with a touch of mystery.'

The Tollund Man

The poem is in eleven four-line stanzas and divided into three sections of five, three and three. The quiet opening line reveals something which Heaney knew almost as soon as he saw the photographs in Glob's book in 1969.

> Some day I will go to Aarhus
> To see his peat-brown head

It is a necessary journey, a pilgrimage. Heaney speaks of having 'vowed to go to pray to the Tollund Man', whom he regards as 'an ancestor almost, one of my old uncles', and the prayer he would pray is that the spirit of the Tollund Man would 'germinate' the murdered victims of Northern violence back to life.
The poem therefore opens up a long perspective, from the pagan, mythological past to a so-called Christian present; it shows, in British poet Blake Morrison's words, that 'some kind of connection exists between Iron Age sacrifices to the Mother Goddess of earth and the violent history of Northern Ireland'.

The language is often spare and simple; in many lines in section 1 the words are often monosyllabic ('Where they dug him out' / 'I will stand a long time' / 'Now his stained face') and the language here is a mourning music. This music is created through the pattern of sounds:

> Some day I will go to Aarhus
> To see his peat-brown head,
> The mild pods of his eye-lids,
> His pointed skin cap.

The writer Michael Parker, in his discussion of these lines, points out that in line 1, no vowel or consonant is repeated, but in lines 2, 3 and 4 a simple pattern of sounds emerges with 's', 'p', 'd', 'i'; Parker suggests that it is 'as if music should be retained solely for the young victim'. You may be impatient with such a detailed and careful analysis of the text but, to do the poem and yourself justice, you must look at the poem's achievement and recognise the poet's technique. Reading a poem aloud will bring you closer to its music. Look at that opening quatrain again:

> Some day I will go to Aarhus

This line clearly expresses Heaney's longing and determination and the lines that follow capture an emotional quality and contain vivid imagery:

> To see his peat-brown head,
> The mild pods of his eye-lids,
> His pointed skin cap.

Heaney's sympathetic imagination is evident in the opening quatrain. Though as yet only viewed in a photograph, Heaney in a phrase such as 'The mild pods of his eye-lids' captures a sense of innocence and gentleness in the Tollund Man. Heaney's eyes look into the eyes of a man who died a violent death and has not been seen for 2,000 years. Though Heaney is writing in the future tense, that imagined encounter is dramatically imagined.

In anticipating the journey that he will some day make, Heaney speaks in a reverent and respectful tone. He will visit the museum, but he will also return to the bog where the Tollund Man was buried. Heaney knows that he 'will stand a long time:

> In the flat country nearby
> Where they dug him out.

Stanzas 2 and 3 record the archaeological details: this dead man's last meal, his nakedness, the rope about his neck.

> His last gruel of winter seeds
> Caked in his stomach,
>
> Naked except for
> The cap, noose and girdle

The winter seeds died with the man. The seeds are also linked with rebirth and the very reason for his death: he was sacrificed to the Earth Goddess to make new growth possible in the spring. 'Caked' and 'Naked' are harsh sounding here; his nakedness makes him an even more vulnerable figure. 'I will stand a long time' looks back to 'Some day I will go to Aarhus', in its stark, bleak simplicity. Its tone is reverential: silence and stillness are called for; Heaney's mood will be a meditative one.

In line 12, Heaney gives us an image of the Tollund Man as one who has entered into a deep and intimate union with this earth spirit. The Tollund Man is mortal; she is immortal. He is

> Bridegroom to the goddess

and her extraordinary force and power is imagined and captured by Heaney in stanza 4:

> She tightened her torc on him
> And opened her fen,
> Those dark juices working
> Him to a saint's kept body.

'Tightened her torc' is a frightening image. The language is economic, compressed and everything usually associated with a torc, an ornamental and precious necklace, such as generosity and gift-giving, is twisted into something destructive and painful. The torc is the rope which is tightened about the man's throat. The contrast between the constricting, suffocating pressure of the noose and the opening fen is dramatic and vivid. The details suggest an almost sexual union between victim and goddess. She opens her fen to receive him.

Heaney compares the Tollund Man to the body of a preserved saint, and in so doing, pre-Christian and Christian are brought together in the description. The earth goddess, having received him, is to hold him forever; the goddess is in control.

The turfcutters, when they came upon the body, came upon a 'trove'. It was originally valuable because it pleased the goddess; it is also valuable because it allows Heaney to think about the past and its violent rituals, the violent present and the connection between the two across thousands of years.

The first section ends as it began, with a controlled, calm, quiet statement:

> Now his stained face
> Reposes at Aarhus.

The verb 'Reposes' suggests resting in peace. The soft 's' sounds and the half-rhyme 'Reposes' and 'Aarhus' bring the first section to a subdued close. The visitor to the museum, the poet Seamus Heaney, may view 'the stained face' at rest now. Knowing its violent history involves the viewer more, in a powerful and complex way.

Section 2 addresses the Tollund Man, but it also speaks of atrocities in the North of Ireland. Heaney says that he 'could risk blasphemy' and pray to this pagan creature as one might pray to a saint. The word 'could' expresses a hesitation; it goes against his own Christian background. Yet his prayer to the Tollund Man would be a prayer that some good might come from the Northern violence. To pray to such a being is viewed as blasphemous by Christians, but Heaney's wish to resurrect the dead in his own part of Ireland is so strong that he thinks that he could risk blasphemy:

> I could risk blasphemy,
> Consecrate the cauldron bog
> Our holy ground and pray
> Him to make germinate
>
> The scattered, ambushed
> Flesh of labourers,
> Stockinged corpses
> Laid out in the farmyards

In this section, the Tollund Man is not spoken of in particular detail, as in section 1; here he is addressed as a spirit or god. Heaney imagines himself thinking and wishing 'the cauldron bog' of Ulster a sacred place, 'Our holy ground'. The Tollund Man was buried as part of a sacred ritual and so the bog, his burial ground, was seen as a holy place. Here the poet wishes the dead to come back to life; wishes the Tollund Man to become a kind, protective presence who might counteract the violence in the North.

His prayer is for the renewal of life, exactly what the Tollund Man was made to die for. And the image Heaney uses is the natural, rural image of the seed. Heaney could pray to

> Him to make germinate
>
> The scattered, ambushed
> Flesh of labourers

of the workers who were brutally murdered in sectarian violence. He prays to the Tollund Man to help Ireland in its time of conflict. Here is an expression of Heaney's religious nature.

The obscenity of the Northern killings is most strongly conveyed in stanza 8. Lines 25 and 26 suggest the violent deaths of many: bodies are 'scattered', 'ambushed', but Heaney also focuses on a specific violent moment.

When Heaney was growing up in the 1950s, the story was still being told of how four Catholic brothers had been massacred by Protestant paramilitaries in the 1920s and the bodies had been dragged for miles along the railway sleepers. (400 people had been killed between 1920 and 1922 and violence and unrest continued for decades.) It is the death of 'four young brothers', which Heaney is referring to here. The details are sickening. The poem does not flinch from reality:

> Tell-tale skin and teeth
> Flecking the sleepers
> Of four young brothers, trailed
> For miles along the lines.

The mutilation is grotesque; 'Flecking' is horrible in its implication. The soft sounds of 'four young brothers' and the idea they represent summon up a picture of family, a future; the long sound of 'trailed' together with the rhymed 'miles' and 'lines' are imitative of their prolonged deaths. 'Stockinged corpses' suggests young men; that the bodies were 'Laid out in the farmyards' makes the poem even more moving: they were prepared for burial in the place where they lived and worked.

'The Tollund Man' was written at a time when the North of Ireland was witnessing a renewed outbreak of violence. Heaney specifically focuses on an episode 50 years before; as a result, his reader is being reminded of sectarian violence past and present. The death of the Tollund Man and these other deaths convey a vast perspective. The reader is being asked to consider the similarities and differences between them.

Section 3 focuses both on the past and future: a day 2,000 years ago when the Tollund man was buried and the day when Heaney will visit the museum in Aarhus. Heaney speaks of his journey to his burial place in the bog as a 'sad freedom'. This phrase 'sad freedom' is a difficult and interesting one. 'Freedom' here has a price; with freedom there is an accompanying sorrow or sadness. The Tollund Man on his way to his execution and burial is described as experiencing a 'sad freedom'; it is 'his sad freedom' and Heaney knows that he will experience something resembling that same emotion when he travels that same road, repeating the names 'Tollund, Grabualle, Nebelgard'. With death, there is a form of freedom for the Tollund Man, but it cannot be separated from sadness. Perhaps Heaney's own 'sad freedom' is the freedom of distancing himself from the Northern situation and the sadness as a result of that.

A strong, close, direct link is felt between Heaney and the Tollund Man: even the rhyme points to this – the 'he' in line 34 and the 'me' of line 35.

The Tollund Man rode a cart to his grave. Nothing is known in fact of how the man was brought to Tollund but Heaney deliberately uses 'tumbril' to rid the moment of any pomp or circumstance; the Tollund Man's journey through the Jutland countryside then prompts Heaney to imagine his own journey through that same countryside when he will some day 'go to Aarhus'.

Heaney will feel himself a stranger as he drives the road the Tollund Man was carried, yet he will share something of the Tollund Man's 'sad freedom':

> Something of his sad freedom
> As he rode the tumbril
> Should come to me, driving,
> Saying the names
>
> Tollund, Grabaulle, Nebelgard,
> Watching the pointing hands
> Of country people,
> Not knowing their tongue.

Listing those placenames is listing the places which are now associated with ancient rituals and death. The list becomes a form of incantation, a poetry in itself. In this imagined future, the people he meets point him towards these places, but he cannot speak their language; he is the outsider, the one who is lost.

Heaney ends the poem by focusing, not on the Tollund Man or on the North of Ireland directly, but on his own strange feelings which he knows he will experience once there:

> Out there in Jutland
> In the old man-killing parishes
> I will feel lost,
> Unhappy and at home.

He has already recognised that these Jutland deaths are different from the deaths in the North of Ireland, yet he knows he will feel bewildered, sad and at the same time he will see similarities between Jutland and his native Ireland. Though 'Out there', he will feel 'lost, / Unhappy and at home.' He has made the poem and in doing so he has confronted violence. In *The Government of the Tongue*, Heaney speaks of how 'the form of poetry itself' can hold 'a higher consciousness' and this was 'an ideal towards which the poets turned' in order to survive what he terms 'the stunting conditions' of Northern Ireland.

In a powerfully effective phrase, Jutland is described as 'the old man-killing parishes' in this final stanza (line 42). The word 'old' denotes as long ago as 20,000 years ago; 'man-killing' is the reality of the Tollund Man's ritualistic death; and 'parishes', meaning community or township, are being destroyed.

The rural settings throughout, the 'flat country' and 'fen' of section 1, the 'labourers' and 'farmyards' in section 2, the country people who will direct Heaney towards Tollund in section 3, also link both communities, those in Jutland and those in Northern Ireland and by implication everywhere.

When Heaney wrote this poem he compared it to a 'coming up into the light'. It clearly marked for him a feeling of release. He has taken on a huge theme. 'The Tollund Man' is both political and personal, public and private; it is a poem that confronts an ugly, human reality. In this poem, Heaney expresses pity for all victims of violence, longs for life not death. It is a sympathetic and imaginative response and by working through his feelings he reaches an understanding in which he is both 'Unhappy and at home', a phrase that points to the possibility of being happy in one's community if the violence did end.

Mossbawn: Sunlight

As title and dedication suggest, this poem celebrates a place and a person. It is unashamedly nostalgic and the poem, as it summons up the past, shifts from the past to the present tense, bringing the moment closer. Heaney has said that in this poem he set out to write from the point of view of the baby within the womb.

The first line sets a mood. It is a short sentence, complete in itself, the shortest in the poem, and all the other, longer sentences in the poem flow from this opening line.

> There was a sunlit absence.

The word 'sunlit' and the 'Sunlight' of the title bathe the moment in warmth. It is a moment of 'absence', not presence, yet the sense of emptiness that absence usually conveys is, in this instance, an emptiness which is filled with the memory of the pump and his aunt. Absence becomes presence.

That opening line also captures stillness, silence, mystery. If there is absence, there is no movement; there is space. Line 1 conveys a mood: Mossbawn in 'long afternoon' sunlight, nothing particular focused on – space, light, warmth, – and then the image of the pump in the yard.

The pump, of course, is a very definite and important presence in Mossbawn. It is the source of water and thereby the source of life. This memory poem celebrates that pump in bright sunlight:

> The helmeted pump in the yard
> heated its iron,
> water honeyed
>
> in the slung bucket

The only person in these lines is the observant poet. The iron heating slowly, the water warming in the bucket, are slow, silent, natural processes. 'Helmeted' in line 2 is not only the pump's shape; it can also mean protective. Without its pump, Mossbawn could not live. Heaney is always alive to the nuances and subtleties of language. The use of 'honeyed' captures the presence of the sun as it warms the water 'in the slung bucket' and gives it a magical touch. 'Helmeted', 'heated', 'honeyed' in lines 2, 3 and 4 are musical in their alliteration and assonance. The sun itself is familiar and domesticated in the image of the 'griddle':

> the sun stood
> like a griddle cooling
> against the wall
>
> of each long afternoon.

The round, golden, cooling griddle bread is a homely image from Heaney's childhood as it stood against the wall. The simile suggests that though time passed ('each long afternoon'), time also stood still ('the sun stood'). The moment was held and stored in memory.

There is a natural development and structure to the poem: the place itself, the farm yard, the sun compared to a cake of bread and then the bread itself, baked by Mary Heaney, the most important presence in the poem. There is a gradual movement from abstract to concrete, from outside, in; and the love is given a tangible reality in the everyday activity of the woman. 'Mossbawn: Sunlight' acquires the lovingly observed detail of a Dutch interior painting: a woman in a kitchen, a domestic activity, window-light transforming the ordinary into something extraordinary and beautiful. This is, without doubt, a beautiful poem and one should never be uneasy or embarrassed about saying so. That its beauty is found in the everyday makes it all the more remarkable.

The word 'So' at line 10 introduces Mary Heaney and it defines the moment. It also confirms her importance in the poem and how the sun is compared to 'griddle' leads naturally to the baking of the griddle bread itself.

Heaney published this poem in the mid '70s when he was in his early thirties. He is thinking back and at first he is thinking in the past tense:

> So, her hands scuffled
> over the bakeboard

Here there is great sense of movement as her hands make the bread. The onomatopoeic 'scuffled' is yet another example of Heaney's fine ear. (The poem in fact celebrates, in passing, what are often termed life's essentials: bread and water.) The short lines run on and create a flowing, complete scene. The poem has very few commas and full-stops, and when used they are used very effectively.

Throughout the poem, the senses are at work in creating atmosphere: the reader sees and hears her hands at work, sees the reddening stove, feels 'its plaque of heat', senses the texture of the 'floury apron', sees the sunlight through the window.

> So, her hands scuffled
> over the bakeboard,
> the reddening stove
>
> sent its plaque of heat
> against her where she stood
> in a floury apron
> by the window.

'Now' at the beginning of line 17 brings the poem from past to present; Heaney repeats 'now' at line 19, giving the moment immediacy. The whole world of the poem is brought closer:

Now she dusts the board
with a goose's wing,
now sits, broad-lapped,
with whitened nails

and measling shins:

Again there is activity and movement – the dusting of the board; then there is stillness, a sense of completion. She 'sits'. The 'goose's wing' was known and used in country kitchens long ago. Heaney is thinking back twenty years or so, but 'goose's wing' is age old and there is something almost timeless about much of the poem.

Mary Heaney is never idealised. She is 'broad-lapped', her nails 'whitened'; she has 'measling shins'. She is a very special presence in the poem and yet her presence makes possible a space, not an empty space, but a space where there is a sense of fulfilment, completion and love. Heaney's recognition of the moment, this spot of time, is a moment of deep insight and understanding. The busyness of baking, the sitting down afterwards lead to this moment, a moment which Heaney calls a space:

Now she dusts the board
with a goose's wing,
now sits, broad-lapped,
with whitened nails

and measling shins:
here is a space
again, the scone rising
to the tick of two clocks.

Heaney has spoken of how sometimes in his work there are 'images of a definite space which is both empty and full of potential. It's a sense of a node that is completely clear where emptiness and potential stream in opposite directions. And I'm delighted to find in one of my favourite earlier poems – "Sunlight Mossbawn" – a line (I don't know where it came from): "Here is a space again".'

The use of the word 'again' in 'here is a space / again' reminds us of other spaces, other such moments. It reminds us of the 'sunlit absence' of the opening line. The woman had made bread and the scone is rising; the poet had made the poem and the words are being marked on the page. The 'tick of two clocks' and 'the scone rising' suggest the passing of time, yet the poem holds the moment forever.

Line 25, 'And here is love', is made possible by line 22, 'here is a space'; one follows on from the other. Like the sunlight, love is everywhere in this poem: it is Heaney's love of place, his love for his aunt, the love she radiates in her everyday life. Love is precious, hidden, found in the most ordinary of places, a farmyard, a kitchen:

> And here is love
> like a tinsmith's scoop
> sunk past its gleam
> in the meal-bin.

Love is compared to a tinsmith's scoop: this symbol with which the poem ends is both the familiar, domestic object used by Mary Heaney when baking and an image of a glowing, buried light. Heaney's Aunt Mary's love is found in the routine of the everyday. Like the scoop's gleam, it is hidden in the ordinary. Though introduced as an image, through simile, the scoop, the actual object, also belongs to the actual setting of the poem. The final image, therefore, is like the first striking image in the poem, the pump.

Hands and touch recur throughout 'Mossbawn: Sunlight', especially in the person of Mary Heaney making bread for the household, and this gives the poem a tactile, sensuous quality. Heaney has remembered the past and made it present. He says 'here is love'; it is before him now and it makes possible the poem.

A close reading of 'Mossbawn: Sunlight' will reveal a masterly control of language. There isn't an obvious rhyme anywhere, yet alliteration, assonance, onomatopoeia, repetition, internal rhymes, structure and feeling make this a perfect poem.

A Constable Calls

This poem, like 'Mossbawn: Sunlight', is a memory poem, but the mood here is very different. It is written in the past tense throughout and begins with accurate description. Heaney is the young observer. At first, it may seem that he is offering no interpretation, no comment, no opinion:

> His bicycle stood at the window-sill,
> The rubber cowl of a mud-splasher
> Skirting the front mudguard,
> Its fat black handlegrips
>
> Heating in sunlight, the 'spud'
> Of the dynamo gleaming and cocked back

And yet even in these six descriptive lines one has a sense of the constable himself. The bicycle 'stood' upright, precise; it is well-equipped and its 'mud-splasher', 'dynamo' and 'fat black handlegrips' suggest control and authority. The very sounds of 'fat black' coming together are threatening. The dynamo 'cocked back' suggests assurance and confidence.

In lines 7 and 8, Heaney attributes a feeling to the bicycle. He imagines

> The pedal treads hanging relieved
> Of the boot of the law

and this signals something of Heaney's private feelings about the constable, who is never given a personal name. The constable cycles his bicycle, pushing the pedals; he does his duty, but the phrase 'the boot of the law' not only refers to the constable's actual boot, but also implies an impersonal, forceful, powerful presence.

Stanza 3 moves indoors to focus on the constable at work:

> His cap was upside down
> On the floor, next his chair.

A welcomed visitor might hang his hat; the constable, for whatever reason, leaves his 'upside down' on the floor. The details now include the man himself. The print of authority is on him. Heaney tells us that though his cap is on the floor:

> The line of its pressure ran like a bevel
> In his slightly sweating hair.

The 'sweating hair' in this instance is yet another small but unattractive detail. He is hot from cycling. There is no mention of him being offered a drink.

We never see the constable's face. He is more symbolic than human. He is there to carry out the law:

> He had unstrapped
> The heavy ledger, and my father
> Was making tillage returns
> In acres, rood, and perches.

The exchange is factual and mathematical. In stanza 4, however, the word 'my' is deeply personal. Compare it to 'His bicycle', 'His cap', 'his belt', 'his cap', 'His boot'. The business being described here is impersonal, matter-of-fact. The constable is anonymous; 'my father' is not.

The constable has been described by the critic Michael Painter as an 'unperson'.

The policeman is portrayed as a 'shadow' being, rather than as an individual. His uniform makes him the embodiment of the Protestant State, and, like his bike, he seems composed of distinctly separate features, a cap, sweating hair, a polished holster, braid cord, a baton-case, a voice without a face.

The real significance of the exchange and its significance for Heaney is captured in the phrase

> Arithmetic and fear.

The meeting is a necessary and an uneasy one. Heaney's father is afraid. He is a Catholic in a predominantly Protestant community, knowing that the people with power, including this constable, are from a different tradition.

In the first poem in the 'Singing School' sequence, Heaney has acknowledged another aspect of this divide when he quotes: 'Catholics, in general, don't speak / As well as students from the Protestant schools.'

Heaney, the boy, does not speak. His thoughts and feelings remain hidden and they are shaped to become the poem itself on the page. Stanza 5, however, continues to record the presence of this constable in their home. What he focuses on are those things for which a constable is known:

> I sat staring at the polished holster
> With its buttoned flap, the braid cord
> Looped into the revolver butt.

The meticulous detail here of 'polished', 'buttoned' and 'Looped' suggest someone in control and command.

When the constable speaks, it is colourless, business-like, perfunctory:

> 'Any other root crops?
> Mangolds? Marrowstems? Anything like that?'

Four utterances. Four question marks. An interrogation. Heaney's father's response – the single, unaccompanied 'No' – is short, impersonal and direct. There is no friendliness between these two men.

Heaney remembers something that his father forgot (or simply chose not) to report and he is full of little fears:

> But was there not a line
> Of turnips where the seed ran out
> In the potato field?

That Heaney should even think such a detail worth reporting is indicative of his unease with the law. It is as if they lived in a state in which every single activity, no matter how small, had to be reported to the authorities. His boyish, fearful imagination worries about the consequences of not telling:

I assumed
Small guilts and sat
Imagining the black hole in the barracks.

Once business is done, there is no sense of small talk. The constable adjusts his baton into position and closes the ledger:

He stood up, shifted the baton-case

Further round on his belt,
Closed the domesday book,
Fitted his cap back with two hands,
And looked at me as he said goodbye.

That the book is referred to here as the 'domesday book' has special resonance when its original and historical meanings are known. The book in which the names are written of all those who have ever lived and died and who will be judged by God is an image that instils a certain fear and a sense of unknowing. The historical meaning of the 'domesday book', as the Great Inquisition, is also relevant here as this is literally what the constable is about, not in eleventh-century England, but in twentieth-century Ulster.

Even a gesture as in line 31, 'Fitted his cap back with two hands', suggests formality, a public persona. He speaks no word to the young boy, but 'looked at me as he said goodbye'. In the final stanza, he is seen as 'A shadow', a darkening presence, and his actions are abrupt and efficient:

He was snapping the carrier spring
Over the ledger. His boot pushed off
And the bicycle ticked, ticked, ticked.

The information has been gathered; again, that boot. It is never spoken of in the poem, but Heaney's small guilt over the line of turnips may now turn to relief and a satisfaction, perhaps, in knowing that the constable hasn't recorded everything exactly. The closing words 'ticked, ticked, ticked' have been compared to the sound of a timed bomb but this might be labouring the interpretation.

'A Constable Calls' speaks of a visit by someone from another tradition, but throughout the poem there is no hint of the personal or of the friendly.

The Skunk

There are very few love poems like this and it is an indication of Heaney's deep love for his wife and her generous spirit that a comparison such as the one used here works so well and so successfully. The skunk is noted for emitting a very offensive odour when attacked or killed; a narrow-minded and humourless woman would be insulted by the comparison. The skunk's less attractive qualities are not dwelt on here, however, and Heaney succeeds in writing a most unusually wonderful, assured, intimate, humorous and erotic love poem.

Heaney, in an interview, speaking of the love poems in *Field Work*, said: '"Love poems" is a terrible phrase; "poems about relationships" is a bit limp too perhaps.., "Marriage poems", call them. There's no reason why benign emotions shouldn't be able to find utterance.'

The poem begins with a description of the skunk, 'Up, black, striped', and gives no indication where this poem will eventually go.

The poem's first words bring the skunk of the title before us. The four adjectives capture the animal's tail; the commas and the use of 'and' give each aspect of the tail a separate focus:

> Up, black, striped and damasked. . .

The unusual simile ought to sound a melancholy, funereal note:

> and damasked like the chasuble
> At a funeral mass

and somehow it does not. It is playfully irreverent. The first line does not tell us what it describes; that is revealed in line 2, but Heaney gives us the thing itself, the tail which is seen before its owner. With marvellous economy that first, long sentence follows the skunk's arrival and movement; it ends with a flourish, an announcement:

> the skunk's tail
> Paraded the skunk.

'The Skunk' is a night-time poem. The word night occurs four times and again in the poem's last word, 'nightdress'. The skunk, which is the main focus of the first two stanzas, is seen as a regular visitor:

> Night after night
> I expected her like a visitor.

Lines 5 to 7 set the scene. Sound and silence, soft light and darkness, the colours orange and green, an evening warmth are all sensuously evoked in this second stanza:

> The refrigerator whinnied into silence.
> My desk light softened beyond the verandah.
> Small oranges loomed in the orange tree.

Line 8 gives us not what Heaney sees but his own inner feeling of unease:

> I began to be tense as a voyeur.

Here the word 'voyeur' signals a change of direction. Heaney is no longer watching the skunk; he is looking into the darkness and seeing his wife. He is 6,000 miles away, but he is now totally preoccupied with her.

At line 9, the poem has shifted into a different mode. Heaney speaks of his wife directly. It may seem as if she is mentioned suddenly, unexpectedly, but Heaney, in line 6, has already told us that he is at his writing desk and that he is writing to his wife back home in Ireland. The skunk is outside his window; Heaney is alone and thinking of his wife.

Not until the final stanza are we told how his mind has worked, how he made the connection between skunk and wife, how it all came back to him 'last night'.

First, he is remembering himself writing love-letters again, now that they are temporarily apart:

> After eleven years I was composing
> Love-letters again, broaching the word 'wife'
> Like a stored cask, as if its slender vowel
> Had mutated into the night earth and air
> Of California.

Distance and absence have sharpened and concentrated Heaney's thinking about the word 'wife'. First, his approaching the word suggests to him 'a stored cask', an image of something precious, matured and self-contained. This becomes an image of their marriage. Then he hears in the word wife, one of the oldest words in the English language, 'its slender vowel'. He sees a cask, hears a sound; next he senses that sound changing into California, its 'night earth and air'. Heaney's wife is in Ireland and the word wife is distanced in the very text by the use of inverted commas; in his mind, the word is changed or mutated into California, a place-name that resonates with significance.

Wife and California both share that assonantal 'if': wif e, Calif ornia. When Heaney wrote this poem California not only meant the spirit of adventure and sunshine, with which the state has always been associated, but more recently the freedom of expression of the 1960s. 'The Skunk' would never have been written if it were not for California. Heaney has frequently said in interviews that his being at Berkeley in the early seventies opened up new poetic possibilities, new freedoms.

Heaney's wife is both absent and present. In her absence, Heaney summons her to heart and mind. The place, its scent, intensifies his sense of longing:

> The beautiful, useless
> Tang of eucalyptus spelt your absence.

A mouthful of wine brings no pleasure. It only reminds him of how she isn't here:

> The aftermath of a mouthful of wine
> Was like inhaling you off a cold pillow.

This last image is one of intense longing; he longs for his wife to be by his side in bed. But he only senses her absence all the more.

Having lost himself to longing Heaney returns to the skunk in stanza 5. He was waiting for her, then forgets the skunk as he thinks of and longs for his wife; then the skunk is before him on the verandah:

> And there she was, the intent and glamorous,
> Ordinary, mysterious skunk,
> Mythologised, demythologised

If the adjectives here are taken separately, they serve not only as a description of an animal but they also honour a woman who is the marriage partner in a steady and mature love relationship: 'intent'; 'glamorous'; 'ordinary'; 'mysterious'; 'mythologised'; 'demythologised' bring together the nature of this marriage. The contradictory descriptions here are realistic and particularly effective. A marriage, because of its long-lastingness, has to have ordinariness and the everyday about it, yet the mysterious and the mythological must also be a part if the relationship is to hold its special qualities.

The skunk is 'snuffing' the boards; it is head-down. The 'snuffing' is 'ordinary' not mysterious, and it is this gesture that leads into the final humorous and very affectionate final stanza:

> It all came back to me last night, stirred
> By the sootfall of your things at bedtime,
> Your head-down, tail-up hunt in a bottom drawer
> For the black plunge-line nightdress.

Here in the intimacy of the bedroom, husband and wife are preparing for bed. They are together again after separation and Heaney now reveals how his wife, 'head-down, tail-up', brings to mind the skunk he used to see 'Snuffing the boards' in California.

Heaney is 'stirred' by the soft sounds of her clothes falling to the ground as 'sootfall'.

The critic Neil Corcoran says of this word: 'it is beautifully accurate in the way it listens to the clothes falling to the bedroom floor, but it also remembers that the clothes are, like all clothes falling from a human body at bedtime, dirty. To be 'stirred' by such a 'sootfall' is to bear witness to the ordinary mysteriousness of a marriage'.

When you read a poem, when you discuss a poem in class or wherever, when you read a critical response, you may not always agree with another person's interpretation. What one must work towards is an intelligent and clear understanding of the text. You can disagree with any viewpoint but your own interpretation should be faithful to what the poet has written. This is often difficult because a poem not only says something, it can also suggest and imply. This is why the reader should make good use of words such as 'perhaps': 'Here the poet, perhaps, is thinking of. . .'

In the passage above, Neil Corcoran interprets 'sootfall' to imply dirty clothes. 'Sootfall' works through both colour and sound. It captures the soft fall of clothes to the bedroom floor and suggests, perhaps, that the clothes are black, and not from dirt! We should ask whether Corcoran's reading of the word 'sootfall' is true to the poem's meaning.

The phrase 'head-down, tail-up hunt' belongs to both wife and skunk, which adds to the gentle humour of the poem. She is hunting for a sexy 'black plunge-line nightdress'; the image of the black chasuble of the funeral mass used to describe the skunk has been replaced by another garment, a real 'plunge-line nightdress'. And the word 'black' used to describe the skunk becomes the black of the nightdress. What began with a funereal image ends with an image of happy, married love and the anticipation, not of 'a cold pillow', but a shared bed.

The Harvest Bow

Stanza 1 belongs to Heaney's father, Patrick Heaney. He is making the harvest bow and Heaney sees this not only as symbolic of the gathered harvest but as a symbol of his father's hidden self. It is autumn, the dying of the year and, like Keat's great ode 'To Autumn', there is a sense of fulfilment, completion, harmony. Keats speaks of 'mellowed fruitfulness'; Heaney speaks of his father's 'mellowed silence'.

> As you plaited the harvest bow
> You implicated the mellowed silence in you

Heaney's father's hands are not only plaiting the actual bow, they also seem to be drawing together, interlacing, the silence within him and implying that silence. In his poem 'An August Night' from *Seeing Things* (1991), Heaney says of his father that 'His hands were warm and small and knowledgeable'.

Heaney's use of the word 'implicated' here is word perfect. Implicated means both to intertwine and to imply. In one word, Heaney has captured both the act and its symbolic significance. It is a 'mellowed silence', suggesting not only the time of year but his time of life.

The long line which flows into the next – throughout this poem there are remarkably few commas to prevent this flowing movement – create a gentle mood in keeping with the autumnal mood of the poem as a whole.

Though the harvest has been cut, the wheat, when made into a harvest bow, gleams. It has a new life; the harvest bow is fashioned

> In wheat that does not rust
> But brightens as it tightens twist by twist
> Into a knowable corona,
> A throwaway love-knot of straw.

The land had produced the harvest and man has now taken that natural product and shaped it into the harvest bow. This is a transforming act, similar to what the artist does when creating a work of art. The tightening twist causes the wheat to brighten; the very phrase that Heaney uses to describe the act is tightly made. The wheat

> brightens as it tightens twist by twist

and the rhyming 'brightens', 'tightens' and the triple alliteration on 't' give the line a charged energy. The action is going on as the sentence is being spoken. It is a line that illustrates well Walt Whitman's understanding of the language of poetry, where one finds 'sounds tuned to their uses'.

In line 5, 'corona' picks up on 'brightens' in line 4 and, by comparing the bow to a small circle of light, Heaney gives it a perfection and beauty. It is a 'knowable corona', something recognised and understood. The harvest bow is something familiar, made each year in autumn, an expression of the season, the passing of time. When Heaney in line 6 also calls it

> A throwaway love-knot of straw

he speaks of its short-lived, temporary nature. It may be viewed as 'throwaway' by its maker; the harvest bow was made each year and in the poem Heaney's father makes no ceremony of giving the harvest bow to his son. But for Heaney it speaks of an unspoken love. Though a 'love-knot', it is a 'throwaway'; yet Heaney does not throw it away. In the final stanza, he tells us that he has pinned it up on his kitchen dresser.

The hands that made the harvest bow are aged hands. Heaney, in stanza 2, remembers them as farmer's hands

> Hands that aged round ashplants and cane sticks

These same hands also 'lapped the spurs on a lifetime of game cocks'. This conjures up a very different image from the hands that plait a harvest bow but Heaney is not romanticising his father; he is merely acknowledging that hands that held a cattle stick or that could send game cocks into a cock fight could also fashion and shape something beautiful like the harvest bow.

Heaney speaks of this ability to make the harvest bow as a 'gift'; the hands now belong to a different order of things as they

> worked with fine intent
> Until your fingers moved somnambulant

First there is the 'fine intent', the careful, concentrated effort, and then a stage where the fingers moved without strain or conscious effort. This is the artistic act itself; it describes the making of harvest bow, the making of the poem itself.

When Heaney holds the harvest bow in his hand he can

> tell and finger it like braille,
> Gleaning the unsaid off the palpable

His father worked in silence, but now what has been unsaid is communicated from father to son in the harvest bow. 'Gleaning' is so naturally appropriate in this context. The harvest gives us the harvest bow and the harvest bow in turn gives Heaney his father's unspoken emotion. Heaney 'gathers in' or gleans from feeling and thinking about this harvest bow the love and fulfilment which the bow symbolises.

In the third stanza, Heaney tells us that within the bow's intricate curves he can see into the past and particularly to another autumn when father and son were walking one evening:

> And if I spy into its golden loops
> I see us walk between the railway slopes
> Into an evening of long grass and midges

Gradually an atmosphere is evoked through detail:

> Blue smoke straight up, old beds and ploughs in hedges,
> An auction notice on an outhouse wall –

There is nothing scenic here, with the abandoned furniture and farm equipment, the buying and selling world of the auction, the outhouse wall, but there is something even more important than place; there is Heaney's warm memory of how special that moment was. 'Blue smoke straight up' is slow, soft and beautiful and the descriptions are sensuous, but this autumn landscape is so totally different from what Keats describes in his ode.

Yet the moment is special, not for what was said, but for what Heaney felt as he walked with his father who wore a harvest bow:

> You with a harvest bow in your lapel,
>
> Me with the fishing rod,

The poem has a present and a past and in line 19 Heaney talks of how, in remembering the past and an evening such as the one he describes, he feels homesick. When the past is described in 'The Harvest Bow' it is always described in the present tense – 'I see us walk' – and when he speaks of his homesickness he gives us a moment ordinary and special in a stanza that is perfectly rhymed. He knows that if he spies into the 'golden loops' of the harvest bow he is

> already homesick
> For the big lift of these evenings, as your stick
> Whacking the tips off weeds and bushes
> Beats out of time, and beats, but flushes
> Nothing: that original townland
> Still tongue-tied in the straw tied by your hand.

'These evenings' of silent companionableness will not last forever; hence his feeling of homesickness. Such evenings are both ordinary and extraordinary.

The ordinariness of the moment is found in 'Whacking', 'weeds', 'bushes', 'beats'. His father 'beats out of time, and beats'. The whacking and beating are violent acts, yet these same hands have delicately fashioned and plaited a harvest bow. In such gestures Heaney gives us two sides of his father's personality.

Not a word is spoken. The sounds are of the stick, whacking and beating, and the stick 'flushes / Nothing'. The nothing here refers to the fact that not a bird or small animal was driven out by the sound of the stick but Heaney implies another meaning:

> Nothing: that original townland
> Still tongue-tied in the straw tied by your hand

The colon here after 'Nothing' suggests a connection between the unsuccessful attempt to find something in the weeds and bushes and the inability to express feelings. Heaney does not speak of his father as 'tongue-tied' but 'that original townland'. It is as if the emotion felt by a people in a townland can be expressed only in the silence of the harvest bow, not in the spoken word. The word 'townland' opens up the poem to include a whole community of country people, a people who gather in the harvest each year and mark that event with the making of a harvest bow.

The poem is the spoken and the written word. Heaney as poet is speaking of his feelings and his love for his father; he is not tongue-tied. In the final stanza, Heaney is in his own kitchen. The poem has moved from Heaney's father's house in Co. Derry, through the landscape of his original townland and then it rests in the contemplation of harvest bow as symbol. Heaney has plaited together remembered moments and the result is a feeling of deep happiness.

The bow is but a 'frail device' but it expresses a complex and interesting idea:

> *The end of art is peace*
> Could be the motto of this frail device
> That I have pinned up on our dresser –

That the motto comes from Coventry Patmore by way of Yeats is significant in itself. It speaks of art's ultimate achievement; it is something understood and longed for by other makers of art in other times. Art makes possible a peace, however momentary. The harvest bow is artefact and the images it has summoned up in the poem, its journey from a father's aged hands to his son's 'deal dresser', lead towards a feeling of love, a feeling of peace. The very act and art of making is peaceful. That it is 'our deal dresser' introduces another relationship also into the poem, that of married love. The love between father and son is now linked with the love between man and wife in the 'frail device' of the harvest bow. The poem ends with an image of the bow as 'a drawn snare':

> Like a drawn snare
> Slipped lately by the spirit of the corn
> Yet burnished by its passage, and still warm.

The bow has snared the corn and yet the spirit of the corn has lately slipped. The corn spirit has departed but its spirit is still seen ('burnished') and felt ('still warm'). What remains, of course, is not the spirit of the corn but the spirit of his father. The spirit of the corn has to slip away; there will be another harvest next year, but the poem itself now holds the warmth of human love. The poem could therefore be read as a poem about continuity. Though there are rusting 'old beds and ploughs in hedges', there will also be a new harvest; the love between father and son makes possible a love between man and wife.

Heaney in this poem displays a great imaginative and sympathetic understanding of his father. This is a poem about inheritance and there is no need for his father to speak words: he has spoken through gesture and through his 'mellowed silence'.

The Underground

This poem remembers an evening from the speaker's honeymoon in London in 1965. The couple are heading to a concert in the Albert Hall. They are late and when they leave the Tube they are rushing down a tunnel, underground. The moment is brought alive with the immediacy of the opening words: 'There we were' and the opening stanza paints a picture of movement, anxiety, disconnectedness. She is 'speeding ahead'; he is following and he thinks of her as someone elusive, someone whom he will never catch up with.

This reference to Greek mythology opens up the experience: a young man and woman, newly married, travelling across London on the Underground in the twentieth century become the figure of a god pursuing a beautiful woman in a Greek or Roman myth. The moment is one of stress, pressure, anxiety and details such as 'japped', 'flapped wild', 'button after button/ Sprang off and fell' convey the speaker's emotional state.

The movement in stanzas 1 and 2 is frantic and frenetic. There is no sense of ease or togetherness which one would usually associate with a honeymooning couple. But a significant change occurs in stanza 3, beginning with its opening line:

> Honeymooning, mooning around, late for the Proms

This paints a more leisurely picture of him and her, and the Hansel and Gretel reference reminds us that the two young children in the Grimms' fairy tale did find their way to safety; they found their way home.

How this poem handles time is interesting. 'There we were' is past tense but at line 10 the story shifts to the present. The speaker is still reliving the past but 'now' brings the moment before us and the speaker, remembering this moment on his honeymoon, travels back in memory and is right there. The sounds of their hurrying in the corridor (the speaker uses 'echoes', a word which remembers another well-known myth) have faded, died and the speaker sees himself as Hansel:

> Retracing the path back, lifting the buttons

There is no reference to the classical music concert in the Albert Hall. We are not told whether they ever got there but there is this powerful, intense image of the two young lovers in the 'draughty, lamplit station'. This is an unglamorous setting – cold, badly lit – and the speaker identifies with the wet train-track. The speaker tells us that he is

> Bared and tense

and eager, focused, intent on listening out for his wife. He has retraced his steps, he has picked up the buttons from her coat. He wants her to join him but he is in such a tense state that he admits that he is

> damned if I look back.

In other words, he is reluctant to turn; he hopes and believes that she will follow. There is also, of course, the other meaning of damned. It could mean the mildest of swear words; it could also mean doomed, destroyed as Orpheus was in the myth. (Eurydice loyally followed Orpheus in that particular Greek myth but Orpheus turned and lost his wife to the darkness of the Underworld forever.) The poem ends without his, or without our, knowing if she has.

He wants her to come; the reader can imagine a happy ending to the episode if she does return to her husband, who has taken care to collect the fallen coat buttons.

In the opening line, the word 'we' occurs – they are together. Then it is 'you' and 'me' but in the final two stanzas 'I' occurs three times. That 'I' is 'all attention' – an 'I' that is nervous, expectant.

It is a very atmospheric, sensuous poem but an unexpected one. Had you been asked to say what you would expect from a honeymoon poem set in London, this might not be what you would imagine.

It is a love poem but a love poem that is rooted in an actual incident, an incident that is frazzled and awkward and tense. That he is waiting for her in the closing line contains the idea of their being together and happy.

The Pitchfork

Manual work has changed through the decades. Many people's work now consists of sitting down to a keyboard and keeping an eye on a screen. Their hands do move across the keys but manual work (*manus* in Latin means hand) traditionally meant a trade. The carpenter or the farmer, for example, would work with instruments and, in this poem, Seamus Heaney describes a farmer's pitchfork and the farmer's understanding of himself in relation to the instrument.

It begins with a very definite statement, a definite understanding of the pitchfork's unique qualities and the farmer's belief that

> Of all implements, the pitchfork was the one
> That came near to an imagined perfection

The speaker here is obviously one who has a deep, close knowledge of the person he is describing. He knows how the man feels when he lifts the pitchfork and pitches. The image

> It felt like a javelin, accurate and light

connects farmer and athlete and transforms what might be seen as ordinary, seasonal farm work into something skilful, graceful, beautiful.

When the speaker describes the farmer wielding the pitchfork in stanza 2, there's a playfulness in the idea of farmer as 'warrior' or 'athlete'. He is neither, but the lightness and grace of the implement allows him to become them. Work can be earnest but the speaker suggests that there are also times of light-heartedness, though whether he is playful or earnest the man using the pitchfork

> loved its grain of tapering, dark-flecked ash
> Grown satiny from its own natural polish.

The description here is tactile and sensuous and it continues through stanza 3 which lists the pitchfork's qualities. Assonance, alliteration, vowel sounds are all used in a list that captures in great detail the numerous features of the implement. The poem at this point becomes a series of adjectives and nouns which bring the pitchfork vividly alive in the reader's mind. Line 12

> The springiness, the clip and dart of it

sums it all up. Stanzas 1 and 2 use the past tense ('came near', 'tightened', 'aimed', 'played', 'loved') but the third stanza seems more immediate, more like the present. The fourth stanza allows us to imagine what might be. The speaker here describes how the user of the pitchfork has a flight of fancy in which he imagines the implement sailing through the air; he 'would see the shaft of a pitchfork sailing past' and the movement would be swift and silent. Its movement would also be like something out of this world – 'Its prongs starlit and absolutely soundless'.

The poem closes not with a physical description but with an idea. He, who uses the pitchfork, has learned to follow the pitchfork, javelin-like, as it soars through the air. The hand has aimed and the mind follows its throw. The pitchfork enters 'an other side', the thrower's imagination sees something close to perfection and the 'opening hand' made it possible.

'So', 'And', 'But' which begin stanzas 2, 4 and 5, are key words in terms of the poem's structure. These announce the development in the train of thought and the poem ends with a sense of release, freedom, triumph.

Lightenings viii

There are two apparently separate and distinct worlds in this poem. Heaney himself has referred to them as 'practical' and 'poetic', but has also spoken of how 'the frontier between them is there for the crossing'. And this is what happens in the poem.

The poem is in four sections. Stanza 1 states the poet's source and announces the setting. It is a self-contained, one-sentence stanza. In stanzas 2, 3 and 4, the sentences flow from one into the other and the sentences are long with the exception of the dramatic 'But in vain' at line 8.

The details in stanza 1 – the monks at communal prayers in the oratory, the ship appearing above them in the air – summon up a gentle, hallucinatory atmosphere. A sound, harsh and clanging, is heard in stanza 2 when Heaney uses words such as 'dragged', 'hooked', 'altar rails'.

The drama of the scene is enacted before the eyes of the monks. Phrases such as 'And then', or the image of 'the big hull rocked to a standstill' and the crewman who 'shinned and grappled down the rope/ And struggled to release it' give the moment its tension and excitement.

The shortest sentence 'But in vain' is both the crewman's and the monks' conclusion. The two separate worlds meet momentarily when the abbot helps the crewman free the ship. The surreal and wonderful image of the ship sailing away is a gentle image, like the image in the opening stanza.

In the closing line, the two different worlds of the poem are reversed. What is everyday and ordinary and familiar for the monks is 'marvellous' to the crewman. In other words, Heaney is reminding us that often the ordinary is seen as ordinary but it can also reveal itself as strange and unusual and wonderful.

A Call

The word 'call' has both everyday and special associations. 'Give us a call' or I'll call you' are familiar utterances. 'To call up' means to be summoned for military service. 'For many are called, but few are chosen' says St Matthew (Ch 22, v. 14) suggests something more important. In The Book of Genesis, The Call of Abraham refers to the command of God to Abraham to leave his idolatrous country.

In Seamus Heaney's poem, 'call' contains both casual and serious meanings. The call here is the phone call home but the speaker also meditates on the idea of a person being called home to God as in the medieval play *Everyman*.

The opening of the poem, it could be argued, isn't poetry; it is ordinary, everyday speech:

> 'Hold on,' she said, 'I'll just go out and get him.
> The weather here's so good he took the chance
> To do a bit of weeding.'

And yet the arrangement of the lines on the page (line 2 is a perfect iambic pentameter) and the overall rhythm create a musical flow.

Following this opening section, the poem shifts to a silent description of the speaker imagining his father at work in the kitchen garden. The four simple monosyllabic words in line 4

> So I saw him

lead us into a detailed description of his father

> Down on his hands and knees beside the leek rig

and his weeding is described using words such as 'touching', 'inspecting', 'separating', 'pulling' which gives the scene an active, on-going feel to it. The frail, little plants are being sorted, separated; some will be discarded so that the others will grow strong and thrive. The speaker imagines all this activity but the sympathetic speaker also imagines how his father feels about this:

> Pleased to feel each little weed-root break,
> But rueful also . . .

This mixture of happiness and sorrow is experienced by the weeder, according to the speaker, because he knows that some plants will live, some will not.

The poem then shifts, in the speaker's imagination, from outdoors back indoors to the hall where he can hear, while he waits,

> The amplified ticking of hall clocks

Clocks, of course, are familiar symbols of the passing of time, our growing old, our inevitable deaths.

The atmosphere in the poem's third section is calm and beautiful. Everything is quiet except for the ticking of the clocks and the sun is catching the mirror and the swinging pendulums. This section like the previous one ends with an ellipsis (the formal name for a series of full-stops). The dictionary tells us that an ellipsis is the omission of words from writing and in this instance those three dots create a silence, a sense of quiet meditation. It reveals a speaker becoming more reflective and allows the reader to follow in that same direction.

The speaker having pictured his father weeding, having heard the ticking clocks, having seen in his mind's eye the unattended phone and the pendulums thinks of death. Death, in this instance, as portrayed in the medieval play *Everyman*. We know not the day nor the hour but we do know that death will come. The speaker's idea of the character Death is a summons, a call.

(And it can be unexpected as in the play where the character Death says to Everyman: 'In great haste I am sent to thee/ From God out of his majesty' and Everyman replies 'What! Sent to me?' And Death says 'Yea, certainly./ though thou have forgot him here,/ He thinketh on thee in the heavenly sphere.')

The poem begins with his mother speaking, it ends with his father speaking. We hear what she says, we do not hear his father but we do hear what the speaker himself almost said. The poem's final line tells us that the speaker 'nearly said I loved him' and this line is on its own. The layout of the poem on the page is effective. The first section is three lines long, the second is seven and the remaining seven lines are divided into four, two, one. This slows down the poem's movement. As the eye and the ear respond to the poem on the page, the poem's emotional mood is created and heightened not only through what is being said but through the arrangement of the lines on the page.

The final line is very simple – eleven words, ten of them monosyllabic – and very complex.

Postscript

This is a get-away-from-it-all poem. It is also a journey poem and the journey is used so frequently by writers as metaphor it may be worth asking if this poem can be read not only as a description of an actual journey but as an image of life's journey.

The title would suggest that it's an afterthought, an aside. It does not announce itself as something of importance and yet the speaker is reminding us that nature is beautiful and revitalising. The poem's opening word reflects this casual, easy-going, welcoming tone. The whole thrust of the poem concerns sharing. Heaney has discovered something marvellous and he wants us to share that same experience.

The words 'out west' suggest the great unknown, the world of adventure ('Go West, young man, go West' was a popular catch-phrase, though the phrase in another context has a darker meaning: in World War I 'going west' meant the end.)

In three sentences, the speaker conveys his enthusiasm for the Burren in County Clare and the poem's opening sentence flows through eleven lines. It is as if the sense of escape, movement, freedom, delight are all contained in the poem's rhythm.

The West of Ireland is most frequently visited during summer, the tourist season, but here Heaney is suggesting that we 'drive out west' into County Clare when the tourists have gone and the 'wing and light are working off each other'. Wind and light are key aspects – movement and colour – and if one were to paint or film the poem's setting it would be a scene beautiful for its greys and whites, the grey of the limestone, the grey of the ocean and inland lake, the white of the wild ocean, and the swans.

'Postscript' is filled with movement – of wind and ocean – but also the car's movement. The speaker is always aware of how he, being in the car, is part of that movement. The poem's first sentence leads us to the swans, their dramatic presence on the lake. Grey stones surround the lake and the lake's surface is 'slate-grey' but the swans are not only 'white on white', the lake is

> lit
> By the earthed lightning of a flock of swans

The image of 'earthed lightning' is one of land and sky. The swans are on the water but we know of course that the air is also their element and the idea of lightning is powerful and exciting.

The movement of the swans contrasts with the movement of the wind and waves. They are floating on the lake and their feathers are

> roughed and ruffling, white on white

These last words are a marvellous example of Heaney's ability to bring language alive and to create a special music. The swans' feathers are roughed up by the strong winds but the ruffling also suggests a more delicate movement; big and little feathers, their smoothness and tranquillity are disturbed.

Heaney economically, in two lines, paints a clear picture of the swans' distinctive movement. Patrick Kavanagh in his poem 'Lines Written on a Seat in the Grand Canal, Dublin' speaks of how 'A swan goes by head low with many apologies' and here Heaney captures the busy, beautiful swans on water:

> Their fully grown headstrong-looking heads
> Tucked or cresting or busy underwater

Anyone who has even seen and watched swans will realise that such lines are sharply observed, accurate descriptions of their individual head and neck movements and the words 'headstrong-looking heads' with its repetition and rhyme confirms the swans' power and dignity. The use of 'or' in

> Tucked or cresting or busy underwater
> gives the line flow, variety.

The opening eleven lines create this magical place in County Clare. At lines 12-13, the speaker offers a word of caution:

> Useless to think you'll park and capture it
> More thoroughly.

This is the shortest sentence in the poem. It is also the only sentence without vivid descriptions and imagery. Having described the experience of driving along the Flaggy Shore, in September or October, Heaney now tells his reader that the best way to experience this is from the moving car. It is a fleeting, beautiful sensation. Park the car and the magic disappears; if the viewer is static, then the pleasure is diminished. It's as if the whoosh of the experience is dependent on movement.

If you park, you are in a particular place. You are here or there, but the poem celebrates the sensation of being transported beyond the here and now: perpetual motion. The experience is both a familiar and mysterious one:

> You are neither here nor there,
> A hurry through which known and strange things pass

There is the known and the strange and both are sensed

> As big soft buffetings come at the car sideways
> And catch the heart off guard and blow it open.

The joy and pleasure, the unexpectedness, the thrill are all contained in these closing lines. The buffetings are 'soft' not dangerous, they come 'sideways' and the final image of the surprised and delighted heart is all the more special because it is caught off guard. The heart blown open, in another context, could be a brutal, violent image, but not here. The poem's final words 'blow it open' convey intense excitement, delight and pleasure.

Tate's Avenue

Here we have four stanzas in which the speaker remembers three different rugs in three different places: the seaside, a riverbank and a back garden in Belfast. And it could be said that he leaves the happiest memory, the best memory until last. This last setting, Tate's Avenue, is the least attractive in terms of location but it is the one which the speaker cherishes most. The 'Not' at the beginning of line 1, the 'Not' at the beginning of line 5, diminish the seaside and the Guadalquivir scenes. What matters most to the speaker is the rug in Tate's Avenue. That scene is given two stanzas; the others are given a stanza each.

The opening stanza tells of the 'first' rug, a 'brown and fawn car rug'. It is never stated but it could be assumed that this is a moment from the speaker's childhood. The details are sensuously described – it is as if the rug itself is 'breathing land breaths'. The rug has been unfolded and it creates a 'comfort zone'. Heaney is well-known as a poet who is alert to language, its various meanings; he loves, for example, reading in a dictionary and being made aware of a word's etymology. Here, he uses what has become a kind of buzz word in the early twenty-first century but he manages to separate it from anything trendy or fashionable and use it in a more authentic way. ('Comfort zone', in fact, is frequently included in a list of the top ten phrases that writers should avoid but Heaney invests the phrase with freshness.) For the child on the rug, it is a comfort zone; a confined, safe place.

If the 'brown and fawn' rug is 'that first one', a child crawling on a rug could be imagined. There is a heightened sense of being in aware of the rug itself but also to the ground beneath. The rug, in the speaker's imagination, is

> breathing land-breaths

and the person on the rug has a sense of the ground beneath as a living presence. Both the person on the rug and the ground breathe. This personification of the world beneath the rug is sensuous and atmospheric. (The word *chthonic* or *chthonian* means relating to or inhabiting the underworld; this is, perhaps, another interpretation; the rug's comfort zone connects and is separate from the land-breaths beneath.)

The second stanza cuts to adulthood and Spain. It's a very different world, more sophisticated, more colourful than the earlier memory. The food and drink suggest an easy, relaxed time. The one thing that connects both scenes is the rug, a different rug, a different place.

The first rug with its 'vestal folds unfolded' suggests innocence, purity; this second rug

> scraggy with crusts and eggshells
> And olive stones and cheese and salami rinds

is a grown-up scene. That they got drunk before the bullfight suggests a kind of easy outlook and an openness to all things Spanish.

Having set these two scenes in the first half of the poem, the speaker, in stanzas 3 and 4, now returns to a time between childhood and adulthood and student days in Belfast. Lovely food and plenty of wine have been replaced by dour, restrictive Belfast where the parks were locked and strict religious codes were supposed to be observed.

The poem ends with a picture of young people in love. It is love's early stages and the speaker creates a setting that is unglamorous and unromantic. But romance, nevertheless, is in the air. In this back yard there is a rug and a young man and woman are together yet separate on the plaid square. There are physical details:

> a page is turned, a finger twirls warm hair

But what is more important is the emotional world. There is a sense of nervous expectation, interest, caution, excitement. The speaker is watching. Sensuous details capture the moment. Line 12 suggests that time has paused:

> And nothing gives on the rug or the ground beneath it.

There is a striking contrast between movement and stillness here: the page being turned, the hair being twirled are keenly observed and 'nothing gives on the rug' suggests that he and she, though content to be there together, are not touching.

This is a personal, private poem and yet it is only in the closing stanza that the speaker uses 'I'.

> I lay at my length and felt the lumpy earth,
> Keen-sensed more than ever through discomfort

The speaker, stretched out on the rug, is keenly aware of his physical self. The lumpy garden beneath the rug heightens his awareness of himself and her. He is keen to make a move and though the rug is not exactly a comfort zone he

> never shifted off the plaid square once.

In the final line, a sentence on its own, he and she become 'we' and the poem ends with an embrace. That final line brings the lovers together and the words convey in their music a harmony:

> When we moved I had your measure and you had mine.

The alliteration here ('moved', 'measure', 'mine') and the assonance ('moved'/'your'/'you'; 'I'/'mine') make for a fine conclusion and the play on 'measure' adds a gentle, humorous touch. To 'get the measure' of someone is to understand them better. Here, 'I had your measure and you had mine' also means that the young man and woman are side-by-side in each other's arms – there is the actual, physical sense of him and her sensing each other's body.

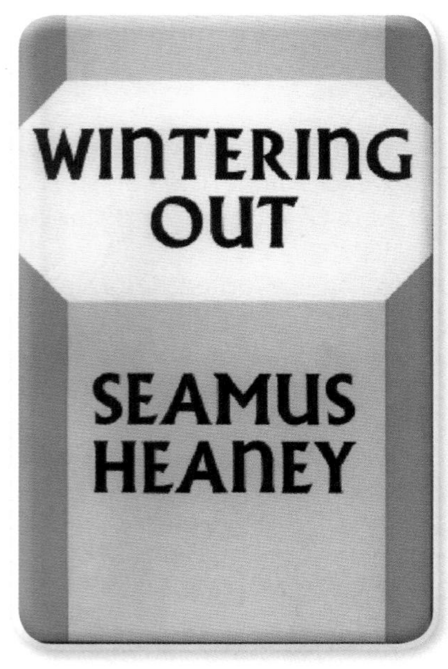

Gerard Manley Hopkins

(1844–1889)

Contents Page

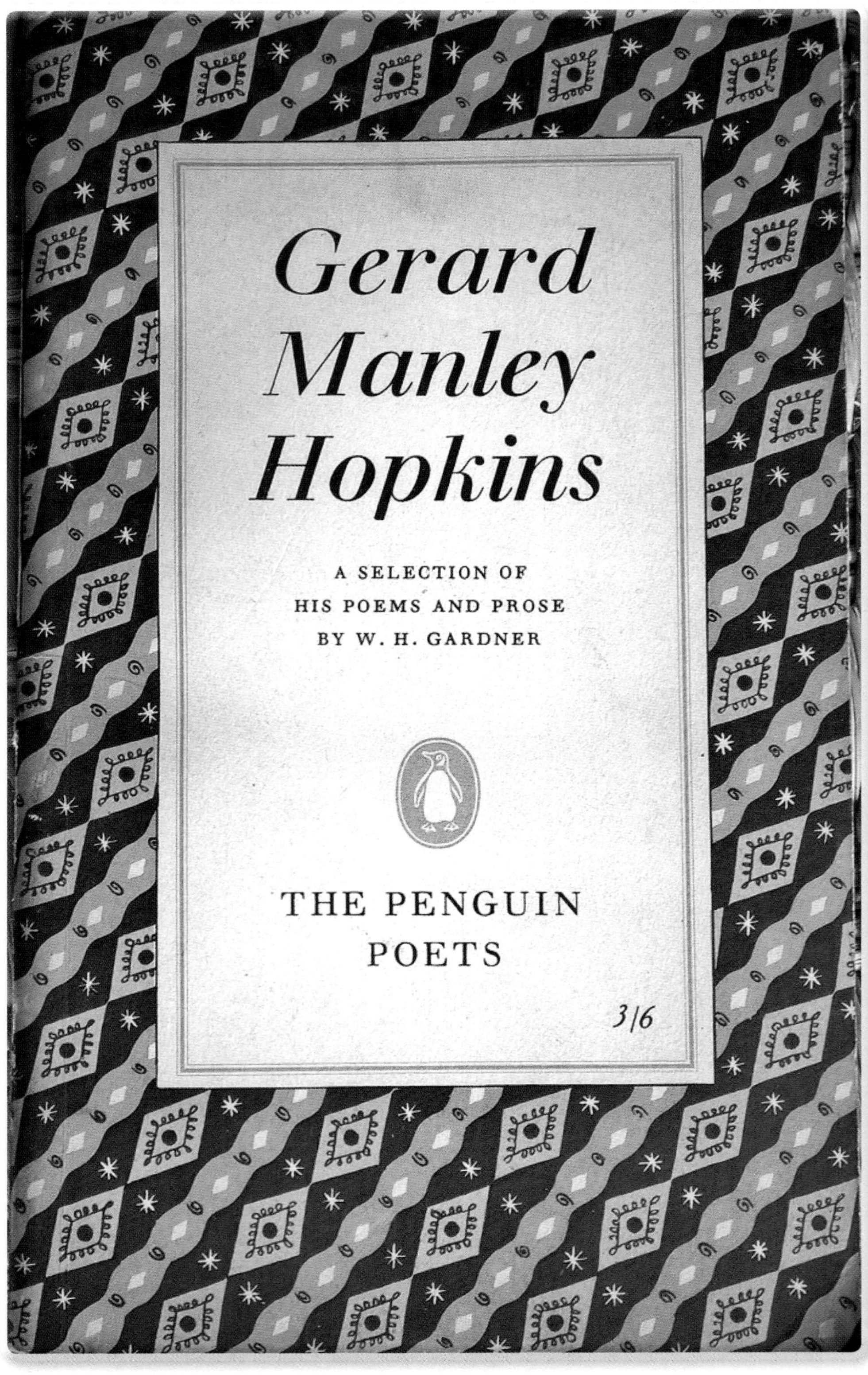
Gerard
Manley
Hopkins
A SELECTION OF
HIS POEMS AND PROSE
BY W. H. GARDNER
THE PENGUIN
POETS
3/6

The Overview

As a member of the Jesuit order, Hopkins was encouraged to frame all academic written work with the mottoes A.M.D.G. and L.D.S. (*Ad Majorem Dei Gloriam:* To the Greater Glory of God and *Laus Deo Semper:* Praise to God Always). His life and work were devoted to God and his poetry is a record of that devotion.

Though he lived and died in the nineteenth century, Hopkins is frequently considered a twentieth-century poet, not because his poems were not published until 1918 but because of their startling and unique style. It has been said that Hopkins was a Victorian in that he was serious, scrupulous, hard-working and set himself exacting ideals, but in his remarkable poetic innovations he was ahead of his time. His poetry was misunderstood, unappreciated, unknown during his lifetime and, even though he had a strong sense of duty and believed in self-sacrifice, he also had an independence of spirit that is evident in his work. He did not write for an audience, nor did he follow the contemporary literary fashion. Hopkins, wrote his American biographer Robert Bernard Martin, 'is constantly more concerned with putting across his perceptions than with fulfilling customary expectations of grammar...most persistent readers of his poems learn to abandon their usual demands of convention in language, in order to enjoy a fuller poetic process than would otherwise be possible.' Coventry Patmore, however, found that Hopkins's poetry had the effect of 'veins of pure gold imbedded in masses of unpracticable quartz'. In Roddy Doyle's novel *The Van*, Darren, studying Hopkins's poetry for the Leaving Certificate, reads one of the poems, wonders when Tippex had been invented and concludes, 'Gerrah Manley Hopkins had definitely been sniffing something. He couldn't write that in his answer though.'

And his poetry, though written in the nineteenth century, had an extraordinarily important influence on twentieth-century poetry. It was not so much that other poets imitated Hopkins; rather they were empowered to develop and explore their own individuality. His style was fresh and free and dazzlingly different. Robert Bridges, Britain's Poet Laureate from 1913 to 1930, was Hopkins's contemporary (both were born in 1844) and friend. One only has to compare these two extracts, opening lines, both from 'nature poems', to realise the remarkable difference between a conventional voice and a truly original one:

> The pinks along my garden walks
> Have all shot forth their summer stalks,
> Thronging their buds 'mong tulips hot,
>   And blue forget-me-not.

> Nothing is so beautiful as spring –
> When weeds, in wheels, shoot long and lovely and lush;
> Thrush's eggs look little low heavens, and thrush
> Through the echoing timber does so rinse and wring
> The ear, it strikes like lightnings to hear him sing.

Hopkins was influenced by Anglo-Saxon or Old English poetry and this is evident in his use of alliteration and kennings. He approved of dialect words such as 'fettle', 'sillion' and invented words such as 'unleaving' and he felt that 'the poetical language of an age should be the current language heightened, to any degree heightened and unlike itself ... The language must divorce itself from such archaisms as "ere," "o'er," "wellnigh"...' An example of such heightening can be seen in Hopkins's recommendation to his poet friend Robert Bridges that the definite article be dropped in 'The eye marvelled, the ear hearkened'. He preferred 'eye marvelled, ear hearkened' which ensured that meanings were compressed. His poetry was not published in book form until after his death and an early reviewer of Hopkins's poetry said that 'You fight your way through the verses yet they draw you on', that the language, at times, created an 'effect almost of idiocy, of speech without sense and prolonged merely by echoes'. But that same reviewer, in 1919, also claimed that Hopkins's poetry contained 'authentic fragments that we trust even when they bewilder us'.

Hopkins preferred kinesis to stasis, movement to stopping; for him, things are more beautiful in movement, as in the flight of the kingfisher, shooting weeds, the windhover, Felix Randal beating iron out, or the mountain stream 'His rollrock highroad roaring down'. And he loved the principle of distinctness in all things; each must be the individual that it is, as in 'As kingfishers catch fire'. Hopkins loved the uniqueness of things, the 'individually distinctive.' He called this quality **inscape**.

Instress was used by Hopkins to convey his understanding of the energy that made possible this uniqueness. ('It is the virtue of design, pattern, or inscape to be distinctive', wrote Hopkins). Michael Schmidt, in his *Lives of the Poets*, sums it up as follows: 'Inscape is manifest, instress divine, the immanent presence of the divine in the object.' Hopkins agreed with Duns Scotus when he praised the individual, not the species, the *haecceitas* (pronounced *hek-sé-i-tas*) or 'thisness' of something.

Hopkins, said Seamus Heaney, is a poet who brings you to your senses. The reader sees and hears the 'hereness-and-nowness' of the moment, but the sounds also match the poem's tone and mood. Hopkins believed that 'my verse is less to be read than heard ... it is oratorical, that is the rhythm is so'.

When Hopkins looks at nature, his involvement with what he sees is total, but it is never a celebration of nature for its own sake; Hopkins saw nature as an expression of God's grandeur. The poetry is inspired by Hopkins's love of God and God's creation. He is a poet of extraordinary highs. The imagination soars in a poem like 'The Windhover' but Hopkins is also a poet who writes the bleakest poetry about the depths of despair in the terrible sonnets.

Biographical Notes

Gerard Manley Hopkins was born at Stratford in Essex on 28 July 1844. He was named Gerard after the saint and Manley was his paternal grandmother's surname and his father's first name. Gerard Hopkins, the eldest child, disliked his middle name and rarely used it except on official occasions. There were nine children in all, though one died in infancy. The family was prosperous, Manley Hopkins being an insurance broker, and in July 1844, at the age of twenty-six, he set up his own company. Though a very active man of business, Manley Hopkins wrote several books, on insurance, on cardinal numbers, on Hawaii, three volumes of poetry, an unpublished novel and newspaper reviews. His father's interest in writing influenced Gerard Hopkins, though their writings were very different.

When Hopkins was eight, the family moved to prestigious Hampstead; the house in Stratford was now too small and an influx of poor Irish into wooden hovels at the back of their house also precipitated the move. Hopkins's lifelong dislike of the Irish may well have begun then. In Hampstead, the family attended St. John's church, where Manley Hopkins became a church warden. Family prayers and night prayers were said at home and Gerard went on to become a Jesuit priest, while his sister Millicent became an Anglican nun.

Hopkins, very slight in build and short, was first taught at home. When he was eight, he began attending Highgate School, where the standards were very high at the time, but hated it. Hopkins boarded for most of the nine years that he spent there and studied English, Latin, history, arithmetic, religion, French, German, drawing, Greek and advanced mathematics. At Highgate, he won the School Poetry Prize when he was fifteen for a poem on the topic of 'The Escorial' (the Escorial being a magnificent palace that was promised by Philip II to St. Laurence if he won the battle at St. Quentin between the French and Spaniards).

Nicknamed 'Skin', (Hop.kin.s = s/kin), he played cricket and swam, was popular and was elected prefect, even though he had very serious disagreements with his headmaster and was whipped. This led to Hopkins becoming a day boy in his final year.

At school, he once drank no liquids for three weeks as part of a bet but also because he had heard of the suffering that sailors sometimes had to endure. His tongue turned black, but he persevered. When the headmaster discovered what he had done he made Hopkins give back the money he had won, though Hopkins argued that this was rewarding the other boy. For this, he was punished by the headmaster.

Academically, he excelled: he won several prizes, including a gold medal for Latin and an Exhibition to Balliol College, Oxford. 'I had no love for my schooldays and wished to banish the remembrance of them', wrote Hopkins several years later, but he enjoyed very much his time at Oxford, the place itself being 'my park, my pleasaunce'. At university, Hopkins met V.S.S. Coles, Robert Bridges and Digby Dolben, and Bridges and Dolben became two of his closest friends; years later it was Bridges who was responsible for publishing Hopkins's poetry in book form, almost thirty years after his friend's death.

At Oxford, where he was studying 'Greats', Hopkins particularly loved boating on the river ('A canoe in the Cherwell must be the summit of human happiness'), swimming and long walks. Hopkins was expected to study Greek and Latin for four years and Scripture for three. He was also expected to write a weekly essay, alternately in Latin and English, on such topics as 'Casuistry,' the 'National Debt' or 'The Origin of our Moral Ideas'.

During his time in Oxford, Hopkins witnessed a division between High Church or Anglo-Catholicism and Broad Church or Liberal religious ideas and in 1863 Balliol was known as a wellspring of such liberal ideas. Broad Church encouraged an examination of traditional definitions; modern scientific and critical studies were applied to the Church's teaching and what was once held as the truth was now being questioned rigorously. Benjamin Jowett, a well-known classicist and Hopkins's first tutor at Balliol, was the most prominent Broad Church figure; Hopkins, being conservative High Church, did not see eye-to-eye with him.

Hopkins frequently attended St. Thomas's Church in Oxford, known for its religious symbols; its Vicar was one of the two first Anglican clergymen to resume Eucharistic vestments since the Reformation. He also admired John Henry Newman, who twenty years earlier, had become a Roman Catholic and had left Oxford. Dr Pusey of Christ Church carried on the High Church tradition which revived many Catholic doctrines and practices which had been abandoned by the Church of England. Those who favoured religious symbols and elaborate ceremony were known as the Ritualists and by 1865 Hopkins, then 21, did not eat meat on Fridays, flogged himself with a whip during Lent and often fasted. A diary entry for 23 January 1866 recorded: 'No verses in passion Week or on Fridays. No lunch or meat on Fridays. Not to sit in armchair except can work in no other way. Ash Wednesday and Good Friday bread and water.'

One of his biographers, Robert Bernard Martin, says that 'It was characteristic of Hopkins that he should espouse unpopular views, suffer for them, and so become even more attached to them', though Martin adds that it is difficult to know whether his behaviour was courageous or stubborn. Hopkins also began going to confession around this time, yet another indication that he was journeying from Anglo-Catholicism towards Roman Catholicism. It is also said that Hopkins decided, while still an undergraduate, to remain celibate and everything would suggest that he did, though many studies of Hopkins's life and work reveal that he was physically attracted to men. Why Hopkins's sexuality should be discussed by his biographers and critics is a question worth asking.

Virginia Ridley Ellis, author of a study of Hopkins, thinks that 'it should be confronted briefly if we are seeking a just view of the whole man behind the poems, and of some of the conflicts and feelings in them.' Ellis thinks that it is possible that 'such inclinations were part of his makeup, and may especially have contributed to Hopkins's sense of "helpless self-loathing" that recurs in his Retreat notes of 1888', but she concludes by saying that she accepts quite literally Hopkins's statement, in a letter to Robert Bridges, that the only person he was in love with was Christ.

Hopkins, as the diary entry quoted above suggests, continued to write poetry at university, and to refrain from writing during Passion Week and on Fridays was a penance. One of his most best-known and best-loved lyrics, 'Heaven-Haven,' dates from this period:

Heaven-Haven
(a nun takes the veil)

I have desired to go
Where springs not fail,
To fields where flies no sharp and sided hail
And a few lilies blow.

And I have asked to be
Where no storms come,
Where the green swell is in the havens dumb,
And out of the swing of the sea.

His journal during his Oxford days included notes for poems and first drafts, notes on architecture, lists of sins, the cost of a haircut, etymologies, drawings, detailed descriptions of what he observed on his walks. One entry reads, 'The water running down the lasher [a country word for weir] violently swells in a massy wave against the opposite bank ... The shape of wave of course bossy, smooth and globy. Full of bubble and air, very liquid. . .' and illustrates Hopkins's love for unusual, accurate, and vivid language. As an undergraduate, Hopkins loved to make up words and his diary contains comments such as the following: '*Crook, crank, kranke, crick, cranky.* Original meaning crooked, not straight or right, wrong, awry. A crank in England is a piece of mechanism which turns a wheel or shaft at one end, at the other receiving a rectilinear force. . .' and this is accompanied by a drawing of a wheel and crank. Hopkins liked to draw and he toyed with the idea of becoming a painter, but rejected it as 'unsafe', for it would involve too great a temptation to be in the presence of natural beauty. Hopkins once admitted to feeling temptation while sketching his friend Baillie and 'evil thoughts' occurred to him while he was drawing; a crucifix once stimulated him in the wrong way.

Such passages, according to Robert Bernard Martin, prove that Hopkins's 'love of getting back to the origins of words was less an archaeological exercise than a real attempt to scrape clean the bones of language and restore its purity'.

In December 1864, Hopkins was one of three Balliol men to win first-class honours in Moderations and in February 1865, aged twenty, he met Digby Dolben, just seventeen, who had left Eton that Christmas and who wanted to study at Balliol the following autumn. This meeting has been described as 'the most momentous emotional event of Hopkins's undergraduate years, probably of his entire life.' Dolben had strong religious opinions, was very attracted to Roman Catholicism, wrote poetry of a religious and erotic nature, and liked outdoor bathing, characteristics which he shared with Hopkins. A month after meeting Dolben, Hopkins translated the following poem from Greek:

> Love me as I love thee. O double sweet!
> But if thou hate me who love thee, albeit
>   Even thus I have the better of thee:
> Thou canst not hate so much as I do love thee.

Although Dolben is not mentioned by name in that and other poems written at the time, it would seem that for Hopkins his friendship with Digby Dolben was particularly close and intense. Robert Bridges, Dolben's cousin, wrote that 'Gerard conceived a high admiration for him' and he also wrote on Hopkins's manuscript of a three-sonnet sequence which dwells on Dolben: 'These two sonnets [I and III] must never be printed.' As to the exact nature of their relationship, there is much conjecture. Some scholars play it down; others think it central to an understanding of Hopkins the man, priest and poet. In his diary and in his poetry, Hopkins reveals a strong physical attraction to Dolben, but whether those feelings were reciprocated one cannot say. Dolben's entry to Balliol was delayed because his knowledge of classics was deemed inadequate. However, Hopkins and Dolben exchanged poems and Dolben promised to send Hopkins a photograph. In March, Hopkins experienced a spiritual crisis and he was advised by his confessor not to write to Dolben; it is thought that the crisis convinced Hopkins to convert to Catholicism. His record of his sins indicates Hopkins's sensuous nature, but he was frightened by temptation and found a release in poetry and religion.

The summer of 1865 was a difficult time for him and at the end of the year he wrote a poem which captured his despondency and despair. It begins:

> Trees by their yield
> Are known; but I –
> My sap is sealed,
> My root is dry.
> If life within
> I none can shew
> (Except for sin),
> Nor fruit above, –
> It must be so –
> I do not love.

Hopkins converted to Catholicism at a time when there was much hostility towards Catholics in Britain. There were fewer than ten Catholics among the student body at Oxford in Hopkins's day and it was stated at an Oxford Union debate 'that all Roman Catholics were an importation from the Devil'. A switch from Anglo-Catholicism to Roman Catholicism would significantly lower his social status and he would be barred from holding a Fellowship at Oxford University. When he did convert, it was much against his family's wishes; he told his parents by letter and 'their answers are terrible', but, in a letter to a friend, he spoke of the importance of 'the Real Presence in the Blessed Sacrament of the Altar. Religion without that is sombre, dangerous, illogical...' He had been attending Mass for some time and spoke to a Roman Catholic priest for the first time during the summer of 1866; he was received into the Church of Rome at the age of twenty-two on 21 October 1866 in Birmingham by Dr John Henry Newman, also a convert from Protestantism and former Oxford academic. Later, he attended Mass in the very church where Newman had attended his last Mass before leaving Oxford in 1846.

His journals from now on contain far more vividly intense passages describing nature. Hopkins crushed earlier preoccupations focusing on male beauty and his love of the beauty of the natural world took their place. Passages such as the following, which describe his walks, indicate Hopkins's brilliant eye for detail: 'Sky sleepy blue ... brow of the near hill glistening with very bright newly turned sods and a scarf of vivid green slanting away beyond the skyline. ... Meadows skirting Sevenbridge road voluptuous green ... Hedges springing richly ... Over the green water of the river passing the slums of the town and under its bridges swallows shooting, blue and purple above and shewing their amber-tinged breasts reflected in the water ... Towards sunset the sky partly swept, as often, with moist white cloud, tailing off across which are morsels of grey-black woolly clouds ...'

During his final year at Oxford, Hopkins was tutored by Walter Pater, essayist and critic, then a young man of 27 and only five years older than Hopkins. Pater and Hopkins spent many hours looking at art and the art of looking in detail becomes more and more evident in Hopkins's own writing; he now focuses on a leaf or a flower with extraordinary precision: 'Alone in the woods ... I have now found the law of the oak leaves. It is of platter-shaped stars altogether; the leaves lie close like pages, packed in and as if drawn tightly to. But these old packs, which lie at the end of their twigs, throw out long shoots alternately and slimly leaves, looking like bright keys', or 'Carnations if you look close have their tongue-shaped petals powdered and spankled red glister ... sharp chip shadows of one petal on another ...'

In June 1867, Hopkins completed his degree, with a First in Greats. He visited Paris that summer and, on returning home, discovered that Dolben had drowned. Dolben, had he lived, would most likely have converted to Roman Catholicism. Shortly after his premature death Hopkins wrote: 'I looked forward to meeting Dolben and his being a Catholic more than to anything ... there can very seldom have happened the loss of so much beauty (in body and mind and life) and the promise of still more.'

From September to the following April, he taught at Newman's Oratory School near Birmingham and that same September Hopkins privately decided to give up writing poetry and to destroy what he had written. This decision has been interpreted to mean that Hopkins was seriously thinking about becoming a priest and, since poetry was so important to him, it would have to be renounced on becoming one.

At the Oratory, Hopkins taught fifth form boys, was in charge of hockey and football, and began taking violin lessons, but was so overworked that he had very little free time. By Christmas he knew that teaching was not for him ('Teaching is very burdensome ... I have not much time and almost no energy – for I am always tired – to do anything on my own account') and did not return to school after Easter. Shortly afterwards, during a retreat at the Jesuit novitiate, he resolved to become a Jesuit priest. July was spent on a walking holiday in Switzerland and on 7 September 1869, at the age of twenty-four, Hopkins entered the Jesuit novitiate, Manresa House, Roehampton, five miles from central London. Jesuits were often ordained at thirty-three, a symbolic age in the life of Christ's ministry; Hopkins had several years of study ahead of him: the novitiate was two years; the juniorate – two years; the philosophate – three years; the theologate – three/four years; the tertianship – one year.

His training was rigorous, disciplined and strict: up at 5.30; prayer and meditation from 6 to 7; breakfast in silence followed seven o'clock mass; pious reading and household chores followed; more spiritual reading, a walk, then gardening and so on. Dinner was also eaten in silence but a novice read aloud from a suitably uplifting book. Special friendships among the novices were not allowed and they were given 'modesty powder', which turned the water opaque, for their baths; letter writing was restricted and all letters were read by his superiors. The life of the trainee Jesuit was a life deliberately without pleasures and Hopkins did penance and engaged in corporal mortification such as scourgings or wearing a chain next to the skin. Between January and July of 1869, Hopkins, as a penance, went about his life with eyes cast down.

For novices, contact with the outside world took the form of catechism classes for Catholic children. In September 1870, Hopkins took his first vows as a Jesuit and was given a new gown, biretta and Roman collar. After Manresa he was sent to the seminary at Stonyhurst, near Blackburn in Lancashire. Here, as in Manresa, baths were allowed once a month and Hopkins followed a rigorous course of study, but Stonyhurst was in the countryside and Hopkins's journals became extraordinarily detailed and vivid. He wrote: 'What you look hard at seems to look hard at you'. And he would gaze intently at a frozen pond or the effect of rain on a garden path. Such focus produced a different kind of writing, and grammatical accuracy was sometimes abandoned for emotional and imaginative intensity, as in the following excerpt from his journal which describes a journey home one evening from confession: 'In returning the sky in the west was in a great wide winged or shelved rack of rice-white fine pelleted fretting'. As has been pointed out, 'In returning' refers to Hopkins himself, not to the sky, as the sentence structure suggests.

Though he had given up writing poetry, he had not stopped thinking in a poetic way and, when he did return to writing poems, phrases from his journals reappear years later in his poetry. The two words most often associated with Hopkins are 'inscape' and 'instress'; two years before he came to Stonyhurst, inscape began appearing in his journals. Impossibly difficult to define in any one way, inscape is the individual, unique, distinctive form, the oneness of something, the unique quality inherent in a person, object, idea. The *Oxford English Dictionary* defines inscape as: 'The individual or essential quality of a thing; the uniqueness of an observed object, scene, event, etc...'. Hopkins also invented the word instress to capture the energy or force which makes possible that inscape; the *Oxford English Dictionary* defines instress as: 'The force or energy which sustains an inscape'. Hopkins believed that, if you study something closely, if you empathise with it, you recognise its inscape and instress. 'All the world is full of inscape', according to Hopkins's journals, and, in a letter to Bridges, he wrote that 'design, pattern or what I am in the habit of calling "inscape" is what I above all aim at in poetry.' When a tree was felled at Stonyhurst, and the felling of trees upset him very much, he felt a great pang and 'wished to die and not to see the inscapes of the world destroyed'. Robert Bernard Martin says that 'To grasp or perceive inscape was to know what was essential and individual in whatever one contemplated. It was a form of identification.'

During the summer of 1872, Hopkins read the medieval Franciscan theologian Johannes Duns Scotus for the first time and this made a huge impact. Duns Scotus believed that the material world symbolised God and Hopkins now felt as if he had been given permission to feel at ease with his love of natural beauty. Up until then, he had felt uneasy if he loved the natural world or a friend, lest it detracted from his primary concern, which was to love God. Now, in loving a flower, he felt that he was also loving its creator. In his poem, 'Duns Scotus's Oxford', written in 1879, Hopkins says that Duns Scotus 'of all men most sways my spirits to peace'.

Hopkins's health in adult life was not good. He suffered from piles and diarrhoea and underwent an operation during Christmas 1872. The following September, by way of granting Hopkins a rest, he was sent back to Manresa House, where, as Professor of Rhetoric, he would teach Latin, Greek and English for a year. It was not a heavy teaching load; he had free days and could visit family and friends, museums and art galleries and was allowed to stay with his family at Hampstead at Christmas. The teaching year left him exhausted and weak and in September he was sent to St. Beuno's College in north Wales to study theology. He was thirty years old and he loved his time at St. Beuno's; the college was situated in a place of great natural beauty and Hopkins liked the Welsh people and began to learn their language. During this time he had not been writing poetry but, in December 1875, a ship, the *Deutschland*, sank off the south-east coast of England, near the mouth of the Thames, and over sixty drowned, including five nuns exiled from Germany. The Rector at St. Beuno's said that he wished someone would write a poem on the subject and Hopkins responded immediately. The result was Hopkins's 280-line poem 'The Wreck of the Deutschland', but it was considered too eccentric, too difficult and unreadable and was rejected by the editor of the Jesuit magazine. Even today, the poem is a challenging but very rewarding one.

Here is but one of its thirty-five stanzas; the tremendous power of the language captures the force and power of the sea and the doomed ship:

Into the snow she sweeps
Hurling the haven behind,
The Deutschland, on Sunday; and so the sky keeps,
For the infinite air is unkind,
And the sea flint-flake, black-backed in the regular blow,
Sitting Eastnortheast, in cursed quarter, the wind;
Wiry and white-fiery and whirlwind-swivelled snow
Spins to the widow-making unchilding unfathering deeps.

It was in this poem that Hopkins also gave full voice to a metrical device that he termed **sprung rhythm**, a term, like inscape and instress, inextricably linked with Hopkins's poetry. Sprung rhythm is also found in Anglo-Saxon and medieval English poetry. 'I do not say the idea is altogether new', he said, 'but no one has professedly used it and made it the principle throughout'; in writing 'The Wreck of the Deutschland', Hopkins commented that 'I had long had haunting my ear the echo of a new rhythm which now I realised on paper.' It is the ear, therefore, which is vital; the rhythm must be heard.

Sprung rhythm, according to Hopkins, 'consists in scanning by accents or stresses alone, without any account of the number of syllables, so that a foot may be one strong syllable or it may be many light and one strong.' The theory is difficult to grasp but the effect is immediate. In a letter, Hopkins explained the idea to his brother: 'Sprung rhythm gives back to poetry its true soul and self. As poetry is emphatically speech, speech purged of dross like gold in the furnace, so it must have emphatically the essential elements of speech. Now emphasis itself, stress, is one of these: sprung rhythm makes verse stressy; it purges it to an emphasis as much brighter, livelier, more lustrous than the regular but commonplace emphasis of common rhythm as poetry in general is brighter than common speech.' In other words, Hopkins preferred sprung rhythm to the more conventional rhythm where the group of syllables forming a metrical unit creates a more predictable movement.

Norman MacKenzie offers the following interpretation of sprung rhythm: 'The name suggests the natural grace of a deer springing down a mountainside, adjusting the length of each leap according to the ground it is covering.' In the manuscript versions of Hopkins's poems, the words are frequently marked with symbols indicating strong stress, weak stress, pause, a drawing out of one syllable to make it almost two, a slurring of syllables and so on. And Hopkins also uses the musical terms 'counterpoint' (cross-rhythm), 'rests' and the terms 'hangers' or 'outriders' (syllables added to a metrical unit or foot but not counted when scanned) to explain and clarify his technique. His friend and fellow-poet Robert Bridges asked why he used sprung rhythm at all and Hopkins replied: 'Because it is the nearest to the rhythm of prose, that is the native and natural rhythm of speech, the least forced, the most rhetorical and emphatic of all possible rhythms, combining, as it seems to me, opposite and, one would have thought, incompatible excellences, markedness of rhythm – that is rhythm's self – and naturalness of expression ...'

Hopkins speaks about sprung rhythm frequently in his journals and letters; sometimes his definitions and commentaries are difficult to grasp, but what has been termed 'the perfect concise explanation' is given by Hopkins himself when he said: '*one stress makes one foot*, no matter how many or few the syllables'.

Though 'The Wreck of the Deutschland' was rejected for publication, it nonetheless encouraged Hopkins to return to the writing of poetry. His health was good, apart from some complaints about indigestion, and he delighted in the Welsh countryside. By the time he left St. Beuno's College, he had written one third of his mature poems, including some of his most famous sonnets: 'Spring', 'The Windhover', 'God's Grandeur', 'As kingfishers catch fire' and the curtal sonnet 'Pied Beauty'. Hopkins published very few of his poems during his lifetime and once, when a friend, Canon Dixon, an Anglican priest, offered to try to publish his poem 'The Loss of the Eurydice', Hopkins forbade it, explaining that it would 'not be so easy to guard myself against what others might say'; he added that Dixon was very welcome to show his poems to anyone 'so long as nothing gets into print.' He did, however, send copies of his poems regularly to Robert Bridges; it is ironic that Bridges, who was once well-known for his poetry and was even appointed Poet Laureate, is now considered the inferior poet, whereas Hopkins, unknown in his lifetime, will always be read. Some years later, in March 1881, Hopkins sent some poems to T. H. Hall Caine, who was gathering together a collection of sonnets, but these were rejected.

In March 1877, Hopkins had exams in moral theology and he had his final exam in dogmatic theology in July. This last, an hour-long oral examination in Latin, did not go well and resulted in Hopkins's not staying on at St. Beuno's as he expected. In September, he was ordained as a priest; none of his family was present at the ordination. A week later, he was ill in bed and he was circumcised. Once recovered, he said goodbye to St. Beuno's and was transferred to Mount St. Mary's College, a Jesuit school, near Chesterfield, Derbyshire, where he taught religion, syntax and poetry. He also heard confessions and gave Sunday sermons. Here, as in Stonyhurst previously, Hopkins was frequently exhausted from being overworked and his health deteriorated; he was unwell during the winter and described his time at Mount St. Mary's as 'dank as ditch-water'. It was not a very productive time for Hopkins poetrywise and in April 1878 he was once again transferred to Stonyhurst for three months to coach the boys for university exams. That summer, Hopkins was appointed assistant priest at the Church of the Immaculate Conception in Farm Street in fashionable Mayfair, London. From Farm Street he went to Bristol to a curacy but was moved to St. Aloysius's church in Oxford after a week. He stayed in Oxford for ten months and was unhappy – 'Often I was in a black mood'; he had little contact with university life and was uneasy among the ordinary town people.

Bedford Leigh, near Manchester, was Hopkins's next destination. There he did parish work for three months and the New Year of 1880 found him in the slums of Liverpool, where he had been appointed curate at St. Francis Xavier's Church. His work there was, in Norman White's words, 'the ordinary parish drudgery – confessions, catechism classes, house and hospital visits, and occasional sermons – in a depressing area.'

Hopkins, though meticulously prepared, was never truly successful in his elaborately written sermons. The sermons preached to the poor people of Liverpool reveal a priest not at ease in the pulpit.

He had little time for writing poetry and, since leaving Oxford, had written only 26 lines: 'Liverpool is of all places the most museless. It is indeed a most unhappy and miserable spot.' Indeed, on 21 April 1880 one of Hopkins's parishioners, Felix Spencer, died of pulmonary consumption in his Birchfield Street slum. Spencer was thirty-one and a horse-shoer or farrier. A week later, on 28 April, Hopkins wrote 'Felix Randal' . He also wrote some music during this time and set some poems by Bridges. His health, once again, was deteriorating. August to October 1881 were spent in St Joseph's parish, Glasgow. He preferred Glasgow slums to Liverpool ones – 'I get on better here, though bad is the best of my getting on.'

Most of Hopkins's time in Scotland was spent in the city but he did get to visit Inversnaid, a small settlement in the Scottish Highlands. It is thought that he wished to see Inversnaid because of Wordsworth's 1807 poem 'To a Highland Girl – At Inversnayde, upon Loch Lomond'. Hopkins's poem 'Inversnaid' was written on 28 September 1881. Apparently Hopkins himself was dissatisfied with the poem; he did not send copies to his fellow-poets Bridges and Dixon, who saw it for the first time after his death.

After Scotland, ten months at Manresa House, Roehampton, awaited the thirty-seven year-old Fr Hopkins. Though ordained in 1877 at thirty-three, Hopkins was now to enter a time of religious meditation and devotional study in the very place where he had begun his novitiate and where, on 15 August 1882, after fourteen years of training, he took his final vows as Spiritual Coadjutor in the Society of Jesus. From Roehampton he went once again to Stonyhurst where he taught the students Latin, Greek and some English. Life weighed upon him at Stonyhurst and Hopkins himself tried to explain his predicament in a letter: 'I like my pupils and do not wholly dislike the work, but I fall into or continue in a heavy state of body and mind in which my go is gone ... I make no way with what I read, and seem but half a man. It is a sad thing to say.' Hopkins was 'always tired, always jaded' and this listlessness made him miserable; during his year and a half at Stonyhurst he completed only three poems. And yet Norman White, in his literary biography of Hopkins, counteracts this image of a man 'in a heavy state of body and mind' and tells of how a former-pupil at Stonyhurst, Alban Goodier, remembered being released from the classroom one day because of toothache and was told to amuse himself in the playground: 'Fr Hopkins came up to the small boy and asked why he was there all alone. Goodier explained, and then Hopkins said: "Watch me." He took off his gown and proceeded to climb up one of the goalposts... Hopkins reached the top of the post and then lowered himself down. He put on his gown and then walked away.'

During the summer of 1883, Hopkins went with his family to Holland for a brief visit. That same summer he met the poet Coventry Patmore at Stonyhurst and their friendship resulted in a correspondence that lasted for several years.

By the following January, Stonyhurst was no longer Hopkins's home: he had been appointed Professor of Greek and Latin Literature at University College, Dublin, which had been founded by John Henry Newman, and lived at 86 St. Stephen's Green, in the heart of the city. Number 86 was dilapidated, with rats in the drains, and Hopkins found Dublin 'joyless' and dirty. The Liffey was used as the public sewer for the city and the poor sanitation, it is thought, may have contributed to Hopkins's early death.

His Greek and Latin classes were small, but Hopkins was also a Fellow of the Royal University of Ireland and the work involved was considerable. He examined candidates from other colleges and these examinations, five or six times per year, resulted in hundreds of scripts each time. In 1887, Hopkins had 1,795 exam scripts to mark, which he did scrupulously, and during his six years in Dublin the number varied from 1,300 to 1,800. 'It nearly killed him', writes Robert Bernard Martin in *Gerard Manley Hopkins: A Very Private Life*: 'Perhaps it did'. He had little success as a lecturer and both lectures and classes were conducted in an uproar. Other accounts suggest that Hopkins's workload was not impossible and that his only sufferings 'were physical and spiritual ones'. One Jesuit, twenty years after his death, said that Hopkins 'was thought by most to be more or less crazy'.

Those six years produced some wonderful celebratory poems such as 'Harry Ploughman' and 'That Nature is a Heraclitean Fire and of the comfort of the Resurrection'; Hopkins saw as much of Ireland as possible and visited Connemara, Castlebar, sailed by the Cliffs of Moher, visited friends at Monasterevan, Enniscorthy and Howth, stayed at the Jesuit school Clongowes Wood College, travelled to England, Scotland and Wales. His time in Ireland also produced his bleakest poems, which Bridges called the 'terrible sonnets', and another critic, W.H. Gardner, called the 'sonnets of desolation'. These dark, desperate sonnets include 'I wake and feel the fell of dark not day', 'No worst, there is none' and 'Thou art indeed just, Lord'. Only one of the eight sonnets is dated; none was read while he lived and, referring to one of them in a letter, he said: 'I have after long silence written two sonnets ... if ever anything was written in blood one of these was'. The literary critic Norman MacKenzie thinks that 'the two sonnets which best qualify for the title "written in blood" are "No Worst" and "I wake and feel the fell of dark, not day"'; Norman White suggests it is 'No Worst'.

Hopkins did not like Ireland. He told Patmore that 'the Irish have little feeling for poetry and least of all for modern poetry'. He felt that he was at a third remove and a line from a sonnet written in 1885 reads: 'To seem the stranger lies my lot'. A letter dated 17 February 1886 bemoans 'three years in Ireland, three hard wearying wasted years' and, in January 1889, Hopkins wrote that 'Five wasted years almost have passed in Ireland'. He had been ill again in the autumn of 1888 and an illness the following spring only made things worse.

On 5 May 1889, he wrote his last letter to his family, in which he joked that his illness at least meant that he would be spared university examining, and concluded: 'I have been in a sort of extremity of mind, now I am the placidest soul in the world. And you will see, when I come round, I shall be the better for this. I am writing uncomfortably and this is enough for a sick man. I am your loving son, Gerard. Best love to all.' Three days later he dictated a letter to his mother in which he explained that 'My fever is a sort of typhoid: it is not severe, and my mind has never for a moment wandered.' Nurses from St. Vincent's hospital came to St Stephens Green and he was moved from number 86 to a better room in 85. He had been ill for nearly six weeks and there were signs of recovery but on 5 June he suffered a relapse. Hopkins was told by Fr Wheeler, who had been looking after him, that he would probably not recover; his parents were sent for. Knowing that he was dying he asked for the Holy Viaticum – the Eucharist given to a person who is dying – and received it several times, the last time on Saturday morning, 8 June. He died that day at 1.30 p.m. The following Tuesday, funeral mass was said at the Jesuit Church, Upper Gardiner St, and he was buried at Glasnevin Cemetery. Inside the main gates and to the left is the communal Jesuit plot. Hopkins's name is one of many at the base of the granite Celtic cross.

•

Bridges felt that 'that dear Gerard was overworked, unhappy and would never have done anything great seems to give no solace ... he seems to have been entirely lost and destroyed by those Jesuits'. The Jesuit obituary offers another view: 'His mind was of too delicate a texture to grapple with the rougher elements of life'. The obituary placed in the newspaper *The Nation* mentioned Hopkins's conversion, his scholarship and his aesthetic faculties, but never referred to what Hopkins is now known for – his poetry.

•

The first edition of Hopkins's collected poetry was published in 1918 and was dedicated by Robert Bridges to the poet's ninety-eight year-old mother. Her son had been dead since 1889. In all, Hopkins left a relatively small number of poems, forty-eight or so; and, though he belongs to the nineteenth century, he is often considered a twentieth-century poet.

POEMS

(Not all of Hopkins's poems can be dated precisely but many of those published here can be dated accurately and, where possible, are printed in the order in which they were written; the first edition of his poems was published in December 1918, twenty-nine years after his death.)

God's Grandeur

The world is charged with the grandeur of God.
  It will flame out, like shining from shook foil;
  It gathers to a greatness, like the ooze of oil
Crushed. Why do men then now not reck his rod?
Generations have trod, have trod, have trod;
  And all is seared with trade; bleared, smeared with toil;
  And wears man's smudge and shares man's smell: the soil
Is bare now, nor can foot feel, being shod.

And for all this, nature is never spent;
  There lives the dearest freshness deep down things;
And though the last lights off the black West went
  Oh, morning, at the brown brink eastward, springs —
Because the Holy Ghost over the bent
  World broods with warm breast and with ah! bright wings.

Glossary

Line 1 charged: according to Hopkins, all things 'are charged with love, are charged with God, and, if we know how to touch them, they give off sparks and take fire, yielding drops and flow, ring and tell of him.'

Line 2 foil: metal (gold, silver, etc.) hammered or rolled into a thin sheet. Here, 'shook foil' is shaken gold foil. Hopkins comments: 'I mean foil in its sense of leaf or tinsel'. Shaken gold foil 'gives off broad glares like sheet lightning and also, and this is true of nothing else, owing to its zigzag dints and creasings and network of small many cornered facets, a sort of fork lightning too' gives off broad glares like sheet lightning.'

Line 4 Crushed: olives or linseed crushed for their oil.

Line 4 men: the poem, like other poems from this period, uses gendered language, referring to 'men' rather than 'people', or humankind.

Line 4 reck his rod: care about, obey his (God's) authority.

Line 6 seared: dried up/withered.

Line 6 bleared: blurred.

Line 8 being shod: wearing shoes.

Line 9 for all this: in spite of all this.

Line 9 spent: exhausted.

Line 13 bent: Michael Schmidt writes that 'bent' relates back to the octave of the sonnet, its metal images contrasting with images of the natural and human worlds.

Lines 9–14: Norman White, Hopkins's biographer, says that the language of the sestet changes from one of urgency and excitement found in the octet to an authoritarian voice in the sestet and that the poem 'finishes with complex imagery of nature's renewing power, hopeful dawn succeeding dark dusk. The Holy Ghost assumes the physicality and tenderness of a bird enlarged to super-terrestrial size.'

Lines 13–14: cf. Genesis I:2 – 'And the Spirit of God moved upon the face of the waters.'

Also, in Milton's 'Paradise Lost', the beginning of creation is described in terms of the Holy Ghost: 'With mighty wings outspread/Dove-like sat brooding o'er the vast Abyss.'

This poem was written at St. Beuno's, Wales, on 23 February 1877. Hopkins included a revised version of the poem in a birthday letter he wrote to his mother in March 1877.

Hopkins told his friend Bridges that the starting point for this poem was the image of gold-foil.

? Questions

1. How would you describe the tone of the opening lines? Which words, in your opinion, best capture that tone? Trace the speaker's tone through the poem and examine how it changes.
2. How does the speaker convey here the grandeur, power and authority of God?
3. Why do you think the one sentence with a question mark is made up of single-sounding or monosyllabic words?
4. The poem both celebrates and condemns. Which is the dominant mood, do you think? Why?
5. How is man (humankind) portrayed in the poem? Which words do you consider most effective in portraying man's presence?
6. Identify important sounds and repetitions in the poem and say why they are effective.
7. Choose four interesting images from the poem and comment on each one.
8. Hopkins is regarded by many as an unofficial patron saint of the green movement. Which poems by Hopkins on your course would support this view?

'As kingfishers catch fire, dragonflies draw flame'

As kingfishers catch fire, dragonflies dráw fláme;
  As tumbled over rim in roundy wells
  Stones ring; like each tucked string tells, each hung bell's
Bow swung finds tongue to fling out broad its name;
Each mortal thing does one thing and the same:
  Deals out that being indoors each one dwells;
  Selves — goes itself; *myself* it speaks and spells,
Crying *Whát I dó is me: for that I came.*

Í say móre: the just man justices;
  Kéeps gráce: thát keeps all his goings graces;
Acts in God's eye what in God's eye he is —
  Chríst. For Christ plays in ten thousand places,
Lovely in limbs, and lovely in eyes not his
  To the Father through the features of men's faces.

Glossary

Line 1 kingfishers: a fish-eating bird with very brilliant plumage.

Line 1 dragonflies: a brilliantly coloured insect; of the phrase 'dragon flies draw flame', Norman H. MacKenzie says: 'The dragonfly jets flame like a blow-pipe, unmistakably itself'.

Line 3 tucked: a dialect word for plucked.

Pied Beauty

Glory be to God for dappled things —
For skies of couple-colour as a brinded cow;
For rose-moles all in stipple upon trout that swim;
Fresh-firecoal chestnut-falls; finches' wings;
Landscape plotted and pieced — fold, fallow, and plough;
And áll trádes, their gear and tackle and trim.

All things counter, original, spare, strange;
Whatever is fickle, freckled (who knows how?)
With swift, slow; sweet, sour; adazzle, dim;
He fathers-forth whose beauty is past change:
Praise him.

Glossary

Title: Pied of various colours (The word 'pied' comes from 'pie' or 'magpie', the black and white bird).

Line 1 dappled: speckled, mottled.

Line 2 couple-colour: two colour.

Line 2 brinded: an older form of brindled, meaning spotted, streaked.

Line 3 rose-moles: pinkish/reddish spots.

Line 3 stipples: dotted, speckled.

Line 4 fresh-firecoal chestnut-falls: typical Hopkins compound words; the chestnuts are being compared to the burning glowing coals. Wind-falls refers to fruit blown from the tree; Hopkins uses the same idea here for the chestnuts: chestnut-falls.

Line 5 pieced: enclosed piece of land.

Line 5 fold: an enclosure for sheep.

Line 5 fallow: land left unsown or uncultivated for a period.

Line 5 plough: plough-land.

Line 6 trades: the various kinds of work associated with the land.

Line 6 gear: tools, machinery.

Line 6 tackle: implements.

Line 6 trim: equipment, fittings.

Line 7 counter: contrasting.

Line 7 spare: restrained.

Line 7 strange: surprising, unusual.

Line 8 fickle: varying, changing.

Line 8 freckled: dappled, spotted.

Line 10 fathers-forth: creates.

Hopkins called this a **curtal** (curtailed, cropped or shortened) sonnet with an abcabc dbcdc rhyme scheme.

It is a tradition in Jesuit schools that all pieces of written work are framed by two statements: A.M.D.G. (*Ad majorem Dei Gloriam* – For the greater glory of God) and L.D.S. (*Laus Deo semper* – Praise God always). Here Hopkins frames his curtal sonnet with similar statements.

? Questions

1. How would you sum up the gist of the poem? Do you think the speaker here convinces his reader that God ought to be praised? Give reasons for your answer.
2. What is man's part in the natural world? Compare and contrast how Hopkins views and portrays humanity in 'Pied Beauty' and 'God's Grandeur'.
3. In the first section (lines 1–6), Hopkins focuses on the particular. Why do you think he speaks about the general in the second part?
4. Comment on the poet's rhythm, assonance and alliteration.
5. Do you think the poem contains a great energy and conviction? Point out words and phrases which capture these.
6. Hopkins's compound words have been called 'miniature poems'. Discuss the compound words in 'Pied Beauty' with this description in mind.

Felix Randal

Felix Randal the farrier, O he is dead then? my duty all ended,
Who have watched his mould of man, big-boned and hardy-handsome
Pining, pining, till time when reason rambled in it and some
Fatal four disorders, fleshed there, all contended?

Sickness broke him. Impatient he cursed at first, but mended
Being anointed and all; though a heavenlier heart began some
Months earlier, since I had our sweet reprieve and ransom
Tendered to him. Ah well, God rest him all road ever he offended!

This seeing the sick endears them to us, us too it endears.
My tongue had taught thee comfort, touch had quenched thy tears,
Thy tears that touched my heart, child, Felix, poor Felix Randal;

How far from then forethought of, all thy more boisterous years,
When thou at the random grim forge, powerful amidst peers,
Didst fettle for the great grey drayhorse his bright and battering sandal!

Glossary

Title: Felix Randal's real name was Felix Spencer. On 21 April 1880, he died, aged thirty-one, of pulmonary consumption after a long illness. Felix, in Latin, means happy.

Line 1 farrier: blacksmith.

Line 1 O he is dead then: this has been printed as 'O is he dead then' in some editions.

Line 3 pining: fading away, wasting away, especially under pain or mental distress.

Line 4 disorders: illnesses.

Line 4 fleshed: inhabited the body; in Elizabethan English, 'fleshed' meant 'to make fierce and eager for combat'.

Line 4 contended: struggled to gain supremacy, attacked.

Line 6 anointed: Felix Randal was given the Sacrament of the Sick, which meant his forehead was touched by the priest's thumb which had been dipped in holy oil.

Line 6 a heavenlier heart: having been anointed, Felix accepted his illness; his heart acknowledged his sins, did penance and prepared for death.

Line 7 sweet reprieve: respite, relief. (Holy Communion?)

Line 7 ransom: redemption, deliverance from sin. (confession and absolution?)

Line 8 all road ever: in whatever way (a dialect phrase from Lancashire in the north of England).

Line 9 us too it endears: it makes us cherish ourselves and be grateful for our health too.

Line 12 boisterous: noisy.

Line 13 random: haphazard, disorganised; this has also been glossed as meaning built with rough, irregular stones.

Line 13 grim: cruel, fierce, severe; grim is also a dialect word for grimy or filthy.

Line 13 peers: equals.

Line 14 fettle: get ready, prepare.

Line 14 drayhorse: dray means a low strong cart for heavy goods; the drayhorse would pull such a cart.

Line 14 sandal: the technical name for a particular type of horseshoe.

It has been suggested that in 'Felix Randal' Hopkins is echoing Ecclesiasticus 38: 'the smith at his anvil is absorbed in his handiwork ... he inclines his ear to the sound of the hammer, and his eyes are on the pattern of the object.'

Norman MacKenzie points out that the poem is structured in such a way that lines 1–4 focus on the wasting body; lines 5–8 on the awakening of the soul; lines 9–11 on the priest/patient relationship in which the patient is as weak as a child; and the final lines offer a dramatic flashback.

The sonnet was written in Liverpool and is dated 28 April 1880.

Questions

1. How would you describe the tone of 'O he is dead then? my duty all ended'? Chart the different feelings expressed by the speaker in this poem. How many can you identify? Does Hopkins feel helpless and unnecessary? Does Hopkins care for his parishioner? Give reasons for your answer.

2. What is the relationship between priest and farrier, between farrier and God? Which one is more important than the other? Why is one more important than the other? Give reasons for your answer.

3. Why do you think Hopkins presents us first with Felix Randal in his prime, then in his sickness and finally in his prime once again?

4. How does Hopkins view Felix Randal's life and death? Comment on the sounds of the poem and discuss how they contribute to the meaning.

5. The poet Eamon Grennan admires the poem for the way in which it manages to treat its subject – the death of a parishioner – in a manner 'both tender and rugged'. Explain how Hopkins achieves both tenderness and ruggedness in 'Felix Randal'.

6. This poem moves from 'a meditative beginning to a fiery ending'. Why do you think Hopkins structured the poem in this way? How would you describe the achievement and the effect of the final line?

Inversnaid

This darksome burn, horseback brown,
His rollrock highroad roaring down,
In coop and in comb the fleece of his foam
Flutes and low to the lake falls home.

A windpuff-bonnet of fáwn-fróth
Turns and twindles over the broth
Of a pool so pitchblack, féll-frówning,
It rounds and rounds Despair to drowning.

Degged with dew, dappled with dew
Are the groins of the braes that the brook treads through,
Wiry heathpacks, flitches of fern,
And the beadbonny ash that sits over the burn.

What would the world be, once bereft
Of wet and of wildness? Let them be left,
O let them be left, wildness and wet;
Long live the weeds and the wilderness yet.

Glossary

Title Inversnaid: on the eastern shore of Loch Lomond in the Scottish Highlands.

Line 1 burn: small stream (Scots word) – coloured brown ('darksome') by the peat/turf.

Line 2 his rollrock highroad roaring down: the stream roars downwards and rocks the stones in its bed. This particular burn is Arklet Water. It flows down from Loch Arklet and enters Loch Lomond near Inversnaid.

Line 3 coop: enclosed space where water is hemmed in by rocks.

Line 3 comb: water combing, cresting over rocks with a 'roping' effect, to borrow a word from Hopkins's journal.

Line 4 Flutes: this has been interpreted as an image from architecture – the fluting on pillars; also, perhaps the music associated with the sound of the flute?

Line 5 fáwn-fróth: the beige or fawn coloured foam or froth.

Line 6 twindles: a word combining twists/twitches and, perhaps, dwindles; twindles, according to Peter Milward, expresses the movement of the froth as it is blown about and forms into smaller bubbles. Norman H. MacKenzie notes that twindles is a Lancashire word and means doubling or dividing in half.

Line 6 broth: disturbed water.

Line 7 féll-: fiercely.

Line 9 Degged: (Lancashire dialect) sprinkled.

Line 9 dappled: variegated, patches of colour and shade.

Line 10 groins: the edge of the stream's path.

Line 10 braes: hillsides.

Line 11 heathpacks: clumps of heather.

Line 11 flitches: brown fronds resembling thin strips of tree trunk; ragged, russet tufts.

Line 12 beadbonny: the mountain ash or rowan tree with its pretty bead-like, red/orange berries (bonny is Scottish for pretty).

Line 13 bereft: deprived of, robbed of.

This is Hopkins's only Scottish poem and was written on 28 September 1881. In a letter to Bridges, he wrote: 'I hurried from Glasgow one day to Loch Lomond. The day was dark and partly hid the lake, yet it did not altogether disfigure it but gave a pensive or solemn beauty which left a deep impression on me.'

? Questions

1. Which words in your opinion best capture a powerful stream rushing downhill? Which words help you see and hear the stream?
2. This poem can be divided into two sections – description and speculation. How does one lead to the other? Why? Give reasons for your answer.
3. 'Hopkins's poetry is noted for its ability to compress ideas and feelings and to express them effectively and succinctly.' Would you agree that this is true of 'Inversnaid'? Which other poems are relevant here? Give reasons for your answer.
4. Write down those words that recur in the poem. Comment on Hopkins's use of repetition and say whether you think it effective.
5. Do you think that this poem is a good illustration of 'wildness and wet'? Why?

'I wake and feel the fell of dark, not day'

I wake and feel the fell of dark, not day.
What hours, O what black hoürs we have spent
This night! what sights you, heart, saw; ways you went!
And more must, in yet longer light's delay.
   With witness I speak this. But where I say
Hours I mean years, mean life. And my lament
Is cries countless, cries like dead letters sent
To dearest him that lives alas! away.

   I am gall, I am heartburn. God's most deep decree
Bitter would have me taste: my taste was me;
Bones built in me, flesh filled, blood brimmed the curse.
   Selfyeast of spirit a dull dough sours. I see
The lost are like this, and their scourge to be
As I am mine, their sweating selves; but worse.

Glossary

Line 1 fell: threat; blow. 'Fell' also means 'mountain' ('By Killarney's lakes and fells...'). Fell has also been interpreted to mean an animal's pelt and that moment when Adam and Eve were expelled from Paradise wearing animal skins. Also, in Exodus 10:21, the plague in Egypt is described as 'a darkness to be felt'.

Lines 7–8 dead letters sent /To dearest him: undelivered letters; perhaps ignored letters? Robert Bernard Martin in his biography of Hopkins says that this echoes an episode twenty years earlier when Hopkins wrote to Digby Dolben (see Biographical Note) frequently, but Dolben hardly replied. Martin also says: 'Hopkins seems deliberately to blur the dividing line between persons and Deity by withholding the capital letter of the pronouns most Victorians used in referring to Christ, as if to indicate the difficulty of distinguishing between his feelings for other men and those for Christ.' (In 'Pied Beauty', however, when God is being praised in the final line, 'Praise him' is written without a capital 'h'.)

Lines 9–14: Norman H. MacKenzie says of the sestet: 'Allusions to the inescapable burden of the Fall and original sin are to be found in curse as well as in sweating: "through thy act," said God to Adam, "the ground is under a curse ... thou shalt earn thy bread with the sweat of thy brow" (Genesis). But instead of being nourished by bread he is being nauseated by a dull dough soured by selfyeast...'

Line 9 gall: bitterness.

Line 9 deep: unfathomable, inexplicable. Originally, Hopkins wrote 'deep decree', then changed it to 'just decree' and finally changed it back to 'deep decree'.

Line 9 decree: command, authority.

Line 11 Bones built in me, flesh filled, blood brimmed the curse: in an earlier draft the line read, 'My bones build, my flesh fills, blood feeds this curse'.

Line 12 Selfyeast of spirit a dull dough sours: Hopkins here feels that his own self is incapable of creating anything wholesome.

This sonnet was written in Dublin and found among Hopkins's papers after his death. Letters Hopkins wrote from Dublin recorded his exhaustion and despair. He was 'continually jaded and harassed'; he speaks of 'a fagged mind and a continual anxiety'. In his private notes, he wrote: 'I begin to enter on that course of loathing and hopelessness which I have so often felt before, which made me fear madness ... What is my wretched life?'

? Questions

1. How does the speaker here create such a bleak effect? Look at what he says and how he says it.

2. 'I' is used eight times. Who is the 'we' referred to in line 2 and the 'dearest him' in line 8? Why is he speaking to himself in this particular way?

3. Outline the progress of thought in the poem. Is there any sense of hope in this sonnet? Give reasons for your answer.

4. What is the effect of so many monosyllabic words?

5. How would you describe the speaker's relationship with God in these 'terrible sonnets' by Hopkins?

6. In the octet the emphasis is on spiritual suffering, in the sestet on the physical. Which one is more vividly conveyed, in your opinion?

7. Though the poem is extraordinarily personal do you think that the speaker's focus includes the suffering and plight of others? What is the effect of this?

'No worst there is none. Pitched past pitch of grief'

No worst, there is none. Pitched past pitch of grief,
More pangs will, schooled at forepangs, wilder wring.
Comforter, where, where is your comforting?
Mary, mother of us, where is your relief?
My cries heave, herds-long; huddle in a main, a chief
Woe, wórld-sorrow; on an áge-old anvil wince and sing —
Then lull, then leave off. Fury had shrieked 'No ling-
ering! Let me be fell: force I must be brief.'

O the mind, mind has mountains; cliffs of fall
Frightful, sheer, no-man-fathomed. Hold them cheap
May who ne'er hung there. Nor does long our small
Durance deal with that steep or deep. Here! creep,
Wretch, under a comfort serves in a whirlwind: all
Life death does end and each day dies with sleep.

Glossary

Line 1 Pitched past pitch of grief: flung forwards into more grief beyond the present suffering.

Line 2 pangs: shooting pain; sudden sharp mental pain.

Line 2 schooled at forepangs: the pangs already experienced teach us or prepare us for the greater pangs to come.

Line 2 wring: squeeze, twist, torture.

Line 5 heave: groan, sigh.

Line 5 herds-long: like a group or a gathering of animals.

Line 5 main: a crowd.

Line 6 wince: flinch.

Line 7 lull: soothe.

Line 8 fell: fierce, cruel.

Line 8 force: (perforce) unavoidably, necessarily.

Line 10–11 Hold them cheap/May who ne'er hung there: those who have not known extreme suffering could dismiss those who are suffering.

Line 12 Durance: endurance.

Line 12 deal with: cope with.

> Aldous Huxley (1894–1963) said of this sonnet: 'Never, I think, has the just man's complaint against the universe been put more forcibly, worded more tersely and fiercely.'

? Questions

1. How does the speaker convey a sense of desolation and finality at the outset?
2. Why is the speaker experiencing such anguish and torment? What is the significance of lines 4 and 5? How does his being a priest contribute to the overall effect of the poem?
3. Which images best capture the poet's pain? Which sounds? What is the effect of the two questions within the sonnet? Are these questions answered?
4. The American poet Adrienne Rich says that, in this sonnet, Hopkins is 'wrestling not just with diction and grammar, end rhymes and metres, but with his own rebellious heart.' Do you think that this is a good description of the poem? Give reasons for your answer.
5. How does the sestet differ from the octet? Which is the more bleak and why? Give reasons for your answer. What comfort does the speaker find in the end?
6. Comment on the imagery of mountains and cliffs in lines 9–10. Do you think such imagery appropriate and effective? Why?

'Thou art indeed just, Lord, if I contend'

Justus quidem tu es, Domine, si disputem tecum: verumtamen justa loquar ad te: Quare via impiorum prosperatur? & c.

Thou art indeed just, Lord, if I contend
With thee; but, sir, so what I plead is just.
Why do sinners' ways prosper? and why must
Disappointment all I endeavour end?
Wert thou my enemy, O thou my friend,
How wouldst thou worse, I wonder, than thou dost
Defeat, thwart me? Oh, the sots and thralls of lust
Do in spare hours more thrive than I that spend,
Sir, life upon thy cause. See, banks and brakes
Now, leavèd how thick! lacèd they are again
With fretty chervil, look, and fresh wind shakes
Them; birds build — but not I build; no, but strain,
Time's eunuch, and not breed one work that wakes.
Mine, O thou lord of life, send my roots rain.

Glossary

Latin epigraph: from Jeremiah XII (Vulgate): 'Righteous art thou, O Lord, when I complain to thee; yet I would plead my case before thee. Why does the way of the wicked prosper? Why do all who are treacherous thrive? Thou plantest them and they take root; they grow and bring forth fruit ...'

Line 1 contend: argue.

Line 7 thwart: frustrate.

Line 7 sots: drunkards.

Line 7 thralls: slaves.

Line 7 lust: desire for sexual indulgence and pleasure.

Line 9 brakes: thickets.

Line 11 fretty: lacy, interlaced; chervil leaves are beautifully cut and ruffled (fretty).

Line 11 chervil: herb – the word 'chevril' means 'the rejoicing leaf'.

Line 12 strain: make a great effort.

Line 13 eunuch: a castrated male. Hopkins sees himself as someone incapable of achieving, producing anything worthwhile. Gus Martin comments: 'having renounced human love for the love of God, Hopkins complains in this dark moment that his life seems both spiritually and physically fruitless'.

This sonnet was written in Dublin on 17 March 1889. Earlier that year, in January, while on retreat at St. Stanislaus's College, Tullamore, he wrote: 'Five wasted years almost have passed in Ireland ... All my undertakings miscarry: I am like a straining eunuch. I wish then for death: yet if I died now I should die imperfect, no master of myself, and that is the worst failure of all. O my god, look down on me.'

Questions

1. 'No worst, there is none' and 'I wake and feel the fell of dark' are powerful expressions of pleading, despair and pessimism. Is the same true of this poem?
2. What is the effect of 'sir'? How would you describe Hopkins's tone here? Is it as if the speaker is in a courtroom pleading his case?
3. In lines 5–14, is the poet's argument a convincing one in your opinion? Give reasons for your answer. Why does the speaker feel alone and isolated?
4. How effective in your opinion is the nature imagery in the poem?
5. How do the line length, punctuation and rhythm contribute to the poem? How would you describe the overall effect of the final line?
6. How is God understood and portrayed in the sonnet? Quote from the poem to illustrate the points you make.

General Questions

A. 'No doubt my poetry errs on the side of oddness ...' was Hopkins's own comment. Discuss this view in the light of your understanding of Hopkins's poetry. In your answer, you should quote from, or refer to, poems by Hopkins on your course.

B. T.S. Eliot thought that Hopkins's language was 'too far from the language of common speech.' Is this a strength or a weakness? In your answer, you should quote from, or refer to, the poems by Hopkins on your course.

C. 'Hopkins in his poetry captures the dizzying heights of delight and the depths of despair.' Would you agree with this statement? Support the points you make with reference to, or quotation from, the poems by Hopkins on your course.

D. 'Hopkins's poetry is both interesting for what he has to say and for the way he says it.' Would you agree with this view? In your answer, you should quote from, or refer to, poems by Hopkins on your course.

E. What aspects of Hopkins's poetry interested you most? In your answer, you should support your discussion by quotation from, or reference to, the poems you have studied.

F. Do you think Hopkins's poetry speaks to readers in the twenty-first century? Give reasons for your answer and support your views with the aid of suitable quotation or reference.

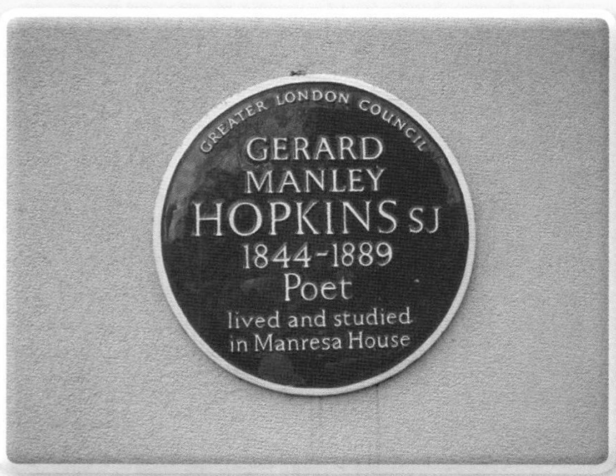

• A plaque to Hopkins in London.

Critical Commentary

God's Grandeur

Hopkins is a poet of extremes. If poets make words work hard then Hopkins makes words work harder than most, whether it is to capture his enthusiasm for God's creation or his despair at feeling estranged from his Creator. 'God's Grandeur' combines feelings of both joy and sorrow. The opening lines are a vivid and marvellous account of the greatness of God. The strong statement of line 1, with its energised verb and alliterative power, is total in its conviction:

> The world is charged with the grandeur of God.

If the above line read 'The world is filled with the grandeur of God', the idea is retained but the power has disappeared. 'Charged' is a scientific term; God's presence is electrifying. Peter Milward, commenting on Hopkins's choice of verb, says that Hopkins 'envisages God not just as present, but as actively present'. In his commentary on the Spiritual Exercises, Hopkins noted: 'All things therefore are charged with love, are charged with God and if we know how to touch them give off sparks and take fire, yield drops and flow, ring and tell of him.'

God's shining light and strength are captured in the natural images of gold foil and crushed olives. The ear immediately picks up on some of Hopkins's most characteristic traits – alliteration and assonance:

> It will flame out, like shining from shook foil;
> It gathers to a greatness, like the ooze of oil
> Crushed.

The sudden lightning flash and the slow process of making oil are two very different movements, but both are expressions of how God's grandeur can be manifested.

The placing of 'Crushed' at the beginning of that next line gives the verb even greater emphasis. This confident mood in the octet ends abruptly when Hopkins asks why God's greatness is not acknowledged or appreciated.

> Why do men then now not reck his rod?

The language has become austere and severe. There is alliteration still ('reck' and 'rod'), but the nine monosyllables that form the question have slowed down the poem's lyrical and dramatic flow. Having already presented the reader with a sense of God's power and might, the question – why do men not honour God? – is all the more effective. The question is awkward to read. It demands pause and attention, and Hopkins in this way is saying that the question is important.

A sense of time past and time passing is contained within the next line, which stresses man's presence on earth. The threefold repetition of 'have trod' creates, according to the British writer James Reeves, 'an overwhelming sense of ceaseless and monotonous effort':

> Generations have trod, have trod, have trod

It feels negative, repetitive and onomatopoeic. The 'trod' sound beats within the line, just as the gesture of trodding can be said to beat upon the earth. Man's presence is further emphasised in the poet's choice of verbs, 'seared', 'bleared, smeared'. The meaning is similar and the sounds are similar; assonance here connects one with the other. Trade and toil are viewed negatively. The earth has been destroyed by man; we have abused the soil to such an extent that it is now 'bare', and that man has lost contact with the earth is suggested in the image of a shoe-covered foot:

> And all is seared with trade; bleared, smeared with toil;
> And wears man's smudge and shares man's smell: the soil
> Is bare now, nor can foot feel being shod.

There is a hopelessness and despair in 'And all' and man's ugly impact is conveyed through the senses, but the sestet offers renewed hope when it turns to God's great ability to renew and awaken the earth. 'Shod' connects and brings us back to 'trod ... trod ... trod' in the earlier line. The first word in the sestet – 'And' – suggests continuity. Hopkins sums up God's greatness in the phrase 'nature is never spent'. Man might destroy nature, has been destroying nature for generations but nature is an expression of God's power and might and, therefore, is never exhausted – 'There lives the dearest freshness deep down things' – and in the sestet we are reminded that God cares for both man and nature.

The imagery of the dawn following the darkest night is a familiar one, but Hopkins makes it his own in a language that is immediate and filled with awe:

> And though the last lights off the black West went
> Oh, morning, at the brown brink eastwards, springs—

The word 'springs', filled with energy and life, placed at the end of the line, is given greater force and that it happens each morning, that it has happened every morning since the beginning of time, even though man has not always respected God's creation, is Hopkins's powerful and effective argument.

The poem ends with the poet's deep belief and explanation for this daily miracle, and in a tone of triumph and appreciation. The Holy Spirit, like a mother bird, cares for and tends to our world.

> Because the Holy Ghost over the bent
> World broods with warm breast and with ah! bright wings.

This final image is one easily pictured. The vastness of the world has become the bird's nest or home – the warmth and brightness contained within the image is reassuring and comforting. The 'bent' world can be interpreted to mean the curved world, or it could also, perhaps, refer to an unnatural or perverted or warped world. In contrast to the harsh-sounding 'bent' is the soft warm sound of 'broods'. The 'ah!' in the final line is filled with wonder and awe.

'As kingfishers catch fire, dragonflies draw flame'

This is a poem that celebrates uniqueness. Hopkins observes in the opening line that we recognise the kingfisher by the sudden flash of brilliant colour, the dragonfly by its jet of flame:

> As kingfishers catch fire, dragonflies draw flame

The bird and insect are but two of several examples given in lines 1–4 that illustrate that each thing, whether animate, inanimate or man-made, has an individual, unique quality. Having considered the unusual and brilliantly coloured world of nature, Hopkins then focuses on the man-made well and the bell. If stones are dropped down a well, each one creates its own sound and makes its own music:

> As tumbled over rim in roundy wells
> Stones ring

The very words describing the act of throwing stones down a well contain their own, appropriate music; 'tumbled' and 'roundy' convey movement and shape, while the alliteration of 'rim', 'roundy', 'ring' and the assonance in 'rim' and 'ring' highlight Hopkins's extraordinary ear.

He lists example after example and the outcome is a varied and wide-ranging list. By line 3 the poet is speaking of how a musical instrument when plucked ('tucked') sounds its unique note and the bell when swung rings out in its own way:

> like each tucked string tells, each hung bell's
> Bow swung finds tongue to fling out broad its name

The different and unique musical sounds here are found in the very verbs that Hopkins has chosen to describe each one: 'tucked' is a contained sound and suggests a hand-held sized instrument; 'swung', 'fling' and 'broad' are expansive and outward sounding. The pacing of 'hung', 'swung', 'tongue' also imitates the bell's sounds – between 'hung' and 'swung' there are two words, between 'swung' and 'tongue' a single word and the quickening rhyme matches the quickening rhythm of the bell.

In four lines, the reader has been asked to consider kingfisher, dragonfly, stones falling down a well, a stringed musical instrument and a ringing bell. Sight and sound play an important part here in our imagining the uniqueness of all these things. The compression and the musical quality of the language are immediately striking.

All of these examples are dazzling and convincing, but Hopkins's purpose in naming them is discovered in line 5. The examples serve as introduction, illustration and explanation. Man is unique too:

> Each mortal thing does one thing and the same.

If one were to simplify these dramatic and arresting lines, it might read as follows. Just as the kingfisher bird is unique because of its flash of fiery colour in flight and the dragonfly is unique because of the way the insect seems to breathe fire and every stone thrown down a well has its own unique, special music, and a stringed musical instrument when played creates its own sound, and every bell that is rung rings out each stroke in its own way, so too does each individual human being have a unique and special quality. The meaning might have been retained in this banal description of Hopkins's poem but the energy and the excitement of the poet's imagination has disappeared in the paraphrase.

The opening lines (1–4) contain, in Norman MacKenzie's words, 'superbly worded examples of how we recognise things in an instant by a characteristic flash of colour or the individual *timbre* of a note.' Lines 5–8 focus on one of God's creations:

> Each mortal thing does one thing and the same:
>   Deals out that being indoors each one dwells;
>   Selves – goes itself; *myself* it speaks and spells,
> Crying *Whát I do is me: for that I came*

These four lines are complex in thought and expression. Teased out, a possible meaning is the following: everything is unique and all things are the same in that all things are unique. Each separate, unique being manifests its unique inner self. Its uniqueness is expressed and I am aware of my own uniqueness. It is why I am here. It is why God created me. In line 7, *myself* is emphasised; in line 8, 'I' is used twice and 'I' also begins the sestet. This progression of thought is in keeping with the poem's theme, which celebrates every unique thing, including the speaker, who has been created in God's image.

Not only is man's uniqueness celebrated, but the speaker recognises a similarity between the unique things already listed and man. Ten lines of this poem – half of the octet and all of the sestet – focus on man and man's intense awareness that he has been created and that he is here for a specific purpose.

The opening words of the sestet indicate how Hopkins wishes to stress this further: 'I say more'. His main theme here, in the closing lines, is that man is made in God's image. Christ, who is both man and God, is present in each one of us and man ought to reflect Christ back to God:

> Í say móre: the just man justices;
> Keeps grace: that keeps all his goings graces;
> Acts in God's eye what in God's eye he is—
> Chríst.

Here, an intricate bond is identified between man and God. Man is capable of acting with Christlike qualities because man's sins have been forgiven, but man is also in constant need of God's graces. Norman MacKenzie sums up this idea when he says that if man 'keeps hold of the grace given him, all his goings, his everyday acts, will be gracious, pleasing to God'.

Christ is present in all men and God the Father sees Christ, his son, who is both God and man, in every man:

> For Christ plays in ten thousand places,
> Lovely in limbs, and lovely in eyes not his
> To the Father through the features of men's faces.

'Ten thousand places' serves as an image of the multitude, while 'plays' adds an attractive sense of Christ's presence in man, a presence of lightness and ease. Christ is present in mankind and the repetition of 'lovely' highlights physical beauty as well as the spiritual. These closing lines praise human beauty, but bodily, mortal beauty is made holy here through the connection Hopkins makes between man and Christ.

'As kingfishers catch fire, dragonflies draw flame' survives only in draft. According to Norman White, Hopkins was dissatisfied with the poem.

Spring

This is one of Hopkins's most famous poems and displays what the poet Elizabeth Bishop called Hopkins's 'emotional rushing effect'. There is no stopping the first stanza. It begins with a strong, powerful, ultimate statement, what Norman White calls 'a burgeoning sound, a hyperbole'.

> Nothing is so beautiful as spring—

The lines that follow illustrate that beauty in a surge of energy, 'by an ecstatic scene of movements, shapes, sounds, textures and colour'. The decisive nature of the words 'nothing' and 'so', and the tone they create, are convincing and the poem illustrates why spring is the most beautiful of all. This poem was written in May 1877, when Hopkins was thirty-three, and, in the words of American academic Virginia Ridley Ellis, is one of those poems by Hopkins that says yes 'wholeheartedly to the resources and richness of natural beauty as it bespeaks and is sustained by divine beauty'.

There is an ecstatic tone throughout the octet and the rhythm is free-flowing. Hopkins's command of alliteration and assonance are very effective in line two, when he offers his first illustration of spring's beauty:

> When weeds, in wheels, shoot long and lovely and lush

Commenting on the verb 'shoot' here, Norman MacKenzie contends that the 'happy rapidity of movement is exaggerated (as in a speeded-up film), after the sluggishness of winter' and lush – meaning succulent or juicy – captures a sense of new life. That Hopkins celebrates weeds, and not flowers for instance, reveals his ability to find beauty in the everyday. In 'Inversnaid', he writes 'Long live the weeds and the wilderness yet'. The weeds are described as 'weeds, in wheels', which is an interesting detail. The phrase might refer to the radiating leaves which are like the spokes of a wheel; it has also been interpreted to refer to the tall grasses wheeling in the breeze; and a third possible meaning suggests 'weeds in wheels' means sprouting at will, spreading here there and everywhere without hindrance, from the Shakespearean use of the word 'wheel' which means 'to roam', 'to wander about'. But whichever meaning you choose, the line certainly conveys movement and energy and something unstoppable.

The imagery is both broad-ranging and precise. The reader is asked to picture the expanse of heavenly blue sky and then to focus in on the little thrush's eggs in the small nest:

> Thrush's eggs look little low heavens

Here, in one line, the poet has created the tiniest detail and a panoramic view side by side and, for Hopkins, it is God their creator that connects one with the other. The poem, having focused on seeing the blue of the eggs and the blue of the sky, then focuses on the sound of the bird's song, in a line that seem to run on and on:

> and thrush
> Through the echoing timber does so rinse and wring
> The ear, it strikes like lightnings to hear him sing

But even the thrush's song is seen in visual terms. Its effect is compared to lightning strikes, and 'rinse' and 'wring' are ringing sounds, echoing each other, just as the trees (timber) are echoing with the sound of birdsong.

A specific tree is then named, and its leaves and blooms are said to brush the descending blue of the sky:

> The glassy peartree leaves and blooms, they brush
> The descending blue

The blue skies, in line 3, were compared to 'low heavens' and here again, in line 7, the sky is referred to as 'descending blue'. Heaven and earth are brought closer here; it is as if heaven is on earth, that spring turns the world into a type of Eden. From the particular and precise detail of the 'glassy peartree', Hopkins then offers a broader picture but an equally effective description of spring when he says:

> that blue is all in a rush
> With richness

The first section ends with a familiar image:

> the racing lambs too have fair their fling.

In eight lines, Hopkins has moved from earth to heaven and from blue sky down to earth again. The verbs create much of the poem's energy and power – 'shoot', 'rinse', 'wring', 'strikes', 'leaves', 'blooms', 'brush' and the abundance and joy and freedom of spring are captured in 'long and lovely and lush', 'echoing', 'lightnings', 'rush with richness', 'racing lambs', 'fling'. The end rhymes also belong to key words, which only adds to the effect: 'lush', 'thrush', 'wring', 'sing', 'brush', 'rush', 'fling'.

The Eden parallel is made explicit in the sestet. Hopkins asks a simple question, a question which sums up all that has been celebrated in the opening lines:

> What is all this juice and all this joy?

And the answer follows immediately:

> A strain of the earth's sweet being in the beginning
> In Eden garden.

But the tone and the rhythm and the imagery are strikingly different in the sestet. Each spring we are offered a glimpse of paradise, of the world as it was before man's fall. The second section contains no evocation of natural beauty, no detail as in the sestet. Seamus Heaney thought that the poem, structurally, is 'a broken arch'. The octave, capturing as it does the essence of spring, is 'description' and 'a delightful piece of inscaping', but the sestet is 'doctrine'.

The feeling of exultation, so wonderfully expressed in the first eight lines, gives way in the sestet to thoughts on how mankind has lost that original joy. The Garden of Eden is echoed each year in the coming of spring, but Hopkins prays that an innocence and inner spring may be preserved in the young.

> Have, get, before it cloy,
> Before it cloud, Christ, lord, and sour with sinning,
> Innocent mind and Mayday in girl and boy,
> Most, O maid's child, thy choice and worthy the winning.

The words here have none of the musical sounds of the octave and 'cloy', 'cloud', 'sour' have negative, not happy, joyful, associations. There is an urgency in 'Have, get'. Mankind no longer lives in Eden; our lives are sour with sinning and Hopkins asks Christ to make possible a spring-like quality in the young. There is a conviction in that final line. Hopkins imagines Christ as a boy (and Mary as a young maid) and he prays to Christ to make possible 'an innocent mind and Mayday' in the young.

The final line is interesting:

> Most, O maid's child, thy choice and worthy the winning

'Most' means best, greatest and most thy choice means thy best choice, the best to be chosen by thee. In other words, Hopkins ends by asking God to look after the young and to keep them innocent. Otherwise, they will become 'sour with sinning'.

The movement of the poem has been from a celebration of the natural joy and beauty of spring to his regret that sinful mankind has lost a quality which is as fresh and as innocent as the season itself.

The Windhover:
To Christ our Lord

This poem was written the same month as 'Spring' – May 1877. It was Hopkins's favourite among the poems he wrote that year and he also described it, on 22 June 1879, as 'the best thing I ever wrote'. The word windhover, another name for a kestrel, is an image in itself. The *Oxford English Dictionary* records that the word was first used in 1674 and the name captures the bird's habit of hovering in the air with its head to the wind. It can be easily seen why Hopkins was attracted to such a word. Like so much of Hopkins's own language, it is an example of compression, intensity and sensuousness.

The sonnet does not look like a conventional sonnet on the page. There are fourteen lines, but the line length is different and illustrates what Hopkins called sprung rhythm. 'The Windhover' also is an excellent illustration of Hopkins's theory of 'inscape' and 'instress': the quintessential nature of the bird and the vital force that created it.

The poem's opening sentence reads as follows:

> I caught this morning morning's minion, king-
> dom of daylight's dauphin, dapple-dawn-drawn Falcon, in
> his riding
> Of the rolling level underneath him steady air, and striding
> High there, how he rung upon the rein of a wimpling wing
> In his ecstasy! then off, off forth on swing,
> As a skate's heel sweeps smooth on a bow-bend: the hurl
> and gliding
> Rebuffed the big wind.

And here is that same sentence in paraphrase:

> This morning I caught sight of a falcon, the darling of the morning, the prince of the kingdom of daylight, a bird which is attracted to the mottled light of the dawn, as it holds itself steady in the sky by its wing movement which serves as a control or guide and then it swoops and sweeps into a gliding movement: its movements force back the wind.

The gist of the poem's opening sentence offers a similar meaning but reading one alongside the other highlights the poet's extraordinary skill in capturing the energy and the delight of the experience. 'I caught' refers to his seeing the bird; the verb is arresting, catching the attention; 'this morning' gives the entire poem immediacy; and 'I caught' could also be said to mean the very act of poem-making. He has captured the windhover in the very words he is putting down on the page.

Alliteration, assonance and the rise and fall of the sentence all convey the marvellous qualities of the bird and its movement. So forceful and effective are those opening lines that it becomes a sentence that communicates without being immediately understood and, once understood, the intricacy of its making highlights Hopkins's skill. The imagery contained in words such as 'minion', 'dauphin', 'wimpling', 'skate's heel', 'bow-bend' allows the windhover to become so much more than a bird in flight. Hopkins gives the word 'Falcon' in line 2 a capital 'F' which looks ahead to the sestet where the falcon becomes a symbol for Christ himself, to whom the poem is dedicated.

'The Windhover' is intensely personal. The opening word is 'I' and the second sentence also focuses on the speaker – 'My'. In 'God's Grandeur', 'Spring' and 'Pied Beauty', Hopkins celebrates and praises God's creation but there is no 'I'. Hopkins is thrilled, excited and moved:

> My heart in hiding
> Stirred for a bird, – the achieve of, the mastery of the thing!

The poem's three exclamation marks, the run-on lines, the end-rhyme and internal rhyme (e.g. 'air'/'there'), the repetition ('off, off') all contribute to the overall effect of the octet. The rhyming scheme in those first eight lines is unusual in that it is without variation - 'king-', 'riding', 'striding', 'wing', 'swing', 'gliding', 'hiding', 'thing' (aaaaaaaa!), but the stanza never reads as dull, predictable or repetitive because of Hopkins's command of rhythm and line break. The use of 'thing' to describe the bird draws attention to the actual and the general – it is the brilliance of this particular bird, but it is also the brilliance of every falcon.

The sestet goes beyond description and, here, the poet gathers together in a series of nouns and adjectives the essential qualities of the falcon as he perceives it.

> Brute beauty and valour and act, oh, air, pride, plume here
> Buckle!

'Brute' and 'beauty' might seem contradictory, but the windhover is both a bird of prey and a beautiful bird. It is capable of dramatic action and movement; it looks proud in its feathered glory. All these qualities are gathered together in line 9 and the word 'Buckle!' at the beginning of line 10, though it can be interpreted differently, suggests an energetic focusing on the various aspects contained within the one bird.

The octet was one of dazzling description; in the sestet, the speaker is more preoccupied with the idea of the bird and this leads to his idea of Christ. The octave is written in the past tense; the sestet is written in the present, which might suggest that Hopkins focuses more intently on the ideas contained in the sestet. The sestet also looks beyond the present to the future (the 'then' in line 10) and allows for the poem's conclusion.

Hopkins's contemplation and meditations in the final six lines move from creature towards creator, from bird to maker. When he contemplates this bird, it prompts Hopkins to speak of the windhover in terms of fire. The linking word 'and' is capitalised for emphasis and signals greater understanding, insight:

> AND the fire that breaks from thee then, a billion
> Times told lovelier, more dangerous, O my chevalier!

The intimacy of 'O my chevalier' expresses Hopkins's love for the falcon and for Christ. Once the significance of the bird is grasped, it is 'a billion/Times told lovelier, more dangerous', and danger becomes an attractive quality.

Norman White says that in the sestet 'the constituents of the falcon's performances are metamorphosed into parts of armour, which the chivalric lord Christ is entreated to buckle on, that he may appear in his glory, the windhover's qualities being merely one minute, exemplary part of the infinitely greater glory of God'. Peter Milward suggests that 'O my chevalier!' may refer 'either to Christ, to whom the poem is dedicated, or to the poet himself, as addressing his own heart, or conceivably to the bird seen as a symbol of Christ', but concludes that it refers to the poet himself for, if the poet is united to Christ in humble service (Hopkins is the 'chevalier' in the service of Christ), then 'the fire of divine love that will break from him will be immeasurably lovelier and more effective – more "dangerous" against his spiritual enemies, the devil, the world and the flesh – than the "brute beauty" he has witnessed in the windhover.'

These are possible interpretations; no one can be said to be definitive but such options allow and invite us to read the text more carefully and to reach an understanding which contributes to the poem as a whole.

The poem ends with two images from nature – a ploughed furrow and burning coals. These images tell of power, force, destruction. The 'sheer plod' of the ploughman and the horse on dull earth reveals a shining quality in that the earth reflects the sunshine and the 'blue-bleak' pieces of live coal, when they collapse, reveal a brilliant fiery gold:

> No wonder of it: sheer plod makes plough down sillion
> Shine, and blue-bleak embers, ah my dear,
> Fall, gall themselves, and gash gold-vermilion.

The speaker is drawing on the understanding reached in lines 9–11: where courage, be it the bird's, Christ's or the heart's courage, leads to action, then 'fire breaks'. Norman MacKenzie thinks that lines 9–11 remind us that 'Fulfilling one's nature reflects the glory of the Creator'.

'No wonder of it' at the beginning of line 12 is further confirmation of Hopkins's belief. Virginia Ridley Ellis thinks that Hopkins here acknowledges 'explicitly and firmly what he has deeply known and implied all along', that there is an important relationship 'between the seemingly drudging servitude of Christ and the true Christian soldier and heroic sacrifice in imitation of Christ'. Hopkins embraces suffering for Christ's sake because it results in glory. The coals sacrifice themselves and 'gash gold-vermilion'; Christ sacrificed himself and made possible the glory of redemption.

The poem's final image is one of triumph, but there is also the contrasting tenderness of 'ah my dear' (a phrase also found in George Herbert's 'Love'). To quote Virginia Ridley Ellis again, the poem ends with 'the final flare and outpouring of love and triumph' and 'Fall, gall' and 'gash' are reminders of Christ's Passion, Crucifixion and Resurrection.

Pied Beauty

This is a shortened or curtal (Hopkins's own term) sonnet: ten and a half lines instead of the conventional fourteen. It resembles 'God's Grandeur' and 'Spring' in that it is another hymn of praise but, whereas man's presence saddens the speaker in these two sonnets, in 'Pied Beauty', man's presence is in harmony with God's creation. It begins and ends with praise and it moves from the past ('brinded', 'plotted', 'pieced', 'freckled') to the present tense ('Praise him').

The variety of the natural world is captured in the first stanza. Following the heightened, praise-filled opening line

> Glory be to God for dappled things—

general description, 'dappled things', is particularised. The speaker lists numerous examples and the images bring together sky, earth and water. The sky is compared to a streaked or brinded cow and the vast expanse of sky is followed by the minute details of the colours of swimming trout.

'Pied Beauty' is another example of Hopkins's mastery of compression. There are only seventy-nine words in all (several are compound-words) and each word, almost, in quick succession presents the reader with another, new idea or image. God is to be praised:

> For skies of couple-colour as a brinded cow;
> For rose-moles all in stipple upon trout that swim;
> Fresh-firecoal chestnut-falls; finches' wings

Here, the eye sweeps and the mind jumps from one world to another. Fallen chestnuts glow with the kind of lustre found in newly burning coals. Tiny details are vividly presented; fish, trees, birds are represented by the trout, chestnuts and finches. Hopkins once said of the bluebell that 'I know the beauty of Our Lord by it', and he could have said the same about everything in the natural world. Everything here is singled out for praise.

In lines 5 and 6, Hopkins looks at man's presence on earth and, unlike 'God's Grandeur', where he laments man's careless disregard for nature, here man is in harmony with God's creation. There is an order and rhythm to man's work:

> Landscape plotted and pieced — fold, fallow, and plough
> And áll trades, their gear and tackle and trim.

Idyllic though it may seem, this is not the Garden of Eden; work after Eden was seen as a curse, but Hopkins sees it as something natural. He tells of how the countryside has been divided and subdivided, and how each section has its own particular, patchworked colouring. The overall image is of a landscape, but the

Between the octave and the sestet, Hopkins has left a space, a space that Edward Hirsch, in this context, sees as a chasm.

The intensity of the experience recorded here is felt in the repetition of 'I' – 'I wake', 'I speak', 'I say', 'I mean', 'I am gall', 'I am heartburn', 'I see', 'I am' – and the images in the sestet, especially, create a sense of physical torment. Line 9 sums up his anguish:

> I am gall, I am heartburn.

The speaker is filled with bitterness ('gall') and a burning sensation and it is God's decision ('decree') that this should be so:

> God's most deep decree
> Bitter would have me taste

A feeling of self-disgust permeates the closing lines as the speaker describes in physical and emotional detail his helplessness and despair:

> my taste was me;
> Bones built in me, flesh filled, blood brimmed the curse.
> Selfyeast of spirit a dull dough sours.

His body, the physical self, is contributing to his spiritual desolation in that it is physically felt: 'Bones built in me, flesh filled, blood brimmed the curse.' In line 12, bread, usually something wholesome and nourishing, is tainted; the image here is of spoilt bread caused by 'selfyeast'. The speaker's spirit has been soured by the body and this leads to self-loathing and self-disgust. Hopkins is a very intense presence in his poetry.

The poem ends with an awareness, not only of the speaker's own plight, but of all who are lost and the speaker realises that the damned in their eternal suffering are worse:

> I see
> The lost are like this, and their scourge to be
> As I am mine, their sweating selves; but worse.

In the darkness, he can 'see' and sympathise. The sonnet, which began in self-pitying mode, moves towards an awareness of others and pities those who are worse off.

The hallmarks of Hopkins's poetry can be found here: the intensity of the felt experience, matched by the intensity of expression; the alliteration and assonance; the importance of the speaker's relationship with God.

'No worst there is none. Pitched past pitch of grief'

The first sentence, in this Sonnet of Desolation, is short. Does it mean that there is nothing worse than this, or does Hopkins mean that he wishes he could say that this is the worst, so that a more intense suffering will not be experienced? Virginia Ridley Ellis points out that this 'first flat, grim statement' is 'often misinterpreted because even careful readers tend to hear what they expect and wish to hear rather than what Hopkins is saying'. Hopkins, Ellis argues, uses 'the superlative only to deny even its bleakest consolation: there will never be a point at which one can at least have the comfort of saying "This is the worst, nothing can be worse than this, it must get better"; one can never say and hope that the worst is "now done".'

The speaker says that he wishes that he had reached the ultimate stage in his grief; a worse state is unimaginable. An early draft of the poem read ''Worst! No worst, O there is none'. In Shakespeare's *King Lear*, Edgar says:

> The worst is not,
> So long as we can say, 'This is the worst'

However, Hopkins, here, seems to long for the worst, so that things cannot get worse. 'Pitched past pitch of grief' suggests the violent motion of being thrown over the edge but there is also the image of being hurled into the pitch dark.

The poem then plunges into even greater despair when the speaker realises that the pangs of suffering will increase. The word order is often deliberately complex as it works towards expressing a particular state of mind. A present pang will have learnt from an earlier pang and, therefore, will be even greater than the intense pain which has gone before is an awkward way of summing up a compressed and complex idea:

> Pitched past pitch of grief,
> More pangs will, schooled at forepangs, wilder wring.

The very sounds here are harsh sounding, severe and the repeated 'p' and 'w' add to the sense of anguish. A pang is a violent though not long-continued pain, but here the idea of never-ending pain in 'More pangs' adds to the trauma. Norman MacKenzie writes: 'The word pangs reminds us of some of the highest levels of pain experienced by human beings ... schooled personifies the pangs into professionally trained torturers.'

In his pain, the speaker looks to his comforter and to the Virgin Mary, but the repeated 'where' suggests that he feels very cut off from them and has been for some time:

> Comforter, where, where is your comforting?
> Mary, mother of us, where is your relief?

These are the only questions in the poem and they are never answered. Instead, the speaker returns to a description and exploration of his pain, until eventually some comfort is found, not in God or Mary, but in sleep.

The poem presents the reader with five extraordinary images of pain and suffering. The words are unremarkable in themselves – herds, anvil, mountains, cliffs, whirlwind – but within the context of the poem they create a bleak and harsh imagery and convey vividly and effectively a powerful sense of the speaker's suffering.

The first of these is the image of huddled masses of animals, referring to Hopkins's cries, and his sorrow is part of a 'world-sorrow':

> My cries heave, herds-long; huddle in a main, a chief
> Woe, world-sorrow

Here 'heave, herds-long; huddle' are not only grouped together in the one line, but the words are linked through alliteration, creating in the mind an image of the speaker's anguished cries of pain coming together. That these cries form a crowd or 'main' is yet another detail adding to the intensity, while huddled animals suggest fear, unease and claustrophobia.

Next is the image of an anvil being struck; 'sing' here is neither musical nor joyful but conjures up what Virginia Ridley Ellis calls 'the music of torment'. There is a force ('Fury') that insists that the pain and suffering continue:

> on an age-old anvil wince and sing-
> Then lull, then leave off. Fury had shrieked 'No ling-
> ering! Let me be fell: force I must be brief.'

The words 'Fury' and 'shrieked' create some of the harshest sounds in the poem and Fury's screeching cry is unrelenting: 'No lingering!', but the word 'lingering' is broken in two at the line-break delaying, briefly, what Fury is not allowing.

There is a different mood at the beginning of the sestet. The huddled, crowded cries and the emotional pain of the octave are replaced by a landscape. The eye imagined the herds and the anvil but the ear registered them. In the closing lines of the sonnet, lines 9–14, the speaker paints the bleakest of landscapes:

> O the mind, mind has mountains; cliffs of fall
> Frightful, sheer, no-man-fathomed.

This is a dramatic landscape and a dramatic picture of the speaker's interior world. 'O' captures the pain of experience, while the image of both mountains and cliffs suggests towering and dangerous terrain. That 'cliffs of fall' ends the line is appropriate. The reader's eye drops to 'Frightful, sheer, no-man-fathomed' on the next line.

At line 10, the speaker is aware that such dramatic imagery may be viewed as excessive, for he says that those who have not experienced such desolation will fail to sympathise or understand:

> Hold them cheap
> May who ne'er hung there.

The speaker is clinging to the precipice, but the pain is so unbearable that it cannot be endured:

> Nor does long our small
> Durance deal with that steep or deep.

'My' cries in line five become 'our' in line 11; the poem opens up to include people other than himself. He is aware of how others suffer too, but the body can only put up with so much physical and mental pain. He speaks to himself, tenderly and caringly, in the final lines:

> Here! creep,
> Wretch, under a comfort serves in a whirlwind: all
> Life death does end and each day dies with sleep.

The comforter and Mary have not answered his cries of anguish and Hopkins turns to the brief respite which sleep brings. It is a temporary release from pain but, nonetheless, a release. There is a pleading, comforting tone and a feeling of exhaustion, but also a feeling of relief that sleep will bring.

'Thou art indeed just, Lord, if I contend'

This is a measured and formal sonnet and, written in March 1889, three months before he died, it is one of Hopkins's last poems. In 'I wake and feel the fell of dark' and 'No worst, there is none', the speaker called on God for help and support, but looked deep into the abyss of himself. Here the speaker is directly addressing God but the speaker's reason is to the fore and the language used in the opening lines is similar to that of a courtroom:

> Thou art indeed just, Lord, if I contend
> With thee; but, sir, so what I plead is just.

'I contend', 'I plead' and 'sir' all suggest a controlled, carefully thought-out argument and yet 'contend' means to strive or fight. The poet does have an argument with God, but he articulates his argument in a coherent and logical manner. In the 'terrible sonnets', the grammar of the poem became as tortured as the thoughts and feelings of the speaker. In this sonnet, not categorised as one of the terrible, Hopkins maintains a rational tone:

> Why do sinners' ways prosper? and why must
> Disappointment all I endeavour end?

He compares himself to others several times throughout the poem, to sinners, to sots and thralls of lust, to the waking natural world of plants and birds. Line 5 contains an interesting argument. Hopkins looks on God as his friend, but he wonders why God treats him so badly; if God were his enemy, he would hardly treat him worse:

> Wert thou my enemy, O thou my friend,
> How wouldst thou worse, I wonder, than thou dost
> Defeat, thwart me?

The stark contrast between friend and enemy within the same line highlights the speaker's sense of confusion and pain. 'O thou my friend' is a heartfelt utterance and Hopkins is not ranting and raving here; instead, he adopts a far more effective, cool and quietly enquiring tone. At line 7 the tone changes. The poet becomes more animated and presents his Lord and master with vivid examples of how everyone and everything seem to thrive, save Hopkins himself. It is ironic that those who indulge in sensual pleasures seem to prosper and flourish, whereas he himself, who devoted his entire life to God, seems to meet with disappointment.

> Oh, the sots and thralls of lust
> Do in spare hours more thrive than I that spend,
> Sir, life upon thy cause.

The sentence structure here, the punctuation and the line-break allow for effective emphases. The tone is still respectful and formal ('Sir'), but there is a more spirited voice heard in that 'Oh'.

The closing lines gather energy, beginning with the urgent 'See', 'look' and the exclamation mark:

> See, banks and brakes
> Now, leaved how thick! laced they are again
> With fretty chervil, look, and fresh wind shakes
> Them; birds build

There is a busyness, movement and continuity here. Spring has come again and nothing is so beautiful as spring, but Hopkins is seeing in nature the opposite of what he feels:

> – but not I build; no, but strain
> Time's eunuch, and not breed one work that wakes

The negatives build up in the final three lines: 'not', 'no', 'not' and the sound of 'strain' make for a different music to the music created in the earlier lines with 'leaved', 'laced', 'fretty', 'fresh', 'shakes'. In 'God's Grandeur', man destroys nature but nature renews itself; here, nature flourishes apart from man.

Birds build and it is part of God's plan. Hopkins feels here that he is building nothing in his own life and the dramatic image of 'Time's eunuch' emphasises the contrast between the natural world and himself. God has made possible the spring; time can bring with it a sense of renewal, but time for the poet means more disappointment.

The words 'and not breed one work that wakes' suggest a self that is dead.

The final line in the sonnet is the poem's shortest sentence. Hopkins's argument has been well-structured, persuasive and well-illustrated, but he is in urgent need of God's help. He asks for this in an immediate, direct way and the final image draws on nature:

> Mine, O thou lord of life, send my roots rain.

The imagery of the opening lines suggests a man pleading before his maker and judge in a courtroom; the poem ends with an image of outdoors and the natural world. Hopkins sees himself as a plant in need of nourishment. He asks his 'lord of life' to send his roots rain.

The poem, Virginia Ridley Ellis points out, 'comes full circle, comes back to God, the only possible centre and source of life'. He begins with 'Thou' and 'Lord' and ends with 'thou lord of life', but between the opening and closing lines 'I' is used six times. It is a poem that focuses on his keenly felt disappointment. The phrase 'all I endeavour' in 'why must/Disappointment all I endeavour end?' is an extreme statement of his plight, but the 'sir' that was used in line 1 becomes the more positive 'lord of life' in the final line.

John Keats

(1795–1821)

Contents	Page

The Overview

All eight poems by Keats are sensuous expressions of intense feeling. 'To One Who Has Been Long in City Pent' celebrates the beauty and freedom of the open countryside, where to see the blue sky and wavy grass and to hear the nightingale's song is to know happiness. Keats writes of the intellectual and imaginative pleasures of reading in 'On First Looking into Chapman's Homer': the imagery in this sonnet is drawn from exploration and discovery. In 'When I have fears that I may cease to be', Keats writes of his 'teeming brain' and the literature he hopes to write: the image of a rich harvest conveys his understanding of the creative process. 'La Belle Dame sans Merci' is atypical of Keats in some ways: he uses the ballad form, a shorter line and a cold, harsh setting. Keats also uses the persona of the knight to tell his story. The sense of longing and the presence of beauty and death, however, are familiar Keatsian themes. The three Odes celebrate music, pictorial art and a season. Each is beautiful. The song of the nightingale and the Grecian urn are untouched by change and death. Autumn is the dying of the year, but it has its own music and beauty. It is man who must accept his own mortality. In one of his final poems, 'Bright star! Would I Were Steadfast as Thou Art', Keats admires the brilliant star but rejects it eventually. He prefers the intimacy and pleasure of a love relationship knowing, however, that to be 'Pillowed upon my fair love's ripening breast' cannot last forever.

John Keats loved the beautiful and his pleasure in the beautiful and immortal found expression in his poetry. The famous opening lines from his long poem 'Endymion' – 'A thing of beauty is a joy forever:/Its loveliness increases; it will never/Pass into nothingness. . .' – sum up Keats's philosophy. Another line, this time from one of his letters, reminds us of Keats's awareness of human powers and gifts: 'I am certain of nothing but the holiness of the heart's affections and the truth of imagination.' He is a poet who loved what life offered and he also loved to share that love with his reader. He felt that 'a poet should not preach but should whisper results to his neighbour.'

It is significant that Keats is admired and remembered primarily for his odes. The ode is essentially a poem of celebration and in his odes, the song of the nightingale, the beauty and mystery of a Grecian urn and the riches of autumn are celebrated in evocative and sensuous language. He hears the song of the nightingale, sees the figures on the urn, senses autumn and plumps the hazel shells, and in his imagination travels beyond the actual and conjures up images and moods associated with all three. Keats is a generous and enthusiastic poet. He shares with us his delight on discovering Homer in Chapman's translation; he thinks of the bees in late autumn and thinks of the season as having 'set budding more,/And still more, later flowers for the bees,/Until they think warm days will never cease. . .'

Beauty is often celebrated, however, against an awareness of transience and mortality. These eight poems by Keats also tell of suffering and death and the human condition. The song of the nightingale must fade though it will be heard by others; the urn becomes a 'Cold Pastoral' but that too will remain, a 'friend to man'. Autumn must give way to winter but, as Keats reminds us in the closing stanza, winter and spring will give way to another autumn eventually.

The sonnet, the ballad and the ode are the poetic forms used in these eight poems and, while Keats is an intensely personal poet, in the ballad 'La Belle Dame sans Merci', his narrative is apparently impersonal. Yet, even here, the preoccupation with beauty and death are typical of his work.

There is a development and progression within the poems, especially within the odes. The eager questioning and engagement with the song of the nightingale and urn give way to a very calm, placid note in 'To Autumn', a poem, unlike the other two odes, without exclamation marks. The suffering which he speaks of ('Where youth grows pale, and spectre-thin, and dies' or 'A burning forehead and a parching tongue') is absent from 'To Autumn', the final ode. The dying of the year is inevitable; Keats writes of it with great calm.

Keats has often been termed 'escapist' ('Away! away! for I will fly to thee'), but he is also a realist. He returns to reality ('to my sole self!') in 'Ode to a Nightingale'; he knows that 'old age shall this generation waste' ('Ode on a Grecian Urn'). He also knows that, though the bright star is beautiful, it is cold and distant and he would prefer the beauty of human love ('Pillowed upon my fair love's ripening breast,/To feel for ever its soft fall and swell'), if only it were 'steadfast' and 'unchangeable'.

• Keats Memorial at Guys Hospital, London where he trained as a surgeon.

Biographical Notes

John Keats was born in London on 31 October 1795 (some biographers suggest 30 October). He was the eldest of five children, one of whom died in infancy. Keats's father ran a livery stables, which allowed him to educate his children well, and when John Keats was almost eight he was sent to be educated in a small private school in Enfield, ten miles outside London, where he was known to be a lively and spirited young boy who liked boxing. Andrew Motion in his biography of Keats says that the 'few specific references he makes to the school imply that when not swimming in the new river, or playing cricket in the fields near by, he spent his time gardening . . . or catching fish.' When Keats was eight, his father fell from his horse and died; his mother remarried and she then died from tuberculosis when he was fourteen. The four Keats children had only their elderly grandmother to look after them and she appointed two guardians and trustees to look after the orphaned children, who had an income of £8,000 (a huge amount at the time) from their grandmother's estate. One guardian died; the other, Richard Abbey, did not act honourably and, as a result, the children were never to experience financial comfort.

John Keats was removed from school in 1810 and apprenticed to his grandparents' doctor in Edmonton. For the next five years, Keats trained to be a doctor, but read extensively in English poetry, especially Spenser (1522–1599). One of Keats's teachers, Charles Cowden Clarke, has given us a famous description of Keats's enthusiasm for the sixteenth-century poet; John Keats, we are told, approached Spenser's *The Faerie Queene* 'as a young horse would through a spring meadow, – ramping.' His response to Spenser's poetry was so enthusiastic and revealed Keats's remarkable empathy so well that when he came across the phrase 'sea-shouldering whales', Clarke tells us that Keats 'hoisted himself up and looked burly and dominant, as he said "What an image that is – sea-shouldering whales."' When he was eighteen, Keats began to write poetry, his first poem being an 'Imitation of Spenser'.

In the autumn of 1815, Keats's apprenticeship came to an end and he began to train as a surgeon at Guy's Hospital, London. He had moved into lodgings in Southwark and he wrote a sonnet contrasting the countryside at Edmonton, Middlesex, with the busy streets of Southwark and its 'jumbled heap/Of murky buildings.' On 5 May 1816, Keats's first published poem 'O Solitude! if I must with thee dwell' appeared and in July of that same year he passed his exams and was granted a licence to practise as a surgeon and apothecary. As his interest in poetry grew, Keats became less interested in medicine. His lecture notes on bone setting are decorated with sketches of flowers and fruits, and he told a friend that 'during the lecture, there came a sunbeam in the room, and with it a whole troop of creatures floating in the ray; and I was off with them to Oberon and Fairy-land.'

Keats could not practise until he was twenty-one, which would be in October 1816. Meanwhile, he went to Margate for two months on holiday – he had never seen the sea until then. From Margate he wrote verse letters, and back in London that October wrote 'On First Looking into Chapman's Homer'. In London, at 76 Cheapside, he shared lodgings with his two brothers George and Tom (John was 21, George 19 and Tom 17; their thirteen-year old sister, Fanny, was at boarding school) and he began to make friends with writers and painters. He continued as a dresser of wounds, but at a meeting with his guardian, Richard Abbey, Keats announced that he did not intend being a surgeon but would rely on his 'abilities as a poet'.

He published his first book of poems in March 1817 – a book that went largely unnoticed – and in May abandoned work as a dresser. He and his brothers moved to Hampstead, a green and airy suburb, thinking that the move would help Tom, who was ill.

Keats found a new publisher and, thinking that great poets wrote long poems, planned to write a four thousand line poem, 'Endymion', based on the Greek myth of the young shepherd boy Endymion who is loved by Diana or Cynthia, the moon. The story can be read as that of the poet in search of beauty. Its first line is one of Keats's most famous: 'A thing of beauty is a joy for ever'.

In April 1817, Keats travelled to the Isle of Wight, to Margate, Canterbury and Hastings, returned to Hampstead and then went to stay with a friend Benjamin Bailey in Oxford, where he worked on 'Endymion'. He finished the poem in Surrey where he had gone to escape London. From here he wrote one of his marvellous letters. Writing to Bailey, he called for 'a Life of Sensations rather than of Thoughts' and he said that 'I am certain of nothing but of the holiness of the Heart's affections and the truth of Imagination – What the imagination seizes as Beauty must be truth'. That same letter also gives us Keats's profound insight on his wish to avoid self-centredness; genius, he felt, requires a 'disinterestedness': 'I scarcely remember counting upon any Happiness – I look not for it if it be not in the present hour – nothing startles me beyond the Moment. The setting sun will always set me to rights – or if a Sparrow come before my Window I take part in its existence and pick about the Gravel.' Keats felt that Shakespeare possessed this gift in an extraordinary way. The writer William Hazlitt said of Shakespeare that he was 'the least of an egoist that it was possible to be. He was nothing in himself; but was all that others were, or that they could become'.

Keats developed this idea further in a letter to his brothers, on 21 December 1817, in which he gives us his theory of **Negative Capability**. Here is how Keats explains it: 'several things dovetailed in my mind, & at once it struck me, what quality went to form a Man of Achievement, especially in Literature, & which Shakespeare possessed so enormously – I mean Negative Capability, that is when a man is capable of being in uncertainties, Mysteries, doubts, without any irritable reaching after fact & reason'. In other words, what Keats admired was a writer's ability to create/enter into a world, an experience or an emotion for its own sake and in doing so the reader is also allowed to experience it fully.

Negative Capability is 'a power of sympathy and freedom from self-consciousness which peculiarly characterises the artist', as *The New Princeton Encyclopedia of Poetry and Poetics* puts it.

In the spring of 1818, Keats got to know Charles Wentworth Dilke and Charles Armitage Brown, who were schoolfriends and had built a double house with a shared garden called Wentworth Place in Hampstead. (Today it is the building most closely associated with Keats and is known as the Keats Museum.) That same year, 'Endymion' was published. Tom's health became worse – in January he was spitting blood; George Keats married and emigrated to the United States. Keats accompanied the newly-weds to Liverpool port in June and then set off with Charles Brown on a walking tour of the Lake District, Scotland and northern Ireland. Bad weather made the journey difficult and Keats suffered frequent colds and sore throats, though on 2 August he and Brown climbed Ben Nevis, the highest mountain in Britain. Keats's health was not good and a doctor in Inverness advised him to return to London at once. He took a boat from Cromarty to London. By then, they had already walked 642 miles.

In London, he discovered that Tom was dying and Keats nursed his nineteen-year-old brother in Well Walk in Hampstead. 'Endymion' received some very negative reviews, but Keats continued to write and began 'Hyperion' around this time. In November, the twenty-three-year old Keats met eighteen-year-old Fanny Brawne, with whom he was to fall in love. On 1 December, Tom died from tuberculosis and Keats soon afterwards went to live in Brown's half of Wentworth Place.

1818–1819 was Keats's magnificent year. In the words of Walter Jackson Bate, it was 'the most productive in the life of any poet of the past three centuries.' He wrote his great odes, poems that confirmed his place among the great English poets. In January 1819, Keats wrote 'The Eve of St Agnes'; in April, 'La Belle Dame sans Merci'; in May, 'Ode to a Nightingale' (written in a single morning), 'Ode on a Grecian Urn' and 'Ode on Melancholy'.

In June, Keats realised that he needed to make money – his guardian had never been generous and George had written from America to say that he was in financial difficulties. Keats planned to write a play – *Otho the Great* – in collaboration with Brown and to do so he went to the Isle of Wight to write. From here, he wrote love letters to Fanny Brawne, to whom he had become engaged and whose family was now renting the other half of Wentworth Place: 'I have two luxuries to brood over in my walks, your Loveliness and the hour of my death.' Brown joined him and later they moved to Winchester, where, that September, Keats wrote 'To Autumn'. He also wrote 'Bright Star! Would I Were Steadfast As Thou Art' sometime during 1819 (and revised it on board ship on his journey to Rome in early autumn 1820).

Back in London, Keats took new lodgings in Westminster, but then returned to live in Hampstead. In February 1820, his health was so bad that he was coughing up blood and his medical background taught him the worst: 'I know the colour of that blood; it is arterial blood; – I cannot be deceived in that colour; – that drop of blood is my death-warrant; – I must die.' He spent two months mostly in bed and then moved to lodgings in Kentish Town a few doors away from an old friend, Leigh Hunt. After another bad haemorrhage, he moved in with Hunt and then stayed with the Brawnes in Hampstead.

A change of climate was thought best and in September John Keats left England for Rome with his friend the artist Joseph Severn. The sea journey took three weeks; in the Bay of Naples they had to wait ten days to fulfil quarantine regulations. They went ashore on 31 October 1820 (Keats's twenty-fifth birthday) and travelled to Rome, but Keats was beyond recovery. He referred to his last months as a 'posthumous existence'. Letters sent to him from England, including letters from Fanny Brawne, remained unopened.

He died on 23 February 1821 and was buried in the Protestant Cemetery in Rome, having lived twenty-five years, three months and twenty-three days. The gravestone bears the following inscription at Keats's request: 'Here lies One Whose Name was writ in Water'. He asked that his unopened letters be buried with him. In what is probably the last letter he ever wrote – to his friend Brown, dated 30 November 1820 – he ends: 'I can scarcely bid you good-bye, even in a letter. I always make an awkward bow. God bless you! John Keats.'

Romanticism

The history of literature is often seen as a series of movements (e.g. Anglo-Saxon or Old English; Medieval or Middle English; Renaissance – Elizabethan, Jacobean, Caroline, Commonwealth; Restoration; Augustan; Romantic; Victorian; Edwardian; Georgian; Modern; Postmodern) and are often discussed as such. Of course this is a very artificial way of looking at literature or art or music. However, there are certain aspects that are characteristic of an age and which separate that age from what has gone before or what follows. If you think of the times you know best – the age in which you live – you will realise that the poem that is being written today is very different from the poem written a hundred or even twenty years ago. Similarly with novels, painting and music. Violence and uncertainty are said to be characteristic of our age. Yes they are, and though it would be a sweeping generalisation and an inaccurate picture of things if it were said of the late twentieth century, the beginning of the twenty-first, that those were the only things to be said about it, violence and uncertainty are undoubtedly striking features of the times we live in.

To understand something of Keats, it is worth knowing something of the thinking and the attitudes of the age in which he lived. Together with Wordsworth, Coleridge, Byron and Shelley, Keats is part of what is now known as the Romantic Movement in poetry. The clichéd version of Romantic is that of moonlight and roses and candlelit dinners for two. Another and more interesting aspect of what

Romantic means, what is known as the Romantic Movement, can be found in painting, music, philosophy, politics and literature, especially towards the end of the eighteenth century and the beginning of the nineteenth. If you listen to a Beethoven (1770–1827) symphony, if you look at a painting by Turner (1775–1851), his 'Rain, Steam and Speed – the Great Western Railway', for example (for which Turner, as every art historian reminds us, leaned out of the train window so as to experience authentically the rain, speed and steam), or if you read a poem by Wordsworth, Coleridge, Byron, Shelley, Blake or Keats, you are experiencing what we now call Romanticism. The Romantic Movement in England is usually thought to date from the 1780s until 1830.

There are many definitions of Romanticism. T. E. Hulme defines it as follows: 'Here is the root of all Romanticism, that man the individual is an infinite reservoir of possibility.' It was a movement that certainly celebrated the individual and, above all else, the individual imagination. John Keats 'loved the principle of beauty in all things' and in his poetry his unique imagination expresses his intense and sensuous delight in things outside himself.

Romanticism is a way of viewing the world, of viewing the self, a way of viewing the relationship between the self and the world. The following lines from Blake's 'Auguries of Innocence' are often quoted as lines that express the Romantic vision:

> To see a World in a grain of Sand
> And a Heaven in a wild Flower
> Hold Infinity in the palm of your hand
> And Eternity in an Hour.

Nature was very important to the Romantic poets, especially to Wordsworth, and many of the finest Romantic meditations take place out of doors (e.g. Wordsworth's 'Tintern Abbey' or Keats's 'Ode to a Nightingale' and 'To Autumn'). M. H. Abrams says in his *Glossary of Literary Terms* that:

> To an extraordinary degree external nature — the landscape, together with its flora and fauna — became a persistent subject of poetry, and was described with an accuracy and sensuous nuance unprecedented in earlier writers. It is a mistake, however, to describe romantic poets as simply 'nature poets'. While many major poems by Wordsworth and Coleridge — and to a lesser extent by Shelley and Keats — set out from and return to an aspect or change of aspect in the landscape, the outer scene is not presented for its own sake, but only as a stimulus for the poet to engage in the most characteristic human activity, that of thinking. The most important romantic poems are in fact poems of feelingful meditation about an important human problem.

POEMS

Dates refer to the year of composition. The poems as they are printed here, are in the order in which they were written.

To One Who Has Been Long in City Pent

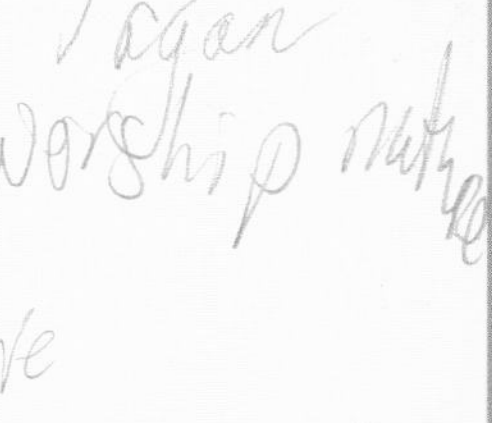

To one who has been long in city pent,
'Tis very sweet to look into the fair
And open face of heaven, to breathe a prayer
Full in the smile of the blue firmament.
Who is more happy, when, with heart's content,
Fatigued he sinks into some pleasant lair
Of wavy grass and reads a debonair
And gentle tale of love and languishment?
Returning home at evening, with an ear
Catching the notes of Philomel, an eye
Watching the sailing cloudlet's bright career,
He mourns that day so soon has glided by,
E'en like the passage of an angel's tear
That falls through the clear ether silently.

Glossary

Title: The title echoes the lines from Milton's *Paradise Lost* (Book IX, line 445–448) – 'As one who long in populous city pent,/Where houses thick and sewers annoy the Air/Forth issuing on a summer's morn to breathe/Among the pleasant villages and farms....' Coleridge also uses the phrase 'in the great city pent' in his poem 'This Lime-tree Bower my Prison'.

Line 1 pent: shut in a confined space.

Line 4 firmament: sky.

Line 6 lair: a sheltered place.

Line 7 debonair: gentle, pleasant, gracious (frequently used by Spenser).

Line 8 languishment: longing.

Line 10 Philomel: the nightingale.

Line 11 career: swift course through the sky.

Line 14 ether: upper air.

This sonnet was written in June 1816, when Keats was twenty, and one month after he had seen a poem of his in print for the very first time. In many ways, it resembles his first published poem in that it focuses on the beauty of nature and the pleasures of escaping the crowded city. He was studying medicine at Guy's Hospital at the time and living in Southwark, described by Keats himself as 'a beastly place in dirt, turnings and windings'. Here Keats is nostalgic for the countryside he knew at Edmonton in Middlesex, where he had been at school. It is significant that, in addition to the joys of nature, Keats also speaks of reading 'a gentle tale of love'. Thus the experience is a combination of natural beauty and the beauty of the imagination.

Questions

1. Though Keats in this sonnet does not describe city life, what does he imply about it?
2. What is the effect of the monosyllabic first line? Why, do you think, is this the only line in the poem where almost every word is a monosyllable?
3. Which words in the opening quatrain capture a sense of release and beauty and freedom? What is the effect of the run-on line or enjambment in the poem?
4. Comment on what Keats sees as perfect happiness (lines 5–8). Why the 'gentle tale of love and languishment'? What does this tell us about Keats?
5. In the closing lines, Keats mentions the song of the nightingale, the sailing cloudlet. What is the poet's mood in these lines?
6. What is the significance of the reference to 'heaven' (line 3) and 'angel's tear' (line 13)?
7. Comment on the structure of the sonnet, paying particular attention to sentence length. Comment too on the musical qualities of the language. How is this music achieved?

On First Looking into Chapman's Homer

Much have I travelled in the realms of gold,
  And many goodly states and kingdoms seen;
  Round many western islands have I been
Which bards in fealty to Apollo hold.
Oft of one wide expanse had I been told
  That deep-browed Homer ruled as his demesne;
  Yet did I never breathe its pure serene
Till I heard Chapman speak out loud and bold.
Then felt I like some watcher of the skies
  When a new planet swims into his ken;
Or like stout Cortez when with eagle eyes
  He stared at the Pacific, and all his men
Looked at each other with a wild surmise –
  Silent, upon a peak in Darien.

Glossary

Line 1 the realms of gold: here it refers to the world of literature (it also refers to the discovery of the New World – El Dorado, the golden land or city imagined by the Spanish conquerors of America).

Line 3 many western islands: Britain and Ireland.

Line 4 bards in fealty to Apollo: poets are bound to Apollo, the Greek sun-god, patron of poetry and music.

Line 6 demesne: estate, region, realm (originally pronounced to rhyme with 'serene').

Line 7 serene: clear, bright expanse of air.

Line 8 Chapman: George Chapman (1559–1634) poet, dramatist, translator of Homer's *Iliad* and *Odyssey*. Chapman's translation was published in 1614.

Lines 9/10: these lines echo a description of Herschel's discovery of the planet Uranus in a book on astronomy which Keats had been given as a school prize in 1811.

Line 11 Cortez: Hernando Cortez (1485–1547), Spanish explorer/conquistador. In 1518, he led an army of 508 men that explored Mexico. In fact, Keats is here confusing Balboa's first glimpse of the Pacific with Cortez's first glimpse of Mexico City. Balboa was the first European to get sight of the Pacific.

Line 14 Darien: the isthmus (narrow neck of land) of Darien joins together North and South America; the old name for the Isthmus of Panama.

This sonnet was written in October 1816 and was first published in the *Examiner*, 1 December 1816. Keats had spent an evening with his good friend and former teacher Charles Cowden Clarke, who had been lent a folio edition of Chapman's translation of Homer. They read aloud from the book and Clarke tells of how Keats responded to certain passages with a 'delighted stare' and 'he sometimes shouted'. When Keats returned to his lodgings at day-break he sat down and composed the sonnet and sent it to his friend Clarke, who received it at ten o'clock.

? Questions

1. This is a Petrarchan sonnet, which means that between the octet and the sestet there is a change in the rhyming scheme signalling a new idea, a development with a new emphasis and energy. This psychological break is known as the turn. The octet rhymes abbaabba, the sestet usually cdcdcd. Why is this sonnet structure particularly suitable for what Keats has to say?

2. Look at the references to time in the sonnet beginning 'Much have I travelled'. Why is the word 'Then' (line 9) so important?

3. What mood or feeling is Keats conveying in the sestet? Which details are particularly effective in creating that mood?

4. What is Keats's tone towards reading in lines 1–4? Towards his reading of Homer?

5. Why do you think Keats chose to say 'looking into' and not reading? Can you suggest why Keats uses many archaic words such as 'goodly,' 'bards,' 'fealty,' in the poem?

6. Keats first compares himself to an astronomer, a watcher of the skies, then to an explorer with his men. Consider the differences between the two types of explorers and say which you think the more effective and interesting of the two.

7. The opening line refers to movement ('travelled'); in the final line there is silence and stillness. Why is this appropriate?

When I Have Fears That I May Cease to Be

When I have fears that I may cease to be
  Before my pen has gleaned my teeming brain,
Before high-pilèd books in charact'ry,
  Hold like rich garners the full-ripened grain;
When I behold, upon the night's starred face,
  Huge cloudy symbols of a high romance,
And think that I may never live to trace
  Their shadows with the magic hand of chance;
And when I feel, fair creature of an hour,
  That I shall never look upon thee more,
Never have relish in the faery power
  Of unreflecting love; then on the shore
Of the wide world I stand alone and think
Till love and fame to nothingness do sink.

Glossary

Title: The title here echoes Shakespeare's Sonnet 12, 'When I Do Count the Clock that Tells the Time', a sonnet which Keats had marked in his own edition of Shakespeare's poems.

Line 2 gleaned: gathered in or collected from.

Line 2 teeming: fruitful, full, prolific.

Line 3 charactery: writing (as used by Shakespeare e.g. 'Fairies use flowers for their charactery', *The Merry Wives of Windsor*, V (v) 77).

Line 4 garners: granaries or store houses.

Line 11 faery: the spelling is Spenserian.

Keats wrote this sonnet in January 1818. It is Shakespearean in form (though there are traces of the octet/sestet structure) and many of Keats's subsequent sonnets were Shakespearean rather than Petrarchan. Keats in a letter once said that he liked to think, if it was not too daring a thought, that Shakespeare was his presiding genius. This sonnet was not published during Keats's lifetime.

Questions

1. What metaphor is used in the first quatrain of the poem for Keats's 'teeming brain'. Is the image an effective one? Give reasons for your answer.
2. The entire poem is made up of one sentence. What is the effect of this?
3. How does Keats give the reader a very strong sense of the passing of time? Comment on the effect of 'when' and 'then'.
4. What kind of writing is Keats interested in? What do you think Keats is referring to in the phrase 'the magic hand of chance'?
5. A new idea is introduced in the third quatrain. Is there any connection between this reference to young loving and what has gone before?
6. Identify Keats's mood in the opening lines of the sonnet and trace his mood throughout the poem. Does the poet's mood change? Which particular words capture this mood best?

La Belle Dame sans Merci

O what can ail thee, knight-at-arms,
Alone and palely loitering?
The sedge has withered from the lake,
And no birds sing.

O what can ail thee, knight-at-arms,
So haggard and so woe-begone?
The squirrel's granary is full,
And the harvest's done.

I see a lily on thy brow,
With anguish moist and fever-dew,
And on thy cheeks a fading rose
Fast withereth too.

I met a lady in the meads,
Full beautiful – a faery's child,
Her hair was long, her foot was light
And her eyes were wild.

I made a garland for her head,
And bracelets too, and fragrant zone;
She looked at me as she did love,
And made sweet moan.

I set her on my pacing steed,
And nothing else saw all day long,
For sidelong would she bend, and sing
A faery's song.

She found me roots of relish sweet,
  And honey wild, and manna dew,
And sure in language strange she said –
  'I love thee true'.

She took me to her elfin grot,
  And there she wept and sighed full sore,
And there I shut her wild wild eyes
  With kisses four.

And there she lullèd me asleep
  And there I dreamed – Ah! woe betide! –
The latest dream I ever dreamt
  On the cold hill side.

I saw pale kings, and princes too,
  Pale warriors, death-pale were they all;
They cried – 'La Belle Dame sans Merci
  Hath thee in thrall!'

I saw their starved lips in the gloam,
  With horrid warning gapèd wide,
And I awoke, and found me here,
  On the cold hill's side.

And this is why I sojourn here
  Alone and palely loitering,
Though the sedge is withered from the lake,
  And no birds sing.

Glossary

Title: There is a French medieval poem 'La Belle Dame sans Merci' by Alain Chartier, written in 1424, from which the title but not the subject matter is taken. The story of a mortal man falling in love with a beautiful woman who is not quite mortal and being destroyed by her is a familiar one. La Belle Dame does not seem sinister, though the knight's love for her has brought him to his woeful and lonely state. The critic David Perkins suggests that this woeful state 'might be attributed to the hopelessness of his love for something superhuman rather than to "la belle dame" herself'.

Line 1 ail: trouble.

Line 1 knight-at-arms: Keats revised the poem and substituted 'wretched wight' for knight-at-arms. Wight is an Old English word for man. The revised version is less medieval in its associations though all scholars think the first version best.

Line 3 sedge: grass-like plant growing in marshes or by water.

Line 13 meads: meadows.

Line 18 fragrant zone: a belt or girdle made of flowers.

Line 21 steed: horse.

Line 26 manna: miraculous substance – 'manna from heaven' – supplied as food to the Israelites in the wilderness (Exodus 16: 14–36). Here it means magical food.

Line 29 elfin: from elf – a supernatural diminutive being, sometimes malignant.

Line 29 grot: grotto or cave.

Line 32 kisses four: in his letter to his brother George, Keats imagines him asking on reading the poem 'Why four kisses?'. Keats playfully answers such a question: 'I was obliged to choose an even number that both eyes might have fair play: and to speak truly I think two a piece quite sufficient – suppose I had said seven; there would have been three and a half a piece – a very awkward affair.'

Line 35 latest: last.

Line 40 in thrall: enslaved.

Line 41 gloam: twilight.

Line 45 sojourn: dwell for a while.

1819 was Keats's *annus mirabilis*, in which he wrote most of his greatest poems. This ballad was written on 21 April 1819 and, though composed in a few hours, it has, in the words of Walter Jackson Bate, 'haunted readers and poets for a century and a half'. Keats included the poem as part of a journal-letter to his brother and sister-in-law in America. The ballad form was unusual for Keats and one of the more effective and striking things about this particular ballad is Keats's use of rhythm. In the final line of each stanza, Keats shortens the metrical line to a four beat, two stress structure.

? Questions

1. What immediate differences do you see between this poem by Keats and the three earlier poems?

2. Outline, briefly, in your own words, the central narrative of the poem.

3. How many speakers are in this ballad? Identify the different voices.

4. What atmosphere is created in the opening three stanzas? Refer to details in the text to support your answer.

5. What is the effect of the shortened fourth line in each stanza?

6. From line 13 to the end of the poem, the knight-at-arms speaks. What did he find so attractive in the lady he met? Why is he suffering? Is there a suggestion that the knight-at-arms is dying? Why does he sojourn in that particular place?

7. How do you respond to, and can you explain, the nightmare element in the poem (lines 33–38)?

8. What is the effect of the medieval allusions in the poem? Comment on the lack of detail in the poem. In your view, is this a strength or a weakness?

Ode to a Nightingale

I

My heart aches, and a drowsy numbness pains
My sense, as though of hemlock I had drunk,
Or emptied some dull opiate to the drains
One minute past, and Lethe-wards had sunk:
'Tis not through envy of thy happy lot,
But being too happy in thine happiness, –
That thou, light-wingèd Dryad of the trees,
In some melodious plot
Of beechen green, and shadows numberless,
Singest of summer in full-throated ease.

II

O, for a draught of vintage! that hath been
Cooled a long age in the deep-delvèd earth,
Tasting of Flora and the country green,
Dance, and Provencal song, and sunburnt mirth!
O for a beaker full of the warm South,
Full of the true, the blushful Hippocrene,
With beaded bubbles winking at the brim,
And purple-stainèd mouth;
That I might drink, and leave the world unseen,
And with thee fade away into the forest dim:

III

Fade far away, dissolve, and quite forget
What thou among the leaves hast never known,
The weariness, the fever, and the fret
Here where men sit and hear each other groan;
Where palsy shakes a few, sad, last gray hairs,
Where youth grows pale, and spectre-thin, and dies;
Where but to think is to be full of sorrow
And leaden-eyed despairs,
Where Beauty cannot keep her lustrous eyes,
Or new Love pine at them beyond to-morrow.

IV
Away! away! for I will fly to thee,
Not charioted by Bacchus and his pards,
But on the viewless wings of Poesy,
Though the dull brain perplexes and retards.
Already with thee! tender is the night,
And haply the Queen-Moon is on her throne,
Clustered around by all her starry Fays;
But here there is no light,
Save what from heaven is with the breezes blown
Through verdurous glooms and winding mossy ways.

V
I cannot see what flowers are at my feet,
Nor what soft incense hangs upon the boughs,
But, in embalmèd darkness, guess each sweet
Wherewith the seasonable month endows
The grass, the thicket, and the fruit-tree wild;
White hawthorn, and the pastoral eglantine;
Fast fading violets covered up in leaves;
And mid-May's eldest child,
The coming musk-rose, full of dewy wine,
The murmurous haunt of flies on summer eves.

VI
Darkling I listen; and, for many a time
I have been half in love with easeful Death,
Called him soft names in many a musèd rhyme,
To take into the air my quiet breath;
Now more than ever seems it rich to die,
To cease upon the midnight with no pain,
While thou art pouring forth thy soul abroad
In such an ecstasy!
Still wouldst thou sing, and I have ears in vain –
To thy high requiem become a sod.

VII

Thou wast not born for death, immortal Bird!
No hungry generations tread thee down;
The voice I hear this passing night was heard
In ancient days by emperor and clown:
Perhaps the self-same song that found a path
Through the sad heart of Ruth, when, sick for home,
She stood in tears amid the alien corn;
The same that oft-times hath
Charmed magic casements, opening on the foam
Of perilous seas, in faery lands forlorn.

VIII

Forlorn! the very word is like a bell
To toll me back from thee to my sole self!
Adieu! the fancy cannot cheat so well
As she is famed to do, deceiving elf.
Adieu! adieu! thy plaintive anthem fades
Past the near meadows, over the still stream,
Up the hill-side; and now 'tis buried deep
In the next valley-glades:
Was it a vision, or a waking dream?
Fled is that music: – Do I wake or sleep?

Glossary

Line 2 hemlock: a plant that can be used as a sedative but is also poisonous.

Line 3 opiate: a drug containing opium that eases pain and induces sleep.

Line 3 to the drains: to the dregs, sediments – leaving nothing.

Line 4 Lethe-wards: towards the river Lethe, whose waters cause forgetfulness in Hades, the Underworld of Greek mythology. The souls in Hades who drank the water would forget their past existence.

Line 5 lot: fortune, destiny, condition.

Line 7 Dryad: a woodland nymph (nymph being a young and beautiful maiden).

Line 11 vintage: a wine of very high quality, usually old.

Line 12 deep-delvèd earth: in a letter written May 1819, Keats speaks of 'a little claret-wine cool out of a cellar a mile deep'.

Line 13 Flora: the Roman goddess of flowers.

Line 14 Provencal song, and sunburnt mirth: that region in southern France and the festivities and celebrations associated with the grape harvest.

Line 15: wine from the Mediterranean region.

Line 16 the blushful Hippocrene: the phrase here is an example of periphrasis (round-about expression) for wine. Hippocrene is a fountain near Mount Helicon, a place sacred to the Muses, and therefore a fountain of inspiration.

Line 25 palsy: loss of feeling and control.

Line 26 Where youth grows pale and spectre-thin and dies: Keats is writing this poem in May 1819; Tom Keats had died from tuberculosis on 1 December 1818. Spectre-thin is ghostly-thin.

Line 29 lustrous: bright, shining.

Line 30 pine: to long for.

Line 32 Bacchus: the Roman god of wine – a beautiful, young man, crowned with ivy and vine leaves and carrying a thyrsus or pine-staff, twined round with ivy and vine leaves. Bacchus is said to possess eternal youth. Often portrayed being drawn in a chariot.

Line 32 pards: leopards.

Line 33 viewless: invisible.

Line 35 tender: gentle, young.

Line 36 haply: perhaps, by chance.

Line 36 Queen-moon: Diana, Roman goddess of light, representative of chastity and hunting.

Line 37 Fays: fairies.

Line 40 verdurous: fresh-green or grass-green.

Line 42 incense: fragrant scent.

Line 43 embalmed: a balm is an aromatic substance, a fragrant and healing ointment; 'embalmed darkness' refers in this instance to a fragrant darkness. 'Embalmed' would also suggest death, an idea explored by Keats in the following stanza.

Line 44 endows: enriches.

Line 46 pastoral eglantine: the sweet briar of the countryside – 'pastoral' evokes an ideal world of pastureland and shepherds.

Line 51 Darkling: in the dark.

Line 53 mused: bemused, muddled, fuzzy.

Line 54 clown: ordinary fellow, countryman.

Line 60 requiem: the requiem sung at Keats's anticipated death.

Line 66 Ruth: in the Bible, Ruth, after her husband died, did not return to her own people but went with her mother-in-law, Naomi, to Bethlehem. There, in an alien country, she became a gleaner in the fields of Boaz. In a lecture entitled 'On Poetry in General', which Keats would have known, William Hazlitt commented that 'The story of Ruth . . . is as if all the depth of natural affection in the human race was involved in her breast'.

Line 69 casements: windows.

Line 70 faery: the spelling is Spenserian and thus summons to mind not only fairy land but the world of Spenser's poetry.

Lines 71/72 forlorn: lost, remote and far away; lonely, desolate.

Line 72 toll: summon.

Line 72 sole: lonely, solitary.

Line 73 fancy: imagination.

Line 75 plaintive: mournful.

Line 75 anthem: a song of praise or gladness; a music with religious associations (echoing the 'requiem' in line 60).

This is the first of the great odes. It was written in May 1819, and was first published in *Annals of the Fine Arts*, July 1819. This would suggest that it is a poem that explores, among other things, the nature of art and the relationship between the different art forms. Many of the odes echo and develop the thoughts in a long letter which Keats had begun to write to his brother George on 14 February but did not send until 3 May. (The printed version of this letter runs to over forty pages and includes the poem 'La Belle Dame sans Merci'). The world has often been called a 'vale of tears', but in this letter Keats prefers to call the world a 'vale of soul-making'. A soul acquires an identity; 'each one is personally itself'. Keats thinks a world of pain and trouble necessary if the intelligence is to become a soul, and he uses the image of a school to explain himself more clearly. The world is the school: the book used in school is the human heart and the soul is like the child who can read the book. The poem can of course be read without reference to the letter, but a careful reading of the poem will reveal many parallels between Keats's ideas in his letters and the ideas in his poetry. Having read the poem (and other poems by Keats), we could ask how Keats's concept of soul-making is revealed to us in the poetry.

Keats was living in Wentworth Place in Hampstead at the time and his friend Charles Brown, with whom he shared a house, has left us this account of the poem's composition: 'In the Spring of 1819 a nightingale had built her nest in my house. Keats felt a continual joy in her song; and one morning he took his chair from the breakfast-table to the grass-plot under a plum-tree, where he sat for two or three hours. When he came into the house, I perceived he had some scraps of paper in his hand, and these he was quietly thrusting behind the books. On inquiry, I found those scraps, four or five in number, contained his poetic feeling on the song of the nightingale.'

Questions

1. An ode is a poem of praise and celebration. In this instance, Keats is celebrating the song of the nightingale and everything that song suggests and symbolises. What is Keats's mood in the opening four lines of the poem? Which words in particular capture that mood?
2. Contrast plays an important part in stanza 1. Discuss how Keats creates this contrast. Look, for example, at words such as 'drowsy numbness' and 'light-winged'.
3. In the poem, Keats longs to escape harsh reality, longs 'to leave the world unseen', and he succeeds for a time. What does he long for in stanza 2? How does Keats succeed in making this so attractive? Which words and phrases are particularly effective?
4. Stanza 3 tells of what Keats has known of human suffering. Which details in particular do you find effective?
5. In the end, it is not an imagined 'draught of vintage' but 'the viewless wings of poesy' that allow him to fly away and enter into the world of the song of the nightingale. In stanzas 4 and 5, Keats describes that world. Comment on the details that you find most effective.
6. In stanza 6, Keats wishes he were dead. Why? What reasons does he give? He also changes his mind in lines 59–60. Why?
7. In stanza 7, Keats thinks of the song of the nightingale heard in other times and other places. What is the effect of stanza 7 within the poem as a whole?
8. What is Keats's mood in the poem's final stanza? Why? What is the significance of Keats telling himself and us that 'the fancy cannot cheat so well'?
9. Keats is known for his sensuousness. Discuss Keats's sensuousness in 'Ode to a Nightingale'.
10. Would you consider this a realistic poem, an escapist poem or a combination of both? Refer to the text in your answer.

Ode on a Grecian Urn

I

Thou still unravished bride of quietness,
  Thou foster-child of silence and slow time,
Sylvan historian, who canst thus express
  A flowery tale more sweetly than our rhyme:
What leaf-fringed legend haunts about thy shape
  Of deities or mortals, or of both,
    In Tempe or the dales of Arcady?
  What men or gods are these? What maidens loth?
What mad pursuit? What struggle to escape?
    What pipes and timbrels? What wild ecstasy?

II

Heard melodies are sweet, but those unheard
  Are sweeter: therefore, ye soft pipes, play on;
Not to the sensual ear, but, more endeared,
  Pipe to the spirit ditties of no tone:
Fair youth, beneath the trees, thou canst not leave
  Thy song, nor ever can those trees be bare;
    Bold lover, never, never canst thou kiss,
Though winning near the goal – yet, do not grieve;
    She cannot fade, though thou hast not thy bliss,
      For ever wilt thou love, and she be fair!

III

Ah, happy, happy boughs! that cannot shed
  Your leaves, nor ever bid the spring adieu;
And, happy melodist, unweariѐd,
  For ever piping songs for ever new;
More happy love! more happy, happy love!
  For ever warm and still to be enjoyed,
    For ever panting, and for ever young –
All breathing human passion far above,
  That leaves a heart high-sorrowful and cloyed,
    A burning forehead, and a parching tongue.

IV
Who are these coming to the sacrifice?
To what green altar, O mysterious priest,
Lead'st thou that heifer lowing at the skies,
And all her silken flanks with garlands dressed?
What little town by river or sea shore,
Or mountain-built with peaceful citadel,
Is emptied of this folk, this pious morn?
And, little town, thy streets for evermore
Will silent be; and not a soul to tell
Why thou art desolate, can e'er return.

V
O Attic shape! Fair attitude! with brede
Of marble men and maidens overwrought,
With forest branches and the trodden weed;
Thou, silent form, dost tease us out of thought
As doth eternity: Cold Pastoral!
When old age shall this generation waste,
Thou shalt remain, in midst of other woe
Than ours, a friend to man, to whom thou say'st,
Beauty is truth, truth beauty, – that is all
Ye know on earth, and all ye need to know.

Glossary

Title: Grecian in this instance means ancient Greece and an urn was a vase with a rounded body, usually with a narrowed mouth and often a foot. It contained and preserved the ashes of the cremated dead. The images on the side of the urn that Keats describes are intensely alive.

Line 1 still: the word here can be interpreted in two different ways – still (as adjective) meaning motionless, and still (as adverb) meaning 'ever' or 'as yet'.

Line 1 unravished: untouched, virginal.

Line 3 Sylvan: literally means belonging to the woods, rural.

Line 7 Tempe: is a valley in Thessaly in Greece.

Line 7 Arcady: a district in Greece associated with music and dancing. Tempe and Arcadia were associated with happiness and a beautiful landscape.

Line 8 loth: reluctant, unwilling.

Line 10 timbrels: the timbrel is an ancient Oriental tabor or tambourine.

Line 13 sensual ear: the ear of sense as distinct from the spirit/the imagination.

Line 14 spirit: inspiration, the poetic imagination, the soul.

Line 14 ditties: dit or ditt was the archaic word for poem; ditty – a little poem set to music.

Line 17 Bold: courageous, assertive.

Line 29 cloyed: wearied, surfeited.

Line 33 heifer lowing at the skies: this detail is to be found on the Elgin marbles.

Line 36 citadel: fortress, especially one guarding or dominating a city.

Line 37 pious: holy – there is to be a sacrifice.

Line 41 Attic: Grecian (Attica was that part of Greece where Athens was located).

Line 41 attitude: here it means the posture given to a figure in statues or painting.

Line 41 brede: brede is an archaic spelling of 'braid', meaning interwoven. Keats may also intend a pun on breed.

Line 42 overwrought: fashioned on the surface of the urn or here, over-excited.

Line 44 tease: entice, mock.

The Elgin marbles, which Keats had seen in the British Museum, the 'View of Delphi with a Procession', a mezzotint after Claude Lorrain, an engraving entitled 'The Sacrifice at Lystra', based on a drawing by Raphael, and a drawing of the Sosibios Vase which Keats himself had made from a book of reproductions all influenced Keats's description of the Grecian urn in this ode. The urn as described is not based on any one Grecian urn or vase; Keats uses a combination of many images from different sources. Though Keats had many painter friends he preferred sculptures or engravings to painting and this ode celebrates the sense of sight. In 'Ode to a Nightingale', Keats hears the immortal song of the bird; in 'Ode on a Grecian Urn', he looks at the immortal work of art. The images on the urn are images of moments of intensity and movement, captured forever. The poem was first published in *Annals of the Fine Arts* in January 1820.

Questions

1. What does one usually associate with the word 'urn'?
2. Keats in 'Ode to a Nightingale', 'Ode on a Grecian Urn' and 'To Autumn' has focused on three different things. Discuss the differences and the similarities among the three.
3. How does Keats begin his 'Ode on a Grecian Urn'? How does it differ from 'Ode to a Nightingale'?
4. List and discuss every description Keats gives of the urn in lines 1–3. Why does Keats think the urn can tell 'a flowery tale more sweetly' than his poem? Discuss here the different art forms and how people respond to them.
5. With lines 5–10, a dramatic change takes place within the stanza. Why and how does that come about?
6. Having entered into the life as depicted on the side of the urn, what does Keats ask? Why?
7. Why does Keats find the images on the urn so attractive? Comment on this in relation to the urn's original purpose.
8. How would you describe the rhythm throughout the ode? Your answer should refer to sound, sentence length, use of punctuation (especially the use of questions and exclamation marks) and repetition.
9. The mood is sometimes meditative, sometimes excited. Which, would you say, is the predominant mood in the poem? Give reasons for your answer and support the points you make with suitable quotation or reference.
10. In the final stanza, why does Keats compare the urn to eternity? And why does he now call the urn 'Cold pastoral!'? What similarities are there between the ending of this ode and 'Ode to a Nightingale'?

Original manuscript by Keats

To Autumn

I

Season of mists and mellow fruitfulness,
Close bosom-friend of the maturing sun;
Conspiring with him how to load and bless
With fruit the vines that round the thatch-eaves run;
To bend with apples the mossed cottage trees,
And fill all fruit with ripeness to the core;
To swell the gourd, and plump the hazel shells
With a sweet kernel; to set budding more,
And still more, later flowers for the bees,
Until they think warm days will never cease,
For summer has o'er-brimmed their clammy cells.

II

Who hath not seen thee oft amid thy store?
Sometimes whoever seeks abroad may find
Thee sitting careless on a granary floor,
Thy hair soft-lifted by the winnowing wind;
Or on a half-reaped furrow sound asleep,
Drowsed with the fume of poppies, while thy hook
Spares the next swath and all its twinèd flowers:
And sometimes like a gleaner thou dost keep
Steady thy laden head across a brook;
Or by a cider-press, with patient look,
Thou watchest the last oozings hours by hours.

III

Where are the songs of spring? Ay, where are they?
Think not of them, thou hast thy music too –
While barréd clouds bloom the soft-dying day,
And touch the stubble-plains with rosy hue;
Then in a wailful choir the small gnats mourn
Among the river sallows, borne aloft
Or sinking as the light wind lives or dies;

And full-grown lambs loud bleat from hilly bourn;
  Hedge-crickets sing; and now with treble soft
 The red-breast whistles from a garden-croft;
   And gathering swallows twitter in the skies.

Glossary

Line 1 mellow: well matured, soft and ripe.

Line 3 Conspiring: acting together towards one end (from the Latin *conspirare*: *con* – together, *spirare*, to breathe).

Line 7 gourd: a large, hard-rinded, fleshy fruit.

Line 8 kernel: the edible part of the nut.

Line 11 clammy: sticky.

Line 13 abroad: over a wide area.

Line 14 sitting careless: sitting without care or at ease.

Line 15 winnowing: separating the chaff or husks from the grain.

Line 17 poppies: associated with sleep.

Line 17 hook: scythe.

Line 18 swath: the sweep of a scythe, the band of grass or corn cut by a scythe.

Line 19 gleaner: one who gathers in handfuls after the reapers.

Line 25 barred: divided into horizontal bars.

Line 25 bloom: here, a verb.

Line 27 gnats: small flies or insects.

Line 28 sallows: willows, especially the broader leaved kinds with comparatively brittle twigs.

Line 30 bourn: boundary, domain, territory.

Line 31 Hedge-crickets: a word invented by Keats. The cricket's song in Keats's earlier poem, 'On the Grasshopper and Cricket', is associated with winter – 'On a lone winter evening, when the frost/Has wrought a silence, from the stove there shrills/The cricket's song, in warmth increasing ever'.

Line 31 treble: high-pitched.

Line 32 garden-croft: a small, cultivated piece of farm land usually adjoining a dwelling.

In the spring of 1819, Keats wrote five odes and Timothy Hilton, in his book *Keats and his World*, says that 'the odes, like so much else that he wrote, are thick with references to his current reading and his life. We can feel the weather in them, for instance, and it comes as no surprise to find that they were written in a beautiful period of spring, a spring that came early in 1819'. In 'To Autumn', Keats celebrates a beautiful September.

In a letter, dated 21 September 1819, Keats describes how he came to write the poem: 'How beautiful the season is now – How fine the air. A temperate sharpness about it. Really, without joking, chaste weather – Dian skies – I never liked stubble fields as much as now – Aye better than the chilly green of the spring. Somehow a stubble plain looks warm – in the same way that some pictures look warm – this struck me so much in my Sunday's walk that I composed upon it.' The last of the great odes, 'To Autumn', was written on 19 September 1819 in Winchester.

Questions

1. Keats is present in all of his poems, but in different ways. In some instances, there is an intense awareness of himself – 'I', 'my' and 'me'. Where is Keats in this poem?
2. The poet Shelley says that 'there is a harmony/In autumn, and a lustre in its sky,/Which through the summer is not heard nor seen.'
   Look and listen to the words, especially in the first stanza, and comment, in detail, on how Keats uses language to create the harmony and music of autumn.
3. What are the characteristics of autumn as revealed to us in this ode? Discuss how Keats personifies the season, especially in stanza 2. Why do you think autumn is viewed as female?
4. How would you describe the movement of this poem? Consider the eleven line stanza, the references to the passing of time, the sounds of the words and their arrangement on the page.
5. In stanzas 1 and 2, the emphasis is on seeing, and in the final stanza on listening. Discuss the imagery in the poem and say why Keats changes from eye to ear in the closing lines.
6. How does Keats involve the reader in this poem?
7. What is the significance of the last line? How do the sounds in words such as 'twitter' and 'skies' echo the sense? Compare these sounds with words such as 'mellow fruitfulness' in line 1.
8. Pick out some examples of accurate, effective words or phrases and discuss them within the context of the poem as a whole. You could begin with 'bosom-friend', 'load', 'plump'.
9. What is Keats's view of the passing of time, dying and death as revealed to us in this poem?
10. Is this a great poem? If your answer is no, please read it again.

Bright star! Would I were steadfast as thou art

Bright star! Would I were steadfast as thou art –
  Not in lone splendour hung aloft the night
And watching, with eternal lids apart,
  Like nature's patient, sleepless eremite,
The moving waters at their priestlike task
  Of pure ablution round earth's human shores,
Or gazing on the new soft-fallen mask
  Of snow upon the mountains and the moors;
No – yet still steadfast, still unchangeable,
  Pillowed upon my fair love's ripening breast,
To feel for ever its soft fall and swell,
  Awake for ever in a sweet unrest,
Still, still to hear her tender-taken breath,
And so live ever – or else swoon to death.

The time of year – late autumn – adds to the atmosphere of loneliness and loss. That closing line in stanza 1 stops the stanza short. The flow that the ear expects, having heard three lines with four beats in each, has now been stopped short. The abrupt 'And no birds sing' (two beats) expresses the knight's loneliness and disappointment.

Though the natural world is dying, part of that world has achieved completion. There is an inner, hidden world – the squirrel's granary is full and the harvest has been gathered in. The world of the knight, however, is one of loss. He looks ill and he feels lost. In stanza 3, the images of the lily and the rose, usually associated with women's beauty, are used to capture the knight's condition.

When the knight tells his story, the lady of the poem, la belle dame, is introduced. The phrase 'I met' suggests something accidental, something that happened by chance, but the woman, it could be argued, has gone in search of the knight and sought him out. Everything about her is flowing and beautiful. She is associated with summer meadows and flowers; her hair is long and her foot is light. The wild eyes, however, give us a sense of her strange and haunting qualities. The language she speaks is 'strange'; she sings a fairy's song but we never hear her directly. We only have the knight's account.

The knight was clearly enchanted from the beginning. He makes her a garland of flowers, a bracelet and a belt (the fragrant zone). He felt that she looked at him 'as she did love'.

A pacing steed is usually ridden by the knight. The clichéd or familiar image is that of the knight in shining armour on horseback. In this version of events, the woman is set on the knight's pacing steed and he tells us that he gazed upon her all day long. The song she sings is enchanting.

All the while, as we read through the poem, the ballad form and its momentum, its narrative and its rhythmic pattern heighten our sense of plot. We know we are going to be told an ending and, of course, the opening three stanzas of the poem have already given us a sense of that ending.

In this poem, the woman seduces the man. She feeds him 'roots of relish sweet/ And honey wild and manna dew'. She tells him that she loves him – 'I love thee true'.

In stanza 8, the setting of the poem moves from the wide open world of meadows, and places where strange and wonderful food can be found, to a grotto or cave. Here words such as 'wept' and 'sighed' darken the once happy, infatuated mood. The knight tells of how he tried to comfort and console this beautiful woman – 'And there I shut her wild wild eyes/With kisses four.'

By stanza 11, the woman is once again controlling the knight – 'she lulled me asleep'. The waking world gives way to dream and the dream gives way to nightmare. The warning cry of 'Ah! woe betide!' suggests danger and terror.

The dream sequence is one of death-pale figures – kings and princes and, presumably, other knights. These others too have been enslaved by la belle dame and they cry out their warning: 'La belle dame sans merci/Hath thee in thrall!' Now the significance of 'sans merci' becomes clear. She is beautiful but she is without pity. Her victims are deluded. The knight speaks of 'starved lips' and open mouths crying out 'horrid warning'.

The poem ends where it began, but line 3 – 'the sedge has withered from the lake' – has become 'the sedge is withered from the lake' in line 47. The present tense as used here has an eerie effect. The knight is one who has escaped the nightmare and yet he can never escape; la belle dame haunts him. The repetition of detail from stanza 1 suggests the knight's inability to escape his aloneness. The final line 'And no birds sing' is powerfully stark and, like all negatives, it emphasises the effect by having the reader imagine its opposite. The positive that is birdsong and everything which that implies is, it would seem, no longer possible.

Ode to a Nightingale

The nightingale was a popular subject for poets. Its song is beautiful and is only heard in darkness (there are no nightingales in Ireland) and the Greek myth of Procne and Philomel, which tells of how the nightingale came to sing such a heartbreakingly beautiful song, adds to the nightingale's memorable and interesting qualities.

Keats in his letters once wrote that 'the world is full of misery and heartbreak, pain, sickness and oppression'. The opening stanza of Ode to a Nightingale certainly suggests misery and oppression:

> My heart aches and a drowsy numbness pains
>   My sense, as though of hemlock I had drunk,
> Or emptied some dull opiate to the drains
>   One minute past, and Lethe-wards had sunk:

This emphasis on the self – 'my heart', 'my sense' – is evident throughout the poem and, though Keats tries to escape the self and reality and enter into the world of the song of the bird, he realises in the final stanza that he is left with an intense awareness of his 'sole self'.

There is a striking contrast in the opening stanza between the mood of the poet and the world of the song of the bird. The first four lines express heaviness, heartache and pain. Keats wants to escape from the world, and the song of the bird symbolises for him a beautiful, harmonious, happy and free sense of otherness. The song seems effortless – 'full-throated ease'. Nowhere in the poem does Keats describe the actual bird; he does not see it, but he hears its song. The title is 'Ode to a Nightingale' ('a' not 'the') and the poem celebrates the song of the nightingale; the bird itself is mortal but its song is immortal, heard in every age.

The poem begins on a low note: 'drowsy numbness', 'dull opiate', 'sunk' capture a sinking, downward feeling. The sounds here are sinking sounds. However, 'light-winged', 'melodious', 'beechen green' and 'singest' provide a striking contrast. The emphasis is first on the self – 'My heart aches' – an inward, self-concerned focus. In lines 5 and 7, the phrases 'thy happy lot' and 'That thou' focus on the very different and contrasting world of the bird.

In the opening line of stanza 2, Keats has abandoned his listlessness and has entered into an extraordinarily imaginative world which has been prompted by the song of the bird. The word 'O' at the beginning of the line and Keats's use of the exclamation mark add to the energy and the tone of longing. The senses of sight and sound are evident in stanza 1. Here the sense of taste is also introduced. The drink Keats longs for is no ordinary wine. It is a drink associated with place, time and season. It is, above all else, a means of escape. The nightingale is not mentioned specifically in this stanza until the very last line, yet every line leads to the world of the nightingale's song. For Keats, the song represents the ideal.

The richness of association ('Flora', 'Provencal song', 'the warm South', 'the blushful Hippocrene'), the sensuous detail ('beaded bubbles', 'purple-stained mouth') and the sense of longing is repeated throughout ('O for a beaker full of the warm South' – 'O, for' in line 11, 'O for' in line 15). In stanza 1, Keats speaks of hemlock; in stanza 2, the 'draught of vintage' is a totally different drink. One destroys, the other brings release, happiness and freedom.

The third stanza returns to the grim reality of life, a world of pain, suffering, death. Keats may wish to escape but it is not easily done. 'The weariness, the fever, and the fret' is what Keats has known. The structure of this third stanza is such that it would seem that the imagination is failing Keats. The word 'Here' in line 24 roots unhappiness in the world of now. The following lines, each beginning with 'Where' and each listing more and more sorrow, make for a very effective rhythmic pattern:

> Where palsy shakes a few, sad, last gray hairs,
>   Where youth grows pale, and spectre-thin, and dies;
> Where but to think is to be full of sorrow
>   And leaden-eyed despairs,
> Where Beauty cannot keep her lustrous eyes,
>   Or new Love pine at them beyond tomorrow.

Beauty and Love are what Keats is searching for. Both, he suggests in the closing lines of stanza 3, cannot exist in a world that is overshadowed by pain and death. The words Beauty and Love are capitalised, personified presences, highlighting their importance.

In stanza 4, Keats enters into the world of the imagination. The first line of the stanza

> 'Away! Away! for I will fly to thee'

echoes the longing of line 11, but has a greater liveliness and energy to it. The god of wine and the 'draught of vintage' are dismissed; Keats will enter into an imagined landscape. We know that he wrote the poem during a warm May morning but Keats has chosen a midnight setting for the ode. The poet tells us that, though the 'dull brain' attempts to draw him back, he flies to this magical and midnight world on the 'viewless wings of Poesy'. Line 35 answers line 31: 'Already with thee! tender is the night'. And lines 36 to 40 describe an unspoilt happiness:

> And haply the Queen-Moon is on her throne,
> Clustered around by all her starry Fays;
> But here there is no light,
> Save what from heaven is with the breezes blown
> Through verdurous glooms and winding mossy ways.

Keats imagines Diana, the Queen-Moon, surrounded by fairies. There is no light, but the darkness is neither frightening nor threatening. And yet there is light, Keats tells us, a magical, heavenly light. The woodland setting is green and winding and mossy – everything is soft and gentle, mysterious and wonderful. The lines 'here there is no light,/Save what from heaven is with the breezes blown' have to be imagined. This is not a scientific description, but a sensuous, imaginative one. There is darkness, yet there is some light. The closing two lines of stanza 4 are not slowed or hindered by punctuation: line 39 flows into line 40, creating a sense of release and relaxation.

In stanza 3, 'Here' referred to the world of suffering. In stanza 4, the same word 'here' (in line 38, 'But here there is no light') refers to a world far removed, a world that the human being can enter into by means of the imagination.

The ode celebrates the song of the bird, more importantly it celebrates the imagination. Keats is at the centre of the poem. The pronoun 'I' is used in every stanza except stanza 3.

Keats uses the five senses (sight, sound, taste, touch and smell) in the ode, but stanza 5 begins with Keats telling us that 'I cannot see what flowers are at my feet'. He then guesses each scent and lists the different fragrances:

> The grass, the thicket, and the fruit-tree wild;
> White hawthorn, and the pastoral eglantine;
> Fast fading violets covered up in leaves;
> And mid-May's eldest child,
> The coming musk-rose, full of dewy wine. . .

The stanza is made up of one long, flowing sentence, and the language, enhanced by alliteration, assonance, onomatopoeia, achieves a beautiful and musical quality. He smells the musk-rose, tastes the dewy wine, hears 'The murmurous haunt of flies on summer eves'.

The word 'embalmed' in line 43 refers to fragrance, but it also suggests death, an idea that Keats returns to in stanza 6. He has already spoken of death in stanza 3. Keats tells us here that he has viewed death as 'easeful'; he has been 'half in love' with death. Here death becomes a means of achieving total happiness. His happiness is so complete that if he were to die, the happiness of the moment would last forever: 'Now more than ever seems it rich to die'. But the 'half in love' is significant. He does not trust it totally, though he describes the imagined sense of release that death would bring – 'To cease upon the midnight with no pain'. Keats, in his use of the phrase 'quiet breath', suggests that he wishes to slip away, to 'cease upon the midnight with no pain'. In contrast, the song of the bird is full, ecstatic. It is pouring forth its soul. If he were allowed to 'leave the world unseen', he would not be united with the bird; the very opposite in fact would occur. By the end of the stanza, he realises that death is not the answer; the nightingale will continue to sing its song and Keats will no longer hear it: 'Still wouldst thou sing, and I have ears in vain –/To thy high requiem become a sod.'

In the seventh stanza, Keats admits to himself that he is mortal, whereas the song of the bird is not. The second half of stanza 4 and all of stanza 5 are at the centre of this poem. Those lines are untouched by sorrow or mortality, except for the phrase 'Fast fading violets', though even this is balanced with 'the coming musk-rose'. However, Keats is enough of a realist to know that the moment that the nightingale's song has made possible cannot last forever. He resents death. F. R. Leavis has described the feeling in lines 61 and 62 as a feeling of 'strong revulsion'. In this seventh stanza, Keats introduces a wonderful temporal perspective into the poem. The actual moment that Keats himself has just imagined and experienced has been experienced by unknown, great ('emperor') and ordinary people ('clown'), and Keats then names a particular person, Ruth. This sense of other places and of other times is a generous and consoling aspect of the poem. Keats is saying that we, though mortal, can all have such moments, which allow us to understand ourselves more fully and to experience a beauty that is all the more precious and valuable because it is shortlived. Such moments allow us to glimpse 'the foam/Of perilous seas, in faery lands forlorn.'

'Ode to a Nightingale' is structured in terms of a journey from the reality of the here and now to the world of imagined perfection and the return to the mortal self. But the experience captured in the poem can never be lost. This poem, like so many works of art, reminds us that, though the artist is mortal, the work of art achieves an immortality. Thus the song of the nightingale can be heard in every age and, once the poem has been made, it too lives in every age. We, the readers of this poem, are mortal too, but we are allowed to enter into the world of immortality when we read the poem, just as Keats did when he shaped and structured it.

In line 70, the word 'forlorn' means far away. The word 'Forlorn!' with which stanza 8 begins strikes a different note. Here it means abandoned, forsaken and lonely. It is the brain, which in line 34 almost prevented him from entering into the world of the imagination, that causes him to return from 'thee to my sole self!' It has been said that the word 'forlorn' has its feet in two worlds, the world of the imagination and the woe of reality. The image of the bell tolling in lines 71–72 suggests the image of death and funeral and echoes the religious imagery of requiem in line 60. This final stanza contains the realisation that the fancy (the imagination) cannot cheat so well. In other words, he feels let down by the imagination because he has had to return to his 'sole self', a self that knows only too well that the song of the bird must fade away.

It is of course significant that the nightingale's song, the plaintive anthem, fades. It does not die nor does it stop. Keats knows that it will be heard again, 'Past the near meadows, over the still stream,/Up the hill-side; and now 'tis buried deep/In the next valley-glades'. Keats describes the song as plaintive, meaning sorrowful or mournful. The emotion is an appropriate one. There is something heartbreakingly beautiful about something that is beautiful but which is also something that must fade away. The magical and beautiful experience is over. He wonders if it was 'a vision or a waking dream?' A vision and dream are closely linked in that both are often associated with the ideal. The word 'waking' in the second last line of the ode reminds us that Keats is back where he began, but of course he has had an extraordinary experience and he has captured it forever in the poem.

Ode on a Grecian Urn

This is titled 'Ode on a Grecian Urn' not 'to' as in the nightingale ode. Stanza 1 begins in a very quiet, meditative mood. The sounds are soft ('still', 'unravished', 'quietness') and the rhythm is slow, capturing a tone of reverence. The word still is interesting because it is ambiguous. Both meanings – 'still' meaning motionless and 'still' meaning 'yet' – add to the mystery of the urn. The artist who created this urn, its maker or 'parent', has long since died, but Keats imagines that the urn has had foster parents, 'silence and slow time' (line 2).

The phrase 'Sylvan historian' in line 3 suggests the urn is a story-teller and it also records the past. The story it tells is a country tale. The urn does not speak; it communicates through images, yet Keats in lines 3 and 4 feels that the urn is capable of telling a story more beautifully than the poet and the poem: the urn can 'thus express/A flowery tale more sweetly than our rhyme'.

With line 5, there is a change of mood. Keats is no longer speaking of the urn as an object that he has spoken about as distant and separate. He has entered into the world of the story as depicted on the sides of the urn. The sentences quicken, becoming shorter, and there are seven question marks, capturing Keats's involvement and his excitement, in the last four lines of stanza 1.

The urn is still, quiet, silent, and yet it is also a warm-blooded, life-filled, energetic, mad, ecstatic presence. In line 6, Keats wonders if the people depicted on the side of the urn are gods or men – 'deities or mortals'. He wonders are they both. The stanza has changed dramatically from a mood of quiet contemplation to that of an excited and stimulated imagination. Keats is not merely describing what he sees on the side of a Grecian urn: he is inventing narratives (the legend that 'haunts about thy shape') and he is involving himself in the stories. He wants to know more and he marvels at the energy and the excitement of it all: 'What men or gods are these?' (line 8), 'What wild ecstasy?' (line 10).

The questioning, with which the stanza ends, subsides and Keats asks no questions in stanzas 2 and 3.

The pipes and timbrels depicted on the urn can be seen but not heard. Keats has imagined the sounds that they make and stanza 2 begins with a reference to the imagined sound which is ideal, perfect. This is why 'Heard melodies are sweet, but those unheard/Are sweeter'. The pipes, though carved in hard marble, have become 'soft', that is soft sounding, because Keats has imagined the pipes playing their music. Keats says to the pipes to play on, but not to play to the ear which is the instrument of the sense of hearing. Play instead to the spirit, and play a music that cannot be heard. That music is even sweeter.

In this second stanza, Keats, having asked for an imagined, ideal and beautiful music, now looks at the images on the side of the urn again and this time in more detail. Stanza 1 gives us a sense of groups – 'deities or mortals', 'men or gods', 'maidens'. He focuses on particular images. First, that of a 'fair youth, beneath the trees' who will sing forever and, second, the image of two young lovers who will love forever. Human love is subject to change, growing old and dying. The love depicted here is forever beautiful and forever young. The use of negatives 'not leave/Thy song', 'Never, never canst thou kiss', 'thou hast not thy bliss', captures the moment's shortcomings. It is a moment frozen in time and there is the happiness of the song and the spring and the anticipation of the kiss. Keats, however, tells the 'bold lover' 'do not grieve'. That special moment will not change. In the real world, Keats knows that 'youth grows pale and spectre thin and dies'. Also, in 'Ode to a Nightingale', Keats speaks of a world where 'Beauty cannot keep her lustrous eyes,/Or new Love pine at them beyond to-morrow'. In the world of the work of art, by contrast, 'She cannot fade. . ./For ever wilt thou love, and she be fair!' After the 'never, never' of line 7, 'yet' in line 8 serves as a turning point. Keats celebrates the immortality of the work of art.

'Happy' is used six times in the first five lines of stanza 3 and the 'Ah' which leads us into the stanza signals Keats's total delight in his vividly imagined eternal spring, eternal music, eternal love, eternal youth. Keats is the outsider, as is the reader. We are outside this intensely happy experience. As human beings, we know that happiness is shortlived, yet the work of art can hold a happy moment forever.

'Happy' is a key-word here. So too is 'for ever'. The 'nor ever' and 'never, never' of the earlier stanza (lines 16, 17) is echoed in the line 'nor ever bid the spring adieu', but the five 'for evers' in lines 24, 26, 27 give a vibrant sense of the now becoming eternal. The repetition, especially in the line 'More happy love! more happy, happy love!', and the exclamation marks heighten the mood. The adjective 'warm' and the verb 'panting' give the scene a powerful, physical touch.

The closing lines of the third stanza acknowledge and accept the mortal, the reality. Keats was twenty-three when he wrote the ode. He knew love (the previous December he had become engaged to Fanny Brawne) and he knew death, having nursed Tom in his final illness, and he returns to a world very different to the world which he has entered into elsewhere in the ode. The phrases 'a heart high-sorrowful and cloy'd', 'a burning forehead', 'a parching tongue' are similar to those lines from 'Ode to a Nightingale' where Keats gives us a vivid sense of his experience of suffering.

The urn is separate, untouched, unmoved by such suffering, but it is Keats's humanity that draws him back, that causes him to return to the real world. We have seen this happen in the nightingale ode. Throughout that poem, there are words and phrases that remind the reader of reality. Less so in the 'Ode on a Grecian Urn', but it is certainly there. The melodist, the music-maker of line 23, is 'unwearied' because he is part of the ideal world; in the real world, Keats knows 'A burning forehead and a parching tongue'. Keats, however, is also saying here that the urn does not know real love, real breathing human passion. The urn, we are told in line 28, is 'far above', at a distance from 'All breathing human passion'. It does not know the disappointment, the anguish, the suffering and the pain that real love may sometimes lead to. Keats, by returning to the world which we know as humans, is recognising and accepting that world with all its limitations. It is not the frozen, perfect moment in time; it is a living, breathing experience which we, because we are human, come to accept. At the beginning of stanza 2, Keats has said that the imagined is better than the real. Similarly, ideal love is above lived love because human love leaves 'a heart high – sorrowful and cloy'd'.

In the fourth stanza, Keats returns to particular details on the side of the urn. He is curious, drawn in. If you were to read the ode omitting stanza 3, there would be no sense of disconnectedness or disjointedness, but you would not have Keats's deep and interesting philosophical reflection on the nature of art and of existence.

The moment that Keats focuses on in stanza 4 is only a moment. There is a priest, a heifer, a procession of people, a ritual. It has no beginning or ending, but Keats, with his extraordinarily sympathetic imagination, wonders where they are going and from where have they come: 'To what green altar, O mysterious priest,/ Lead'st thou that heifer lowing at the skies, And all her silken flanks with garlands dressed?' The image, like all other images on the urn, is carved in marble, but Keats's choice of word here gives the image a living, breathing, flowing presence: 'green', 'lowing', 'silken'. This third scene is one which is most remote from Keats's own world and Keats goes beyond what is portrayed before him. He feels sorry for the 'little town by river or sea shore,/Or mountain-built with peaceful citadel,/

Is emptied of this folk, this pious morn?' Keats is empathising with the place, now something inanimate without its people, just as he has already empathised with the urn by entering into the world that was carved on its side.

The little town will be desolate, but Keats then gives us an even more interesting idea. This little town will never know the reason for its loneliness, why its streets 'for evermore/Will silent be'. This is a different form of 'forever'. It is not the intensely happy and excited forever of stanza 3. The people of the town have wandered into the work of art; there they will remain for ever. They have disappeared from the town and are forever captured on the urn. In one way, the desolate town is similar to human beings who can witness the happiness of the young lovers in art but can never know that immortal love for themselves.

The stillness in the closing lines of stanza 4 is in marked contrast to the frenzy of earlier sections. The very sounds in lines 35 to 40 and the rhythm create a haunting silence. Keats displays a tender concern for the town's loneliness.

With the first line of the final stanza, Keats steps back and looks at the urn as a whole. The tone here is typical of the ode: 'O Attic shape! Fair attitude!'; it is a tone of praise, awe and admiration, but the word 'shape' is strikingly impersonal, considering that the urn was viewed by Keats in line 3 of stanza 1 as a 'sylvan historian'. Keats has distanced himself from the particular when he speaks of 'marble men and maidens overwrought'. Yet again, however, in line 43, the single detail of the 'trodden weed' somehow alters the still marble form; it becomes a living tableau. But Keats continues to draw himself away. The very first words in the poem are 'Thou still unravished bride of quietness' and line 44, 'Thou, silent form, dost tease us out of thought', is similar in its effect. Both lines are regarding the urn as a whole object, not as a series of intricate, lively scenes. The urn is as mysterious as eternity. It has drawn Keats into its mystery. The word 'tease' means entice. In other words, it has drawn an imaginative response from Keats, not a rational one. 'Tease' can also mean 'to mock' and the urn, as a 'foster-child of silence and slow time', does present us with mystery: the mystery of death (the ashes within the urn), the mystery of the work of art that lives in every age (the images on the urn), the mystery of the artist who has lived and died.

The phrase 'Cold Pastoral!' is dismissive, but it does not come as a shock or surprise. Keats in lines 29 and 30 has already recognised the inevitable distance between the work of art and the human being. Keats knows that 'old age shall this generation waste'. He and all others will die, but the urn will remain for others to look on and to experience.

The word 'Cold' is perfectly appropriate: the urn is made of marble and was originally intended to contain the ashes of the dead; the figures on the urn are still, unmoving. Yet so many details from the text up to now suggest warmth and a living presence. Keats cannot stay within the imaginative world that has been prompted by his viewing of the urn. Both 'Ode to a Nightingale' and 'Ode on a Grecian Urn' acknowledge and reveal beauty and, inevitably, recognise that the human being cannot dwell with beauty forever.

The phrase that Keats now uses to describe the urn is 'a friend to man'. It is a friend because it tells a story that enhances life; yet it also, because of its very purpose, reminds us of death. It is immortal and the different stories that are depicted on its side – an ideal rural paradise, music and song, passionate young love, ritual and ceremony – are things which we as humans value.

The final two lines of this particular ode have puzzled readers for generations. The 'sylvan historian', the urn, says to man: 'Beauty is truth, truth beauty'. The urn itself is beautiful and it contains a truth, a truth that even when it involves sorrow can be beautiful. But the two ideas contained in the 'Beauty is truth, truth beauty' can be read as separate statements, one an aesthetic judgement, the other a moral one: if something is beautiful it contains a truth; whatever is true is beautiful. Who is speaking these last two lines? There is no original manuscript in existence for this poem and the first printed version in 1820 was as follows:

> 'Beauty is truth, truth beauty,' – that is all
> Ye know on earth, and all ye need to know.

If this is how Keats intended the poem to be read it means that the words 'Beauty is truth, truth beauty' are spoken by the urn and addressed to man, and Keats himself perhaps is addressing his fellow man in ' – that is all/Ye know on earth, and all ye need to know.' The 'Ye' here is not in keeping, however, with Keats's own sense of 'ours' when he speaks of mankind's suffering. Robert Gittings in his edition of Keats's *Complete Poems* says that the following interpretations are possible: 1. Both lines are spoken by the urn, and addressed to man; 2. the lines are spoken by the poet to the urn; 3. the lines are spoken by the poet to the figures on the urn; 4. 'Beauty is truth, truth beauty' is spoken by the urn, and the remainder is the poet speaking to his readers; 5. 'Beauty is truth, truth beauty' is spoken by the urn and the poet then addresses the urn, not mankind. There was another printed version of the poem in 1820 and four contemporary transcripts of the text. All five omitted the inverted commas here.

The reading which argues that the urn speaks the words 'Beauty is truth, truth beauty' is certainly a valid one. Keats does say immediately before that line when he is addressing the urn 'Thou shalt remain . . . a friend to man, to whom thou say'st'. This is significant in that the urn did not communicate in words but in images up to now. It was also described as a 'silent form'. When it speaks it says two things and they are both true.

The preferred interpretation of these lines is as follows: In both lines, the urn is speaking to men. The urn is immortal and it is a friend to mortal man. Keats gives the urn these words which remind all of us, including Keats, that the urn itself, an object from ancient Greece, captures beauty and truth. The nineteenth-century critic Matthew Arnold says of these lines:

> For to see things in their beauty is to see things in their truth, and Keats knew it. 'What the Imagination seizes as Beauty must be Truth,' he says in prose; and in immortal verse, he has said the same thing – 'Beauty is truth, truth beauty, – that is all/Ye know on earth, and all ye need to know.' No, it is not all; but it is true, deeply true, and we have deep need to know it.

T. S. Eliot felt that the line 'Beauty is truth, truth beauty' is 'a serious blemish on a beautiful poem, and the reason must be either that I fail to understand it, or that it is a statement which is untrue'. Another critic, Arthur Quiller-Couch, thought the last two lines of the ode 'a vague observation – to anyone whom life had taught to face facts'. You will have your own opinion, and it is impossible to say which one is the definitive interpretation.

The ode finishes on an extraordinary still note. The words with which the poem ends are the words which the urn has 'spoken' and will 'speak' in every generation, words which remind us of the power and importance of the work of art. Keats, both in the nightingale ode and in 'Ode on a Grecian Urn', though creating beautiful worlds, always returns to reality. The 'hungry generation' in 'Ode to a Nightingale' and 'this generation waste' in 'Ode on a Grecian Urn' reveal a mind that can recognise reality. That Keats can create for us worlds other than the real and the transient is part of his greatness as a poet.

On a lighter note, here is a spoof version of Keats's 'Ode on a Grecian Urn':

Round Vase
Gods chase
What say?
What play?
Don't know.
Nice though.

To Autumn

The nightingale is female and the Grecian urn is an 'unravished bride'. In 'To Autumn', Keats once again focuses on a female presence. Each of the other odes had ten-line stanzas. Keats introduces a variation here – there is an extra line which is appropriate in a poem which celebrates the lingering season.

In the earlier odes, Keats is very much a presence within the poem, as can be seen from the use of 'I', 'my', 'me' ('I' is used nine times in 'Ode to a Nightingale'). In 'To Autumn', it is as if he has allowed the season itself to speak and has absented himself; there is no personal pronoun, and yet, of course, Keats is everywhere in the poem. It is his sensibility, his imagination and his sensuous evocation of the season which make the poem possible. The achievement of 'To Autumn' is most clearly seen when it is read as the final ode in a sequence.

Sensuousness is one of Keats's hallmarks as a poet and it has been pointed out by the literary critic Douglas Bush that the three stanzas of 'To Autumn' contain sensuous imagery with a different emphasis in each stanza. The first is mainly to do with touch, the second with the visual, and in the final stanza the world of the poem is conveyed through the ear.

The opening line of 'To Autumn', 'Season of mists and mellow fruitfulness', differs considerably from the opening lines in the other two odes. In 'Ode to a Nightingale', the focus is on the suffering self: 'My heart aches'; in 'Ode on a Grecian Urn', it is on the otherness of the urn, its separateness: 'Thou still unravished bride...'; in 'Ode on Melancholy', Keats is urging himself, another, the reader, not to commit suicide: 'No, no, go not to Lethe'. Here, in 'To Autumn', there is a wonderful sense of having entered into, having become part of, the season itself. That opening line offers a sense of completion: it sums up the qualities of the season, its landscape and its produce: 'Season of mists and mellow fruitfulness'.

The first eleven lines of the poem speak of ripeness and fulfilment. Everything is in harmony: the season itself and the sun are bosom-friends. Keats speaks of how the fruit trees are loaded and blessed by the autumn sun. Autumn is the season closest to winter and is often associated with the beginning of the year's end, but for Keats the sun is 'to set budding more,/And still more, later flowers for the bees'. The mood is one of excess; in this first stanza, there is no suggestion that it will ever fade away. The phrase 'budding more', followed by 'and still more', suggests an endless pleasure. The bees are deceived. Keats tells us that they 'think warm days will never cease'. The verbs 'load', 'bless', 'bend', 'fill' 'swell', 'plump', 'o'er-brimmed' all create the sense of an ongoing, enriching process. There is a great deal of quiet activity. The first stanza consists of one sentence, a sentence which, as we read it, records the fullness of autumn. Keats knows, and we know, that autumn will end but it is as if he is saying that there is no need to go into that.

In the second stanza, autumn is personified as 'sitting careless on a granary floor' or 'on a half-reaped furrow sound asleep'. The harvest is not done and autumn itself, though described as harvester and reaper, is lingering. She is neither harvesting nor reaping. There is very little movement. Autumn's scythe (hook) spares the next swath. It is autumn, a time of change leading to inevitable decay, but here autumn sits still.

The image of autumn as gleaner who 'dost keep/Steady thy laden head across a brook' and the image of autumn as patient watcher by the cider-press are also images of silence and stillness. The phrase 'last oozings' refers both to something almost over and to very, very slow movement, the pressing of the apples into cider. These are the apples that weighed down the 'mossed cottage trees' in line 5. But there is no hurry. Keats never once laments the fact that autumn will soon give way to winter. In the nightingale and Grecian urn odes, he was intensely aware of happiness and its opposite. Here, it is the beauty and music and harmony of autumn which holds him. 'To Autumn' is a poem where Keats's theory of Negative Capability is demonstrated fully.

Keats does not look ahead to winter. Instead, he goes back to spring, autumn's origin. Stanza 3 introduces this idea. The first line of the third stanza, contains two questions. But these questions do not trouble Keats: 'Where are the songs of Spring?' he asks, only to let them be: 'Ay, where are they?' There is no need to think of the songs of spring. Four months earlier, in May, he did think of the song of the nightingale, a song of spring, but that was another occasion and he celebrated it in a separate poem.

In line 24, he turns to autumn and listens to its music. The poem's movement is from visual to aural. Autumn is not spring, but he knows that 'thou hast thy music too'. The closing lines of the poem are a symphony of autumn's music: 'the wailful choir' of the gnats; the sound of 'the light wind' as it 'lives or dies'; the 'loud bleat' of the full-grown lambs; the song of the hedge-crickets; the 'treble soft' of the red-breast; the twitter of the 'gathering swallows'. The music is sad: 'wailful' and 'mourn' in line 27 tell us that. The gnats mourn the end of the year and they mourn their own brief lives. Their music rises and falls. The phrase 'sinking as the light wind lives or dies' is of a very different texture to the abundance and excess of the first stanza, only 20 lines before. Yet the final music in the poem is not wailful or mourning; it is the music of song and treble soft. The swallows are gathering either because it is the day's end or for migration. The music of the song of the nightingale allowed Keats to forget suffering and death momentarily. Keats listens with a very attentive ear to the music of autumn and the music itself is not a means of escape. In thirty-three lines, Keats has captured the essence of autumn. It charts the dying of an autumn day ('the soft-dying day') and the dying of the year.

The autumn of the final stanza is different from the autumn of the opening lines. In stanza 3, the harvest's done: 'the next swath and all its twined flowers' have become 'the stubble-plains' touched with 'rosy-hue'. Change has come about, imperceptibly, inevitably: 'while', line 25, leads to 'then', line 27, until 'now' is reached in line 31. Yet Keats even gives the dying day a sense of new beginnings. The 'barred clouds bloom the soft-dying day'. He also, in line 30, speaks of 'full-grown lambs' which bring us back to spring and the beginning of the year.

The structure of the poem allows the imagery to speak for itself. It is, of course, how Keats viewed that particular autumn, September 1819, but those very images draw the reader in. Autumn reveals itself. It is as if there is no intermediary. The poem, according to the poet Sean Lysaght, embodies the truth that the poet 'does not have to parade his/her own private emotions to write effectively. At this late stage in his career, with the knowledge that he is soon going to die, Keats transcends the psychological drama of the Odes by writing a poem descriptive of the dying year. His art achieves great serenity here; at the same time it communicates the full pathos of his personal situation.'

The season of spring in 'Ode on a Grecian Urn' did not end because it is part of the work of art. The 'happy boughs' never shed their leaves. Here the spring which he mentions in the final stanza has given way to summer and autumn, and winter must follow. Of all the odes, the subject matter of 'To Autumn' – the season itself – is the most familiar and the most immediate. It is a poem that speaks to everyone who knows the seasons and, if you consider Keats's own belief that there are four seasons in the mind of man, this poem takes on an added poignancy. He wrote it when he was twenty-three. He would be twenty-four that October and two years later he was dead.

Sensuousness is one of the striking qualities in Keats's work. So too is his love for the beautiful, which is often expressed against the overshadowing reality of suffering and death. Matthew Arnold, in an essay published in 1888, said: 'The thing to be seized is that Keats had flint and iron in him . . . indeed nothing is more remarkable in Keats than his clear-sightedness, his lucidity.' Here Arnold is recognising that, though Keats is sensuous and passionate, he also views the world honestly. Keats knows that moments of intense pleasure and happiness do not last.

Bright Star! Would I Were Steadfast as Thou Art

What strikes the reader immediately in this sonnet is the contrast and the distance between the high, bright star and the human being on earth. The first two words, 'Bright star!', and that exclamation mark, focus on the far away. In the first line, Keats expresses a longing to be steadfast like the star. But, having highlighted this particular quality, Keats immediately expresses some reservations. The word 'not' at the beginning of line 2 indicates his reservation. Though the steadfastness is a quality that he admires, he does not want to experience the star's loneliness and its sense of distance, its sense of being separate and apart.

Keats's fine imaginative powers are clearly seen in the first eight lines of this Shakespearean sonnet. This poem is charged with imagery. The star is splendid, brilliant and magnificent, but it is detached and alone. Keats wants to be and does not want to be like the star. It is hermit-like in its loneliness. The phrases 'watching, with eternal lids apart' and 'sleepless' give the star a human quality, but it is an unattractive human quality. Though what the star sees is beautiful – the cleansing tides and the new-fallen snow – it knows no ease or rest. Planet Earth in this poem is beautiful. 'The moving waters' and 'the new soft-fallen mask/Of snow upon the mountains and the moors' create a sense of varied landscape (seashore, steep slopes and level land), and the sounds here, moving waters, snowfall, are quiet and gentle. Everything associated with Earth in the poem is in a state of flux. The tides rise and fall and the image of cleansing waters suggests flux, change, renewal; the snow falls, but it is only a 'mask', without steadfastness.

At the beginning of the third quatrain, Keats emphasises again that the star is being rejected: 'No' in line 9 echoes the 'Not' of line 2. The star is steadfast; it looks upon a cold beauty (the night, the water, the snow-covered landscape) and the poem, consisting of a single sentence, moves towards the warm, living, transient world of human love. Keats longs for the 'still steadfast, still unchangeable', but prefers the sweet unrest of love to the cold and lonely unchanging world of the bright star. In this, it resembles 'Ode to a Nightingale' and 'Ode to a Grecian Urn' especially. Both odes express a longing for otherness, but in both Keats accepts that it is impossible to dwell in an ideal world permanently.

The song of the nightingale and the world depicted on the side of the urn were at a remove from reality. In 'Bright Star', Keats chooses the world of 'breathing human passion': in lines 10 and 11 he describes the soft, warm, gentle intimacy between lovers: 'Pillowed upon my fair love's ripening breast,/To feel for ever its soft fall and swell'. The phrase 'fall and swell' describes movement, movement of the tide in line 5, the movement of the human breath. And 'ripening' also suggests maturing, changing. It is this which Keats ultimately prefers. The warmth of this shared experience is all the more effective when contrasted with the cold isolation of the bright star.

The moment of human love is cherished by Keats. He wants the sensuous experience (the sensuousness of 'pillowed', ripening', 'soft fall and swell') to last forever. Sleep would deny him that pleasure: Keats longs to remain 'awake for ever in a sweet unrest', and it is unrest because he knows that human love cannot remain unchanged. It is not steadfast and unchangeable like the star.

If it were possible to hear his love's 'tender-taken breath' forever (and the repetition of still at the beginning of line 13 emphasises his desire), 'Still, still to hear her tender-taken breath' would be to 'live ever'. Elsewhere in Keats's poetry, we have seen that he knows that the beautiful moment cannot be held forever. It must end and, when it cannot last, then the only other choice is to 'swoon to death'.

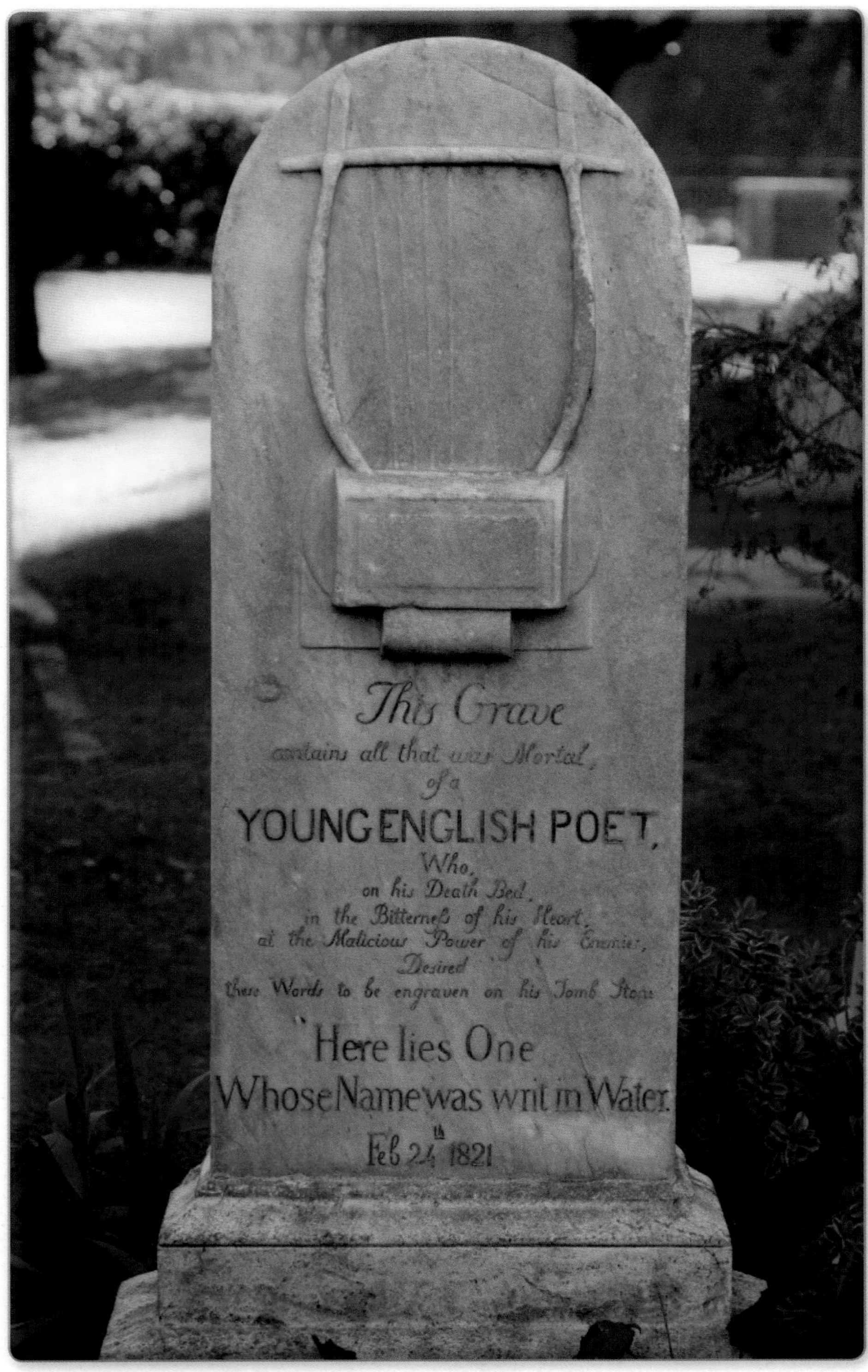

• The grave of the English poet John Keats in Rome.

Sylvia Plath
(1932–1963)

Contents Page

The Overview

Biographical detail poses a problem for some readers of a poet's work. How much is there to know? How much should one know? The poet Thom Gunn argues that the making of poems is not the equivalent of turning out clay pots: poems are rooted in and tell directly or indirectly of a life. People who have never read a Sylvia Plath poem know that she killed herself (at 30; she had attempted suicide in 1953 when she was 21) and somehow her death has come to overshadow and dominate the life. In Plath's case, the life is so emotionally complicated and complex that a fuller understanding and appreciation of the poems are possible when they are read against the life. That life was, in Sylvia Plath's own words, 'magically run by two electric currents' and these she named 'joyous positive and despairing negative'; her poetry reflects those charged opposites.

These ten poems by Plath were written within the space of seven years. The first, 'Black Rook in Rainy Weather', was written when she was 24; she wrote the final one, 'Child', on 28 January 1963, two weeks before she died. The poems describe the natural world and the domestic world but, whether Plath is writing about a black rook, a pheasant, an elm tree, poppies in July, bees, or her child, she is primarily writing about herself, her emotional, psychological, imaginative states. Her choice of subject matter is significant but how she responds to that subject matter equally so. In Edna Longley's words, 'Plath speaks for the interior workings of the unconscious forces'.

Her poetry has urgency and intensity. It has been termed hysterical and self-dramatising but such descriptions ignore the clear-sighted understanding she has of a situation and the carefully shaped poems on the page. She does write of troubled emotions. the darker side of life, her own experiences. Ted Hughes told Eavan Boland that Sylvia Plath's face changed in absolutely every single moment of expression. She did know extremities and, if her work is more pessimistic than optimistic, more shaded than light, she herself defended it as follows: 'Don't talk to me about the world needing cheerful stuff! What the person out of Belsen — physical or psychological – wants is nobody saying that the birdies still go tweet-tweet, but the full knowledge that somebody else has been there and knows the worst, just what it is like. It is much more help for me, for example, to know that people are divorced and go through hell, than to hear about happy marriages.' (Letter to her mother 21 October 1962) She believed that her own disappointments, pain and suffering were valid subjects for poetry.

'She loved nature and weather and children and poetry and had this tremendous spirit', says Eavan Boland, and this is evident in many of the poems here. In 'Black Rook in Rainy Weather', there is a focused, intense concentration on the natural world. She chooses to write about what many would consider dull and unattractive, but Plath is hopeful that the scene before her will afford her a sort of miracle.

The everyday can glow unexpectedly; ordinary moments are made holy. In a voice that is low key, she longs for such moments. The voice is sometimes nervous, edgy as in 'Pheasant', but her fear relates to the human threat – 'You said you would kill it this morning / Do not kill it' – and, within the same poem, there is the hymn of praise for this unusual bird: 'It's a little cornucopia'. The voice here is ultimately protective. There is also in Plath a lyrical, tender voice, especially in her poems about motherhood: 'Morning Song' and 'Child' are wonderful expressions of love.

'Morning Song', 'Finisterre', 'Mirror', 'Pheasant', 'Elm', 'The Arrival of the Bee Box', in Seamus Heaney's words, reveal 'the terrible stresses of her own psychological and domestic reality'. If she writes about a dramatic landscape, as she does in 'Finisterre', we see that landscape as Plath sees it. She brings to it, just as every viewer would, her own preoccupations and concerns. Anne Stevenson, in her book *Bitter Fame: A Life of Sylvia Plath*, writes that Plath's 'raw-edged response to personal sorrows and joys, her apprehensions of the world's horrors and injustices, as well as its beauty, were excessive to an unusual degree'.

Asked once about the importance of poetry, Plath said: 'I am not worried that poems reach relatively few people. As it is, they go surprisingly far – among strangers, around the world, even. Farther than the words of a classroom teacher or the prescriptions of a doctor; if they are very lucky, farther than a lifetime.' She wanted her poetry to mirror the life lived, its ordinariness and its extraordinariness, so much so that Plath once famously said that she wanted to get a toothbrush into a poem and that she was interested in writing about 'The real world. Real situations, behind which the great gods play the drama of blood, lust and death'.

Her mother, Aurelia Plath, said that Sylvia Plath 'made use of everything and often transmuted gold into lead . . . These emotions in another person would dissipate with time, but with Sylvia they were written at the moment of intensity to become ineradicable as an epitaph engraved on a tombstone'. But on the page the thoughts and feelings are shaped and crafted. The Irish poet Eavan Boland speaks of Plath's 'great élan, her handling of the line, her very unusual take on language and image – all of those things have become coded into the poetry that we now have. She is a very defining poet'. Robert Lowell spoke of Plath's 'perfect control, like the control of a skier who avoids every death-trap until reaching the final drop' and Michael Schmidt says that it 'is hard to imagine a poetry more forcefully stamped with a personality and voice'.

Biographical Notes

Sylvia Plath was born on 27 October 1932 in Boston, Massachusetts. Her father Otto Plath, from Grabow in Prussia, had emigrated to America when he was 16. He studied languages (he could speak five) and biology, zoology and entomology (study of insects); he became a professor and entomologist and, when he was 43, he married one of his students, 22 year-old Aurelia Schober, a second-generation Austrian, who also had a Germanic background. Sylvia was their first-born and, according to her mother, she tried to speak when she was eight weeks old. A brother, Warren, was born in 1935, when Sylvia was two and a half.

It was an academic home. Aurelia hoped to write one day and Otto was devoted to his teaching and research. In 1934, Otto Plath published a scientific study *Bumblebees and their Ways*, a work which Otto had researched and which Aurelia had helped him write. There followed a major article called 'Insect Societies'. Aurelia read to the children – rhymes, fairytales, poems and then Dr Seuss, A.A. Milne, J.R.R. Tolkien, Robert Louis Stevenson, Kipling, Lamb's *Tales from Shakespeare.*

Sylvia went to school at four, performing extraordinarily well from the beginning. When she was young the family lived in a house outside Boston on the harbour. In September 1938, just before her sixth birthday, a vicious hurricane tore through the district. When the Plaths emerged after the storm, the sight of the destruction marked an important episode in Sylvia Plath's life: she wrote a poem about it years later.

In the late 1930s, Otto Plath was not well but refused to consult a doctor until his leg became discoloured after stubbing his toe. Diabetes was diagnosed; his leg had to amputated and he died a week after Sylvia's eighth birthday. When Aurelia told her daughter, who was sitting up in bed reading, she said 'I'll never speak to God again' and hid beneath a blanket.

Aurelia took a job, first teaching, then devising medical-secretary courses, and the family moved house to Wellesley when Sylvia was ten. Plath later wrote: 'My father died, we moved inland. Whereupon those nine first years of my life sealed themselves off like a ship in a bottle – beautiful, inaccessible, obsolete, a fine, white flying myth.' Though she had been getting A grades, she repeated a year at school, joined the Girl Scouts, the basketball team and the school orchestra (she played viola). English and art were her best subjects.

Sylvia Plath had been writing poems since the age of five and she published her first poem in the Boston Herald when she was eight; she introduced it: 'I have written a short poem about what I see and hear on hot summer nights'. During adolescence she wrote rhymes, began a diary and published poems and drawings in the school magazine. 'Writing' says Anne Stevenson, one of her biographers, 'soon became as natural to her as eating.' She also read voraciously. By the age of 12 she had read *Gone with the Wind* three times, reading it this time in two days. The young Sylvia Plath was ambitious and self-obsessed. At 17 she wrote in her diary: 'I have a terrible egotism. I love my flesh, my face, my limbs with overwhelming devotion . . . I think I would like to call myself "The girl who wanted to be God"'.

After high school, Plath won a scholarship to Smith College at Northampton, Massachusetts. She began there in September 1950 and studied English, art, botany, history and French; she worked hard and began to make a reputation for herself as a published writer. She was on the editorial board of the *Smith Review*; she wrote for newspapers and she wrote short stories and poems. One of her stories won a $500 first prize in *Mademoiselle* and she became more determined than ever to succeed as a writer.

During her third year at Smith, she was anxious that she might not earn an A average and wrote in her journal: 'if ever I have come close to wanting to commit suicide, it is now'. But she drove herself to do well. During the Smith years she heard Robert Frost and W.H. Auden read their work at the college and spent a summer in New York working for *Mademoiselle*, during which she interviewed Elizabeth Bowen. Her only novel *The Bell Jar*, which was published under the name Victoria Lucas in 1963, tells the story of a young and talented woman who spends a summer in New York working for a magazine. Like the character Esther Greenwood in the novel, Sylvia Plath was given to extraordinary mood swings. That summer Plath had also applied to attend Frank O'Connor's summer writing class at Harvard and submitted sample work. She returned home from New York to discover she had been rejected and she took it badly. Her mother noticed 'a great change in her; all her usual *joie de vivre* was absent.' She contemplated suicide, underwent electroconvulsive therapy and at her lowest she hid herself in the basement and swallowed forty sleeping tablets. She was missing for two days; the Boston papers carried headlines: 'Beautiful Smith Girl' or 'Top Ranking Student at Smith Missing'. She had been in a coma but vomited up the pills. She was hospitalised and later transferred to a psychiatric hospital, where she stayed for almost four months. The electroshock treatment and daily psychotherapy sessions at McLean Hospital had a profound effect on Plath. She had very supportive friends and visitors but, on her 21st birthday, 27 October 1953, her mother brought her yellow roses, Sylvia Plath's favourite flowers, and she threw them into the wastepaper basket.

She returned to Smith and during her final year had an intense relationship with Richard Sassoon, a distant relation of the poet Siegfried Sassoon. Meanwhile, she was winning several literary awards and honours, including a Fulbright scholarship to study at Cambridge. She graduated in 1955. Soon after, Sassoon, like other boyfriends she had had, declared his love for her and was rejected.

Once again, she turned to writing. That August several of her poems were published; to date she had written over two hundred. In September Plath, almost 23, sailed for England and Cambridge on the *QE II*.

The two Fulbright years at Cambridge, according to her mother, were 'the most exciting and colourful' of Sylvia's life. Her first letter home from Cambridge described it as 'the most beautiful spot in the world'. Plath decided against studying for a PhD and devoted her time to wide reading as a background to her own creative writing. She joined the Dramatic Club, wrote for the *Varsity* paper and travelled to Paris and Nice (where she visited the Matisse chapel and in a postcard home said of the visit that it was 'about the most lovely in my life'). She also suffered mood swings and consulted the university psychiatrist; her journals reveal despair and anger. She wrote: 'A Life Is passing. My Life.'

On Saturday, 25 February 1956, Plath saw the psychiatrist and felt better. That same day, she bought a new literary magazine which contained some poems by someone called Ted Hughes. That evening Plath went to a party to celebrate the new publication and it was there she met Hughes for the first time, the man who was to become the most important in her life. Both were passionate about poetry and both were determined to become writers.

By mid-April, Sylvia Plath and Ted Hughes were falling in love. She had renounced her old lovers and 'took up Ted', whom she described to her mother, in a letter dated 17 April 1956, as 'the strongest man in the world...brilliant poet whose work I loved before I met him, a large, hulking, healthy Adam...with a voice like the thunder of God – a singer, story-teller, lion and world-wanderer, a vagabond who will never stop.' They were both writing many poems and, by the end of April, Sylvia declared that 'within a year I shall publish a book of 33 poems which will hit the critics violently...My voice is taking shape, coming strong. Ted says he never read poems by a woman, like mine; they are strong and full and rich...they are working, sweating, heaving poems born out of the way words should be said...' Sylvia sent her carefully typed poems to English and American magazines. Now she began to do the same with Ted Hughes's. They planned to marry in June, choosing Bloomsday, 16 June, and wishing to keep it secret; Plath's mother and brother were, apart from bride and groom, the only ones who knew. Plath and Hughes, who had known each other for less than four months, were married at the church of St. George the Martyr in Bloomsbury. Plath intended a big second wedding in America. Meanwhile, she felt that if it were known that she had married, Cambridge might think that she wouldn't be able to concentrate on her studies during her final year and that she might lose her scholarship; she would complete her studies in Cambridge and Hughes was going to teach English in Spain for a year, an idea later abandoned.

They both went to Spain for the summer and settled in Benidorm, then a quiet fishing village. 'You Hated Spain', the title of a Ted Hughes poem, sums up Plath's opinion of the country; she thought it hot, violent and found the bull-fighting repulsive, and yet she could write that 'Every evening at dusk the lights of the sardine boats dip and shine out at sea like floating stars.' They both worked hard at their writing. Ted wrote to his parents telling them of his marriage and, when

Plath and Hughes returned to England in August, they stayed at Hughes's family home in Yorkshire. When Plath returned to Cambridge, Hughes stayed on in Yorkshire but did some work for the BBC in London. Plath's poems were being accepted by American publications but she was suffering 'hectic suffocating wild depression'. In October, she told the Fulbright Commission that she had married, only to discover that it did not affect her scholarship; nor was Newnham, her Cambridge college, annoyed by the announcement. Plath and Hughes then took a flat in Cambridge and began their life together. Hughes taught at a boys' school and Plath continued to send his poems to magazines. In fact, it was Plath who helped Hughes get his first book, *The Hawk in the Rain*, published; she had entered it for a contest at Harper's and the judges were W.H. Auden, Marianne Moore and Stephen Spender. When he won she was thrilled, claiming that 'We will publish a bookshelf of books between us before we perish' and have 'a batch of brilliant healthy children'.

After Cambridge, Plath and Hughes lived in America: Plath took up a teaching job at her old college, Smith, in 1957. She enjoyed the work but they were anxious about their writing careers and, during one of her lows, Plath believed that she couldn't write, couldn't teach, couldn't think and all the time wanted to be the perfect wife, perfect teacher, perfect writer. She taught three days a week; the rest of the time she devoted to her own writing; she was working twelve hours a day. Hughes took a job at the University of Massachusetts at Amherst, early in 1958, but they both decided that, when summer came, their own work had to come first and they would give up teaching.

By late 1957, when *The Hawk in the Rain* was published in England and America to critical acclaim, it was becoming clear to Plath that her husband was regarded as the better poet. Hughes's poems were being published in prestigious magazines, hers were being rejected, and their relationship suffered. On her last day of teaching in May, Hughes had promised to meet her when class was done; he never showed and Plath came upon him with a Smith student. Hughes denied her accusation but Plath did not believe him. That evening in her journal she declared that she would not commit suicide because of it. A week later they had a violent exchange and fought physically: Plath sprained her thumb and Hughes ended up with Plath's fingernail marks on his face. And yet, the marriage survived.

In June 1958, Plath learned that *The London Magazine* took two of her poems, including 'Black Rook in Rainy Weather', and she was particularly thrilled when *The New Yorker* accepted two poems the same month. Hughes and she moved to Boston in September, where they devoted themselves to writing, but, by October, worried about money, she found a job as part-time secretary at Massachusetts General Hospital's psychiatry clinic where, after her breakdown, she had been admitted in June 1953. Work did not allow her to write as much as she hoped and she became, once again, depressed. She was disappointed that she couldn't become pregnant, was disgusted by Hughes and went into therapy. There she explored the relationship she had with her mother, who had not approved of Plath quitting her job at Smith. Plath felt that this implied that her mother did not believe she could earn a living by her writing. In turn, she believed that she had to write to defy her mother. She quit the secretarial job and wrote her best short story 'Johnny Panic and the Bible of Dreams', which has as its subject matter mental illness and suicide.

Both Plath and Hughes were profiled in *Mademoiselle* in January 1959. Plath spoke of how 'Both of us want to write as much as possible' and the magazine printed her poem 'The Times are Tidy'. But their marriage was not as happy as that profile would suggest. They quarrelled again. Hughes was completing a second collection; Plath signed up for a creative-writing seminar at Harvard run by the poet Robert Lowell, whose poetry was remarkable for its intense examination of immediate personal situations. One of his books was called *Life Studies* (1960) and, in one of his poems, 'Epilogue', Lowell asks 'Yet why not say what happened?' Plath's own poetry now began to probe deeply; she was determined to write a poetry that was 'grim' and 'antipoetic'. She wrote about her mother, her husband and her dead father, whose grave she visited.

To earn money Plath took another part-time secretarial job, this time at Harvard, but Hughes was awarded a Guggenheim grant and they were both offered residencies at the artists' colony at Yaddo, New York State. After Boston and before Yaddo, they toured America, visiting Michigan, Montana and Utah; in California they visited Plath's aunt Frieda. At Yaddo, in the autumn of 1959, Plath and Hughes lived a disciplined writing life. Some of Plath's poems were accepted for publication; some were rejected. To help themselves write, they would hypnotise each other, try stream of consciousness experiments, mind control, concentration exercises involving deep breathing and free association. For Plath, the results were good: on one day alone, 19 October, she wrote two poems, including 'The Colossus', which became the title poem in her first collection, published in October 1960.

Thanksgiving was spent with Mrs Plath at Wellesley. Sylvia Plath was now five months pregnant and they stayed on at Wellesley until early December when they sailed from New York for England. They visited Hughes's parents at Heptonstall for Christmas; by February had moved into a rented flat in Chalcot Square in London and on 1 April 1960, Plath, hypnotised by Hughes to minimise the pain, gave birth to their first child, a daughter, Frieda. A second pregnancy miscarried on 6 February 1961 and in her poem 'Parliament Hill Fields', written five days later, the 'you' to whom she speaks is the dead foetus. 'Morning Song', written on 19 February 1961, hints at both birth and miscarriage.

Plath worked every morning, seven days a week, on her novel *The Bell Jar*. Mrs Plath visited England during the summer and she looked after Frieda, while Plath and Hughes went to France and later to Devon to look for a house in the country. They found and bought Court Green, their ideal house, outside the village of North Tawton near Dartmouth. Part of the house dated from the eleventh century; it was on three acres and it adjoined an ancient church and graveyard. They sublet their London flat to a young Canadian poet and his wife, David and Assia Wevill, and, on 31 August 1961, Plath, Hughes and Frieda moved to Devon. In the middle of August, she discovered that she was pregnant and on 22 August wrote in her diary that she had finished *The Bell Jar*.

It was in Court Green in Devon that Plath began to write the poems for which she is best known; she would be dead eighteen months later. Their life in Devon followed a pattern. Plath would write in the morning, Hughes in the afternoon and both looked after Frieda. In the evenings they read. In September alone, Plath wrote four poems, one of these being 'Finisterre', and in October another four, including 'Mirror'. She became involved in the life of the village, attending the Anglican Church for a while, and joined a mothers' group which held monthly meetings.

Their second child, Nicholas, was born at home on 17 January 1962 and left her exhausted. In March she summoned up extraordinary energies and wrote 'Women Waiting', a poem, almost four hundred lines long, for three voices, set mainly in a maternity ward. On 25 March both children were baptised and Frieda attended Sunday school.

Hughes worked in the garden; Plath took up horse-riding. She wrote five poems in April, including 'Pheasant' and 'Elm'. 'Pheasant', according to Ronald Hayman, protests 'against Ted Hughes's predatoriness towards animals and birds. Feeling privileged to be visited by the majestic pheasant which was pacing through the uncut grass by the elm on the hill, she pleads with him not to kill it.' 'Elm', dated 19 April 1962, is considered to be the best of the April poems.

The Wevills visited on a week-end in May. Assia Wevill, who had been born in Germany, was aged 34. This was her third marriage and she now found that she was attracted to Hughes. Plath disliked what she saw and became nervous and suspicious. They had been married six years but, by the Monday, Hughes was involved with Assia Wevill; that summer Ted Hughes frequently spent time in London and, when he and Plath were together at Court Green, there were arguments. On 7 June, in one of her letters home, she told her mother that 'This is the richest and happiest time of my life' and in a letter dated 15 June: 'Today, guess what, we became beekeepers!', an event she would capture four months later in her poem 'The Arrival of the Beebox'. Yet in July Plath wrote 'The Other', 'Words heard, by accident, over the phone' and 'Poppies in July', poems documenting the changing nature of her relationship with Hughes. Plath's mother visited and sensed a marriage under strain. In early August, Mrs Plath returned to America; when she said goodbye to Plath, Hughes and the children at Exeter station, she was saying goodbye to her daughter for the last time. Plath's poem 'Burning the Letters', written 13 August 1962, records how she went to Hughes's desk and destroyed many of his papers, and on 27 August she wrote to her mother telling her that she was 'going to try to get a legal separation from Ted'.

Plath and Hughes agreed to a trial separation: he would spend some time in Spain with Assia Wevill and Plath wanted to spend some time in Ireland. That September Plath and Hughes left the children with a nanny and travelled to the West of Ireland, where they stayed with the poet Richard Murphy at Cleggan. They visited Inishbofin and Murphy remembers the journey: 'We sailed to Inishbofin, a passage of six miles across open water with a strong current and an ocean swell. Sylvia lay prone on the foredeck, leaning out over the prow like a triumphant figurehead, inhaling the sea air ecstatically.' They visited Yeats's Tower at Ballylee and Thomas Kinsella joined them at Murphy's cottage. Hughes then went to visit the artist Barrie Cooke in Co. Clare and Plath went to Dublin, where she stayed with Thomas Kinsella and his wife, before returning to Devon. Back at Green Court, she received a telegram from Hughes in London and realised that he had left for good.

Hughes's family was upset by the separation. Ted Hughes now lived in London and agreed to pay maintenance. Plath became deeply depressed, lost weight, began to smoke and took sleeping pills. It was a fruitful time in terms of poetry, however. On 26 September she wrote a poem in which she addresses Nicholas, to whom Hughes had not warmed. In 'For a Fatherless Son', Plath tells her son that he 'will be aware of an absence, presently,/ Growing beside you, like a tree,/ A death tree...' In October, an extraordinarily creative time, she wrote twenty-five poems, sometimes one a day. She wrote to her mother: 'Every morning, when my sleeping pill wears off, I am up about five, in my study, with coffee, writing like mad – have managed a poem a day before breakfast'. She planned to return to Ireland from December to February: 'Ireland is heaven, utterly unspoiled, emerald sea washing in fingers among green fields, white sand, wild coast, cows, friendly people, honey-tasting whisky...' At the end of October, she wrote one of her most famous poems, 'Lady Lazarus', which contains the lines: 'I am only thirty/ And like the cat I have nine times to die... Dying/ Is an art, like everything else./ I do it exceptionally well.' Hughes and Plath agreed to a divorce; Plath abandoned plans to visit Ireland again but she rented a flat in London, at 23 Fitzroy Road, in a house in which W.B. Yeats had once lived, a fact which thrilled her – 'my work should be blessed.'

Back in Devon, she gathered together her recent poems and arranged them into what would become her second collection, *Ariel and Other Poems*. She sent her poems out, only to discover that most of them were rejected. She herself thought these recent poems her best and, despite the rejections, she continued to write through November. In December she disposed of the bees, closed up the house, left Court Green and moved into the upstairs flat at 23 Fitzroy Road on 12 December 1962. Hughes saw Plath and the children but they spent Christmas visiting friends, while Hughes went to Spain on holiday.

January 1963 was one of the worst in living memory, the coldest in England since 1947. It snowed heavily and it was bitterly cold. In London, hospitals were crowded and the number of suicides increased significantly. Plath and the children had flu; the heating did not work properly; the power failed. In mid-January, *The Bell Jar* was published under the pseudonym Victoria Lucas and it received good reviews, even though American publishers turned it down. Towards the end of January she began to write poetry again. 'Child', a poem on motherhood, is dated 28 January 1963.

But by February the strain was taking its toll: the extreme cold, the exhaustion of looking after two small children, the marriage breakdown proved too much. She and the children had stayed with some friends across town for a weekend early in February. On Sunday afternoon, having slept and rested, Plath asked to be driven home. She wept most of the way but could not be persuaded to return to her friends. That evening Plath put the children to bed, wrote letters and taped a note which read 'Please call Dr Horder' to the pram in the hall. Towards dawn she prepared some food and left it by her sleeping children. She opened the window in their bedroom, closed the door and sealed the room with tape and towels. Then she sealed herself in the kitchen, opened the oven door, knelt down beside it and turned on the gas. She died on Monday, 11 February 1963. In her desk lay the finished manuscript of *Ariel and Other Poems* which contains 'Edge', thought to be the last poem Plath wrote. 'Edge' is dated 5 February 1963; it begins

> The woman is perfected.
> Her dead
> Body wears the smile of accomplishment...

Sylvia Plath is buried in Heptonstall, Yorkshire. On her tombstone (since removed) were carved the words (from the *Bhagavad Gita*) 'Even amidst fierce flames the golden lotus can be planted.'

The Irish poet Eavan Boland chose Sylvia Plath as 'the giant at my shoulder' in a radio programme of the same name. Here is how Boland described her:

> 'She used to get up at four a.m. in the morning, work and she said she used to hear the glassy music of the milk bottles, the blue hour between the glassy music of the milk bottles and the baby's cry. Plath died in mid-sentence, in process. When you think about how her work is going to fare I have absolutely no doubts that within poetry she is going to be somebody who defined a subject matter and considerable amount of play and surrealism. She is a very essential poet, let alone woman poet. The legend of Plath as a dark and driven and unstable young woman is a tremendous simplification of her work. Her work will endure where poetry endures and I want it to endure as language, music, challenge, poetry and not as legend.'

Dido Merwin, who knew Sylvia Plath in London, says that she was 'brilliant, articulate, overtly ambitious, energetic, efficient, organized, enviably resourceful in practical matters, blessed with a hearty appetite and (as she said herself) "an athletic physique which I possess and admire,"' she seemed infinitely stronger than she actually was. It was Plath's 'carefully projected All-Aroundness that provided the camouflage.'

POEMS

Dates refer to the year of composition. The poems as they are printed here, are in the order in which they were written.

Black Rook in Rainy Weather

On the stiff twig up there
Hunches a wet black rook
Arranging and rearranging its feathers in the rain.
I do not expect a miracle
Or an accident

To set the sight on fire
In my eye, nor seek
Any more in the desultory weather some design,
But let spotted leaves fall as they fall,
Without ceremony, or portent.

Although, I admit, I desire,
Occasionally, some backtalk
From the mute sky, I can't honestly complain:
A certain minor light may still
Lean incandescent

Out of kitchen table or chair
As if a celestial burning took
Possession of the most obtuse objects now and then —
Thus hallowing an interval
Otherwise inconsequent

By bestowing largesse, honor,
One might say love. At any rate, I now walk
Wary (for it could happen
Even in dull, ruinous landscape); sceptical,
Yet politic; ignorant

Of whatever angel may choose to flare
Suddenly at my elbow. I only know that a rook
Ordering its black feathers can so shine
As to seize my senses, haul
My eyelids up, and grant

A brief respite from fear
Of total neutrality. With luck,
Trekking stubborn through this season
Of fatigue, I shall
Patch together a content

Of sorts. Miracles occur,
If you care to call those spasmodic
Tricks of radiance miracles. The wait's begun again,
The long wait for the angel,
For that rare, random descent.

Glossary

Line 8 desultory: disconnected.

Line 10 portent: omen; significant sign of something to come.

Line 15 Lean: a variant reading is Leap.

Line 15 incandescent: shining brightly.

Line 17 celestial: heavenly, divine.

Line 18 obtuse: dull, insensible.

Line 19 hallowing: making holy.

Line 20 inconsequent: irrelevant; disconnected.

Line 21 largesse: plenty.

Line 23 Wary: cautious; watchful against deceptions.

Line 24 sceptical: questioning; critical.

Line 25 politic: cautious, wise.

Line 31 respite: temporary relief.

Line 37 spasmodic: in fits and starts; jerky.

Line 38 radiance: beaming light.

Line 40 that rare, random descent: echoing perhaps The Acts of the Apostles 2, when the Holy Ghost descended upon the Apostles; in art this was often portrayed in the form of a dove: 'And suddenly there came a sound from heaven as of a rushing mighty wind, and it filled all the house where they were sitting. And there appeared unto them cloven tongues like as of fire, and it sat upon each of them.'

Questions

1. Why do you think the speaker is drawn to the black rook? Does the speaker enjoy watching the rook? How can you tell?
2. What sense do you get of the speaker's mood from your first reading of the poem? Which words or phrases give you a sense of that mood?
3. 'I do not expect a miracle' (line 4) and yet 'Miracles occur' (line 36). What do you think the poet means by miracles in this poem?
4. How is this a poem about the extraordinary in the everyday? Show how the poem captures the ordinary and the extraordinary. What makes the ordinary special? Quote from the poem to support your discussion.
5. What, in your opinion, does the poet mean by 'love' (line 22)? How would you describe a state of 'total neutrality' (line 32)? Why does the speaker fear such a state?
6. The poet speaks of 'fatigue' in the closing lines of the poem. How would you describe the tone? Is it optimistic or pessimistic?
7. Do you think this is a poem that describes life as you know it? As most people know it? Give reasons for your answer.
8. Choose any three details from the poem which you found interesting and give reasons for your choice.
9. What is the significance of 'The wait's begun again' (line 38)? What do the words 'angel' and 'rare' suggest?
10. In her journals, Sylvia Plath, referring to 'Black Rook in Rainy Weather', speaks of a 'glassy brittleness'. What do you understand by that phrase? Do you recognise that quality in this particular poem and in other poems by Plath?

The Times Are Tidy

Unlucky the hero born
In this province of the stuck record
Where the most watchful cooks go jobless
And the mayor's rôtisserie turns
Round of its own accord.

There's no career in the venture
Of riding against the lizard,
Himself withered these latter-days
To leaf-size from lack of action:
History's beaten the hazard.

The last crone got burnt up
More than eight decades back
With the love-hot herb, the talking cat,
But the children are better for it,
The cow milks cream an inch thick.

Glossary

Line 2 the stuck record: when the needle becomes stuck in the groove on a vinyl record on a turntable. The poem was written in 1958, long before CDs and downloads. An image of being stuck in a groove; an image of no change.

Line 4 rôtisserie: a cooking device for roasting food on a revolving spit.

Line 11 crone: withered old woman.

Line 13 love-hot herb: herb used as a love potion?

Questions

1. What sense of present times is conveyed in this poem? What does the phrase 'stuck record' suggest?

2. Look at the images in stanza 1. What atmosphere is created through these images? Why should the hero be considered 'unlucky'?

3. Does the poet, in your opinion, like the times referred to? Give reasons for your answer. How would you describe those times politically?

4. If the present is spoken of in terms of times being tidy, how would you describe the past as described in lines 11–13?

5. What is meant, in your opinion, by the last two lines? Is the speaker pleased with the change?

6. How does the speaker view the world of the fairy tale?

Morning Song

Love set you going like a fat gold watch.
The midwife slapped your footsoles, and your bald cry
Took its place among the elements.

Our voices echo, magnifying your arrival. New statue.
In a drafty museum, your nakedness
Shadows our safety. We stand round blankly as walls.

I'm no more your mother
Than the cloud that distills a mirror to reflect its own slow
Effacement at the wind's hand.

All night your moth-breath
Flickers among the flat pink roses. I wake to listen:
A far sea moves in my ear.

One cry, and I stumble from bed, cow-heavy and floral
In my Victorian nightgown.
Your mouth opens clean as a cat's. The window square

Whitens and swallows its dull stars. And now you try
Your handful of notes;
The clear vowels rise like balloons.

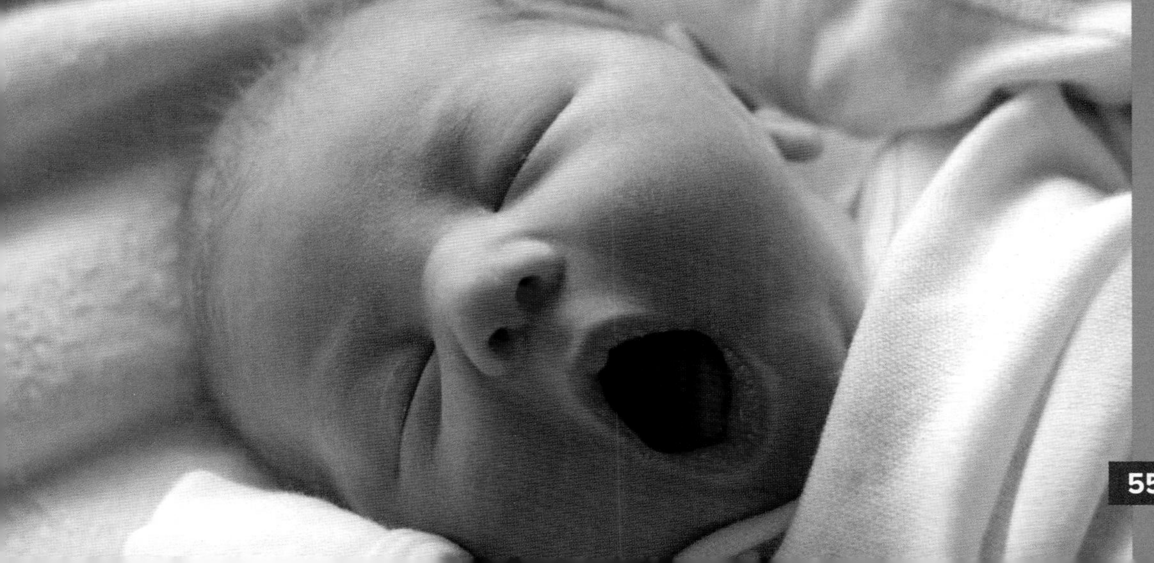

Glossary

Line 1 you: Frieda Rebecca – Plath and Hughes's daughter, born 1 April 1960 at home in their Chalcot Square flat in London.

Line 6 Shadows: casts a shadow?

Line 8–9 the cloud that distills a mirror to reflect its own slow/ Effacement at the wind's hand: the cloud drops rain which forms a puddle and the puddle reflects or mirrors the cloud as it is blown apart by the wind; an image of the relationship between parent and child.

Line 11 flat pink roses: on the wallpaper.

Line 13 cow-heavy: in this instance, a reference to her breasts heavy with milk.

Plath had miscarried on 6 February 1961; soon afterwards, she wrote 'Morning Song', a poem, which, in Anne Stevenson's words, speaks 'in curiously similar imagery both of birth and miscarriage. The tenderness "Morning Song" evinces for the baby acts at a distance: "I'm no more your mother/ Than the cloud that distills a mirror to reflect its own slow/ Effacement at the wind's hand. The child is a "new statue" in a "drafty museum" in which "We stand round blankly as walls".'

The three-line stanza used here was to become a feature of many of Plath's poems

Questions

1. Do you think the opening image is an effective one? Explain your answer.
2. What is suggested by the words 'among the elements'?
3. How does the poet see her relationship with her daughter? Which lines best convey that relationship? Examine the image of the cloud in the third stanza. What is its significance? What does it suggest about the relationship between mother and child?
4. 'Slapped. . . bald cry. . . our voices echo . . .' Trace the different sounds in the poem and comment on their effect.
5. Do you like this mother and daughter poem? Is it typical or atypical, usual or unusual? Give reasons for your answer.
6. This has been called a 'chill and beautiful poem.' Can you suggest why?

Finisterre

This was the land's end: the last fingers, knuckled and rheumatic,
Cramped on nothing. Black
Admonitory cliffs, and the sea exploding
With no bottom, or anything on the other side of it,
Whitened by the faces of the drowned.
Now it is only gloomy, a dump of rocks —
Leftover soldiers from old, messy wars.
The sea cannons into their ear, but they don't budge.
Other rocks hide their grudges under the water.

The cliffs are edged with trefoils, stars and bells
Such as fingers might embroider, close to death,
Almost too small for the mists to bother with.
The mists are part of the ancient paraphernalia —
Souls, rolled in the doom-noise of the sea.
They bruise the rocks out of existence, then resurrect them.
They go up without hope, like sighs.
I walk among them, and they stuff my mouth with cotton.
When they free me, I am beaded with tears.

Our Lady of the Shipwrecked is striding toward the horizon,
Her marble skirts blown back in two pink wings.
A marble sailor kneels at her foot distractedly, and at his foot
A peasant woman in black
Is praying to the monument of the sailor praying.
Our Lady of the Shipwrecked is three times life size,
Her lips sweet with divinity.
She does not hear what the sailor or the peasant is saying —
She is in love with the beautiful formlessness of the sea.

Gull-colored laces flap in the sea drafts
Beside the postcard stalls.
The peasants anchor them with conches. One is told:
'These are the pretty trinkets the sea hides,
Little shells made up into necklaces and toy ladies.
They do not come from the Bay of the Dead down there,
But from another place, tropical and blue,
We have never been to.
These are our crêpes. Eat them before they blow cold.'

29 September 1961

Glossary

Title: Finisterre literally the end of land: Land's End. The Finisterre/Land's End in this instance is not the well-known tip of Cornwall but westernmost tip of Brittany which Plath had visited the previous year. Plath and Ted Hughes also visited Berck-Plage where soldiers who had been wounded in the Algerian war were recovering in a sanatorium. Line 7 may refer to this.

Line 3 Admonitory: warning.

Line 10 trefoils: plants with flowers and leaves consisting of three little leaves like clover.

Line 13 paraphernalia: odds and ends; 'ancient paraphernalia' here may be a reference to a belief that souls became mists.

Line 19 Our Lady of the Shipwrecked: the Virgin Mary, who prayed for those who were shipwrecked.

Line 36 crêpes: small dessert pancakes (and an indication that the setting is French).

Ronald Hayman says of 'Finisterre': 'Beyond the admonitory black cliffs at the end of the land in 'Finisterre', the faces of the drowned are whitening the unbounded sea.

Questions

1. In the first stanza, how does the poet suggest that the headland or promontory Finisterre is dangerous, frightening, powerful? Quote from the poem to support the points you make.

2. Plath sees the rocks and the 'sea exploding' in terms of 'messy wars'. Do you think this is an effective metaphor?

3. In line 10, the speaker focuses on the trefoils. Does this change the poem? What does the speaker associate with these plants?

4. Discuss how the speaker links the mists with souls. Do you think it is an interesting and convincing image?

5. The only instance in the poem where the poet speaks in an 'I' voice is lines 17–18. How would you describe what is happening here? What does it reveal of the speaker?

6. The third stanza portrays a monument to Our Lady of the Shipwreck. How does the poet imagine her? Which details help us see Our Lady of the Shipwreck clearly? How would you describe her? Why is the reference to 'marble sailor' and 'peasant woman' interesting?

7. The poem ends with a voice other than the poet's, a voice directed at the tourist. What is the effect of this? Why do you think the speaker in lines 31–35 emphasises a different place, 'another place, tropical and blue'? What does such a detail introduce into the poem?

8. Comment on the poem's closing line. Do you think it is effective?

9. Do you think 'Finisterre' a personal or impersonal poem? Give reasons for your answer. What does 'Finisterre' reveal to us about Sylvia Plath?

10. Elizabeth Hardwick said that, in Plath's poetry, the sea imagery was 'not particularly local but rather psychological.' Discuss this statement in the light of your reading of 'Finisterre'.

Mirror

I am silver and exact. I have no preconceptions.
Whatever I see I swallow immediately
Just as it is, unmisted by love or dislike.
I am not cruel, only truthful—
The eye of a little god, four-cornered.
Most of the time I meditate on the opposite wall.
It is pink, with speckles. I have looked at it so long
I think it is a part of my heart. But it flickers.
Faces and darkness separate us over and over.

Now I am a lake. A woman bends over me,
Searching my reaches for what she really is.
Then she turns to those liars, the candles or the moon.
I see her back, and reflect it faithfully.
She rewards me with tears and an agitation of hands.
I am important to her. She comes and goes.
Each morning it is her face that replaces the darkness.
In me she has drowned a young girl, and in me an old woman
Rises toward her day after day, like a terrible fish.

23 October 1961

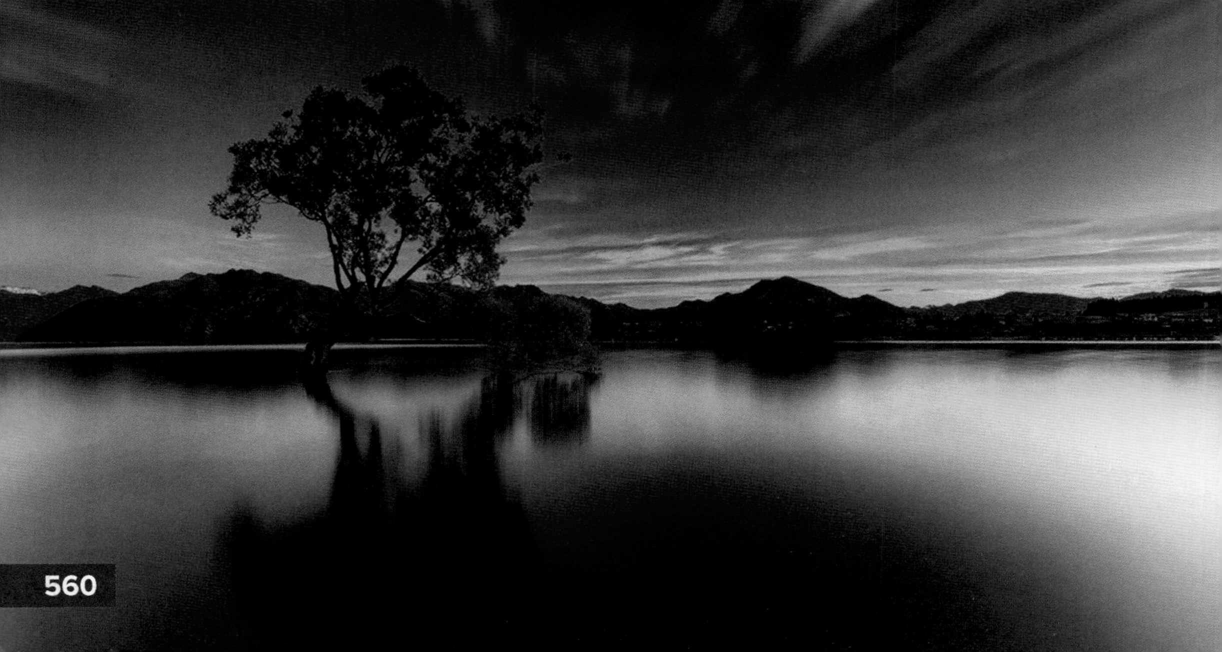

Glossary

Line 1 silver: this has been interpreted by some readers as a play on Sylvia.

Line 1 preconceptions: pre-formed ideas; thoughts already formed.

Line 11 reaches: range, scope.

Line 14 agitation: disturbance.

'Mirror' was written four days before Plath's twenty-ninth birthday.

Ronald Hayman comments: 'the looking-glass measures the movement towards death...she empathises with the looking-glass which always swallows what it sees, but unlike the moon and the candles, which are both romantic, it tells the truth. The woman who looks in the mirror every day has drowned a young girl in it and sees an old woman rising towards her like a terrible fish.'

Questions

1. The speaker here is the mirror. What does it say of the woman who looks in the mirror? If the woman spoke, how different would it be?
2. How would you describe the attitude of the mirror in the first section (lines 1–9)? Which words best express that attitude in your opinion?
3. Do you think that the image of the lake (line 10) is an interesting one? Give reasons for your answer.
4. Why are the 'candles or the moon' seen as 'liars'? What relationship exists between the mirror and the woman?
5. Which words suggest unease, fear, terror? Discuss the effectiveness of the simile in the final line.
6. Plath uses no rhyme here. What would rhyme have contributed? Do you think rhyme would have been appropriate?
7. Comment on the poet's frequent use of 'I' and its effect.

Pheasant

You said you would kill it this morning.
Do not kill it. It startles me still,
The jut of that odd, dark head, pacing

Through the uncut grass on the elm's hill.
It is something to own a pheasant,
Or just to be visited at all.

I am not mystical: it isn't
As if I thought it had a spirit.
It is simply in its element.

That gives it a kingliness, a right.
The print of its big foot last winter,
The tail-track, on the snow in our court—

The wonder of it, in that pallor,
Through crosshatch of sparrow and starling.
Is it its rareness, then? It is rare.

But a dozen would be worth having,
A hundred, on that hill — green and red,
Crossing and recrossing: a fine thing!

It is such a good shape, so vivid.
It's a little cornucopia.
It unclaps, brown as a leaf, and loud,

Settles in the elm, and is easy.
It was sunning in the narcissi.
I trespass stupidly. Let be, let be.

7 April 1962

Glossary

Line 1 You: possibly her husband Ted Hughes.

Line 3 jut: sharp forward movement, projection.

Line 7 mystical: spiritual, seeking union with God.

Line 12 court: the space enclosed by walls/buildings; the poem was written at Court Green in Devon, the home that Plath and Hughes and baby daughter moved to on 31 August 1961. Court Green had three acres of lawn, garden and orchard.

Line 13 pallor: paleness.

Line 14 crosshatch: shading by intersecting sets of parallel lines – here, a reference to the marks made by the birds in the snow.

Line 20 cornucopia: abundance, plenty.

Line 23 narcissi: in spring, thousands of daffodils and narcissi would bloom around Court Green; the place was famous for them.

Questions

1. How does the poet achieve an edgy and direct feeling in the opening lines? Look at the short sentence in line 2 and words such as 'kill', 'startles', 'jut', 'pacing.'
2. Why is the speaker so pleased with the pheasant? List those qualities and details that she finds attractive. What fascinates her about the bird?
3. The speaker denies the mystical, a belief in the divine. Are you, as reader, convinced that she is not mystical?
4. Which words best describe the 'rare' and 'vivid' pheasant in your opinion?
5. How would you describe the two different moods in the closing line?
6. Consider the use of long and short sentences and their effect in the poem.
7. Both 'Black Rook in Rainy Weather' and 'Pheasant' are poems that focus on birds. Compare the two poems and examine the effect both birds have on the speaker. Which one did you prefer and why?
8. How would you describe the differences between the 'you' and the 'I'? Do you think this poem can be read as a commentary on the differences between male and female?

Elm

For Ruth Fainlight

I know the bottom, she says. I know it with my great tap root:
It is what you fear.
I do not fear it: I have been there.

Is it the sea you hear in me,
Its dissatisfactions?
Or the voice of nothing, that was your madness?

Love is a shadow.
How you lie and cry after it
Listen: these are its hooves: it has gone off, like a horse.

All night I shall gallop thus, impetuously,
Till your head is a stone, your pillow a little turf,
Echoing, echoing.

Or shall I bring you the sound of poisons?
This is rain now, this big hush.
And this is the fruit of it: tin-white, like arsenic.

I have suffered the atrocity of sunsets.
Scorched to the root
My red filaments burn and stand, a hand of wires.

Now I break up in pieces that fly about like clubs.
A wind of such violence
Will tolerate no bystanding: I must shriek.

The moon, also, is merciless: she would drag me
Cruelly, being barren.
Her radiance scathes me. Or perhaps I have caught her.

I let her go. I let her go
Diminished and flat, as after radical surgery.
How your bad dreams possess and endow me.

I am inhabited by a cry.
Nightly it flaps out
Looking, with its hooks, for something to love.

I am terrified by this dark thing
That sleeps in me;
All day I feel its soft, feathery turnings, its malignity.

Clouds pass and disperse.
Are those the faces of love, those pale irretrievables?
Is it for such I agitate my heart?

I am incapable of more knowledge.
What is this, this face
So murderous in its strangle of branches?—

Its snaky acids kiss.
It petrifies the will. These are the isolate, slow faults
That kill, that kill, that kill.

19 April 1962

Glossary

Title: Elm the wych elm featured here grows on the shoulder of a moated prehistoric mound outside the house where Plath and Ted Hughes lived in Devon. Sylvia Plath declared Court Green and the surrounding countryside a veritable Garden of Eden but Anne Stevenson points out in *Bitter Fame: A Life of Sylvia Plath* that 'it came complete with a serpent. Sylvia herself identified it the following April, jotting hastily on a draft of her poem "Elm": "the stigma of selfhood".'

The wych elm has a rough bark, branches are fan-like and leaves are large, double-toothed, dull-green colour, and rough to the touch; brownish flowers appear in March. On good soil the wych elm may attain a girth of fifty feet.

***dedicatee:* Ruth Fainlight** – American poet; she married the novelist Alan Sillitoe.

Line 1 tap root: the main root and the strongest; it grows straight down.

Line 8 How you lie and cry after it: in *Ariel* and in the *Collected Poems* there is no full-stop after 'it'; however some editions include a full-stop at the end of line 8.

Line 10 impetuously: violently, rapidly, suddenly.

Line 15 arsenic: a violent poison; here 'the fruit of it: tin-white, like arsenic'; may be a reference to hailstones.

Line 16 atrocity: violence, cruelty.

Line 18 filaments: fibres.

Line 19 clubs: the branches are like sticks, thicker at one end, and weaponlike.

Line 23 being barren: the moon, like a sterile woman, can give no life.

Line 24 radiance: light.

Line 24 scathes: harms, injures.

Line 26 flat, as after radical surgery: the moon is compared to a woman after a mastectomy operation, flat-chested.

Line 27 endow me: have given me your qualities.

Line 33 malignity: danger, evil.

Line 35 irretrievables: things impossible to restore.

Line 40 snaky acids: snake-like poisons.

Line 41 petrifies: stupefies, turns to stone.

On a draft of 'Elm' Plath wrote 'Elm/ Jealousy/ Stigma (of selfhood)/ Pheasant'.

Ted Hughes, in a note, says of 'Elm': The house in Devon 'Court Green' was overshadowed by a giant wych-elm, flanked by two others in a single mass, growing on the shoulder of a moated prehistoric mound. This poem grew (twenty-one sheets of working drafts) from a slightly earlier fragment:

She is not easy, she is not peaceful;
She pulses like a heart on my hill.
The moon snags in her intricate nervous system.
I am excited, seeing it there.
It is like something she has caught for me.

The night is a blue pool; she is very still.
At the centre she is still, very still with wisdom.
The moon is let go, like a dead thing.
Now she herself is darkening
Into a dark world I cannot see at all.

These lines were a premature crystallisation out of four densely crowded pages of manuscript. In her next attempt, some days later, she took them up and developed out of them the final poem 'Elm'.

One of her biographers, Ronald Hayman, sees 'Elm' as a 'death-oriented' poem: 'The tree expects her to be scared of the bottom which it knows with its great tap root, but she isn't scared, she says: she has already been there.

The memory of electro-convulsive therapy helps her [Plath] to empathise with the great tree which has suffered the atrocity of sunsets and been scorched to the root. The first person singular refers to both her and the tree when she speaks of being terrified of the malign dark thing that is sleeping in her. She can feel its soft feathery turnings all day, and in the strangle of branches is a murderous face which petrifies the will.'

? Questions

1. In 'Elm,' as in 'Mirror', the poet does not speak in her own voice. As a reader, how do you react to such poems? (Prosopopoeia is the technical term for this – when a writer has an inanimate object speak in a human voice.)
2. What is your initial, overall impression of what the elm tree says of itself? Do you think this elm in any way compares with the Tree of Knowledge in the Garden of Eden?
3. Examine how the speaker refers to 'I' and 'you'. Is one the tree, the other the poet? Are 'I' and 'you' one and the same at any point in the poem?
4. What do you understand by 'I have been there'? Are there similarities between the tree and the poet?
5. Trace and examine the various sounds in the poem beginning with the sound of the sea (line 4), the sound of hooves (line 9), the sound of poisons (line 13). What do these sounds contribute to the overall effect of the poem?
6. How would you describe the words which make up this poem? Consider such words as 'gallop', 'atrocity', 'burn', 'drag'. Is the dominant impression one of harshness? Nervousness? Unease? Terror?
7. Why do you think the speaker says at line 37, 'I am incapable of more knowledge'. Comment on the final line in the poem.
8. Discuss how 'Elm' is a poem that explores suffering.
9. Reread the final three stanzas. Why are the clouds (line 34) so significant? How does the speaker view them? Why is her heart agitated? Comment on the face which has replaced the 'faces of love'. How did this come about? How would you describe the speaker's mood in the closing two lines of the poem?
10. It has been said of Sylvia Plath that she 'carried a concentration-camp around in her mind.' Does such a description fit any of the poems on your course?

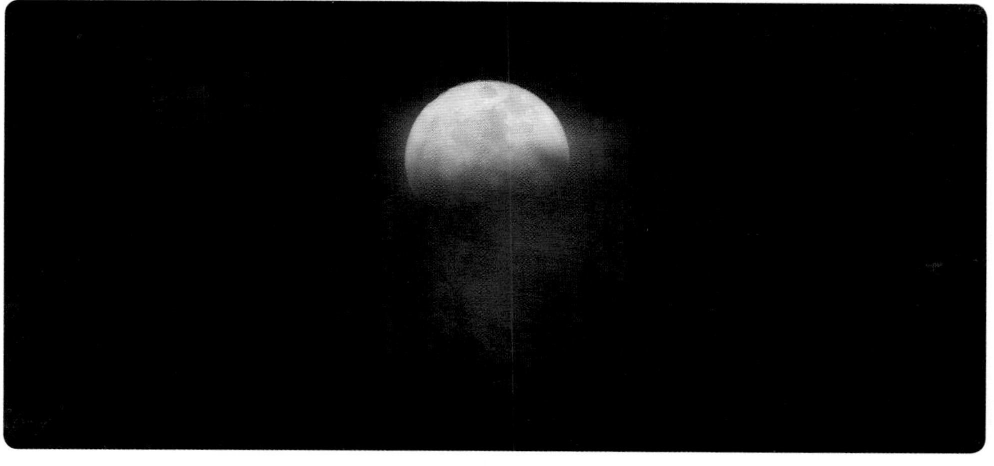

Poppies in July

Little poppies, little hell flames,
Do you do no harm?

You flicker. I cannot touch you.
I put my hands among the flames. Nothing burns.

And it exhausts me to watch you
Flickering like that, wrinkly and clear red, like the skin of a mouth.

A mouth just bloodied.
Little bloody skirts!

There are fumes that I cannot touch.
Where are your opiates, your nauseous capsules?

If I could bleed, or sleep! —
If my mouth could marry a hurt like that!

Or your liquors seep to me, in this glass capsule,
Dulling and stilling.

But colorless. Colorless.

20 July 1962

Glossary

Title: Poppies – cornfield flowers usually red but also white and yellow; opium poppy associated with drug-induced sleep – opium is extracted from white poppy seeds.

Line 10 opiates: drugs, narcotics.

Line 10 nauseous: sickening.

Line 10 capsules: little gelatine containers holding medicine.

Line 13 glass capsule: a bell jar perhaps.

Line 14 dulling and stilling: Anne Stevenson comments that when Plath was depressed 'there was a turning in on herself, a longing for nonbeing, "dulling and stilling" as in "Poppies in July."' This is one of only three poems Plath wrote in July 1962 (the others are 'The Other' and 'Words heard, by accident, over the phone'); all are directed at Assia Wevill, with whom Ted Hughes was having an affair. 'Poppies in July' is the least explicit. In Ronald Hayman's words, 'Assia's presence can be felt only indirectly, but it seems to be contributing to the appearance of the poppies, which are like little hell flames, wrinkly and clear red, or like the skin of a bloodied mouth.'

Questions

1. The title indicates that this is a poem about flowers in summer. Is it what one would expect of a poem on such a topic? When does the reader first realise that it is not a typical poem?

2. How would you describe the mind of the speaker in this poem? Which details support your opinion? What is the effect of the exclamation marks?

3. How are the poppies described by the speaker? List the different images and say whether you think there is a connection or similarity among them.

4. Does the speaker's mood change as you read through the poem? How would you describe the mood in the closing line?

The Arrival of the Bee Box

I ordered this, this clean wood box
Square as a chair and almost too heavy to lift.
I would say it was the coffin of a midget
Or a square baby
Were there not such a din in it.

The box is locked, it is dangerous.
I have to live with it overnight
And I can't keep away from it.
There are no windows, so I can't see what is in there.
There is only a little grid, no exit.

I put my eye to the grid.
It is dark, dark,
With the swarmy feeling of African hands
Minute and shrunk for export,
Black on black, angrily clambering.

How can I let them out?
It is the noise that appalls me most of all,
The unintelligible syllables.
It is like a Roman mob,
Small, taken one by one, but my god, together!

I lay my ear to furious Latin.
I am not a Caesar.
I have simply ordered a box of maniacs.
They can be sent back.
They can die, I need feed them nothing, I am the owner.

I wonder how hungry they are.
I wonder if they would forget me
If I just undid the locks and stood back and turned into a tree.
There is the laburnum, its blond colonnades,
And the petticoats of the cherry.

They might ignore me immediately
In my moon suit and funeral veil.
I am no source of honey
So why should they turn on me?
Tomorrow I will be sweet God, I will set them free.

The box is only temporary.

4 October 1962

Glossary

Line 10 grid: wire network.

Line 13 swarmy: swarm-like – as in a large, dense group.

Line 22 Caesar: Roman ruler.

Line 29 colonnades: long column-like flowering branches.

Line 32 moon suit: the boiler-suit, worn by Plath as protection when tending bees, is like that worn by an astronaut.

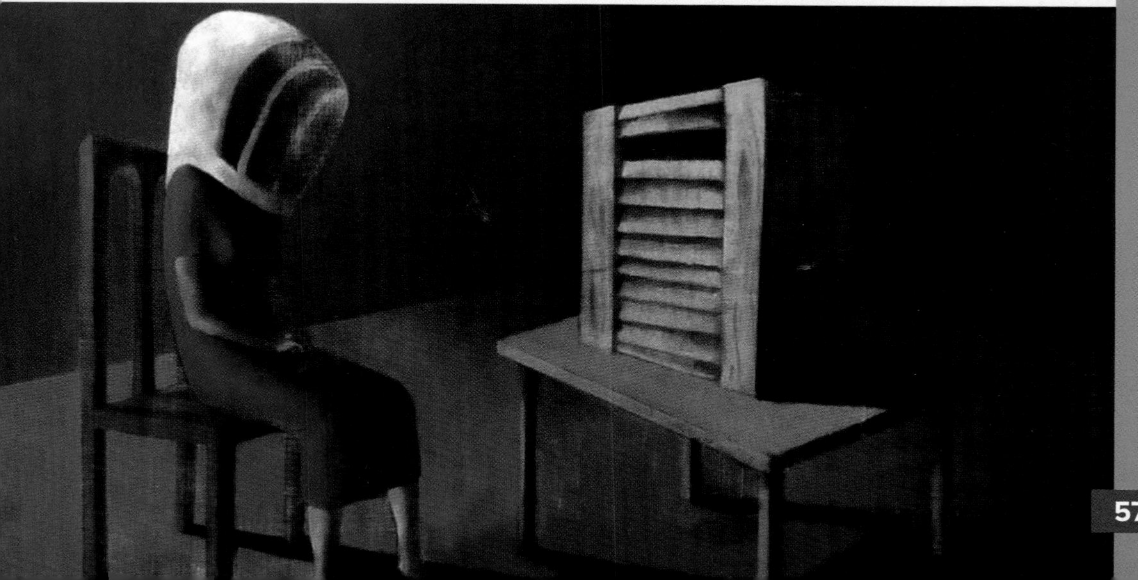

Questions

1. Would you consider this a memorable poem? Give reasons for your answer, supporting the points you make by quoting from the text.
2. How would you describe the speaker's reaction to the bee box? Fascination? Unease? Fear? Look at each stanza in turn. How does she portray herself?
3. Discuss how Plath creates a dramatic atmosphere in 'The Arrival of the Bee Box'. Which words and phrases are particularly effective?
4. What has this poem to say about power and control? Consider the significance of 'Caesar' and 'sweet God'.
5. In this thirty-six line poem, the speaker uses 'I' eighteen times. Consider the 'I' phrases in sequence. Read them aloud. What is the effect of the poet's use of 'I' here?
6. Choose three interesting images and say why you found them so.
7. Is the subject matter of bees in a bee box something that you would associate with Plath? Compare and contrast this poem with other poems by Plath that focus on nature – 'Black Rook in Rainy Weather', 'Pheasant', 'Elm', 'Poppies in July'. Is Sylvia Plath a typical nature poet?
8. Comment on the way the poem is shaped on the page. In your answer, you should consider Plath's use of the long and short line, her use of repetition, the stanza divisions and the final, separate line.
9. Of this poem, Nuala Ní Dhomhnaill says: 'The poem fairly buzzes with energy, not the least of which is the energy of simple, colloquial words and phrases – "coffin of a midget," "a square baby," "I have simply ordered a box of maniacs," yet the whole is greater than its parts.' What, in your opinion, is the 'whole' of the poem?
10. Compare and contrast Elizabeth Bishop's poem 'The Fish' and Sylvia Plath's poem 'The Arrival of the Bee Box' as poems that explore the significance of power and control.

Child

Your clear eye is the one absolutely beautiful thing.
I want to fill it with color and ducks,
The zoo of the new

Whose names you meditate—
April snowdrop, Indian pipe,
Little

Stalk without wrinkle,
Pool in which images
Should be grand and classical

Not this troublous
Wringing of hands, this dark
Ceiling without a star.

28 January 1963

Glossary

Line 5 Indian pipe: leafless American plant with single flower resembling a tobacco pipe.

Line 6/7 Little/Stalk: small stem of plant.

Line 9 classical: beautiful, noble.

Line 10 troublous: full of troubles, disturbed.

Ronald Hayman, in *The Death and Life of Sylvia Plath*, sums up this poem as follows: '[Plath's] frustrated yearning for domestic happiness is tenderly expressed in 'Child', which juxtaposes darkness and lamentation with beautiful young eyes which ought to be feasted on colours and ducks.'

Sylvia Plath's son, Nicholas, was born on 17 January 1962.

This poem, dated 28 January 1963, was written just two weeks before Plath died on 11 February 1963.

Questions

1. How would you describe the speaker's tone in the poem's opening line? Why do you think it is the longest line in the poem?

2. The American essayist and poet Henry David Thoreau said that 'every child begins the world again'. Do you think the speaker here conveys a similar idea? Give reasons for your answer.

3. There is a clear difference between the world of the child and the speaker's world. Which words best capture that difference, in your opinion?

4. What mood is created by the images in the poem's final stanza? Do you think this is an optimistic or a pessimistic poem?

5. What effect did this poem have on you? Of the poems by Plath on your course, which one did you like best? Admire the most?

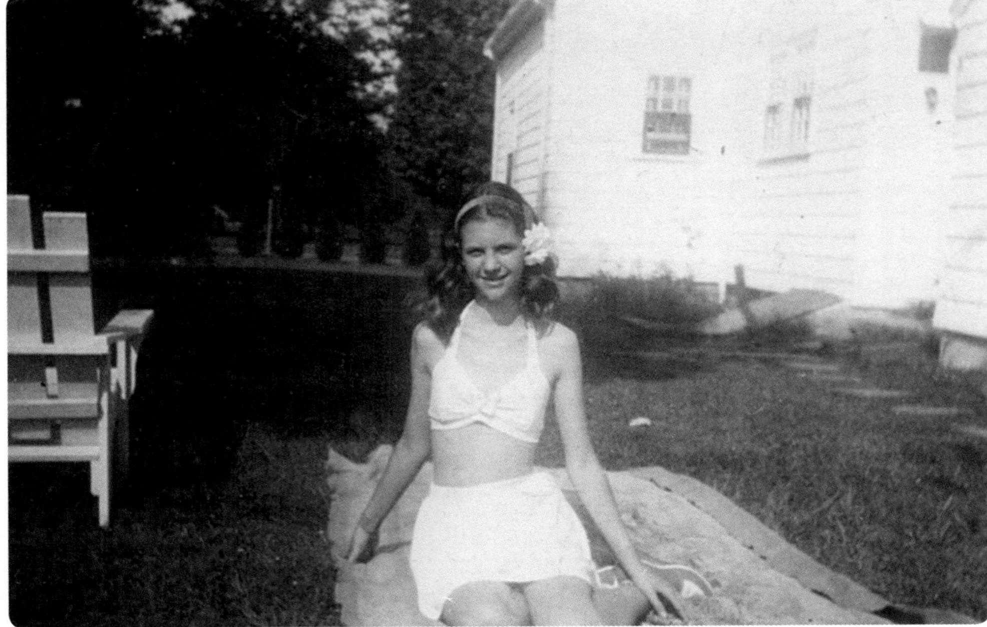

Sylvia Plath as a teenager.

> I am silver and exact. I have no preconceptions.

Its impersonal statement-like tone changes in line 2 and the mirror becomes all-devouring, ruthless:

> Whatever I see I swallow immediately
> Just as it is, unmisted by love or dislike.
> I am not cruel, only truthful —
> The eye of a little god, four-cornered.

Anyone who looks in the mirror at a particular moment in time is swallowed up. That moment can never come again and, therefore, the mirror tells the story of our transient nature. The mirror can be passive (it reflects) or active (it swallows) but 'Most of the time I meditate on the opposite wall'.

The mirror emphasises its truth-telling qualities. If the viewer thinks it is being shown cruel reality the mirror reminds us that 'I am not cruel, only truthful'.

The constant gaze of the mirror suggests an unchanging state:

> Most of the time I meditate on the opposite wall.
> It is pink, with speckles. I have looked at it so long
> I think it is a part of my heart.

However, the view is altered by faces and darkness:

> But it flickers.
> Faces and darkness separate us over and over.

There is, therefore, constant movement and change. It is also emotionless. The mirror captures the world 'unmisted by love or dislike'.

In the second stanza, the first word registers a more particular emphasis. The focus has shifted from the general to the particular:

> Now I am a lake.

The image of the lake suggests hidden depths, danger. The mirror may still be silver and exact but now, instead of returning the image it reflects, the voice of the mirror in stanza 2 speaks of how a woman who looks in the mirror looks inwards and downwards:

> Now I am a lake. A woman bends over me,
> Searching my reaches for what she really is.

The mirror tells a truth deeper than surface reality. It is possible for the woman to see herself in the mirror 'for what she really is': once a young girl and one day she will, inevitably, see herself as an old woman. The speaker dismisses candles and the moon. They do not reveal the truth in the way the mirror does. Their light is deceptive and, unlike the mirror, they do not reflect the woman 'faithfully'. However, the harsh reality brings little comfort; the mirror is rewarded for telling the truth 'with tears and an agitation of hands'. The woman is clearly distressed but the mirror also knows that:

> I am important to her.

This woman returns to the mirror again and again – 'She comes and goes'. The closing lines speak of how daily the darkness gives way to the woman's ageing face. Youth must give way to old age; the word 'rises' in this context has a sinister quality and the final line contains a disturbing and unusual image of old age as 'a terrible fish':

> Each morning it is her face that replaces the darkness.
> In me she has drowned a young girl, and in me an old woman
> Rises toward her day after day, like a terrible fish.

The mirror is a lake and out of its depths this terrible fish rises up. The passing of time is captured in phrases such as 'over and over', 'comes and goes', 'Each morning', 'day after day'. The tone in the closing lines remains impersonal; the speaker states the harsh facts. The mirror reminds us of our mortality.

Pheasant

There is an urgency here from the outset. The speaker is addressing someone directly. The message is urgent; the sentence structure is urgent. In 'Black Rook in Rainy Weather' Plath valued the bird for what it was and for what it might offer. Here the speaker's tone is, at first, an order ('Do not kill it'), then explanation ('It's a little cornucopia') and finally a plea ('Let be, let be').

The poem refers to an earlier moment in the opening line and leads immediately to the present moment:

> You said you would kill it this morning.
> Do not kill it.

And for the remainder of the poem the speaker gives many reasons why the pheasant should be spared.

The speaker is both surprised and frightened by the pheasant:

> It startles me still

Then, in language that imitates the bird's abrupt, jutting movements, we are given a sense of its presence as witnessed by the poet:

> The jut of that odd, dark head, pacing
>
> Through the uncut grass on the elm's hill.

The speaker thinks that the bird bestows something special:

> It is something to own a pheasant,
> Or just to be visited at all

And then the poet highlights all of the pheasant's special qualities, its 'kingliness', its 'rareness'.

Plath rejects any suggestion of the divine when she says:

> I am not mystical; It isn't
> As if I thought it had a spirit.

And explains that:

> It is simply in its element.

She remembers the pheasant in last winter's snow, its impressive big footprint, compared to the sparrow's and the starling's prints.

The poem celebrates the pheasant and charts the poet's pleasure in seeing the bird. For her it is 'a little cornucopia', a sign of abundance and plenty. The poem remembered the bird in the snow but it ends with the immediate April present, the bird settled in the elm tree and sunning in the narcissi. The poet sees herself as an intruder in the pheasant's world ('I trespass stupidly') and ends with the repeated plea of 'Let be, let be'.

That the speaker is convinced that she is right and that the person whom she addresses in lines 1 and 2 is wrong can be seen in the very direct, clear statements such as 'It is something to own a pheasant', 'It is rare', 'It is such a good shape', 'It's a little cornucopia'. The poem is framed by short dramatic sentences 'Do not kill it.' and 'Let be, let be.'

The mood at the outset is edgy, uneasy, nervous, but becomes more confident as the speaker expresses the belief that the bird does not deserve to be killed. The admission that the speaker feels somehow inferior in the presence of this kingly, rare bird captures a mood of humility, and the words 'Let be, let be' indicate a calming and hopeful mood.

Elm

Plath has created a poem in which the deep-rooted elm speaks. It speaks of itself, its life, its experiences, its suffering; but Plath also has the elm tree speak, as it were, to Plath directly, and at one stage in the poem the voice of the elm changes to the voice of a woman. The tree becomes the woman and the woman becomes the tree; they seem to inter-penetrate each other.

Plath's poetry has been called the poetry of extremity and 'Elm' is a poem that speaks of knowing 'the bottom', of reaching an extreme. Martin Booth says that Plath's poetry 'has a beautiful weirdness to it, an inviting malevolence, that the world is dark . . . and it seeks to set a mood as much as tell you something concrete.' The mood in 'Elm' is one of the most striking things about it; the poem creates feelings of suffering and despair. The psychological states explored and described in the poem are captured through haunting and memorable imagery and, because it examines the unconscious as well as the conscious, it is not always possible to grasp exactly what the poet means in every line.

When we read the opening lines, Seamus Heaney says, 'the owls in our own tree branches begin to halloo in recognition'; in other words we can sense what the poet is speaking of, though we may not be able to describe it. The voice in the opening lines tells of a deep dark sense of its own self. It has known the bottom, has plunged the dark depths. The elm knows no fear but it knows that 'you' (the reader? Plath?) fears the bottom:

> I know the bottom, she says. I know it with my great tap root:
> It is what you fear.
> do not fear it: I have been there.

There is a chilling quality to these opening lines. 'I know . . . ', 'I know. . . ' announces the tree's dark knowledge. The only comfort offered to one who fears 'the bottom' is contained in the line 'I do not fear it: I have been there'. The 'great tap root' is a physical image for a journeying deep into the ground; it could become an image for the individual journeying deep within itself.

The elm speaks in the voice of a woman ('she says'), and, though the tree is featured as a powerful physical entity, it is also associated with states of mind. It is this psychological exploration that gives the poem its power and which forges the connection between elm tree and the 'you' of the poem.

The speaker tells of madness and the transient nature of love in stanzas 2 and 3. The tone is matter-of-fact 'Love is a shadow') and pitying or gently mocking perhaps ('How you lie and cry after it').

> Is it the sea you hear in me,
> Its dissatisfactions?
> Or the voice of nothing, that was your madness?
>
> Love is a shadow.
> How you lie and cry after it
> Listen: these are its hooves: it has gone off like a horse.

The image of the sea and the image of the horse's hooves are images of powerful movement and in Plath's imagination the tree seems to contain these. The elm tree is portrayed as a restless force and it becomes the galloping horse. The tree sees itself as moving 'impetuously' in darkness, and the woman experiencing the absence of love knows no comfort:

> All night I shall gallop thus, impetuously,
> Till your head is a stone, your pillow a little turf,
> Echoing, echoing.

With 'your head' and 'your pillow', the focus shifts again to the human figure, the 'you' of line 2; it is as if there is a powerful link between the tree and the person to whom the tree speaks: both know turmoil and disturbing experiences. For the woman, love has disappeared and she is left suffering ('your head is a stone, your pillow a little turf'). The repeated 'echoing' intensifies the pain.

The tree then speaks of 'the sound of poisons', the rain, the hush that follows, and the impression is one of cold, harsh, violent offerings:

> Or shall I bring you the sound of poisons?
> This is the rain now, this big hush.
> And this is the fruit of it: tin-white, like arsenic.

At times, the poem speaks in the voice of the tree and the poet. Seamus Heaney points this out: 'The elm utters an elmy consciousness, it communicates in tree-speak: "This is the rain now, this big hush". But the elm speaks poet-consciousness also.' At times we are listening to the elm describing its being a tree and at other times we hear the voice of a woman describing her own dark and troubled interior world. When the tree, for example, speaks of how it has been burnt and scorched by sunsets it tells of a natural phenomenon but it could also serve as an indirect reference to Plath's own experience of electro-convulsive therapy.

For Heaney 'What is exciting to observe in this poem is the mutation [change/ alteration] of voice; from being a relatively cool literary performance, aware of its behaviour as a stand-in for a tree, it gradually turns inward and intensifies'.

The tree can speak of its experiences as a tree, of rain and sunsets, of violence and pain:

> I have suffered the atrocity of sunsets.
> Scorched to the root
> My red filaments burn and stand, a hand of wires.

External forces cannot allow the tree to remain a spectator or bystander. The tree must respond; it must call out, must shriek:

> Now I will break up in pieces that fly about like clubs.
> A wind of such violence
> Will tolerate no bystanding: I must shriek.

The storm and even the sunset are destructive; the only release comes in crying out.

It is difficult at times to separate tree and woman. The following lines seem to refer to the tree:

> The moon, also, is merciless: she would drag me
> Cruelly being barren.
> Her radiance scares me. Or perhaps I have caught her

Here, the tree, having suffered sunsets and storm, now suffers because of the moon; it is an image of the cruel moon being caught in the branches of the elm. The image of the moon as wounded female figure, diminished and flat as after a mastectomy, emerges in the following lines:

> I let her go. I let her go
> Diminished and flat, as after radical surgery.
> How your bad dreams possess and endow me.

Here, the tree accuses the woman of transferring her bad dreams onto it; the tree has taken on, has been endowed with the woman's attributes.

The tenth stanza is an expression of fierce longing, but the cry in search of love is seen in terms of an owl, who inhabits the elm, seeking out its prey with destructive 'hooks':

> I am inhabited by a cry
> Nightly it flaps out
> Looking, with its hooks, for something to love.

The poem is at its most personal in stanza 11. It is as if the voice of the elm tree fuses with the voice of the woman:

> I am terrified by this dark thing
> That sleeps in me;
> All day I feel its soft, feathery turnings, its malignity.

At one level, it is the owl sleeping within the tree, but it can also be interpreted as the dark, frightening unknown with the woman. This recognition of danger and evil ('malignity') frightens. It is a sleeping 'thing' but also moving, turning.

The final three stanzas describe passing and disappearing clouds and the speaker asks if they are the pale faces of love, faces that can never be found again. The speaker is troubled and agitated. A language that was predominantly statement at this point becomes questioning:

> Clouds pass and disperse.
> Are those the faces of love, those pale irretrievables?
> Is it for such I agitate my heart?

And if the elm is a tree of knowledge the speaker is incapable of more:

> I am incapable of more knowledge.

Knowledge is rejected here, presumably, because it is hurtful: the knowledge that the faces of love have disappeared and will never return.

The final image in the poem is one of a murderous face and 'its snaky acids kiss'. The faces of love, like the clouds, have disappeared and in their place is this murderous face. This could be a reference to the serpent in the tree of knowledge which has been depicted with a human face. This face is caught within the branches and the effect on the speaker is one of terror. The tone is nervous and abrupt:

> What is this, this face
> So murderous in its strangle of branches?—

The face that the speaker now sees is petrifying. Her imagination has created this face within the elm tree. It is of her own making, born out of her inner self, and she ends with the realisation that such moments are dangerous and destructive:

> What is this, this face
> So murderous in its strangle of branches?—
> It petrifies the will. These are the isolate, slow faults
> That kill, that kill, that kill

The poem ends with an admission that such imaginings are deadly. They are destructive. They are born of herself and, though they are 'isolate, slow', there is something inevitable about them. They are faults 'That kill, that kill, that kill', a line which has a chilling, doomed quality to it.

Each of the three-line stanzas contains a short line and a variable longer line. The use of long and short lines gives the poem an uncertain structure mirroring, perhaps, the unease within the poem.

'Elm' is a poem which, in Seamus Heaney's words, comes from a place of suffering, 'from the ultimate suffering and decision in Sylvia Plath'. It is a difficult and complex poem and, like the state of unease and agitation which occasioned it, it would be impossible to simplify.

Poppies in July

The title announces summer flowers, but by the end of the poem's first line the flowers have acquired a dangerous and sinister quality. The speaker sees them as 'little hell flames'. The poppies are untouchable; if the poet puts her hands among the flowers, they have no effect:

> Little poppies, little hell flames,
> Do you do no harm?
>
> You flicker. I cannot touch you.
> I put my hands among the flames. Nothing burns.

The repeated 'little' in the opening line suggests tenderness but 'hell flames' alters the image and creates a sense of evil. Putting her hands among the flames suggests a impulse for self-inflicted suffering but 'Nothing burns'.

The poppies are exhausting and unattractive. Other images follow, unusual or unattractive or both:

> And it exhausts me to watch you
> Flickering like that, wrinkly and clear red, like the skin of a mouth.
>
> A mouth just bloodied.
> Little bloody skirts!

All description is subjective and the way Plath sees these poppies in July reveals something of Plath's frame of mind. Why should these poppies be unattractive, dangerous and fascinating to her? She does not tell the reader. The link made in the poem between the wrinkly, clear red poppies and an injured mouth presents the reader with the presence or the possibility of physical violence.

There is a shift in focus from line 9. The poppies are no longer before us but the speaker wishes for the drugged state the poppy is associated with. Violence or sleep are seen as preferred states to her present one. The speaker longs for escape and the opiates of the poppies are seen as a means of releasing her into a numbed, inert state where everything would be 'colorless. Colorless'.

In the opening stanzas, the poppies are alive and colourful, flame red and bloody and flickering, but their constant movement and colour are rejected for a world drained of colour and inert. The poem moves quietly towards a death-wish. Plath writes that the opiates are 'nauseous'; she is not blind to the sickening quality of the drug and yet she chooses it, which suggests her determination and desperation.

The question marks and the exclamation marks indicate a fascination (line 2), a feeling of repulsion (line 8), a desperation (line 10) and an intense longing (lines 11 and 12).

The Arrival of the Bee Box

The subject matter or the little drama of this poem is straightforward: 'I have ordered a box of bees for a beehive in the garden'. What is remarkable and interesting about this poem, like so many of Sylvia Plath's poems, is her response and reaction to the box of bees when it is delivered. There is no other person mentioned in the poem and the experience of viewing the swarm of bees is fascinating, compulsive and intense.

The poem begins in a matter-of-fact way:

> I ordered this, this clean wood box

However, Plath's individual and unusual way of viewing things can be seen in the imagery, a mixture of domestic and eerily strange. This clean wood box is:

> Square as a chair and almost too heavy to lift.
> I would say it was the coffin of a midget
> Or a square baby
> Were there not such a din in it.

The 'coffin', 'midget', 'square baby' all suggest the negative, the abnormal. The bee box, within three lines, has become something strange and sinister. The first stanza works on the eye and the ear: lines 2–4 give us the shape, line 5, with its onomatopoeic 'din in it', gives us the sound.

Though the box is locked, it is dangerous and most of the poem records Plath's total fascination with the trapped bees: 'I can't keep away from it'. There is no escape, but the speaker describes how she is drawn to the world of the bees within the box. The language is stark, straightforward, as in:

> There are no windows, so I can't see what is in there

But then, in a series of powerful images, the bees become imprisoned, badly treated Africans and a Roman mob. Her thinking about them as black slaves prompts her to free them ('How can I let them out?'):

> I put my eye to the grid.
> It is dark, dark,
> With the swarmy feeling of African hands
> Minute and shrunk for export,
> Black on black, angrily clambering.

The repetition in 'dark, dark' and 'Black on black', the sensuous details of 'swarmy' and 'shrunk', the energy of 'angrily clambering' create a hidden, claustrophobic scene of heat, dark oppression and helpless desperation. With the question 'How can I let them out?' comes a different tone. There was a distancing in the opening lines; gradually the speaker is more and more involved.

The noise terrifies her and the image of the bees as an unruly Roman mob suggests chaos and danger. She saw them as Africans; she hears them as Romans:

> I lay my ear to furious Latin.
> I am not a Caesar.
> I have simply ordered a box of maniacs.

It is then that she reconsiders her role. Though she saw them as frighteningly noisy, she now views herself as all-powerful and determining:

> They can be sent back.
> They can die, I need feed them nothing, I am the owner.

With these statements, she imagines herself playing at Caesar. She is in total control. The bees are entirely dependent on her and a more caring note is introduced:

> I wonder how hungry they are.
> I wonder if they would forget me
> If I just undid the locks and stood back and turned into a tree.
> There is the laburnum, its blond colonnades,
> And the petticoats of the cherry.

There is also a wonderful sense of the bees in their element – not unnaturally locked in a square box – but free to visit the glorious and lyrical laburnum and cherry trees. The contrast between the confined, crowded world of the box and the freedom that is possible causes the speaker to dwell on how it is possible for her to play 'sweet God'. She is 'not a Caesar' and therefore incapable of controlling a Roman mob but she is empowered and capable of releasing the bee prisoners: 'Tomorrow' 'I will set them free'.

Here the speaker is active, not passive. The speaker's presence is felt throughout: ten sentences begin with 'I' and 'I' is used eighteen times in all. She in control, not a victim, and the furious, frantic energy of the bees will end because of her. The poem explores the possibility of power and control and the poem concludes: 'The box is only temporary'.

Sylvia Plath's father, a distinguished entomologist, who died when she was eight, had written a standard work on bees: *Bumblebees and Their Ways*. Even the subject matter of a poem such as 'The Arrival of the Bee Box' would have special significance and resonance for Otto Plath's daughter.

Child

It is difficult not to read Sylvia Plath's poems in the light of her life and death. Knowing that she wrote 'Child' on 28 January 1963 and that she died, two weeks later, by her own hand on 11 February 1963 at the age of thirty, the poem becomes charged with a heartbreaking sadness. It is one of the last things Plath wrote (she wrote eight other poems after 'Child') and one of the most poignant. It celebrates her child; it expresses her love for her child and it tells of her own disturbed, troubled state.

The poem begins with an image of beauty, health and happiness. The tone is immediate and involved. The longest line in the poem, the opening line, expresses total joy. There is a longing to give:

> Your clear eye is the one absolutely beautiful thing.
> I want to fill it with color and ducks,
> The zoo of the new

The poem becomes a collection of nursery toys, beautiful things, most of its one sentence offering a sense of the child's potential, its life ahead. 'The zoo of the new' is effective in summoning up a sense of delight and excitement, just like the delight and excitement in a young child on visiting a zoo. This is what should be, the poet is saying; this is what she wants: delights and wonders, those things that will bring happiness.

> Whose names you meditate—
> April snowdrop, Indian pipe

Life's fragile beauty is contained in the image of the snowdrop; the image of the 'Little/ Stalk without wrinkle' suggests newness and freshness. The mother sees her child as a pool:

> Pool in which images
> Should be grand and classical

The poem so far paints a hopeful picture of child and childhood, but it ends with a dark and agitated reflection in the pool of childhood. It is how Plath sees herself, projecting her anxieties and sorrows on to the child. The child should only see things that are noble and dignified:

> Not this troublous
> Wringing of hands, this dark
> Ceiling without a star.

In contrast with the life-enhancing words and images in the earlier part of the poem, these final words are negative and grim. The speaker undoubtedly loves her child but seems helpless and unable to protect it from harm.

Prescribed Poetry
at Leaving Certificate Higher Level

The "new" poetry course was first examined in 2001. Below are the eight poets prescribed, each year, since then. Names in bold indicate the poets on the exam paper that particular year. [In 2009, a Paper II exam paper was inadvertently handed out to a group of pupils when they ought to have been given Paper I. The four prescribed poets were seen by that group and as a result a substitute Paper II was sat on a Saturday morning and at a cost of one million euros. Originally the paper carried Larkin, Longley, Mahon and Rich. In the substitute paper, Longley was replaced by Montague.]

2001 **Bishop** Boland Dickinson Heaney **Keats Larkin Longley** Shakespeare.

2002 **Bishop Boland** Dickinson Heaney Keats Larkin **Longley Shakespeare**.

2003 Bishop **Donne Frost Heaney** Hopkins Mahon **Plath** Yeats.

2004 Dickinson Frost Heaney **Hopkins Kavanagh Mahon Plath** Wordsworth.

2005 **Boland Dickinson Eliot** Heaney Kavanagh Longley Wordsworth **Yeats**.

2006 **Bishop Donne** Eliot **Hardy** Hopkins **Longley** Plath Yeats.

2007 Bishop Donne **Eliot Frost** Kavanagh **Montague Plath** Yeats.

2008 Boland **Donne** Frost **Larkin Mahon** Montague Plath **Rich**.

2009 **Bishop Keats** Larkin [Longley*] Mahon **Montague*** Rich **Walcott**.

2010 Boland **Eliot Kavanagh** Keats Longley **Rich** Walcott **Yeats**

2011 **Boland Dickinson Frost** Hopkins Kavanagh Rich Wordsworth **Yeats**.

2012 Boland Heaney Frost **Kavanagh Kinsella Larkin** Plath **Rich**.

2013 **Bishop Hopkins** Kinsella **Mahon Plath** Rich Shakespeare Wordsworth.

2014 Bishop **Dickinson** Heaney Kinsella **Larkin** Mahon **Plath Yeats**.

2015 Dickinson Donne **Frost Hardy Montague Ní Chuilleanáin** Plath Yeats

2016 **Bishop Dickinson Durcan Eliot** Larkin Ní Chuilleanáin Plath Yeats

2017 **Bishop Boland Donne** Durcan Eliot Hopkins **Keats** Plath

2018 Boland Durcan **Frost** Hopkins Keats **Larkin Montague Ní Chuilleanáin**

2019 Bishop Heaney Hopkins Kennelly Lawrence Ní Chuilleanáin Plath Yeats

2020 Boland Dickinson Durcan Frost Lawrence Ní Chuilleanáin Rich Wordsworth

2021 Bishop Boland Durcan Frost Heaney Hopkins Keats Plath

2022 Bishop Dickinson Keats Kennelly Lawrence Rich Wordsworth Yeats

Questions from Past Papers

Elizabeth Bishop

- 'From the poetry of Elizabeth Bishop that you have studied, select the poems that, in your opinion, best demonstrate her skilful use of language and imagery to confront life's harsh realities.'

Justify your selection by demonstrating Bishop's skilful use of language and imagery to confront life's harsh realities in the poems you have chosen. [2017]

- 'Bishop uses highly detailed observation, of people, places and events, to explore unique personal experiences in her poetry.'

Discuss this statement, supporting your answer with reference to the poetry of Elizabeth Bishop on your course. [2016]

- 'Bishop's carefully judged use of language aids the reader to uncover the intensity of feeling in her poetry.'

To what extent do you agree or disagree with the above statement? Support your answer with reference to the poetry of Elizabeth Bishop on your course. [2013]

- 'Elizabeth Bishop poses interesting questions delivered by means of a unique style.'

Do you agree with this assessment of her poetry? Your answer should focus on both themes and stylistic features. Support your points with the aid of suitable reference to the poems you have studied. [2009]

- 'Reading the poetry of Elizabeth Bishop.'

Write out the text of a talk that you would give to your class in response to the above title.
Your talk should include the following:
- Your reactions to her themes or subject matter.
- What you personally find interesting in her style of writing.

Refer to the poems by Elizabeth Bishop that you have studied. [2006]

- 'The poetry of Elizabeth Bishop appeals to the modern reader for many reasons.'

Write an essay in which you outline the reasons why poems by Elizabeth Bishop have this appeal. [2002]

- 'Introducing Elizabeth Bishop.'

Write out the text of a short presentation you would make to your friends or class group under the above title. Support your point of view by reference to or quotation from the poetry of Elizabeth Bishop that you have studied. [2001]

Eavan Boland

- 'Boland makes effective use of symbols and metaphors to explore personal experiences and deliver penetrating truths about society.'

To what extent do you agree or disagree with this statement? Support your answer with reference to the poetry of Eavan Boland on your course. [2017]

- 'Boland's reflective insights are expressed through her precise use of language.'

Write your response to this statement, supporting your answer with suitable reference to the poetry on your course. [2011]

- 'The appeal of Eavan Boland's poetry.'

Using the above title, write an essay outlining what you consider to be the appeal of Boland's poetry. Support your points by reference to the poetry of Eavan Boland on your course. [2005]

- 'Write a personal response to the poetry of Eavan Boland.'

Support the points you make by reference to the poetry of Boland that you have studied. [2002]

Paul Durcan

- 'Durcan takes a narrative approach to explore a variety of issues in poems of great emotional honesty.'

Discuss this statement, supporting your answer with reference to the poetry of Paul Durcan on your course. [2016]

Robert Frost

- 'From your study of the poetry of Robert Frost on your course, select the poems that, in your opinion, best demonstrate how the poet helps us to understand the darker aspects of his poetic vision through his effective use of poetic narrative and dramatic scenes.'

Justify your selection by demonstrating how Robert Frost helps you to understand the darker aspects of his poetic vision through his effective use of poetic narrative and dramatic scenes in the poems you have selected. [2018]

- 'Frost communicates rich insights into human experience using language that is both accessible and appealing.'

Discuss this statement, supporting your answer with reference to the poetry of Robert Frost on your course. [2015]

- 'Frost's simple style is deceptive and a thoughtful reader will see layers of meaning in his poetry.'

Do you agree with this assessment of his poetry? Write a response, supporting your points with the aid of suitable reference to the poems on your course. [2011]

- 'Robert Frost – a poet of sadness?'

Write an introduction to the poetry of Robert Frost using the above title. Your introduction should address his themes and the impact of his poetry on you as a reader. Support your points with reference to the poems you have studied. [2007]

- 'We enjoy poetry for its ideas and for its language.'

Using the above statement as your title, write an essay on the poetry of Robert Frost. Support your points by reference to the poetry by Robert Frost on your course. [2003]

Seamus Heaney

- 'Dear Seamus Heaney . . . '

Write a letter to Seamus Heaney telling him how you responded to some of his poems on your course. Support the points you make by detailed reference to the poems you choose to write about. [2003]

Gerard Manley Hopkins

- 'Hopkins's innovative style displays his struggle with what he believes to be fundamental truths.'

In your opinion, is this a fair assessment of his poetry? Support your answer with suitable reference to the poetry of Gerard Manley Hopkins on your course. [2013]

- 'There are many reasons why the poetry of Gerard Manley Hopkins appeals to his readers.'

In response to the above statement, write an essay on the poetry of Hopkins. Your essay should focus clearly on the reasons why the poetry is appealing and should refer to the poetry on your course. [2004]

John Keats

- 'Keats uses sensuous language and vivid imagery to express a range of profound tensions.'

To what extent do you agree or disagree with this statement? Support your answer with reference to the poetry of John Keats on your course. [2017]

- 'John Keats presents abstract ideas in a style that is clear and direct.'

To what extent do you agree or disagree with this assessment of his poetry? Support your points with reference to the poetry on your course. [2009]

- 'Often we love a poet because of the feelings his/her poems create in us.'

Write about the feelings John Keats's poetry creates in you and the aspects of the poems (their content and/or style) that help to create those feelings. Support your points by reference to the poetry by Keats that you have studied. [2001]

Sylvia Plath

- 'Plath makes effective use of language to explore her personal experience of suffering and to provide occasional glimpses of the redemptive power of love.'

Discuss this statement, supporting your answer with reference to both the themes and language found in the poetry of Sylvia Plath on your course. [2014]

- 'Plath's provocative imagery serves to highlight the intense emotions expressed in her poetry.'

To what extent do you agree or disagree with this assessment of her poetry? Support your answer with suitable reference to the poetry of Sylvia Plath on your course. [2013]

- 'The poetry of Sylvia Plath is intense, deeply personal, and quite disturbing.'

Do you agree with this assessment of her poetry? Write a response, supporting your points with the aid of suitable reference to the poems you have studied. [2007]

- 'I like (or do not like) to read the poetry of Sylvia Plath.'

Respond to this statement, referring to the poetry by Sylvia Plath on your course. [2004]

- 'If you were asked to give a public reading of a small selection of Sylvia Plath's poems, which ones would you choose to read?'

Give reasons for your choices supporting them by reference to the poems on your course. [2003]

The Unseen Poem

Part II

Part II

Approaching the Unseen Poem

Every poem, to begin with, is an unseen poem. When approaching a poem, it is useful to ask some very basic questions, such as: Who is speaking in the poem? What is being said? What prompted the poet to write the poem? What struck you first about this particular poem? What do you think of the opening? The Ending? Does the poet use unusual words, images or repetition?

The following is an outline of a step by step approach to the unseen poem on the page.

The shape of the poem on the page

This is often the very first thing you will notice about the text. Certain forms are recognised immediately, for example the fourteen-line sonnet or the sestina. Other poems may have a less definite shape, and that is also an important aspect of those poems. George Herbert (1593–1633) used very specific designs in some of his poems:

Easter Wings

Lord, who createdst man in wealth and store,
Though foolishly he lost the same,
Decaying more and more
Till he became
Most poor:
With thee
O let me rise
As larks, harmoniously,
And sing this day thy victories:
Then shall the fall further the flight in me.

My tender age in sorrow did begin;
And still with sicknesses and shame
Thou didst so punish sin,
That I became
Most thin.
With thee
Let me combine,
And feel this day thy victory;
For, if I imp my wing on thine,
Affliction shall advance the flight in me.

A modern writer who uses the same device is the American poet John Hollander. His poem 'Swan and Shadow' would lose its impact if it were printed as follows:

> Dusk Above the water hang the loud flies Here O so gray
> then What a pale signal will appear When Soon before its shadow
> fades Where Here in this pool of opened eyes. . .

This is how it should be:

Swan and Shadow

Dusk
Above the
water hang the
loud
flies
Here
O so
gray
then
What A pale signal will appear
When Soon before its shadow fades
Where Here in this pool of opened eye
In us No Upon us As at the very edges
of where we take shape in the dark air
this object bares its image awakening
ripples of recognition that will
brush darkness up into light
even after this bird this hour both drift by atop the perfect sad instant now
already passing out of sight
toward yet untroubled reflection
this image bears its object darkening
into memorial shades Scattered bits of
light No of water Or something across
water Breaking up No Being regathered
soon Yet by then a swan will have
gone Yes out of mind into what
vast
pale
hush
of a
place
past
sudden dark as
if a swan
sang

Shape here is so obviously of particular importance, but every poem has been shaped in a special way by means of line number, line length, rhyme and so on. Shakespeare wrote a 154 sonnet sequence; when Romeo and Juliet meet for the very first time in Shakespeare's play, they speak a sonnet between them. Elizabeth Bishop's 'The Prodigal' consists of two sonnets.

The Title

After the look of the poem on the page, the title is the next thing to be noticed. The American poet Emily Dickinson wrote 1,775 poems, but gave none of them titles. However, most poems have a title. What does the choice of title tell us about the poem? When we get to know the poem better we can then think about how effective and suitable the title is. Michael Longley's poem 'Carrigskeewaun' celebrates the place of the title, but each stanza is also given a title.

Consider the following titles. What do they reveal, or not reveal, suggest, imply, announce? Does the title win the reader's attention?

'The Dream of Wearing Shorts Forever' (Les Murray); 'Finale' (Judith Wright); 'Red Roses' (Anne Sexton); 'Red Sauce, Whiskey and Snow' (August Kleinzahler); 'Death of an Irishwoman' (Michael Hartnett); 'Hitcher' (Simon Armitage); 'Fifteen Million Plastic Bags' (Adrian Mitchell); 'For Heidi with Blue Hair' (Fleur Adcock); 'Wanting a Child' (Jorie Graham); 'SOMETHING FOR EVERYONE!!!' (Peter Reading); 'Phenomenal Woman' (Maya Angelou); 'The Hunchback in the Park' (Dylan Thomas); 'Depressed by a book of Bad Poetry, I walk Toward an Unused Pasture and Invite the Insects to Join me' (James Wright); 'Logan' (Catherine Phil MacCarthy); 'Ode on a Grecian Urn' (John Keats); 'Love' (George Herbert and Eavan Boland); 'The Armadillo' (Elizabeth Bishop); [r-p-o-p-h-e-s-s-a-g-r] (E E Cummings); 'Tea at the Palaz of Hoon' (Wallace Stevens); 'Church Going' (Philip Larkin); 'The Black Lace Fan My Mother Gave Me' (Eavan Boland); 'From a Conversation During Divorce' (Carol Rumens)

Language/Vocabulary

The language of poetry is the language of the age in which the poem is written. If someone today wrote a poem using 'thee' and 'thou' it would not convince; if someone today wrote exactly as Keats did, that poem would be dismissed as inauthentic. The poet writes in a language different from his or her predecessors and the poet today is less restricted in terms of subject matter. There is no word today, no emotion, no topic deemed unsuitable for poetry. Sylvia Plath once said that she wanted to get the word 'toothbrush' into a poem, meaning that she felt that there was nothing too ordinary or mundane for the poet to write about.

Yet the magic of poetry is such that each of the poets in this collection – though they span four centuries and all write in English – has a distinctive, unique voice. Their choice of words is part of this unique quality.

Ask yourself how you would describe a poet's vocabulary, his or her choice of words? This may be difficult to do at first. The task is easier if you look at opposites: is the language unusual or ordinary? Formal or colloquial? Does the poet invent new words? And, if so, what does this tell us about the poet? Is the language concrete or abstract? Are the words drawn from Anglo-Saxon, Latin, Anglo-Irish? Are there words on the page from the world of Greek Myth / Science / The Bible? Are there particular words that you would associate with particular poets? And how is the language of poetry different from the language of prose?

The following illustrates some interesting differences between the language of prose and the language of poetry. The first is a newspaper article which, according to his biographer Lawrance Thompson, inspired Robert Frost's poem 'Out, Out—'. The second is the poem itself. A discussion of the similarities and differences between the two should sharpen an awareness of language.

Sad tragedy at Bethlehem
Raymond Fitzgerald, a Victim of fatal accident

Raymond Tracy Fitzgerald, one of the twin sons of Michael G. and Margaret Fitzgerald of Bethlehem, died at his home Thursday afternoon, March 24, as a result of an accident by which one of his hands was badly hurt in a sawing machine. The young man was assisting in sawing up some wood in his own dooryard with a sawing machine and accidently hit the loose pulley, causing the saw to descend upon his hand, cutting and lacerating it badly. Raymond was taken into the house and a physician was immediately summoned, but he died very suddenly from the effect of the shock, which produced heart failure . . .

(From *The Littleton Courier*, 31 March 1901)

'Out, Out —'

The buzz saw snarled and rattled in the yard
And made dust and dropped stove-length sticks of wood,
Sweet-scented stuff when the breeze drew across it.
And from there those that lifted eyes could count
Five mountain ranges one behind the other
Under the sunset far into Vermont.
And the saw snarled and rattled, snarled and rattled,
As it ran light, or had to bear a load.
And nothing happened: day was all but done.
Call it a day, I wish they might have said
To please the boy by giving him the half hour
That a boy counts so much when saved from work.
His sister stood beside them in her apron
To tell them 'Supper'. At the word, the saw,
As if to prove saws knew what supper meant,
Leaped out at the boy's hand, or seemed to leap —

He must have given the hand. However it was,
Neither refused the meeting. But the hand!
The boy's first outcry was a rueful laugh,
As he swung toward them holding up the hand
Half in appeal, but half as if to keep
The life from spilling. Then the boy saw all —
Since he was old enough to know, big boy
Doing a man's work, though a child at heart —
He saw all spoiled. 'Don't let him cut my hand off —
The doctor, when he comes. Don't let him, sister!'
So. But the hand was gone already.
The doctor put him in the dark of ether.
He lay and puffed his lips out with his breath.
And then—the watcher at his pulse took fright.
No one believed. They listened at his heart.
Little — less— nothing! — and that ended it.
No more to build on there. And they, since they
Were not the one dead, turned to their affairs.

The importance of vocabulary is also clearly seen in the following two poems. They share the same title and they both say something similar. One was written – the original spelling is retained – at the beginning of the sixteenth century (and supposedly tells of Thomas Wyatt's sorrow on being forsaken by women friends, including Anne Boleyn, who left him for Henry VIII); the other was first published in 1979.

They flee from me, that somtime did me seke

They flee from me, that somtime did me seke
With naked fote stalkyng within my chamber.
Once have I seen them gentle, tame, and meke,
That now are wild, and do not once remember
That sometyme they have put them selves in danger,
To take bread at my hand, and now they range
Busily sekyng in continuall change.
  Thanked be fortune, it hath bene otherwise
Twenty tymes better: but once especiall,
In thinne aray, after a pleasant gyse,
When her loose gowne did from her shoulders fall,
And she me caught in her armes long and small,
And therwithall, so swetely did me kysse,
And softly sayd: deare hart, how like you this?
It was no dreame: for I lay broade awakyng.
But all is turnde now through my gentlenesse,
Into a bitter fashion of forsakyng:

And I have leave to go of her goodnesse,
And she also to use newfanglenesse.
But, sins that I unkyndly so am served:
How like you this, what hath she now deserved?

– Thomas Wyatt (1503–42)

They flee from me that sometime did me seek

At this moment in time
the chicks that went for me
in a big way
are opting out;
as of now, it's an all-change situation.
The scenario was once,
for me, 100% better.
Kissing her was viable
in a nude or semi-nude situation.
It was How's about it, baby?
Her embraces were relevant
and life-enhancing.

I was not hallucinating.
But with regard to that one
my permissiveness
has landed me in a forsaking situation.
The affair is no longer on-going.

She can, as of now, explore new parameters
How's about it? indeed!
I feel emotionally underprivileged.
What a bitch!
(and that's meaningful).

– Gavin Ewart (1916–95)

Punctuation

All poets are wordsmiths and punctuation is an aspect essential to poetry. Sometimes its absence is deliberate, as in the poems by Emily Dickinson. The frequent use of the full-stop will naturally slow down a line. In his poem 'Laertes', Michael Longley uses only one full-stop and that is at the end because, in his own words, he 'sustained the sentence from the first word right the way through'. Philip Larkin's 'MCMXIV' is also a one-sentence poem.

The full-stop, comma, colon, exclamation mark, question mark, dash, bracket, ellipsis and italics are just some examples of punctuation and their use are important aspects of a writer's style. You will meet with all of these in the prescribed poems. If you are aware of their importance and significance when you come to read the ten Emily Dickinson poems on your course, for example, consider the significance of how each poem ends: two with a full-stop, seven with a dash, one with a question mark. A poem that ends with a full-stop achieves a sense of closure; the dash often creates the opposite effect.

Rhyme

Rhyme, for centuries, has been one of the most distinguishing characteristics of poetry, though poetry without a regular rhyming scheme is not necessarily a poem without music. Blank verse, which is unrhymed iambic pentameter, for example, achieves rhythm and cadence without end rhyme. Internal rhyme and cross rhyme are also important features in poetry.

The run-on line is deceptive in that often a very rigorous and regular rhyming scheme is not apparent. 'Child of Our Time' by Eavan Boland has a very disciplined and regular end rhyme, but Boland's mastery of rhythm and the flowing line is such that a careless reader might think that the poem has no rhyming scheme.

Rhythm

Rhythm is movement. We are all familiar with rhythm. The individual day, the seasons of the year, the sound of the sea all have their own rhythm or movement. The Dublin poet Paula Meehan believes that our sense of rhythm dates from the time spent in the womb – the regular heartbeat of the mother and our own heartbeat give us an inbuilt rhythmic pattern.

Cadence

Cadence, a musical term, is difficult to define, yet it is easily recognised. A dictionary definition speaks of the rise and fall of words. If you consider the following short extracts, you can hear this rising, falling sound and it is a very effective means of capturing a mood:

Brightness falls from the air,
Queens have died young and fair,
Dust hath closed Helen's eyes.

(from 'Song' by Thomas Nashe, 1567–1601)

It was evening all afternoon.
It was snowing
And it was going to snow.

(from 'Thirteen Ways of Looking at a Blackbird'
by Wallace Stevens, 1879–1955)

Only the groom, and the groom's boy,
With bridles in the evening come.

(from 'At Grass' by Philip Larkin, 1922–85)

The cadence here creates a mood: in the first an elegiac feeling, in the second a melancholy one, the third a peaceful, tranquil one. The sounds of the words, the arrangement of the words in the line, the use of repetition, for example, create these cadences.

Line break and line length

These are other important aspects of the total impact of the poem. It would be a worthwhile and interesting exercise to think about line break in a poem you are not already familiar with. Here are two poems called by William Carlos Williams minus capital letters, punctuation, line break. How do you think it ought to be arranged on the page?

the red wheelbarrow

so much depends upon a red wheelbarrow glazed with rain water beside the white chickens

to a poor old woman

munching a plum on the street a paper bag of them in her hand they taste good to her they taste good to her they taste good to her you can see it by the way she gives herself to the one half sucked out in her hand comforted a solace of ripe plums seeming to fill the air they taste good to her

The poet Denise Levertov says that 'there is at our disposal no tool of the poetic craft more important, none that yields more subtle and precise effects, than the linebreak if it is properly understood'. Levertov illustrates her point by taking four lines from the William Carlos Williams poem 'To a Poor Old Woman', mentioned above, in which the old woman has been eating plums:

They taste good to her
They taste good
to her. They taste
good to her.

Each word here has a special emphasis because of its place in the line. If Williams had written of the plums that:

> They taste good to her
> They taste good to her
> They taste good to her

it would be a very different and less effective piece. Levertov's commentary (see below) on the four lines from Williams is worth reading, for it shows a mind keenly alert to the power of language.

But first, look again at the four lines that Williams wrote:

> They taste good to her.
> They taste good
> to her. They taste
> good to her.

Levertov observes: 'First the statement is made; then the word good is (without the clumsy overemphasis a change of typeface would give) brought to the center of our (and her) attention for an instant; then the word taste is given is given similar momentary prominence, with good sounding on a new note, reaffirmed – so that we have first the general recognition of well-being, then the intensification of that sensation, then its voluptuous location in the sense of taste. And all this is presented through indicated pitches, that is, by melody, not by rhythm alone.'

The nuts and bolts of poetic language belong in the study of metre, which is the study of sound patterns and measured sounds. Every syllable is long sounding or short and the way such sounds are arranged is an intrinsic part of poetry. When you come to read Shakespeare's sonnets, you will discover that each one is written in a five foot line, each foot consisting of one unaccented syllable followed by an accented one (the iambic pentameter). This is not as complicated as it sounds. The glossary at the back of this book provides a detailed note on metrics.

Imagery

If you say the words traffic-jam, strobe lighting, town, river, hillside, elephant, images form one after the other in your mind, all in a matter of seconds. Many of the words in the English language conjure up an image on their own. Every noun does, for example. However, there is a difference between the image prompted by the word 'tiger' and the phrases 'roaring like a tiger', and 'he's a tiger'. Here tiger becomes simile and metaphor. Symbol is another familiar and powerful technique and symbol occurs when something in the poem such as a tiger in a cage is both actual and means something beyond itself. For example, a caged animal is just that, but it can also stand for the death of freedom. 'The Armadillo' in Elizabeth Bishop's poem of the same name is both actual and symbolic.

And in 'The Harvest Bow' Seamus Heaney writes of how the bow made by his father is an actual object, but it also becomes a symbol of his father's life and work as a farmer, the season itself, and a work of art.

Tone

What is being said and how it is being said are very important. Think for a moment of the sentence: 'Please leave the room'. Tone, or the attitude of the speaker, can make a huge difference here. First try saying that sentence four different ways simply by emphasising a different word each time. Then, if you introduce a note of anger or exhaustion or apathy or urgency into your voice, the sentence takes on a different meaning. In poetry, tone is the attitude the poet/speaker has towards the listener or reader. Tone can be formal or casual/off-hand, serious or tongue-in-cheek, superior or prayer-like, profound or simple and so on.

Mood

A tone can create a mood or atmosphere. Mood is the feeling contained within the work and the feeling communicated to the reader. In 'Sonnet 29' by Shakespeare, the mood at first is one of loneliness and dejection. The speaker feels worthless: 'I all alone beweep my outcast state'. However, the mood is triumphant and exultant in the closing couplet. Shakespeare, remembering his friend and the love that they share, feels an immense emotional richness. In Eavan Boland's poem 'This Moment', the mood throughout is one of expectation and mystery.

Allusion

This is when one writer refers to another writer's work, either directly or indirectly. When an allusion is used, it can enhance or enlarge a topic or it can serve as an effective contrast. When Keats mentions 'the sad heart of Ruth' in 'Ode to a Nightingale', he is referring to a sorrow from a very different time. The moment in the Bible and the moment that the poem focuses on are brought together, one enriching the other, through allusion.

Onomatopoeia

Listen out for the sounds. Read the poem aloud and the onomatopoeic words will clearly reveal themselves. Keats's 'Ode to a Nightingale' contains one of the finest examples of words imitating the thing they describe: 'The murmurous haunt of flies on summer eves'.

Other Aspects To Keep In Mind

Beginnings and Endings

Think about the following examples of opening and closing lines. What do these openings reveal to us of the poets? The situation in which they find themselves? Their tone/mood? Does the poet use the run-on line or punctuation in an interesting way?

Beginnings

'This Italian earth is special to me
because I was here in a war
when I was young and immortal.'

– Harvey Shapiro, 'Italy 1996'

The sunset's slow catastrophe of reds
and bruised blues
leaches the land to its green and grey.

– Robin Robertson, 'Tryst'

That God-is
Light smile of your arms
One second before
I'm in them.

– Ruth Padel, 'Being Late to Meet You at the Station'

never in all my life have I seen as handsome a rat as you.

– Christopher Logue, 'Rat, O Rat . . .'

Endings

And I let the fish go.

– Elizabeth Bishop, 'The Fish'

Never such innocence again.

– Philip Larkin, 'MCMXIV'

To the children, to a bewildered wife,
I think 'Sorry Missus' was what he said.

– Michael Longley, 'Wounds'

And reaching into my pocket in Dublin for busfare home
I found handfuls of marvellous, suddenly worthless coins.

– David Wheatley, 'Nothing to Declare'

For thy sweet love remembered such wealth brings,
That then I scorn to change my state with kings.

– William Shakespeare 'Sonnet 29'

Responding to the Unseen Poem

A Blessing

Just off the highway to Rochester, Minnesota,
Twilight bounds softly forth on the grass.
And the eyes of those two Indian ponies
Darken with kindness.
They have come gladly out of the willows
To welcome my friend and me.
We step over the barbed wire into the pasture
Where they have been grazing all day, alone.
They ripple tensely, they can hardly contain their happiness
That we have come.
They bow shyly as wet swans. They love each other.
There is no loneliness like theirs.
At home once more,
They begin munching the young tufts of spring in the darkness.
I would like to hold the slenderer one in my arms,
For she has walked over to me
And nuzzled my left hand.
She is black and white,
Her mane falls wild on her forehead,
And the light breeze moves me to caress her long ear
That is delicate as the skin over a girl's wrist.
Suddenly I realise
That if I stepped out of my body I would break
Into blossom.

James Wright (1927–80)

It is important that we re-read the poem a few times. A poem usually consists of sentences or sections and, having read the poem through several times, it might be useful to approach the poem a sentence or a line or two at a time.

The shape of the poem seems to be irregular. There is no obvious rhyming scheme. The poem contains twelve sentences, some long and flowing, others equally effective because they are short. The lines are of uneven length and the final line is the shortest.

Wright calls his poem '*A* Blessing' not '*The* Blessing', which would imply something more specific. If the moment that he writes about is 'a' blessing, it means that there are other such moments also. The blessing experienced in this particular moment, however, is the particular focus of this poem. A blessing has religious and holy connotations and it is a special moment for the poet, though the setting is not a place associated with a conventional religious experience.

The poem begins in a matter-of-fact way – 'Just off the highway' – and the American city and state are named. A 'highway' suggests reinforced concrete, the man-made, busyness, speed, but the second line is soft and natural and beautiful, capturing, as it does, a world 'Just off the highway'. It is twilight, a time of fading light and shadows; the quaint, old-fashioned phrase 'softly forth' contains gentle sounds and the grass contrasts with the highway itself.

The use of the word 'And' at the beginning of line 3, which is also the beginning of a new sentence, leads us further into the poem. The first thing that Wright tells us about the ponies is that their eyes 'darken with kindness' and that they are Indian (Native American) ponies. Their mystery and their nature are conveyed in the words 'darken' and 'kindness'; that they are Indian might be significant. Modern America as symbolised by the highway is very different from the Native American traditions.

'Gladly' and 'welcome' suggest how Wright feels as both he and his friend are approached by the ponies.

The human and the animal world meet when 'We step over the barbed wire'. Wright speaks of the ponies being alone. Their happiness is vividly conveyed in a phrase: 'They ripple tensely'.

There is no sound mentioned. The image Wright uses – 'They bow shyly as wet swans' – is elegant and graceful and beautiful. The three short sentences in lines 11–12, each following the other, are effective. They are both the poet's accurate observation and his conclusions:

> They bow shyly as wet swans. They love each other.
> There is no loneliness like theirs.

The loneliness that the poet speaks of here is a different kind of loneliness, a loneliness that does not frighten or destroy.

The moment passes and the ponies are 'At home once more', happy to be visited and happy to feel at ease 'munching the young tufts of spring in the darkness', a phrase that contains sensuous, evocative details.

The final part of the poem, the last three sentences, focuses on the speaker. 'I', absent from the poem so far, is now used four times. 'I would like to hold the slenderer one in my arms' is Wright's response when his left hand is nuzzled ('ripple';'munching';'nuzzle' add to the sensuousness of the experience). It is clearly a very personal and beautiful moment that the poet is recording. He moves from the very emotional/subjective response to objective description in the lines:

> She is black and white,
> Her mane falls wild on her forehead

He then returns to the intense emotion of 'the light breeze moves me to caress her long ear'. The image of the 'skin over a girl's wrist' is echoing the earlier image of the swans. Both are graceful and slender and delicate. The moment of insight comes and it comes 'suddenly':

> Suddenly I realise
> That if I stepped out of my body I would break
> Into blossom.

The final image is inspired by the natural world and, just as a blossom unfolds naturally and beautifully, Wright, in choosing this image, is giving us a very vivid description of a complex, metaphysical/spiritual moment. It is a poem of longing and here the word 'break', so often associated with destruction, is used with opposite effect. The word 'break' is also placed appropriately at the line break.

•

The above is but a beginning. However, gradually, with each re-reading, you can enter more fully into the poem. If, for example, you focus on the mood of the poem would one word sum up the mood or does the mood change and how would you describe that changing mood? What is the dominant mood of this poem?

Are the verbs or adjectives or sound of particular importance? What if the images were removed? What would the poem lose?

Your own response to a poem on the page should focus on **Theme** and **Technique**. Hundreds of poems may share a similar theme, but every true poet has his or her own individual way of viewing and expressing an idea, his or her own individual way of mastering technique.

Sample Answer on the Unseen Poem

Your response need not be long, but it must be personal. You must engage with the text. And quote little details throughout your answer to support the points you make. The examiner is told to watch out for FOUR things: the candidate's awareness of the poem's

- **Pattern** (or structure)
- **Imagery** (the word pictures painted by the poet and the impact/effect such images have on you, the reader)
- **Sensuousness** (the world as evoked or brought to life through sight, smell, hearing, taste, touch)
- **Suggestiveness** (what personal thoughts, ideas, feelings are prompted by this particular poem)

And, yes, the first letter of the four aspects listed here, as outlined by the Examinations Commission, form an unfortunate and unforgettable acronym: P.I.S.S. But there you go. Did the powers that be think of that at the time?

Here is a poem that could appear as an Unseen Poem and there follows an answer written in exam conditions that earned twenty marks out of twenty.

In this poem, Alistair Elliot celebrates the ordinary things in life.

A Northern Morning

It rained from dawn. The fire died in the night.
I poured hot water on some foreign leaves;
I brought the fire to life. Comfort
spread from the kitchen like a taste of chocolate
through the head-waters of a body,
accompanied by that little-water-music.
The knotted veins of the old house tremble and carry
a louder burden: the audience joining in.

People are peaceful in a world so lavish
with the ingredients of life:
the world of breakfast easy as Tahiti.
But we must leave. Head down in my new coat
I dodge to the High Street conscious of my fellows
damp and sad in their vegetable fibres.
But by the bus-stop I look up: the spring trees
exult in the downpour, radiant, clean for hours:
This is the life! This is the only life!

Question

Write a personal response to this poem, highlighting aspects of it that you liked and/or disliked.

Answer

(Written by Bethany Hart, a Leaving Cert pupil in exam conditions)

On first reading this poem, I did not particularly like it but when I looked closer, the poem opened itself to me, and I can now see that it is intelligent, lyrical and atmospheric. I think the first three lines have a beautiful rhythm; the words are mostly monosyllabic and Elliot creates a steady pace, which suits the relaxed mood of the poem. I liked the image of pouring 'hot water on some foreign leaves' because I found it quirky and different. It seems that in order to celebrate the ordinary things in life, the poet is exaggerating and lyricising them so that making a cup of tea sounds like a beautiful song.

I like how the poet uses rich images such as 'a taste of chocolate' and 'I brought the fire to life' to create a warm atmosphere. The poem is very sensuous in this way; the poet wants to engage his reader's senses with these images.

In the second stanza the poet brings a contrast to the warm feeling previously created. He comments on the happiness that the human race experiences 'with the ingredients of life', describing the world as 'lavish' and 'the world of breakfast as easy as Tahiti'. It seems to me that the poet wants us to return to basics and appreciate the little things. He describes the people around him as 'damp and sad', which not only contrasts with the previous stanza but also with the statement that 'people are peaceful in a world so lavish'. I think the poet is commenting on the fact that possessions do not affect how long happiness lasts.

The final moment in the poem is my favourite moment. It is a sentence of complete exultation and celebration. Elliot describes 'the spring trees' in the 'downpour', as at their best, at their highest, at the moment when the rain is feeding them and bringing life to them. I think he means to tell us that we should be like these spring trees and exult in the things that make us 'radiant' and bring us life.

Appendices/Glossary

Part III

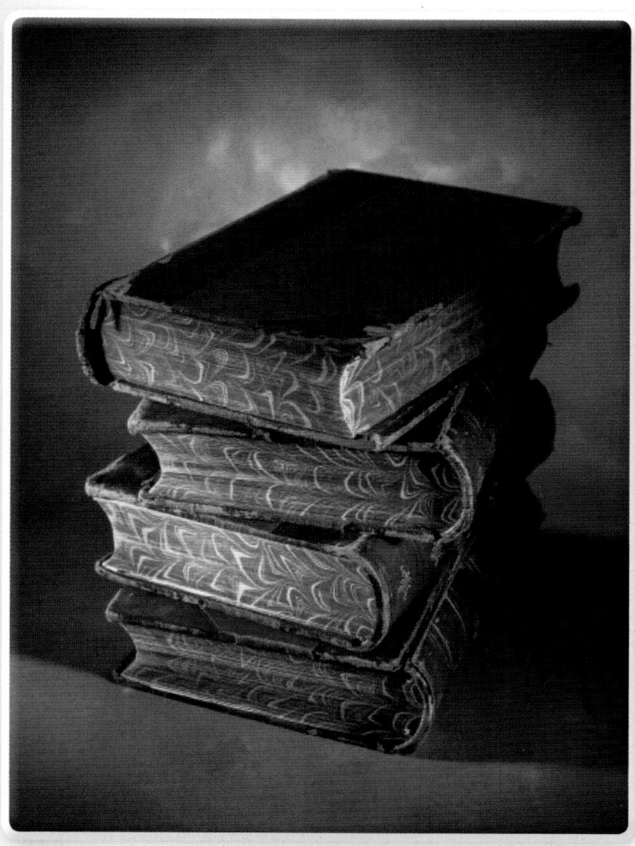

Contents Page

Appendix I

Responding to a Poem – Some Exercises and Strategies

Some Questions to Ask

- Who is speaking? (the poet/a persona/an inanimate object/an animal?)
- What is being said?
- What occasion prompted the poem/why was it written?
- How does the poem begin?
- How does it end? (Write down the opening and closing lines and comment on the style)
- Which line/section captures the gist of the poem?
- Which image is the most effective/striking/memorable?
- What struck you first about a particular poem?
- What struck you while re-reading the poem?
- Comment on the shape of the poem.
- Are the lines regular in length?
- Comment on the stanza divisions.
- Does the poem belong to a particular genre? – sonnet/sestina/ballad/lyric/epic/ode...?
- Comment on the punctuation in the poem. What would the page look like if only the punctuation remained? (e.g. poet's use of question marks, dashes, commas, and where these occur in the line)
- Ask if the poet uses (i) alliteration (ii) assonance (iii) onomatopoeia (iv) end-rhyme (v) internal rhyme (vi) metaphor (vii) simile (viii) repetition (ix) rhyme scheme (x) run-on lines.
- Comment on the title of the poem.
- If you were to paint this poem, what colours would you use?
- If this poem were a piece of music, how would you describe it? Which musical instrument(s) would suit it best?
- Draw three pictures or images that you see with your mind's eye when reading or thinking about this poem.
- Say from which source the poet has drawn these images – from nature, art, mythology, science . . .
- Which is the most important word/line in the poem? Justify your choice.

SAMPLE ANSWER

'Hopkins's poetry is both Original and Engaging.'

Original means unique, original means rare, original means memorable. Hopkins is all three and reading his poetry I discovered that I was being drawn in, I was becoming more and more involved and engaged with the work. It is a challenging and complex poetry, but it is also very rewarding. Hopkins's originality is clearly seen in everything he writes and I found that I was connecting more and more with the work the more I reread the poems.

'Spring' is one of Hopkins's signature poems and he writes about the season in an original way. He uses hyperbole to express his total admiration for the opening up of the year. 'Nothing is so beautiful as spring'. Hopkins's originality is immediately seen in the details, the alliteration, the surging rhythm:

> When weeds in wheels shoot long and lovely and lush

There is an exuberance here as Hopkins celebrates new life. He paints a picture of bird's eggs and the vastness of a blue sky. He brings them together brilliantly – 'Thrush's eggs look little low heavens' and he also includes the sounds of spring. The reader is drawn in and is charmed by the idea of the thrush's song. A truly original touch is found in the way Hopkins compares the sensation of hearing the song to a lightning strike. 'It strikes like lightning to hear him sing.'

There is a terrific energy in the octet – words such as 'The glassy peartree leaves and blooms' or 'the racing lambs too have fair their fling', the repeated 'blue', the word 'leaves' as a verb give the poem originality and freshness.

But one of the most original ideas that I've ever come across is found in the second stanza. Hopkins asks a question and answers it, and the use of the question here engages the reader. 'What is all this juice and all this joy? A Strain of the earth's sweet being in the beginning . . . ' He clearly adores spring and for him it is an echo, melody or 'strain' of paradise. Every spring we are given a glimpse of what The Garden of Eden was like - 'the earth's sweet being in the beginning'. Hopkins says 'Eden garden' not The Garden of . . . – another original touch. The reader is also drawn in and engaged because this idea is a serious, challenging and an attractive one. As is the final idea in the sonnet. Every child is innocent, every child contains a spring-like quality, a Mayday but as we grown up we become 'sour with sinning'. For Hopkins this can be avoided through Christ. If we follow Christ he is saying we will steer clear of sin. There's an inviting and engaging idea.

'The Windhover' is a difficult, complex poem. It swoops and dives and there isn't an unnecessary word on the page. Everything is compressed and captured in an original and engaging way. Hopkins says 'I caught' not 'I saw' and the description of the bird as 'morning morning's minion' and 'dapple-dawn-drawn Falcon' paint interesting pictures in my mind. The lines flow with such rhythm, the exclamation marks, the immediacy of the emotion strike me as original. He has succeeded brilliantly in capturing 'the achieve of, the mastery of the thing!' And the word 'windhover' is a kenning, a word that brings two words together to create a new original one containing a new, fresh idea.

But most original and engaging of all is the way he ends the poem. The windhover in the morning sky is identified as having a 'brute beauty' and then the mind jumps to a ploughed field and 'blue bleak embers'. And yet it all makes sense. We imagine these things and we can, through Hopkins's original way of seeing, make interesting connections.

The poem is dedicated 'To Christ our Lord' and the final line suggests Christ's courage and sacrifice as he dies and makes possible the resurrection, as he falls and yet creates 'gold-vermilion'. A really fascinating, engaging and original way of thinking.

Another indication of Hopkins's originality are the terms Inscape and Instress. These words were invented by Hopkins to explain how the mystery and essence of God is evident everywhere in creation. Inscape is the unique, essential quality in everything, the oneness of something which proves Hopkins's interest in what is original. And the power that makes or fuels that creative process is Instress. Hopkins himself says that instress is 'the force or energy that sustains an inscape'. 'God's Grandeur' is one of the best illustrations of Hopkins's theories of both inscape and instress.

The opening line captures God's force and power [instress]: 'The world is charged with the grandeur of God'. This poem certainly engages and amazes me. And I like how 'charged' can be read in two ways. It can mean 'powered' or it can mean 'responsible for'. Here is a poet writing in 1877 and yet he is saying something that we need to hear in the twenty-first century. We are destroying the planet – 'all is seared with trade; bleared, smeared with toil'. I'm really engaged here and connect with the ideas. Hopkins is ahead of his time. We experience both inscape and instress when we are somehow stopped in our tracks and some special feeling takes over. We are moved. We see, we feel, we gain a deeper understanding. Hopkins's poetry does just that.

My favourite Hopkins poem is 'Felix Randal'. It's a sonnet but doesn't look like a conventional sonnet – another typical, original, Hopkins touch and it seems to me that he writes about death in an unusual and interesting and engaging way. At first Hopkins seems distant, cool, remote: 'O is he dead then?' But he isn't. He has such a deep faith that he knows that Felix Randal is being cared for by God and that God began looking out for the farrier 'some months earlier'.

Even the colloquial expression 'Ah well, God rest him all road ever he offended' shows originality. Hopkins uses a familiar, ordinary Lancashire saying [Hopkins wrote the poem in Liverpool where Randal was a parishioner]. 'Felix Randal' also contains one the most beautiful and true observations that I've ever come across.

'This seeing the sick endears them to us, us too it endears' is a very engaging idea. We can connect with it so easily. Hopkins expresses great tenderness and love towards Felix Randal and even though it is about death the poem's final three lines blaze with life.

It's an original touch. Hopkins brings the reader back to Felix's glory days in his 'random grim forge'. This 'big-boned, hardy-handsome man, powerful amidst peers' is beating out iron. But Hopkins doesn't put it that way. Instead we have the original touch. Felix is fettling for 'the great grey drayhorse his bright and battering sandal!'

And then there are the 'Terrible Sonnets'. These are bleak and black and terrifying but very involving and engaging. You are drawn in by the anguished voice, by the despair. When Hopkins says

> O the mind, mind has mountains, cliffs of fall
> Frightful, sheer. No-man fathomed

I was immediately engaged. And to describe the mind as a steep, dangerous, frightful place is not only original but unforgettable. Hopkins is so direct and honest here. It is like reading a very private diary. To use a cliché, you can feel his pain. When he speaks of 'black hoürs' he uses an accent [the umlaut] over hoürs to drag out the never-ending loneliness. His poetry is like a musical score. Or when he uses a word like 'fell' in 'I wake and feel the fell of dark', the fact that 'fell' can mean both 'threat' and 'mountain' engages the reader and the fact that there are two meanings makes for an original reading experience. Hopkins makes you think and he makes you imagine.

Another original aspect is Hopkins's image of 'dead letters sent/To dearest him that lives alas! away'. The idea of Hopkins writing a letter and getting no reply is a striking and immediate image of how Hopkins feels abandoned by God in this bleak hour. And when he describes himself as tasting himself and how that taste was bitter is another original image. 'God's most deep decree/Bitter would have me taste: that taste was me'. It is easy to sympathise and to engage with Hopkins here.

Even if I saw a poem by Hopkins that I hadn't seen before, there are things in a Hopkins poem that might help me guess that it's one of his – alliteration, compression, a rhythmic flow [what he calls sprung rhythm], a deep engagement with God. His originality and the way he brings the reader on board, the way he engages the reader are remarkable. I think Hopkins will stay with me long after the Leaving Cert.

Glossary of Literary Terms

ACROSTIC: this is when the first letter in each word at the beginning of a line or stanza spells out a word, name or title. For example:

Man
Is
Never
Dead

ALLEGORY: the word allegory comes from Greek *allos*, 'other', and *agoreuein*, 'to speak'. In literature, an allegory is a work which has a surface meaning and another, deeper, meaning; in other words it can be read at two levels. An example would be George Orwell's *Animal Farm*. It is a story about a group of animals and can be read as such, but it also charts certain events in Eastern European and Russian politics.

ALLITERATION: when two or more words in close connection begin with the same letter or sound and affect the ear with an echoing sound. Examples include the childhood doggerel, 'Betty bought a bit of butter but the butter Betty bought was bitter'. Dickinson uses alliteration as in 'Berries of the Bahamas – have I –/But this little Blaze . . .'; or Larkin in 'The Whitsun Weddings' - 'A slow and stopping curve southwards we kept'; or Seamus Heaney's 'to the tick of two clocks'.

ALLUSION: this is when a writer deliberately introduces into his/her own work recognisable elements from another source. This may be a reference to a well-known character, event, or place or to another work of art. For example, in her poem 'Love', Eavan Boland never names Virgil's Aeneas but the reader is expected to identify 'the hero . . . on his way to hell' as an allusion to Book VI of *The Aeneid*.

AMBIGUITY: when language is open to one or more interpretations based on the context in which it occurs. Ambiguity can be intentional or unintentional. An example would be the opening line of Keats's 'Ode on a Grecian Urn': 'Thou still unravished bride of quietness' – where the word 'still' can mean 'without movement, silent' or 'as before, up to the present time'.

ANAGRAM: this is when a rearrangement of the letters in one word or phrase results in a new word or phrase, as in 'listen' into 'silent', 'now' into 'won'.

ANAPHORA: when a word or phrase is repeated for effect at the beginning of lines, clauses or sentences. The Bible contains many examples, as in the Book of Ecclesiastes: 'A time to be born, and a time to die. A time to plant, and a time to pluck up that which is planted.' In Shakespeare's Sonnet 66, ten of the fourteen lines begin with 'And'.

ANTITHESIS: in Greek, 'antithesis' means 'opposition'. Antithesis occurs when contraries are placed side by side, as in T.S. Eliot's 'We are the hollow men/We are the stuffed men' from 'The Hollow Men'; or Samuel Johnson's 'Marriage has many pains, but celibacy has no pleasures'; or in Shakespeare's Sonnet 116 'Whose worth's unknown, although his height be taken'.

ARCHAISM: in Greek, the word means 'old-fashioned', and an archaism is when a writer or speaker deliberately uses a word or phrase no longer in current use, for example, 'oft', 'morn', 'thy'. Keats's use of 'faery' in 'Ode to a Nightingale' is an example.

ARCHETYPE: the word comes from Greek meaning 'original or primitive form' and archetypes can take the form of symbols, characters, images or events which we respond to in a deep and meaningful way. For example fire, the dark, the sun, the father, the mother, snake, birth, death, the young man setting out on a journey, the young man from the country first arriving in the city all come under the heading archetype.

ASSONANCE: in Latin, 'assonare' is 'to answer with the same sound'. Assonance is when vowel sounds are repeated in a sequence of words close to each other. For example, in W. B. Yeats: 'I hear lake water lapping with low sounds by the shore'.

AUBADE: in French, 'aubade' means 'dawn'. The aubade is a celebratory morning song or a lament that two lovers must part.

BALLAD: a simple and memorable song that tells a story in oral form through narrative and dialogue. It is one of the oldest forms of literature and was originally passed on orally among illiterate people. Ballads often tell of love, courage, the supernatural. Ballads usually are written in four-line stanzas with an abcb rhyme, and often have a refrain. The first and third lines are usually four stress iambic tetrameter, the second and fourth lines are in three stress iambic trimeter. For example:

> There lived a wife at Usher's Well
> And a wealthy wife was she
> She had three stout and stalwart sons,
> An sent them o'er the sea.

Other examples of ballad include Keats's 'La Belle Dame sans Merci' and the anonymous 'Frankie and Johnny'.

BLANK VERSE: this is unrhymed iambic pentameter and is often used in long poems and dramatic verse. One of the earliest examples of blank verse in English is to be found in Henry Howard Surrey's translation of Virgil's *Aeneid*, which was published in 1540. Shakespeare, Milton, Wordsworth, Robert Frost all wrote in blank verse.

CADENCE: the word 'cadence' means 'the fall of the voice' and refers to the last syllables in a pattern of words. Cadence is difficult to define, and yet it is easily identified or, more accurately, easily heard. When Philip Larkin writes at the end of 'At Grass

> With bridles in the evening come

we know that the sounds have been arranged in a particularly effective way on the page. For example, he puts the verb at the end which is not usual in English (it is a Latin form), but the effect is musical and beautiful and very different from 'Come with bridles in the evening', which says exactly the same thing. Cadence is found especially in Biblical poetry, free verse, prose poetry. Ezra Pound in *Make It New* (1934) urged poets to 'compose in the sequence of the musical phrase, not in sequence of a metronome'.

CAESURA: a caesura is a pause which usually occurs in the middle of a line and is caused by rhyme, punctuation or syntax. For example, Boland uses the caesura for effect in the closing lines of 'The Pomegranate':

> The legend will be hers as well as mine.
> She will enter it. As I have.
> She will wake up. She will hold
> the papery flushed skin in her hand.
> And to her lips. I will say nothing.

CARICATURE: from an Italian word meaning 'to exaggerate'. When a character's personality or physical feature is portrayed in a distorted manner, the result is a caricature. The cartoonist's work is almost always a caricature.

CLICHÉ: a phrase which has through overuse become familiar and jaded. The word cliché originally referred to a plate used in printing which produced numerous identical copies. Clichés were once original and interesting uses of language but now, though it is difficult to do so, they are best avoided. Examples include 'a clear blue sky', 'go haywire', 'hard as a rock', 'stand up and be counted', 'tough as nails'.

CLIMAX: climax comes from a Greek word meaning ladder and a climactic moment is one when there is intensity. In a Shakespearean play, for example, there is often a climax in Acts III and V, when the audience's interest is at its height. In Shelley's sonnet 'Ozymandias' the lines 'My name is Ozymandias, King of Kings,/Look on my Works, ye Mighty, and despair!' form a climax.

CLOSURE: the way a poem, novel, play, etc. ends and how the author achieves the sense of an ending. For example, Shakespeare in his sonnets uses a rhyming couplet; Philip Larkin in 'The Explosion' places a single line between eight three-line stanzas.

COMPARATIVE LITERATURE: the study of the relationships and similarities between different literatures by writers from different nations or peoples – e.g. you can read *Great Expectations* by Charles Dickens and *Cat's Eye* by Margaret Atwood and examine and analyse both as 'coming of age' novels or *Bildungsroman* (an upbringing or education novel) – one about a boy in the nineteenth-century in England, the other about a girl growing up in Canada in the twentieth century. Ian Reed states that 'Unless we compare things, we cannot see things either wholly or fully'; and Michael Lapidge says: 'The comparative approach is instinctive to human intelligence. From our very infancy we learn by comparing like with like, and by distinguishing the like from the nearly like, and the other.'

CONCEIT: conceit comes from a Latin word meaning 'to seize' and the literary conceit occurs when a writer expresses an idea in which an interesting connection is made between two distinct things. For example, when a writer compares his state of love to that of a ship in a storm or when John Donne (1572–1631) likens the souls of two lovers to a compass:

> If they be two, they are two so
>   As stiffe twin compasses are two,
> Thy soule, the fixt foot, makes no show
>   To move, but doth, if the other doe.

Dr Johnson described the conceit most associated with the seventeenth-century Metaphysical poets as 'a kind of *discordia concors* [a harmony of opposites]; a combination of dissimilar images, or discovery of occult resemblances in things apparently unlike . . . The most heterogeneous ideas are yoked by violence together'. In Seamus Heaney's poem 'Valediction', the poet uses the conceit of a ship at sea to express his own inner feeling.

COUPLET: two lines of rhymed or unrhymed verse which follow the same metre. Eavan Boland's 'The War Horse' is written in couplets. The heroic couplet is made up of iambic pentameter lines which rhyme in pairs.

CRITICISM: the evaluation, interpretation and discussion of a work

CROSS RHYME: (or interlaced rhyme) this occurs when a word at the end of a line rhymes with a word in the middle of a following line.

ECPHRASIS: also spelt *ekphrasis* (meaning 'description' in Greek); it is a poem that describes a work of art, e.g. Keats's 'Ode on a Grecian Urn' or Bishop's 'Poem' or Derek Mahon's 'Courtyards in Delft'.

ELEGY: elegy comes from the Greek word meaning lament. The elegy is usually a long, formal poem that mourns the dead. Gray's 'Elegy in a Country Churchyard' is one of the more famous. Also, Whitman's elegy for Abraham Lincoln, 'When Lilacs Last in the Dooryard Bloom'd' and W. H. Auden's 'In Memory of W.B. Yeats'.

ELISION: this occurs when a syllable is omitted or when two syllables are slurred together to form one. For example, in Shakespeare's sonnet:

> Th' expense of spirit in waste of shame

Or in Elizabeth Bishop's 'Questions of Travel':

> blurr'dly and inconclusively

END RHYME: this is when the words at the end of lines rhyme.

ENJAMBMENT: also known as the run-on line, enjambment occurs when a line ending is not end stopped but flows into the following line. For example these lines from Michael Longley's 'The Greengrocer':

> He ran a good shop, and he died
> Serving even the death-dealers
> Who found him busy as usual
> Behind the counter, organised
> With holly wreaths for Christmas,
> Fir trees on the pavement outside.

EPIGRAM: a short witty well-made poem. Coleridge defined the epigram as follows and the definition is itself an epigram.

> 'What is an epigram? A dwarfish whole
> Its body brevity, and wit its soul'

Another example would be the epigram called 'Coward' by A. R. Ammons: 'Bravery runs in my family.'

EPIPHANY: a moment of illumination, beauty, insight. For example, the closing lines of Elizabeth Bishop's 'The Fish' or the final stanza of Seamus Heaney's 'Sunlight'.

EYE RHYME: (also known as sight-rhyme) eye-rhyme occurs when two words or the final parts of the words are spelled alike, but have different pronunciations as in 'tough/bough', 'blood/mood'.

FEMININE ENDING: (also known as 'light ending') the feminine ending is an unstressed syllable at the end of a regular metrical line and is added for its musical quality. This feminine ending makes for a falling foot.

FEMININE RHYME: words of two (or more) syllables which rhyme. Shakespeare's sonnets 20 and 87 use feminine end rhymes throughout.

FOOT: a metrical unit of measurement in verse and the line can be divided into different numbers of feet as follows:

one-foot line	:	monometer
two-foot line	:	dimeter
three-foot line	:	trimeter
four-foot line	:	tetrameter
five-foot line	:	pentameter
six-foot line	:	hexameter
seven-foot line	:	heptameter
eight-foot line	:	octameter

Once a line is divided into feet, each foot can then be identified as containing a distinctive metrical pattern. For example, if a foot contains one weak and one strong stress (U –) that foot is an iamb or an iambic foot. If there are five iambic feet in a line, it is known as an iambic pentameter. The following are the most common forms of metrical foot – the stress pattern is given and an example:

iamb (iambic)	:	◡ – (hello)
rochee (trochaic)	:	– ◡ (only; Wallace; Stevens)
anapest (anapestic)	:	◡ – (understand)
dactyl (dactylic)	:	– ◡ ◡ (suddenly; Emily; Dickinson)
spondee (spondaic)	:	– – (deep peace)

FREE VERSE: on the page, free verse is unrhymed; it often follows an irregular line length and line pattern and is unmetered. Free verse depends on rhythm, repetition or unusual typographical and grammatical devices for effect.

FULL RHYME: (also known as perfect rhyme or true rhyme) when the sound or sounds in one word are perfectly matched by the sounds in another. For example, soon and moon, thing/spring, mad/bad, head/said, people/steeple, curious/furious, combination/domination.

HAIKU: the word 'haiku' in Japanese means 'starting verse', and the haiku is a sixteenth-century Japanese form of lyric poem of seventeen syllables in three lines of five, seven and five syllables respectively. Originally, the haiku had to follow certain rules: it had to have nature imagery, a reference to a season, a reference to a religious or historical event; had no rhyme; had to create an emotional response in the reader; and it had to capture the essence of its theme in an insight. The seventeenth century Japanese poet Basho wrote many fine haikus. Here are some modern ones:

1.1.87
Dangerous pavements.
But I face the ice this year
With my father's stick.
– Seamus Heaney

This is a haiku.
Five syllables and then foll
ows seven. Get it?
– John Cooper Clarke

To write a haiku
In seventeen syllables
Is very diffic.
– John Cooper Clarke

HALF RHYME: (also called slant-rhyme, near-rhyme, off-rhyme, half-rhyme, partial rhyme, imperfect rhyme) half-rhyme occurs when two words have certain sound similarities, but do not have perfect rhymes. Half-rhymes often depend on the same last consonant in two words such as 'blood' and 'good' or 'poem' and 'rum'. Emily Dickinson, Hopkins, Yeats, Dylan Thomas, Elizabeth Bishop and many other poets use half-rhyme.

HYPERBOLE: in Greek, the word 'hyperbole' means 'an overshooting, an excess' and hyperbole is the deliberate use of exaggeration or overstatement for dramatic or comic effect. For example, in 'The Daffodils' Wordsworth is using hyperbole in 'Ten thousand saw I at a glance'. The opposite of hyperbole is litotes.

IAMB: the iamb is a metrical foot made up of one unaccented syllable followed by an accented one (◡ –). The word 'today' or 'forget' or 'hello' are examples of the iamb.

IAMBIC PENTAMETER: the word pentameter is Greek for five measures and is used to describe a line of verse containing five metrical feet. The iambic pentameter is the most commonly used meter in the English language and there's a very simple reason for this: the length of an iambic pentameter line is the length of time most of us can hold our breath. Blank verse, which Shakespeare used in his plays, is unrhymed iambic pentameter. There is a old girls' skipping chant which goes 'I must, I must, I must, improve my bust' and it is a perfect example of iambic pentameter. So too is a sentence such as 'You make me sick, you make me really sick' or 'My birthday is the twenty-sixth of May'. The iambic pentameter could be represented as follows:

daDA daDA daDA daDA daDA or (◡ – | ◡ – | ◡ – | ◡ – | ◡ –)

Obviously, when you read a line of iambic pentameter, you do not exaggerate the stress, just as we do not exaggerate the stress on a vowel sound in our everyday speech. In the poem, however, the underlying structured pattern creates a music and a flow that is heard in the ear. If you look at and read lines such as the following from Eavan Boland's 'The Pomegranate', you will see and hear them as iambic pentameters:

I climb the stairs and stand where I can see (line 26)

The rain is cold. The road is flint-coloured (line 43)

Not every line in a poem that is written in iambic pentameter will follow the iambic pentameter pattern. If that were the case, the sequence of stresses could have a crippling effect. The rule for poets seems to be that they will use a rule, knowing that it can be broken or abandoned when necessary. The best judge, in the end, is the ear rather than a book on metrics.

IMAGE: in literature, an image is a picture in words, and similes, metaphors and symbols all offer the reader word-pictures as in

'his brown skin hung in strips
like ancient wallpaper,
and its pattern of darker brown
was like wallpaper:
shapes like full-blown roses . . .'
– Elizabeth Bishop 'The Fish'

' . . . where the ocean
Like a mighty animal
With a really wicked motion
Leaps for sailor's funeral . . .'
– Stevie Smith 'Deeply Morbid'

Ezra Pound defined the image as 'an intellectual and emotional complex in an instant of time' and this definition reminds us that the image involves the head and the heart. Our intellect creates the picture and our emotions are also involved in determining our response to it, and all of this takes place in an instant of time. Single words such as 'snow', 'rat', 'velvet', 'isolation' and so on present us with images of our own making. The poet, in creating a successful image, allows the reader to see something in a new and interesting way.

IMAGERY: the pictures presented in a work of literature which communicate more fully the writer's intention. For example, the predominant imagery in a play by Shakespeare may be light and darkness and these images become powerful ways of portraying characters, moods, the play's structure.

IN MEDIAS RES: in Latin, the phrase means 'in the middle of things', and, when a work is said to begin immediately or abruptly and without introduction, then it is said to begin *in medias res*. For example, Seamus Heaney's poem 'St Kevin and the Blackbird':

> And then there was St Kevin and the blackbird.

INTERNAL RHYME: this is a rhyme which occurs within the line to create a musical or rhythmical effect, as in Elizabeth Bishop's 'Filling Station', where 'taboret' (American pronunciation) and 'set' and the repeated color form an internal rhyme:

> Some comic books provide
> the only note of *color* —
> of certain *color*. They lie
> upon a big dim doily
> draping a tabor**et**
> (part of the s**et**), beside
> a big hirsute begonia.

INTERTEXTUALITY: the term was coined by Julia Kristeva in 1966. It refers to the interdependence of literary texts; any one text does not exist in isolation, but is linked to all the texts which have gone before. All texts define themselves against other texts, either through differences or similarities.

IRONY: there are two kinds of irony: verbal irony, when something is said and the opposite is meant; and irony of situation, the classic example being the story of Oedipus.

KENNING: a word invention frequently found in Old Norse and Anglo-Saxon or Old English in which two ideas are joined to form a condensed image. For example, 'whale road' or 'swan's path' for sea; 'sky-candle' for the sun. Gerard Manley Hopkins uses kennings in his poetry, calling the kestrel a 'windhover', for example.

LITOTES: litotes is the technique whereby you say something positive by contradicting a negative. A famous example is when Saint Paul said of Rome: 'I am a citizen of no mean city'; in other words he is saying that he is a citizen of a magnificent and great city. If you say of someone that he/she is not bad-looking' you are using litotes.

LYRIC: from the Greek word for lyre, a stringed musical instrument. The lyic poem was originally sung and accompanied by the lyre. Lyric now means a personal, concentrated, musical, short poem. Helen Vendler says 'Lyric is the genre of private life: it is what we say to ourselves when we are alone.' Examples include Ben Jonson's 'Song: To Celia', 'Fern Hill' by Dylan Thomas, Michael Longley's 'Amish Rug'.

MASCULINE RHYME: when stressed monosyllabic words rhyme.

METAPHOR: when a direct link is made between two things without using 'like' or 'as'. Metaphors are often more powerful than similes. 'You're an angel' is more effective than 'You're like an angel'; 'He blazed a trail through the town' is a metaphor which gives a vivid image of a person directly compared to fire – colourful, exciting, dangerous.

METRE: the word metre comes from the Greek word for measure and there are different ways of identifying the metre in a poem:

(a) by the number of stressed syllables in a line: STRONG-STRESS METRE
(b) by the number of stressed and unstressed syllables in a line: ACCENTUAL-SYLLABIC METRE
(c) by the number of syllables in a line: SYLLABIC METRE
(d) by the duration of short and long syllables in a line: QUANTITATIVE METRE

Do not worry overmuch about the technicalities of metre. I. A. Richards compared metre in a poem to a frame around a painting. It is obviously important but the poem can be appreciated and understood without a thorough knowledge of every technical term in the book. Metre can appear too artificial if overemphasised. When you speak or write, you do not always plan a metrical pattern in your speech, yet the words you speak and the order in which you speak them often make for an effective sound-pattern. The metrical pattern is important, but your ear and your command of language allow you to communicate effectively. In poetry, metre is very important; it is one of poetry's most distinguishing features.

METRICS: the composing or study of the rhythmic pattern in verse. The theories relating to these.

MOOD: this is the feeling contained within a poem and the feeling communicated to the reader. If someone walked into a room containing several people and angrily shouted at you to 'Get out of here at once!', the TONE of voice used would be an ANGRY, COMMANDING one and the MOOD within the room might be one of UNEASE. Do not confuse TONE and MOOD. Tone has to do with the expressing of an attitude; mood has to do with feeling.

MOTIF: motif comes from Latin and means 'to move'. Motif means a theme, a technique, an event, a character which is developed and repeated in a work. For example, in Shakespeare's *Macbeth*, light and darkness become a motif. In literature in general, there are certain motifs such as the *Carpe Diem* (Seize the Day) motif, which means to make the most of a situation. In Michael Longley's poetry, the relationship between father and son, be it between Longley and his own father or that between Odysseus and Laertes, becomes a motif.

MYTH: a story of strange, unusual, supernatural happenings of unknown authorship which was passed on to future generations in an effort to explain origins and natural events.

NEAR RHYME: (also known as slant-rhyme, partial-rhyme, oblique-rhyme, half-rhyme) near-rhyme occurs when two words sound approximately the same and are placed within the poem for musical effect. Emily Dickinson frequently used near-rhyme such as in 'song'/'tongue'.

NEGATIVE CAPABILITY: a phrase used by John Keats (1795–1821) in a letter dated 21 December 1817; it refers to a power of sympathy and a freedom from self-consciousness. In the letter he wrote that the true poet is one who is 'capable of being in uncertainties, Mysteries, doubts, without any irritable reaching after fact and reason'. Keats, by way of illustration, spoke of a sparrow picking among the gravel outside his window, and his observation of the sparrow was so intent and interested that he became that sparrow.

OBJECTIVE CORRELATIVE: the term was first used by Washington Allston in 1850 in *Lectures on Art* and later by T. S. Eliot in his study of *Hamlet*. The phrase refers to how the objective or external world can produce an emotion in the viewer; how there is a correlation between the object and the viewer. Similarly, if a writer uses certain details, descriptions in his/her work, a specific emotional response will be evoked in the reader.

OCTAVE/OCTET: an eight-line stanza. In a Petrarchan sonnet, the fourteen lines are divided into octet and sestet. The octet often poses a question and this is answered in the sestet.

ODE: a poem of celebration and praise. John Keats wrote some of the most famous odes in the English language.

ONOMATOPOEIA: in Greek, 'onomatopoeia' means 'the making of a name' and onomatopoeia refers to words whose sounds imitate what is being described. For example, 'buzz', 'slap', 'cuckoo', 'gargle'.

OTTAVA RIMA: an Italian eight-line stanza in iambic pentameter with an abababcc rhyming scheme.

OXYMORON: (in Greek, the word means foolishness) oxymoron refers to a figure of speech in which contradictory and opposite aspects are linked. It is similar to paradox, but the oxymoron is contained within a phrase, the paradox within a statement. Examples of oxymoron include 'cruel kindness' and 'thunderous silences'.

PALINDROME: in Greek the word palindrome means 'running back again'. A palindrome is a word, a line of verse or a sentence which reads the same way backwards and forwards: e.g. 'Dad'; 'noon'; 'Madam, I'm Adam'; 'Was it a cat I saw?'. The following refers to Napoleon: 'Able was I ere I saw Elba'. Other examples are: 'Sums are not set as a test on Erasmus'; and 'A man, a plan, a canal – Panama!'

PARADOX: a paradox is when language expresses a truth in what seems, at first, to be a contradiction. For example, Wordsworth's 'The child is father of the man' or Shakespeare's line in *Julius Caesar*: 'Cowards die many times before their deaths'.

PARODY: this is when a well-known work is deliberately imitated in a mocking or humorous way. The reader is expected to be familiar with the original work, if the parody is to be effective.

PATHETIC FALLACY: this term was coined by John Ruskin in 1856 and it refers to the writer's technique of attributing human feeling or behaviour to nature. For example, in 'Lycidas' John Milton says of the flowers 'And Daffadillies fill their cups with tears'.

PATHOS: the word *pathos* in Greek means 'suffering' or 'passion'. Pathos is a deep, sympathetic feeling which the writer summons up in the reader or audience. The final line of Seamus Heaney's poem, 'Mid-term Break' is an example: 'A four foot box, a foot for every year.'

PENTAMETER: this is a line of poetry which is made up of five metrical feet. The iambic pentameter (◡ –/◡ –/◡ –/◡ –/◡ –) is the most commonly used meter in the English language.

PERIODS OF ENGLISH LITERATURE: the following is an outline of the periods into which English literature has been divided by literary historians, though the exact dates sometimes vary:

450 – 1100	Old English or Anglo-Saxon period
1100 – 1500	Middle English or Medieval English period
1500 – 1660	The Renaissance
1558 – 1603	Elizabeth the First's reign Elizabethan
1603 – 1625	Jacobean (after James I)
1625 – 1649	Caroline age
1649 – 1660	Commonwealth period/Puritanism
1660 – 1798	Neo–Classical period
1660 – 1700	The Restoration
1700 – 1745	Augustan Age (the Age of Pope)
1745 – 1798	Age of Sensibility (the Age of Samuel Johnson)
1798 – 1832	Romantic Period
1832 – 1901	Victorian period
1901 – 1914	Edwardian
1910 – 1936	Georgian
1914 – 1970s	Modern English
c. 1970s –	Postmodern

PERSONA: in Latin, the word *persona* means person or mask, and the persona is the speaker in a work such as poem or play who is different from the poet or playwright. The list of characters in a play used to be given under the heading *Dramatis Personae* (the dramatist's persons). In Michael Longley's poem 'Self-Heal' and in 'Wedding-Wind' by Philip Larkin, the voice is that of a female persona.

PERSONIFICATION: this occurs when a writer gives human qualities to inanimate objects or abstractions. For example, if one said that the clouds were in a rage that would be personification.

POETIC LICENSE: when rules are broken, when facts are ignored, when logic is abandoned all for the sake of the overall effect. Emily Dickinson abandons conventional grammatical rules with poetic license. Or Eavan Boland mixes Greek and Latin names in her reference to the myth of Ceres and Proserpine/Demeter and Persephone.

PUNCTUATION: in Latin, the word *punctus* means 'to point' and punctuation indicates speed, flow, emphasis, direction, the emotional charge of language and so on. The following are the more familiar forms:

comma	,	a slight pause
semicolon	;	a longer pause or a division between clauses
colon	:	a long pause; introduces a list, explanation or quotation
full-stop	.	indicates a full stop at the end of a sentence; also used at the end of certain abbreviated words (e.g. Prof. and ad. but not Mr because Mr in the abbreviated version ends with the same letter as the word in full does)
ellipsis	...	indicates that something is missing or is being omitted
dash	–	used to indicate a break in a sentence or elsewhere
hyphen	-	connects compound words

quotation marks	' '	are used to indicate quoted material
	" "	indicate a quotation within a quotation or something of a false or spurious nature
slash	/	indicates a line ending
exclamation mark	!	used for emphasis or to express emotion
question mark	?	suggests puzzlement, confusion, a need for information
parentheses	( )	used in an aside
brackets	[ ]	indicates an editorial comment
italics	*italics*	used for emphasis, foreign words

PUN: a play upon words alike or nearly alike in sound, but different in meaning. A famous example is the dying Mercutio's line in *Romeo and Juliet* (III i): 'Ask for me tomorrow and you shall find me a grave man.'

QUATRAIN: in French, 'quatrain' means a collection of four, and quatrain, in English, refers to a poem or stanza of four lines, usually with alternating rhyming schemes such as abab, aabb, abba, aaba, abcb.

REPETITION: repeated sounds, words, structures is a feature of all poetry to a lesser or greater degree. Repetition has many effects such as emphasis, music, surprise, predictability. Paul Durcan's use of repetition in 'Going Home to Mayo, Winter, 1949' or Elizabeth Bishop's use of repetition in the closing lines of 'The Fish' are significant and effective.

RHYME: when a sound is echoed creating a music and order within the work.

RHYME SCHEMES:

Couplet	aa
Triplet	aaa
Ballad stanza	abab
Limerick	aabba
Ottava Rima	abababcc

RHYTHM: the work in Greek means 'flowing'. Rhythm refers to how the words move or flow.

ROMANTICISM: Romanticism and the Romantic Movement belong to a period in English Literature in the late eighteenth century and the beginning of the nineteenth. Some date the beginning of the movement from the beginning of the French Revolution in 1789; others from 1798 when Wordsworth and Coleridge published *Lyrical Ballads*. The movement ended in the 1830s (Victoria became queen in 1837). The movement began as a reaction to the formality and restraint of neo-classicism in the preceding age. The Romantic Movement focused on the individual's feelings and imagination. The child was valued for its innocence and society was regarded as a corrupting influence. The Romantic poet wrote about his own thoughts and feelings (Wordsworth, speaking of *The Prelude*, said that 'it was a thing unprecedented in literary history that a man should talk so much about himself') and celebrated nature over city life and civilisation. Samuel Johnson, in the eighteenth century, had said that 'The man who is tired of London is tired of life'; the Romantics often found their inspiration in nature.

RUN-ON LINE: this is the same as enjambment. See above.

SARCASM: not to be confused with IRONY, sarcasm is a crude and obvious method of expressing apparent praise when the opposite is meant.

SENSIBILITY: the sensitivity and quality of a person's mind, the capacity of feeling or emotion.

SENTIMENTALITY: an expression of feeling which is excessive, indulgent, immature.

SESTET: a group of six lines, usually the final six lines in a sonnet where the fourteen line poem is divided into eight (octet) and sestet.

SESTINA: a complicated poetic form in which the poem consists of six stanzas of six lines each followed by three-line stanza. The same six end-words occur in each of the first six stanzas and form a definite pattern. The final stanza also contains the six key-words. Elizabeth Bishop's 'Sestina' is an example.

SIMILE: from the Latin word for 'like', the simile is a figure of speech in which one thing is compared to another, using the words 'like', 'as', 'as if'. For example:

> When I was small I swallowed an awn of rye.
> My throat was like standing crop probed by a scythe.
> – Seamus Heaney 'The Butter-Print'

SONNET: a fourteen line poem, usually in iambic pentameter.

STREAM OF CONSCIOUSNESS: the phrase was invented by the nineteenth-century American psychologist William James to describe the writer's attempt to imitate or capture every thought, impression, memory, feeling and so on in an individual consciousness, as they happen. The most famous example of stream of consciousness is found in the closing forty pages of James Joyce's *Ulysses*. Here Joyce has entered into Molly Bloom's consciousness. Her thoughts and ideas flow through the reader's mind, and Joyce abandoned all conventional punctuation to give the passage immediacy. Here is an excerpt:

> I love flowers Id love to have the whole place swimming in roses God of heaven theres nothing like nature the wild mountains then the sea and the waves rushing then the beautiful country with fields of oats and wheat and all kinds of things and all the fine cattle going about that would do your heart good to see rivers and lakes and flowers all sorts of shapes and smells and colours springing up even out of the ditches primroses and violets nature it is as for them saying theres no God I wouldnt give a snap of my two fingers for all their learning why dont they go and create something I often asked him atheists or whatever they call themselves go and wash the cobbles off themselves first then they go howling for the priest and they dying and why why because theyre afraid of hell on account of their bad conscience ah yes I know them well who was the first person in the universe before there was anybody that made it all who ah that they dont know neither do I so there you are they might as well try to stop the sun from rising tomorrow the sun shines for you he said the day we were lying among the rhododendrons on Howth head in the grey tweed suit and his straw hat the day I got him to propose to me yes first I gave him the bit of seedcake out of my mouth and it was leapyear like now yes 16 years ago my God after that long kiss I near lost my breath . . . . .

STYLE: the manner of writing or speaking, e.g. the way a writer uses words may be direct or convoluted or vague or inaccurate or florid . . . . 'Style most shows a man, speak that I may see thee' (Ben Jonson)

SUBJECT MATTER: this refers to the actual material spoken of in the work. For example, a poet might write about a cluttered room which is the subject matter of the poem, but the theme of the poem could be the confusion felt because a relationship has ended. In Elizabeth Bishop's poem 'Filling Station', the subject matter is an oily, dirty, petrol (gas) station but the poem's theme is human endeavour, dignity, love.

SUBLIME: in Latin, this means high, lofty, elevated. The sublime in literature refers to moments of heightened awareness, intense feeling. The closing lines of James Wright's poem 'A Blessing' are sublime.

SURREALISM: Surrealism is a movement in art and literature which sought to release and express the creative potential of the unconscious mind. It frequently contains the irrational juxtaposition of images. The Uruguayan-born French writer Isidore Lucien Ducasse's (1846–1870) description of 'the chance meeting on a dissecting-table of a sewing machine and an umbrella' has been frequently quoted as a definition of surrealism. Salvador Dali's paintings are examples. The surreal is literally 'above the real'. In writing, the surreal occurs when conventional modes are broken, and dreamlike or nightmarish or seemingly unrelated images are juxtaposed. In Michael Longley's poem 'The Linen Workers', the opening lines have a surreal quality: 'Christ's teeth ascended with him into heaven:/ Through a cavity in one of his molars/The wind whistles; he is fastened for ever/By his exposed canines to a wintry sky.'

SYMBOL: a symbol is a word, phrase or image which represents something literal and concrete, but also suggests another source of reference. In everyday life, a piece of coloured cloth is just that, but that same cloth can be a country's flag. It is both object and symbol. Similarly in literature: in Shakespeare, the King is a male character, but he is also the symbol of power, authority and God's presence on earth. The use of symbol is a powerful device because of its rich, complex associative qualities. In Michael Longley's poem 'The Civil Servant', the smashing of the piano is a symbolic act.

SYNAESTHESIA: in Greek, *synaesthesia* means 'to feel or perceive together', and it is when one sensory perception is expressed in terms of a different sense. For example, when an image is experienced through two senses at the same time, as in:

> a loud red coat
> purple stained mouth

SYNECDOCHE: this is a figure of speech in which a part stands for the whole. For example, 'sail' stands for ship; 'hired hands' or 'all hands on deck' means hired persons.

TETRAMETER: the word *tetrameter* in Greek means four measures and the tetrameter is a four foot, four stress line. These feet can be iambic, trochaic and so on. The iambic tetrameter is the second most widely used form in English poetry, the most common being the iambic pentameter.

THEME: theme comes from a Greek word meaning 'proposition', and the theme of a work is the main or central idea within the work. Theme should be distinguished from subject matter. For example, the subject matter of Philip Larkin's 'Church Going' is visiting churches, but the theme of the poem is our natural fascination with religion, its power, effect and future.

TONE: the tone is the attitude conveyed by the writer. From the writer's tone of voice, the reader can identify the attitude of the writer towards his/her subject matter and/ or audience. A tone can be reverent, angry, disrespectful, cautious, dismissive, gentle, reserved, slangy, serious.

TRIMETER: the word *trimeter* in Greek means 'three measures' and the trimeter line is a three foot line. The trimeter is used in nursery rhymes and in many songs, such as Sir Thomas Wyatt's 'I will and yet I may not'.

TROCHEE: the trochee is a two syllable foot. The first syllable is long or stressed, the second is short and unstressed (◡ –). Examples are 'pushing', 'running'. It is known as the falling foot, opposite to the iambic foot, which is a rising foot.

VERSE: verse comes from the Latin word 'to turn' or 'a line or row of writing'. Verse can now refer to a line in a poem, a stanza, a refrain or a passage from the Bible. Verse can also refer to an entire poem based on regular meter or a poem that is lacking in profundity.

VILLANELLE: the word comes from Italian *villanella*, a rustic song or dance. At first, a villanelle was called such because of its pastoral subject and the use of a refrain. Later, the villanelle followed a strict pattern and became a poem of five three-line stanzas and a concluding quatrain, with only two rhymes throughout. The intricate rhyming scheme is as follows: aba, aba, aba, aba, aba, abaa. Examples of the villanelle are Dylan Thomas's 'Do Not Go Gentle Into That Good Night' and 'One Art' by Elizabeth Bishop.

VOICE: this is the distinctive utterance of a writer; it is the sounds we hear when we read or listen to the poem. In other words, a writer's ability to use words in such a way that a reader can recognise that writer's unique quality. T. S. Eliot identified three voices in poetry:

1. the poet in silent meditation
2. the poet addressing an audience
3. the voice of a dramatic character or persona created by the poet

Acknowledgements

The publishers would like to thank the following for permission to reproduce copyright material in this book.

Poems

Faber and Faber for 'The Forge', 'Bogland', 'The Tollund Man', 'Sunlight', 'A Constable Calls', 'The Skunk', 'The Harvest Bow', 'The Underground', 'The Pitchfork', 'Lightnings viii', 'A Call', 'Tate's Avenue' and 'Postscript' by Seamus Heaney.

Faber and Faber for 'Black Rook in Rainey Weather', 'The Times are Tidy', 'Morning Song', 'Mirror', 'Finisterre', 'Pheasant', 'Elm', 'Poppies in July', 'The Arrival of the Bee Box' and 'Child' by Sylvia Plath.

Carcenet Press for 'The War Horse', 'Child Of Our Time', 'The Famine Road', 'The Shadow Doll', 'White Hawthorn', 'Outside History', 'The Black Lace, 'This Moment', 'The Pomegranate' and 'Love' by Eavan Boland.

Penguin Random House for 'Nessa', 'Girl with Keys to Pearse's Cottage' and ''Windfall', 8 Parnell Hill, Cork' by Paul Durcan.

New Directions Publishing Corporation for 'To a Poor Old Woman' and 'The Red Wheelbarrow' by William Carlos Williams.

Wesleyan University Press for 'A Blessing' by James Wright.

Haughton Mifflin Harcourt for 'The Voice You Hear When You Read Silently' by Thomas Lux.

The publishers have tried to make every effort to trace and acknowledge the holders of copyright materials included in this book. In the event of any copyright holders having been overlooked, the publishers will be pleased to come to a suitable arrangement at the first opportunity.

Notes

Notes